Assessment and Selection
in Organizations

Assessment and Selection in Organizations

Methods and Practice for Recruitment and Appraisal

Edited by

Peter Herriot

Birkbeck College,
University of London

Section Editors

Pieter J.D. Drenth
Robert A. Roe
Alan Jones
Ivan T. Robertson
Victor Dulewicz

JOHN WILEY & SONS
Chichester · New York · Brisbane · Toronto · Singapore

Copyright © 1989 by John Wiley & Sons Ltd.
Baffins Lane, Chichester
West Sussex PO19 1UD, England

Other Wiley Editorial Offices

John Wiley & Sons, Inc., 605 Third Avenue,
New York, NY 10158-0012, USA

Jacaranda Wiley Ltd, G.P.O. Box 859, Brisbane,
Queensland 4001, Australia

John Wiley & Sons (Canada) Ltd, 22 Worcester Road,
Rexdale, Ontario M9W 1L1, Canada

John Wiley & Sons (SEA) Pte Ltd, 37 Jalan Pemimpin 05-04,
Block B, Union Industrial Building, Singapore 2057

Library of Congress Cataloging-in-Publication Data:

Assessment and selection in organizations: methods and practice for
　　recruitment and appraisal / edited by Peter Herriot.
　　　　p.　cm.
　　Bibliography: p.
　　Includes index.
　　ISBN 0 471 91640 4
　　　1. Employee selection.　2. Employment tests.　3. Recruiting of
　　employees.　I. Herriot, Peter.
　　HF5549.5.S38A87　1989
　　658.3′112—dc20　　　　　　　　　　　　　　　　　　89-14712
　　　　　　　　　　　　　　　　　　　　　　　　　　　　CIP

British Library Cataloguing in Publication Data:

Assessment and selection in organizations: methods and
　　practice for recruitment and appraisal.
　　1. Personnel. Assessment
　　I. Herriot, Peter
　　658.3′125

　　ISBN 0 471 91640 4

Typeset by Inforum Typesetting, Portsmouth
Printed and bound in Great Britain by Courier International Ltd, Tiptree

Contents

Section 3: The Tools of Selection

Section 4: Selection in Specific Areas

Section 5: Performance Appraisal and Counselling

List of Contributors

JEN A. ALGERA
Eindhoven University of Technology, Faculty of Industrial Engineering and Management Science, PO Box 513, 5600 MB Eindhoven, The Netherlands.

DAVID ARIS
Adviesbureau Psychotechniek, Drift 10, 3512 BS Utrecht, The Netherlands.

DAVID BARTRAM
Ergonomics Research Unit, The University of Hull, 26 Newland Park, Hull HU5 2DW, UK.

F. BARWELL
Health Service Management Centre, University of Birmingham, Park House, 40 Edgbaston Park Road, Birmingham B15 2RT, UK.

ROWAN BAYNE
Psychology Department, Polytechnic of East London, The Green, Stratford, London E15 4LZ, UK.

GERSHON BEN-SHAKHAR
Department of Psychology, The Hebrew University of Jerusalem, Jerusalem 91905, Israel.

CHARLES E. BETHELL-FOX
Hay Management Consultants Ltd, 52 Grosvenor Gardens, London SW1W 0AU, UK.

GERRIT BOERLIJST
Technische Hogeschool Twente, Dedrijfskunde, Postbus 217 7500, AE Drienerlo, Enschede, The Netherlands.

MARK COOK
Centre for Occupational Research Ltd, 14 Devonshire Place, London W1N 1PB, UK.

H. PETER DACHLER
Hochschule St Gallen, Guisanstrasse 11, CH 9019 St Gallen, Switzerland.

PAUL DOBSON
Centre for Personnel Research and Enterprise Development, The City University Business School, Northampton Square, London EC1V 0HB, UK.

SYLVIA DOWNS
Pearn Kandola Downs, Windsor House, 12 High Street, Kidlington, Oxford OX5 2DH, UK.

RUSSELL J. DRAKELEY   *Craig, Gregg and Drakeley Associates, 14 Grange Gardens, Pinner, Middlesex HA5 5YE, UK.*

PIETER J.D. DRENTH   *Department of Psychology, Free University, 1081 de Boelelaan, 1081 HV, Amsterdam, The Netherlands.*

VICTOR DULEWICZ   *The Management College, Greenlands, Henley-on-Thames, Oxon RG9 3AU, UK.*

ROB T. FELTHAM   *NFER–Nelson, Darville House, 2 Oxford Road East, Windsor, Berkshire SL4 1DF, UK.*

CLIVE FLETCHER   *Department of Psychology, University of London Goldsmiths' College, New Cross, London SE14 6NW, UK.*

LYNDA GRATTON   *London Business School, Sussex Place, Regents Park, London NW1, UK.*

MARTIN A. GREUTER   *Adviesbureau Psychotechniek BV, Drift 10, 3512 BS Utrecht, The Netherlands.*

JOHN D. HANDYSIDE   *57 Gloucester Road, London SW7 4QN, UK.*

N. M. HARDINGE   *Headquarters Royal Air Force Support Command, Brampton, Huntingdon, Cambridgeshire PE18 8QL, UK.*

PETER HERRIOT   *Department of Occupational Psychology, Birkbeck College, University of London, Malet Street, London WC1E 7HX, UK.*

WILLEM K.B. HOFSTEE   *Department of Psychology, University of Groningen, Grote Markt 31-32, NL 9712 HV Groningen, The Netherlands.*

PAUL A. ILES   *School of Management, The Open University, 1 Cofferidge Close, Stony Stratford, Milton Keynes MK11 1BY, UK.*

PAUL G.W. JANSEN   *Industrial Psychology Branch, PTT Telecom, Postbus 30 000, 2500 GA's-Gravenhage, The Netherlands.*

ALAN JONES   *Senior Psychologist (Naval Division), Ministry of Defence, Old Admiralty Building, Spring Gardens, London SW1A 2BE, UK.*

RICHARD MACDONELL   *Department of Business and Management Studies, University of Salford, Salford M5 4WT, UK.*

PETER J. MAKIN   *School of Management, UMIST, PO Box 88, Sackville Street, Manchester M60 1QD, UK.*

GEERT MEIJBOOM   *Provinciale Gelderse, Energie Maatschappij, Arnhem, The Netherlands.*

KLAUS MOSER   *Institut für Agrarsoziologie, Landwirtschaftliche Beratung und Angewandte Psychologie, Universität Hohenheim, Postfach 70 05 62 (430), 7000 Stuttgart 70, Federal Republic of Germany.*

SUSAN NEWELL — *Aston University Management Centre, The Triangle, Birmingham B4 7ET, UK.*

GEORGE PENNEY — *National Computing Centre, Oxford Road, Manchester M1 1BD, UK.*

STEVE E. POPPLETON — *Psychology Department, Wolverhampton Polytechnic, Wilfruna Street, Wolverhampton WV1 1LY, UK.*

JOSE-MARIA PRIETO — *Department de Psicologia Diferencial y Psicologia del Trabajo, Universidad Complutense, Campus de Somosaguas, 28023 Madrid, Spain.*

ROGER PRYOR — *Interactive Skills Ltd, Cygnet House, Market Place, Henley-on-Thames, Oxon RG9 2AH, UK.*

IVAN T. ROBERTSON — *Department of Management Sciences, UMIST, PO Box 88, Manchester M60 1QD, UK.*

ROBERT A. ROE — *Department of Social Sciences, Tilburg University, Hogeschoollaan 225, Unit P, Room 811, Postbox 90153, 5000 LE Tilburg, The Netherlands.*

HEINZ SCHULER — *Institut für Agrarsoziologie, Landwirtschaftliche Beratung und Angewandte Psychologie, Universität Hohenheim, Postfach 70 05 62 (430), 7000 Stuttgart 70, Federal Republic of Germany.*

JEROEN J.J.L. SEEGERS — *GITP/FOCUS, Bergen Dalseweg 127, Postbus 9043, 6500KC, Nijmegen, The Netherlands.*

VIVIAN J. SHACKLETON — *Aston University Management Centre, The Triangle, Birmingham B4 7ET, UK.*

SYLVIA SHIMMIN — *Department of Behaviour in Organizations, University of Lancaster, Gillow House, Bailrigg, Lancaster LA1 4YX, UK.*

MIKE SMITH — *Manchester School of Management, UMIST, PO Box 88, Sackville Street, Manchester M60 1QD, UK.*

PAUL VAN DER MAESEN DE SOMBREFF — *Rijks Psychologische Dienst, Postbus 20013, 2500 EA's-Gravenhage, The Netherlands.*

P. SPURGEON — *Health Service Management Centre, University of Birmingham, Park House, 40 Edgbaston Park Road, Birmingham BI5 2RT, UK.*

PAUL THORNE — *Bristow Design Systems Ltd, 50/54 Southampton Row, London WC1B 4AR, UK.*

JAMES WALKER — *City University Business School, Northampton Square, London EC1V 0HB, UK.*

RICHARD S. WILLIAMS — *Middlesex Business School, Middlesex Polytechnic, The Burroughs, Hendon, London NW4 4BT, UK.*

KAREL DE WITTE   *Centre for Organizational and Personnel Psychology, Catholic University of Leuven, Tiensestraat 102, 3000 Leuven, Belgium.*

CHARLES J. DE   *Department of Psychology, Catholic University of Nijmegen,*
WOLFF   *Montessorilaan 3, 6400 HE Nijmegen, The Netherlands.*

General Introduction

PETER HERRIOT

THE TARGET AUDIENCE

This book is aimed primarily at practitioners—people who are engaged in assessing other people at work. We expect it to be of use to human resource professionals, be they employed by organizations or working as consultants. The book is not, however, a manual: it does not give practical instructions about how to carry out assessments. Rather, it suggests the general principles which should underlie professional practice, based upon sound research. There is a crying need for authoritative and disinterested comment when several unsound and un-proven assessment tools are being marketed aggressively in Europe and America.

This latter comment implies a world-wide market, and indeed, that is the intention. Readers will note immediately, however, that this is a European and not an American volume; there are no transatlantic contributors. We believe that there can be and should be a specifically European contribution to the theory and practice of assessment, although most of the published research is American. Indeed, a skim through the references will indicate a marked transatlantic bias, indicating the great debt we owe our American colleagues.

There are, nevertheless, some important European contributions which are worthy of emphasis. In the Netherlands, for example, psychologists have had a considerable influence on employment legislation, with the consequence that the preservation of the privacy of the applicant is a major concern. In Spain, similar very strong links with Government have resulted in well-organized and powerful professional associations of human resource specialists. In the United Kingdom, an emphasis on organizational cultures has resulted in the widespread use of tools, such as the repertory grid, to tap assessment dimensions specific to the organization. So we hope that our European readership will extend to Americans who will find something different from the Old World; perhaps a willingness to tackle problems as they come, warts and all.

THE CONTEXT

However, there are several other much more important reasons than the existence of some get-rich-quick charlatans for the production of this book. We are in the process of several major contextual changes which combine to place assessment in the forefront of organizational concern.

The first of these is the new emphasis on 'human resources'. The old word 'personnel', with its connotations of administrative procedures and low status, has been replaced in many organizations by this new label. This may be more than a purely cosmetic change. The idea that 'the people make the place' (Schneider, 1987) has been gathering momentum since the popular management texts of the 1980s such as *In Search of Excellence*, by Peters and Waterman (1982). The concept that there has to be proper policy making in the human resources area has caught on. So has the feeling that human resource policies have to be tied in with overall corporate strategy in a systematic way. As a consequence, recruitment, selection, and career development systems as a whole have come under scrutiny. Many of these systems have developed historically, like Topsy, with bits being bolted on in reaction to some internal or external event. Their overall design and their compatibility with each other is now the major concern. Organizations are looking proactively at longer term policy, and away from the quick technological fix, the magic tool which will solve this or that immediate problem.

Apart from the general managerial climate in the best run companies, what are the other events in the outside world which are forcing this reappraisal? First, there is a major demographic trend which should totally revolutionize our thinking about recruitment and selection. In the 1990s, there will in general be a seller's rather than a buyer's market for scientific and professional labour. Across Europe, but particularly in Germany and in the United Kingdom, there will be a marked decrease in the number of young people entering the labour market. There is no reason to suppose that governments with a strong ideological orientation towards decreasing public expenditure will succeed in producing more graduates. Hence there will be competition for highly educated people, especially scientists and engineers. For the emphasis in the 1990s will be on quality and effectiveness of goods and services, rather than on the productivity and efficiency of the 1980s. And to ensure quality you need good research and development, design, and production. Organizations are left with the major problem of recruiting and retaining precisely those types of employee who are in the shortest supply.

This will have profound effects upon the design of recruitment and career development procedures. Instead of the organization selecting the applicant, the position will be reversed; the applicant will in general be selecting the organization. Hence applicants will have to be treated as equals; since they have the market power, organizations will have to surrender their administrative power. They cannot afford to continue assessing individuals without explaining what it is they are assessing, why they are assessing it, and handing over the data to its owner (the applicant). In the same way, retention of scarce human resources will also become a major concern. Individual as well as organizational needs will have to be assessed, and psychological contracts agreed by means of negotiations.

There are other external events in the 1990s which will affect the human resources climate. Employment legislation will probably be enacted for member states of the European Community which will contain far stricter provisions regarding discrimination than those currently in force in individual nations. Similarly, legislation regarding safeguards to applicants' privacy and their rights to be informed of the results of assessments may well be promulgated. Together with the increased transferability of labour across national boundaries, these legislative developments will have profound effects.

THE PLAYERS

How are we facing up to these challenges, those of us who are engaged in the business of assessment? The answer appears to be that we are facing in several different directions, depending upon where we are coming from. And the contents of the book faithfully reflect this confusion.

Who are the players, and why are they so much at odds with each other? First come the academic psychologists, with your editor claiming the front position for his own particular tribe. Most, but by no means all, of the contributors to the handbook are academics. However, most academics in the area of assessment engage in consultancy, so the distinction between academics and practitioners is blurred at the edges. Then there are practitioners, some of whom are consultants, while others are employed by organizations as human resource specialists.

All of these different groups of players come to the problem of assessment from their own point of view. One set of academics trace their origins to the study of individual differences, and to its application by such as F.W. Taylor and Munsterberg in the early years of this century. They perceive performance at work as the result of the individual's characteristics. Emboldened by their use of the validity generalization technique, some of them go so far as to minimize the effect of organizational context upon performance. It is all a result of the individual's capacities, and what is more, of his or her general intellectual ability rather than of specific aptitudes. While these psychologists have in general been responsible for the development of the most effective tools of assessment, they have tended to adopt an entirely technological perspective. Assessment is considered by these psychologists to be of the individual by the organization, and employees will be more effectively selected or promoted as a consequence of the technical qualities of the tools used.

Another theoretical viewpoint has informed some of the other academic contributors of this book. Coming from social psychology, they concentrate upon the social relationship between applicants and employees and the organization. Hence they treat the recruitment and selection procedure as a two-way process. Also, they are interested in more general social phenomena, such as the organizational culture, as the setting for assessment activities, and social trends regarding individuals' rights and the meaning of work.

Consultants, of course, vary in their points of view too. Some have great expertise in particular forms of assessment, for example, aptitude tests or assessment centres. Others have a more organizational perspective, perceiving selection and appraisal systems as a whole rather than as isolated sets of methods or instruments. The former are sometimes apt to apply their favourite tool whatever the problem. The latter are not always as familiar with the tools of their trade as they might be. But consultants differ from academics in that they have to handle relationships with their clients. Hence they have to be aware of organizational culture and processes in order to maintain satisfactory relationships; in particular, they often have to deal with the uncomfortable situation of having employees and employers as clients simultaneously.

Organizational members who have contributed to this book come with yet another point of view. From the perspective of the personnel department, assessment is just one of the many battlegrounds of organizational power politics. It is, nevertheless, one of the areas in which they possess expert power, and so it is a good weapon to use in furthering the interests of their department. For personnel people, the organizational perspective is crucial; the very idea of the use of a particular technique regardless of organizational context is ludicrous. On the contrary, their emphasis is upon the development of systems appropriate to the organization. Many of them are coming to realize that organizations are changing so rapidly that the traditional methods of job analysis are no longer appropriate. Systems have to be adaptive, since jobs can no longer be construed as static sets of tasks.

So the book's structure reflects these different points of view. We start by trying to put assessment into its contexts, both historical, economic, demographic, and cultural. Assessment is not a historic technology but an organizational activity rooted in the way organizations and societies have developed. In Section 2 we consider the design of selection procedures in the light of these contexts. In Section 3 we return to the traditional tools of selection, and emphasize that the evidence about how valid they are continues to be of vital importance. Their uses may change as people assess themselves rather than are assessed by others; but the quality of the instrument matters whoever uses it. Section 4 looks at selection in different occupational categories. For far too long, psychologists have behaved as though manufacturing industry were the sole sort of organization in existence; now they realize that many of the assumptions about assessment made upon that basis do not generalize across the board. Finally, in deference to the career development dimension of assessment, we look at appraisal in Section 5. If the retention and flexible use of scarce human resources is an imperative of the 1990s, then sound methods of assessing for directions of self-development are vital.

I owe a huge debt to Elspeth Ross for coordinating the whole enterprise; to the section editors for their enthusiasm and expertise; to the authors for their speed of response and international spirit of cooperation; to Wiley for their encouragement and skill; and to Barbara Herriot for pretending that I wasn't any busier than usual!

REFERENCES

Peters, T.J., and Waterman, R.H. (1982). *In Search of Excellence*. Harper and Row, New York.

Schneider, B. (1987). The people make the place, *Personnel Psychology*, **40**, 437–53.

Section 1: The Context

Introduction to Section 1: The Context

Pieter J. D. Drenth

In this first section an attempt will be made to place the process of assessment and selection in a broader contextual framework. Several authors will discuss various dimensions of this context and together they will demonstrate that taking it into account is a necessary condition for a fuller understanding of the phenomenon being studied in this handbook.

There was a time when psychological selection was treated in a rather isolated way. The psychologist stood at the entrance of an organization and advised, or in many cases even determined, who had to remain outside and who could enter. Admittedly this approach has been a very fruitful stimulant for the creation and production of numerous assessment instruments and tests as well as for the development of advanced psychometric theories and models, but at the same time it has failed to throw much light on the complex and dynamic processes of decision making underlying the selection of personnel.

A number of elements can be used to illustrate the importance of this 'contextualization'.

In the first place it became clear that good selection, even based upon a correct assessment of strengths and weaknesses of the candidate, can never be realized without a proper insight into the criterion for which the selection had to take place. This meant first of all a development and elaboration of methods of function and task analysis for selection purposes.

It turned out that in many cases global criteria might not be such a good choice. People can qualify for a job for a variety of reasons and a more nuanced definition of a 'good worker' seemed to be needed. Accordingly, multidimensional criteria were called for.

But more fundamental questions posed themselves. Why is selection research restricting itself primarily to traditional production and output criteria? Why are not other criteria such as work satisfaction or indicators of the well-being of the worker being used more often? It seemed that the selection psychologists too easily confined themselves to the classical, economic–rationalistic conceptions about work performance and contributions of people to organizational goals.

This decrease in the isolation of selection and the increased attention to the importance of the proper choice and definition of the criterion has clearly widened the scope of selection psychologists and furthered their integration in the organizational personnel policy at large.

A second widening of this scope was encouraged by the increasing realization that selection is only one way, and often not the most appropriate way, of eliminating the discrepancy between capacities and characteristics of the potential labour force on the one hand and the physical, mental and social requirements posed by the organization on the other. Improvement of the match between employee and function can be achieved in at least two other ways. Firstly, through training. Training is based upon the assumption that a human being is changeable and can adjust to external requirements, whereas selection starts from the assumption that it is more efficient to try to identify and to choose the well-qualified candidates by assessing the relevant stable and permanent characteristics of the individual. It will be obvious that both approaches may be useful and that a combination of both views will lead to more satisfactory results than either one separately.

The second alternative approach is through changing or adjusting the task. Too often the tasks, their content, their physical and social requirements, the utilization of tools and machines needed, are such that it would prevent even the best selected worker from performing satisfactorily. Work design, work structuring and proper distributions of tasks between men and machines can sometimes be more helpful than selection and training of personnel.

One could carry this argument even further and challenge, as some people do, the basic assumptions underlying the classical selection tradition as such. Conceiving an organization as a dynamic and flexible entity to be developed and to be given meaning *vis-à-vis* an ever changing and ambiguous environment and as a system in which the members, interacting with each other and with the environment, define reality rather than start from it leaves little room for the classical selection paradigm. In the latter the organization is seen as a given, stable, well established system with predetermined objectives and predefined criteria for 'good' and 'unsatisfactory' behaviour. In the former conception of an organization there is little room at all for a separation of the 'good' and the 'bad', the 'men' and the 'boys' prior to the entry into the organization. It should be replaced by an approach in which assessment, training and organizational development are combined into an integrated well balanced human resource and development policy.

A third way in which the selection was taken out of its isolated position was the general decision-making approach to problems of personnel allocation. In this approach first of all a clear distinction was made between *probabilities* of certain outcomes of personnel decisions on the one hand (often to be determined by the—psychological—predictors) and the *values* of these outcomes (being a result of a subjective evaluation by key figures in the system) on the other. It also stressed the need to specify all kinds of parameters that have to be taken into account, such as: the seriousness (in terms of costs) of wrong decisions (both the accepted unsatisfactory employees and the rejected good ones); the proper balance in the avoidance of false positives and false negatives; the importance of antecedent probabilities and selection ratios, and the like. Of particular importance in this respect is to take into account the labour market. Changes in requirements of abilities, skills, knowledge and appearance result from economic and technological developments. And those changes often take place at a very rapid pace nowadays. It will be clear that these changes can alter the antecedent probabilities and the selection ratios dramatically, and, consequently, the success ratio of selection. Personnel selection specialists should have sufficient insight in the present and future labour market dynamics in order to adapt their selection strategy accordingly.

A fourth factor in the widening of the scope of the selection psychologist is stimulated by what may be called the awakening of the applicant. The classical selection paradigm with the prevalence of the interests and values of the organization can no longer be taken for granted. The unilateral approach had to be replaced by an approach in which it is emphasized that selection decisions are bilateral in nature. A match has to be created between two 'systems'—the individual and the organization—each with its own input, expectations and needs. More and more often the 'rights' of the applicants are being acknowledged: rights to receive a humane and fair treatment; rights to be properly informed about both the requirements and rewards of the organization and the procedures of making the selection decisions; rights to be protected from unjustifiable violation of confidentiality and invasion of privacy, from the unnecessary use of disguised techniques and questionnaires and from discriminatory effects as a result of assessment or selection.

Particularly this last issue, the possible bias or discrimination in selection, has received wide and critical attention both in Europe and in the United States. Criticism includes the accusation that psychological tests provide less opportunity to members of linguistic and cultural minority groups to show potential abilities, and, therefore, contribute to an unfair and discriminatory treatment of the latter. Whether or not this claim can be substantiated or denied, it proves sufficiently that selection theory and practice, because of its societal and political impact, should be designed and evaluated within a larger moral and legal framework and in view of possible societal consequences.

A fifth and final point to be made in this respect is the growing awareness of the fact that selection cannot be isolated from other measures and provisions within the general personnel policy of a company. Selection is preceded by advertisement and recruitment and immediately followed by treatments such as introduction and training. Moreover, many pieces of information utilized in selection are derived from data collected in other phases of the career of employees, including performance appraisal, task analysis, promotion and career opportunities within the company, reward systems, etc. It would be extremely unwise to treat selection as an isolated phenomenon and to dissociate it from the general organizational personnel system. Selection should be conceived as a first and integral phase in the total career guidance system of personnel in the organization.

The authors in Section 1 address themselves to the various issues indicated above. Each one of them discusses a particular facet of the wider context in which assessment and selection should be placed.

Richard Williams starts off by showing that changes and developments in the job market do have a clear impact on patterns of employment and, consequently, on recruitment and selection.

In the second chapter Gerrit Boerlijst and Geert Meijboom depict assessment, which they describe as the central issue in matching the indiviudal and the organization, within the more general framework of a theory of career development.

In the third chapter Peter Dachler questions the applicability, the usefulness and the acceptability of the classical selection paradigm based upon the prediction of how well a person will perform on a specific, predefined job in a given unchanging organization.

In the fourth chapter Pieter Drenth, in discussing the issues of possible discrimination of psychological testing, shows that the criteria 'maximal effectiveness' and 'equal opportunities' are incompatible and that it is a policy decision to what extent both goals should be met in a possible compromise.

Charles de Wolff challenges in the fifth chapter the classical selection model and its psychological assumptions, such as the identifiability of permanent personality traits with sufficient predictive power, and the availability of relevant stable organizational criteria to be used for the selection decisions.

In the sixth chapter Paul Jansen demonstrates that information or computerization creates a new set of functions for which different abilities are needed. Among others a greater stress on fluid mental abilities and personality traits such as flexibility and decisiveness is required.

In the seventh and final chapter of this section Sylvia Shimmin puts the selection practice in a wider European context. This chapter illustrates that broader constellations of societal factors clearly affect the practice of selection across the continent.

Together, these authors depict convincingly that the 'contextualization' of selection is a *sine qua non* for a full appreciation of not only the techniques, but also the organizational and societal impact of psychological assessment and selection.

Chapter 1.1

Patterns of Employment and the Job Market

RICHARD S. WILLIAMS

Middlesex Business School, Middlesex Polytechnic, The Burroughs, Hendon, London NW4 4BT, UK

INTRODUCTION

This chapter will provide an overview of some of the main changes to have taken place in job markets, patterns of employment and work organization. Where data are available certain of the major trends within Europe will be described with, by way of comparison, some illustrations from Japan and the United States. It should be noted, however, that there are many problems in making international comparisons of labour force data. As Walsh and King (1986) point out, for example, custom and practice in the compilation of labour force data vary from country to country both in respect to what data are collected and how; accordingly, the evidence presented should be taken as being indicative of broad trends. Also, certain developments are less well documented than are others and information about how widespread some of the working patterns are is not readily available. Consequently, it is the nature of the working practices which will be described rather than their extent. However, the purpose here is not so much to explain as rather to describe so as to give an overview of the range of contemporary employment and working patterns.

Some of the changes have implications of various kinds for recruitment and selection—both what an organization looks for and the methods used. Not all of the consequences are new—though working patterns are changing many are long-established—but some of them have increased in importance. These implications will be briefly introduced here with the themes being developed more fully in later chapters.

Handbook of Assessment in Organizations   Edited by P. Herriot
© 1989 John Wiley & Sons Ltd

THE LABOUR FORCE

Table 1 shows the size of the employed labour force in several European and other countries; it also indicates trends over a ten-year period (1974–83, where possible), activity rates and unemployment rates. As can be seen, most countries have shown some increase in the size of their employed labour force but in four countries there has been a drop.

Table 1   Labour force trends, activity rates by gender, and unemployment rates

| | Employed labour force (000s) | Labour force trend (%) | Activity rates | | Unemployment | |
			Men (%)	Women (%)	Rate (%)	Change (%)
Belgium	3667	−5.5	78.7	50.2	14.0	213.7
Denmark	2420	1.2	87.6	74.2	11.0	152.1
France	21729	0.4	77.2	56.1	9.7	154.6
W. Germany	25187	−5.2	79.1	49.4	8.6	111.0
Greece	3509	7.5	79.3	40.0	8.5	487.5
Ireland	1125	5.4	87.1	37.9	16.0	190.4
Italy	20921	4.5	79.5	40.2	10.2	94.5
Japan	57330	9.5	88.4	57.2	2.6	56.0
Luxembourg	158	1.7	86.6	41.8	1.9	900.0
Netherlands	5038	6.4	68.9	34.3	14.0	219.2
Norway	1957	20.0	87.7	60.3	3.0	52.5
Portugal	4038	1.9	88.4	55.1	7.9	50.0
Spain	11237	−15.9	83.7	34.7	20.1	364.2
Sweden	4224	6.6	87.2	78.8	3.1	104.5
UK	24027	−5.0	86.1	59.9	13.0	261.6
USA	103033	15.7	87.0	64.3	7.4	7.7

Source: Walsh and King (1986).

What the overall figures conceal are gender variations in activity rates. Indeed, one of the most significant trends to have taken place in the past decade or so has been the marked increase (in many countries) in the number of women in the labour market, with some decline in men's participation. None the less, the activity rates for men are higher than those for women, in some countries the rate for men being double that for women.

Perhaps the single most important implication of the change in the gender make-up of the labour force is that it reinforces the already existing need for equitable selection as between the sexes. What this means for employers in practice is already well documented (see Chapter 1.4 in this volume).

Another of the more important trends has been the increase in rates of unemployment. Despite the different ways in which unemployment figures are calculated, the data in Table 1 give a reasonable impression of the developments which have taken place. In all of the countries listed there has been an increase in unemployment both in the rate and in numbers. Again, there is considerable variability in the rate, between 2 and 20 per cent, and in the extent of change over a ten-year period. Even countries where there is a relatively low rate of unemployment have shown a substantial increase in the numbers unemployed; the most striking example of this is Luxembourg.

More recent figures indicate that unemployment rates have continued to increase in certain countries whereas in others they appear to have declined. One factor, which seems likely to have played a part in reducing levels of employment, has been the introduction, in some countries, of special employment and training measures. In this regard a particular area of concern, throughout Europe, has been the transition from education to employment. The European Community has a programme of projects concerned with this transition and two elements have a particular relevance to assessment. First, there is the work which has been done to identify the 'competence'—skills, abilities, personality traits, attitudes, and knowledge—required in the adult world. Second, there have been developments in methods of assessment. In particular, there has been increasing recognition that traditional educational assessment, with its emphasis on knowledge, neglects the other competences. There has been some move towards assessment based on records of personal achievement, for example (European Community, 1985).

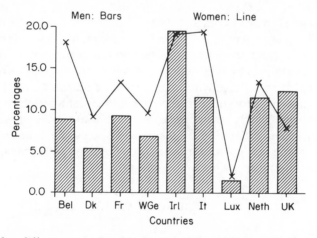

Figure 1 Gender differences in levels of unemployment for several countries. [EEC Labour Force Survey; IDS (1987).]

In the same way that there are gender differences in activity rates so too are there such differences in levels of unemployment. Figure 1 shows data for a number of European countries for August 1987. As can be seen, the difference is slight in some countries and in Ireland and the United Kingdom the rate is higher for men that it is for women. Typically, however, the proportion of unemployed women is greater than that of men.

So, as the 1980s come to a close there remains an over-supply of labour. For most occupations, therefore, there is less of a recruitment problem whereas selection difficulties may have been heightened. As Lewis (1985) points out, 'In practical terms, attracting applicants is less of an issue, but administration and deciding whom to offer employment to are more difficult with large numbers'. This position is reversed for those occupations where skill shortages remain.

One trend in Britain, attributed in part to rising unemployment, has been the greater use of informal methods of recruitment (Ford *et al.*, 1986; Wood, 1986); word-of-mouth recruitment is an example. Such methods undoubtedly have advantages for the employer—they are relatively cheap, the employer will not be deluged with a large number of applications, and so on. But certain categories of employee may be disadvantaged by the use of word-of-mouth recruiting. For example, where the existing workforce is predominantly white or male (or both) the existing composition is likely to be maintained by the use of word-of-mouth; in consequence, the employment prospects of women and members of ethnic minority groups will suffer. This is a disturbing aspect of the apparent increase in the use of this method.

To the extent that the economic environment remains harsh for many employers, redundancy will continue to be a phenomenon in the 1990s. Thus, there remains the question of how this employment (rather, unemployment) decision will be made. Probably, employers will seek to avoid the decision by relying on natural wastage, redeployment (where it is possible) and last in–first out. But these devices will not always work and in such circumstances it is far from clear how the decision is made in practice. For example, a survey by the British Institute of Personnel Management (1980) reported that organizations claimed that work performance was a major criterion in selecting senior executives for redundancy. However, the researchers were able to find few examples of rigorous procedures being used to identify those who might be made redundant. And this begs the question about what procedure is to be used: the existing performance appraisal system, perhaps? Clearly, the danger here is that using the appraisal system in this way may lead to inflated assessments with the possible consequence that the appraisals become less useful for other (developmental) purposes, thereby discrediting the scheme as a whole.

HOURS OF WORK

The 'normal' working week

The first point to make is that there are problems in defining what is the normal working week or day (and this difficulty becomes all the greater as we see more and more variations in working patterns). Thierry and Jansen (1984) give some of the history of working hours but for present purposes it is more appropriate to indicate briefly current patterns. Within many European countries the 'normal' working week is about 40 hours; others show some variation from this norm, the United Kingdom and Denmark being lower and Greece and Ireland higher. Some comparative data from Income Data Services (IDS, 1986) suggest that in the United States the average number of hours worked each week is much the same as the 'norm' for Europe, whereas in Japan the figure is quite a bit higher—on average 46 hours a week.

Table 2 Trends in part-time and full-time employment

	% growth 1973–83 FT	% growth 1973–83 PT	PT as % of total employment (1973)	PT as % of total employment (1983)	% Growth rates 1973–83				Proportion of women			
					Females FT	Females PT	Males FT	Males PT	1973 FT	1973 PT	1983 FT	1983 PT
France	0.2	100.1	5.1	9.6	3.2	104.5	–1.4	80.1	29.6	93.7	36.0	84.6
W. Germany	–4.0	65.4	7.7	12.6	–3.8	65.2	–4.0	68.5	30.9	92.0	30.9	91.9
Japan	6.2	26.6	13.6	15.8	4.8	32.2	6.9	13.8	35.0	82.7	33.1	72.8
Netherlands	–6.0	453.6	4.4	21.0	–2.7	436.4	–6.9	525.8	20.1	80.9	20.8	78.4
Sweden	–2.0	37.2	16.2	24.3	8.9	32.6	–6.4	68.2	29.9	87.4	32.2	84.2
United Kingdom	–6.7	21.9	15.3	18.9	0.8	18.2	–9.5	66.1	26.7	92.3	28.9	89.6
United States	14.8	19.7	14.3	14.1	32.9	23.9	5.7	11.2	33.3	66.3	38.5	69.3

Source: Neubourg (1985).
FT full time.
PT part time.

Part-time working

In a recent review Neubourg (1985) has shown that over a ten-year (1973–83) period part-time employment has increased in many countries in Europe, Japan and the United States (see Table 2). There are variations from country to country, and indeed there are within-country variations according to the employment sector being considered. However, it seems clear that part-time working has increased at a faster rate than has full-time employment, the latter having dropped in some countries. Furthermore, part-time working has increased both for men and for women, but again with some variation across countries.

A particularly noticeable feature of part-time working is the large proportion of women found therein. Thus, the data reported by Neubourg (see Table 2) show the share of women in full-time and part-time employment and it can be seen that women comprise the large majority of part-time workers. As compared to men women dominate part-time employment by a factor of between two and four, depending on the country. The distribution of men and women in part-time and full-time employment is shown in a slightly different way in a recent EEC Labour Force Survey (IDS, 1987): of the men in employment well over 90 per cent, typically, are employed full time. For women, however, there is much greater variability across countries as the data in Figure 2 show.

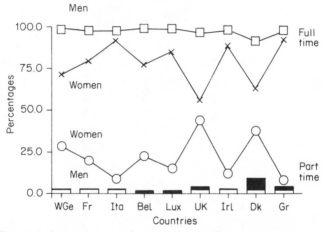

Figure 2   Full-time and part time employment by gender in several European countries. [EEC Labour Force Survey; IDS (1987).]

It should also be noted that the participation rate of married women is greater in part-time employment than it is in full-time employment. For example, in France 63 per cent of women workers in full-time employment were married and the comparable proportion for those in part-time employment was 79 per cent. The 1983 figures (Neubourg, 1985) for some other European countries were:

W. Germany	FT: 51%	PT: 86%
Netherlands	FT: 38%	PT: 79%
United Kingdom	FT: 56%	PT: 84%

What all these gross figures imply are patterns of occupational segregation. These have existed for decades, with women most commonly employed in a narrower range of occupations than are men and more women than men usually being found at the lower organizational levels. Such segregation is widespread: for example, reported by Davidson (1987) as occurring throughout EEC countries, Australia and the United States.

Earlier, the recruitment and selection implications of women in the labour force were touched on; but there may also be other assessment implications—for example, in appraisal schemes and assessment for promotion. This certainly will be the case for many women in full-time employment and, again, the practical actions that employers need to take are well documented; the volume edited by Davidson and Cooper (1984), for example, reviews many of the issues pertaining to the employment of women in various countries around the world. But women in part-time employment may find themselves not subject to any formal assessment of their performance at all. Often, part-time workers are not covered by appraisal schemes; in consequence, training and development needs are not considered and women may be disadvantaged in terms of their career progress. This disadvantaging effect may be reinforced by the move towards employment patterns which draw a distinction between 'core' and 'periphery' staff, as described in the next section.

EMPLOYMENT AND WORKING PATTERNS

'Core' versus 'periphery'

The watchword for the 1980s, and for the foreseeable future, has become 'flexibility'. One element of this flexibility is the distinction now being drawn between 'core' and 'periphery' staff. Those in the 'core' will be the key staff on whom the organization depends for its future. They are likely to be employed on relatively 'permanent' contracts and will be eligible for career development opportunities not only of the kind traditionally available, i.e. upward advancement, but also lateral movement. Indeed, there will be the expectation that those in the 'core' must be functionally flexible—retraining and redeployment will be the normal pattern for 'core' employees. For these people it is likely that the traditional sorts of assessments will still be needed; after all, there will be decisions to be made about promotion and about job transfers. But, being key staff adds to the importance of these decisions and this implies that a reliance on appraisals and interviews is misplaced. The use of more rigorous methods, such as psychological tests and simulations, would therefore seem to be justified.

Those in the 'periphery', proportionately a larger group than the 'core', will be of two broad kinds. There will be some who will be employed on a relatively permanent basis like those in the core. These will be workers in low skilled jobs where there is often a high level of turnover, this turnover giving the organization the flexibility it needs to manage employment levels. For these staff the assessment demands will not be particularly great. Indeed, so far as appraisal is concerned the current performance of such staff typically is not appraised at present and it is hard to envisage that this will change. And there seems not to be a need to assess future potential given that these staff probably will not have any advancement opportunities.

The second group of 'periphery' workers comprises those working according to a variety of contractual arrangements with time being the key factor. Thus, this category will include part-time workers, job sharers, those on short-term or fixed-term contracts, and the like. Sub-contracting, the use of temporary staff agencies and various consulting arrangements also come into this category.

Although there is some dispute (ACAS, 1987; IDS, 1988a,b; Marginson and Sisson, 1988) about the prevalence of these forms of employment and working (at least in Britain) they are none the less sufficiently common for the assessment needs to be already well recognized. For some groups it appears that no need for assessment is seen. Part-time workers are a good example. Though an initial selection decision has to be made, it is likely that after that no formal assessment of performance will be made. This tends to be the case in the United Kingdom, part-time employees typically being excluded from appraisal schemes. And it is likely that this situation will only change as and when more part-time employment becomes available at higher levels within organizations. There is little evidence to suggest that this will happen, although it is possible that one force for such change will be pressure from women (who presently dominate part-time employment) seeking career development opportunities while wishing to work still on a part-time basis.

One consequence of the division into 'core' and 'periphery' is that the 'periphery' may serve as a route into the 'core', in other words an extended recruitment and selection mechanism. This may operate, for example, with certain specialist staff initially employed on a temporary contract or part-time basis. Thus, it may be a way of 'trying out' staff; if they perform satisfactorily (or better) they may be offered employment within the 'core'. What remains a matter for speculation, however, is how the assessment will be made; probably not using a formal scheme. If this is what happens the danger will be much as with the use of word-of-mouth recruiting, namely that certain groups will be disadvantaged.

Perhaps one of the major changes in employment has been the increase in different types of working pattern. Some patterns are long established, such as *shift working*, although we have seen different shift systems being introduced over the years. Kogi (1985) reports a considerable increase in the incidence of shift work over a period of 50 years or so with a rise during more recent years being particularly noticeable in developing countries.

Also long established is *overtime*, i.e. working time which is longer than the norm agreed by contract. The incidence of this has tended to fluctuate somewhat according to the prevailing economic conditions but the general trend appears to be towards employers endeavouring to decrease overtime. *Temporary work* has had its peaks and troughs. In the recessionary years it declined somewhat in the United Kingdom but there are some signs of a resurgence. This may have something to do with the shift towards 'core' and 'periphery' employment patterns.

Then there are working patterns with a somewhat shorter history: *flexible working hours* are one example. The idea is that employees work the same total number of hours as is the norm but they are given some choice over when the hours are worked. An employee could work more than the norm in one day, say ten rather than eight hours, and so build up a number of extra days' holiday. There usually are agreements to regulate the procedures to be followed.

A rather different kind of flexibility is the *compressed working day and working week*. Included in this heading are such practices as four- or four-and-a-half-day or four-night working weeks, 'job-and-finish' (i.e. a set amount of work is to be done and when it is complete the worker leaves), and annual hours.

Yet another kind of flexibility is with respect to the place of work. A well established example is *homeworking*. This traditionally is associated with light assembly and craft occupations, predominantly employing women, but the advent of new computer-based information technology allows for the extension of homeworking to new groups of employees. Indeed, they may not necessarily be employees in the traditional sense, their services being retained perhaps on some other kind of contractual basis, such as consultancy. Thus, homeworkers would be part of the organization's 'periphery'. Various managerial and professional occupations may well be affected by this development.

One illustration of this is the 'networking' project in Rank Xerox in the United Kingdom (Judkins, West, and Drew, 1985). Judkins and others define 'networking' as 'a system of work in which selected and trained volunteers leave their parent company and found their own business, which then contracts to provide specified services to the parent company among other clients, and uses a microcomputer link to do so'.

How are the volunteers selected? The selection procedure has a number of interesting elements. One is that it is a mutual process between the parties involved—the 'networker', his or her manager, support staff (if any) and the networker's spouse or partner (if there is one). All must agree to the shift to becoming a 'networker'. Other 'networkers' also are involved; they discuss the prospective 'networker's' business idea. Though their assent is not required, this discussion may reveal a project which should be rejected. Third, psychological tests are used with confidential feedback being provided to the prospective 'networker'.

As well as being interesting from a selection point of view—especially the mutuality of the process—this project also is interesting because 'networking' can be seen as a new form of work organization; this is the subject of the next section.

CHANGES IN WORK ORGANIZATION

During the course of this century many changes in job design and work organization have been seen. Scientific management, job rotation, job enlargement and job enrichment (whether on an individual or group basis) represent the main themes. But there have been other developments. For example, there are different organizational forms like 'networking'; another is the matrix form. As discussed in Chapter 5.7, this has implications for appraisal. Where the individual has more than one boss, as in a matrix organization, there is a case for 'multiple appraisal' which involves all parties who can make an informed assessment of the individual's performance. In this way appraisal also may become a more mutual process involving not only line managers but also the individual appraisee and perhaps subordinates.

In recent years, perhaps the greatest impact on work organization derives from the increasing use of computer based technology in an ever-widening range of jobs at many different levels. There are examples of jobs having been enhanced, in the senses of using more skills or using higher level skills (or both), and there are examples of de-skilling having resulted. However, it should be recognized that the changes in the design of jobs do not necessarily result from the technology itself but rather from management decisions about how the technology is to be used. The main points to note here are that changes in work organization have resulted and that these changes have altered skill requirements. There consequently may be new assessment needs. (See Chapter 1.6 for a more detailed discussion.)

CHANGES IN PEOPLE'S ATTITUDES

A final issue to be considered concerns changes in people's attitudes and expectations, in particular expectations about the work they wish to do, about their career progress, and about the balance that they wish to achieve between their work and non-work lives. (Much interesting evidence on these points is to be found in the report of the Meaning of Working International Research Team, 1987.) The plans that people have about these matters are important for organizations as they may have implications for the employment decisions, such as redeployment or relocation, which employers may wish to take.

There are a number of aspects to this general issue. For example, the increased number of women in employment has brought more and more dual-career couples. In the traditional family it was the man's career decisions which were paramount but now, and in the future, there will be many more cases in which either or both spouses may be faced with important career decisions having family implications. Employers will need to be sensitive to these matters; indeed, there is the implication that employment decision making, especially in regard to job transfers, has to be a more mutual process than traditionally has been the case. In other words, employment decisions will become negotiated decisions (Herriot, 1984; Schein, 1978) and this means that employers will have to take much more care to find out about the career aspirations of their employees (and prospective employees).

To reinforce this point it is worth noting that there is greater advocacy today of career self-development (Fletcher and Williams, 1985) and there is some suggestive evidence that people wish to have more say in the decisions that are made about their careers. So, not only will employers' information seeking need to be more thorough, but also their information sharing will have to increase too. These actions have to be taken if there is to be a better match between what is desired by workers and what employers are able (or willing) to provide.

REFERENCES

ACAS (1987). *Labour Flexibility in Britain: The 1987 ACAS Survey*. Advisory, Conciliation and Arbitration Service, London.

Davidson, M. (1987). Women and Employment. in P.B. Warr (ed.), *Psychology at Work*. Penguin, Harmondsworth, Middx, pp. 223–46.

Davidson, M.J., and Cooper, C.L. (eds) (1984). *Working Women: An International Survey*. Wiley, Chichester.

European Community (1985). *Transition of Young People from Education to Adult and Working Life: Interim Report 1985*. European Community, Brussels.

Fletcher, C., and Williams, R. (1985). *Performance Appraisal and Career Development*. Hutchinson, London.

Ford, J.R., Bryman, A., Beardsworth, A.D., Bresne, M., Keil, E.T., and Jenkins, R. (1986). Changing patterns of labour recruitment, *Personnel Review*, **15**, 14–18.

Herriot, P. (1984). *Down from the Ivory Tower*. Wiley, Chichester.

Incomes Data Services (1986). International working time cuts more apparent than real, *IDS International Report*, **264**, 6–7.

Incomes Data Services (1987). EEC Labour Force Survey, *IDS European Report*, **283**, 6–7.

Incomes Data Services (1988a). Flexible Working, *IDS Study* **407**.

Incomes Data Services (1988b). Re-organising Working Time, *IDS Study* **417**.

Institute of Personnel Management (1980). Executive Redundancy, IPM Information Report No. 30, Institute of Personnel Management, London.

Judkins, P., West, D., and Drew, J. (1985). *Networking in Organizations*. Gower, Aldershot, Hants.

Kogi, K. (1985). Introduction to the problems of shift-work, in S. Folkard and T.H. Monk (eds), *Hours of Work*. Wiley, Chichester.

Lewis, C. (1985). *Employee Selection*. Hutchinson, London.

Marginson, P., and Sisson, K. (1988). The management of employees, in P. Marginson, P.K. Edwards, R. Martin, J. Purcell, and K. Sisson (eds), *Beyond the Workplace: Managing Industrial Relations in the Multi-establishment Enterprise*. Basil Blackwell, Oxford.

Meaning of Working International Research Team (1987). *The Meaning of Working*. Academic Press, London.

Neubourg, C. de (1985). Part-time work: international quantitative comparison, *International Labour Review*, **124**, 559–76.

Schein, E. (1978). *Career Dynamics*. Addison-Wesley, Reading, Mass.

Thierry, H., and Jansen, B. (1984). Work and working time, in *Handbook of Work and Organizational Psychology*. Wiley, Chichester.

Walsh, K., and King, A. (1986). *Handbook of International Manpower Market Comparisons*. Macmillan, London.

Wood, S. (1986). Personnel management and recruitment, *Personnel Review*, **15**, 3–11.

Chapter 1.2

Matching the Individual and the Organization

GERRIT BOERLIJST[1] and GEERT MEIJBOOM[2]

[1]*Technische Hogeschool Twente, Dedrijfskunde, Postbus 217 7500, AE Drienerlo, Enschede, The Netherlands*
[2]*Provinciale Gelderse, Energie Maatschappij, Arnhem, The Netherlands*

INTRODUCTION

Developments in society in technical, socio-cultural and economic fields have always had an influence on activities of theory development and research within the domain of social sciences. This is especially true when we are concerned with the relationship between individual and work context. Results of empirical social scientific research have, in their turn, led to changes in people's opinions and perceptions of work and work behaviour. The evolution in thinking about critical human success factors for work organizations, starting from the restricted perception of 'social engineering' towards the broad and maybe euphoric view of 'development of human resources' (Peters and Waterman, 1982; Fombrun, Tichy, and Devanna, 1984; Hall and Goodale, 1986; Schein, 1978), can only be understood against the background of historical movements and changes which have taken place in the structure of society at large and in the way in which the accompanying models of man have changed during the last 50 years.

There has been a growing awareness within organizations, that the continuance of their business depends to a large degree on the quality of the 'human resources' and also the quality of the management thereof. Human resources management implies conscious and specific directing of human effort in the short and long term. 'Assessment' can be seen as a central issue, namely as an important condition for influencing and organizing human behaviour in the

Handbook of Assessment in Organizations   Edited by P. Herriot
© 1989 John Wiley & Sons Ltd

direction of the objectives of the organization (as well as in the direction of those of individual job incumbents).

Within the context of the work organization the term 'assessment' indicates, in its broader sense, collecting and processing relevant information in a systematic and reliable manner with a view to realizing and maintaining adequate matching between the organization and its surroundings on the one hand (external matching) and between the sub-systems of the organizations on the other hand (internal matching). Assessment activities form an essential part of the integral management process, directed to the development, implementation and execution of the performance strategy of the organization.

Evans (1986) distinguishes the following types of important matching processes:

- '. . . matching resource capabilities and limits with environmental opportunities and risks' (strategic management);
- '. . . achieving congruence between task, technology, attitudes and roles' (job design);
- '. . . fitting the right people into the right jobs' (performance management);
- '. . . and doing this at the right time' (career management).

In the context of this handbook, 'assessment' refers to the performance and flexibility of individuals within the organization and to all the relevant related person and organization variables, with a view to the realization of a desired match between individual and organization for the short and/or long term.

In the following section we will circumscribe our theme 'Matching the individual and the organization' more thoroughly.

DEFINING THE DOMAIN

The relationship between the individual and the organization in an historical perspective

Throughout the ages people have performed work and have always been fully aware of this. The evaluation of human work has undergone an evolution in the course of time. In successive societies, such as we meet in the development of Western civilization, human work has been experienced in different ways. Work has been successively considered as a curse, a stultifying activity, a punishment from God, a duty, and finally as an occupation with its own intrinsic value (Nosow and Form, 1962).

The phenomenon of the division of work is as old as work itself, but up to the middle of the eighteenth century it had never been the object of what we nowadays refer to as rational–empirical scientific thinking. In medieval times we find a dominating economy which the German economist Sombart (1863–1941) refers to as *Bedarfsdeckungswirtschaft*. This economy was geared to satisfying the requirements of everyone according to his or her position and status in society. The primary classification principle for social stratification in this feudal society was not work, but property. Nosow and Form (1962, p. 9) say the following about this: 'To ask men in such underdeveloped traditional societies why they work is similar to asking why they stay alive. This is not true for modern industrial man. To ask him what he seeks from his work is to ask a reasonable question, for work has more meaning than mere survival or maintaining tradition.'

The change in the evaluation of work as an intrinsic useful human and societal activity dates from the late Middle Ages. From that time onwards the traditional division of work gradually makes way for a professional division of work on an economic basis—a change towards an *Erwerbswirtschaft* (Sombart), in which production is for profit and for an anonymous market.

With the rise of modern capitalism at the end of the eighteenth century, the professional division of work was further institutionalized. Industrial organization came into prominence, with its rationally planned, hierarchically structured, functional division of work and with a strict separation between capital and labour. The issue of matching individual and organizational objectives and needs dates from this time.

The development of the professional division of work forms the causal background for some socio-scientific schools of thought. The economist Adam Smith, with his major work *An Inquiry into the Nature and Causes of the Wealth of Nations* (1776), provided the impulse for the creation of organizational sociology and the well-known doctrine of 'scientific management'. Smith was particularly interested in the technique of the production process, whereby productivity, and therefore also profits and prosperity, could be improved by means of drastic task specialization. The French sociologist Durkheim focused attention on the social results of the professional division of work for society. In his book *De la Division du Travail Social* (Durkheim, 1893), he laid the foundations of what was later called 'occupational sociology'.

The attempts by the British scientist Francis Galton (1822–1911) to explain differences in professions and statuses of professions in terms of parental inheritance of personal 'occupational characteristics' have led to the creation of 'differential psychology', in which 'trait theories' play an important role. Miller (1974) stresses the fact that trait theories are mostly based upon 'matching models'. Within the context of those theories one thinks in terms of possibilities to match person traits with the demands of life, or, more specifically, with the demands of an occupation or job. Trait theories have found their practical application value in career counselling and personnel selection.

The present-day Western concept of work has an economic and social foundation. The economic basis lies in the fact that the level of prosperity of individual and society is dependent on the outcomes of work productivity on a national scale. Society expects from its individual members and groups a substantive contribution to the production process of goods and services with a view to maintaining and promoting a socially acceptable and desired standard of life. The social basis of the Western concept of work is founded on the fact that individuals and groups within society derive their basic values and objectives largely from their role and position in the work process. The profession, the job, the position and the working environment are among the main sources from which people derive their social security, status, prestige and scope to develop their abilities.

Just as society—and at intermediate level the work organization—makes requirements and has expectations of human work behaviour, in the same way individuals make requirements of their work context and have personal expectations with regard to it. Each individual aims at specific, individual objectives in the production process in the light of his or her ideas about personal contentment and development.

The following present-day developments, trends and conditions in society make high demands on the individual and on the work organization in terms of flexibility, adaptability and coping with uncertainties:

– Developments in the area of information and computer technology.
– Multiformity and differentiation of consumer needs.
– A rise in the average level of education of the labour market.
– Changes in the work ethos with the accent on 'quality of life'.
– A continuing increase in the average age of the working population and an increase in the number of women in the working population (Fombrun, 1984).

Present-day society has a complex and turbulent character, with a strong dynamic influence on the interacting relationship between the individual and the organization.

Two dimensions of matching: performance and flexibility

Webster's English College Dictionary (Gay *et al.*, 1984) defines the word 'match' as follows:

– to find a counterpart for;
– to fit together or make suitable for fitting together.

We state that these meanings are applicable to the relationship 'individual–organization' as well. We then can define a good matching as a real or at least expected congruence between known and relevant qualities of both parties, qualities they need for reaching their respective, and sometimes common, aims and objectives.

The concept 'matching' encompasses a more passive and a more active connotation.

In its more passive sense, 'matching' means taking a *decision*, based on a one-off assessment of the situation, to reach a 'goodness of fit' between individual and organizational needs and possibilities. Such a decision involves an once-only 'informed choice' (Brousseau, 1983), and most often it's the result of compromises (Taylor and Pryor, 1985). The example is 'personnel selection and placement', but also other so-called 'career decisions' belong to this category.

In its more active connotation, matching means an *intervention*, aimed at the accomplishment of a 'good fit' not only in the short but also in the long run. In this case the term 'good fit' refers to the active adjustment of the individual to the organization or vice versa.

In both above-mentioned meanings of matching, an aspiration to stability is expressed. Organizations as well as personnel are seen as more or less stable entities, that are not expected to change dramatically in the course of time.

Most existing matching methods have *stability of work performance* as their aim. They are in line with a relatively static and deterministic picture of the world, in which a certain invariance and stability are attributed to human being and environment; a picture in which *predictability* and *certainty* are dominating concepts. The roots of this paradigm reach far back into the nineteenth century.

Nowadays the view is gaining ground that this static picture on which the matching paradigm is based, is inadequate and offers insufficient guarantees for the survival of organizations and the people involved. Our present-day society is no longer characterized by stability, relative homogeneity and certainty. On the contrary, the ever increasing speed of change has resulted in the need for people and organizations to adapt continuously in a flexible way. Product life cycles are becoming shorter all the time and performance criteria and working techniques are out of date almost from one day to the next. Traditional planning and prognosis models are no longer seen as valid instruments for the long-term prediction of the future.

Flexibility is the strategic objective which society imposes on itself and its individual members. Flexibility is considered as a new effectiveness criterion—alongside performance—for the individual and the work organization. Achieving a greater flexibility of individual and organization forces a reconsideration of the traditional 'matching paradigm'. It is now assumed that people and organizations are dynamic entities which are changing all the time, intentionally or unintentionally.

Flexibility encompasses two essential matching targets:

1. *Achieving flexibility of performance* by means of organizing a continuous process of mutual matching and adjustment to changing situations and needs.
2. *Achieving flexibility of human resources* in order to create potential matching possibilities in the still unknown future. What this involves is the stimulation of a wider availability of people on the basis of *exploration* of new, unused competencies of people.

Both targets ask for an integrated process of continuous assessment and intervention, both by the organization and its individual members.

The present-day relationship between the individual and the organization is characterized by its symbiotic and dynamic nature (Von Glinow *et al.*, 1983; London and Stumpf, 1986). Organizations and individual employees are interdependent in their aspiration to their own specific objectives. This relationship has at the same time a dynamic character because the needs and objectives of both parties are constantly subject to changes. Changes are a result of developments in the environment and of the processes of internal learning, growth, stagnation and ageing.

The term 'flexibility for the future' refers indirectly to time-related concepts such as 'development' and 'change'. Here we have to face the problem, whether development and change in organizations and/or individuals are predictable or not. This depends on the possibility or impossibility of uncertainty reduction with respect to events and processes in the future.

MATCHING AND THE PROBLEM OF UNCERTAINTY: STRATEGIC HUMAN RESOURCE MANAGEMENT

For managers uncertainty implies future situations and circumstances by which their organizations might be influenced in a positive or negative manner. In essence the problem of change over a period of time is explicitly formulated in most corporate strategies today and expressed by the term 'flexibility'.

Flexibility can be described as the capacity an organization possesses to adjust in an adequate and effective manner to external and internal changing demands and needs. Nowadays flexibility in many cases is interpreted as 'adjustment by innovation', especially focused on organizational work behaviour and organizational 'capacities' (human, technological and financial resources) (Kanter, 1983).

Strategic management is the answer many companies have developed to the problem of uncertainty. Strategic management essentially involves two different but related processes of adjustment: external and internal.

External adjustment refers to the managerial task of matching organizational and work behaviour to external situations and developments. Internal adjustment refers to matching organizational resources to new or changed strategic targets. One essential organizational capacity involves 'human resources'. Management of human resources in terms of managerial effectiveness (flexibility and competitive performance) and psycho-social effectiveness (equity, improved human relations and the quality of working life) is a core target in the strategy of many organizations today (Evans, 1986; Fombrun, Tichy, and Devanna, 1984; Hall and Goodale, 1986). Human resource management has become an integrated part of general strategic management. Practically, this means that human resources are objects of management interventions, i.e. adjustments at the strategic, tactical and operational level (Devanna *et al.*, 1984). A basic, underlying assumption of strategic human resource management is that the organizational needs, in terms of human competencies, and the needs of individual employees, in terms of career development, are continuously changing. Career management therefore is a core dimension of human resource management which implies: career analysis, career development policy, career planning, career counselling and career controlling (monitoring). The 'Human Resource Development and Planning Model' as constructed by Schein (1978) is an example of how these career-oriented activities—from an organizational as well as an individual point of view—can be logically and sequentially integrated.

MATCHING AND DEVELOPMENT

The traditional definition of matching is—as we mentioned earlier—the once-only determination of the degree of congruence between relevant characteristics of the individual and the work organization, on the basis of which both parties decide by mutual consent to enter into a work relationship for a certain time. In this sense matching is primarily a staffing issue for the organization and an issue of choice of profession, or choice of career for the individual. The purpose of matching is to make an effective contribution to the 'quality of organizational and individual life'. The primary concern here is with the quality of the performance or the performance outcomes.

In accordance with this conception, the so-called 'match-makers' (i.e. management and individual) work from the assumption that the relevant properties and characteristics of the individual and organization respectively have a rather static and unchanging character. Work organizations are looked upon as closed, social systems operating more or less independently of the environment. The perception of the development of the individual has been grafted onto the biological developmental model which so powerfully dominates Western civilization. Three developmental phases can be broadly distinguished in this model: growth, maturity and decline (Harris, 1957). The period of maturity is presented in this model as a period of relative stability and it is this phase in the course of human life in which individuals are actively involved in the labour process.

The current views and perceptions relating to the functioning of social systems, including work organizations, and to the course of personal development, do not correspond any longer with these static and deterministic conceptions of social reality. Work organizations are better seen as open systems, which maintain a constant relationship of exchange with the environment within which they operate. Organizations are continuously moving and changing. Their development takes on an increasingly unpredictable character.

Since the rise of social gerontology (Birren, 1959; Birren and Schaie, 1977, 1985) the perception has gradually dawned that people go through numerous developmental stages throughout the entire course of their life—from birth to death. Within the realm of psychology and sociology this has provided the impulse towards a lifespan view of human development (Baltes, Reese, and Lipsitt, 1980; Honzik, 1984; Datan, Rodeheaver, and Hughes, 1987).

Performance and attitudes are no longer the exclusive loci of concern. The relationship between individual and organization can no longer be understood from a static matching perspective only. The objectives, quality and strategies of matching must also be viewed in the light of developments and changes. Human behaviour—in terms of task performance or self-perception—is continuously subject to changes as a result of time-bound effects of developments in human attributes and attributions, and of developments in jobs and work contexts. The term 'career development' is introduced to refer to the development of dynamic person–job relationships. Like 'matching', 'career development' also has two meanings (Boerlijst, 1984):

1. Career development as an unfolding process which appears in our range of vision by continuously observing the ongoing actions and interactions of individuals and their work environment, as well as their effects upon the

individual. This is the more passive connotation. A more active interpretation is given in (2).

2. Career development as a set of strategic processes of individual or organizational interventions (cognitive, behavioural, environmental) to create continuously effective person–job relationships, effective both from the perspective of the individual and from the organization (Hall, 1976; Hall and Goodale, 1984; London and Stumpf, 1986; Latham, 1988).

The organizational career theme and the issue of career development have achieved fame above all through the work of Hall (1976), Schein (1978), and van Maanen (1977). Sad to say, theory development and research in this field is characterized by a great heterogeneity in career concepts, extreme fragmentation of knowledge available and a relative lack of systematic research into career development from an interactional perspective (Vardi, 1980; Boerlijst, 1984). Recent surveys in the field of career development and career management can be found in the work of Gysbers *et al.* (1984), Hall and Associates (1986), Hall and Goodale (1986); Schein (1986), and Boerlijst and Aite-Peña (1988).

Matching targets

Traditional matching models are primarily based on short-term targets: the achievement of performance desired by the organization and of an involvement aspired to by the individual or a commitment in relation to a current work context. It is in effect a 'psychological contract' (Schein, 1970, 1978), because the matching relationship is defined in psychological terms (abilities, needs, attitudes). A typical example of such a matching model is the Work Adjustment theory of Lofquist and Dawis (Dawis and Lofquist, 1984). In this model two matching processes are expected. The first concerns the realization of a consonance between capacities ('abilities') of the individual and needs ('ability requirements') of the organization, and the second between the 'needs' of the individual and the 'reinforcer system' of the organization. The success of both processes is just a question of getting a 'good fit' between individual and organization. The criterion of success is that both parties have to feel satisfied by each other (de Wolff and van den Bosch, 1984).

When we consider matching in the light of developments and changes in personal abilities, needs, performance criteria and other personal and organizational characteristics, then we are not only involved in the short-term objectives, but also in matching targets in the long term. Matching processes have in this case, as was said before, an interventional character, with the aim of steering the development of individuals and their organization in a preferred direction.

From the perspective of the organization, matching has in this case the objective of creating favourable conditions for the continuous development of human competencies (abilities, skills, knowledge) and the continuous maintenance of those competencies with a view to future performance. The matching targets here are performance and adaptability.

From the perspective of the individual, matching has the objective of creating favourable conditions for need satisfaction and building a personal identity or self-reliance.

With some adaptation to the table that Hall (1984) applied to the mapping of targets of development we can classify the matching objectives as follows:

	Locus of Concern	
Time-frame	*Task*	*Self*
Short term	Performance	Need fulfilment
Long term	Adaptation	Identity

In the following paragraphs, we will discuss a number of theoretical orientations in relation to these four targets. These orientations can be roughly divided into two groups (Super, 1981; Sonnenfeld and Kotter, 1982):

1. *Traditional matching theories.* In these theories, the accent lies on the short-term targets of 'performance' and 'need fulfilment'. This group of theories can be further subdivided into three main types: differential theories (emphasis on aptitudes and personality traits); situational theories (emphasis on socio-economic structure or socialization process) and the phenomenological theories (emphasis on self-concepts and congruences).
2. *Developmental theories.* In these theories, the emphasis lies on the long-term targets of 'adaptability' and 'identity' in relation to life-stages. The pragmatic aim here is on the one hand the prevention or correction of incongruences between individual and work context and on the other hand the identification of potential, new matching possibilities. The present-day career development models have evolved in particular from the domain of career-choice psychology and sociology. Dissatisfaction with the 'one-choice-at-a-time' theories has been the stimulus for the development of theoretical concepts in the 1940s and 1950s, in which career choice is seen as a life-long process (Super, 1980, 1981; Osipow, 1983; Zytowski and Borgen, 1983; Holland, 1985a). It is not surprising, therefore, that the focus in these models is directed above all to the development of individual cognitive career concepts. On the one hand, these theories deal with attitudes and cognitions relating to personal development and growth (self-concept, ego-image, self-worth, competence, identity and motivation) (Hall, 1976; Schein, 1978; Helbing, 1987). On the other hand, they concern the more objective, work-related features (work interests, advancement, promotion, salary increases, power, prestige status) (Van Maanen and Schein, 1977; Bartol, 1981). From within the domain of personnel selection, few attempts have been made up to now to develop career models relating to the cognitive capacities of people (Fossum *et al.*, 1986). Within this domain, there still generally prevails the dominating idea that the development and growth of the cognitive capacities—in particular the intellectual abilities—take place before reaching adulthood, after which stabilization occurs followed by a

phase of general decline (Botwinick, 1967). Results of recent life-psychological and gerontological research show that personal cognitive development is more dependent on environmental peripheral conditions, including experiences, than on a 'natural' restriction imposed by the physical age of individuals (Baltes, Dittmann-Kohli, and Dixon, 1984; Baltes and Kliegl, 1987).

For the purpose of the discussion, we have restricted ourselves to two theoretical angles of approach, differing in content. From the locus of concern 'Task' we look at the theoretical views relating to people's intellectual abilities. From the locus of concern 'Self' we have chosen theoretical orientations relating to cognitive career concepts (self-concepts) which individuals hold or develop. The underlying rationale for the choice is twofold:

1. People's intellectual abilities have always been seen as crucial determinants for the work performance. As a result of the present-day turbulent developments in society, 'performance obsolescence' and 'performance innovation' are topical issues for the individual and the organization (Fossum *et al.*, 1986). These issues acquire even greater significance when we view them in the light of the increasing ageing of the working population in Europe, the United States and Japan, that we have to face during the next three decades (Doeringer, Rhodes, and Schuster, 1983; Sinick, 1984). Recent theoretical views and attitudes concerning the development of people's intellectual capacities offer interesting and challenging points of departure for theory and practice.
2. Theoretical models and instruments derived from them, which are based on or inspired by the phenomenological-oriented self-concept theory, occupy a dominant position in the present-day career psychology and career counselling practice (Super *et al.*, 1963; Super, 1981; Helbing, 1987; Boerlijst and Aite-Peña, 1988).

Matching and performance

We will now review the matching relationship individual–organization from the perspective of the organization, focusing on the cognitive qualities of people in relation to job performances.

Prediction of the future work behaviour of individuals on the basis of cognitive test performances has always been one of the 'core activities' of work and organizational psychologists. The significance of psychological tests for issues of selection and staffing has been amply discussed in psychological literature (among others Schmidt *et al.*, 1985). Therefore, in this chapter we are not dealing with the many psychometric theories, for instance the theory of intelligence, which have been developed over the past decades, or the numerous tests which are applied in practice in selection and career guidance.

Matching processes of individuals and organizations very often take place on the basis of individual cognitive (and other) test results. It is assumed then that test performances are good predictors of the performance of the required tasks and of the associated problem-solving tasks in day-to-day work practice. In the test situation, the cognitive problem issues as well as the possible solutions to them (or strategies for solution) are mostly standardized and sometimes pre-scribed. The individual can only make a choice from given alternatives.

The premise here is that test performances and problem-solving strategies and solutions can be generalized for different tasks in the work context.

From an interactional or transactional view on (the development of) human behaviour, we must query this way of thinking. On the contrary, this view takes it for granted that individuals in interaction with their direct surroundings are constantly interpreting their own situation in a subjective and idiosyncratic manner and that those interpretations are co-determiners of the behaviour and the situation (Rodeheaver and Datan, 1985). A given real-life problem changes in accordance with the reaction of the individual and this opens possibilities for new, idiosyncratic ways of relevant problem-solving behaviour. The same tasks or task structures can therefore result in different performance or different idiosyncratic solution strategies. In other words the desired performance within the same position or job can be achieved by means of different problem-solving strategies. Differences between individuals in job performances are therefore not only based on differences in cognitive abilities (and other personal characteristics), but also on differences in problem-solving style.

On the basis of the above, we can conclude that the classical test situations in which individuals are placed, give an inadequate representation of the dynamic interaction processes as we meet them in reality within work organizations. In this test situation, the accent lies on the test results and the problem-solving strategies are taken as constants. The selection of individuals on the basis of differences in personal characteristics should therefore be complemented with test results in which differences in problem-approaching strategies and problem transformation capacities can be expressed. The development of a dynamic test programme, in which the setting of the task or problem changes on the basis of interventions by the individual himself, is perhaps possible with the help of a computer (see Chapter 3.7). The development of a dynamic, inter-active com-puter test program in which 'real-life organizational problems and settings' are simulated, offers interesting future perspectives for selection application (Sternberg, 1986).

Matching and need fulfilment

A breakthrough in the traditional 'trait-performance' orientation occurred in the 1950s and 1960s with the appearance of numerous publications in the ield of job motivation. Motivation theories have resulted in the view that people's achieve-ments are not only dependent on individual differences in abilities, but also on the degree of congruence between the subjective esteem of the work itself, the work environment, and work experiences; in short, the degree of individual job satisfac-tion (French, Rodgers, and Cobb, 1974; Kahn, 1981; Kleiber and Maehe, 1985). Job satisfaction has an influence not only on performance but also on many other variables such as absenteeism and turnover (Mowday, Porter, and Steers, 1982).

The degree to which individuals are satisfied with their job or position is dependent on a complex of factors (Brousseau, 1983): current motives and abilities, task characteristics, organizational context, the duration of the performance of the function, the influence of work experience on personal characteristics, the type of career that is aimed at and the degree to which the job or position in question fits into that particular career concept. Brousseau (1983, p. 37) concludes therefore that '. . . the "goodness fit" between a person and a job is likely to change with the passage of time as the person accumulates experience in a job and moves into new career stages'.

In the present-day matching theories and developmental theories, the theoretical concept which is receiving a lot of attention is the so-called 'self-concept', which is the image or the esteem that individuals have of themselves or attribute to themselves (Helbing, 1987). The self-concept is an important motivating factor in the choice of a profession or work environment and in personal career development.

The self-concept theory has a phenomenological basis and has acquired fame within the realm of career-choice psychology and career-choice practice through the work of Super (1980, 1981, 1986) and Holland (1966, 1976, 1985a). The axiom of this theory is—as Super (1981, p. 32) comments himself—a simple one: '. . . matching one's picture of oneself against one's picture of people in occupations that one knows and in which one is interested'.

Holland's theory is a further elaboration of the self-concept philosophy. This theory is representative of classical 'matching theory'. It has a great influence nowadays on the practice of vocational counselling. This influence is due to the fact that, on the basis of this theory, Holland has also developed a psychometrically satisfactory career-interest questionnaire, the Self-Directed Search (SDS) (Holland, 1985b). Holland's career-choice theory is a personality theory, based on the assumption that differing personality types feel themselves attracted to, or are especially suited to, typical work environments. Besides this, the degree of congruence between person orientation and work environment seems to be not only significant for the choice of a profession or career, but also for a number of other dimensions, like job performance and persistence, job satisfaction, stability of choice, etc. (Spokane, 1985).

Research, however, has shown that the congruence realized at the beginning of the career does not have a constant character. Adler and Aranya (1984), in research among accountants, found that in later stages of their career they started to display significant deviations from Holland's 'ideal' personality type. It is quite possible that Holland's theory—and this also applies in general to trait factor models of vocational behaviour—has taken insufficient account of the empirical fact that personality characteristics, such as for example cognitive style, can change in the course of a career (Kolb and Plovnick, 1977) and that the requirements and expectations as set by the work situation, can be different in distinct phases of the career (Schein, 1978). In a critical comment, Super (1981) refers to the methodologically weak basis on which the work of Holland and most of his followers is based: the predictors and the criteria both refer to preferences. Super concludes (p. 33): 'What most of the earlier research has therefore done is to establish not the validity of the theory but the relative stability of vocational preferences, not the ability of vocational interests or preferences ("personality type") to predict the occupation ("environment") actually chosen, entered, or pursued over a period of time but only expressed preferences at a somewhat later date.' According to Super longitudinal research designs are a necessary condition of the testing of the validity of the self-concept theory in general and of the congruence theories in particular.

Matching and adaptability

From a dynamic matching perspective a continuous adjustment is required between the cognitive qualities of the individual and the knowledge, skills and abilities which are required for an adequate job performance. Incongruences between the individual and the organization on these factors result in 'obsolescence' in the view of Fossum *et al.* (1986): 'Obsolescence occurs when the person requirements of a job which are demanded by its tasks, duties, and responsibilities become incongruent with the stock of knowledge, skills, and abilities currently possessed by the individual; given that the knowledge, skills, and abilities were previously congruent with job demands.' Fossum *et al.* describe a large number of organizational and individual factors which have an influence on performance obsolescence. One of the factors which we will concentrate on predominantly here is 'age'.

An attitude which is prevalent within our society and within work organizations is that persons are not capable of further development after reaching adulthood, because their learning abilities and learning capacities are no longer sufficient. It is assumed that the cognitive development of people is characterized by a relatively fast increase in all kinds of cognitive abilities, followed by a gradual decrease when growing older. Recent research, however, has shown that a decrease in performance of older people is more related to particular circumstances which occur relatively more frequently in their case (for example, a poor state of health, deficiencies or gaps in their education) than to a decline in cognitive functions (Labouvie-Vief, 1985; see also Birren, Cunningham, and Yamamoto, 1983). To some extent, then, measured age differences turn out to be generation differences.

Until comparatively recently, for the determination of cognitive abilities especial attention was paid to particular forms of formal, logical reasoning. These are forms of reasoning which usually receive the greatest attention in the education of young people and which can be seen as basic elements for intelligent functioning (ability to make associations, to classify, and such like). Each person develops these abilities to his own distinctive level, which can be assessed by observing the average degree of difficulty of the tasks and problems which the person in question is able to solve. They are also the forms of reasoning which are called upon in normal intelligence tests. It is important to know that most people are able to keep these developed abilities at their distinctive average level for virtually the whole of their working lives, but they are more likely to arrive at their maximum or peak performances at an earlier rather than a later age. As far as these functions are concerned, the 'reserve capacity' usually declines on growing older. During recent years, more attention has been given to forms of reasoning which rise above this 'school' type of intelligence and which, in fact, can be exploited better by older than by younger people (Commons, Richards, and Armon, 1984; Commons *et al.*, 1986).

Moreover, greater emphasis is laid on the development of experiential knowledge, the development of expertise in the performance of a profession or function, and the development of wisdom in solving social problems or in evaluating one's own and other people's actions and such like. Interesting elaborations of this can be found for example in Dittmann-Kohli and Baltes (1985), Smith, Dixon, and Baltes (1986), and Baltes and Kliegl (1987). The interesting point in these aspects of intelligent functioning is the fact that they can, to some extent, continue to develop for many years and that they allow the possibility of applying compensations where particular forms of reasoning and thinking fall short or display shortcomings (Munnichs *et al.*, 1985; Labouvie-Vief, 1985; Datan, Rodeheaver, and Hughes, 1987, p. 167 ff.). It is clear that adults and the elderly have in principle numerous possibilities of continuing to develop during the course of their career (according to Morrison and Hock, 1986), of finding compensations for abilities and skills which decline with the years, and of facing new situations. The problem, however, is that too little attention has been paid up to now—also on the part of the individuals concerned, in fact—to the deliberate stimulation of methods of thinking and feeling which are often characterized by society as 'soft', but which are essential if one is to deal adequately with complicated tasks and problems in daily life.

The significance of 'learning through experience' for cognitive and perhaps also social and emotional development, is still insufficiently realized and exploited in the normal training methods of work organizations. Some mechanisms which are appropriate for this, such as job rotation, 'sabbaticals' in a completely different environment, preparation for another career, for example a second or lateral one, are generally considered as less opportune than training courses for particular skills, 'on-the-job' training, and such like.

Matching and identity

Research and theory development relating to careers—and in particular the psychological aspects of careers—have been initiated and stimulated particularly from the quarters of occupational sociology and vocational psychology. Sociologists' interest in working careers is geared in particular to studying socialization processes in the context of the profession and the organization (Van Maanen, 1975; Raelin, 1984; Jones, 1986). The influence of the system of values and norms operative within the work organization on the 'performance' of the individual and the organization is a current topic in organizational sciences.

Present-day discussions on the subject of achieving innovation and flexibility of the work organization have resulted in the theme 'organization culture' acquiring a central position in processes of strategic management (Peters and Waterman, 1982; Kanter, 1983; Mintzberg, 1983; Schein, 1985; Frost, 1985).

The socialization research has given the stimulus to the development of the so-called 'career stage models' (Super *et al.*, 1957; Schein, 1978; Dalton, Thompson, and Price, 1977; Hall, 1976; Levinson, 1986). A career stage model is a representation of a working career with successive phases (partly overlapping), which are differentiated by their unique 'biosocial development tasks'. Adaptation to these 'developmental demands' is on the one hand a condition for the further development of the individual and on the other hand the result of an individual development process.

Theoretical concepts relating to human development within career psychology have been predominantly derived from the self-concept paradigm. Super (1957) defines the individual development in terms of 'career maturity' of the behaviour of the individual in the direction of a specific identity of his or her own (self-concept). Schein (1977, 1978) maintains an occupational self-concept which he calls 'career anchor'. A career anchor is an interconnected pattern of self-perceived talents, motives and values and this self-concept has an influence on the subsequent direction, stability and integration of the individual career. Career anchors are the result of work experience, which means the interaction between individual and organization during the first phases of the career. A career anchor evolves on the basis of a continuous match between abilities, motives and values of the individual on the one hand and the available career opportunities on the other hand. Schein (1978) has formulated five types of career anchors, dominated by security, technical/functional competence, managerial competence, creativity and autonomy. For the determination of one's own career anchor Schein has developed a 'Career Anchor-analysis form'. DeLong (1982) has refined the career anchor model by the addition of three other potential career anchors: identity, service and variety. In addition he has designed a questionnaire—the Career Orientation Inventory—for the purposes of empirical research into the validity of career anchors.

An interesting theoretical point of contact with career anchors is offered by Driver's 'career concept model' (Driver, 1979, 1982). Driver himself speaks of a 'preliminary map' and of a 'conceptual roadguide' (p. 81). This model is based on the assumption that individuals have different ideas as to how their careers should develop (see also: Olson, 1979; Prince, 1979). The career concepts have a motivational basis, whose substance corresponds to Schein and DeLong's career anchors. In fact, they are strategic concepts within the 'personal career policy' (Boerlijst, 1984, Boerlijst and Aite-Peña, 1988). The career concept expresses a career strategy which the individual aspires to for the purpose of the implementation (and development) of his own identity concept (self-concept). The model describes four 'ideal' career concepts.

1. The *linear career concept* (vertical mobility in the hierarchy of the organization and oriented towards the acquiring of power and success).
2. The *steady state career concept* (lifelong commitment to a function or function domain and oriented towards security and the further development of specific skills and knowledge, in short, of expertise).
3. The *spiral career concept* (series of infrequent but important changes in a new

professional field or area of function and oriented to personal growth and identity).
4. The *transitory career concept* (frequent changing of functions without any consistency in direction and oriented to independence and novelty).

The integration of models relating to career concepts, career anchors and career stages into a general career model, opens up possibilities of answering the question: What type of job sequences are necessary to promote individual development within the various types of careers? (Brousseau, 1983).

MATCHING AND ASSESSMENT IN THE FUTURE

It is to be expected that in the coming decades the management of organizations will attach ever increasing importance to the stimulation of a continuous process of 'dynamic' matching between individual and organization. The rapid changes in the requirements of, and concessions to, the market, call for large capital investments in flexible production systems as well as in human ingenuity. These investments have to be recovered at an ever increasing speed. Many companies and organizations go all out to be ahead of their competitors in order to 'stay in the market' whatever the cost. The risk of a limited success or a complete failure must be reduced to the minimum. There is a growing awareness that this is only possible when the 'human resources' in the organization are equal to this task and will continue to be so.

There will be a growing demand for methods of career intervention and counselling to stimulate the development of transferable expertise in very different experiential problem areas. The inevitable increase in average age of the working population also means that ways of avoiding 'obsolescence' of older employees and management must be further and better explored. For people's productivity to be maintained throughout their working lives, there will have to be an increase in their versatility to solve new and still partly unknown problems of 'modern times'. It goes without saying that they will have to be able to switch jobs and careers more than has been necessary up to now. Multiple and lateral careers will probably become generally accepted. An important condition is that preparation for such a multiple career prospect must be approached in a well-considered manner suited to a person's abilities and experiences. Such a preparation must start early in one's career and must not stop too early, as is now often the case. The organization's present and future needs of a functional contribution of its 'human resources' must be taken into account.

Assessment will most likely play an increasingly important role. The costs of investments in the development of careers throughout the working period can easily start to rocket. The motives and potentials of people and their organizations will have to be constantly and thoroughly reviewed, in order to keep the match between the two as close as is feasible. In particular, assessment will play a part in the evaluation of 'dynamic' career intervention methods and in the selection of the most suitable people for a particular career development programme. In this connection it is interesting to note the previously mentioned development of interactive computerized test programs, in which a person is confronted with a set of problems in a simulated organization. The programs permit the 'organization' to act and react as realistically as possible to the actions and reactions of the person in question to the problems presented to him or her. Such test programs offer the facility to determine to what extent individuals are capable of controlling or manipulating a problem situation that is partly caused by their own reactions to earlier problems. It can be seen whether people are able to correct their own 'wrong' reactions, and so on. The simulation of interpersonal relations, not only in the cognitive, but also in the emotional or affective sphere, and in which matching or collision between parties is the issue, remains a bottleneck situation. Time will tell whether satisfactory and valid assessment methods in this field can be developed.

REFERENCES

Adler, S., and Aranya, N. (1984). A comparison of the work needs, attitudes, and preferences of professional accountants at different career stages, *Journal of Vocational Behavior*, **25**, 45–57.

Baltes, P.B., Dittmann-Kohli, F., and Dixon, R.A. (1984). New perspectives on the development of intelligence in adulthood: Toward a dual-process conception and a model of selective optimization with compensation, in P.B. Baltes and O.G. Brim Jr (eds), *Life-span Development and Behavior*, Vol. 6, pp. 33–76. Academic Press, New York.

Baltes, P.B., and Kliegl, R. (1987). Theory-guided analysis of mechanisms of development and aging through testing-the-limits and research on expertise, in C. Schooler and K.W. Schaie (eds), *Cognitive Functioning and Social Structure over the Life Course*, pp. 95–119. Abler, Norwood, NJ.

Baltes, P., Reese, H.W., and Lipsitt, L.P. (1980). Life-span developmental psychology, in M.R. Rosenzweig and L.W. Porter (eds), *Annual Review of Psychology*, **31**, 65–110.

Bartol, K.M. (1981). Vocational behavior and career development, 1980: a review, *Journal of Vocational Behavior*, **19**, 123–62.

Birren, J.E. (1959). Principles of research on ageing, in J.E. Birren (ed.), *Handbook of Ageing and the Individual: Psychological and biological aspects*. University of Chicago Press, Chicago.

Birren, J.E., Cunningham, W.R., and Yamamoto, K. (1983). Psychology of adult development and aging, in M.R. Rosenzweig and L.W. Porter (eds), *Annual Review of Psychology*, **34**, 543–75.

Birren, J.E., and Schaie, K.W. (eds) (1977, 1985). *Handbook of the Psychology of Ageing*. Van Nostrand Reinhold, New York.

Boerlijst, J.G. (1984). Career development and career guidance, in P.J.D. Drenth, H. Thierry, P.J. Willems, and Ch. J. de Wolff (eds), *Handbook of Work and Organizational Psychology*, Vol. 1, pp. 313–43. Wiley, New York.

Boerlijst, J.G., and Aite-Peña, A. (1988). Loopbaanontwikkeling en loopbaanbegeleiding. [Career development and career guidance.] To be published in P.J.D. Drenth *et al.* (eds), *Nieuw Handboek Arbeids- en Organisatiepsychologie* [New Handbook of Work and Organizational Psychology], Van Loghum Slaterus, Deventer.

Botwinick, J. (1967). *Cognitive Processes in Maturity and Old Age*. Springer, New York.

Brousseau, K.R. (1983). Toward a dynamic model of job–person relationships: Findings, research questions, and implications for work system design, *Academy of Management Review*, **8**, 33–45.

Commons, M.L., Richards, F.A., and Armon, C. (eds) (1984). *Beyond Formal Operations: 1. Late adolescent and adult cognitive development*. Praeger, New York.

Commons, M.L., Sinnott, J., Richards, F.A., and Armon, C. (eds) (1986). *Beyond Formal*

Operations: 2. Comparisons and applications of adolescent and adult developmental models. Praeger, New York.

Dalton, G.W., Thompson, P.H., and Price, R. (1977).' Career stages: A model of professional careers in organizations, *Organizational Dynamics*, **6** (3), 19–42.

Datan, N., Rodeheaver, D., and Hughes, F. (1987). Adult development and aging, in M.R. Rosenzweig and L.W. Porter (eds), *Annual Review of Psychology*, **38**, pp. 153–80.

Dawis, R.V., and Lofquist, L.H. (1984). *A Psychological Theory of Work Adjustment.* Univ. of Minnesota Press, Minneapolis.

DeLong, T.J. (1982). Re-examining the career anchor model. *Personnel*, **61**, 50–62.

Devanna, M.A. *et al.* (1984). A framework for strategic human resource management, in C. J. Fombrun, N.M. Tichy, and M.A. Devanna (eds), *Strategic Human Resource Management.* Wiley, New York. pp. 33–57.

Dittmann-Kohli, F., and Baltes, P.B. (1988). Toward a neofunctionalist conception of adult intellectual development: Wisdom as a prototypical case of intellectual growth, in C. Alexander, E. Langer, and M. Oetzel (eds). *Higher Stages of Human Development: Adult growth beyond formal operations.* Oxford University Press, New York.

Doeringer, M., Rhodes, S.R., and Schuster, M. (1983). *The Aging Worker.* Sage, Beverly Hills, California.

Driver, M.J. (1979). Career concepts and career management in organizations, in G.L. Cooper (ed.), *Behavioral Problems in Organizations.* Prentice-Hall, New York.

Driver, M.J. (1982). Career concepts—A new approach to career research, in R. Katz (ed.), *Career Issues in Human Resource Management.* Prentice-Hall, Englewood Cliffs, NJ, pp. 23–32

Durkheim, E. (1893, repr. 1960). *De la division du travail.* PUF, Paris.

Evans, P.A.L. (1986). The strategic outcomes of human resource management, *Human Resource Management*, **25**, 149–67.

Fombrun, C.J. (1984). The external context of human resource management, in C.J. Fombrun, N.M. Tichy, and M.A. Devanna (eds), *Strategic Human Resource Management.* Wiley, New York, pp. 3–19.

Fombrun, C.J., Tichy, N.M., and Devanna, M.A. (eds) (1984). *Strategic Human Resource Management.* Wiley, New York.

Fossum, J.A., Arvey, R.D., Paradise, C.A., and Robbins, N.E. (1986). Modeling the skills obsolescence process: A psychological/economic integration, *Academy of Management Review*, **11**, 362–74.

French, J.R.P., Rodgers, W.L., and Cobb, S. (1974). Adjustment as person–environment fit, in G. Coelho, D. Hamburg, and F.J.C. Adams (eds), *Coping and Adaptation.* Basic Books, New York.

Frost, P.J. (ed.) (1985). *Organizational Culture.* Sage, Beverly Hills, California.

Gay, H. *et al.* (eds) (1984). *Longman–Webster English College Dictionary.* Longman, Harlow.

Gysbers, G. *et al.* (1984). *Designing Careers.* Jossey-Bass, San Francisco.

Hall, D.T. (1976). *Careers in Organizations.* Goodyear, Santa Monica, California.

Hall, D.T. and Associates (1986). *Career Development in Organizations.* Jossey-Bass, London.

Hall, D.T., and Goodale, J.G. (1986). *Human Resource Management: Strategy, design, and implementation.* Scott, Foresman, Glenview, Illinois.

Harris, D.B. (1957). Problems in formulating a scientific concept of development, in D.B. Harris (ed.), *The Concept of Development.* University of Minnesota Press, Minnesota.

Helbing, H. (1987). The Self in Career Development. Ph.D. thesis, Amsterdam.

Holland, J.L. (1966). *The Psychology of Vocational Choice.* Blaisdell, Waltham, Massachusetts.

Holland, J.L. (1976). Vocational preferences, in M.D. Dunnette (ed.), *Handbook of Industrial and Organizational Psychology.* Rand-McNally, Chicago, pp. 521–70.

Holland, J.L. (1985a). *Making Vocational Choices: A theory of careers*, 2nd edn. Prentice-Hall, Englewood Cliffs, New Jersey.

Holland, J.L. (1985b). *The Self-Directed Search: Professional—Manual.* Psychol. Assess. Resourc., Odessa, Florida.

Honzik, M.P. (1984). Life-span development, in M.R. Rosenzweig and L.W. Porter (eds), *Annual Review of Psychology*, **35**, 309–31.

Jones, G.R. (1986). Socialization tactics, self-efficiency, and newcomers' adjustments to organizations, *Academy of Management Journal*, **29**(2), 262–79.

Kahn, R.L. (1981). *Work and Health*. Wiley, New York.

Kanter, R.M. (1983). *The Change Masters*. Simon & Schuster, New York.

Kleiber, M.L., and Maehe, M.L. (eds) (1985). *Advances in Motivation and Achievement*. Vol. 4: *Motivation and adulthood*. Jai Press, Greenwich, Connecticut.

Kolb, D.A., and Plovnick, M.S. (1977). The experiental learning theory of career development, in J. Van Maanen (ed.), *Organizational Careers: Some new perspectives*. Wiley, New York.

Labouvie-Vief, G. (1985). Intelligence and cognition, in J.E. Birren and K.W. Schaie (eds), *Handbook of the Psychology of Aging*, 2nd edn. Van Nostrand Reinhold, New York, pp. 500–30.

Latham, G.P. (1988). Human resource training and development, in M.R. Rosenzweig and L.W. Porter (eds), *Annual Review of Psychology*, **39**, 545–82.

Levinson, D.J. (1986). A conception of adult development. *American Psychologist*, **41**, 3–13.

London, M., and Stumpf, S.A. (1986). Individual and organizational career development in changing times, in D.T. Hall and Associates (eds), *Career Development in Organizations*. Jossey-Bass, London, pp. 21–49.

Miller, C.H. (1974). Career development theory in perspective, in E.L. Herr (ed.), *Vocational Guidance and Human Development*. Houghton Mifflin, Boston.

Mintzberg, H. (1983). *Power in and around Organizations*. Prentice-Hall, Englewood Cliffs, New Jersey.

Morrison, R.F., and Hock, R.R. (1986). Career building: Learning from cumulative work experience, in D.T. Hall and Associates (eds), *Career Development in Organizations*. Jossey-Bass, London, pp. 236–73.

Mowday, R.T., Porter, L.W., and Steers, R.M. (1982). *Employee Organization Linkages: The psychology of commitment, absenteeism, and turnover*. Academic Press, New York.

Munnichs, J., Mussen, P., Olbrich, E., and Coleman, P. (eds) (1985). *Life-span and Change in a Gerontological Perspective*. Academic Press, New York.

Nosow, S., and Form, W.H. (1962). *Man, Work and Society: A reader in the sociology of occupations*. Basic Books, New York.

Olson, T. (1979). Career concepts and decision styles. Paper given at the National Academy of Management Meeting, Atlanta, 1979.

Osipow, S.H. (1983). *Theories of Career Development*, 3rd edn. Prentice-Hall, Englewood Cliffs, New Jersey.

Peters, T., and Waterman, R.H. (1982). *In Search of Excellence: Lessons from America's best-run companies*. Harper & Row, New York.

Prince, B. (1979). An investigation of career concepts and career anchors. Paper given at the Western Academy of Management Meeting, Portland, Oregon, 1979.

Raelin, J.A. (1984). An examination of deviant/adaptive behaviors in the organizational caucus of professionals, *Academy of Management Review*, **9**, (3), 413–27.

Rodeheaver, D., and Datan, N. (1985). Gender and the vicissitudes of motivation in adult life, in M.L. Kleiber and M.L. Maehe (eds), *Advances in Motivation and Achievement*, Vol. 4: *Motivation and adulthood*. Jai Press, Greenwich, Connecticut, pp. 169–87.

Schein, E.H. (1970). *Organizational Psychology*. Prentice-Hall, Englewood Cliffs, New Jersey.

Schein, E.H. (1977). Career anchors and career paths: A panel study of management school graduates, in J. Van Maanen (ed.), *Organizational Careers: Some new perspectives*. Wiley, New York.

Schein, E.H. (1978). *Career Dynamics: Matching individual and organizational needs*. Addison-Wesley, Reading, Massachusetts.

Schein, E.H. (1985). *Organizational Culture and Leadership*. Jossey-Bass, San Francisco.

Schein, E.H. (1986). A critical look at current career development theory and research, in D.T. Hall and Associates (eds), *Career Development in Organizations*. Jossey-Bass, London.

Schmidt, F.L., Pearlman, K. *et al.* (1985). Forty questions about validity generalization and meta-analysis, *Personnel Psychology*, **38**, 697–799.

Sinick, D. (1984). Problems of work and retirement for an aging population, in G. Gysbers *et al.* (eds), *Designing Careers*, Jossey-Bass, San Francisco, pp. 532–57.

Smith, J., Dixon, R.A., and Baltes, P.B. (1986). Expertise in life planning: A new research approach to investigating aspects of wisdom, in M.L. Commons, J.D. Sinnott, F.A. Richards, and C. Armon (eds), *Beyond Formal Operations: 2. Comparisons and applications of adolescent and adult developmental models*. Praeger, New York.

Sonnenfeld, J., and Kotter, J.P. (1982). The maturation of career theory, *Human Relations*, 19–46.

Spokane, A.R. (1985). A review of research on person–environment congruence in Holland's theory of careers, *Journal of Vocational Behavior*, **26**, 306–43.

Sternberg, R.J. (1986). The future of intelligence testing. *Educational Measurement: Issues and Practice*, **5**, 19–22.

Super, D.E. (1957). *The Psychology of Careers*. Harper, New York.

Super, D.E. (1980). A life-span, life-space approach to career development. *Journal of Vocational Behavior*, **16**, 282–98.

Super, D.E. (1981). A developmental theory: implementing a self-concept, in D.H. Montross and C.J. Shinkman (eds), *Career Development in the 1980s: Theory and practice*, pp. 28–42.

Super, D.E. (1986). Life career roles: Self-realization in work and leisure, in D.T. Hall and Associates (eds), *Career Development in Organizations*. Jossey-Bass, London, pp. 95–119.

Super, D.E., Crites, J.O., Hummel, R.C., Moser, H.P., Overstreet, P.L., and Warnath, C.F. (1957). *Vocational Development: A framework for research*. Teachers College Press, New York.

Super, D.E., Starishevsky, R., Matlin, N., and Jordaan, J.P. (eds) (1963). *Career Development: Self-concept theory*. College Entrance Examination Board, New York.

Taylor, N.B., and Pryor, R.G.L. (1985). Exploring the process of compromise in career decision making. *Journal of Vocational Behavior*, **27**, 171–90.

Van Maanen, J. (1975). Police socialization: A longitudinal examination of job attitudes in an urban police department, *Administrative Science Quarterly*, **20**, 207–29.

Van Maanen, J. (ed.) (1977). *Organizational Careers: Some new perspectives*. Wiley, New York.

Van Maanen, J., and Schein, E.H. (1977). Career development, in J.R. Hackman and J.L. Suttle (eds), *Improving Life at Work*. Goodyear, Santa Monica, California.

Vardi, Y. (1980). Organizational career mobility: An integrative model, *Academy of Management Review*, **5**, 341–55.

Von Glinow, M.A., Driver, M.J., Brousseau, K., and Prince, J.B. (1983). The design of a career oriented human resource system, *Academy of Management Review*, **8**, 23–32.

Wolff, Ch. J. de, and Bosch, G. van den (1984). Personnel selection, in P.J.D. Drenth, H. Thierry, P.J. Willems, and Ch. J. de Wolff (eds), *Handbook of Work and Organizational Psychology*, Vol. 1. Wiley, New York, pp. 289–312.

Zytowski, D.G., and Borgen, F.H. (1983). Assessment, in W.B. Walsh and S.H. Osipow (eds), *Handbook of Vocational Psychology*. Erlbaum, Hillsdale, New Jersey.

Chapter 1.3

Selection and the Organizational Context

H. PETER DACHLER

Hochschule St Gallen, Guisanstrasse 11, CH 9019 St Gallen, Switzerland

INTRODUCTION AND OVERVIEW

It has been a relatively long-held view that selection of employees for work organizations, their training and development be conceptualized and implemented by taking into account specific characteristics of the organization. This is in addition to the specific job requirements which people need and will need in the future (Goldstein, 1986; Hall and Goodale, 1986; Schneider and Schmitt, 1986). One can therefore approach this chapter from two very different perspectives. The more traditional and perhaps less risky approach would be to review the various organizational characteristics, from organizational structure, reward patterns, leadership styles to the climate of an organization, which together with the specific characteristics of jobs, are thought to interact with individual attributes, in determining employee effectiveness and therefore need to be considered in the selection and employee development process.

Another approach would be to look at the problem of selection and development as fundamentally a problem of dealing with *change*. Such change refers not only to what organizations are and do within their ever-changing environment, but also to *changing perspectives* of what is the nature of organizations and what is the nature of individuals in organizational settings. In the latter sense of change, we are referring to the changing meaning and practice of employee selection and development in a dynamic organizational context (Benson, 1983). Reviews of the organizational factors that play a crucial role in selection and development already exist (e.g. Hall and Goodale, 1986; Schneider and Schmitt, 1986). Moreover, the *meaning* of selection within the context of very dynamic and complex organizations needs to be brought into sharper focus. Therefore, this chapter will take the

Handbook of Assessment in Organizations   Edited by P. Herriot
© 1989 John Wiley & Sons Ltd

second and perhaps more risky approach. While we will give the issue of selection central attention, in the context of the problem of change all the development activities concerning people, careers and new assignments are also addressed. Therefore, from the point of view taken in this chapter we will often talk of selection and development as issues belonging together.

We will start out with a brief review of the basic assumptions that are made traditionally when considering selection within the context of organizations. Then we will critically evaluate them in the light of *changing perspectives* of the nature of organizations and the increasing complexity and ambiguity that organizations, and especially future organizations, are likely to experience.

A further section then briefly reviews the possible consequences for selection and development conceptions and practices that derive from new requirements of future organizations and alternative assumptions about the nature of organizations and individual differences.

Selection and development within dominant assumptions of organizations and their members

The assumptions to be reviewed in this section are crucially important. This is because they underline those concepts and techniques which are considered useful and meaningful with respect to the 'human resource' problems that are encountered by today's organizations (Benson, 1983; Dachler and Enderle, in press). Furthermore, the increasingly dynamic environment of organizations as well as rapid changes within organizations pose special problems for selection, placement, personnel and career development issues. Hence, these fundamental assumptions also have a crucial bearing on the way we conceptualize and deal with change in practice.

The currently accepted selection and appraisal paradigm is a direct reflection of well-ingrained assumptions about the nature of organizations and people acting in organizational contexts. Therefore, we will briefly review these implicit selection-relevant assumptions concerning the fundamental characteristics of organizations as well as those regarding individual differences.

The main thesis of this chapter maintains that a reassessment of these implicit assumptions is a precondition for developing alternative conceptions regarding the selection and development process in organizations and consequently for designing alternative selection and development processes for work organizations. The development of such alternatives has become an urgent necessity, because the traditional assumptions inherent in the selection and development paradigm have emerged from organizational structures of the past. Such structures are supported with methods that make sense to those people who have constructed the organizations we encounter today. However, their perspectives may no longer 'fit' all the demands facing organizations of the future. This future, which is not predictable in specifics, will nevertheless most certainly involve an increased organizational complexity through much denser interlinkages among organizations of various kinds and across national boundaries. This will result in greater ambiguity and more rapid change in organizational life (Morgan, 1987).

Such developments and their concomitant propensity for rapid change make current assumptions that made sense in the past appear constraining and greatly reduced in their meaning and usefulness. More importantly, current assumptions make it very difficult to ask fundamentally new questions because such questions may not be meaningful or even recognizable within the dominant selection paradigm. But fundamentally new questions need to be asked in order to open up new perspectives and more meaningful selection practices within the organizational realities that are unfolding.

It should be remembered that the American management and organizational design perspectives which have evolved strongly since the Second World War, and have to a considerable extent been copied by a large proportion of European work organizations, are a particular consequence of unique circumstances during the height of America's economic power. The United States, especially after the Second World War, possessed an immense internal mass market which led to an emphasis on mass production with a labour pool that was and still is relatively under-qualified and under-educated. It is therefore not surprising that under those circumstances American management philosophy embraced the technocratic idea of highly differentiated division of labour, specialization and a rather centralized and redundant hierarchy of authority. Over-controlling by concentrating on those aspects that can be quantified (as if qualitative aspects could be ignored without risk), American management techniques effectively handled the mass production process with under-qualified employees.

Currently there exists increasing saturation of traditional mass markets and a growing development towards internationalization of markets. Moreover there is a growth of quality consciousness, not only price consciousness, and an increasing importance of market niches because of increasingly specialized customer needs. Consequently, organizations are faced with demands for an enormous *flexibility* and a much more complex and technically driven production and service process. All of this argues against an analytical, *a priori*, structured system of statically defined job requirements, whose incumbents need to be pushed and pulled by professional managers and supervisors, who see one of their main functions as keeping the analytically well-designed organizational machine functioning as flawlessly as possible. Thus, the changes of the last ten to fifteen years may require different perspectives on organizing and therefore different perspectives on the employee selection and development problem. American principles of management, including principles of organizational structure and function, can be questioned when one compares their success with that of their major competitors in the face of the fundamental economic and social changes that have taken place. This decreasing success is certainly an important signal that some of the implied assumptions regarding organizations and people, which made sense in the context of past circumstances, are losing some of their usefulness with respect to the challenges of unfolding events and circumstances.

Assumptions about the nature of organizations that guide dominant selection and development practices

Researchers as well as practitioners in selection and development emphasize the point that it is, ultimately, the individuals in organizations that make things happen. Although this assumption is logically correct, since without individuals there can be no organization, the specific way in which one *interprets* the statement that individuals make things happen, is of crucial importance. The traditional image of what an organization is finds its reflection in some form of organization chart. An organization chart shows individual positions or jobs, each held by a person with (hopefully) the appropriate knowledge, skills and abilities that are required by the particular demands of the position as well as the demands of the more immediate organizational environment. Positions are arranged in line with the organizational objectives according to the well-established principles of division of labour and hierarchy of authority. We will briefly discuss the important assumptions which are relevant to selection and which are implicit in such a conception of organizations.

Individual as the main unit of analysis

The basic unit in organization charts as well as in most of the theories of organizational behaviour is the single individual. While it is recognized that individuals in organizations interact with each other to determine many organizational and environmental factors that, in turn, affect them (Dachler, 1985, Preglau, 1980; Schneider, 1983a), it is nevertheless assumed that the aggregation of the personal attributes and individual behaviours constitutes the properties and behaviours of organizations as a whole. In other words, organizational effectiveness and survival is seen as a function of the (usually linear) aggregate of individual qualifications (knowledge, skills and abilities) and the enhancing or constraining effects of organizational factors on individual performance. These factors include supervision, climate, the nature of the tasks, etc. This basic perspective is well illustrated in one of the well-known textbooks on staffing:

> A subtle but important distinction has been introduced—the distinction between predicting and understanding the behavior of *individuals* and predicting and understanding the behavior of people in the *aggregate* . . . [This distinction] . . . refers to the idea that staffing researchers are always concerned with making a choice from a pool of applicants and the challenge is to make the best choice — to choose the best individual. At the same time, however, staffing researchers need to maintain an organizational perspective and be sensitive to the *cumulative* [emphasis by HPD] effects of [selection] decisions on the functioning of the organization, in the aggregate (Schneider and Schmitt, 1986, p. 21).

Implied in these statements is also the idea that selection takes care of one precondition of effective performance, namely the 'best' or optimal individual knowledge, skills and abilities, whereas the more motivation-based aspects of performance depend on the characteristics of the organizational environment, such as leadership, job characteristics, communication structures, or organizational climate, once the individual has been selected.

Researchers like Schneider (1983a, 1983b) have pointed out that by integrating organizational characteristics into the job analysis it should be possible to select poeple not only on the basis of their knowledge, skills and abilities that are required by the immediate tasks contained in a job, but also with respect to individual personality and attitude characteristics which better fit established climates, leadership styles and reward systems that exist in an organization. While this is an important idea with respect to incorporating motivational issues into the selection process, the assumption is still that it is the interaction of *personal*, relatively enduring characteristics with certain identifiable organizational factors which *determines* effective performance of *individuals* in organizations. Furthermore, selecting for motivation has not been an area in which commonly used selection techniques have been overly successful. This is most likely due to the implicit assumption that motivated performance is a consequence of quantitatively measurable individual attributes (e.g. motive, needs, values, expectations) in interaction with predetermined characteristics of the *immediate* environment of a *specific* job (e.g. task characteristics, supervision on the job, expectations regarding rewards for job performance, etc.).

Note that job and organizational characteristics are assumed to be relatively stable and objectively identifiable. It is this assumption which makes the idea sensible, that through the selection process one can optimally match the characteristics of individuals to the objective reality of analytically defined jobs and their organizational environments. If organizations change, the whole process of job analyses and identification of (probably different) required employee attributes needs to be repeated in the hope that for a while organizational and job characteristics will remain stable for the selection and development process to work efficiently. In the light of increased dynamic changes, and changes 'out of the blue' (Morgan, 1987, p. 12) that organizations are increasingly experiencing, this selection and development perspective may have a rather conservative and stifling effect on dealing with unexpected, unpredictable and constant change.

A direct consequence of conceptualizing organizations as structured aggregates of identifiable, single individuals, is that organizations, in line with the meaning of a traditional organization chart, focus on single jobs or job categories which all have their individually identifiable functions within the rational principle of division of labour and hierarchy of authority. Jobs are coordinated based upon the *implicit* conception that individuals and their job-related functions need to be centrally controlled with various mechanisms. Within such a conception of structure it is assumed that higher authority often needs to interfere specifically with the activities of individuals, and that in general the primary function of organizing is to overcome and rectify individuals' human fallibility in their respective jobs. Crucial for selection and development is the underlying assumption that the multiple *tasks* which need to be accomplished and coordinated towards the overall objectives of the organization are best packaged into jobs with rationally established job descriptions that have to be met by the corresponding optimal qualifications of individuals. *Selection therefore focuses above all on the prediction of how well a person will perform on a specific, predefined job.*

Especially in view of increasingly ambiguous and unstructured problem situations with which future organizations are faced, it becomes more difficult to organize towards the complex and often ambiguous future objectives on the basis of the traditional means–ends rationality, through analytically planned and structured job classes and job hierarchies. Furthermore, the idea that certain decision competencies can be unambiguously and reliably assigned, _a priori_, to certain jobs or certain positions of authority is becoming increasingly problematic (Dachler, 1986). It is increasingly difficult to assign complex, unstructured and dynamic problem situations rationally and analytically to predefined and stable job descriptions. Problems increasingly cut across many jobs and their respective individual encumbents. Problems to be acted upon are usually not 'God-given', but emerge from social–political negotiation, from influence, and from social or collective construction of reality processes. Such processes make it impossible to know in any reliable, 'objective', or deterministic manner which person has made what decision, within what job, at what time, to result in which organizational outcome.

Rather, the meaning of problems is defined by a variety of people, who, based upon their own reality, their own implicit theories, values and interests, negotiate various problem definitions as well as alternative potential solutions. Problems as well as derived solutions are mostly emergent phenomena rather than an outcropping of rational, reductive analyses (Berger and Luckmann, 1966; Dachler, 1985; Daft and Weick, 1984; Gergen, 1982; Probst, 1987; Weick, 1979). Problems increasingly transcend individual jobs, and changing problem _meanings_ constantly involve different patterns of jobs and people. Hence the emphasis on selecting people with the _primary_ focus on successful performance within a job already predefined and well anchored in the organization chart needs to be strongly questioned.

To summarize, it is becoming increasingly apparent that large and complex organizations, in contrast to mom and pop stores or smaller firms, such as the early Apple or Nixdorf computer firms, can no longer be understood appropriately by visualizing an additive increase of effectiveness by additional hiring of people who have the optimal characteristics for the requirements of, _a priori_ defined, individual jobs. This is because the additive aggregation of individual characteristics and behaviours essentially ignores the contribution of the complex networks of _relationships_ among people and groups within organizational settings. _The focus on individual qualifications with respect to successful performance in a predefined job, begs the question of what and how each of the interdependent jobs contributes to the overall performance of an organization._ In other words, even if theoretically one could imagine an organization in which all members perform optimally in their respective jobs, this in itself cannot guarantee that the organization as a whole also performs optimally. Organizational effectiveness is more than the sum of individual job performances, precisely because complexly interwoven relationships and the fundamental relatedness of organizations are crucial processes. Current selection and development models have failed to take them into account. This brings us to the second implicit assumption regarding the nature of organizations which drives the dominant perspective of employee selection and development.

Neglected aspects of relationships

Although relationships among people and groups in organizations are a traditional concern of organizational psychology, and have received some attention in
selection research (e.g. De Wolff and Van den Bosch, 1984), crucial aspects of
relational processes have so far played a negligible role in employee selection. A
closer look at the *underlying assumptions* that are made regarding the nature of
relationships will show that employee selection and development has ignored
fundamental concepts regarding *complex networks* of relationships in organizations.

In psychology, in general, and organizational psychology, in particular, relationships are primarily conceptualized analogously to physical relationshps. A
chemical reaction, for instance, which represents complex relationships among
chemical elements, is defined by the attributes of the interacting elements as well
as by some preconditions, such as the necessary temperature, pressure, or purity
of the element. Very similar is the traditional conception of relationships among
people or groups.

Relationships are defined by either the attributes and behaviours of the
individual actors or by the aggregate characteristics of the interacting groups.
Power relationships, or leader–member relations for instance, are researched on
the basis of resources, personal characteristics and behaviour patterns of the
powerful and subordinate interaction partners (Dachler, 1988). With such a
conception, however, little is said about the *relationship itself*. For instance,
theorists such as Bateson (1972, 1980) or Watzlawick, Beavin and Jackson (1967)
have pointed out that relationships are essentially communication processes
which include a *content level* as well as a *relationship level*, the latter informing how
the content level is to be understood within the *context of the relationship*. The *nature*
of relationships is an emergent property of interpretation processes that are based
upon *implicit* rules, norms, goals, interests and values which define the *meaning* of
relationships. De Wolff and Van den Bosch (1984) and Herriot (see Chapter 2.5)
have already pointed out that the selection process moves through different
phases, involving different processes and that, in general, the selection process is
more complex than some of the traditional models imply.

It should also be remembered that the human process of knowing in general is
an interpretation-driven *construction of reality process*. Implicit cognitive *preconceptions* (involving such concepts as mental maps, implicit theories, behavioural
scripts, values and interests) guide what through *exploratory perception* and
information-seeking *actions* is selected out of the potentially unlimited information available in the 'world out there'. Without such preconceptions of what is
expected to be known or what is *sought* to be seen, the 'world out there' is simply an
ambiguous, unrelated, buzzing confusion (cf. von Glasersfeld, 1985; Neisser,
1976; Weick, 1979). In relationships, therefore, actors relate to each other on the
basis of constructed realities involving their own identity, the content or problem
issues under consideration, their opposite actors and the overall social context in
which the interaction occurs.

Consider the group think phenomena which Janis (1972) pointed to, or the

construction of mental prisons in which individuals and groups encase themselves in interactions (Smith, 1982), or the power and politics in organizational
decision making that Pettigrew (1973), Pfeffer (1981) and others attempted to
describe. One should also remember the often observed barriers in communication and mutual understanding between, for example, marketing and production
departments, both of which 'see' the 'reality' of some problem situation from a
very different perspective. It should be clear that such relational problems simply
vanish into explanatory insignificance, if addressed *solely* on the basis of the
attributes (knowledge, skills and abilities) and specific behaviours of 'one individual at a time' (cf. Gergen and Davis, 1985).

This by necessity short and sketchy excursion into the nature of relationships
was intended to draw attention to the fact that traditional selection and development perspectives within their implicit set of assumptions construe a rather
simplistic image of the wide ranging phenomena involved in complex organizational relationships. For instance, a well-executed job analysis obviously takes
into consideration the kind of interpersonal, intragroup and intergroup relationships in which the various tasks to be performed in a given job are embedded.
From such an analysis inferences are then made about the necessary qualifications
of the job holder that allows him or her to handle these relationships successfully.
One might decide that such a person requires gregariousness, sensitivity to
political and human relations processes, good negotiation skills, etc. In this way
the network of relationships in which a job incumbent is embedded gets reduced
to particular enduring individual characteristics through which relationships with
others can be 'successfully' handled.

Relationships, however, are essentially communication processes that involve
a high degree of complex interpretation and social construction of reality processes. Hence the idea of selecting people on certain single and isolated dimensions defined *a priori*, that are thought to be 'possessed' by people, in fact obscures
or ignores social and political processes that are inherent in the design, control
and development of *organizations as wholes*. Therefore, crucial aspects of organizational performance processes may at best be ignored and at worse be hindered or
unwittingly directed towards undesirable or dangerous ends.

Assumptions about the nature of individual differences that guide dominant selection and development practices

Employee selection and development are 'problems' because of the fact that
individuals differ on many characteristics. They are problems also because
different tasks in organizations require different qualifications for successful
performance. However, they become problems in need of some solution only
through the meaning that is attached to them, that is, how in the context of any
given period of history or in a particular cultural, economic and social set of
circumstances such factual experiences are interpreted. Individual differences
have occupied the interest of social observers and those who saw the practical
consequences of such differences since the beginning of 'conscious' mankind.
However, the interpretation of what individual differences mean, what their

origin is, and what practical consequences derive from them, has changed in important aspects from the ancient Greeks, through Darwin, to early attempts by researchers like Galton, Pearson, Binet, Simon and Cattell (e.g. Schneider and Schmitt, 1986, p. 6 ff.). Therefore, it is important to look at current interpretations of individual differences and their underlying assumptions that serve as the basis for the dominant selection and development practices.

Within the long tradition of individual-difference-based employee selection and development one of the main assumptions concerns the idea that human beings can be reduced to relative independent traits, attributes, skills and abilities which can then be reliably and validly measured, in the sense that the measured quality of such attributes reflects as closely as possible the objective reality of the person who is being assessed. This assumption is, of course, in line with the idea that jobs contain relatively clear tasks, specified *a priori* from whose characteristics one can deduce isolated personal attributes that are required for successful performance on that job.

What remains unclear in this view of assessment is whether the personal attributes in question or the tasks that define a particular job are all that 'objective'. That is, employee attributes, such as decisiveness, competitive aggressiveness, leadership skills, tolerance for ambiguity, etc., are only linguistic or mental tools that have been invented to explain a certain set of behaviours which are thought or felt to be related to each other, and which as an aggregate seem to have certain effects. Most if not all of these dimension labels are therefore a result of our interpretations that we attach to many relational problems. These interpretations are not figments of our imagination, but are usually more or less ambiguous conventions which within some time period have been experienced as useful or meaningful in dealing with our everyday world in line with our goals and interests. This does not in any way deny that human attributes can be usefully measured. It simply means that there is no such thing as an objective trait called interpersonal skill, or aggressiveness, or decisiveness, or lack of self-confidence, etc., which a person possesses to various degrees as might be the case when we talk about physical characteristics, such as height and weight. Furthermore, the way we isolate one individual attribute as distinct from another attribute is in fact our own social construction. It simply reflects a particular way in which some set of behaviours is interpreted or explained to give an overall meaning to what otherwise would be isolated acts.

It might well be useful, for example in a selection situation, to distinguish the human relations orientation of a potential employee from his or her interpersonal and leadership skills. Nevertheless, one need not be an experienced psychologist to reinterpret such constructs so that, for instance, all three of these dimensions become part of one overall dimension; or out of the *three* dimensions we construct *seven* seemingly independent traits; or alternatively we retain the original three labels—human relations orientation, interpersonal and leadership skills—but give them a very different meaning by changing the definition of what we mean by each label. Thus, both the assumption of an independent identity of each attribute as well as the assumption that employee attributes are objectively possessed by the candidates are an output of our inherent capability to *interpret* or assign some meaning to the observations we make around us.

Furthermore, lately a number of researchers (Gergen, 1984; Gergen and Davis, 1985; Smith, 1972) have raised some interesting and revolutionary questions. They refer to attributes of interacting individuals, which we see reflected in specific behaviours or utterances, or in the absence of certain behaviours or utterances, and suggest that these are *interpreted* as some personal attribute, primarily on the basis of the relational or social context in which the social exchange takes place. Whether some act is considered aggressive or playful and whether a person is seen as aggressive or gregarious, depends on the interpretation of, or the particular meaning attributed to, the social context. This question is not restricted to momentary attribution or person-perception issues in a given social situation (cf. Hamilton, 1976). It is also relevant to attributes that are experienced as enduring characteristics of some person, such as consideration in the case of a supervisor or extroversion in the case of a sales person, for example.

Consider the case in which a leader is assessed as a task-oriented, controlling and highly structuring person. Leaders in Western society often have to legitimize their function, based upon the assumption that leading involves moving, creating, accomplishing objectives, designing new structures and outcomes. Furthermore, self-conceptions of leaders often contain the implicit theory or implicit assumption that the ultimate 'force' by which things are moved, created, accomplished and designed resides within the person who is assigned to a leadership position. This 'force' is based on the greater energy, knowledge, sense of responsibility, etc., that leaders attribute to themselves (and other observers attributionally support) in comparison to those people who are led. Such constructed (or interpreted) realities emerge from and are supported by the norms, rules and values that have evolved historically in Western cultures and societies *and* within the grown structures and processes of particular organizations with respect to leadership relations. These provide the social–cultural, interpretative context in which leaders have to construct their own identity. Through such an implicit self-understanding leaders are more likely to look for the kind of information that indicates and helps understand subordinates as in need of moving, as requiring structuring, as not being as independent and responsible as the leader attributes to him- or herself, and so on. It is such information which helps legitimize the socially constructed self-conception of many leaders (Dachler and Dyllick, 1988). As a consequence, subordinates, based upon the signs, symbols and communications which the leader employs as meaningful within his or her implicit self-conception, are more likely to interpret themselves as less competent and less active. Alternatively, they select themselves out of such a leader relationship, leaving those that 'fit' the leader's self-conception and, obviously, the kind of organizational context in which such a self-conception continues to make sense.

Thus, the assumption that individuals possess certain enduring characteristics which *cause*, in interaction with job and organizational variables, successful performance on some specific job, is a limiting conceptual basis for employee selection and development practices. Rather, so-called individual attributes are really the consequence of relationships and the meanings that are put upon them.

People may be seen to differ on certain characteristics depending on different outcomes of such mutual social construction of reality processes within complex organizations. Furthermore, such socially constructed realities may also have a bearing on what human attributes are interpreted as leading to effectiveness *within a given interpretation of leader–follower relationships*. Such relationally driven interpretation processes simply cannot be accommodated within the traditional *implicit assumptions* that guide employee selection and development practices.

To summarize, the implications of these arguments are that within a perspective of individual differences as *emergent phenomena* from complex networks of relationships, the traditional assumptions regarding enduring individual traits that can be selected to fit certain *a priori* established requirements of some job, may only contribute to *short-term* job effectiveness. Traditional practice limits the selection process to the immediate and defined demands of a given job and focuses only on those attributes that are relevant to the tasks as they are currently defined without incorporating the social–political processes on the basis of which jobs get their ever changing *meaning*. Consequently, the *overall potential* of applicants for future tasks and for various future career paths is neglected. In today's increasingly dynamic organizations it is the future potential of applicants, not only the immediate short-term success, with which selection and development must concern itself.

SOME CONSEQUENCES FOR SELECTION AND DEVELOPMENT PRACTICES

We have attempted briefly to outline and critically discuss some of the conceptual bases for current selection and development practices as a means of showing that crucial aspects of a rapidly changing organizational world are not given sufficient attention and at times are being overlooked. More importantly, we have tried to argue that some of the selection practices currently used may in fact impede some crucial organizational processes and changes that are most likely required for the effective handling of problems that organizations in the (near) future most likely will face. The crucial message in these arguments is that selection and development processes, and the implicit assumptions on which they are based, are an *integral part of the organizational phenomenon as a whole*. They cannot be dealt with as a separate function, which, although affected by other organizational variables, can be understood by removing them analytically from the overall patterns of processes within organizations as a whole. In this section we would like to illustrate some neglected aspects of the employee selection and development processes which become apparent on the basis of the alternative assumptions we have pointed to and will elaborate further, regarding the nature of organizations and the meaning of individual differences.

It may be helpful first to point out that the following arguments are based on an important distinction that needs to be made regarding the nature of jobs. While the fundamental concerns of this chapter *in principle* relate alternative perspectives about selection and development to all kinds of jobs, at this point of our understanding it is useful to make a distinction between two different categories of jobs. First, there are rather structured jobs, that are less embedded than others in the complex relational networks of organization, and that are relatively less prone to quick and constant change. Second, there exist jobs that, because of their strong relational embeddedness, are more ambiguous and unstructured in nature. Prime examples of the former jobs are those strongly attached to the structure and goals inherent in standard procedures, like accounting jobs, or to the structure of technical processes. In such cases, the problems to be dealt with are relatively unambiguous, the range of solutions is relatively restricted, and the meaning of such jobs and their objectives is more clearly defined and relatively less prone to change based upon relationally driven interpretational processes.

On the other hand, in an increasingly interdependent and service-oriented economy, there are multitudes of jobs and job categories, which, because of their embeddedness in complex intra- and interorganizational relationships, change their *fundamental meaning* relatively rapidly. This can occur because goals and objectives are changed or they are redefined so that their meaning changes. It can also happen because some patterns of tasks within a job suddenly are seen as absolutely crucial, even though at another time these same tasks are given a low priority, since they did not seem to be dealing with issues seen as in need of immediate solution. Moreover, based upon frequent restructuring attempts of organizations, integral tasks within a job are reassigned to other jobs, or eliminated altogether, while completely new tasks may be incorporated into an existing job. Thus, while there are certainly some *aspects* of any job that remain stable over relatively long times, the *overall meaning* of jobs may certainly change. This may imply changes in what is meant by successful performance on the job and the qualifications needed to be able to reach success in that job. It is for these kinds of less structured jobs, with ambiguous goals, which are found at all levels of the organizational hierarchy, that the following suggested changes in selection and development practices are particularly relevant.

Towards a more holistic assessment of employees

We have argued earlier that the different employee characteristics which are used in selection are simply convenient interpretative labels through which we attempt to assemble into meaningful 'pieces' the complex web of interrelated thinking, feeling, intuiting and behaving patterns of what we interpret to be successful or qualified employees. The question was raised whether it is meaningful to '*split up*' a job candidate on the basis of some category system, defined *a priori* into different dimensions, which are then attempted to be assessed, as if each dimension were a separate and distinct attribute that can be placed into an importance hierarchy according to its 'causal' contribution to job success. The meaning of any employee characteristic is always embedded in a network of many other characteristics, precisely because we cannot interpret something like decisiveness on its own. We have at the same time to consider implicitly the candidate's self-confidence, his or her work and life experiences so far, the way he or she takes initiative and the way a candidate thinks, analyses, structures and interprets problems and makes decisions in a particular social–cultural context. In other words, a given employee characteristic derives its meaning from the 'nomological network' of *implicit theories* about human behaviour in general.

There is another aspect which gets far too little explicit attention. The way in which required employee attributes are *selected* and *defined* for measurement in the selection process cannot solely be a reflection of the analytically derived requirements of the respective jobs. Instead, it must *also* be a reflection of the overall personnel policies, organizational strategies, and the culture and historically grown 'identity' of a company. Since the 'collective' performance of an organization must be more than simply the (linear) aggregate of performance on the various jobs in a company, and since collective performance is also a reflection of various social–political processes that run their course within the relational networks within and between organizations, employee attributes must clearly relate to more than just performance on a predefined job.

For instance, suppose a company recognizes that it must drastically increase its overall flexibility in order to respond more efficiently to dynamic market forces. In addition to considering changes in its structure, in its personnel policies, in its management philosophy, and in its overall strategies, some consideration must also be given to new requirements for employees within the context of changes in strategies, personnel policies, etc., over and above the requirements of the specific tasks contained in the various job descriptions. One might want to consider, for example, whether the general *idiosyncrasies* of employees should be given a chance to work, rather than trying to orient employees to one company way of doing things, in order to increase the potential alternatives that are brought to bear in solving problems. One might also want to *create* the preconditions so that people in different functional areas must confront and learn from each other, so that people start thinking independently beyond their own job responsibilities towards overall company objectives, and so that people can 'learn' the meaning of their role and function from their own experiences rather than such meaning being imposed by their supervisor or by the formal structure, and so on. What is implied with this example is that in this case one is actually not just dealing with some additional isolated skills and abilities of people, but with more global or holistic considerations regarding people, such as alternative ways of thinking, other world views, other *implicit* rules about the meaning of relationships within the organization, and so on. There is actually a large variety of possible ways of thinking, feeling, intuiting and behaving that can lead to successful performance. At any given time, some patterns emerge as significant, as useful and success related depending on the way people interpret their world within the network of social–political relationships.

Thus, over and above specific skills and abilities that may be required by the structural characteristics of the tasks and the immediate social environment of a job, there are many general 'patterns' which are part of the 'whole' person and which lose their fundamental meaning when one attempts to reduce such patterns to single dimensions for ease of quantitative measurement. Therefore, selection processes in principle may require a more *holistic assessment* of employees. Using the metaphor of a picture, it is the total picture and not the sum of its 'measurable' features that should be the output of selection processes. The sum of the individual features is always less than the meaning or the 'message' that the total picture of a candidate provides. Practitioners and selection specialists may argue that, while the total person comes to work, it is only certain aspects of that person which are relevant to the organization. This is of course an argument which makes sense only within a mechanistic perspective of organizations in which one 'sees' specially designed parts (i.e. jobs, functions), that in their causal interdependence accomplish some objectives. But it is precisely the *collection of total persons* which in social interaction, through communication and interpretation of their mutual organizational world, can have such a strong bearing on the way organizations design, control and develop themselves.

Selection processes cannot *over the longer range* assess how well or badly a candidate will perform in a job or in his or her work career, in the same sense that one tries to appraise the actual and specific performance of a person in a particular position at a particular time. Rather, it is the *future-oriented potential* of a candidate that needs to be assessed, i.e. the extent to which that differentiated but whole picture which emerges from the assessment process fits the *general implicit conceptions* an organization has (or should develop) regarding its employees in the context of the overall company strategies, its history and culture, in addition to the specific momentary requirements of a given job.

The call for a holistic assessment of employees in the selection and development process, rather than a reductionistic, purely statistical process of measuring artificially isolated characteristics of employees, is based upon the earlier discussed ideas regarding organizational effectiveness as a result of *changing interpretations* of problem-related *job patterns*. With more holistic assessment of employees it becomes possible to 'pool' employees within a personnel information system according to their *differentiated overall potential*, their career interests and their development progress. Such 'employee pools' can then be used for flexible assignments throughout a company and for flexible future development with respect to different career paths and changing demands on the organization. While information banks regarding available skills and abilities within an organization are in use, the problem is always that in trying to find the 'right' person for some assignment one essentially has to 'assemble' such a person from isolated dimensions, ranging from aspects of intelligence to social characteristics, such as interpersonal or communication skills. Whether one can get an overall 'picture' of a person is highly questionable, without information regarding the complex *interdependence* of the various measured dimensions and without those aspects that were not assessed, because they were not considered important for the requirements of some specific job.

Let us briefly describe an example in which a more holistic selection process turned out to be necessary as a consequence of changes that had occurred in an organization. We refer to one of our research projects on the relationship between the way supervisors and managers implicitly construct their own identity and the way they construct their social context in an organization (Dachler and Dyllick, 1988). We found that, depending on the ways in which managers constructed their own reality as leaders, organizational processes could emerge through which function-specific jobs were in fact integrated. For example, ever changing demands on one organization required a considerable flexibility in marketing and production processes.

Identity as a leader means the way one implicitly understands oneself as a leader and what leadership is, what it can and cannot do, and what it should do. The chief executive's identity as leader was that of an indirect manager, according to the motto: 'cultivate certain *processes* and let them *ripen*'. He allowed processes to develop by which individuals *in* marketing jobs were 'thrown together' with individuals *in* production jobs. After a while both sets of people not only ceased to think of themselves as either marketing or production employees, but began to be able to *think* in terms of the perspectives of the other function. Solutions then emerged from the *integrated reality* of the marketing and production functions. Marketing people could more fundamentally understand the problems of the world of production and vice versa, so that the individuals from either functional area could help in designing solutions for interrelated marketing and production problems. An enormous effort over considerable time was necessary to bring such processes to bear fruit. Therefore, a crucial question emerged whether a more holistic selection and development process could not from the start help in contributing towards such an integrated decision process, rather than selecting and developing individuals on the basis of specific traits for marketing or production jobs defined *a priori*. Such a holistic selection process was instituted for certain areas in the company by designing various assessment processes, including the fact that the groups in which a candidate would work started to act as assessors and different assessment and decision *phases* were designed into the overall selection process.

The role of organizational development processes in selection and development

As was pointed out earlier, it has long been argued that employee selection cannot be effective, if it is conceptualized and implemented apart from the organization as a whole. However, we have tried to show that contrary to the current selection paradigm, individual attributes as well as the meaning and nature of jobs are in good part a result of social interpretation processes. These emerge out of patterns of relationships, rather than existing objectively within general, relatively stable, laws of organizations whose meaning is definable independently of our enquiry and knowing processes. Within such a perspective the idea that employee selection must be an integral part of *organizing* takes on a somewhat different meaning.

The criterion problem

This has been a central issue in selection and development since the beginning of establishing systematic employee selection and development systems. From the beginning, measurement–technical issues of validity and reliability constituted the centre of attention with respect to the criterion problem and most often are still the main issues of concern. More effort has traditionally been invested in the measurability of the criterion than in its *fundamental meaning*. There is a frequently made distinction between the actual criterion (that aspect of job performance which is actually measured) and the rather unfortunate expression of the 'ultimate criterion' (unfortunate because it implies a definition, *a priori knowable* of global success on a job). Such a distinction points to the often considerable discrepancies between the meaning of success that is implied by what performance aspects are *actually* assessed and the *general*, often vague and difficult to specify *overall conception* of successful performance. Most suggestions of reducing these discrepancies have focused on technical solutions in the measurement process (e.g. Cascio, 1987; Schneider and Schmitt, 1986). This implies that the problem lies in the *not yet perfect* measurement process of an assumed 'objective', *a priori* knowable and relatively clearly definable construct of success. The more sophisticated and complete the criterion measure is, the more closely the 'ultimate' criterion can be measured.

Such a positivist perspective simply ignores or unwittingly avoids taking seriously the fact that it may be very difficult, if not impossible, unambiguously to find or see objective, stable, and in their meaning consensually agreed upon, performance criteria. As has already been pointed out, performance (individual as well as collective) has become much more complex and ambiguous. Over and above the more narrow and specific knowledge, skills and abilities required by the technical nature and structure of a given job, increasingly demands are heard for 'softer' employee characteristics, such as initiative, creativity, organizational commitment, independence, entrepreneurship, flexibility, etc. In addition, one hears pleas for fundamental changes in the way employees think and are motivated: synthetic instead of analytic thinking; long-term, strategic problem-solving processes rather than short-term, particularistic approaches to problem definitions and their solution; thinking innovatively beyond the particularistic interests of the immediate job objectives and the quarterly assessed profitability of performance; a focus on the contribution towards more global departmental, division or company strategies and policies, rather than only towards the specific objectives of a given job (e.g. McCaskey, 1982; Morgan, 1987; Kotter, 1978). If one looks at such requirements for members of complex and dynamic organizations, it becomes clear that first of all, the conception of success has more to do with a different way of thinking and knowing about the organizational world than with additional single human traits and behaviours, *a priori* specifiable. Also implied is a move away from primarily quantitative output-oriented conceptions of success, like profits, numbers of employees trained, units produced, etc., towards the *kind of processes by which outputs are accomplished*. Longer term success is often not only dependent on the *amount* of output but on the process by which that output is achieved. Quality, in particular, is heavily dependent on not only efficient, i.e. cost-effective processes, but also on the particular way of thinking about, handling, coordinating, conceptualizing, rethinking, questioning, redefining and recreating the various tasks, resources and people that constitute the processes which lead to a high quality output.

This is precisely why future selection processes need to focus increasingly more on the *holistic potential* of new employees, so that selection provides answers not solely on how well a prospective employee is likely to produce certain quantifiable outputs in a particular job for which he or she is being recruited, but also on what overall potential a candidate has to contribute to and further *develop particular ways in catalysing the multifaceted organizational processes*. In addition, selection processes must also contribute towards usable answers about the potential of prospective organization members to grow, develop and adapt with respect to *different possible* career paths within an organization.

It must at this point also be stressed, that what is *meant* by successful performance in a given job or with respect to collective performance is not something that can be answered analytically only in terms of unambiguous causal relationships. Instead, 'success' is also an emergent, in part self-organizing result of complex social interaction and interpretation processes (Daft and Weick, 1984; Morgan, 1986; Weick, 1979). Very often, job analysis procedures use job incumbents and other experts (e.g. supervisors) to help in defining both the job requirements as well as the necessary individual attributes which are necessary for successful performance in a job of interest. Far too little attention, however, is paid in such approaches to the fact that 'experts' *interpret* the meaning of a job, and therefore its crucial task and individual requirements, from their own particular socially constructed reality. If one took experts with a marketing perspective to define the meaning of certain production jobs and vice versa, a very different meaning would emerge, with different priorities in tasks and therefore different required individual characteristics of the job incumbent. The fact that jobs are increasingly embedded in complex networks of relationships would imply that there is a *variety of 'experts'* that have some implicit conception of what a given job has to accomplish and what success or effectiveness in that job entails. Of course, these implicit conceptions are in part a reflection of: (*a*) the way each actor in the network interprets his or her own work reality; (*b*) the particular relationship he or she has with his or her job and the organization as an institution as well as other related jobs and job incumbents in the network; and (*c*) the implicit organizational culture and history-derived norms and rules that provide the social–cultural context of the multiple relationships in the network.

For example, there is good reason to argue that the recent validity generalization studies (e.g. Schmidt and Hunter, 1981), which show that *well-established tests* of cognitive abilities reliably predict criteria of individual performance in a wide range of jobs and in different situations, simply reflect a social reality that has been socially constructed in the United States and, most likely, in most Western industrialized societies. First of all, these results are based upon *a particular kind of conception* of 'analytic' intelligence (among other potential conceptions) on which 'well-established tests' of cognitive abilities are normally based. Secondly, a large variety of jobs in Western cultures have implicitly been 'upgraded' in their (social) importance by implicit theories that postulate a requirement for an academic kind of analytic intellectual skills. Performance appraisers have correspondingly learned to watch for the kinds of behaviours which are commonly attributed to what is understood as an analytic type of cognitive skills. Since candidates are selected *and* evaluated on such skills, simply because 'success' has been socially constructed to be dependent on an academic type of cognitive skills, the validity generalizations only reflect this current construction of reality. These studies cannot imply that they reflect some 'God-given', objective reality with which we have to live, as if they demonstrated some unalterable natural law! On the contrary, it is high time to reflect upon whether such a construction of work reality in so many cases still meets our goals and values within an ever changing, and in its course unpredictable, world. One can certainly imagine other conceptions of intellectual abilities that perhaps come closer to the 'practical intelligence' and to the synthetic and holistic thinking which one can observe among some managers, for example, who are faced with a great deal of ambiguity and complexity (McCaskey, 1982).

The recognition that organizations are not by definition, on the basis of some objective reality of social nature, only a feat of rationally derived social engineering, but are also an emergent consequence of implicit social–interpretative or social–construction processes, might suggest an alternative focus in dealing with the criterion problem. Given social design processes within organizations which implicitly affect not only the meaning of jobs and what is considered successful performance in jobs, but also what attributes of people are interpreted as meaningful and as success related, the question arises whether one could use organizational development-oriented approaches (e.g. Argyris and Schön, 1978; Checkland, 1981; Cummings, 1980) to define job criteria and the potential of employees for longer range success within the organization. Organizational development processes in this context are understood to be any endeavour which contributes to *greater reflection* about assumptions, implicit rules and preconceptions that guide the interaction process within the relational networks. Reflection processes are seen as those that would allow all actors within a relational network to define, *explicitly* and *collectively*, the meaning of objectives and tasks which constitute job patterns, including the nature of effectiveness. In this way, the job analysis process would explicitly and systematically acknowledge and integrate the various political interests and values of 'stakeholders' in certain job patterns. The variety of different constructed realities of actors in the relational network could thereby be more systematically integrated. While the specifics of such an approach to the criterion problem need a great deal of research and development work, one would clearly not have to start from the beginning. Within the organizational development literature, the literature on alternative, democratic approaches to organizational design (Bernstein, 1976; IDE, 1976; Zwerdling, 1978), on soft systems methodology (Checkland, 1981), on quality of work life and emancipatory work design (Emery and Trist, 1973; Hackman, 1975; Hackman and Oldham, 1974; Walker, 1974; Ulich, Grosskurth and Bruggemann, 1973), and, of course, on aspects of selection and training (e.g. Hall, 1986; Schneider, personal communication), there is already a large variety of potentially interesting suggestions and approaches. Some of these have already been implemented, if not always systematically researched.

From such an approach to the criterion problem a hitherto somewhat ignored potential of selection might also be realized. *Selection could be thought of as primarily a development tool.* The objective then in selection is no longer to evaluate *only* potential candidates with respect to characteristics that are thought to be prerequisites for successfully meeting the demands of a particular job. Rather the selection process should provide a broad base of information regarding areas of pronounced and less pronounced characteristics, on the basis of which the potential for various longer term career paths can be evaluated and development processes can be instigated towards current as well as future demands within an organization.

Such development processes need to work out a common consensus of successful performance, that has a meaning not only for the narrow tasks of a given job, but also with respect to the company culture, its strategies and management philosophy. Through such a process more meaningful performance dimensions could be selected. Furthermore, a more 'consensually validated' process could be designed to determine which, in a given company perspective, are crucial individual attributes that should be *assessed* in the *selection process and further developed* within the company. Such an organizational development process, although without doubt demanding and costly, can be cost-effective. On the one hand, more meaningful *flexible* performance criteria for selection and performance appraisal could be developed. At the same time, on the other hand, organizations are encouraged to work out openly and explicitly, and therefore *better understand*, their conception of performance. As a consequence one can better avoid leaving such conceptions at the implicit level with all its inherent dangers of 'sweeping troublesome issues under the rug'. One can also avoid creating many misunderstandings through the ubiquitous ambiguity surrounding the conception of successful performance in the context of the organization *as a whole*. In this way, a company can also build-in a rather flexible process of constantly reinterpreting what it means and *needs* to mean by successful performance in view of a highly dynamic and ambiguous organizational world.

For instance, it is becoming increasingly clear that organizations, especially large organizations, can no longer see themselves as purely *economic units* in the context of a national or international economy. In today's highly organized and organizationally interrelated Western societies it becomes clear that, whether organizations like it or not, they are also crucial *societal* units with enormous impacts on society that go far beyond economic criteria. Outputs of work organizations also include fundamental human and social issues, such as the way employees see themselves as individuals and as working employees, the way they see the meaning of work, loyalty to the company, the meaning of work careers. Also involved are issues outside of the work organization, such as the meaning of education, the meaning of being a male or a female, the meaning of families and children, the way we live or should not live, and so on. Furthermore, the success of a company can no longer be assessed by ignoring its ecological impact, as the experiences of the atomic power or the chemical industries have clearly shown. It is simply no longer acceptable to have organizations concentrate their interpretation of their identity, and therefore the meaning of successful performance only within broad economic concepts. This is not simply an issue of ethics, but an absolute requirement for broader organizational as well as long-term economic survival. *What work organizations socially construct as powerful members of our societies are later societal preconditions within which they have to survive.* For instance, in the trend of corporate mergers and overhead value analyses, reductions in workforce are often carried out with a 'book-keeper rationality'. Within such processes employees start constructing different realities regarding company loyalty, commitment, long-term investments in quality, and the meaning of higher level management, and may begin to develop short-term perspectives of work. Those realities form the socially constructed environment which work organizations collectively designed for themselves and for which they carry the responsibility as well as the consequences.

Thus, when the implicit theories about successful performance and its interdependent dimensions are constructed for selection and other personnel decisions within organizations as a whole, an explicit reflection process is necessary. Mandated instructions from above, which are always prone to mis- and reinterpretations as they 'move' through the company, usually fall short. Mutually carried out negotiation and communication processes with all relevant actors need to be explicitly carried out. Through these processes, an attempt is made to integrate the various individual and group realities into a socially constructed meaning of successful performance over and above the narrow demands of specific jobs.

These arguments are all based upon the well-supported assumption that what ultimately ends up in the *definition* of successful performance has a crucial influence on what gets emphasized in an organization and *what does not*! In other words, the established definitions of performance expectations send out crucial signals throughout the organization about what needs to be emphasized and what seems less important, and can be more or less ignored. Thus, very narrowly defined performance criteria for specific jobs can easily counteract broader, company philosophy and strategy-related performance expectations. Therefore, an explicit collective process in defining global performance expectations, which allows a clearer understanding of these expectations and their meaning within the company culture, is required. New realities can thereby be created. The establishment of the meaning and usefulness of broad performance expectation cannot be left either to a powerful coalition or to chance. Powerful coalitions act within their own particular reality, which is no truer or better than many of the different realities that have been constructed within organizations as a whole. The myth of the more knowledgeable and truer realities of powerful coalitions has contributed to long-term disasters, such as the missed opportunities of the Swiss watch industry or the enormous difficulties for American companies to adjust quickly to an export and quality-conscious market. Through the hierarchical structuring and centralization of decision competencies a lot of potential variety is lost in bringing to bear different perspectives on apparent problem situations and therefore opportunities are lost in developing alternative solution approaches.

The predictor problem

Within the perspective taken in this chapter, the meaning of the term predictor is ambiguous. Selection is seen more as a developmental tool, that provides information about the longer range potential of prospective employees rather than short-term prediction about successful performance on some particular job.

As was shown earlier, the concentration on finding single, *a priori* definable human traits which can be unambiguously measured as a means for predicting a higher probability of success on a particular job to a great extent avoids tackling a complex problem. This is that such traits are in large part interpretative labels from which certain beliefs, perceptions and behaviours are deduced as indicative of some trait. Furthermore, the traditional 'predictor mentality' in selection ignores and prevents a more fundamental understanding of the fact that individuals do not *possess* personal attributes, but that we experience attributes as interpretative outcomes within the context of the network of relationships in which employees carry out their jobs. If we take seriously that the goal of selection is primarily a developmental one, then it would be rather useless to have the selection process provide only information regarding how 'good' or 'bad' a candidate is on some trait. If a person gets the feedback that he or she has rather limited organizing skills, then that person has really received very little useful information. He or she gets no information about the specific behavioural and thinking processes which characterize what are *seen* as chaotic organizing processes. And that is precisely the information a person would need (and the organization would need) in order to figure out what potential he or she might have for different kinds of jobs and different kinds of work careers and how he or she should direct his or her development activities.

The great difficulty, however, is to define a given individual characteristic in such a way that these behaviour or thinking patterns can be specified. Within a particular context of social reality, they can be logically and reliably subsumed under the implicit conception of a given trait label. In other words, specific behaviours observed during the assessment in the selection process must be *interpreted* as indicative of one or the other of the traits used in the selection process. And here lies the major problem.

Traditional selection procedures 'solve' this problem by relating the scores of exhibited behaviour on some measuring instrument to the scores of some norm group in order to gauge the extent to which a person has shown a certain characteristic. It is clear that such statistically derived information simply accepts the usually very narrow and often vague interpretation inherent in the way a measure was constructed and in the way a particular norm group was established. Thereby many other possible interpretations are neglected, which may have a much greater relevance to the existing reality of the organization in question.

For instance, in the process of designing a measure of initiative for supervisors, some conceptualization of what 'initiative' means needs to be invented. One can do that according to some theory in the literature. However, one has to explicitly recognize that such a 'theory' is only *one* possible interpretation of initiative, regardless of how much empirical research has been conducted regarding the validity of that theory. Another, and from our perspective more sensible, approach, is to have the organizational process 'define' initiative, by using participant observation, by looking at existing leadership documents in the company or by conducting 'open' interviews *throughout* an organization, for example. In so doing, one will most likely come to understand better what within a particular organization is meant by supervisory initiative. Further, one will realize that this meaning has a great deal to do, for instance, with the way supervisors and managers in that organization implicitly define themselves as leaders, as we have tried to illustrate earlier. Some may implicitly understand themselves as the origin of action, as one of the main causes of movement and change in their area of responsibility, as movers and shakers, who activate people and restructure situations. Out of such a self-identity of leadership they interpret as initiative people actively taking charge, engaging themselves frequently in group discussions, or forcefully promoting their own point of view in competition with those of others. This is certainly one way of interpreting initiative, one that makes sense in the male-oriented perspective of Western societies.

But what about an employee from whom one does not hear that much in a group setting, who quietly but actively listens to the various points of view and at the crucial moment makes an integrative suggestion or provides a summary conception of the problem under discussion? His or her intervention may initiate certain processes in the group from which a solution emerges that seems meaningful and acceptable to the group. Such a person takes initiative, not by trying to dominate the action process primarily from his or her point of view, but by trying to be the origin of some action or outcome, by catalysing a certain way of thinking or initiating certain processes by which a meaningful solution can emerge from the group. It takes a very different kind of supervisory self-image, a different leader reality, in order to interpret initiative in the way described above.

Based on the arguments made so far, it becomes questionable whether even with the most sophisticated *traditional* job analyses methods it is possible to define objectively some employee characteristic *without* getting into rather *subjective interpretation processes* through which the specific meaning of some required employee characteristic is established in behavioural terms. Any behaviour that occurs in a contextual vacuum is completely ambiguous. The same behaviour can signify very different characteristics depending on the total context in which it occurs, and depending on the overall significance that is attributed to the relevant organizational context. Thus, the overall culture and management philosophy of a company, its strategic perspective and general history will have a bearing on whether an employee characteristic, such as initiative, is seen as 'moving and shaking' or as 'initiating processes and cultivating them'. Rationally and analytically it would be impossible to decide on the one or the other perspective as being better, truer, or more successful, since we could never know specifically the various rules, images and preconceptions which enter into such an interpretation. But one can certainly activate the processes and systematically support them, through which a meaningful and company-relevant definition can be negotiated and renegotiated throughout the company.

Thus, with respect to establishing the behavioural definition of many employee traits to be included in the selection process, it may not suffice to take such definitions *only* from the 'shelves' of pre-established lists of traits and their particular definitions through the corresponding measurement method. Instead, through trying to make explicit the social–political interpretation and communication processes which implicitly occur in all organizations, we may be able to establish behavioural definitions of employee characteristics which fit or are meaningful in the context of the overall company management culture and philosophy.

CONCLUSIONS

We have tried to show that by questioning the implicit assumptions underlying the traditional selection models, alternative perspectives of organizations and individual differences can emerge. These are not truer or more valid in the sense of being closer to some ultimate objective reality, but they may be more meaningful with respect to problems that complex organizations, and particularly future organizations, most likely will face. The aim could not be to provide new ready-made answers to the question of selection in the organizational context. Instead we tried to point to a different way of thinking both about the way we know and understand the phenomena of employee selection and development as well as about the social technology that we construct to implement the selection and development decisions in organizations.

We have for space reasons deliberately neglected to discuss in detail possible alternative 'instrumental' approaches to employee selection. We have pointed to the potential of systematically incorporating organizational development processes into the design of selection and development systems without, however, being able to discuss the possible 'tools' in detail. At this point, we would also like to point out that the whole assessment centre philosophy, as well as many of the instruments that have been developed within that philosophy, seems much more adapted to the perspective taken in this chapter than the formal, mainly quantitative–statistical measurement and validation approach in the traditional selection models. As a matter of fact, many of the central ideas in this chapter have been developed in designing and implementing assessment centres in work organizations (Dachler, 1987).

REFERENCES

Argyris, C., and Schön, D.A. (1978). *Organizational Learning: A theory of action perspective.* Addison-Wesley, Reading.

Bateson, G. (1972). *Steps to an Ecology of Mind.* Ballantine Books, New York.

Bateson, G. (1980). *Mind and Nature.* Bantam Books, New York.

Benson, K. (1983). Paradigm and praxis in organizational analysis, in L.L. Cummings and B.M. Staw (eds). *Research in Organizational Behaviour*, vol. 5. Jai Press, Greenwich, pp. 33–56.

Berger, P.L., and Luckmann, T. (1966). *The Social Construction of Reality.* Doubleday, New York.

Bernstein, P. (1976). *Workplace Democratization. Its internal dynamics.* Kent State University Press, Kent, Ohio.

Cascio, W.F. (1987). *Applied Psychology in Personnel Management*, 3rd edn. Prentice-Hall, Englewood Cliffs.

Checkland, P.B. (1981). *Systems Thinking, Systems Practice.* Wiley, Chichester.

Cummings, T.G. (1980). *Systems Theory for Organizational Development.* Wiley, Chichester.

Dachler, H.P. (1985). Allgemeine Betriebswirtschafts- und Managementlehre im Kreuzfeuer verschiedener sozialwissenschaftlicher Perspektiven [Organization and management theory at the crossroads of different perspectives in the social sciences], in

R. Wunderer (ed.). *Die Betriebswirtschaftslehre als Management- und Führungslehre.* Poeschel, Stuttgart, pp. 203–35.

Dachler, H.P. (1986). Toward a systemic perspective of participation and industrial democracy. Invited address to the division of organizational psychology of the International Association of Applied Psychology at the 21st International Congress of Applied Psychology, Jerusalem, July 1986.

Dachler, H.P. (1987). Proper use of assessment techniques. Questions from practitioners to human resource specialists. Plenary talk given at the First European Congress on the Assessment Centre Method, Amsterdam, November 1987.

Dachler, H.P. (1988). Constraints on the emergence of new vistas in leadership and management research: An epistemological overview. In J.G. Hunt, B.R. Baliga, H.P. Dachler and C.A. Schriesheim (eds). *Emerging Leadership Vistas.* Heath, Lexington.

Dachler, H.P., and Dyllick, T. (1988) 'Machen' und 'Kultivieren': Zwei Grundperspektiven der Führung [Doing and cultivating: Two basic Perspectives of Leadership], *Die Unternehmung,* **4.**

Dachler, H.P., and Enderle, G. (1989). Epistemological and ethical considerations in conceptualizing and implementing human resource management, *Journal of Business Ethics.* (in press).

Daft, R.L., and Weick, K.E. (1984). Toward a model of organizations as interpretation system, *Academy of Management Review,* **9** (2), 284–95.

Emery, F.E., and Trist, E.L. (1973). *Towards a Social Ecology.* Tavistock, London.

Gergen, K.J. (1982). *Toward Transformation in Social Knowledge.* Springer, New York/Heidelberg.

Gergen, K.J., and Davis, K.E. (eds) (1985). *The Social Construction of the Person.* Springer, New York/Heidelberg.

Gergen, K.J. (1984). Toward self as relationship. Plenary talk given at the Conference on Self and Identity, Cardiff, Wales.

Glasersfeld, E. von (1985). An introduction to radical constructivism, in P. Watzlawick (ed.). *The Invented Reality.* Norton, New York, pp. 17–40.

Goldstein, I.L. (1986). *Training in Organizations: Needs assessment, development, and evaluation,* 2nd edn. Brooks/Cole, Monterey.

Hackmann, J.R. (1975). On the coming demise of job enrichment. In E.L. Cass and F.G. Zimmer (eds). *Man and Work in Society.* McGraw-Hill, New York, pp. 97–115.

Hackman, J.R., and Oldam, G.R. (1974). *The Job Diagnostic Survey.* Yale University Press, New Haven.

Hall, D.T. (1986). Dilemmas in linking succession planning to individual executive learning, *Human Resource Management,* **25,** 235–65.

Hall, D.T., and Goodale, J.G. (1986). *Human Resource Management—Strategy, design and implementation.* Scott Foresman, Glenview.

Hamilton, D.L. (1976). Cognitive biases in the perception of social groups, in J.S. Carroll and J.W. Payne (eds). *Cognition and Social Behaviour.* Erlsbaum, Hillsdale, pp. 81–93.

IDE – International research group (1976). Industrial democracy in Europe (IDE): An international comparative study, *Social Science Information,* **15,** 177–203.

Janis, I.L. (1972). *Victims of Group Think.* Houghton Mifflin, Boston.

Kotter, J.P. (1978). *Organizational Dynamics—Diagnosis and Interventions.* Addison-Wesley, Reading.

McCaskey, M.B. (1982). *Managing Change and Ambiguity.* Pitman, Marshfield.

Morgan, G. (1986). *Images of Organizations.* Sage, Beverly Hills.

Morgan, G. (1987). Riding the cutting-edge of change. A study of emerging managerial competencies. Working Paper Series, York University, Faculty of Administrative Studies, York, Ontario.

Neisser, U. (1976). *Cognition and Reality.* Freeman, San Francisco.

Pettigrew, A.M. (1973). *The Politics of Organizational Decision Making.* Tavistock, London.

Pfeffer, J. (1981). *Power in Organizations.* Pitman, Boston.

Preglau, M. (1980). Organisation, Führung und Identität [Organization, leadership, and identity], in J. Morel, T. Meleghy, and M. Preglau (eds). *Führungsforschung—Kritische Beiträge*. Hogrefe, Göttingen, pp. 133–69.

Probst, G.J.P. (1987). *Selbstorganisation—Ordnungsprozesse in sozialen Systemen aus ganzheitlicher Sicht*. [Selforganization—Ordering processes in social systems from a holistic view.] Paul Parey, Berlin/Hamburg.

Schmidt, F.L., and Hunter, J.E. (1981). The future of criterion-related validity, *Personnel Psychology*, **33**, 41–60.

Schneider, B. (1983a). Interactional psychology and organizational behavior, in L.L. Cummings and B.M. Staw (eds). *Research in Organizational Behaviour*, vol. 5. Jai Press, Greenwich, pp. 1–32.

Schneider, B. (1983b). An interactionist perspective on organizational effectiveness, in D. Whetten and K.S. Cameron (eds). *Organizational Effectiveness: A comparison of multiple models*. Academic Press, New York.

Schneider, B., and Schmitt, N. (1986). *Staffing Organizations*, 2nd edn. Scott Foresman, Glenview.

Smith, K.K. (1972). An intergroup perspective on individual behaviour. In J.R. Hackman, E.E. Lawler, and L.W. Porter (eds). *Perspectives on Behavior in Organizations*. McGraw-Hill, New York, pp. 359–72.

Smith, K.K. (1982). *Groups in Conflict—Prisons in disguise*. Kendall/Hunt, Dubuque.

Ulich, E., Grosskurth, P., and Bruggemann, A. (1973). *Neue Formen der Arbeitsgestaltung*. [New forms of work designs.] Europäische Verlagsanstalt, Frankfurt/Main.

Walker, K.F. (1974). Workers' participation in management: Problem, practice and prospect. *International Institute of Labor Studies (IILS) Bulletin*, **30**, 3–35.

Watzlawick, P., Beavin, J.H., and Jackson, D.D. (1967). *Pragmatics of Human Communication: A study of interactional patterns, pathologies, and paradoxes*. Norton, New York.

Weick, K.E. (1979). *The Social Psychology of Organizing*, 2nd edn. Addison-Wesley, Reading.

Wolff, Ch.J. de, and van den Bosch, G. (1984). Personnel selection, in P.J.D. Drenth, H. Thierry, P.J. Willems and Ch.J. de Wolff (eds). *Handbook of Work and Organizational Psychology*. Wiley, Chichester.

Zwerdling, D. (1978). *Democracy at Work*. Association for Self-Management, Washington, DC.

Chapter 1.4

Psychological Testing and Discrimination*

PIETER J.D. DRENTH

Department of Psychology, Free University, 1081 de Boelelaan, 1081 HV, Amsterdam, The Netherlands

INTRODUCTION

The discussion on the question whether psychological tests contribute to an increase or decrease in discrimination against minority groups is in Europe quite recent (Drenth, 1987). This discussion has already been conducted in the United States for several decades. Even early in the 1960s Gross (1962) and Black (1962), for example, accused the tests of measuring knowledge and capacities which the advantaged groups (the 'white middle class citizens') were better able to evolve and develop, thus leading to discrimination against minorities. At the same time, minority groups voiced the opinion that test usage should be positively assessed because the assessments would then be based on one's real capacities and not on several biases and prejudices (see, for instance Brim, 1965). To a certain extent, there is a long-standing tradition of avoiding the use of verbal tests for groups with differing linguistic and ethnic backgrounds because of the discriminatory effect that verbal tests could have. Already in the First World War an alternative to the verbal 'Army alpha' was developed. The non-verbal 'Army beta' was to make a 'fairer' distinction between more or less intelligent recruits in the multilingual America of that period.

As has been said, this issue has never, until recently, taken a central place in Europe, at least as far as large-scale application is concerned. The quantitatively large increase in the number of foreign native speakers and immigrants in many European countries has made the problem more acute in Europe as well. There

---

* This chapter is an adaptation of an earlier article in *Gedrag en Organisatie* (1988).

Assessment and Selection in Organizations   Edited by P. Herriot
© 1989 John Wiley & Sons Ltd

was a branch of psychology in which some interest in the subject existed; cross-cultural psychology. However, this branch has until recently played only a modest role in Europe. The European psychology was 'Western'. Knowledge of the psychology of other peoples did exist (the Netherlands and England, for example, have always been countries of travellers and merchants), but this knowledge was more anecdotal and not systematic. Here also a change has taken place, partly due to recent increases in mobility and immigration.

Placing Yugoslav, Turkish and Moroccan applicants in industry, schools and training grew from an incidental to a frequent and complex problem. Realization grew that use of the same tests, instruments of assessment and norms would lead to severe difficulties and could no longer be justified.

There was also a growing realization that in principle there was no difference between intercultural differences and intersubcultural differences. In other words, within one culture the same problems can be encountered as between cultures. Psychometrically seen, the problems of comparisons between test results of applicants from an urban against a rural environment, from blue collar against a civil service background is basically no different or more difficult than that concerning a comparison between Surinam and Frisian or Turkish and Scottish test groups. Also in the first comparisons the question arises: may I use the same test and if so, under what conditions?

It goes without saying that these problems with respect to minorities in European countries take on an additional political and emotional character. Minority groups justifiably ask for special attention to 'unbiased' assessment and treatment. It is also reasonable that psychology be asked to investigate whether the use of psychological tests not only avoids an obvious unfair treatment of minority groups in selection or placement in industry and government but that these tests also actively promote a fair treatment of such groups.

'FAIRNESS' OF TESTS

The question we now arrive at is what is termed as 'fairness' or its opposite 'bias' in test usage (Clearly, 1968; Cole, 1981). As has been said, this topic has long been under discussion in American selection psychology. This is understandable. The ideology of equal opportunity, formally supported by the 'Civil Rights Act' of 1964, has placed this issue in the centre of attention. In the United States, one encounters large ethnic and cultural minority groups in which, at least until recently, the 'opportunities' in education and vocations were hardly 'equal'. In addition, in the American selection process, whether for industry or education, formal test use has always prevailed over the subjective, intuitive test usage that has been more popular in Europe. There is, of course, no reason to assume that possible 'test bias' would play a more modest role in clinical test use. However, it is more difficult to detect this and it remains implicit.

The popular logic behind 'test bias' is as follows: The average test, either through form or content (or both), measures something which is present to a greater extent in an advantaged (e.g. white) than in a deprived (e.g. black) part of the population and, as such, has a discriminatory effect with regard to the latter group. In view of this, suggestions are often made to ban the test. This rigorous step is not unlike the ancient practice of slaying the bearer of bad tidings.

It may be a fruitful approach to try to analyse concepts like 'fairness', 'test bias' and 'discrimination' in some more detail. It can be argued that the test as such can never be discriminatory. A test only brings something to the surface, provides a score or a score profile. What can be discriminating, however, is an interpretation of the test (of such score or profile) or the use of the test.

DISCRIMINATION IN TEST INTERPRETATION

One can speak of a discriminatory character of test interpretation when differences in intelligence test scores are seen as differences in genetically determined intelligence potential. This inborn potential, or 'Intelligence A' as defined by Vernon (1969), is a postulate that has never been measured nor is ever likely to be measured. In any operational measurement of intelligence, at least by means of psychological tests, the result remains an indication of what Vernon calls 'Intelligence B', the phenotypical aspect of cognitive capacities. This is always a product of the interaction between genetically determined aptitudes on the one hand, and environmental influences and experience on the other.

On the other hand it is apparent that one type of intelligence test, in terms of its psychological meaning, could be closer to 'Intelligence A' than another; in other words, one test is geared more to the genetically determined component of intelligence than the other.

In fact tests can be placed on a continuum (see Table 1) with at the one end, tests for 'Intelligence A' as defined by Vernon, the hereditarily determined cognitive ability. At the other end of the continuum one finds tests measuring cognitive aptitudes or achievements which are pre-eminently determined by environmental or cultural factors (including educational). A history test or mathematics examination can be seen as examples of the latter. Between both extremes are tests for which a varying degree of cultural dependence has been demonstrated or may be assumed.

Table 1 Spectrum of intellectual/cognitive abilities and measurement devices

	Intellectual/cognitive abilities	Measurement devices
A.	Intelligence potential	Culture-free tests
B.	General intelligence General ability	Intelligence test batteries (g-score or sum score)
C.	Educational/vocational aptitudes	Aptitude tests
D.	General educational insight	General educational insight tests
E.	General educational achievement	General achievement tests
F.	Specific educational or training achievement	Specific achievement/performance tests

One sees that the influence of culture and environment increases in the spectrum presented in Table 1 the further one departs from level A and the more one approaches level F. It should be noted that it concerns a smooth transition. Nevertheless, an important distinction can be made between A, B and C on the one hand, and D, E and F on the other. The first group is 'prospective' and has a primarily predictive function. The latter group is 'retrospective', and has an evaluation function with regard to a previous learning process.

For a long time the illusion has existed in psychology that the so-called 'culture-free' test is able to measure 'Intelligence A'. In the meantime, it has become apparent that much experience with the so-called culture-free tests has not substantiated the expectation of being able to operationalize and maintain the idea of culture-free testing. Culture-free intelligence remains an immeasurable postulate and tests that purport to be culture free cannot substantiate their pretensions (Dague, 1972).

One could even go a step further and ask if the elimination of culturally bound variance from a test does not at the same time remove the most crucial aspect from the concept of intelligence. In any event, this is true of the element of language, in most cultures the most obvious means of communication through which concepts are formed and problem solving is learned. In other words, it is not at all disastrous that the attempts to construct culture-free tests have been unsuccessful. The latter would have been instruments which, in the first place, lack the capacity to contribute to knowledge of the essentials of intelligence, formed by both culture and environment and, in the second place, fail to provide a significant and practically useful relationship with many relevant criteria—certainly criteria within the education system.

Of course, it cannot be denied that some tests are more difficult to use in cultural comparison research than others. Tests such as the WAIS or the Stanford–Binet are by form and content so culturally determined that they are of no use in such comparison investigations. Translations impair the possibility of comparison for other reasons. In other words, tests are more or less faced with undesired cultural dependency affecting their usefulness in intercultural comparisons. However, as has been pointed out, not all culturally bound test variance is undesirable because this points to a relevant, culturally bound concept.

Let us now systematically summarize what has been said so far. The total variance in an intelligence test can be seen to comprise the following four components:

1. A component determined by 'Intelligence A' (hypothetical, immeasurable).
2. A component determined by culturally bound intelligence (desired culturally bound variance).
3. A component determined by undesired, usually culturally determined skills (which we wish to eliminate).
4. An error component (which we wish to keep as small as possible).

As has been said, the aptitudes responsible for component 3 are strongly determined by culture, training or environment; to be able to read, write, to follow instruction in the language used, to count. Also, test attitudes, motivation, concentration, fear, the tendency to provide socially desirable answers and such like, are strongly environmentally determined. When measuring intelligence, the aim is to ensure that these 'skills' play as small a role as possible. In the first place (see van der Flier, 1972) this can be assisted by extensive instruction and exercise; secondly, through carefully selected test procedures and conditions; thirdly, by statistical correction with partial correlation techniques; and, fourthly, by a selection of the test items which do not require these types of skills.

A final solution is to limit the use of the test to those sections of the population where it has been shown or where it can be assumed that the skills concerned will not display the (undesired) variance. For example, a written intelligence test for a normal Dutch population shows no differences with regard to the skills 'to be able to read Dutch' or 'to be able to write Dutch'. These skills have been sufficiently learned in that population to no longer display any variance. In an immigrant group of applicants this could be an incorrect assumption. In this case, the test would measure the factor 'to be able to read and write Dutch' instead of 'intelligence'; an example of undesired variance. For this group the 'intelligence test' should not be used for determining intelligence.

From describing the possibility of discrimination in the interpretation of tests, we move on to the question of possible discrimination in test usage.

DISCRIMINATION IN THE USE OF TESTS

The chances of discrimination in test usage occur mainly in the area of selection. By employing tests (minority) groups who gain lower scores have less chance of being selected and—according to a widely held view—are thus discriminated against.

Let us consider this matter further. We assume that the tests used are reliable and objective and contain a sufficient degree of validity. This means that reasonable relationship exists between the test scores and later performance (training performance, work performance) so that those who are appointed on the grounds of, for example, high scores, also have a greater chance of success in the function for which they are selected.

With regard to this selection, there are two strategies which can be distinguished in view of our problem. We shall attempt to see to what extent discrimination occurs in these strategies.

Maximization of efficacy

In the first place, the strategy aiming at maximization of efficacy. This strategy is geared to equal chances of success of all those investigated in the function for which selection is being made. It is therefore based on maximizing validity.

When does discrimination occur in this process? Not when lower scores on the selection tests for all applicants alike (whether they come from majority or minority groups) are coupled with lower scores in later performance in the function. In other words, if selection test scores for various groups of applicants equally reflect later performance, there is no discrimination, even if the *average* test score for one group is lower than for the other. Given in statistical terms, this means that there is no discrimination if the regression lines for the two groups coincide (as illustrated in Figure 1).

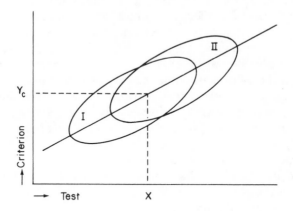

Figure 1

Discrimination takes place when a difference in test performance between two groups does not coincide with an analogous difference in the criterion performance. Statistically seen, this occurs when the regression lines do not coincide. An example is given in Figure 2.

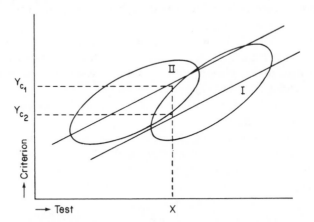

Figure 2

We see again, that the average test score for Group II is lower than for Group I, but this is not to be found analogously in the criterion performance. An example of this situation could occur in the case where an immigrant group (II) could be disadvantaged by a (language or cultural) handicap, which in reality is of lesser importance or is compensated. It is important that the concept discrimination is used here to show that one and the same cut-off score on the selection test predicts a higher criterion score for one (discriminated) group than for the other (advantaged) group. In such a situation different cut-off scores for the different groups should be applied.

Note that this must be empirically demonstrated and not merely assumed. Cronbach (1972) presented the situation shown in Figure 1 (no discrimination) as most commonly occurring when referring to comparisons between the relationships between tests and school performance for black and white pupils in the USA. He states that when discrimination occurs, then it is the white pupils that are more likely to be affected; that is, language and cultural handicaps play an even greater role in education than in the test!

In this way, the term 'discrimination' is psychometrically defined and the problem appears to be solvable along psychometric lines. However, it is not as simple as this. There are at least two more flies in the ointment.

Firstly, a part of the problem seems to be pushed aside; to the criterion. Suppose a test correlates with the criterion (later performance in training or function). Suppose, however, that later criterion performance is an unfair reflection of one's capabilities (for example, by prejudiced assessment or because immigrants have less chance to display good learning or work performance due to a language handicap). Thus the criterion will contain an amount of 'bias' which then also will be reflected in the (correlating) tests. The removal of this form of discrimination will have to occur therefore via a 'purification' or 'fairer' content of the criterion measure.

Secondly, the maximization of validity gives rise to more direct questions. The inclusion of variables such as sex, socio-economic class, ethnic grouping, religion, etc., as predictors can in themselves be beneficial to validity. But, is this justifiable? This would mean direct discrimination, even though legitimate within the model! Moreover, 'neutral' predictors such as motivation, attitudes, knowledge, language fluency, etc., may increase validity on the one hand, but on the other, could be correlated with the previously mentioned variables. Could we not then speak of 'indirect' discrimination?

In this connection two submodels can be distinguished within the model of the maximization of efficacy:

1. In the first place, *unqualified individualism*. In this approach, everything which increases the validity is acceptable, either as a predictor or as a moderator: test scores, knowledge, questions on personality, biographical information including variables such as sex, ethnic grouping, etc. The legitimacy is found in the aim: maximization of equal opportunities on the criterion performance. If belonging to an immigrant group decreases the chance of success, then this should be included in the multiple regression with a negative weight.

2. The second approach, called *qualified individualism*, deems as unacceptable the direct discrimination of women, minorities, the socio-economically weak, which could be the result of unqualified individualism. These types of demographic or sociological variables should therefore not play a direct role in selection, neither as predictor nor as moderator, even if they increase the

predictability of the criterion performance. On *a priori* grounds, the social or demographic groups which may not be discriminated against are established, and belonging to this group may not be considered as a (dichotomous) variable to be included in the prediction formula. Direct discrimination is therefore avoided. Maximizing validity is attempted but not by including direct discrimination parameters. However, indirect discrimination is not eliminated. Valid predictors which in turn could correlate with the factors just mentioned are included in the regression formula.

Maximization of equal opportunities in selection

Besides maximizing the efficacy, the selection strategy can also be geared towards the maximization of equal opportunities in selection.

As a first example selection by means of lottery can be mentioned. Following this 'strategy' everybody has an equal chance to be accepted indeed. A totally unreliable test has the same effect: chance determines the selection. It is clear that what suffers here is the efficacy; i.e. the improvement of the average training performance or work performance by selecting those who have a greater chance of performing successfully.

In addition, four strategies can be mentioned which are aimed at some efficacy in terms of better performance of those selected as compared to the average performance of all candidates, but, at the same time, which strive for an increase of equal opportunity in selection for various groups.

1. The principle of 'weighted lottery', as used for example in the admission of medical students in the Netherlands. Selection is still a matter of lottery, but the chances of 'having luck' increase with a higher grade point average of the applicant.
2. What could be called *corrected individualism*. In this strategy, all predictors are corrected for their relationship with the possibly discriminating variables. Through partial correlations the valid predictors are purified of their discriminative effects. This can, of course, be at the expense of validity.
3. Selection from each category for which it is decided to avoid discrimination (women, minority groups) of a percentage in proportion to the percentage of that category in the group of applicants. Of course, this can have a negative effect on the efficacy as well.
4. A proposal to select from the categories as mentioned in 3 (above) a percentage in proportion to the percentage of *successful* representatives of those categories among the applicants (based on previous research). This proposal has been made by Thorndike (1971) and Cole (1973). This can also be disadvantageous for the efficacy, although to a lesser extent than the proposal mentioned in 3 (above).

There is now considerable agreement that the aims of maximizing efficacy (validity) and maximizing equal opportunity are in conflict. In other words, there is no perfect objective solution to the problem of discrimination in selection, in which preference is still given to those candidates who are more likely to perform successfully. Making subjective decisions regarding the relative importance of both aims is unavoidable. The decision maker must, it seems, indicate how much validity he or she is willing to sacrifice in order to create equal opportunities. This has been quantitatively expressed in the utility models of, for example, Darlington (1971), Gross and Wen-Huey (1975), Petersen and Novick (1976) and Van der Flier and Drenth (1980).

A rough but in many cases pragmatic approach is followed in the so-called quota system. In each case a certain percentage of the minority groups concerned is accepted, even though some of them may have less chance of success than some of those rejected from the majority group. The level of the percentage is some-times empirically defended (see under 3 and 4 above), but arises mainly from intuition or on the basis of negotiations or a political choice.

CONCLUSION

Two issues become clear from what has been said in the foregoing. Firstly, it is incorrect to accuse the test as such of being discriminatory. It is only in the interpretation or the use of the test data that discrimination can occur.

Secondly, in selection intended to choose those who have the best chance of later success, the possibility always exists that members of minority or immigrant groups have less chance to be selected than members of majority groups and the indigenous population. This is inherent in, and a consequence of, the above-mentioned purpose of selection.

If one wishes to offer better chances to the minority groups, then this will usually be at the expense of the efficacy. Basically, it will be a policy decision which balances between 'equal opportunity' and 'efficacy' in the given circum-stances and within the economic and political conditions which will be preferred.

REFERENCES

Black, H. (1962). *They Shall not Pass*. Random House, New York.

Brim, O.G. (1965). American attitudes towards intelligence tests, *American Psychologist*, **20**, 125–30.

Clearly, T.A. (1968). Test bias: prediction of grades of negro and white students in integrated colleges, *Journal of Educational Measurements*, **5**, 115–24.

Cole, N.S. (1973). Bias in selection, *Journal of Educational Measurements*, **10**, 237–55.

Cole, N.S. (1981). Bias in testing, *American Psychologist*, **10**, 1067–77.

Cronbach, L.J. (1972). Judging how well a test measures, in L.J. Cronbach and P.J.D. Drenth (eds), *Mental Tests and Cultural Adaptation*. Mouton, The Hague.

Dague, P. (1972). Development, applications and interpretation of tests for use in French-speaking Africa and Madagascar, in L.J. Cronbach and P.J.D. Drenth (eds), *Mental Tests and Cultural Adaptation*. Mouton, The Hague.

Darlington, R.B. (1976). A defense of rational personnel selection, and two new methods, *Journal of Educational Measurements*, **13**, 43–52.

Drenth, P.J.D. (1987). Intelligence tests in education, evaluation and selection, in Ç. Kağiçibaşi (ed.), *Growth and Progress in Cross-cultural Psychology*. Swets & Zeitlinger, Lisse.

Drenth, P.J.D. (1988). Psychologische selectie en discriminatie, *Gedrag en Organisatie*, 1(3), 12–22.

Flier, H. van der (1972). Evaluating environmental influences on testscores, in L.J. Cronbach and P.J.D. Drenth (eds), *Mental Tests and Cultural Adaptation*. Mouton, The Hague.

Flier, H. van der and Drenth, P.J.D. (1980). Fair selection and comparability of testscores, in L.J. Th. van der Kamp, W.F. Langerak, and D.N. de Gruijter (eds), *Psychometrics for Educational Debate*. Wiley, London.

Gross, M.L. (1962). *The Brain Watchers*. Random House, New York.

Gross, A.L. and Wen-Huey, Su (1975). Defining a 'fair' or 'unbiased' selection model: a question of utilities, *Journal of Applied Psychology*, **60**, 345–351.

Petersen, N.S., and Novick, M.R. (1976). An evaluation of some models for culture-fair selection, *Journal of Educational Measurements*, **13**, 33–39.

Thorndike, R.L. (1971). Concepts of culture-fairness, *Journal of Educational Measurement*, **8**, 63–70.

Vernon, P.E. (1969). *Intelligence and Cultural Environment*. Methuen, London.

Chapter 1.5

The Changing Role of Psychologists in Selection

CHARLES J. DE WOLFF

Department of Psychology, Catholic University of Nijmegen, Montessorilaan 3, 6400 HE Nijmegen, The Netherlands

INTRODUCTION

The history of personnel selection is dominated by the 'individual differences' paradigm. For a long time work psychologists were primarily concerned with 'differential psychology', trying to identify, describe and measure differences in aptitudes, traits and interests. On the one hand they studied jobs, trying to find out what job incumbents were required to do, and on the other hand they selected or devised tests for measuring the required qualities.

This approach has been rather successful, particularly in the first part of this century. In the First World War tests were already used on a large scale in the US military forces. In the Second World War this happened on an even larger scale. Thorndike (1949) mentions in the introduction of his well known textbook that 'hardly a man of the 14 000 000 who served the nation during that period failed to have his career affected in some measure by selection and classification tests devised and administered by personnel psychologists'.

When Thorndike published his book he was rather optimistic. He predicted 'a rich future for psychologists using tests for selection and classification of personnel'. He had good reasons to be proud. The 'Army Air Force Psychology Program' was especially successful. Individuals selected with the help of selection procedures designed by personnel psychologists did much better than unselected individuals. Correlations between tests and criteria were substantial.

Thorndike was well aware that selection is a complicated process. In the introduction to his book he points out that he wants to 'attempt to provide a

---

Assessment and Selection in Organizations   Edited by P. Herriot
© 1989 John Wiley & Sons Ltd

guidebook to show the way that must be travelled in developing a selection program and to point out some of the rocky spots and morasses which lie in wait for the unwary'. He also made a distinction 'between "self styled psychologists," "personnel experts" and other quacks, and the reputable worker in the field, who is continuously concerned with testing, verifying and improving the adequacy of his procedures'. Thorndike believed in a professional approach, which was based on the measurement of individual differences. He and his colleagues developed a mature selection technology, which had much appeal. In the period between the late 1930s and the early 1950s not only methods for statistical analysis, job analysis and test constitutions were developed, but also instruments were designed and information about validity was disseminated. Buros published his *Mental Measurement Yearbooks*, Lindquist edited the *Educational Measurement Handbook* (1951), Personnel Psychology published the *Validity Information Exchange*. Psychologists, not only in the United States but also in Europe were highly impressed and adopted this technology on a large scale, for application not only in organizations, but also in educational institutes.

At that time there was a strong belief in individual differences, not only among psychologists, but also among clients. Cowley (1928) wrote a review article about management selection that stated: 'the approach . . . perhaps must always be through the study of traits'. And also in the 1950s and 1960s psychologists were convinced that differences in performance should be attributed to individual differences. As a consequence personnel selection was defined as a prediction problem.

Thorndike also strongly realized that psychologists were dependent on others for the continuing support of their activities (p. 312): 'A basic fact that every personnel psychologist needs to appreciate . . . is that the broad administrative decisions which determine the conditions under which he is to work will be made not by him but by his administrative superiors. Some person or persons in the top level of management will have the power to decide that there is to be a personnel selection program and that psychological tests are to be used.'

For a long time psychologists saw themselves as professionals who could assist management in the decision-making process about selecting individuals from among applicants or of determining to which possible job category a particular individual should be assigned.

So it was during the 1940s and 1950s that a clear role for the personnel psychologist was established. He or she was someone using tests to measure individual differences, in order to predict future performance, and assisting management in the decision-making process. In that period psychologists were rather optimistic about the contributions they could make to achieve organizational goals. Many were excited about the new technology. Selection had become a science, and was no longer an art. It was an activity requiring scientific rigour.

What made psychologists even more optimistic was the idea of an iterative process. By improving the tests and by adding new predictors to test batteries, validities could be improved. By increasing efforts better predictions could be made. So a bright future looked to be ahead.

Unfortunately reality was different. Although the new technology was widely applied there were many problems which were unforeseen at that time. Those problems partly had to do with the paradigm, and partly they stemmed from society. Psychologists had defined selection as a prediction problem. In doing so they had isolated one particular problem, and had disengaged it from other problems. In the course of time they learned that important aspects had been overlooked.

PROBLEMS IN SOCIETY

Within society several issues were raised during the 1960s and 1970s. These concentrated on dignity and discrimination.

This concern started in the early 1960s with publications like *The Tyranny of Testing* (Hoffman, 1962), *The Brain Watchers* (Gross, 1962) and *The Naked Society* (Packard, 1964). Psychological testing was strongly attacked. In 1965 the US Senate and the House of Representatives set up committees for a congressional inquiry in testing. The chairman of the committee explained in the *American Psychologist* (November 1965) why the House Hearings were held '. . . the Federal Government has been engaged in . . . searching the minds of Federal employees and job applicants through personality testing'. Applicants and employees 'resent the questions and admit quite freely that their answers were those they thought would get them the job or promotion' and 'There is little or no effective appeal procedure for our citizens, who wish to challenge personality testing as an invasion of privacy. . . .' Psychologists defended themselves by pointing out that they were not interested in the answers to individual questions, but in the relationships with a criterion. But the committee did not accept that argument.

It was not only in the United States that applicants felt abused. In the Netherlands in 1971 questions were asked in Parliament about psychological testing. The Government set up a committee (the Hessel Committee) to study selection procedures. The final report was published in 1977. The committee based its recommendations on two principles:

1. The criterion for selection is the applicant's suitability for the job.
2. All parts of the procedure should be consistent with human dignity.

The committee also recognized a number of rights for applicants, i.e. the right of confidential treatment of data, the right to lodge complaints, the right to privacy, the right to a fair chance to be engaged and the right to information.

Another issue discussed at that time was the imbalance between employers and applicants. Employers can afford to pay consultants, or hire specialists to assist them in the decision-making process. But applicants have to do it all by themselves. In this view psychologists were seen as servants of management. At that time there was also much mistrust about management. As a consequence selection was also looked upon with suspicion. Psychologists started to concentrate on other issues (e.g. participation). In some countries, such as Italy, psychological selection literally disappeared.

The other issue receiving much attention, particularly in the United States, was discrimination. In 1964 the US Congress passed the Civil Rights Act, in which a separate paragraph was dedicated to 'Equal Employment Opportunity' (EEO). In the following years more detailed prescriptions were issued by the EEO Commission and the Office of Federal Contract Compliance, among others *Guidelines on Employment Testing* was published (1966). This created the possibility of exercising sanctions against employers who discriminate against minorities.

The effect of this legislation on selection psychology was enormous. Ash and Kroecker (1975) mention that in the early 1970s some 70 000 claims per year were lodged with the EEO Commission, of which 15–20 per cent concerned discrimination on account of an unfair use of tests.

Psychologists were unprepared. During the 1960s there was hardly any discussion about this issue. During the 1970s it required immediate attention. It also introduced many legal aspects. It is now common that in literature on selection reference is made to court cases (e.g. Schneider and Schmitt, 1986).

In Europe there has also been concern about employment opportunities for minorities, but the impact of legislation is in no way comparable to what occurred in the United States.

In this respect it is worth while to note the conclusion of the US National Academy of Sciences:

> The Committee has seen no evidence of alternatives to testing that are equally informative, equally adequate technically, and also economically and politically viable . . . and little evidence that well-constructed and competently administered tests are more valid predictors for a population subgroup than for another; individuals with higher scores tend to perform better on the job regardless of group identity (National Academy of Sciences, 1982, p. 144).
>
> (Quoted from Schneider and Schmitt, 1986.)

The examples mentioned above show that selection issues, and activities of psychologists, evoked reactions from society. They also led to government intervention, e.g. in a form of legislation. This had a tremendous impact on the development of the subject. Many psychologists changed their interests and took up other subjects. The interest in doing selection research diminished considerably. At universities selection became a neglected subject. A number of practitioners continued to work in this area, but in general there was a substantial reverse. It is only in the past few years that interest at universities started to grow again.

PROBLEMS WITH THORNDIKE'S APPROACH

In the course of time psychologists discovered a number of problems about Thorndike's approach. They can be grouped in three categories: technical problems; problems about assumptions; and problems related to the interaction between organization and applicant.

Practical problems

The high expectations psychologists held immediately after the war did not come true. Much progress was made in test construction; better tests became available; many studies were executed. But correlations between combinations of tests and criteria were not as good as was hoped for. At the end of the 1960s Rundquist (1969) wrote that there appeared to be a ceiling. For predicting training criteria correlations did not exceed 0.50, and for job performance, measured by supervisor ratings, 0.35. So the idea that by improving instruments, and by adding new tests to the battery, correlations would improve did not materialize.

Furthermore, Thorndike's approach could in many cases not be applied. It required the use of fairly large samples to establish a good combination of tests, but often such samples were not available. Even in large organizations where thousands of applicants were tested every year there were often only a few vacancies for a certain category of positions. For example, the present author worked during the 1960s in an organization employing some 17 000 individuals, but there were some 1000 different jobs. As a consequence test results could not be related to criteria in the way prescribed by Thorndike. Many psychologists used clinical methods in such a situation.

Nor was it easy to define populations. Positions bearing the same title might involve different tasks (e.g. cranedriver could mean someone operating a crane capable of handling 500 kilos, or one for ten tonnes).

Psychologists discovered that criteria could only partially be predicted. Objective measures are often not available, and if they are, they often have limited validity (in the example above the amount transported by a cranedriver might have more to do with the crane than with the cranedriver). The most used measures are ratings by supervisors. But they have limited reliability, and it has been demonstrated that the major part of the variance cannot be predicted by psychological tests (de Wolff, 1963, 1967).

Problems about assumptions

In his book Thorndike assumed that there is an ultimate criterion, and that this can be measured. This criterion is related to the total contribution individuals make to the organization during their period of employment. 'Such a criterion is almost always multiple and complex' (Thorndike, 1949). Thorndike was well aware of the difficulties of measuring such a criterion. 'It is rarely, if ever, available for use in psychological research.' At best one can measure 'intermediate criteria'.

This line of reasoning assumes that, when the prediction is made, the demands that will be made upon an individual during employment are known. The literature on open systems theory shows that this is not a realistic assumption. Organizations operate in a turbulent environment, and as a consequence demands change, skills and knowledge become obsolete, and new skills and knowledge have to be acquired. Thorndike's model fits in a closed system approach, but not in an open system one. When there is a good intermediate criterion, like there was in the Second World War with pilot training, it is applicable. But when one selects individuals for a career, and future demands are not known, the ultimate criterion cannot be predicted. Furthermore, it was assumed that demands could be established through job analysis, specifying tasks which constitute the total work assignment of a single worker. For many positions this is not the case. A manager, operating in an expanding organization has to meet other demands than a manager who has to execute a downsizing operation. When one has to merge two organizations tasks are different from when quality circle programmes have to be set up: requirements are contingent upon the situation.

An important assumption of Thorndike's approach is that performance is determined by individual differences. There is, however, now a vast literature showing that other variables are also important determinants. It is commonly accepted that performance has multiple determinants, e.g. motivation, training, leadership, and working conditions. This has several consequences. If there are multiple determinants performance can only be partially predicted by tests. But it is also likely that selection procedures might affect other determinants, e.g. motivation. Job involvement (Mowday, Porter and Steers, 1982) appears to be influenced by the way organizations socialize employees, and structure the staffing process.

If there are multiple determinants performance can be improved not only through selection but also through other interventions (e.g. training).

The interaction between organization and applicant

The selection situation is not a neutral one. For both the applicant and the organization there is much at stake. Through employment individuals can acquire many rewards like income, social contacts, security, promotion and recognition. And the impact individuals have on organizational performance is often perceived to be large. So the organization is very eager to recruit a capable individual. Both parties often try to have alternatives, i.e. other job offers or other candidates. Parties also try to influence one another, to sell only strong points and to play down weak aspects. In such a negotiating process Thorndike's approach is usually not much help. If a clear relationship between tests and performance on the job has been demonstrated this might be useful for explaining to an applicant why he or she is accepted or rejected. But if such information is lacking, e.g. because of small numbers, or because tests have low validity, it is difficult to explain the decision-making process to candidates. The concepts used for constructing tests are different from the ones used in communication between applicants and organizations.

Furthermore the approach assumes that the employer can make a choice, and that the decision is accepted by the applicant. But applicants often also have a choice. They can turn down the offer, and stay where they are, or accept another offer. There is not one decision-making process, but there are two. And these two processes are interrelated. Thorndike's approach does not cover this aspect.

Neither does the approach appreciate the processes going on prior to the decision making. When candidates are already employed by the organization they may deliberately strive to gain a promotion. Sometimes there is competition, and in the interaction between candidates it can gradually become clear who is most qualified (or accepted by the individuals who have to do with that decision).

Becoming a leader is usually the result of a social process, and not of computing a test score.

A DIFFERENT APPROACH TO SELECTION

Thorndike's approach appears to be applicable in cases where there is a well-defined and measurable criterion, and when there are many more applicants than vacancies. In other cases other approaches are needed. And even when the model is applicable there is need for additional activities. Actually such other approaches have emerged; there are psychologists who have adopted a different role in assisting organizations in staffing problems. In this final part of the chapter we will describe a different approach and the consequences for the psychologists' role.

When a vacancy occurs in an organization, management is usually confronted with a very complex problem which can be approached in very different ways. A first question is should one try to fill the vacancy or try to reorganize so that the work can be done with lower costs. If one decides to look for applicants the next question is: What are the job requirements and what are the rewards which can be offered and what is the best way to recruit applicants? Has one to look for applicants in the organization (internal recruitment) or outside the organization (external recruitment)? And how should one try to get in contact with applicants: through advertisements in journals (which journals?), through consultants (head hunting), through campus recruitment? Should it be a position with tenure, or should one try to hire someone temporarily?

As soon as individuals have applied for the job there are other questions: how to conduct interviews, and how to compare applicants. Should psychological tests be administered?

Most managers are only occasionally involved in staffing problems. Usually only a few vacancies occur per year. So it is common that they seek advice and the help of professionals. This can be someone from the personnel department or an external consultant. Often such a professional is a psychologist. There is even a kind of specialization. Hiring production workers or clerical staff is different from recruiting an executive officer. If one considers reorganization, so that a vacancy is not to be filled, one might have a different consultant than when one wants to recruit applicants for a particular training programme.

So staffing is a complex problem requiring extensive expertise. Psychologists with a training in personnel psychology and broad experience in this field can be highly regarded consultants.

More narrowly defined the selection problem is a decision analysis. Whom should be hired and whom should be rejected by management? But also should an applicant accept or reject an offer? This implies a, usually lengthy, exploration process. Both the organization and the applicant have to explore the costs and benefits of particular alternatives. The organization is primarily interested in the qualifications of candidates. Do applicants meet job requirements? Applicants are interested in the rewards offered. To what extent do these rewards meet their particular needs? Usually both the organization and the applicant have to consider alternatives. There are other applicants, and there might be other job offers. So the selection process requires appraisal and negotiating. Basically parties explore to what extent fruitful collaboration is possible. Do they have joint interests, and can they meet the other party's expectations?

To complicate this, in the decision-making process all kinds of political arguments might be involved. An organization might feel (or is!) obliged to give priority to female candidates or candidates belonging to minority groups. Or, when there is a merger involved, the management might feel obliged to appoint candidates from both organizations. Appointments are very important rewards, so the way one fills a vacancy might have an important impact on the motivation of other employees.

Psychologists who act as consultants have three kinds of contribution to make.

1. They can assist in structuring procedures.
2. They can facilitate the exploration process.
3. They can advise management.

Structuring staffing procedures

Large organizations will develop formal procedures. How to recruit, how to select, how to provide information to applicants, etc. Smaller organizations will often use the service of a consultant. Psychologists can assist managers in setting up such procedures. This might include training of managers, i.e. how to conduct an employment interview, how to develop job requirements, etc. A central issue is exploration. Procedures should be set up in such a way that both parties have the opportunity to explore the situation and to exchange views. Information can be prepared in advance (hand-outs, reports): it should be presented at the appropriate moment. In the first stage of the process other information is needed (e.g. information about job context and working conditions) than in a later stage (e.g. detailed information about employment conditions).

Facilitating the process

During the selection process, there often is a need for a third party, who assists both the manager and the applicant in their exploration process. Usually a systematic analysis is required to establish what costs and benefits are involved. What are the job requirements, and what are the rewards? What is it an applicant seeks in a job? Through interviews a professional can assist a party in conceptualizing the problem, to find ways to collect appropriate information, to appraise information, and to decide what alternative is to be preferred. There are many pitfalls. Decision makers are easily biased, and through skilful questioning a psychologist can help to develop a more realistic solution.

Assisting management in the decision-making process

The final responsibility for the decision-making process is with management. If, for whatever reason, mistakes are made, management will be confronted with the consequences and has to remedy this. So a psychologist can give professional advice, but does well to leave the final responsibility with the manager. It is common, particularly when important hiring decisions have to be made, that a number of people are involved in the decision-making process. This might be higher managers or representatives of employees. During a meeting decisions are made. In discussions consultants can offer opinions and point at issues which deserve consideration.

The relationship with the applicant is different. Consultants are paid by management, and it is expected that they have their loyalty with the organization. Codes of ethics prescribe the conduct of a psychologist in his relationship to a client, e.g. the Dutch code prescribes that the psychologist makes explicit what his role is in the procedure, and what the rights are of the applicant. It also mentions that the applicant might require from the psychologist that the results of a psychological testing procedure are presented to the applicant first. So in an interview with the consultant an applicant might ask for information, and discuss issues which he or she feels to be important. The decision to accept or reject a job offer is usually something the applicant does at home.

This approach is based on different assumptions. It is no longer assumed that future performance in all cases can be predicted with a reasonable amount of accuracy on the basis of individual differences. Instead, the approach capitalizes on improving the fit between the organization and the individual, on self-selection and on improving work commitment. It is also assumed that organizations can improve performance through other means (training, leadership, better structures, etc.), and that such means can be tailored to the needs of a particular individual.

The exploration process will give both parties a better understanding of the costs and benefits involved; and will lead to more congruence between abilities and job requirements and rewards and the needs of individuals (Lofquist and Dawis, 1969). During the process it also becomes more clear how the other party appraises the solution. Both parties make explicit what their goals are, and how they feel these goals can be attained. So there is a goal setting process also. The process stimulates auto self-selection. It is assumed that individuals seek positions which are congruent with their capacities, and where there is congruence between rewards and needs. When they find such a position they will remain, there will be more job satisfaction and the organization will be more pleased with the performance (Lofquist and Dawis, 1969).

Finally, the staffing process is actually the beginning of work socialization. The individual is confronted with the goals and values of the organization, and has to make up his or her mind to what extent he or she is prepared to work for the organization. Acceptance leads to work commitment, which in turn leads to lower turnover of staff.

This approach is not new. It is practised by many psychologists. But the assumptions have not been made explicit in the literature on selection. The assumptions have, however, been used in other areas, and evidence has been reported to support these theories.

There still is plenty of room for doing research in this respect. Now there is more interest in European universities in the organizational entry process it must be hoped that more studies will be reported trying to establish relationships between structure and process variables and commitment and performance.

CONCLUSION

It is not assumed that this approach entirely replaces the classical one. Where there are large numbers of positions, and when the required performance is well understood, Thorndike's model is still useful. It is also possible to use a combination of approaches, i.e. predicting future performance, structuring procedures and facilitating exploration processes. In practice this will mean that Thorndike's approach will be more used in mass selection (e.g. for training programmes). Structuring and facilitating will be found particularly in selection for managerial and high level staff positions, although the principles can be applied for almost all positions.

REFERENCES

American Psychological Association (1966). *Standards for Educational and Psychological Tests and Manuals*. APA, Washington D.C.

Ash, P., and Kroecker, L.P. (1975). Personnel selection, classification and placement, *Annual Review of Psychology*, **26**.

Buros, O.K. (ed.) (1938). *The 1938 Mental Measurements Yearbook*. Gryphon Press, New York (also published in 1941, 1949, 1953, 1959, 1965, 1972 and 1979).

Commissie Hessel (1977). *Een sollicitant is ook een mens*. (An applicant is also a human being.) Staatsuitgeverij, The Hague.

Cowley, W.H. (1928). Three distinctions in the study of leaders, *Journal of Abnormal and Social Psychology*, **23**, 144–57.

Equal Employment Opportunity Commission (1966). *Guidelines on Employment Testing Procedures*. Equal Employment Opportunity Commission, Washington D.C.

Equal Employment Opportunity Commission (1970). *Guidelines on Employee Selection Procedures*. Federal Register.

Gross, M.L. (1962). *The Brain Watchers*. Random House, New York.

Hoffman, B. (1962). *The Tyranny of Testing*. Crowell, Collier, New York.

Jansen, A. (1979). *Ethiek en praktijk van personeelsselectie*. (Ethics and practice of personnel selection.) Kluwer, Deventer.

Lindquist, E.F. (ed.) (1951). *Educational Measurement*. American Council on Education, Washington D.C.

Lofquist, L.H., and Dawis, R.V. (1969). *Adjustment to Work*. Appleton, New York.

Mowday, R.T., Porter, L.W., and Steers, R.M. (1982). *Employee–Organization Linkages*. Academic Press, New York.

National Academy of Sciences (1982). *Ability Testing: Uses, consequences, and controversies*, Vol. 1. National Academy Press, Washington D.C.

Packard, V. (1964). *The Naked Society*. McKay, New York.

Rundquist, E.A. (1969). The prediction ceiling, *Personnel Psychology*, **22**, 109–16.

Schneider, B., and Schmitt, N. (1986). *Staffing Organizations*. Scott, Foresman, Glenview.

Thorndike, L.J. (1949). *Personnel Selection: Test and measurement technique*. Wiley, New York.

Wolff, Ch.J. de (1963). *Personeels beoordeling*. (Personnel appraisal.) Swets & Zeitlinger, Amsterdam.

Wolff, Ch.J. de (1967). *Het criterium probleem*. (The criterion-problem.) Kluwer, Deventer.

Wolff, Ch.J. de, and Bosch, G. van de (1984). Personnel selection, in P.J.D. Drenth, H. Thierry, P.J. Willems, and Ch.J. de Wolff (eds.), *Handbook of Work Organizational Psychology*, Vol. 1. Wiley, Chichester.

Chapter 1.6

New Technology and Selection

PAUL G. W. JANSEN

Industrial Psychology Branch, PTT Telecom, Postbus 30 000, 2500 GA's-Gravenhage, The Netherlands

INTRODUCTION

'New technology' has become almost equivalent to the use of modern 'high-tech' computers, or to 'computerization'. Computerization refers to processing information, whether in quantitative (digital) or qualitative (analogous) form, (note that analogous information may be processed digitally, and vice versa), with the aid of automata in which there is a virtual distinction between a *control* unit (the central processing system) and a *data* unit (the memory). In a so-called 'Neumann computer' input is stored and subsequently retrieved at appropriate moments in the computing process, which is controlled by a central processing unit. The distinction between data and control is virtual in the sense that there is no intrinsic difference between these two components of a computerized system: it is just a matter of denotation, and subsequent operation, that decides which part of the information tells the computer how to process the remaining (data) part.

In the field of computer systems developments have been rapid, with about every decade a new generation of computers: from 1950 the first radio tube-based systems became available; starting from about 1960 transistor-based systems were in operation; from 1970 computers were constructed via integrated circuits; and in the 1980s we see both the introduction of networks of personal computers and the integration of telecommunication (telephone, telex, telegraph, etc.) and automation into 'telematica' or 'telegration'—transport of speech and data via the same network. From about 1990 the introduction may be expected of parallel processing systems instead of the former sequential systems. These so-called 'non-Neumann' or 'fifth generation' computers are of use in solving elaborate (and mostly

Assessment and Selection in Organizations   Edited by P. Herriot
© 1989 John Wiley & Sons Ltd

iteratively constructed) problems where even today's high speed 'number crunchers' are much too slow for practical applications, e.g. in the field of weather forecasting (cf. Paddon, 1984).

The availability of more sophisticated systems of information processing generally has had the following effects on task characteristics: on the one hand management of the information flow going into and out of the computer has become of the utmost importance (informatization, p. 95 below), and on the other hand production processes have become more and more under the, sometimes tight, control of systems (automation, p. 97 below). A third effect is that a whole class of new tasks or functions has arisen pertaining to the development, implementation, and maintenance of computer technology and usage (computing functions, p. 99 below). The distinction between informatization on the one hand and automation on the other hand can also be found in the work of Buchanan and Boddy (1983, p. 5); there it is denoted as computer aided 'administration' versus computer aided 'manufacturing'.

Generally, computerization is associated with informatization, and not with the effect of automation of job elements. But it was only the development of the former that enhanced the sophistication of the latter, although in its basic form (e.g. the conveyor belt or assembly line) automation goes back as far as the Taylor production systems of the 1920s. Especially the refinement of feedback control, which on the one hand can be described as the ability of the production worker to self-regulate his work flow, and on the other hand as the opportunity to fine-tune the production process to the characteristics of the individual worker, was only possible on account of computerization. Therefore, one of the outcomes of the implementation of new technology for task characteristics, and therefore for selection, will be treated below under the heading 'automation'. However, in the majority of cases computer systems in the sense described above seem absent. In such cases, the computer is reduced to a rather closed circuit of robotized components of the working process, into which working man is fitted tightly— and consequently over which the worker has little control. The latter is transferred to either a unit of the system, or to a newly created function (and eventually, of course, to the computer expert).

As a consequence, the system bears little resemblance to the personal computer, or even to the mainframe which, generally, will constitute the basic experience with new technology of most readers. Personal computers, psychologically, have the status of a pocket calculator: they yield information on account of which, indeed, some action *must* be taken, but they have no actual supervision on the way the working day is structured. In the latter respect, they have, psychologically, less controlling influence than a desk agenda (although they do have some impact, and increasingly so, on the content of these functions as will be explained below). The effects of informatization, automation, and the new set of computing functions on procedures of selection are treated in Effects on Selection, p. 100. Finally, notions are offered of a more general, and speculative, nature.

EFFECTS ON FUNCTIONS

It seems that the conclusion of Turner and Lawrence (1965), that task characteristics are essentially determined by technological factors, still holds good. In this line, two consequences of the introduction of new technology on functions may be, generally, distinguished: you may be involved since you are *using* new technology, or you are committed to the *implementation* or maintenance. Moreover, the new technology may be used actively by you (as a subject), or you may feel you are used by it passively (as an object). The first is referred to as informatization, the latter as automation. This distinction, of course, is of a rather black and white nature. It is of use in the treatment below (where it will be shaded to a more realistic tinge of grey consequently). Computing functions pertaining to implementation and maintenance of new technologies are treated on p. 99.

Informatization

Toffler (1980) has described the coming of modern society in terms of three 'waves': the first wave consists of the agricultural revolution, which started some 10 000 years ago, and essentially consists of the increasing potential to feed more people from the harvest of fewer acres. The Industrial Revolution, which started at the end of the eighteenth century, constituted the second wave; characteristic of it are for instance the concentration of work, and therefore of workers, in huge plants or factories, the utilization of all kinds of machines, and the rationalization of the production process by differentiation over a vast assembly line. The third wave is characterized by the coming of a society that is based on new technologies, the key-word of which is 'information'. It is the information age, characterized by computerization. (A similar kind of analysis, pertaining in particular to large business corporations, is found in Drucker, 1988.)

Since computers process information at high speed and high accuracy, computerization has the effect of presenting almost immediately answers to questions that are as reliable and specific as both the formulation of the problem and the layout of the memory allow. Moreover, modern telecommunication systems make it possible to have access to information that is physically located (stored) at virtually every place on earth. In the last decade, attention has been devoted to implementing parts of the human information processor in the computer, e.g. by programming heuristic rules by means of which large, fuzzy problems can be reduced to smaller well-defined sub-problems. Processing data in a computer by means of such internalized human problem solvers, of course, makes demands on the user. For instance: what is the effect on function demands, and thus on personnel selection, of building expert systems in which a *specific* part only of cognitive knowledge is represented (both pertaining to well-organized sets of information and to well-defined rules of manipulating them)? Does this imply that the expert can be replaced by a 'team' of an expert computer and a layman worker? Or, conversely, will this result in the human worker being called upon to make use of his or her most powerful ability: *reasoning* with information, instead of locating, memorizing, and retrieving it?

Rasmussen, Duncan, and Leplat (1987) stipulate that new technology, i.e. computerization and increasing levels of automation, put greater demands on the problem-solving skills of operators. What is more, the problem-*finding* part of the problem-solving cycle becomes essential. By application of skills in diagnosing situations for problem cues, the right questions should be asked at the right times (and accordingly, proper actions should be taken).

Thus, greater demand is put on human information processing which, in terms of personnel selection would imply that more is required of the cognitive abilities of applicants. According to Toffler (1985) more is required of the capacity of workers to manipulate 'materials' of a symbolic nature. For example, signals of a calamity (e.g. a fire) are presented to a desk operator in the control room of a chemical plant, in the form of a red light, or a pointer on a dial-plate instead of yellow flames and grey smoke.

In this respect, new technology not only implies an upgrading in intellectual demands that are required by a well-functioning system, but also a relative dominance of 'fluid' cognitive abilities over more 'crystallized' intellectual skills. That is, psychological capacities that are critical to 'education permanente' within the function (e.g. analytical thinking, reasoning) are required more than performances that are the result of past learning at school and experience at work (cf. Stern, 1987, p. 3). This is even reinforced by the higher rate at which previously learned knowledge wears out in the information age: approximately two-thirds of the technological processes that will be used in the year 2000 are yet unknown at the present moment, and approximately fifteen years after school education has been completed, half of the knowledge has already become obsolete.

Another characteristic of the impact on work process of new (computerized) technology is that feedback can be obtained on actions almost instantly (Vijlbrief, Algera, and Koopman, 1985), either from the real world or from the system, in which the former is simulated with a high degree of fidelity. As a result of this, the user is immediately confronted with the results of his actions, and may, therefore, for the first time ever perceive these as outcomes that are directly related to *his* operations. That is, whereas in the past real world feedback loops might take months or even years, they encompass only minutes, or at the most some hours, in the simulation model. In this way aspects of financial management, e.g. of a large company, could be learned.

Finally, in an environment that is constantly changing on account of input/output flows and feedback loops, the only centre of stability may be the human factor itself . . .

Thus, we have problem solving, learning ability, problem finding, internal control, and flexibility as the key function requirements in highly informatized organizations. The users should be able to perceive the right bit of information at the right time, to process it and to be still independent enough from irrelevant features of the computerized system to make their own inferences—which then are to be put back in the same, or other technological systems, or are passed on to co-users, as the case may be.

On a wider scale the claim on such person characteristics is reinforced by the expectation, of, e.g. Toffler (1985), that informatization may hasten the substitution of bureaucracy as a principle of organization by '*ad-hoc* cracy'. In the latter, the structure of, e.g. a business corporation changes periodically as a result of innovations in production processes, fluctuating marketing prospects and a relative increase in providing service as opposed to producing goods. As a result, more stress is put on imagination, decisiveness and the ability to learn *fast*.

Automation

At lower levels in the organization, implementation of new technologies may result in the benefits of informatization being outweighed by the drawbacks of automation. In other words, the users may perceive themselves and their jobs as victims of new technology. Generally, computerization is associated with informatization, and much less with automation. In the last case, the term robotization (Weinstein, 1981) is preferred, which again seems to carry positive overtones of giving life to dead systems instead of taking life from living workers, that is, from their functions—although below we will also describe more optimistic scenarios for the future effects of automation.

Specifically, at lower levels in the organization, implementation of new technology may have two effects: either the *production* process is automated, or *control* over production is automated. In the first case, the human functions that remain are those that pertain to controlling the automated process. Typically, the resulting jobs are characterized as: monotonous work, vigilance tasks, and requirement for large tolerance of stress. Moreover, often the functional distinction between the processes of primary production and control is paralleled by a physical distance: control is executed in a control room that is located far away from the floor where the actual production takes place. The controller communicates with the production unit via intermediary systems as for instance consoles, terminals, dial plates, key pads, etc. In the second case, it is control that is automated, and remaining human functions are situated at the level of primary production. Again, routine and monotony may be typical task characteristics. In this case, however, tolerance for external control, e.g. by a non-human computer system, is also required. A recent study from the Dutch research association 'TNO', under commission by the Netherlands Ministry of Social Affairs, indicates that, generally, automation does not alleviate monotonous work (TNO, 1988). Although by automation certain monotonous tasks in the production setting are spared to labourers, they mostly are replaced by other monotonous (control) functions. In the same study it is estimated that still in 1986 there were about 250 000 workers in the Netherlands who conducted monotonous work. The latter is characterized by the performance of *simple* operations at *rapid* pace in *short* time.

Conversely, the investigation reveals that some functions get more interesting, i.e. they get enriched on account of new possibilities that are offered by automation. That dull monotonous work is not a necessary outcome of automation has for instance been put forward by Toffler (1985). This author describes the impact of informatization on primary production as 'de-standardization': automation makes it possible to produce variable amounts of various products for all kinds of varieties of consumers each with specific 'tastes' (Quinn, Baruch, and Paquette,

1987, p. 30). Thus, automation makes it possible to return as it were to the nineteenth century 'arts and crafts' artisan who manufactured in his own way products that always were unique. In this manner, it can be considered a beneficial effect of automation that it makes it possible to meet the highly individualized demands of today's consumers. In this view, complete automation is viewed as essentially being in conflict with current demands for flexibility, total quality control, and tailor-made production.

In an interesting overview of the impact of technological changes on work in areas dominated by women, the same conclusion is reached (Hartmann, Krant, and Tilly, 1986). There is no one-to-one, direct translation of technological innovation into 'revolutionized' working conditions. The outcome of changes in technology depends on other factors, especially the ways in which they are implemented. In this respect, technological innovation can have different impacts on different occupational groups. And, finally, to illustrate this point of view we quote from Young, Levi, and Slem (1987, p. 53): 'Technological change will cause major changes in the way organizations operate: their design and culture, professional roles and job designs, and human resources policies and practices. Changes are inevitable, but whether they improve or damage the quality of work life in organizations is a question of management.' This is also the principal argument of Buchanan and Boddy (1983, pp. 7–8), who in their own words presented 'the first major report of a research study of the effects of computing and information technology on jobs and organizations' (p. 3). One of the reasons why the introduction of new technologies did not immediately lead to increases in production in the United States, is that production conditions were not adapted correspondingly: the old Taylor-based production organization, which is characterized by a sharp division between labour/production and maintenance/control, was essentially preserved. At present, it seems that it is realized that new production systems cannot function optimally without commitment of the production workers. Thus, the aim should not be to increase production by automation alone, but by the combined efforts of automation, team work, job involvement, etc. One of these 'etceteras' is the integration of production and control into one and the same job, that is performed by a relatively autonomous *team* of workers. As Sell (1987, p. 345) argues, although by automation previous job demarcations become inappropriate, this has not necessarily to lead to the instalment of monotonous jobs. New technology makes the way free for job enrichment, by integrating manufacture and inspection (using modern micro-electronic devices) into the same function. However, as Sell remarks, this may lead to union resistance. For, by integrating management/control and worker/production, certain class-determined conflicts of interests may be blurred. In order to 'survive' in the age of informatization, unions will have to find ways of 'new cooperation' or 'union management' in which part of the negotiating autonomy is given up, that is, transferred to local factory representatives (e.g. the Netherlands 'works councils').

Computing functions

Computerization has given way to a whole new class of 'computing functions'. As Buchanan and Boddy (1983, p. 7) put it on account of several case studies: technological change tended to be accompanied by the establishment of new 'support' departments or groups responsible for planning, programming and maintaining the new machines.

Following the alternation of generations of computer technology, the human functions that are connected to the development, implementation and maintenance of computers change rapidly also. For instance, the development of high level programming languages has eliminated to a large degree the burden of meticulously programming, step by step, a problem. Such programming required previous detailed analysis into a seemingly endless chain of very simple, even dull, basic operations like add, subtract, store, and retrieve. Just because of these new technological opportunities, it has become more or less a matter of ideology, or 'task', as to which style of programming should be preferred. On the one hand, it is possible to describe (or even *pre*scribe) computer programming as a sort of higher mathematics in which a theorem (the problem) is solved by a program that can be *proved* to lead to a solution in terms of the conditions in which the initial problem was framed (Browning, 1985; Dijkstra and Fijen, 1984). On the other hand, programming may be viewed as a trial and error process: 'raw' versions of the program are simply 'kicked' into the computer, to see if it works. In several cycles the program is debugged until it functions acceptably well according to the specifications of the user. In the latter case, the goodness of a program is decided by the pragmatic definition of what are its workable outputs.

Of course, both views on ideal styles of programming have a repercussion on the function profile of the ideal programmer. In the first case analytical capacities may be essential, but in the second the ability to accept an error as something that is unavoidable, something even that is to be welcomed since it leads to possibilities of improving the program becomes critical.

In the second case, also, the ability to have a general outline of the solution is more important than being able to translate this rough overall picture into clearly delineated steps of the program.

Of course, in practice, programming will generally be a mixture of both styles, or they are incorporated (and divided) into two different functions: the information analyst (or functional designer) versus the application programmer. To illustrate the rapid development in the field of computing functions, and corresponding difficulties of ascertaining function *content* from function *designation* alone, we refer to initiatives of the Netherlands Society for Computing (Nederlands Genootschap voor Informatica, 1986) to take stock of all existing functions in computing. A first report dates from 1982, a second revised edition already appeared in 1986! The Netherlands Postal and Telecommunications Services commissioned a study of the existing and the recommended nomenclature for computing functions, as well as of existing and recommended types of training courses. In the final report (Roebersen, 1987) several kinds of difficulties with the prevailing terminology for computing functions are mentioned. As an example, the one function 'application programmer' is found to be either denoted as 'programmer', or as 'systems analyst', or as 'assistant systems analyst'. In the same way a senior operator (the person who coordinates the work of a team of operators) is denoted as a 'shift leader' or a 'system manager'. Conversely, it is found that the latter title, i.e. 'system manager', can refer to three different functions in computing: 'production supervisor', 'senior operator' or 'data manager'. In sum, the class of computing functions is characterized by :

- a dynamic set of functions: functions (dis)appear suddenly, or change completely in content as a result of the rapid alternations of technological innovations;
- a fuzzy set of function denotations.

For both reasons, it is not as straightforward as it may appear, to answer in the context of selection the question what, generally, is the dispositional profile of a 'good programmer'.

EFFECTS ON SELECTION

Generally, the design of a selection procedure is decided by three different kinds of considerations:

1. A scientific or rational argument focusing on what are the most efficient means (in terms of the highest predictive validity for the lowest price) for assessing the future job success of a present-day job applicant.
2. A political or managerial perspective concentrating on what are the guidelines, derived from a set of political or managerial principles, for selection practices (e.g. the principle of equal opportunities may be formulated as the requirement for quota selection).
3. A cultural or corporate image deriving from what are generally, and mostly implicitly, accepted in the organization as 'good' practices of human resources management (e.g. in some companies it is 'not done' to apply psychological tests in selection—simply because it was 'never done').

The latter two considerations more or less constitute conditions within which selection may be carried out by the specifications as obtained from scientific/ rational arguments. For instance: with the rise of new computer technology, it may be *culturally* necessary to abandon 'old-fashioned' paper-and-pencil tests and to resort to computerized testing although from a scientific or rational point of view nothing may be gained by this: computerized testing may not yield better predictions of job success and it may be a lot more expensive, but it does send the message to job applicants that the company surely is 'high-tech'. Thus, although it may well be that programming capacities can be assessed reliably well (as measured by the first type of criterion) in classical ways, it may from a cultural or corporate image point of view still be advisable to select applicants for computing functions via the most sophisticated computer equipment.

This shows that new technology can affect selection in at least two ways: first, as a result of informatization or automation function requirements change, and therefore selection criteria, and operational measures of them, alter (see below). Second, modifications in selection instruments can result from new technological opportunities only, which are implemented both for reasons of efficiency and on account of corporate image considerations (see p. 103 below).

For more in-depth discussions of actual examples of selection procedures, the reader is referred to Section 4 (especially Chapters 4.1 and 4.8).

Changes in selection criteria

As was described above, new technology, generally denoted as 'computerization', affects the content of functions in at least two ways: informatization and automation. *Informatization* requires more of the 'higher' cognitive abilities of the worker; problem finding, permanent learning, imagination, fluid intelligence are becoming key-words in this domain. Generally, the capacity to learn fast is becoming more important than the amount of knowledge that already has been 'crystallized' in rather rigid patterns of reasoning about problems or of handling them. The question is whether these intellectual demands can be, or are, measured by traditional intelligence tests. This is a matter that is not decided yet, also not in a negative sense (contrary to popular, and may be also scientific, belief). Although intelligence tests do have a rather old-fashioned appearance, they have an important feature: exactly because of the often criticized content-irrelevance to actual tasks to be performed in the job at issue, and also since item content in intelligence tests is distinct from learned knowledge, these tests may measure the ability to pick up new cognitive operations fast. That is, it may well be that traditional intelligence tests are of a much more 'fluid' nature, and are becoming more so by becoming more 'obsolete' than, e.g. college grade point averages.

In that case, the intelligence test is not applied as a measure of past learning, but of the ability to learn fast. An indication for this may be the finding that ability tests generally are the best predictors of job performance (evaluated according to scientific/rational criteria only), even in the case of jobs that are already affected by new technology.

For example, Schmidt, Gast-Rosenberg, and Hunter (1980) presented an overview of validities of two aptitude tests for computer programmers, by means of validity generalization (see Chapter 3.3 for meta-analytic results for different instruments of selection). Criteria were measures of proficiency (ratings of overall job performance) and of training results (final course grades). For proficiency criteria, validity was on average about 0.40, and for training criteria 0.70. Note that in this particular case a 'classic' aptitude test firstly has high validity for a 'computerized job', and secondly is especially good at predicting *learning ability* in the new job. This result was confirmed, on a larger scale, by the study of Pearlman, Schmidt, and Hunter (1980).

In another study (Schmidt, Hunter, and Caplan, 1981) the 'trans-situational generalizability' of the validities of a set of cognitive tests and a weighted biographical information blank for performance criteria for two job groups in the petroleum industry was investigated. For both job classes, operations and maintenance, cognitive tests did have substantial estimated true predictive validity (around 0.25), whereas the true validity of the biographical data was estimated essentially zero.

Nevertheless, when item-content, either for rational or for cultural reasons may be a hindrance to applying standard intelligence tests to predict function proficiency, another approach would be to simulate key intellectual job tasks in a selection instrument. Again, such a situational measure of analytical thinking, problem solving, etc., may well turn out to be a paper-and-pencil test.

The greater demands on flexibility, cooperation, and interpersonal or social behaviour that are caused by informatization (because of work being 'organized' more according to an *ad-hoc* cracy instead of a bureaucracy; Drucker, 1988, p. 47 stipulates the 'greater emphasis on individual responsibility for relationships and for communication') constitute an additional argument for applying selection instruments of a simulational nature: when there is no relevant prior work history (since history is becoming old too fast), or when quality of functioning in prior positions cannot be assessed reliably (because of the relative instability of the function elements), one has to resort to generating relevant behaviour by simulating critical elements of the function at issue. Assessment of the applicant's set performance then can be paralleled by self-assessment of the candidate who is confronted with his own behaviour in the simulation situation.

Still, when function content is getting more and more dynamic, it may be that assessment of critical behavioural samples via situational tests may not be generalizable enough to make predictions of job success over a sufficiently long period of time. In such cases, prediction of future job proficiency necessarily cannot be very specific. Instead of focusing on specific samples of behaviour, as determined by specific job elements, it is in such cases advisable to direct the content of predictions to more general, not situationally specific, *styles* of functioning. An example is the several styles of leadership as distinguished in the literature, e.g. 'participative' or 'initiating structure' (Campbell *et al.*, 1970), although we realize that the concept of style as a situationally independent personal characteristic is an issue of debate. We believe that in contingency models, like for instance Fiedler's (1967), the concept of 'situation' is treated in a sufficiently ample way to allow generalizations of the kind as described above. 'Style' of functioning may be generalizable over situations, whereas actual elements of previous job behaviour may not be.

Another consequence of the permanent dynamics of functions in settings of informatization, is that it is always necessary to explore the actual behavioural content of the function at issue in case of an assignment for a specific procedure. Both because of the fuzzy definition of computing functions (p. 100), and on account of the rapid changes in functions that are subject of ongoing informatization, it is not possible for the organization to rely on 'timeless' manuals of job descriptions.

Thus, informatization implies that it is, for prediction purposes in the context of selection, not meaningful to concentrate on isolated elements of the job that are to a high degree situationally specific. Instead, one should search for trans-situational, that is more abstract, *modes of behaviour*. The higher level of abstraction, that will become visible even in the language that is employed in the selection context, represents the price that is paid for generalizability over a number of specific tasks. In this respect, new technology in the sense of informatization may have a peculiar effect on the vocabulary that is used in formulating predictions about future functioning. Moreover, to obtain predictions about behaviour in a highly dynamic environment over periods of, on average, two years the selection psychologist has to resort to domains of behaviour that can be expected to remain relatively meaningful when actual function content changes.

As described above, the impact of *automation* on jobs is twofold: either control or maintenance is separated from production, and one of the two is automated; or both are integrated into one enlarged, or enriched function. In the latter case, more is required of the job applicant. Self-reliant functioning, instead of taking orders from and relying on, e.g. a foreman, becomes more important. Moreover, internalization of control within one's function requires the flexibility and self-discipline of critically monitoring the quality and output of one's work.

In the first case, either control or production is automated, and the worker either produces in conditions of automated control, or controls a fully automated process of primary production. In these cases, stress tolerance, the ability to endure external control of a non-human origin, and resistance to monotony and routine are likely function requirements. In a number of recent studies the impact of the use of new office technologies in terms of the contribution to occupational stress is examined (Amick and Östberg, 1987; Czaja *et al.*, 1987). More and more the 'design', both physical and psychological, of the office environment is found to be important. This holds even more in the case of so-called 'computer-mediated home-based office work', in which especially women are employed (Christensen, 1987).

It may in a number of situations not be realistic to assume that such demands can be reliably and satisfactorily met by applicants. Then, instead of selecting persons for functions, it may be wiser to adapt function conditions to the characteristics—and thereby the limits—of human behaviour. For instance, Rasmussen, Duncan, and Leplat (1987) stipulate that, since making mistakes belongs to the normal range of human behaviour, it may, even from a rationally economic point of view, be better to change tasks in such a way that they become more error tolerant (see also Willems, 1984, p. 248). Another example, pertaining to the assessment of capacities for computing functions, is the recent discipline of 'software ergonomics': developing computerized systems in such a manner that they fit the (im)possibilities of the human worker as information processing agent.

Changes in selection methods

Technological innovation presents new opportunities for selection methodology. The latter may actually be used both for reasons of efficiency (e.g. shorter testing time) and on account of considerations of corporate image (e.g. making a first good impression on function applicants by applying high tech selection equipment).

In both respects the best example of changes in selection methods on account of computerization, is computerized testing. Since this topic is extensively discussed in Chapter 3.5, we confine the treatment here.

Computerized psychological testing began in the early 1960s (Johnson, Giannetti, and Williams, 1979). Computers were used to score and interpret standard psychological tests, as for instance the MMPI (Dunn, Lushene, and O'Neil, 1972) and the WAIS (Elwood, 1969; Elwood and Griffin, 1976). A reason for administering tests by means of terminals and keyboards is that it opens the way to apply modern item response theory-based scoring models instead of classical test theory (Guion, 1987). Also, with computerized testing it is possible to record all kinds of extra information on (the) testing behaviour that was previously not attainable (e.g. latencies, cf. Stout, 1981). Most current applications of computerized testing are confined to the field of cognitive or intelligence tests.

But, computerized testing seems to be especially of interest for personality assessment (e.g. Suziedelis, 1983). To date, most applications are found in a clinical setting. For instance, Angle *et al.* (1977) describe the administration of a large battery (3000 items) of specific behavioural statements by means of a computer. In this way it is possible to, firstly, roughly scan a wide array of problem areas of a client and, secondly, focus on behavioural difficulties in a specific problem area. Most clients appeared to prefer this kind of computer-aided behavioural assessment to a human interviewer. On account of the large computerized data basis, in this way a behavioural analysis of the client can be made, and essentially an ideographic 'picture' of the client can be drawn that generally is much more reliable than the information which is gathered by a human assessor.

Space (1981, p. 600) concludes that by using in this way the computer as a diagnostician, the testing situation becomes 'a very rich source of behavioural data'. Ideographic data, reflected in behaviour unique to a given subject, may be more accurately identified by computer techniques than by clinical assessment.

Thus, given the same information as a human assessor, the computer is more reliable, and most often does well or better in diagnostic classification of the behavioural pattern of the testee. However, it seems that these techniques of behavioural assessment are not transferred from the clinical area to the domain of personnel selection. A behavioural item bank directed at, e.g. all bits of management behaviour, which would be of use to draw an inventory of and weight *past* behaviour, seems not to exist at present.

In our opinion computerized large-scale biographical questionnaires might be a significant contribution of new technology to personnel selection (see also Chapters 3.4 and 3.10).

To date it is still uncertain what will be the general impact of computerized testing on the design and implementation of instruments of personnel selection. Partly, this is caused by a, still, relative lack of experience with real-world applications. Besides, many applications are both very test and equipment specific, so that they are not open to comparative research on the relative merits of the system. It is clear, however, that testing by a computer poses some intriguing questions on the status of the instrument of measurement. For instance, it may well be that a 'mere' change in the way a test is administered implies an essential modification of the validity of the instrument: a terminal test may be *essentially* different from a paper-and-pencil test. Moreover, it may from a political or cultural point of view not be acceptable, both to the testee and to the organization, to reduce the testing time to, e.g. half an hour by a sophisticated computerized adaptive intelligence battery, when previously it took about half a day to reach the same kind of reliability in the estimated test score.

DISCUSSION

Although developments in the field of computer technology have gone fast in the first four generations of its existence (see above), it seems that arrival of the fifth generation, that of parallel computers, is taking longer than expected.

At the international congress 'Frontiers in Computing' (1987) it was reported that progress of a Japanese project of building a computer with at least 1000 processors operating in parallel in 1992, is getting slower and slower. Especially the construction of a general purpose computer (that is, a computer that is not specifically built and programmed for one type of problem solving in one restricted area of application) poses difficulties. Particularly, these pertain to the exponentially increasing complexity of the system, for instance to the development and usage of a parallel programming language.

It seems that it is only feasible to program in a parallel way, what in *reality* functions as parallel processes. On account of the limited capacity of the human mind to perform parallel processing, it is only feasible to separate into independent components (which subsequently can be processed in parallel in the computer) what in fact is parallel. Thus, although informatization makes all sorts of fluid abilities critical, it may well be that there is in this respect a limit to the programming and information capacities of human users. As a consequence, also in the field of informatization the ergonomic side of personnel selection (as reported above for automation) will become more important.

In this regard it is a problem that implementation of new technologies in many cases still is a prerogative of technicians. Understandably, they rely on a more or less common-sense implicit psychology in their work. But, as Blackler and Oborne (1987) put it: 'the strategy of reducing (by new technology) the number of people involved in work requires us to pay *more*, not less, attention to human factors'. It is self-evident that with the ongoing implementation of new technologies, either as informatization or as automation, more, and not less, attention will have to be paid to personnel selection. And it may be reassuring that, although developments in computer technology have been rapid, the rate of changes in actual work processes was found to be comparatively slow and *evolutionary*, not *revolutionary*, by Buchanan and Boddy (1983, p. 240) in a number of case studies.

REFERENCES

Amick, B.C., and Östberg, O. (1987). Office automation, occupational stress, and health, *Office: Technology and People*, **3**, 191–209.

Angle, H.V., Ellinwood, E.H., Hay, W.M., Johnson, Th, and May, L.R. (1977). Computer-aided interviewing in comprehensive behavioural assessment, *Behavior Therapy*, **8**, 747–54.

Blackler, F., and Oborne, D. (eds) (1987). *Information Technology and People: Designing for the future*. The British Psychological Society, Leicester.

Browning, C. (1985). *Guide to Effective Software Technical Writing*. Prentice-Hall, Englewood Cliffs, NJ.

Buchanan, D.A., and Boddy, D. (1983). *Organization in the Computer Age. Technological imperatives and strategic choice*. Gower, Aldershot.

Campbell, J.P., Dunette, M.D., Lawler, E.E., and Weick, K.E. (1970). *Managerial Behavior, Performance and Effectiveness*. McGraw-Hill, New York.

Christensen, K.E. (1987). Impacts of computer-mediated home-based work on women and their families, *Office: Technology and People*, **3**, 211–30.

Czaja, S.J., Cary, J.M., Drury, C.G., and Cohen, B.G. (1987). An ergonomic evaluation of traditional and automated office environments, *Office: Technology and People*, **3**, 231–46.

Dijkstra, E.W., and Fijen, W.H.J. (1984). *Een methode van programmeren*. (A method of programming.) Academic Service, The Hague.

Drucker, P.F. (1988). The coming of the new organization, *Harvard Business Review*, **66**, 45–53.

Dunn, T.G., Lushene, R.E., and O'Neil, H.F. (1972). Complete automation of the MMPI and a study of its response in latencies, *Journal of Consulting and Clinical Psychology*, **39**, 381–7.

Elwood, D.L. (1969). Automation of psychological testing, *American Psychologist*, **24**, 287–9.

Elwood, D.L., and Griffin, R.H. (1972). Individual intelligence testing without the examiner: reliability of an automated method, *Journal of Consulting and Clinical Psychology*, **38**, 9–14.

Fiedler, F.E. (1967). *A Theory of Leadership Effectiveness*. McGraw-Hill, New York.

Frontiers in computing. International Conference in Computer Science. Amsterdam, December 1987.

Guion, R.M. (1987). Changing views for personnel selection research, *Personnel Psychology*, **40**, 199–213.

Johnson, J.H., Giannetti, R.A., and Williams, Th.A. (1979). Psychological systems questionnaire: An objective personality test designed for on-line computer presentation, scoring, and interpretation. *Behavioral Research Methods & Instrumentation*, **11**, 257–60.

Hartmann, H.I., Krant, R.E., and Tilly, L.A. (eds) (1986). *Computer Chips and Paperclips: Technology and women's employment*, Vol. I. National Academy Press, Washington D.C.

Nederlands Genootschap voor Informatica (1982; 2nd revised edition 1986). *Functies in de informatica* (Functions in computing). Rapport van de Werkgroep Functie-ordening van het NGI, Amsterdam.

Paddon, D.J. (1984). *Supercomputers, Parallel Computers*. Oxford University Press, Oxford.

Pearlman, K.P., Schmidt, F.L., and Hunter, J.E. (1980). Validity generalization results for tests used to predict job proficiency and training success in clerical occupations, *Journal of Applied Psychology*, **65**, 373–406.

Quinn, J.B., Baruch, J.J., and Paquette, P.C. (1987). Technology in services, *Scientific American*, **257**(6), 24–32.

Rasmussen, J., Duncan, K., and Leplat, J. (eds) (1987). *New Technology and Human Error*. Wiley, Chichester.

Roebersen, G.J. (1987). *Informaticafuncties en -opleidingen*. (Computing functions and -education.) PTT Concernstaf Sociaal-Strategisch Beleid. The Hague, The Netherlands.

Schmidt, F.L., Gast-Rosenberg, I., and Hunter, J.E. (1980). Validity generalization results for computer programmers, *Journal of Applied Psychology*, **65**, 643–61.

Schmidt, F.L., Hunter, J.E., and Caplan, J.R. (1981). Validity generalization results for two job groups in the petroleum industry, *Journal of Applied Psychology*, **66**, 261–73.

Sell, R. (1987). Book review, *Journal of Occupational Psychology*, **60**, 344–5.

Space, L.G. (1981). The computer as a psychometrician. *Behavior Research Methods & Instrumentation*, **13**, 595–606.

Stern, E. (1987). Functions of working life as a learning opportunity. *News* (European Centre for Work and Society), No. 14 (Dec), 3–6.

Stout, R.L. (1981). New approaches to the design of computerized interviewing and testing systems, *Behavioural Research Methods & Instrumentation*, **13**, 436–442.

Suziedelis, A. (1983). Psychotron—a new technique for personality research. Paper presented at the Third European Meeting of the Psychometric Society, Jouy-en-Josas, France, 8 July.

TNO (1988). *Monotone arbeid nu en straks* (Monotonous work now and later). Bureau Humanisering van Arbeid, Delft, The Netherlands.

Toffler, A. (1980). *The Third Wave*. Morrow, New York.

Toffler, A. (1985). *The Adaptive Corporation*. McGraw-Hill, New York.

Turner, A.N., and Lawrence, P.R. (1965). *Industrial Jobs and the Worker. An investigation of response to task attributes*. Harvard University, Boston.

Vijlbrief, H.P.J., Algera, J.A., and Koopman, P.L. (1985). Management of automation projects. Paper presented at the second West-European Conference on the Psychology of Work and Organization, Aachen, West Germany, 1–3 April.

Weinstein, M.B. (1981). *Android Design. Practical approaches for robot building*. Howard W. Sams, Indianapolis.

Willems, P.J. (1984). Human engineering—ergonomics, in P.J.D. Drenth, H. Thierry, P.J. Willems, and Ch.J. de Wolff (eds), *Handbook of Work and Organizational Psychology*, Vol. I. Wiley, New York, pp. 235–56.

Young, A., Levi, D., and Slem, Ch. (1987). Dispelling some myths about people and technological change, *Industrial Engineering*, **19**, 52–5, 69.

Chapter 1.7

Selection in a European Context

SYLVIA SHIMMIN

Department of Behaviour in Organizations, University of Lancaster, Gillow House, Bailrigg, Lancaster LA1 4YX, UK

INTRODUCTION

The definition of 'company policy' was once described as being either so precise that it was restricting or so loose that it was meaningless. Similarly, the notion of a European context runs the risk of being defined too narrowly or too broadly for practical purposes. It may be that there are as many European contexts as there are countries or that, among these different settings, there are one or two common strands which make a discernible context. To speak of *a* European context as if it were a single entity is probably misleading, particularly as the word European itself covers many viewpoints. A publication, *Work Psychology in Europe*, by the Polish Academy of Sciences (1980) covered eighteen countries, including the Soviet Union, Poland, Bulgaria and other Eastern European countries, as well as the Scandinavian countries of Norway, Sweden and Finland. An informal network of European professors of work and organizational psychology (ENOP) was established in 1981 and also adopted an encompassing perspective, but its membership has tended to be greater in Western European countries than in those in the Eastern bloc. This broad political distinction allows for some overlap, but could well result in differing traditions of theory and practice. Latterly, Europe is seen by many as synonymous with the European Economic Community, which gives yet another perspective as, with the exception of Denmark, it ignores Scandinavia, as well as Switzerland, and includes, at least potentially, part of what was formerly seen as Asia Minor. From this viewpoint, a European context would not include some of the more politically and economically stable countries of the Continent, but would include others of a more volatile nature.

Handbook of Assessment in Organizations   Edited by P. Herriot
© 1989 John Wiley & Sons Ltd

In whatever way the boundaries are set, there will be some differences between countries, given the 'marvellous and often bewildering diversity of forms, ideas and institutions' noted by Hakel (1981) when giving an American's view of work psychology in Europe. There are, however, some broad constellations of factors—political, social and economic—affecting the practice of selection across the Continent that can be identified and it is these which are addressed in this chapter. The intention is to focus upon the influences which shape the climate of opinion and set the parameters to the situations in which selection takes place, rather than to deal with the methodology of selection which is covered in other chapters.

AN ERA OF CHANGE

Patterns of work and the structure of employment are changing rapidly throughout Europe. In countries such as Portugal and Spain there has been an accelerating change from a primary agrarian economy to a growing industrial and service economy, while the manufacturing base and traditional heavy industries in regions such as the north of England have declined. Technological innovations are affecting all sectors of employment, making a large number of skills no longer relevant, requiring people to supervise machinery and equipment rather than to operate it and to change jobs or to learn new techniques a number of times in their working lives to keep pace with the rate of change. In contrast with the situation in the older industries, where selection was concerned with matching past performance to a defined job which an individual could hold until retirement, the emphasis today is on estimating a person's probable adaptability and ability to learn new skills and new tasks. This poses several problems for selectors. Are they to select for short-term proficiency and accept the possibility of high levels of turnover if employees cannot cope with job changes? Are they to select for longer term adaptability to change and, if so, how well can the nature of these changes be foreseen and how do the selectors assess the degree of adaptability needed? To what extent is this a matter of training? In some countries, notably in West Germany, generic vocational training and re-training schemes are seen as a major factor in responding to the changing demands of employment.

Another change of significance in recent decades is the growth in protective legislation conferring legal rights and entitlements upon employees and, directly or indirectly, increasing the influence of the State on personnel policies and practices. The 'right to work' is a fundamental concept in the European Social Charter and in the Constitutions and Labour Codes of the European Socialist countries. Historically, one of the reproaches levelled against capitalist economies by Socialists is that private ownership and the profit motive operate with a reserve army of unemployed and it is the excess supply of labour over demand which underpins the very notion of vocational selection. Although not as restricting on managerial initiative as in the Soviet Union, in which Gutsenko and Zharkov (1982) note the limiting effect of labour legislation which regulates in great detail not only the grounds for dismissal but also the transfer of workers to other jobs on the initiative of management, the trend towards similar protective laws is apparent in the European free market economies. In recent decades these have introduced what could be called 'rights within work' relating to matters such as welfare, benefits, minimum terms of notice, compensation for redundancy and protection against unfair dismissal. In some instances, the stimulus for legislation of this kind has come from external bodies such as the International Labour Office or the European Economic Community, but they also reflect the changing ethos within member states towards a more egalitarian society. As a result, 'matters which were once entirely within the sphere of managerial prerogatives or, to some extent, shaped by collective bargaining are now directly regulated by a host of legal rights and duties' (Hepple, 1981).

In discussing what is meant by the 'right to work', Hepple points out that the phrase may indicate a right against the State, that is an abstract background right requiring the State to maintain a policy of full employment; a right against employers to be engaged and to remain continuously employed; and a right against trade unions so that one can be employed while remaining outside union membership. The emphasis on the concept of such rights is on the role and position of the individual as distinct from that of the organization. This trend towards strengthening the rights of the individual concerning recruitment and selection practices and job tenure has extended through the 1960s, when labour was in such short supply that companies competed to attract applicants and personnel selection was a misnomer (Holdsworth, 1983), to the 1980s, which have been characterized by high levels of unemployment and the need for labour flexibility and adaptability to deal with new technology.

The implications for personnel management of this changed environment have been described by van Ham, Paauwe and Williams (1986). In their view,

> . . . a personnel manager today is seldom confronted with a simple and clear-cut selection situation. The present economic malaise, characterised by a low turnover rate and a host of provisions protecting the individual against redundancy at a time when the pace of technological change has never been greater, has resulted in any new employee not being appointed so much for one particular job, but rather for a series of jobs over a number of years; jobs that may well succeed one another, but which do not necessarily imply any promotions.

They maintain that this calls for a different type of selection from the prevailing go/no-go approach, based on relatively 'hard' data pertaining to a specific job, and concentrating instead on applicants' adaptability, social and personal values, trainability and other factors. To this end, they suggest that a gradual entry into service (e.g. through probationary periods of initial fixed-term contracts) would be helpful and, at the other end of the scale, a gradual exit from employment should occur rather than sudden and complete severance.

Comments of this kind have also to be seen in the context of the increased participation of married women in the labour force, frequently on a part-time basis, and of the pressures exerted by, and on behalf of, women generally for equality of opportunities and treatment. In Switzerland, where women were enfranchised much later than in other countries, it is interesting to note there are the beginnings of affirmative action programmes, modelled primarily on those in the United States, and Dachler (personal communication) writes of the implications for selection of a new (1988) marriage law. This gives the wife the right, formerly exclusively that of the husband, to co-determine the geographical location of the family home and what will be done with the family income. It also guarantees her the right to work without a veto on her employment by her husband. Within the EEC, while there has been less harmonization of labour law overall than the founders of the Community envisaged, in terms of workers' rights perhaps the most influential have been the law protecting EEC workers from discrimination on grounds of nationality and Article 119 of the Treaty of Rome on equal pay for men and women. As a result, selection procedures are subject to legal constraints such as those embodied in the UK Sex Discrimination Act and Race Relations Act. These present employers with the major challenge of 'ensuring that selection for jobs and for promotion should be both within the law and effective in getting the most suitable people' (Pearn, Kandola and Mottram, 1987).

Alongside the increasing concern for fairness and avoidance of bias in selection there has been a growing emphasis on democratization of the process, both in the form of more interactive procedures and constructive feedback to candidates and, in countries such as the Netherlands and West Germany, in the co-decision rights of Works' Councils in formulating the regulations of principles of personnel selection (Koopman-Iwema and Flechsenberger, 1984). Anderson and Shackleton (1986) summarized the general position which, to some degree, has permeated most countries of Europe, when they said that 'overall the trend has been one of a growing emphasis of research into the perceptions, attitudes, reactions and rights of the applicant in the recruitment process. This trend is also indicative of the ethical ramifications and implications for personnel specialists being seen to be working *with* applicants rather than *on* applicants.' However, as de Wolff and van den Bosch (1984) noted, there is hardly any professional literature on participation in engaging personnel or, as discussed below, on how selection is undertaken in many instances, or by whom.

SELECTION PRACTICES

Although industrial and organizational psychologists have a long-established claim to the field of selection, they have no monopoly of the domain. Their role is often marginal and unprotected by law and they have no redress when, and if, other selection practitioners use dubious or irrelevant procedures. Currently, there appears to be no pressure from interested bodies such as trade unions to investigate the process of selection and, in most European countries, there is much less research on the topic being carried out in universities or other institutes than formerly. In France, for example, there is no systematic research at present on the evaluation and assessment of normal adults (Levy-Leboyer and Sperandio, 1987). Certainly there is no European equivalent of Project A, sponsored by the United States Army Research Institute, in which large, diverse samples of men and women from the major ethnic groups in nineteen occupations are being studied longitudinally with a view to 'designing and engineering new solutions to the problems of assessing people and allocating them to positions' (Hakel, 1986).

To some extent, this lack of research may be the result of changing values. During the 1960s and 1970s students of work psychology showed increasing reluctance to be employed in, or on behalf of, industry (de Wolff, Shimmin and de Montmollin, 1981), although the situation has now changed in many European countries where work and organizational psychologists are in a favourable position in the labour market. There is also the gap between, and the contrasting outlook of, those who are primarily scientists and those who are essentially practitioners. The latter frequently work for clients who are prepared to take on trust the procedures used, without enquiring whether any attempts have been made to validate them, while the former have always been concerned by the problems of, and the importance of, validation.

Formal data on selection practices, as distinct from research, are hard to obtain. Personal communications from colleagues in different parts of Europe suggest a diversity and, in some instances, an unsatisfactory situation. In Switzerland, there are hardly any regulations concerning the selection process and any procedure deemed effective and reasonable by the employer is used. This may include graphology and astrology. For occupations in which there are federal apprenticeship schemes leading to a federally approved final certificate, employers tend to rely on the certificate as the main selection tool. But, in all cases, no systematic validation is undertaken. The public sector in France, with a previously strong tradition of psychometrics, is no longer to the fore in this respect and some industries are now using graphologists as selectors, as are the recruitment and consultancy agencies which seek to obtain good staff for small enterprises. Belgium has sought to regulate selection procedures by law, but has not yet drafted a satisfactory format. In Italy, where selection tests (and attitude surveys) were forbidden by the law on the rights of workers (Statuto dei lavoratori) in 1970, personnel selection and assessment are a matter for unions and personnel managers, not psychologists. Wood (1986), in reporting an Anglo-German research study, described the pragmatic nature of the selection criteria adopted by organizations faced with skill shortages. Although not conforming to the recommendations of the textbooks, he noted that the procedures used were not necessarily *ad hoc*, casual, inefficient or devoid of rationality. Be this as it may, the practice of selection may often leave much to be desired and, as Robertson and Makin (1986) observed of management selection in the United Kingdom, the message does not appear to have reached practitioners that psychological research and theory have much to offer. Perhaps this is because they do not perceive psychology as offering anything that will enhance significantly their commercial success.

The time-scale of developing and validating a selection procedure is probably one reason why so little systematic validation takes place. Another is that, until comparatively recently, there was less awareness of the cost-benefit of labour and a tendency to view employees as interchangeable to a large extent. Furthermore, subjectivity in selection as represented by interviewer bias, the applicant's having the right connections and/or having or holding the right opinions, and other forms of nepotism may be socially deplored but may also be tolerated within an organization or community. Interviews remain the most widely used procedure, despite their known drawbacks, which may not be as serious as some critics have suggested if they adhere to certain conditions and procedures (Drenth, 1988).

With regard to psychological testing, social, economic, political and religious influences underlie the broad distinctions which can be made in Europe between the predominantly Catholic South and the mainly Protestant North and between the capitalist West and the Socialist East. Thus, in Spain, where the Catholic Church tends to disapprove of psychological tests, the unions favour their use in selection as preferable to patronage and nepotism. In Sweden, psychologists tend to be critical of tests and to spend less time on them than their colleagues elsewhere because of their social and ethical implications (Poortinga *et al.*, 1982). Throughout Europe, however, there has been a marked trend over the years to import tests from other countries, especially the United States, which has had a profound influence on selection methods in many European countries. The success with which these tests have been adapted, translated, revised and standardized for use in different contexts is hard to assess, but the observations of Sandor Klein (1987, unpublished), a Hungarian psychologist, may be pertinent here. In his view, it is *beliefs* about the effectiveness of the procedures used, rather than the procedures themselves, that determine how selection is undertaken. Thus, if an approach is believed to have predictive value, it is found to have predictive value by those who advocate it.

Klein's comments may have been influenced by the lack of control over tests which prevails in his country. As he wrote in the *Newsletter of the International Test Commission* in 1980:

> There is not an institutionalised form of test edition in Hungary even today. Single psychologists and institutions have produced a number of different versions or translations of foreign tests . . . and in most cases they spread without appropriate Hungarian standards. A number of tests are available only by acquaintance in a home-made form. Tests manufactured in such a way can be acquired by almost everybody. . . .

While this is an extreme example, it shows why psychologists have been concerned to promote professional competence in selectors and to exert, where possible, some quality control in the use of tests. As indicated earlier, European psychologists have not been able to claim exclusive rights in this respect and, although their training and the codes of ethics of their professional associations influence their own conduct, they cannot sanction what others do. Ultimately, practice is largely a matter of personal integrity, knowledge and experience.

Whereas to some psychologists the validity of psychometric tests is of crucial importance, to others the tests are suspect on grounds such as the invasion of privacy. The final report of a government appointed commission in the Netherlands to examine selection procedures, published in 1977, had the title 'An applicant is also a human being'. This described a number of rights the commission considered an applicant should have. These were: the right to a fair chance to be engaged; the right to information, including information about the procedure, the job itself, the work organization, information gathered about the applicant and reasons for rejection; the right to privacy, tempered by admissible violation where the information sought has a bearing on the job; the right to confidential treatment of personal data; the right to an instrumentally efficient procedure which is valid and reliable; the right of an applicant to lodge a complaint about his/her treatment and/or the selection decision, together with the recommendation that those carrying out psychological selection tests should be subject to legal disciplinary measures. Although the government did not enact the findings of the commission, its recommendations were incorporated in part or in whole in the codes of practice of such bodies as the Dutch Institute of Psychologists and the Dutch Association for Personnel Officers.

The growing awareness of the importance of the individual and of what he or she should be entitled to, whether as an applicant or as an employee, signifies greater accountability towards those about whom data are obtained and decisions taken. It includes the recognition that human resources are not, like material resources, totally at the disposal of an organization, but are capable of change and development and may acquiesce or object to personnel decisions that affect them. Dunnette and Borman (1979) pointed out that the focus of psychological texts and books on personnel management is invariably on institutional selection decisions, rather than on decisions by individuals as to whether or not to accept a particular job offer or to remain with an organization following re-location or placement. They noted the 'frequent incompatibility' between these two categories of decision and commented that 'locating and selecting the most qualified persons for available jobs will almost always yield quite different placement decisions from locating the most qualified jobs for particular persons'.

There is, therefore, now much more consideration of selection from the candidate's viewpoint than formerly. Ekvall (1980) has described the situation in Sweden as follows:

> The advance of industrial democracy has resulted in a situation where decision making for personnel selection purposes is increasingly made by large groups of persons within a company and not simply by the heads of personnel departments or by top management. Thus, for example, employee representatives are now present when psychologists report on the results of testing. Furthermore, the persons being tested have been made more aware of issues and have been given greater control of what happens to the results. An applicant who undergoes psychological testing is allowed nowadays—amongst other things—to be informed of the results before the employer is given this information. He has the possibility of backing out and having his results—the test protocols—destroyed, if he wishes. It is also possible for him to have consultation with the psychologist, using the results as a basis for discussion. This consultation can often be characterised as vocational guidance.

The same conditions apply also in the Netherlands and although they represent what is probably an ideal, rather than a reality, in other parts of Europe, the view of selection as a social process in which people are assisted to become more aware of themselves and their potential is gaining ground. Emphasis is placed on facilitating self-selection on the basis of realistic job previews, which may take the form of trainability testing in specific skills (Robertson and Downs, 1979) or the situational exercises and multiple approach of assessment centres. Williams

(1984) pointed out that assessment centres are more likely to provide conditions that favour valid self-appraisal than more traditional selection procedures, not least because they allow participants to experience a sample of the organizational climate in which they would be operating and, hence, to assess its compatibility or incompatibility with their own norms and values. He suggested that the Pre-Regular Commissions Boards in the British Army serve this function of facilitating self-selection, even though their primary purpose is to enable candidates to be assessed by external observers. More research into the processes of self-appraisal in the context of assessment centres may well lead to further developments of this kind in the future.

THE EUROPEAN VIEW OF SELECTION

This chapter has argued that there are changing economic conditions and changing social values which have disrupted traditional notions of organizations, work, employment and, hence, of selection and training. These changes have had most effect within organizations, including the establishment and strengthening of the rights of people within employment through specific labour legislation. What has tended to lag behind is the practice of personnel selection, although professional codes of practice have been painstakingly revised and re-written in many countries. This is due largely to the persistence of traditional approaches which define selection as a prediction problem confronting managers responsible for choosing or deploying their subordinates, a view that is being challenged from many quarters. Technological change, on the one hand, and legal requirements, on the other, impel a move towards selecting people who are adaptable and capable of responding appropriately to new tasks and training opportunities and away from matching applicants' existing skills to well-defined (and relatively unchanging) jobs.

Selection in Europe is not undertaken solely or wholly by, or with the aid of, psychologists. The situation varies between countries and between organizations of different size. Some multinational corporations use experts from their parent company to select on the same basis in different countries, while small enterprises often lack expertise in this area. What seems apparent is that there is a broad consensus among professional and academic psychologists, irrespective of language and country, about the role they could and should play in personnel selection, what they should be promoting and how they should go about it. Their ability to achieve their desired end, however, is limited by scarcity of resources. There are insufficient trained psychologists either for the volume of personnel selection work or to keep up to date with developments in salient aspects such as psychometric testing. Research in the field is also under-subscribed and under-utilized.

As in the United States, where the advent of legally enforceable requirements relating to psychological testing led to re-examination of the tests commonly in use and the manner in which they are used, so in other countries in which employers can be called upon to justify the use of a test, such as the United Kingdom, complex practical, technical and legal issues may arise. It seems likely that the American experience, whereby legislation led some organizations to support large-scale and carefully planned selection research programmes and others to withdraw entirely from using psychometric tests, will be paralleled in Europe.

In several countries, independent consultants and practitioners, with varying qualifications, are active in assisting in or undertaking selection on behalf of organizations. It is not clear if their clients always understand the ramifications of the procedures used or if they grasp any proper reservations that may be expressed by their advisers about norms, validity, reliability and interpretation. At this level, the preferred prejudices of the organization are probably paramount and it may well be that external consultants are chosen on the basis of those whose findings are likely to concur with what key members of the organization think. There is certainly much anecdotal evidence to this effect, although documented and systematic data on the matter are lacking.

What is more substantial is wide agreement on the need for more democratization of the selection process, by giving greater consideration to the candidate's viewpoint, by involving workers' representatives in determining the procedures to be used, by encouraging self-appraisal and self-selection, by making more flexible and interactive use of different techniques, and so on. How this is to be achieved depends to a large extent on the prevailing social and legal climate, but the aim is common in seeking to select applicants who will most benefit both themselves and the organization by becoming employed. The approach rests more on social and developmental psychology than on differential psychology. It is associated with a systems perspective that sees recruitment, selection, induction, training, career development, etc., as integral parts of the total process whereby an organization interacts with, and responds to, its environment. There is also increased concern about the fairness of, and avoidance of, bias in selection procedures on the part of psychologists and members of society alike, as well as pressure to associate workers in enterprise decisions that, traditionally, were the prerogative of management. The emphasis given to these aspects of the selection process varies in different countries.

These strands together delineate the contextual climate of selection in Europe. They cohere in as much as psychologists and other professionals throughout the Continent share the same perceptions of the current situation. At one level, the picture is kaleidoscopic and fragmented; but, at another, there are common views and shared standards that transcend national boundaries. With the growth of the formal and informal associations and networks that now characterize the European scene, an extension of converging approaches may be anticipated in the years ahead.

REFERENCES

Anderson, N., and Shackleton, V. (1986). Recruitment and selection: A review of developments in the 1980s, *Personnel Review*, **15**(4), 19–26.

Drenth, P.J.D. (1988). De Waarde van het Selectie-interview. *Gedrag en Organisatie*, **1** (3), 12–22.

Dunnette, M.D., and Borman, W.C. (1979). Personnel selection and classification systems, *Annual Review of Psychology*, **30**, 477–525.

Ekvall, G. (1980). Industrial psychology in Sweden, in X. Zamek-Gliszezynska (ed.). *Work Psychology in Europe*. Polish Scientific Publishers, Warsaw.

Gutsenko, K., and Zharkov, B. (1982). Judicial protection of labour rights in the USSR, *International Labour Review*, **121**(6), 731–45.

Hakel, M.D. (1981). Challenges of diversity: An American's view of work psychology in Europe, in C.J. de Wolff, S. Shimmin, and M. de Montmollin (eds). *Conflicts and Contradictions—Work Psychologists in Europe*. Academic Press, London.

Hakel, M.D. (1986). Personnel selection and placement, *Annual Review of Psychology*, **37**, 351–80.

Ham, J. van, Paauwe, J., and Williams, R. (1986). Personnel management in a changed environment, *Personnel Review*, **15**(3), 3–7.

Hepple, B. (1981). A right to work? *Industrial Law Journal*, **10**, 65–83.

Holdsworth, R. (1983). Personnel selection, in A.P.O. Williams (ed.). *Using Personnel Research*. Gower Press, London.

Klein, S. (1980). Uses of test methods in Hungary, *Newsletter of the International Test Commission, and of the Division of Psychological Assessment of the IAAP*, No. 14.

Koopman-Iwema, A.M., and Flechsenberger, D. (1984). Works' Councils: the Dutch and German case, in A.M. Koopman-Iwema and R.A. Roe (eds). *Work and Organisational Psychology—European Perspectives*. Swets and Zeitlinger, Lisse.

Levy-Leboyer, C., and Sperandio, J-C. (1987). *Traite de Psychologie du Travail*. Presses Universitaires de France, Paris.

Pearn, M., Kandola, R., and Mottram, R.D. (1987). *Selection Tests and Sex Bias: The impact of selection testing on the employment opportunities of women and men*. Equal Opportunities Commission Research Series, HMSO, London.

Polish Academy of Sciences (1980). *Work Psychology in Europe*. Polish Scientific Publishers, Warsaw.

Poortinga, Y.H., Coetsier, P., Meuris, G., Miller, K.M., Samsonowitz, V., Seisdedos, N., and Schlegal, J. (1982). A survey of attitudes towards tests among psychologists in six Western European countries, *International Review of Applied Psychology*, **31**, 7–34.

Robertson, I.T., and Downs, S. (1979). Learning and the prediction of performance: development of trainability testing in the United Kingdom, *Journal of Applied Psychology*, **64**, 42–50.

Robertson, I.T., and Makin, P.J. (1986). Management selection in Britain: A survey and critique, *Journal of Occupational Psychology*, **59**(1), 45–57.

Williams, A.P.O. (1984). The neglected process of self-selection. *Proceedings of the 26th Annual Conference of the Military Testing Association*.

Wolff, C.J. de, Shimmin, S., and Montmollin, M. de (1981). *Conflict and Contradictions—Work psychologists in Europe*. Academic Press, London.

Wolf, C.J. de, and Bosch, G. van den (1984). Personnel selection, in P.J.D. Drenth, H. Thierry, P.J. Willems, and C.J. de Wolff (eds). *Handbook of Work and Organisational Psychology*, Vol. 1. Wiley, Chichester.

Wood, S. (1986). Personnel management and recruitment, *Personnel Review*, **15**(2), 3–11.

Section 2: The Selection Process

Introduction to Section 2:
The Selection Process

Robert A. Roe

This section deals with personnel selection as a process, i.e. a series of activities developed in order to identify suitable applicants and choose those who are expected to contribute optimally to the organization's goals. The selection process is approached from a dual perspective. A number of chapters take the perspective of 'what ought to be done', or in other words how to devise selection procedures and how to carry them out. Other chapters concentrate on 'what is actually done', i.e. how procedures are composed and what happens in practice.

Publications on selection, throughout the years, have generally stressed the first perspective, dealing with principles of job analysis, test construction, regression analysis, validation, utility assessment, etc. Meanwhile most practitioners in the recruitment and selection field have followed the second perspective, concentrating on the optimization of traditional procedures, searching the commercial market for 'new tools', and trying to find out what their colleagues in other firms or consultancies are doing. There has been comparatively little research on actual selection practices; and the results that are available usually lack important detail, such as which types of tools are used for which type of job opening, the frequency of use, methods followed in interpreting tests, etc. Furthermore, there is comparatively little systematic knowledge about the antecedents and consequences of certain ways of recruiting and selecting people. At the same time it can be noted that practitioners have shown limited interest in sound principles of developing procedures, and hardly any readiness to apply those principles in their work. It seems that both domains, i.e. that of research and development in selection methods, and that of recruitment and selection practice, have developed largely independently, resulting in a remarkable discrepancy between present-day theory and practice.

Many reasons can be given for this development. A trivial one is that for a long time publications on selection methodology, especially by psychologists, have stressed the separate tools of selection, particularly the psychological 'test', rather than the logic and organization of the overall selection process. And when selection procedures were indeed being discussed, quite often a narrow, psychometric perspective was adopted. Only recently have researchers started to show interest for 'selection procedures', as integral structures of activities that do not merely cover the administration of a testing programme, but encompass every activity that is involved in selecting applicants. As will be shown in this section, this approach sheds light on a number of new aspects of selecting people, simultaneously altering the view of many other aspects, such as predicting work behaviour, taking decisions on the basis of uncertain information, or assessing utilities, which have been known for a longer time. For example, changing the focus from one selection instrument to a series of successively administered instruments, that are only partially accounting for a final selection decision, evokes all kinds of questions about establishing norms, setting cut-offs, assessing validity and utility, etc.

Even if future research and development attention would focus on integral procedures rather than on tests, one cannot expect practitioners simply to adopt available scientific methods and knowledge. Most likely a discrepancy will continue to exist. A situation like this is not unique to the field of personnel selection, however. In almost every domain, even in engineering, there is a large gap between the level of the techniques that are in current use, and the level of the technology. Transfer of knowledge from research and development laboratories to the practitioners' workshops takes time, and depends on many factors, including the (continued) training of professionals, product development activity leading to the production of usable methods and tools, product qualities such as price, time usage, user friendliness, etc. Besides, there are factors relating to the context of use that may prohibit, or hamper, the acceptance of technical innovations.

By pursuing this analogy a little further and looking into these factors in more detail, one may start to understand better the discrepancy between 'is' and 'ought' in personnel selection. Training is an important factor for the personnel specialist. As scientific knowledge is growing fast, and professionals cannot be expected to keep up to date, some recurrent training is definitely required in order to keep up. Apart from this, training is essential for relating the idiom of selection technology to that of selection practice.

The product development function, i.e. converting technological knowledge into usable artefacts, has been fulfilled only to a very limited degree within the personnel selection field. The only type of product that has been developed in great variety and at an extensive scale, is the test. It is remarkable that the test, which indeed can be considered as a complete, ready-to-use artefact embodying knowledge that was previously only available to psychometric experts, has gained wide-scale acceptance. Job analysis techniques are another, but less impressive example. Other tools and methods should be developed in the future as well, bringing new items of knowledge within the reach of the professional. It seems that computerized decision support systems have a great potential applicability here.

Which product qualities are critical for acceptance of tools and methods by professionals is largely unknown. The time involved in learning to use, and in making use of the product might appear to be an important factor, as personnel selection activities tend to take place under strict time constraints. Price may be less important, as long as the expenditure can be spread over a large number of administrations. User friendliness is an aspect that has often been overlooked within the selection domain, even in earlier tests with their sometimes complex scoring templates, and cumbersome scoring routines. Especially in developing a new generation of tools and methods, one should pay great attention to the 'user interface', trying to minimize the effort that users have to spend on operating the instrument.

Finally, there are the conditions under which selection professionals are working. The features of selection procedures and the properties of the aids used determine to a large degree the content of the professional's job, as well as his or her status and income. Changes in selection methodology have the potential to affect these working conditions, and therefore sometimes are met by total resistance. Except for those cases in which principles of organizational change are adequately used, the selection specialists may effectively oppose innovations.

Without doubt there are still other factors to be mentioned. Two of them are particularly interesting, as they are typical for the psychological aspects of personnel selection. The first one is that practically every person, professional selectors included, suffers from common sense. This means that one is subjected to phenomena like first impression, contrast effects, sympathy, etc., which have been well identified in years of research on selection interviews and attribution processes. Moreover, there is the illusion of certainty in judging other people, which minimizes the need for supplementary, objective information. The second factor has to do with the felt need for improving the quality of judgements and decisions about applicants. The illusion of certainty, or the lack of doubt, experienced by many professionals may be seen as determinant. The absence of effective scrutiny by candidates, and their later managers, certainly plays a role as well. It is noteworthy that an external condition, such as equal employment legislation in the United States, has made the need for quality to be felt much more strongly.

Many of the factors listed here are addressed, in one way or another, by the chapters within this section. The 'ought' and the 'is' perspective are both exposed, as well as confronted with one another. This makes this section a fascinating one for those readers who are interested in understanding and/or bridging the gap between selection theory and selection practice.

Chapter 2.1 by Roe, 'Designing Selection Procedures', takes the technology of personnel selection as a starting point. His contention is that selection specialists should focus on the concept of 'selection procedure', and should strive to develop selection procedures in a systematic way, taking account of all kinds of practical, as well as scientific requirements and constraints. His description of the development method, which is based on the design cycle from engineering, is followed by an example from a (re)design project carried out in a selection consultancy.

Greuter and Algera, in Chapter 2.2, 'Criterion development and job analysis', elaborate the idea of designing selection procedures. They concentrate on two particular functions of the selection procedure, i.e. gathering information about jobs and predicting performance of applicants on the job. They start with an overview of criterion concepts, and continue to discuss the use of job analysis as an aid in developing procedures. Their chapter contains a comprehensive review of job analysis methods and techniques that are relevant for selection.

Two essential components of any personnel selection procedure are the predictive performance model and the decision-making model. In Chapter 2.3, 'Performance modelling for personnel selection', Greuter shows how the design cycle concept can be applied to the construction of a prediction model. After having mentioned a number of major design considerations, he describes the steps to take when defining the model's content (i.e. criterion and predictor variables) as well as its format and structure (i.e. the pattern of their interrelationships). His treatment is completed by a review of both traditional and recent techniques for estimating the prediction model's parameters, and for evaluating its validity. Decision models are not treated in this section. They can be developed in an analogous way, however.

Once the selection procedure is developed, the selection process can start. Selection is usually preceded by some type of recruitment activity. This activity is treated by De Witte in his Chapter 2.4, 'Recruiting and advertising'. The author sets out with a discussion of what applicants and recruiters do during the recruitment phase, including searching and decision making. Next he gives a brief review of studies on the effectiveness of recruitment channels. The remainder of the chapter is devoted to a presentation of results from research on the effectiveness of the personnel advertisement as a recruitment channel.

The selection process itself implies a series of contacts and exchanges between the candidates and the organization. This aspect is highlighted in Herriot's Chapter 2.5, 'Interactions with clients in personnel selection'. It is indicated that the behaviours of both parties during their interaction affect mutual expectations and decision making, partly inadvertently. Furthermore, a series of suggestions is given, based on the research literature, about how to improve communication between candidates and organization, and how to optimize selection outcomes.

Selection activities are being performed by people in organizations, usually specialists working in personnel departments or consultancy agencies. Aris in Chapter 2.6, 'The organization of a psychological consultancy', presents a systematic description of the many factors that have to be taken into account in running a consultancy that specializes in personnel selection. Much of what he describes is also valid for the operation of testing departments in industrial firms. He stresses the importance of establishing and maintaining good relationships with client organizations and with candidates. Furthermore, he reviews a great number of practical issues that relate to office management, financial administration, analysis of business data, and finally research and development.

Shackleton and Newell take a different perspective. Chapter 2.7, 'Selection procedures in practice', is essentially a review of studies on what actually happens in personnel selection. They start with an overview of selection processes in terms of subsequent activities developed by the organization. Next they consider a number of selection instruments, including the interview, references, psychological tests, assessment centres, as well as biodata and graphology. They present scarce research evidence on the factors that determine the actual composition of selection procedures. The chapter is concluded by a discussion of differences between actual and recommended selection practice.

The final chapter, by Iles and Robertson, deals with the general question of how personnel selection procedures, as actually used in practice, affect candidates. As discussed in Chapter 2.8, 'The impact of personnel selection procedures on candidates', selection can have both beneficial and adverse impacts. The authors review research evidence with regard to fairness and bias, as well as the perceived infringement on clients' rights. Furthermore, they summarize the results of recent research on cognitive and affective reactions of candidates to recruitment, as well as to the use of interviews, work samples, assessment centres, and other methods. This chapter also contains a conceptual model, based on research by the authors, which hypothesizes how certain effects on candidates are brought about.

Chapter 2.1

Designing Selection Procedures

ROBERT A. ROE

Department of Social Sciences, Tilburg University, Hogeschoollaan 225, Unit P, Room 811, Postbox 90153, 5000 LE Tilburg, The Netherlands

INTRODUCTION: A TECHNOLOGICAL VIEW OF SELECTION

Personnel selection has a long history. Since the early work of Münsterberg and others, numerous methods, techniques and tools have been developed, and a large volume of data has been assembled regarding the differential characteristics of people and the way in which they relate to job performance. It is remarkable that though considerable knowledge on selection has thus been obtained throughout the years, little attention has been paid to the way in which the available knowledge can be used in the development of selection procedures for specific positions within organizations. The same is true for the structuring of the development process itself.

In practice it is left to the personnel specialist to set up procedures according to his or her own preference. There are hardly any conventions to follow. With regard to specific components of selection procedures such as psychological testing and medical examinations a few prescriptive models exist. The prevailing model with regard to psychological testing (cf. Thorndike, 1949; Cascio, 1978) is one which focuses on selection as prediction. This 'classical model' includes such steps as: analysing the job, choosing criteria to predict, choosing predictors, carrying out a validation study, and composing a predictive test battery. A limitation of models such as these is that they relate only to a part of the total selection procedure. The design of the overall selection procedure is far beyond their scope. Moreover, these models tend to present a narrow view of the problem. The classical model, for example, reduces selection to prediction, leaving out aspects that relate to the management of the selection process, such as decision making, negotiation between employer and applicant, costs and benefits, or to the societal context of selection,

Assessment and Selection in Organizations   Edited by P. Herriot
© 1989 John Wiley & Sons Ltd

such as legal regulations, labour market conditions, etc.

The purpose of this chapter is to show that a more systematic and comprehensive approach to the design of selection procedures is possible by adopting a 'technological' perspective. This means that we will conceive of our knowledge on personnel selection as part of technology in general, i.e. the science of realizing certain objectives by using available knowledge as well as solution oriented methods.

Technology relates to 'science' in the stricter sense of the word in that it uses the same type of methods and knowledge about reality. The major difference lies in the fact that it aims at creating new phenomena, or changing existing reality, rather than explaining existing phenomena. Its main criterion is goal effectiveness rather than truth. Another difference is that it may combine elements of different fields of science, e.g. behavioural, economic, physical, or political, depending on the problem area.

Technology is not identical to merely solving isolated problems. It provides a basis for technical solutions by offering general concepts and principles, as well as an appropriate methodology, i.e. the 'design methodology'.

Speaking of a 'selection technology' means on the one hand that we consider all our knowledge that relates to selection, ranging from differential psychology and psychometrics to decision theory, economics, ethics, and law (cf. Roe, 1983; Muchinsky, 1986; Guion and Gibson, 1988; also other chapters of this book), as a general database upon which we should draw when developing selection procedures. On the other hand it means that we are ready to accept real-life selection problems of organizations, prepared to develop the optimal solution for every specific case. The objective is thus to bridge the gulf between theoretical knowledge and practical problems leaving both sides intact, i.e. without distorting practical problems in order to let them obey theoretical constraints, or without forcing theory to be mutilated according to the constraints of practice. This, as will be shown, is feasible by adopting the design methodology.

In this chapter we will first give a description of design methodology and discuss in general terms how it can be applied in the process of developing selection procedures. Next we will focus on the major functions of selection procedures: information gathering/giving, prediction, and decision making, and indicate how they can be achieved in various components of selection procedures. We will discuss some major design options, leaving a more detailed discussion to subsequent chapters. Another topic deals with general considerations about the composition of selection procedures in terms of people, means and time. Finally, we will illustrate the technological approach by presenting some data on a project that aimed at re-design of selection procedures in a consultancy office.

THE DESIGN CYCLE CONCEPT

Design methodology comes from the engineering sciences. It is basically a set of principles for defining, shaping and maintaining a technical product. Fundamental to design methodology is the so-called 'design cycle' concept (Eekels, 1983), which specifies a number of steps that have to be taken within the frame of an

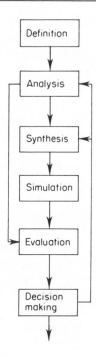

Figure 1   Design cycle

iterative process. The design cycle has been depicted in Figure 1, and will be discussed below.

It should be noted that the design cycle concept can be applied to any type of product, e.g. an aircraft, a chair, or a hair pin. Talking about personnel selection the product to be designed may be a psychological test, a job analysis instrument, or an integral selection procedure. We will focus on the selection procedure as the artefact to be produced, noting that its separate components can be developed in an analogous way. Our description thus relates directly to selection procedures. The steps of the design cycle are the following:

1. *Definition*   As a first step, one should define the purpose of the selection procedure and determine the functions which it should fulfil in its given context. Generally speaking selection procedures should serve to collect relevant information, make predictions of performance, evaluate performance, take decisions, and finally inform people involved. The functions that a procedure should have are context-dependent, e.g. they will be different for procedures used within companies and those used by consultancy agencies. In order to identify the functions one should interview future users of the procedure, and other people that are involved.
2. *Analysis*   From the functions to be fulfilled one has to derive requirements that the procedure should meet. These may relate to the input data (what is and is not available), the prediction, the decision (or recommendation), the communication with the people involved, etc. Furthermore, the constraints

should be specified. Usually there are limitations regarding time and use of resources. But there may be other constraints as well, e.g. with regard to the nature and duration of the transformation process, the interface to the organization's overall employment policies, ethical standards, etc. In principle the requirements and constraints should be set by the future users of the procedures, and other people involved. They belong to the conceptual world of the organization, not to that of the selection specialist. The selection specialist, however, can assist in operationalizing the requirements and constraints into design criteria.

3. *Synthesis* The next step is making a design, i.e. creating a preliminary selection procedure or adapting an existing procedure in such a way that it can fulfil the desired functions while staying within the limits of the constraints. Synthesis is essentially a creative activity, as the solution that is produced cannot be derived from available knowledge by deduction. However, it certainly implies an intensive use of both substantive knowledge about people and their behaviour, as well as methodological knowledge about tools and techniques, and designing as such (choosing or constructing elements, assembling parts, etc.). The result of synthesis is a description of the selection procedure.

   Synthesis may start with writing specifications, i.e. technical properties that the procedure to be designed should possess, such as a minimal predictive validity. Specifications can be seen as partial solutions to the design problem, chosen to meet specific requirements or constraints.

4. *Simulation* This step comes down to testing the operational, predictive, and economic properties of the selection procedure, i.e. duration, capacity, validity, effectiveness, utility and costs, etc. Simulation can either be done on an empirical basis by running experimental try-outs, such as validation, or by using models. Examples of simulation models are the Taylor–Russell tables, the Curtis and Alf tables, and the Cronbach–Gleser formulae for estimating utility.

5. *Evaluation* Once the properties of the selection procedure are known one can proceed to assess their value for the user, taking the requirements and constraints as a reference point. This step should answer the question whether the procedure as a whole is, or is not, sufficiently satisfactory.

6. *Decision making* Finally, a decision has to be made, either accepting the selection procedure for operational use, or rejecting it. In case of rejection one may continue with step 3, trying to modify and thereby improve the previous solution. Eventually, when errors or insufficiencies in the programme of requirements and constraints show up, one may return to step 2 and start with reformulating requirements and constraints first.

The principle of iteration is typical for designing: usually, the proper solution is found only after a number of efforts. This follows from the nature of designing as a reductive rather than a deductive process. Logically speaking, several solutions are feasible. Therefore, it is virtually impossible to determine the best solution in a single round.

An important implication is that the design cycle can equally well be applied to the design of completely new procedures as to the re-design of existing procedures. There is no sharp distinction line between design and re-design.

Of course, the 'design cycle' only gives the basic structure of the design process (cf. Eekels, 1983). In practice this process is far more complex, as there are several consecutive processes starting with a global design and proceeding in a step-by-step manner towards a completely detailed design. During specific phases of the whole process a number of parallel design processes may take place, directed at the creation of separate components, such as a job analysis method, an interview schedule, or a predictive performance model.

MAJOR FUNCTIONS OF SELECTION PROCEDURES

Though selection procedures may have many different functions to fulfil, the following four functions are most commonly found (cf. Roe and Greuter, 1989):

1. *Information gathering*: obtaining information about job openings, job content, job requirements, etc., and on physical, behavioural and biographical characteristics of applicants.
2. *Prediction*: transforming information on (past or present) applicant characteristics into predictions about their future behaviour, and the resulting contributions to organizational goals.
3. *Decision making*: transforming predictive information on applicants into a preferred action.
4. *Information supply*: producing information on applicant characteristics, predicted behaviours, plans for action (decisions), etc.

These functions can be materialized in a number of ways. Below will be mentioned some major design options that exist for each of these functions. Making a choice among these design options is decisive for the remainder of the design activity. Examples of this will be given in some of the chapters to follow.

The information-gathering function

In order to be able to select employees for positions in organizations, one should dispose of relevant information about the organization: the position, the employment conditions, etc., on the one hand; and information on the applicants on the other hand. Gathering such information can be seen as an essential function of selection procedures.

The main choices to be made with regard to the information-gathering function concern the content areas to be covered and the format of the information. Once a choice has been made on these two points, one can continue to look for specific techniques and instruments to be employed.

Information about the organization

Content areas that one might want to cover are:

- nature of the organization, location of the organization;
- type of position, context of the position, career ladders;
- number of vacancies (to be expected/when);
- to-be-performed roles/tasks/activities/duties and future roles and responsibilities;
- factors influencing performance/success: social, leadership, technical, working conditions, working hours (shifts);
- behavioural and personal requirements and constraints;
- time constraints: date and desirable duration of employment, interval between application and hiring;
- type of contract, labour conditions, working hours;
- policy directives with regard to personnel policy.

The types of information to be included, and those to be disregarded, have to be assessed carefully. There is a strong tradition in personnel selection to focus upon job content and corresponding behavioural and personal requirements. These types of information are indeed crucial for the prediction function (see below), as they help to define or operationalize criteria and predictor variables. One should, however, avoid limiting oneself to these aspects because of mere routine. Other aspects, e.g. factors of a political or cultural nature, may be equally important for adequate selection, and hence should be identified during the stage of designing procedures.

With regard to the type of *method* there is a kind of continuum, ranging from completely free format to fully structured. Structured methods are generally more effective, because they leave less room for overlooking certain points. Also they have the advantage of greater processing efficiency. The Position Analysis Questionnaire, and the Occupation Analysis Inventory can be mentioned as examples (see Chapter 2.2).

Applicant information

Here the main *content* areas are:

- cognitive and psychomotor aptitudes;
- cognitive abilities;
- psychomotor abilities;
- character traits;
- interests and values;
- knowledge and skills;
- biographical characteristics, including educational and work experience, age, sex;
- application motives;

- career preferences and goals;
- needs and demands for working conditions, salary, career options;
- availability (hours and periods).

The type of information needed depends partly on the labour market situation, and the bargaining position of the organization and the candidates, and partly on the nature of the position to be filled, more particularly the criteria that have to be predicted.

With regard to the *method* there is a great number of possibilities. These include: application letters, application forms, employment interviews, references, educational qualifications, work samples, psychological tests for various mental abilities, aptitudes, skills, etc., situational tests, assessment centres, biographical inventories, rating scales, medical check-ups, selection interviews, etc.

The choice among these options depends in the first place on the content covered, but at the same time it is associated with choices on prediction and decision making (see below). Also of importance are cost–benefit considerations, i.e. the relationship between the effort involved in obtaining the information and its usefulness.

The prediction function

Decisions about hiring and classifying applicants are based on expectations about their future behaviours and the resulting contributions to the realization of organizational goals. Therefore, some type of prediction activity is necessary, deriving expectations about future behaviour from past or present characteristics of the applicants. There are two main prediction principles, i.e. the sign approach and the sample approach (cf. Wernimont and Campbell, 1968).

The sign approach is based on the 'deductive–nomological' principle (cf. Stegmüller, 1974): when, for a given set of people, a certain law states that a relationship exists between a characteristic A and a certain type of behaviour E, one can deduct from this law the prognostic proposition that a person who possesses A will show behaviour E. This is true not only for a deterministic law, but also for probabilistic laws, which assign a probability to the relationship between A and E (Roe, 1983). Within the sign approach the characteristic A is generally considered as a trait (i.e. something the individual *has*), while E is a behaviour (something the individual *does*). Once the relationship between A and E has been hypothesized and sufficiently supported by empirical evidence, one can consider A as a 'sign' for the appearance of behaviour E.

The sample approach rests on the principle of generalization: when a person behaves in manner E at a given occasion defined by time and place, it is concluded that he or she will behave identically on other occasions belonging to the same universe, i.e. an occasion at another place or time. No trait concepts are involved in this approach; one generalizes directly from behaviour to behaviour (from what someone *does* to something else he or she *does*).

The two approaches differ not only in their underlying epistemological basis, they also lead to a different type of diagnostic process and to the use of different instruments. Figure 2 shows the diagnostic process corresponding to the sign approach. The process has two phases. First, there is an analytical or 'downward phase' in which one tries to identify useful diagnostic indicators. This phase starts with a description of the organization's goals and requirements with regard to the job. Next, conceptual criteria are specified, corresponding to relevant dimensions of work behaviour and performance results. On the basis of knowledge from differential psychology (cf. the 'laws' referred to above) conceptual predictors are chosen. These predictors can be conceived of as personality traits. Finally, the conceptual predictors, which have a well-defined theoretical status, or construct validity, are operationalized by choosing, or developing, certain operational predictors, such as cognitive tests, personality inventories and rating scales.

In the second or 'upward phase' the order is reversed. One starts with administering the operational predictors. Next one makes inferences on applicants' traits (conceptual predictors) and work behaviours (conceptual criteria). And, finally, conclusions are drawn about predicted job success in terms of contributions to the fulfilment of the organization's goals and requirements.

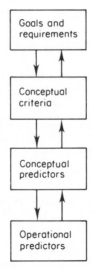

Figure 2   Diagnostic procedure in case of the sign approach

Figure 3 gives in a comparable way the diagnostic process for the sample approach. Again one starts with goals and requirements, but now the second step consists of defining the domain of tasks corresponding to the position involved. From this domain a sample of tasks is drawn, which is finally operationalized in some 'content oriented device', such as a work sample, a biographical inventory, a situational test, etc. The results obtained after having administered the instrument are interpreted in terms of the performance on the task sample, the total task domain, and finally job success.

These two approaches can be implemented in two different ways, i.e. by clinical methods or formalized methods. The combination leads to four

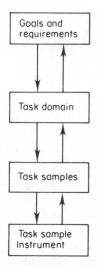

Figure 3   Diagnostic procedure in case of the sample approach

different forms of prediction (Roe, 1983; see also Figure 4):

1. *Prediction on the basis of a nomological model*   The model contains a formalized specification of the relationship(s) between one or more predictor variables, operational measures of traits, and one or more criterion measures.
2. *Prediction on the basis of a domain sampling model*   'Content oriented devices' are used to measure past or present performance; scores are generalized in a formal way (i.e. statistically) to future performance estimates, e.g. using confidence intervals.
3. *Clinical prediction based on predictor comparison*   The scores of applicants on predictor variables are compared in order to find those with the best overall profile; it is assumed that this person's performance on the job will be best.

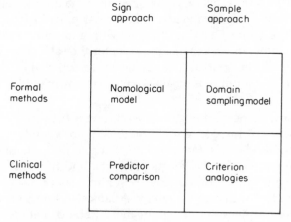

Figure 4   Different approaches to prediction

4. *Clinical prediction based on criterion analogies*   The work performance of applicants in similar situations is analysed in order to draw analogies; thus an idea of future performance is derived from past performance.

Decision-making function

Expectations about the applicants' future work behaviour do not constitute the end result of selection activity but are merely a basis for deciding whom to accept or reject, or whom to place in certain positions. Generating decisions, or at least ideas about decisions that should be taken if other things were equal (pre-decisions or recommendations), is therefore another important function that selection procedures should fulfil.

There are several ways in which the decision-making function can be implemented. First of all there are various 'decision strategies' from which one can choose. These strategies can best be described by adopting a general framework for decision analysis that is found in decision theory. This framework includes:

– possibilities for action (e.g. accepting, rejecting, allocating);
– outcomes defined by conditions such as better or worse performance as indicated by criteria, and action possibilities;
– utilities and probabilities assigned to those outcomes.

Generally speaking a strategy is a way of weighting utilities and probabilities of outcomes, and finding the optimal action.

Some well-known strategies for decision making under risk and uncertainty as defined by decision theory are:

1. *Maximization of expected utility*   The optimal action is the one which has the highest expected utility over various outcomes; this implies averaging of utilities after weighting by probability.
2. *Maximin*   The optimal action is the one with a maximum utility for the worst possible outcome; this means avoiding the risk of bad results.
3. *Maximax*   The optimal action is the one with a maximum utility for the best possible outcome; this means taking risks for the sake of best results.
4. *Minimax regret*   The optimal action is the one for which the difference between highest and lowest utility is smallest, which is a way of playing safe.

The choice for any of these strategies depends on the organization's goals and the nature of the job. An entrepreneurial firm looking for a product designer may be inclined to take the risk of a failure while trying to find the talented artist who helps to create real new forms for its products, and thus opt for the maximax strategy. A hospital attracting nursing personnel may rather want to avoid any risks and choose for the maximin strategy. A bank selecting high school graduates may prefer those applicants for whom the difference between good and bad performance is small, meaning that they can neither be expected to be brilliant nor to be a great failure. This equals to the minimax regret strategy. Many larger organizations prefer maximization of expected utility (cf. Conbach and Gleser, 1965), which gives the best average results over a larger number of decisions.

Apart from strategies there is a choice to be made between informal and formal decision making. The use of an analytical scheme as described above, along with algorithmic rules for establishing optimal solutions, typifies formal decision-making methods. Opting for such an approach towards the decision-making function in personnel selection leads to the development of decision models. The various strategies can be used in an informal, judgemental way as well, however, and this seems to happen most often in practice.

Information supply function

A final function of selection procedures is to supply information about examination results obtained by applicants, their expected performance, (pre)decisions taken, etc., to those who are using the procedure and to others involved. Among them one finds line managers and personnel managers who have final responsibility for hiring people. Among the other people who have to be informed there are the applicants.

The *contents* of the information may include:

- demands made by the applicants;
- descriptions of characteristics of the applicants;
- expected performance of applicants, including uncertainties;
- (pre)decisions reached, either conditioned or unconditioned, regarding suitability for a job or career;
- risks and potentialities, etc.

With regard to the communication *medium* one has to make a choice between oral presentation in special sessions, or by telephone, and written reports. The *form* can be either a narrative or a standardized description.

Functions and procedures

Given the options outlined above there are indeed various ways in which a selection procedure may fulfil the aforementioned functions. Which options one should choose, and in what way they should be implemented depends on many considerations, which relate to the requirements and constraints on the one hand, and to the technical possibilities and limitations of various solutions on the other hand.

The simpler procedures concentrate all the functions in a single technique, such as a selection interview. The more advanced procedures tend to cover a number of clearly distinguishable components:

- Information gathering procedures, which include the use of job analysis techniques, application forms, work samples, tests, interview schedules, etc.

- Predictive performance models, either embodied in prediction formulae, prediction tables and charts, or in clinical inference procedures.
- Decision models, such as compensatory or disjunctive decision algorithms, with corresponding decision analysis forms, sets of utility formulae, decision tables and charts.
- Information supply procedures, such as reporting, structured oral feedback procedures, giving views or reports, etc.

COMPOSING SELECTION PROCEDURES

At the level of specific selection procedures there are numerous ways to build composites from the available elements and components. What is the optimal procedure ultimately depends on the requirements and constraints specified at the beginning of the design process. However, there are a number of general considerations that play a role in finding the final shape for the selection procedure.

1. *Effectiveness considerations*   Selection procedures should yield the right type of information and lead to correct decisions. This has implications for the instruments to be used. On the one hand instruments should give adequate information about particular criteria, on the other they should have a maximum level of predictive validity.
2. *Efficiency considerations*   Every step taken within a selection procedure and any instrument used may add to the procedure's utility as well as to its costs. Benefits and costs may increase at a different rate, however. Quite often utility levels off when procedures are made more comprehensive, while the costs rise continuously. Thus it makes sense to look after the utility–cost ratio in composing selection procedures. There are two major ways to increase the utility–cost ratio. The first one is to cut the costs through a reduction of test length, and/or duration of the procedure. The second one is to introduce multiple stages, which implies bringing down the number of applicants to be considered and hence leads to a reduction of total costs. This is particularly valuable when the selection ratio is small. One may optimize net utility by placing the cheaper instruments at the beginning of the procedure and the more expensive ones at the end (even though this may imply a lower validity at the earlier stages).
3. *Ethical considerations*   Information gathering about applicants almost automatically implies a certain intrusion of privacy for the applicant. In order to protect the person's privacy one may look for instruments which, other things being equal, are least intrusive and offer least possibilities for disclosure of personal information. In a multi-stage procedure one may start with instruments that only assess public information (e.g. a limited application interview), and place more 'sensitive' instruments (e.g. personality tests) at the end.

   Another factor to consider is discrimination. Avoiding discrimination may require the introduction of parallel procedures of information gathering and processing for distinct groups.

4. *Managerial considerations* Carrying out selection procedures requires a number of different activities. As discussed in Chapter 2.7 there are certain requirements to be met which relate to the managerial point of view. For example, it may be necessary to standardize the length of interviews and tests, to put activities in certain order for reasons of optimizing the use of personnel, or to use standardized objective instruments in order to reduce labour costs.

DESCRIBING THE SELECTION PROCEDURE

The final product of the design process is a description of the integral selection procedure, which makes clear what activities should be undertaken, by whom, at what moments, which instruments should be used, etc.

We recommend that two documents are prepared:

1. A technical report giving the specifications of the procedure. This report should include:
   (a) a flow description of the procedure, which lists the activities in their chronological order, as well as their logical relationships;
   (b) a description of techniques and instruments used for gathering and supplying information, including references to data on construct or content validity and reliability;
   (c) a description of the prediction model and/or decision model, including data on predictive validity and utility.
2. A user manual containing directives for a proper use of the procedure. This manual should include:
   (a) a description of staff and facilities needed;
   (b) instructions on the administration of the procedures;
   (c) work aids such as forms, checklists, norm tables, etc.

In addition to these documents the various techniques and instruments should be made available, in order to put the selection procedure into operation.

When a set of procedures is developed for different jobs or job categories one should also describe the overall framework, both in the format of technical specifications, and that of a manual.

EXAMPLE OF (RE)DESIGN OF SELECTION PROCEDURES

The design methodology which was described above, has been applied in a project that aimed at the improvement of existing selection procedures used by 'Adviesbureau Psychotechniek', a Dutch consultancy agency. The project, which started in 1984, was carried out in an 'organizational development' style. While a project group played a directing and coordinating role, the total staff of the agency met at regular times in order to discuss the results and prepare decisions and plans. Working groups consisting of staff members were charged with specific tasks, such as defining job requirements, designing administrative work flows, etc.

In the course of time the following steps have been undertaken:

1. Using a method for describing the flow of information at several stages of personnel selection consultation, an extensive analysis was made of the *functions* of the selection procedures. In addition, a compilation was made of *requirements and constraints* as seen by 'relevant parties' (managers from the selecting organization, applicants, unions, etc.). The resulting document, called 'Programme of requirements' listed approximately 90 items, divided over seven parties. Included were such items as:
   - the procedure should produce a conclusion and a recommendation that are clear, correct, and informative;
   - the procedure should fit into the personnel policy procedures of the employer;
   - the procedure should produce information relevant for individual career planning;
   - candidates should be treated correctly and with due personal attention;
   - the intrusion of privacy should be limited as much as possible;
   - candidates should have the opportunity to prevent reporting to the employer;
   - the procedure should be non-discriminatory towards sexes, racial groups, different age groups, etc.;
   - the procedure should be complaint-proof;
   - there should be a non-restrictive procedure for filing and handling complaints;
   - the procedure should offer meaningful and challenging tasks to the staff;
   - the scientific basis of the procedure should be acceptable to current standards;
   - the procedure should be cost-efficient and competitively priced.
2. Next, a detailed *description* was made of the major procedure for the examination of applicants and the consultation of client organizations, which had been in use for several years. The result was laid down in a technical report as mentioned before.
3. The existing procedure was *evaluated* by the entire staff of the agency during a special half-day session. The evaluation was performed on the basis of the 'Programme of requirements', by three groups of staff members, each of which was focusing on a particular aspect of the procedure. The same groups participated in a half-day brainstorming session generating possible solutions for the problems identified earlier. In total 159 problems were identified, while 205 suggestions for improvements were generated. Afterwards these problems and suggestions were condensed and listed in an eight-page summary document.

   The categories covered were:
   - tests and other instruments;
   - contacts with client organizations;
   - processing of test data;
   - consultation and reporting;

- treatment of candidates;
- internal organization.

4. A special one-day meeting with staff of the agency was devoted to the formulation of needs for research and development, on the basis of the problems and suggestions for improvement gathered in the previous phase. In this way a *design programme* was defined, the so-called 'Development plan'. This plan contained specifications of the future selection procedure, and developmental activities that should be undertaken. From this general master plan a 'Workplan for 1985' was derived. It was laid down in these plans:
   - that jobs would have to be classified in a new job categorization system;
   - that the set of instruments (tests, work samples, etc.) would be updated according to current psychometric standards;
   - that a new protocol for interaction with candidates would have to be made;
   - that modules of predictive instruments would have to be formed for each of the job categories;
   - that new procedures would have to be designed that would incorporate the modules;
   - that a new work process would have to be set up for the agency as a whole in order to accommodate the new procedures.

5. The workplan was carried out to a large degree by a number of working groups from the staff. This implied a series of design activities, including *synthesis* and *simulation*. Two of the planned activities could be finished completely in 1985. The other items recurred in the 'Workplan for 1986', which was drawn up at the end of the year. This plan added:
   - the design of new job analysis instrument, aiming at a better communication with the client organization on the one hand and an unequivocal identification of psychological job requirements (i.e. relevant personal characteristics) on the other hand;
   - a try-out of the integral revised selection procedure.

6. In the course of 1986 the remainder of the development activities were carried out, using the design approach again. For example, the job analysis instrument was constructed in a number of iterations on the basis of a separate 'programme of requirements'. After a try-out, in fact an empirical *simulation*, in the fall of 1986, the procedure was *evaluated* against the original programme of requirements at the end of that year. It appeared that the majority of items was indeed met. Next it was *decided* to implement the new procedure with all relating administrative routines at the beginning of 1987. The 'Workplan for 1988' focused on a number of remaining problems, like the development of rating scales for job analysis and personality assessment, as well as an improvement of prediction and decision making, and refinement of the instruments.

This is where the project is now. It has produced a large number of changes in the agency's method.

CONCLUSION

It seems that the technological approach does indeed offer a more systematic and comprehensive framework for the development of personnel selection procedures than more traditional approaches. The adoption of the design cycle concept clarifies several points. First of all, it becomes much clearer that both functional requirements and practical constraints do play an essential role. In fact, they appear to be fundamental to the design and re-design of any procedure. Secondly, it becomes clear that systematic evaluation and decision making are crucial steps in the development process. One can observe both the progress made and the steps that are still to be taken. Finally, one sees that (re)designing a selection procedure may be a complex process that takes a lot of time and effort, while still retaining an orderly character.

REFERENCES

Cascio, W.F. (1978). *Applied Psychology in Personnel Management*. Reston, Virginia.

Cronbach, L.J., and Gleser, G.C. (1965). *Psychological Tests and Personnel Decisions*, 2nd edn. University of Illinois Press, Urbana, Illinois.

Eekels, J. (1983). Design processes seen as decision chains: their intuitive and discursive aspects. *Proceedings of the International Conference on Engineering Design*, Copenhagen.

Guion, R.M., and Gibson, W.M. (1988). Personnel selection and placement, *Annual Review of Psychology*, **39**, 349–74.

Muchinsky, P.M. (1986). Personnel selection methods, in C.L. Cooper and I.T. Robertson (eds.), *International Review of Industrial and Organizational Psychology*. Wiley, Chichester, pp. 37–70.

Roe, R.A. (1983). *Grondslagen der personeelsselektie*. Van Gorcum, Assen.

Roe, R.A. (1984). Advances in performance modeling: the case of validity generalization. Paper presented at the symposium 'Advances in Testing'. Acapulco, Mexico, 6 Sept. 1984.

Roe, R.A., and Greuter, M.J.M. (1989). Developments in personnel selection methodology, in R.K. Hambleton and J. Zaal (eds.), *Advances in Testing*. Kluwer, Deventer.

Stegmüller, W. (1974). *Probleme und Resultate der Wissenschaftstheorie und Analytischen Philosophie. Band I: Wissenschaftliche Erklärung und Begründung*. Studienausgabe Teil 5. Springer, New York.

Thorndike, R.L. (1949). *Personnel Selection*. Wiley, New York.

Wernimont, R.F., and Campbell, J. (1968). Signs, samples and criteria, *Journal of Applied Psychology*, **52**, 372–6.

Chapter 2.2

Criterion Development and Job Analysis

MARTIN A. GREUTER[1] and JEN A. ALGERA[2]

[1]*Adviesbureau Psychotechniek B.V., Drift 10, 3512 BS Utrecht, The Netherlands*
[2]*Eindhoven University of Technology, Faculty of Industrial Engineering and Management Science, PO Box 513, 5600 MB Eindhoven, The Netherlands*

INTRODUCTION

Criterion development and job analysis are two of the more traditional themes within the context of personnel selection. Developing and applying selection procedures cannot be accomplished without some form of criterion development and job analysis, no matter how rudimentary. Their relevance was long ago pointed out by Freyd (1923) in explaining the basic principles of 'measurement in vocational selection' (see Guion, 1976). According to Freyd the process of building and applying selection devices consists of ten steps. The first step comes down to conducting a job analysis. Job analysis should lead to the identification of relevant traits that are necessary for successful job performance. In conducting a job analysis, the job content must not be analysed in a superficial, global way but 'a more or less protracted, objective and systematic study of the behavior of individuals actually engaged in the particular activity' is called for (cf. Guion, 1976, p. 782). The second step in Freyd's scheme is aimed at identifying and operationalizing relevant criteria and can be labelled as a criterion development phase. In a next step required abilities and other person characteristics must be specified, an activity that is nowadays usually regarded as an integral part of job analysis procedures. Another example illustrating a long-standing interest in job analysis, can be found in the work of Münsterberg. In 1911 Münsterberg developed a work sample for selecting tram crews. In the work sample traffic situations were simulated on a map by using figures and letters to represent traffic participants as pedestrians, cars and horse-drawn vehicles. By moving the map

Assessment and Selection in Organizations   Edited by P. Herriot
© 1989 John Wiley & Sons Ltd

behind a little window, applicants could be confronted with alternative traffic situations. As Münsterberg has amply described, this ingenious device is developed on the basis of an extensive, thorough, real-life study of driving behaviours of tram conductors, to pick up the right type of traffic situations to simulate in the exercise.

More recently, the still growing interest in *assessment centres* has accentuated the relevance of job analysis and criterion development. For purposes of assessment centres, job analysis has at least two specific objectives (cf. Thornton and Byham, 1982). First, the job analysis is designed to identify clusters of activities (so-called 'behavioural incidents') that constitute important aspects of the job at hand and that can be simulated in one or more AC exercises. Second, job analysis helps to determine the attributes required to carry out the job effectively. As we shall point out below, these latter two objectives can be considered as a general pay-off of job analysis.

In this chapter the main emphasis is placed upon job analysis as a tool for obtaining information about job openings and as a means for developing selection oriented predictive performance models, thus contributing to the predictive function of personnel selection. While doing this, we will give detailed treatment of some recent developments with regard to synthetic validity, validity generalization and job analytic procedures for deriving work samples, because most of the scientific research and thinking about job analysis is devoted to these three topics.

As far as the structure of this chapter concerns, we will start with an introductory section about criterion concepts and their role in personnel selection (p. 144). Subsequently, we will give a review of the basic functions of job analysis as applied in the context of personnel selection (p. 152). This section serves as a guiding structure for the remainder of the chapter, because further sections elaborate some parts of these basic functions. On p. 154 job analysis procedures are considered as information gathering devices that can be applied for obtaining job relevant information about the vacancy at hand. The penultimate section explains how job analysis procedures serve to develop selection oriented performance models that are necessary for predicting the future job success of applicants. We end with some final comments concerning directions for future research and the use of job analysis in practice.

CRITERION CONCEPTS AND THEIR ROLE IN PERSONNEL SELECTION

In the history of industrial psychology a great deal of discussion has always been accorded to the criterion problem. Jenkins published in 1946 an article with the title 'Validity for what?', indicating that one cannot apply tests in a meaningful way by simply interpreting test scores without reference to external criteria to which they relate. Since no one would seriously consider arguing against this statement, it is surprising to see how little development effort is directed at constructing and operationalizing multiple criteria throughout the years. Even now, Jenkins's position that 'psychologists in general tend to accept the tacit assumption that criteria were either given by God or just to be found lying about . . .' (1946, p. 43), meaning that convenient availability of a criterion was more important than its adequacy, seems to hold as a general evaluative statement concerning the interest that is devoted to multiple criteria development nowadays: supervisory ratings continue to be the most typical measures of criterion performance. For example, Lent, Aurbach and Levin (1971a) found that supervisory ratings were used in 879 instances out of 1506 references to criteria. Results of a review by Monahan and Muchinsky (1983) show a consistent decline of supervisory ratings as the sole measure of job proficiency, but they still are the most frequently used methods of evaluating criteria. Furthermore, most of these ratings are of an overall, global nature. Lent, Aurbach and Levin (1971b) found that of a total of 406 validity studies reviewed, 344 (84.7 per cent) used only one overall criterion.

In this section we would like to pin-point some of the major developments in the field of criterion theory and development. We will start with a brief account of the meaning and definition of a criterion. In the next paragraphs we will highlight some major developments in the field of criterion development and theory. We will do so without having the intended purpose of being thoroughly exhaustive. The interested reader is referred to Smith (1976), Roe (1983) and Cascio (1987) for a more elaborate and systematic evaluation of the field. In the context of this chapter we will confine ourselves to a discussion of the controversy between multidimensional and unidimensional criterion concepts (p. 148), the classification of criteria and the development of taxonomies (p. 148), the incidence and meaning of so-called dynamic criterion (p. 150) and utility analysis (p. 151).

Defining criteria

Before continuing to explain the role of criteria in personnel selection, it is instructive to define what a criterion is.

Brogden and Taylor state that the criterion should measure the contribution of the individual to the overall efficiency of the organization (1950a, p. 139). A definition comparable to those of Brogden and Taylor has been given by Ghiselli and Brown: 'By criterion is meant any attribute or accomplishment of the worker that can be used as an index of his serviceability or usefulness to the organization that employs him' (1948, p. 62). Finally, Nagel has noted that 'for a given activity, the criterion is an index by which we can measure the degree of success achieved by various individuals' (1953, p. 272). All these different definitions converge to essentially one central meaning of the criterion concept: a criterion as a measure of success for a given activity.

Success criteria may in principle be related to different groups of activities as defined at various levels of abstraction. Figure 1 shows a hierarchically ordered series of activities ranging from minuscule muscle actions to broad descriptions of occupational activities. A lower level is implicated by activities at a higher level. For example: writing a report concerning the suitability of a job applicant (recruiting and selection officer) includes more specific activities such as writing, correcting, analysing and compiling (test) data, etc.

In the context of personnel selection elemental motions or muscular actions are usually not seen as relevant criteria to predict although on the other hand they are

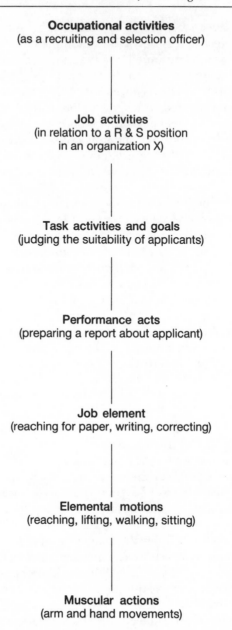

Occupational activities
(as a recruiting and selection officer)

Job activities
(in relation to a R & S position
in an organization X)

Task activities and goals
(judging the suitability of applicants)

Performance acts
(preparing a report about applicant)

Job element
(reaching for paper, writing, correcting)

Elemental motions
(reaching, lifting, walking, sitting)

Muscular actions
(arm and hand movements)

Figure 1 A hierarchy of performance activities

not formally or fundamentally excluded (after all, one might be trying to predict the actions of a rope-dancer or triathlete). Job elements, a term introduced by McCormick (McCormick, Jeanneret and Mecham, 1972; see also McCormick, 1976), are commonly denoted by the use of action verbs (writing, reaching, negotiating, instructing, etc.). Usually, they do not constitute criteria that are individually predicted, but they may form the basic elements for a more encompassing grouping into categories of performance acts or even task activities. With this latter two categories we arrive at the type of criteria that are, in our opinion, of particular relevance to personnel selection. There is some dispute, however, whether performance and task dimensions within the same job are to be described separately. It has been argued that within job differences do not moderate test validities. Following this line of argument one could confine oneself to criteria at a global job or occupational level. We shall return to this important topic later.

Requirements for deriving operational criteria

Thorndike has introduced the notions of ultimate versus substitute criteria. The ultimate criterion is the complete, final goal for performance in a particular type of job. It represents the true order of success in the job activities; it can only be stated in very broad terms. Instead of trying to accomplish the almost impossible task of predicting the ultimate criterion one proceeds in practice by predicting a more concrete, substitute criterion of success. The distinction between ultimate and substitute criterion has pointed at the relative value of a diversity of performance measures and introduced the notion of criterion *relevance*: the extent to which an index of success as applied is related to the true order of success in a given activity.

'Relevance' can be considered as a first requirement for operationalizing a criterion (cf. Smith, 1976). The measures of a criterion should be neither contaminated with irrelevant variance nor be deficient in the sense of missing important objectives or aspects of the performance domain under study. These situations can be referred to as 'criterion contamination' and 'criterion deficiency' respectively (Brogden and Taylor, 1950a).

In addition to relevance, two additional requirements must be put forward: reliability and practicality (cf. Smith, 1976; Roe, 1983). In general, reliability pertains to the (lack of) agreement between different performance evaluations at different periods of time and/or with different although apparently similar measures (equivalent measures). In the context of human performance measurement the concept of reliability refers to at least two different aspects: (1) the variability of the performance behaviours at hand (performance reliability); and (2) the reliability of their operational indicators (measurement reliability). Regarding the first point, it is important to reiterate that performance criteria serve as a set of predicted outcomes in personnel selection; an implicit requirement is that such performance behaviours must be reliable (in the sense of 'stable') over a certain period of time, if prediction is to succeed. With this objective in view, it is remarkable how little research attention has been devoted to the assessment of performance stability. We will refer to the stability of performance at a latter moment (see p. 150). As far as the reliability of performance measures is concerned, much more research has been conducted, especially into the homogeneity of a set of performance measures or the consensus between various raters such as supervisors, peers and the job incumbents themselves.

The third requirement for criteria (practicality), expresses that a given criterion can be made available in an economic way and does have enough transparency and acceptability to those who want to use it for making decisions.

Multidimensionality

The idea that for a given performance domain a diversity of 'substitute' performance measures can be formulated, is indicative of the multidimensional nature of performance behaviours. An overwhelming majority of studies involving statistical analyses of sets of criterion measures (i.e. factor analysis) finds that these analyses rarely yield one single factor. Job performance tends to be complex and multidimensional, i.e. reflects various independent aspects (e.g. Smith, 1976). The multidimensionality is at the heart of a classical problem in the field of criterion development and theory: how many criteria should be utilized? Should one confine oneself to a single, overall measure or should one operationalize multiple criteria?

As has been pointed out above, the concept of a single criterion appears to be inconsistent with the available empirical evidence that shows that various performance measures are not redundant, but reveal different aspects of the same performance domain. Also, it seems logically unproductive to consider performance success as a unitary concept for different persons in the same job: Ghiselli (1960) points out that two persons may achieve the same overall performance with different performance strategies, a phenomenon which he labels as individual dimensionality. Henceforth, evaluation of individual performance should be made on the basis of different aspects.

This plea in favour of a multidimensional criterion seems to prohibit the use of a single, overall criterion, but in fact this is not the case. The issue of a multidimensional versus one overall criterion has been shown by Schmidt and Kaplan (1971) to be a pseudo-controversy. Both approaches can be of value: multiple criteria are called for when *predicting* future work behaviour, and a single overall criterion is necessary when one wants to arrive at a final *decision* about applicants (for example: acceptance or rejection). In most instances the best strategy is to combine these two approaches: at first a multiple criterion set is to be constructed because a multiple criterion is more informative and helpful when choosing and validating predictors. Also, relations between predictor and criterion variables can be more easily interpreted in a theoretical frame. The various sub-aspects can subsequently be combined in a composite score following some sort of a combination rule (unit weighting scheme: differential weighting). In doing this, the original performance scores can be converted to some underlying utility dimension (cf. the dollar criterion approach of Brogden and Taylor, 1950a).

Classification of criteria

As has been argued vehemently by various authors (cf. Smith, 1976; Dunnette, 1976; Fleishman and Quaintance, 1984; Roe, 1983), the study of performance cannot proceed systematically when one does not have any means of classifying the numerous performance behaviours involved in various occupations, jobs or organizations. One of the few attempts to arrive at a general classification or taxonomy for performance criteria has been made by Smith (1976). She has developed a classification scheme in which three dimensions seem to cover most criteria:

1. *The time-span covered*: criterion measures can be obtained either very soon after actual on-the-job behaviour has occurred or many years afterwards.
2. *The specificity desired*: some criteria refer to specific instances of behaviour, while others give rise to a global estimate (see also Figure 1).
3. *Degree of closeness to organizational goals to be approached*: criteria range from the description of actual behaviour, through the evaluation of immediate results, to estimates of the pay-off for the organization.

The voluminous research programme of Fleishman has also contributed considerably to the process of taxonomy construction. In his book *Taxonomies of Human Performance* (cf. Fleishman and Quaintance, 1984) several bases for the classification of work performance are discussed. In the (1) 'behaviour description approach', categories of activities are formulated based upon observations and descriptions of what job incumbents actually do while performing a task: emphasis is placed upon a description of overt behaviour as manifested. The (2) 'behaviour requirement approach' is based upon the cataloguing of behaviours that *should* be emitted or are assumed to be required in order to achieve the desired criterion level of performance. In the (3) 'ability requirements approach', tasks are described in terms of the abilities that a given task requires of the individual performer. Finally, work performance can be classified on the basis of (4) task characteristics. In this approach the task is depicted as a set of conditions that elicits and stimulates performance. Work performance can be described in terms of these 'triggering' events, placing emphasis on such aspects as task instructions, motivational contingencies, etc.

Which descriptor type one must choose in a specific instance, depends upon the purpose of application. As we shall demonstrate later on, in the context of personnel selection the first three alternatives (behaviour description, behaviour requirement and ability requirements approaches) do constitute viable options for classifying performance criteria. Nevertheless, important distinctions do exist between these three alternatives and there is no logical reason whatsoever to assume that these various job descriptions converge to comparable criterion structures and job families (see, for example: Cornelius, Carron and Collins, 1979; Stutzman, 1983; Algera and Greuter, 1989). This latter observation makes the choice of the right type of job descriptor a crucial aspect in developing criteria (see also p. 158 below).

The classification of criteria cannot be viewed as an end in itself, but it should always be related to the intended purpose, i.e. application of a criterion taxonomy to personnel selection. As such, it has been noted that criteria are to be connected with individual as well as with situational determinants in an integrated performance model (see, for example: Dunnette, 1963; James, 1973; Smith, 1976; Roe, 1983). A general criterion model has been proposed by James (1973). His model can be seen as a generalized version of a criterion model presented by Campbell *et al.* (1970) concerning managerial effectiveness. Three classes of variables are included: criteria (behavioural criteria as well as end results), organizational and situational characteristics and individual differences. The main point of James's argument is that such an integrated approach can at best be accomplished through the theory and technology of construct validation. In his review, construct validation is considered as the only adequate method to find out what is really being measured by criteria. Multiple measures of all kinds of performance behaviours should be used and be studied in their relationships to one another: ratings, objective measures of performance, abilities, motivation and satisfaction, situational parameters, organizational outcomes, etc. In this way criterion development becomes in essence an act of theorizing about work performance and its determinants.

Dynamic criteria

As has been just noted, criteria can be dynamic, i.e. they can change over a certain period of time. The concept of dynamic criteria is introduced by Ghiselli (1956) and refers to changes in the factorial structure over time. A well known example, illustrating a special kind of criterion dynamics (i.e. differential validities), can be found in a study by Ghiselli and Haire (1960) of taxi drivers. This study shows changes in the level of validity of an identical predictor against the criterion 'received fares', dependent upon the moment of criterion measurement. Barrett, Caldwell and Alexander (1985) have re-examined this concept by evaluating three types of dynamic criteria:

1. changes in group average performance over time;
2. changes in validity over time; and
3. changes in the rank order of individuals on the criterion.

Their review (NB: a narrative review, *not* a meta-analysis) does not support a conclusion of extensive changes in average performance over lengthy time-spans. Also, there are few indications in favour of the type of differential validities that were found in the Ghiselli and Haire study of taxi drivers: only 28 of such cases (including the study of Ghiselli and Haire) could be identified among a total of 480 paired coefficients from twelve studies. As a result of the small sample size in some of the studies (subgroup Ns as low as 20–30 are reported) the power is in some instances relatively low, however. The evidence for the third position, changes in the rank order on the criterion, looks somewhat more impressive, although it should be noted that the number of studies is limited here. All in all, the review of Barrett *et al.* offers some support for the conclusion that dynamic phenomena with regard to criteria are more or less exceptional although not impossible.

Criterion development and utility measurement

As is stated very clearly in the views of Brogden and Taylor (1950a), Ghiselli and Brown (1948) and several others, the ultimate criterion represents some overall index of usefulness indicating the individual's contributions to the goal of the organization. If one takes this overall index to be a financial one, utility theory comes into play and may be considered as an integral part of criterion development.

Utilities can be attributed to performance levels on the basis of some sort of utility function. When an algebraic format is adopted for this utility function, this comes down to specifying the function $U = f(Y)$, wherein U stands for a score on a utility dimension (expressed in dollars or some other currency, if one selects a financial variable), Y represents a criterion construct and f denotes an appropriate function.

The utility approach of Brogden, Cronbach and Gleser is, at this moment, by far the most popular method in the field of industrial and organizational psychology (see Brogden and Taylor, 1950a; Cronbach and Gleser, 1965). In this context we would like to point to the progress that has been made in estimating an important parameter of the Brogden/Cronbach/Gleser model, the SD_y of performance scores expressed in dollar values. For more than twenty years the application of utility models has been hampered because it seemed an impossible task to estimate this SD_y parameter, but in recent years several strategies have been proposed. For a review of such models as the 40–70 per cent rule, CREPID-procedure and the percentile method of Schmidt *et al.* (1979) the reader is referred to Cascio (1982); see also Cascio (1987). Although these estimating procedures make utility analysis available as a tool for a broad spectrum of human resources accounting problems and also make it very convenient to interconnect criterion and utility theory, it has at least one serious drawback: hardly anyone discusses the tenability of the assumptions on which the Brogden/Cronbach/Gleser model is based: utility functions are assumed to be linear, utilities for rejecting employees are considered to be zero and the net gain in utility is expressed as contrasted with an *a priori* procedure of random selection. As far as these assumptions do not hold, estimated utility gains will be more or less in error. A viable alternative may be found in the use of assumption-free models as the cost accounting approach of Brogden and Taylor (1950a: the so-called dollar criterion) or Roche (1961: standard costing method). Also, a usable, assumption-free method has been proposed by Vrijhoff, Mellenbergh and Van den Brink (1983). Although this method has been developed for educational pass–fail decisions, it seems equally applicable to personnel selection problems.

Another disenchanting point of criticism has been voiced on the basis of a Monte Carlo study by Alexander and Barrick (1987). In this study exceptionally large standard errors of utility estimates are reported. If the goal is to get accurate estimates, there is still a long way to go!

FUNCTIONS OF JOB ANALYSIS

Job analysis is used for many different purposes in personnel management. According to Levine (1983; see also Levine *et al.*, 1983), no less than eleven objectives can be identified: personnel selection is another field of application (but an important one!) in the same way as training, job evaluation, performance appraisal, job design, manpower planning, efficiency/safety policies, etc.

Although some methods and instruments pretend to be suited for a diversity of purposes, the evidence shows that job analysis methods must be perceived as differentially effective for various human resources objectives (Levine *et al.*, 1983). As far as personnel selection is concerned, content and structure of job analysis techniques are dictated by the nature of (selection) specific problems that can eventually arise during the selection process. According to Roe (1986) the main functions that selection procedures should fulfil can be described as follows (see also Chapter 2.1. of this handbook):

1. *Information gathering* Obtaining information about job openings, job content and other characteristics of the organization on the one hand, and physical, biographical and behavioural characteristics of the applicant on the other hand.
2. *Prediction* Transforming information on (past or present) applicant characteristics into predictions about their future behaviours, and the resulting contributions to organizational goals.
3. *Decision* Transforming predictive information on applicants into a preferred action.
4. *Information supply* Producing information on applicant characteristics, predicted behaviours, plans for actions (decisions) and communicating this to managers.

The functions of job analysis can be tied in with these general selection processes: job analysis procedures are especially helpful during the information gathering phase, as far as the description of the job content and the derivation of required attributes is concerned. Besides, job analysis techniques particularly serve the prediction function by identifying critical elements in the prediction model: criterion and predictor variables.

Referring to Figures 2 and 3 of Chapter 2.1 of this handbook, the following steps are in order:

At first the job content must be precisely described in terms of *goals and requirements*. As a part of this process references are given to such questions as: How is the job at hand related to departmental and organizational goals and structures? Is it really necessary to fill the vacancy? If so, what are the main activities and goals?

Next, *criteria* are specified. These criteria correspond either to relevant *task domains* or to more or less abstract *behavioural dimensions*. Task domains are usually chosen as a relevant basis for the description of criteria when one considers the use of some sort of job sample technique (more generally speaking: a content based selection device) for the screening and selection of applicants. Behavioural dimensions are called for if one opts for the measurement of relevant human attributes: capacities, personality traits or other stable characteristics.

Both approaches will be analysed in terms of their consequences for criterion development and predictor selection on p. 165 below. At this moment we will restrict ourselves to presenting an example of task dimensions versus behavioural dimensions within the same job, in this particular instance a nursing job in a mentally retarded facility (see Figure 2). The 28 task dimensions were derived from a set of 115 task statements of a tailor-made job inventory. The behavioural dimensions mentioned in Figure 2 are produced by following the methodology of Behaviour Observation Scaling (BOS).

1. **Task dimensions** (adapted from Stutzman, 1983, p. 507)

    1. Feed residents who need help
    2. Cook meals/serve meals
    3. Clean/make up beds
    4. Do laundry
    5. Daily living care (grooming–dressing)
    6. Care/regulate residents' property
    7. Inventory, non-medical
    8. General clerical
    9. Dealing with non-ambulatory residents
    10. Control of residents
    11. Transport/escort residents
    12. Drive
    13. Staff–supervisory communications
    14. Staff–staff communications
    15. Employee orientations
    16. Supervision of employees
    17. General assessment of mood, emotional condition and activity level
    18. Supervision of residents
    19. Staff–resident interactions
    20. Administer/give medication
    21. General nursing care
    22. Reporting/recording/writing
    23. Assess general physical condition
    24. Inventory, medical
    25. Emergency care
    26. Teach/train residents
    27. Safety, security of residents
    28. Safety, security of physical plant

2. **Behavioural dimensions** (adapted from Greuter, 1988b, p. 143)

    1. Cooperation (working together as a team)
    2. Showing understanding and apprehension of mentally/physically retarded persons
    3. Educational/pedagogical activities
    4. Providing medical and nursing attendance
    5. Working attitude (positive orientation toward work; punctuality)
    6. Social accomplishment and proficiency
    7. (Short term) Work planning (autonomous work planning)
    8. Stability
    9. Creativity
    10. Organizational adjustment

Figure 2 Task and behavioural dimensions for a nursing professional in a mentally retarded facility

As a third step *predictors* are identified. These predictors are either sample type predictors (content based selection devices) or attribute type predictors (capacities, personality traits, other characteristics).

The next activity consists of finding predictor instruments: relevant tests, interviews, task sample devices.

After the administration of tests, interviews and other predictor instruments the whole process is again repeated, but now in a reversed order (see Chapter 2.1). Finally, the predicted job success can be evaluated in terms of the tasks and goals of the job as originally specified.

In applying the procedure as outlined, several instruments are needed:

1. Tasks and goals can be identified by applying *descriptive job analysis procedures*, for example job inventories, critical incident technique, etc.
2. Conceptual criteria can (again) be found with the help of *job analysis techniques*.
3. The gap between job content (tasks and goals) and conceptual predictors (human attributes) can be bridged by so-called *ability oriented job analysis techniques*. In this way one evades the identification of intermediary conceptual criteria.
4. Predictors can also be derived from the content of criteria: in order to achieve this objective, *rules of correspondence* are needed that stipulate the relationships between each criterion aspect and predictors. In the case of the sample approach these rules are relatively straightforward, because predictor and criterion content stem from the same domain. With the sign approach, things are more complicated, however. But again, *job analysis techniques* may fulfil an important role in solving this dilemma.
5. For the operationalization of criteria and predictors *existing tests or instruments* can be used. If these instruments are not available, one is committed to the alternative of constructing them oneself. In this respect, the BARS/BOS methodology (Behaviourally Anchored Rating Scales/Behaviour Observation Scales) can help us arrive at operationalizations of conceptual criteria.

    In case of the sample approach, we point out that job analysis procedures may be of central importance for constructing sample type predictors (see also below).
6. Predictor and criterion scores are linked by means of a *prediction model*. In defining the elements of the prediction model job analysis again comes into play. The penultimate section of this chapter explains how this contribution is achieved.

As is abundantly clear from the above account, job analysis techniques do play an important part in developing selection procedures. In the following sections we will explore the role of job analysis in more detail. We will do so by inspecting the contribution of job analysis to the information gathering phase and the predictive function of personnel selection more closely.

JOB ANALYSIS AS AN INFORMATION GATHERING DEVICE

Job analysis is pre-eminently suited as a tool for gathering information about the job vacancy and the organizational context.

Ryan and Sackett (1987) conducted a survey of a segment of the Division of

Industrial and Organizational Psychology of the American Psychological Association. Several questions focused on the type of information typically gathered about the organization and job before conducting a selection procedure. Their results show that the most common categories of information sought are: job descriptions and specifications, climate/culture conditions, performance standards, prevailing management philosophy, intended usage of the assessment information, management style of immediate supervisor, reasons for successes or failures of past incumbents, industry and structure. Information about *organizational conditions* was most commonly obtained by interviewing organization members and through informal means such as conversations. Information about *job vacancies* was typically obtained through written job descriptions and oral descriptions by contacting individuals and/or position supervisors. Most of these descriptions are of a narrative nature. Remarkably, less than 40 per cent of the sample used a formal job analysis method.

The Ryan and Sackett study demonstrates the importance of job analytic procedures as a tool for formulating the selection problem in a clear and precise manner. At the same time this survey illustrates that much of the information gathering goes on in an unsystematic way, without some formalized job analytic procedure. Below we will discuss some possibilities for structuring the information gathering process by the use of job analysis. With this end in view, we will attend to type of job information sought, degree of specificity of the job information, methods of data collection, and sources of job information. We will conclude this section with some comments about the legal assessment of job analytic procedures, thus illustrating a frame of reference for evaluating the quality of job information.

Type of job information

Job analytic procedures do vary in the types of information that are elicited by the job analyst. This has been persuasively argued by Fleishman and Quaintance (1984) by identifying various approaches to classifying work performance: (1) behaviour description; (2) behaviour requirements; (3) ability requirements; and (4) task characteristics (see above, p. 149). As has already been briefly mentioned, the first three categories do provide for the most relevant job information in the context of personnel selection.

Within the *behaviour description approach* (1) a further subdivision can be made between work-oriented and worker-oriented job analysis methods.

Work- or job-oriented methods lead to a description of work activities in terms of the technological activities and relevant jargon of the job under study. Job-oriented methods may reflect such items as purpose, procedures, resources and materials, levels of responsibility, job-specific equipment (machines, apparatus, tools and instruments), specification of desired end results (products, services), etc. It results in a specific and detailed description of jobs that is uniquely informative about the job to be analysed, but this specificity makes it at the same time difficult to make comparisons between jobs. Because the content of work-oriented procedures is highly job specific, one is committed to develop specific job inventories for each job at hand. A noticeable exception is the Occupation

Analysis Inventory of Cunningham *et al*. (1983). This instrument contains individual work elements that fall into five generalized categories: information received, mental activities, observable behaviour, work outcomes and work context. Although the items in these subsections are formulated in a specific, detailed way to achieve as much specificity in occupational description as possible, they seem to retain their applicability to a wide spectrum of occupations.

Worker-oriented methods result in a description of generalizable human behaviours, such as decision making, communicating, advising, instructing, negotiating, reasoning with various materials, etc. A classical example of this approach is the Position Analysis Questionnaire of McCormick (McCormick, Jeanneret and Mecham, 1972). The PAQ consists of 187 worker-oriented job elements, organized into six categories of dimensions: information input, mental processes, work output, relationships with other persons, job context and other job characteristics (specified work pace, amount of job structure, etc.). Broader categories of work behaviours have been derived using principal component analysis. An overall or general analysis was carried out as well as separate analyses of the PAQ subdivisions. Furthermore, research efforts included also the derivation of job dimensions from human attribute data. With regard to this latter aspect the PAQ can also be classified as an abilities-oriented job analytic procedure (see p. 165).

It should be noted that distinctions between work- and worker-oriented methods are not always clear-cut. Sometimes, questionnaires contain statements of both a work- and a worker-oriented nature. As an example we point to a group of job analysis instruments that have been developed for a more or less homogeneous group, i.e. management positions. As a rule, questionnaires such as the Executive Description Questionnaire of Hemphill (1960), Supervisor Task Description Questionnaire (Dowell and Wexley, 1978), Management Position Description Questionnaire (Tornow and Pinto, 1976), etc., must be considered as job specific (thus work oriented) devices but a closer inspection of the item content reveals that a lot of the items can be described as worker oriented as well.

Following the *behaviour requirement approach* (2) several methods do exist that have at least some relevance for personnel selection problems. In this respect we would point to the Task Strategies Approach of Miller (1971; see also p. 174) and the Job Element Method of Primoff (1955; see also Fleishman and Quaintance, 1984, p. 114).

The Critical Incidents Technique (CIT) of Flanagan (1954) can be reckoned among the more popular methods in this category. According to the CIT format critical incidents of inferior, average and superior performance are collected by means of a series of (individual or group) interviews with job incumbents or other job experts. These incidents are then grouped into more encompassing behavioural dimensions. The CIT also offers good prospects for operationalizing performance dimensions in relation to performance appraisal systems (cf. Caroll and Schneier, 1982).

Ability-oriented job analytical procedures (3) try to capture the job content in terms of trait requirements: capacities or personality traits that can be considered as necessary conditions for adequate performance. Trait requirements are directly derived from job content without specifying conceptual criteria first. An example of this approach can be found in the Minnesota Job Requirements Questionnaire (Desmond and

Weiss, 1973, 1975), which asks job incumbents and superiors for the incidence of the type of reasoning problems that are used to define aptitudes: the MJRQ leads to an estimate of the extent in which GATB dimensions are relevant for successful performance (for example: estimates of V-, N-, S-, P-factors are made).

The most systematic work that has been published in this domain is that of Fleishman with respect to the Task Abilities Scales (TAS: see Fleishman and Quaintance, 1984). Here the job analyst should indicate for a fixed set of ability factors to which degree they are supposed to play a role in the job. The scales are anchored with examples of tangible behavioural incidents which were found by empirical research and expert studies (see also p. 174).

It should be noted that the ability-oriented approach is sensitive to judgemental and attributional errors. The type of interpretational processes required is sometimes very indirect and difficult to accomplish. For example: it may not be very problematic to postulate the importance of a verbal reasoning factor for journalists, writers and librarians, but what traits can be inferred as relevant for such occupations as those of clinical analysts, metal workers, computer programmers, managers, etc.? The kind of inferences to be made, may bear a close resemblance to the sort of attributional processes that are reported in the literature about person perception, for example: in observing job incumbents while performing, the job analyst may exaggerate the preponderance of individual capacities as determinants of critical, error-prone activities, or he or she may play down the importance of individual differences because 'everybody seems to manage this part of the job very well'. This job analysis-specific manifestation of the so-called 'fundamental attributional error' is just one example, but other attributional errors (i.e. job stereotypes) may hamper the process of analysing jobs as well. For example, in accordance with attribution theory one may hypothesize that high and low job performers may be generating different task information and ability requirements, because jobs are perceived and valued differently.

The derivation of attribute requirements can probably be improved by such measures as the training of job analysts (Hahn and Dipboye, 1988) and providing detailed and complete information about the job at hand (see, e.g. DeNisi, Cornelius and Blencoe, 1987). It also seems that the inference of trait requirements can be better done for well defined, homogeneous subtasks than for the job as a whole (Cornelius and Lyness, 1980). Scale interventions can offer partial solutions at most, in our opinion. In this respect the kind of scales as developed by Fleishman for the Task Abilities Scales do deserve merit, because the aspects to be rated are defined in a clear and concrete manner. Also, scale points are anchored by means of daily instances or activities that can be widely recognized. An example of the TAS is given in Figure 3.

Degree of specificity of job information

In personnel selection it is usually emphasized that detailed or molecular job information is needed to get an adequate picture of the job under study and to infer required capacities and traits on the basis of this information. However, studies that have used the validity generalization approach of Schmidt and

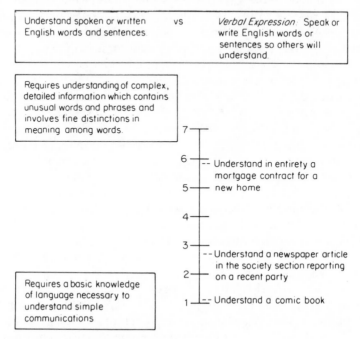

Figure 3   An example of the TAS: definition and ability rating scale for Verbal Comprehension. (From Fleishman and Quaintance, 1984, p. 319)

Hunter have cast some doubt on the use of molecular job analysis methods. The general finding has been that fine grained, detailed job analyses tend to create the appearance of large differences between jobs that are not of any practical significance in selection (see, for example, Pearlman, Schmidt and Hunter, 1980; Schmidt, Hunter, and Pearlman, 1981; Schmidt *et al.*, 1985).

It should be explicitly emphasized, however, that these observations are made within the context of validity generalization. Within the validity generalization approach of Schmidt and Hunter (1977, 1981) validity coefficients relate to global performance ratings in very broad job categories. For example: one of the groups is 'clerical occupations', which includes secretaries, stenographers, typists and typewriting machine operators, interviewing clerks, file clerks, duplicating machine operators and tenders, mailing and miscellaneous office machine operators, stenographers and typing, filing and related occupations not elsewhere classified. It is evident that for analysing job content for such broad categories holistic, global techniques of job analysis are sufficient. They give the required information at lower costs than more detailed methods (cf. Cornelius, Schmidt and Carron, 1984). As a matter of fact, it has even been suggested that the job title by itself would give sufficient information for identifying relevant predictors and estimating validities within a database.

Secondly, when only overall performance ratings are used, it is sensible to use molar job analysis methods without reference to specific tasks, duties and behaviours. As Tenopyr and Oeltjen (1982) have pointed out, the usage of overall criterion measures may give rise to extensive generalizability because of the general factor underlying these kinds of ratings (due to halo effects). More specific criteria may be associated with relatively more situation- or task-specific variance in the distribution of observed validity coefficients. In these instances molecular job analysis methods would be called for. Fleishman and Quaintance (1984) state that better control over the measurement of criterion performance will make it possible to show that task differences can moderate test validities. As long as it is considered necessary or profitable, a more prolonged and detailed job analysis can be carried through in order to arrive at better predictions and higher utilities.

As an illustration, we will elaborate on one of these studies a little bit further (thereby following the reproduction by Fleishman and Quaintance, 1984, p. 432). The task which is involved in the job of navy sonar operators consists of an auditory signal identification. Subjects were to determine the identity of a variety of complex sounds representing various types of ships. Each time a signal was presented, subjects had to determine whether it belonged to a cargo ship, warship, submarine or lightship. Signals were to be identified under nine different task conditions that differed from each other with respect to signal duration and signal-to-noise ratio. A battery of 24 specifically selected tests (covering well-established factors in the perceptual and cognitive ability domains) was administered to all subjects prior to their involvement in the auditory signal identification criterion task. From this battery an auditory perceptual ability factor was extracted that correlated most strongly with criterion performance. However, loadings on this auditory perceptual factor increased in magnitude as signal durations grew shorter and signal-to-noise ratios became smaller. In other words the contribution of this ability factor to performance increases as the criterion task becomes more difficult. It is noteworthy that these changes in the validity of the predictor set would remain unnoticed when a more global criterion measure had been used.

Still another argument favouring detailed job analysis methods has been put forward by Cornelius, Carron, and Collius (1979). They make a distinction between selection systems to be developed for selecting applicants who are expected to demonstrate task performance almost immediately (e.g. typists) and selection systems that are constructed for selecting applicants in settings that require training (e.g. managerial trainees). Cornelius *et al.* (1979) propose a task-oriented job classification approach in the former situation, while in the latter situation an ability- or aptitude-oriented job analysis (i.e. a more global job analysis) would be appropriate. In the former situation the selection system would be more directed at tapping task-related performance styles using simulations, work samples, situational interviews, etc. In the latter situation the selection system is oriented at measuring abilities and aptitudes of a far more general nature. This distinction made by Cornelius *et al.* may serve to illustrate a more general principle underlying the use of job analysis: when one considers the use of sample type predictors, specific and detailed job analysis information is needed. With sign type predictors (e.g. aptitude and trait measurements) it is advisable to abstract from specific tasks and duties, in order to arrive at more generalized performance dimensions that may be connected, at least in principle, with relevant attribute requirements.

All in all, a general directive concerning the appropriate specificity of job analysis information, cannot be given and *should* not be given. The choice of a job analysis method must be appropriate to the selection dilemma at hand: What criteria are to be predicted? What predictor instruments are considered (signs or samples)? How much time and money may be devoted to developing and applying job analysis methods?

Methods of data collection

To collect relevant job information, several methods are available:

1. *Interview* This is probably the most widely used method. In the survey of Ryan and Sackett (1987), around 80 per cent of the respondents used an interview to obtain organizational or job information. Interviews can be held with job incumbents, supervisors, personnel managers, etc. As far as form and structure are concerned, individual as well as group interviews can be considered. Also, a so-called 'technical conference' (conference with experienced personnel) can be held. The interview can also be easily reconciled with the technique of critical incidents, as has already been pointed out. With respect to interview structure a semi-structured approach is advisable. However, the survey of Ryan and Sackett suggests that much of the interviewing takes place on an informal basis.
2. *Observation* Information gathering by means of observational activities of the job analyst him- or herself is appropriate for short cycle jobs, that remain relatively unchanged over (shorter) time periods and are dominated by physical activities and routines that are easily observable. A serious drawback of observation may be that relevant or critical work episodes do not occur within the observational periods. To optimize the representativeness of the sampled job behaviours, some form of time sampling can be applied, as is done in the more or less traditional time studies or work sampling approaches. To facilitate the process of periodic registration of work behaviour, devices such as video cameras can be used. An excellent review of these methods can be found in McCormick (1979).
3. *Questionnaires* Questionnaires can be subdivided into structured versus open-ended questionnaires, depending upon the amount of structure that is permitted while responding.

   A number of structured questionnaires have already been mentioned: the Position Analysis Questionnaire, Occupation Analysis Inventory, Minnesota Job Requirement Scale, etc. This listing can easily be expanded with a series of other instruments and inventories (see for example: Fleishman and Quaintance, 1984). The advantages of a structured format are obvious: they are practical and economical to administer and they lead to quantified job descriptions that are amenable to various statistical procedures and computerized data processing.

As an example of a semi-structured method we would like to point at diaries and similar devices. According to the diary method it is necessary to keep written records of the daily work activities as registered on a periodic base (e.g. an hourly basis). In accordance with the critical incidents technique, critical behaviours (demonstrating very good or very poor performance) can be recorded. Diaries can be described as rich, though not very cheap, sources of information.

4. *Relevant work records* In addition to one of the foregoing methods one can also make use of existing documents and records such as task instructions, performance records, maintenance records, design information (blueprints), etc.
5. *Introspectional analysis* By letting the job analysts perform the job by themselves, they can find to their own cost which critical difficulties do exist and what kinds of attributes are required to reach adequate performance levels. Although this method has some face validity, it cannot be recommended: learning experiences do not always generalize across persons; beginners' problems may be exaggerated, job identification can turn out to be either too low or too high, etc.

The choice of a specific data-collection method determines for a large part the degree of quantification that is realized at the end. This may range from strictly qualitative as characterized by typically verbal, general narrative job descriptions, to rigorously quantitative statements of the type that are made available by structured questionnaires such as the PAQ and others.

Sources of job information

Job incumbents, supervisors, personnel managers, as well as trained job analysts can each be called in to provide information about the job at hand. In view of this variety of possible agents important questions concern the reliability (inter-rater agreement) and validity of these rater sources.

Studies into the reliability and validity of job information have been confined to structured job analysis instruments, and more particularly to the Position Analysis Questionnaire (PAQ). Although agreement between and within different types of raters tends to be rather satisfactory in a number of studies (e.g. Crowley, 1981; Sackett, Cornelius and Carron, 1981; Jones *et al.*, 1982; Schmitt and Fine, 1983), alarming findings have been reported by Smith and Hakel (1979). In their study reliability and validity (judge convergence and prediction of present pay level) were determined for each of four analyst sources: job incumbents, supervisors, job analysts and a comparison group of college students. Strangely enough, correlations between ratings obtained from expert judges (incumbents, supervisors, analysts) and those from 'naive' raters (the group of college students relying only on job titles or brief job descriptions) also reached the same high levels (0.89–0.94). This suggested that if students who are in no sense familiar with a job, can provide ratings that are highly correlated with those of experts, the PAQ may reflect only common knowledge about jobs: the PAQ is only measuring some sort of job stereotype. Cornelius, Schmidt, and Carron (1984) have replicated the Smith and Hakel study, using a more appropriate method for calculating the convergence between expert and naive raters (i.e. computing correlations within the same job and averaging across all jobs instead of correlating mean PAQ values across jobs as was done by Smith and Hakel). This latter study reported correlations in the fifties instead of in the nineties, suggesting that the PAQ seemed to be able to provide at least some substantial information about jobs beyond what must be qualified as common knowledge or job stereotypes. Arvey *et al.* (1982) manipulated the amount of job information and the degree of job interest exhibited by incumbents. Both types of manipulations had only very minor effects on the PAQ and no effects on the Job Diagnostic Survey. That job analysts were not biased by incumbents' positive or negative statements about the job, is probably reassuring. However, the fact that no effects resulted from giving more information is more problematic and underlines the Smith and Hakel conclusion that raters may well be responding on the basis of some sort of job stereotype.

A study of DeNisi, Cornelius and Blencoe (1987) seems to moderate some of these criticisms. As a first point they signalled that the number of PAQ items rated as 'does not apply' (DNA) distorts the true extent to which expert and naive raters agree. Because the PAQ is designed to be used with virtually any job, some items are almost always rated as 'does not apply' by the analyst. Harvey and Hayes (1986) showed that if approximately one-fifth of the items are rated as 'does not apply', the correlation between two PAQ profiles could be as high as 0.50, even if the other items have been filled in on a completely random basis. All in all, this study suggests that expert and naive raters are probably not equivalent after all. Agreement between expert and naive raters is at least partly artificial and may be reduced by applying the PAQ more selectively to jobs. The agreement may be further reduced by more extensive training of job analysts. A study by Hahn and Dipboye (1988) shows that trained subjects demonstrate less leniency and more variance in evaluating 23 jobs on ten dimensions. Furthermore, the most accurate results come from subjects that have received training as well as full information about the job to be analysed. Training seems to facilitate the absorption of job relevant information, or putting it another way: the effects of giving information are enhanced by training raters in handling this information accurately.

In our opinion the issue of job stereotypes deserves much more attention than it has been given thus far. One of the major shortcomings is that job stereotypes are not addressed directly but inferred from the agreement between naive and expert raters. It is not clear what kinds of stereotypes are active. Do sex-linked job stereotypes exist? Are stereotypes bound to other characteristics such as age, ethnic origin, physical appearance, etc.? In the field of job evaluation there is evidence that trained job analysts are aware of judgemental errors in evaluating jobs with high (manipulated) pay levels as opposed to those with low pay levels (Mount and Ellis, 1987).

Legal assessment of job analysis instruments

Since the early 1970s, in the United States a strong emphasis has been put on the construction of content based selection devices such as work samples, situational interviews, and some types of biographical questionnaires (e.g. Pannone, 1984). Partly, the popularity of content based selection devices can be attributed to the relatively high validities of this type of instrument (see Schmitt, Gooding and Kirsch, 1984; Muchinsky, 1986), but this is not the only reason. An equally important aspect concerns the solid reputation of these methods in court. Job analysis fulfils a key position in court procedures. Thompson and Thompson (1982) present a set of standards which delineates the components of a job analysis necessary to withstand legal scrutiny. Tasks, duties and activities must be identified, suggesting work-oriented job analysis procedures. Terms used by the courts which denote types of information to be described through job analysis are: elements, aspects, characteristics, aptitudes, knowledge, skills, abilities and critical incidents. Data should be collected from several up-to-date sources: interviews with job incumbents, supervisors and administrators; training manuals, observations, questionnaires, etc. A high level of expertise of the job analyst is strongly valued by the court, though it is not sufficient to prove that an adequate job analysis has been performed. All in all, court procedures are suggestive of job analysis methods that produce detailed, minute descriptions of jobs.

Hogan and Quigley (1986) noted that at least three questions regarding job analysis arise in court cases. The first is whether a job analysis has been completed at all. The second concerns the material adequacy of the job analysis. The third asks whether the method selected is appropriate for the validation strategy subsequently used.

Naturally not having conducted a job analysis (first question) is an obvious disadvantage. The accuracy of job information (second question) has received differential attention by the courts. Sometimes, job analysis is given a general and superficial review, but it can also be scrutinized carefully. For example, in *Berkman* v. *City of New York* (1982, cited by Hogan and Quigley, 1986, p. 121), the court recognized inter-rater correlation coefficients as an indicator of the degree of consensus between raters. Also, agreement between five different job analysis methods, illustrating convergent validity, has been considered by the court.

The third issue relates to the adequacy of the job analysis method with respect to validation strategy. Hogan and Quigley (1986) discuss the case of *United States* v. *New York*, a case in which knowledge, skills, abilities and traits were identified by job analysis as critical in the performance of a trooper. However, deriving these attributes was judged to be inappropriate for conducting a content validity study as was originally planned. In *Berkman* v. *City of New York*, already briefly mentioned above, the appropriateness of the job analysis method was also attended to by the court, which determined that a criterion-referenced validation study was the correct strategy to use given an ability-oriented job analysis.

Although the above-mentioned examples illustrate an increasingly more pervasive and detailed inspection of job analysis with some expanding interest in technical matters, we are still not convinced that judgements relate adequately to substantial matters, beyond a simple, intuitive rule that 'good looks go for a long way on the stage'. Also it should be emphasized that the examples described above indicate the state of affairs in the United States. In most other countries, including most European countries, there is still a long way to go. In the Netherlands, for example, relevant jurisprudence is totally absent. Some global directives concerning the usage of job analysis methods have been laid down in professional codes for psychologists and personnel managers. Furthermore, some individual organizations have agreed upon some minimal rules governing the supply of information about jobs and attribute requirements to applicants, for example as part of a (more encompassing) institutional code. This usually bears no legal status outside of the organization, and is the result of a collective labour agreement. To our knowledge, things are not much better regulated in other European countries, although some variations in relevant legislation do exist. One of the major reasons that has prevented the settlement of some minimal arrangements, relates, as far as we can see, to conceptual difficulties encountered when one tries to formulate some requirements, for example: What is the best way to operationalize reliability and validity? What constitutes the 'expertise' of a job analyst? How does one evaluate the quality of narrative job information? What kind of information about jobs is required considering the intended usage of job analysis (i.e. applying job analysis in the context of personnel selection)?

SPECIFYING PREDICTION MODELS BY JOB ANALYSIS

Job analysis may serve to define a relevant prediction model for the selection problem at hand.

Two critical observations must be added to this statement. At first, job analysis does not help in every stage of the model building process. As is shown in Chapter 2.3 of this handbook, the process of building predictive performance models consists of several steps. For example: defining the model's content (specifying criterion and predictor variables); specifying structure and format of the relationship between the model elements; estimating parameters; and, finally, evaluating the predictive qualities of the model. If necessary, the whole process or some parts of it can eventually be repeated until the final results seem satisfactory. Job analysis comes primarily into play in the first stage of this process: specifying the content of the model, i.e. criterion and predictor variables. Secondly, it should be emphasized that job analysis does not form the sole basis for identifying conceptual criteria and predictors. One can also rely on results of meta-analysis or on explorative validation studies (Roe, 1983). Nevertheless, job analysis is the predominant method in our opinion. Also, it must be realized that meta-analysis and explorative validation studies each imply some sort of job analysis techniques.

As has been briefly pointed out before, predictions can be predicated upon 'signs' or 'samples'.

Within the sign approach, performance is modelled in an abstract manner. The model is based upon empirical or theoretical hypotheses (or 'educated guesses', when relevant data are lacking) with regard to relatively stable person characteristics. Because work performance and individual traits are interconnected by hypotheses, individual characteristics measured by tests or other instruments can be regarded as 'signs' or 'indicators' of future work performance.

In the sample approach stable traits are not included explicitly in the prediction model, but this method is based on the behavioural consistency between test performance and job performance. Prediction is accomplished by statistically generalizing from a sample to a population, i.e. from performance on some sort of work sample to performance behaviours in the relevant task domain.

As far as the use of job analysis is concerned, different requirements are made by the sign and sample approach. This crucial observation lies at the root of what will be argued in this section: the need to differentiate between job analysis methods in terms of their model-building capacities for sign or sample type prediction will be continuously underlined. We shall first discuss how conceptual criteria can be identified by means of job analysis techniques. Subsequently, the process of identifying conceptual predictors is discussed: some general principles are laid down and it is discussed how sample type and sign type predictors can be derived from job content.

Identifying conceptual criteria by job analysis

If predictions are to be based on signs, more abstract and general criteria should be chosen. In this way it is realized that criteria can be applied to a broader category of jobs than the job under study. Furthermore, it must also be possible to relate these criteria to existing psychological theory about individual differences. If the last requirement is not fulfilled, it becomes a hard task to generate plausible hypotheses concerning relevant capacities and personality traits. Viewed in these two perspectives, the best results can be obtained from a worker-oriented job analysis.

Despite various critics, the Position Analysis Questionnaire still seems to be the most promising candidate. Studies into the 'job component validity' (see McCormick, Jeanneret and Mecham, 1972; McCormick, DeNisi and Shaw, 1979) do lend some support for the idea that PAQ dimensions can be meaningfully related to human attributes, i.e. at least to cognitive capacities as measured by the General Aptitude Test Battery (GATB). In the first study (McCormick *et al.*, 1972) multiple correlations are reported between 0.59 and 0.80 with a median of 0.71. The latter study (McCormick *et al.*, 1979) reveals values between 0.30 and 0.83 with a median of 0.73, although there are criticisms to be made of these studies.

Another well known example can be found in the Functional Job Analysis method (FJA) of Fine (1963, 1974; see also Fleishman and Quaintance, 1984, pp. 108–13). Fine analysed a total of 4000 job descriptions in order to derive critical worker behaviours. In his terminology a 'worker behaviour' is defined by an action verb and one or more objects. Together with some specified outcomes (products or purposes) worker behaviours can be laid down in short sentences (e.g. negotiates about the price in order to get a profit; listens to the engine to decide upon what causes the malfunction, etc.), that form the basic descriptive components of Fine's job analysis. Furthermore, the FJA allows for an evaluation of so-called worker functions. Fine establishes that what workers do, they do in relation to Data, People and Things. For example, in relation to Data, the worker functions include: compare, copy, compute–compile, analyse, innovate–coordinate and synthesize. These functions are hierarchically ordered and higher worker functions include those of a lower level: if a job includes 'compiling data', it is assumed it also includes lower worker functions such as comparing and copying. Figure 4 illustrates the Data, People and Things dimensions as developed by Fine.

Job-oriented methods often result in a specific and detailed description of jobs that is not easily fitted to more abstract performance models and individual difference variables. As has already been observed on p. 155, a notable exception is the Occupation Analysis Inventory of Cunningham *et al.* (1983). As in the case of the PAQ, correlations between job dimensions and GATB tests were determined following the job component model of McCormick as explained above. Multiple correlations reached reasonably high values, that were all statistically significant ($P < 0.01$).

In applying the sample approach (work samples, situational tests, situational interviews, etc.) very detailed job information is needed (see also p. 159 concerning the specificity of job information). Job content must be defined exhaustively so that no parts are missed in simulating the job. Moreover, it must be realized that the predictive qualities of samples derive from a point-to-point correspondence between predictor and criterion: as predictor and criterion sets have more points in common, their validities are higher (see Asher and Sciarrino, 1974). All in all, a job-oriented analysis seems to be necessary in order to acquire a complete understanding of the job. Preferably, different data collection methods (especially interviews and observation) should be deployed in conjunction and various job agents should be used (job incumbents, supervisors).

The Critical Incidents Technique (CIT) of Flanagan (1954) seems to be the most frequently mentioned method for identifying conceptual criteria when constructing work samples (cf. Dunnette, 1976; Landy and Farr, 1983). The CIT produces detailed and more abstract job information simultaneously: the incidents themselves offer a rich source of very concrete and detailed performance behaviours of a *work*-oriented nature. By grouping these behavioural incidents into more encompassing and somewhat abstract behavioural dimensions, one discovers the type of *worker*-oriented dimensions that are more typical of a sign type prediction model and can be connected to individual capacities and traits.

Identifying conceptual predictors by job analysis

As has been observed before, the choice of conceptual predictors lies at the root of a crucial selection dilemma: what Xs must be used to predict criterion performance following the prediction formula: $Y = f(X)$?

The choice of predictors can best be based on the content of criteria as defined in an earlier stage. Thus, criteria serve a dual purpose: they show what kind of performance behaviours are to be predicted and at the same time, they point out potentially relevant predictors.

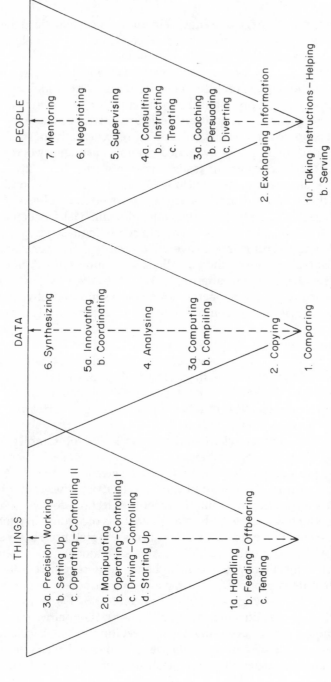

Figure 4 Working functions of the Functional Job Analysis method. (From Fine, 1983.)

Sample type predictors

As far as content concerns, it does not seem unduly problematic to derive sample type predictors, because criteria and predictors are conceptually similar and belong to the same domain. However, the population of tasks should be defined in relevant terms and a sampling procedure must be laid down in which criteria are specified for judging the representativeness of content validity of the resulting predictor instrument. At first sight these objectives do not seem to be difficult to realize, but in fact, some quite arbitrary decisions have to be made concerning the choice of appropriate dimensions for judging representativeness. For example, the predictor instrument can be evaluated in terms of adequacy of time sampling (Are the most time consuming tasks represented in the instrument?), task relevance (Are all relevant tasks included?), criticalness of suboptimal performance (Are those tasks included that lead to deleterious effects if performed incorrectly?), task difficulty (Are the more difficult tasks adequately represented?), etc. A pragmatic strategy may be to combine these various dimensions according to some algorithm into an overall composite index. For example, Cascio (1982) proposes a composite index, called Task Importance Value, in which: (1) time spent, (2) importance, (3) consequences of errors and (4) level of difficulty are taken together following a simple additive/multiplicative rule. Task activities with high composite scores are eligible for simulation by work samples.

An index for quantifying the content validity of the resulting instrument is the content validity ratio (CVR) of Lawshe (1975). This index is a linear derivative of the proportion P that expresses the number of judges that have agreed upon qualifying some work sample activity as a dominant activity of the job under study ($P = N_e/N$ wherein N_e = number of judges that sees a particular activity as essential; N = total number of judges).[*]

Despite the apparent simplicity of the derivation of job samples, there is not much literature illuminating systematic procedures for analysing job content and transforming job content into content-based selection devices. A noticeable exception is a recent article by Schmitt and Ostroff (1986). These authors propose a series of steps in developing content-oriented selection devices. The first step consists of conducting a rather elaborate job analysis procedure in which different techniques are taken together. This procedure is adopted from Levine (1983) and is called C-JAM (Combination of Job Analysis Methods). Task statements are generated in two meetings with job incumbents. After several revisions a final set of task statements is proposed, that have been grouped in major performance dimensions. Next, meetings are held to generate KSAOs (Knowledge, Skills, Abilities, Other personality characteristics) and questionnaires are administered to rate the importance of task dimensions (resulting in the calculation of 'Task Importance Values') and KSAOs. Finally, several content-based selection tests are constructed tapping especially those task dimensions with Task Importance

---

[*] NB: CVR = 2P–1

Values. In the research example provided by Schmitt and Ostroff concerning a selection procedure for an emergency telephone operator, several work samples (spelling test, telephone call recording task, typing test, monitoring task), a situational interview and a telephone call simulation were constructed. All of these instruments were evaluated in terms of content validity using the procedure of Lawshe (1975) mentioned above. Except for one dimension, all major task dimensions were sufficiently represented in the test materials. Estimates of inter-rater reliability were usually in the area of 0.60. Unfortunately, no evidence of predictive validity was presented. Still, the Schmitt and Ostroff procedure is creditable for the systematic way by which sample type predictors are derived from job content. Furthermore, by also generating relevant KSAOs, it bridges the gap between signs and samples.

Sign type predictors

The derivation of predictors becomes more complex in the case of sign type predictors. Now, criteria and predictors are not conceptually similar, but they relate to different conceptual systems, concerning work performance behaviour and individual differences respectively: two different worlds of human behavioural taxonomies as Dunnette (1976, p. 477) so aptly puts it. The problem to be solved is to find a way to link these two different systems.

As far as job analysis is concerned, this linkage process can be accomplished by the methods which are summarized in Figure 5. These approaches can be distinguished from each other by differentiating between methods that require only molar job information about the *job as a whole*, as opposed to those that demand molecular job information about *job aspects*.

Choice of predictors is based on:

Job as a whole	*Relevant job aspects*
(Clinical methods) (1)	(Clinical methods) (1)
Rational validity (2)	Decision trees (5)
Ability-oriented job analysis (3)	Attribute rating (PAQ, OAI) (6)
Job classification for validity	Synthetic validity (7)
generalization (4)	Experimental/correlational approaches
	(Fleishman) (8)
	Theoretically based job analyses (9)

Figure 5   Deriving sign type predictors by job analysis procedures

Below, we will briefly summarize each of the methods mentioned in Figure 5.

Deriving predictors from the job as a whole.   Some methods for deriving conceptual predictors do not require detailed job information but can be carried out on the basis of very brief job specifications containing sometimes not much further information than a job title. These methods include clinical methods (1), rational validity (2), ability-oriented job analysis (3) and job classification for validity generalization (4).

Clinical methods (1).   Probably, most of the inferences are made on an informal clinical basis. In this process the selecting agent may have only global job information or very detailed molecular information. It is not clear how attribute requirements and corresponding predictors are chosen. This may well be a process that is governed by job stereotypes, unrealistic expectations regarding desirable applicant characteristics, etc.

Since no formal attempt is made to analyse systematically the job except for making some clinical impressions, there is no guarantee whatsoever that predictors are chosen that will optimize procedural validity, that consensus will exist between judges, and that the same results will be produced for comparable instances or at later moments.

Rational validity (2).   Experienced researchers in the field of personnel selection seem to be able to make accurate estimates of the validity of predictors. Schmidt *et al.* (1983) describe a procedure in which experts are supplied with job information (job title and an additional job description) and are then required to make validity estimates for various predictors. The resulting coefficients are termed 'rational validities'. According to Schmidt *et al.* (1983) the combined judgement of 20 experts yields a validity estimate as accurate as a criterion-related validity study with $N = 981$. Experts with less experience, although 'trained professionals in the field of personnel selection', do perform considerably less well but still the combined judgement of 20 persons is as accurate as a local validity study with a sample size of 217 (Hirsch, Schmidt and Hunter, 1986). From a logical point of view it does not make sense to make use of expert judgement if sufficient data about jobs are available. In this case one can better consult the relevant literature or databases directly (by performing a meta-analysis, for example). When such data are lacking, expert opinion seems useless because the 'expertness' is apparently not anchored in valid data. In this latter case an empirical exploration may be required.

Ability-oriented job analysis (3).   This job analysis technique can probably be qualified as the most popular method for deriving sign type predictors, because it constitutes a cheap and easily administered approach. At this moment, we will give no further treatment of this group of methods. The reader is referred to p. 156, where the basic rationale underlying these methods, and some disadvantages that pertain to the attribution of relevant attributes to performance behaviours, is discussed.

Job classification for validity generalization (VG) purposes (4).   Job classification decisions underlie nearly all personnel functions (e.g. grouping jobs for validity generalization, performance appraisal, training need analysis, etc.). In designing selection or promotion systems, it must be decided whether job groups or job families can be formed for use with a single set of predictors. As such, it does not necessarily preclude the analysis of jobs on a molecular level as is suggested by the positioning in Figure 5. Since a comprehensive review of Pearlman (1980) suggests that broader, molar job analysis methods will suffice in demonstrating job similarities or differences for validity generalization purposes (and that's the viewpoint considered here), job classification has been listed in Figure 5 as a molar approach, through which predictors are derived by analysing the job as a whole.

Secondly, it may seem odd to consider job classification as an approach for deriving predictors since, after all, jobs can be grouped without any reference to relevant predictor sets. It is important, however, that any job classification must not be regarded as an end in itself but must be related to the intended purpose or objective of the grouping system (cf. Pearlman, 1980). For a job classification to be meaningful for personnel selection purposes it should have reference to predictor validities in one way or another: the grouping of jobs should be such that it moderates test validities, that is 'groupings within which specified test validities will generalize and between which such validities will not generalize' (Pearlman, 1980, p. 18). Viewed from this perspective, job classification is almost tautological to choosing predictors: if one determines what job categories are to be formed and to what category a new job belongs, it is also clear which predictor instruments are to be chosen.

In classifying jobs three issues are important (Pearlman, 1980). First, as has been pointed out above, the resulting job classification should contribute to the objective as originally specified, in this case grouping jobs for validity generalization. Secondly, jobs can be classified on the basis of job-/work-oriented data, worker-oriented data, attribute data or on some overall measuring device for the job as a whole (e.g. job title). As has been briefly mentioned above, the choice of one of these job descriptors as a basis for classification is an extremely important one, because resulting job groupings may vary as a function of the descriptor type, as is demonstrated in a study of Cornelius, Carron and Collius (1979). In this study seven nominally different foreman jobs in a chemical processing plant were analysed by using three different types of descriptors but holding constant the type of (hierarchical) clustering algorithm. It turned out not only that the number of similar foreman jobs differed according to the type of job descriptor but also there were differences relating to which jobs were most similar. A third issue in job family construction pertains to the grouping method used. We tend to heartily agree with Pearlman's observation that discussions on the best grouping method are far less important than more substantive issues in job family development (i.e. type of job descriptor chosen).

On the basis of a review of differential effects of various job descriptors, Pearlman concludes that validities are generalizable within job families (p. 21). Furthermore, he argues that job groups based on either human attribute requirements or some overall, global index ('job title') are likely to prove more useful for both theoretical and practical applications. However, a number of comments seem to be in order here (see also Algera and Greuter, 1989). First we reiterate some of the remarks that have been made before, especially those concerning the required specificity of job analysis information (1) since very broad job categories are used for validity generalization purposes global analysis methods suffice to decide whether a given job belongs to a certain category and (2) the use of overall criterion measures may inadvertently give rise to extensive generalizability and mask potential task or situational moderators within the same job category.

In addition to these two points, a crucial question is whether validity generalization procedures as proposed by Schmidt and Hunter (1977, 1981) are sensitive enough to detect moderators within the data set used. As evidenced in a number of Monte Carlo simulations (Osburn *et al.*, 1983; Sackett, Harris and Orr, 1986; Kemery, Mossholder and Roth, 1987; Spector and Levine, 1987) power is unacceptably low. Small true differences in validities will not be detected regardless of mean sample size and number of studies in the meta-analysis. Even moderate true differences will stay unnoticed when sample sizes and number of studies are small (see Sackett *et al.*, 1986).

Other problems with the Schmidt–Hunter procedure are: residual variance seems consistently underestimated (Roe, 1984; Jansen *et al.*, 1986); robustness issues with respect to correction for attenuation and restriction of range are ignored (Jansen *et al.*, 1986); the hypothetical distributions for criterion reliability, predictor reliability and restriction of range (assumed by Schmidt and Hunter, because real values of reliabilities and restriction of range are rarely reported in validation studies) are in error because they result in either an overestimation of artefactual variance (Pease and Switzer, 1988); finally, the level of true validity seems to be overestimated (Jansen *et al.*, 1986). All in all, in spite of a considerable research effort on validity generalization, there is still doubt on the adequacy of the method. As a consequence the quality of the databases that have been created, cannot be completely relied upon when choosing predictors.

Deriving predictors from job aspects.   In contrast to the aforementioned methods the following approaches do rely on more specific job information pertaining to job aspects of a work- or worker-oriented nature.

Decision trees (5).   For some of the abilities of the Task Abilities Scales of Fleishman (see p. 157) decision trees have been developed. This implies that the analyst can confine him- or herself to a series of dichotomous (yes/no) decisions in order to determine whether a given ability factor is relevant. An example of such a decision tree is presented in Figure 6. We judge the usage of decision trees as very instructive indeed because they tell the job analyst in a step-by-step manner how the rating process should be carried out. The steps to be taken are very small and do not represent inferential leaps of the kind that can hardly be bridged.

Attribute ratings (PAQ, OAI) (6).   In developing the Position Analysis Questionnaire (PAQ) and Occupation Analysis Inventory (OAI) arrangements are made for obtaining ratings of attribute requirements from job experts (mostly psychologists). According to McCormick, Jeanneret and Mecham (1972, p. 394), an attribute is somewhat akin to the concept of a worker trait. Some of the attributes can be referred to as abilities or aptitudes. Others are referred to as situational attributes (e.g. working alone, time pressure, complexity of duties, etc.). The various attributes are rated in terms of their relevance for each of the worker elements in the PAQ or OAI. This rating process ends up with an 'attribute profile' for each job element. Unfortunately, neither the PAQ nor the OAI provides rules for the choice of predictors in a specific instance: 'rules of corre-

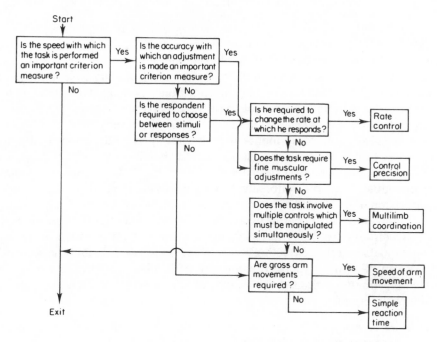

Figure 6   A decision flow diagram for ability identification. (After Fleishman and Quaintance, 1984.)

spondence' between job data structure and attribute requirements are not presented.

Greuter (1988a) has developed a set of attribute weights for a relatively small set of 50 worker elements (intellectual activities, contacts, supervising, etc.) and 33 situational elements (stressors, climate variables, leadership climate). For each of these elements the relevance of a fixed set of 24 abilities/aptitudes and 37 personality traits was determined by conducting a rating experiment with eight industrial psychologists. Results indicated that reliabilities of mean attribute ratings were satisfactory: an average inter-rater correlation coefficient of 0.84 was computed for the derivation of aptitudes/abilities and of 0.77 for the group of personality traits. As a next step a matrix with mean attribute weights was composed, that enables one to determine the required attribute profile for the job to be analysed: in order to determine the attribute requirements in a specific instance, the vector of job data scores is post-multiplied with the constructed matrix of mean attribute weights. Deriving the attribute profile uniformly from the job data as illustrated above, may lead to a set of predictors that maximizes composite validity, because subjective inferences are suppressed. In a study of Sparrow *et al.* (1982), a set of five predictor instruments was chosen following a comparable algorithm as was used by Greuter (1988a). The concurrent validity of two of these measures with overall job performance was extremely high (R = 0.91), suggesting that a component strategy, as explained above, can be a useful approach for selecting predictors. Unfortunately, sample size was very small (N = 14).

Synthetic validity (7). The concept of synthetic validity has traditionally been defined as: 'the inferring of validity in a specific situation from a logical analysis of jobs into their elements, a determination of test validity for these elements, and a combination of elemental validities into a whole' (Balma, 1959, p. 395). It is evident from this definition that job analysis plays a major role, namely in the determination of the relevant job components. According to Hamilton and Dickinson (1987), job components may be specified with a job analysis as behaviours, traits, abilities or skills, provided that the elements used can be conceived as determinants of behaviour. For each of these elements validity estimates must be made, rationally or empirically. The validity of the overall procedure can be calculated by such methods as the J-coefficient of Primoff (1955).

The rationale of the J-coefficient possesses great potential for choosing predictors when an empirically based validation study is not feasible, or when a relevant database for conducting some form of meta-analysis is lacking: the concept can be applied most conveniently with adequate sample sizes, inadequate performance ratings (or no ratings at all), new jobs without incumbents, rapidly changing jobs, etc.

Experimental/correlational studies (8). Fleishman has conducted a number of studies that are relevant for deriving predictors when detailed job information is available. Among others he estimated the predictive validity of some of the ability scales of the TAS (Theologus and Fleishman, 1973; see also Fleishman and Quaintance, 1984, pp. 321–7). First, a panel of nine judges was asked to rate descriptions of a series of 38 experimental tasks, on each of the Task Abilities Scales. Next, predictive validity of the scales was estimated by whether the judges' ability ratings were correlates of actual task performance. A multiple regression was performed for each task, in which mean ability ratings were the predictor variables and task performance was the criterion. In selecting ability scales for use as predictors relevant requirements were: (1) high scale-reliabilities, (2) high variability in mean ratings across tasks and (3) ability–performance relationships that could be considered inherently 'logical'. Finally, a set of three predictors was derived (Gross Body Coordination, Manual Dexterity and Arm–Hand Steadiness) that resulted in a multiple correlation coefficient of 0.64 (corrected for small sample sizes). Other examples of comparable studies can be found in Fleishman and Quaintance (1984).

As was true for the attribute requirement approach discussed above the Fleishman study also seems to underline the critical importance of selecting predictors in a rational and logical fashion: in this way the validity of the predictor set seems to be optimal.

Theoretically based job analysis (9). Another method for identifying predictor constructs proceeds by way of a theoretical analysis: the job at hand is analysed by referring to categories or elements that come from some sort of theoretical system model. As an example we like to point at the Task Strategies Approach (TSA) of

Miller (1971; see Fleishman and Quaintance, 1984, pp. 127–9). The theoretical rationale underlying Miller's TSA, is that of an information-processing model. The activities proposed by Miller refer to covert, internal cognitive processes. The worker is seen as an operator with a minimum of four system functions: input reception, memory, processing and output effectors. The human information processor must scan the environment to detect task-relevant cues, eventually filter these cues and identify message entities or other patterns. In the next stage short-term and long-term memory are activated to make comparisons, to store information on a temporary or long-term base, etc. Situational and task cues are interpreted and decided upon, including activities such as counting, computing, planning, problem solving. Finally, an appropriate response is chosen.

From the above-mentioned methods for identifying relevant predictor constructs, the last category (theoretically based job analysis methods) seems to be particularly promising, because it stipulates *why* required attributes are relevant for adequate job performance. All the other methods can be characterized as black-box approaches because they only state which predictors may be appropriate given some type of criterion or set of criteria.

A FINAL COMMENT

If one inspects the literature concerning job analysis procedures, it turns out that three topics seem to exhaust the domain of practical and scientific endeavours at this moment: (1) job classification for validity generalization; (2) synthetic validity; and (3) job analysis as evaluated in court proceedings (highlighting the construction of sample type predictors). In reviewing recent developments in these three fields, we were not convinced that the available research is heading in the right direction.

As far as job classification for validity generalization purposes is concerned, we have already pointed at some statistical and technical overkill at the expense of more substantial matters. Moreover, as far as more substantial matters regarding the choice of an adequate job descriptor are considered, it is done by evaluating validity generalization (VG) data-banks that cannot be relied upon. With respect to synthetic validity some excellent progress has been made in delineating procedures for estimating several components of the J-coefficient (see Hamilton and Dickinson, 1987), but, again, the influential role of job descriptor type is overlooked or for the greater part neglected (cf. Algera and Groenendijk, 1985). Finally, with regard to legal perspectives on the use of job analysis, it has been noted that legal criteria are at odds with evidence from the VG approach, because the court requires detailed job information and molecular job analysis approaches (e.g. Cornelius, Schmidt and Carron, 1984). It seems to us, however, that legal and professional criteria pertain to different functions of job analysis. In court decisions emphasis has been put on aspects of what we have been labelling as the information gathering function of job analysis (What data collection methods are deployed? What agents are used? etc.), while professional and scientific debate is primarily oriented at the contribution of job analysis to the predictive function of personnel selection. Although these two functions are related in a logical and practical sense they do not pose identical or even comparable demands on the process of job analysis, or to state it more bluntly: in our opinion, it is not sufficient to restrict the scope of job analysis activities to those that are necessary for serving the predictive function. Applicants as well as other relevant persons of the client system, are entitled to get as much information as possible in order to build up a clearer picture of the job at hand.

As contrasted to the aforementioned subjects (job analysis for validity generalization, synthetic validity, legal perspective), other relevant questions have not been given much attention.

Of particular importance is research concerning the identification of relevant trait requirements for performance behaviour patterns. This point has been delineated as the main dilemma to be solved in every selection procedure. Although job analysis does not constitute the sole method for identifying relevant traits or predictors, it is indeed a very important one and mostly the only method that can be carried out in practice because relevant data necessary to apply alternative approaches (meta-analysis, exploratory validation) are frequently not available. We wish to make a plea for the use of job analytic procedures that derive predictors as correlates from job sub-aspects, not from 'job as a whole'. It was already noted that theoretically oriented instruments are of critical importance, because they describe the *process* of performing. In addition, the attribute requirement approaches of McCormick, Cunningham and Fleishman may prove worth while in bridging the gap between performance behaviours and individual differences. This group of methods can easily be reconciled within a synthetic validity strategy: although it has not been worked out for the Position Analysis Questionnaire, Occupation Analysis Inventory or any other instruments, attribute weights that are until now being scaled according to some Likert-type format, can be expressed as validity coefficients by using a synthesizing procedure as the J-coefficient.

Another neglected issue touches upon the already briefly mentioned role of situational moderators of the relations between job content and attribute requirements. Most job analysis methods are strictly job-oriented. They focus on job content and aspects of the organizational context are not systematically analysed, except for some characteristics (mostly physical) of the immediate job context. This can be seen as an important omission for at least two reasons: at first, as the survey study of Ryan and Sackett (1987) shows, informational items regarding various organizational conditions are valued as eligible and informative aspects by various participants of the selection process, including psychologists. Secondly, some situational variables may turn out to be moderators for ability–performance relationships, although some may consider this alternative as a fundamental and empirical impossibility (cf. Schmidt, Hunter and Pearlman, 1981; Schmidt *et al.*, 1985). Of course, it must be emphasized that not every situational aspect may serve as a potential moderator. Precedence must be given to those situational variables that make an environment appropriate or inappropriate for the manifestation of a certain ability or trait, that is: environmental conditions that either demand exercise of a quality, making it important for effective performance, or constrain exercise of the quality, making it incompatible to effective performance (cf. Forehand, 1968). Greuter (1988b) has developed a preliminary taxonomy for classifying these variables, denoted as Selection Oriented Situational (SOS) predictors. Relevant categories in the SOS taxonomy (with a total of 28 aspects) are: role-defining properties (work load, role ambiguity, role conflict); intrinsic job factors (variety, identity); extrinsic factors (rewards); climate and culture variables; physical and social working conditions; and various constraints impinging on the process of work planning and performing (cf. Peters and O'Connor, 1980).

As a final point, more research should be devoted to the development of such cognitively oriented job analysis methods as the Task Strategies Approach of Miller (see p. 174). Cognitive operations come into play in a rapid and pervasive way in a variety of jobs. This makes it productive to look at task performance as a sequence of information processing activities. Information processing theory may be called in to construct a theoretical account of what happens between the presentation of a task stimulus and the observed response. It may be instructive to apply such a cognitive information processing approach, as a sort of try-out, to the job of job analyst, because this may reveal substantial evidence concerning the act of analysing jobs as an information gathering process. Following such an approach the job analyst can be depicted as an information processor with several input functions (input selection, filtering, detecting, channelling, searching, etc.), memory and processing functions (categorizing, storing, transmitting, interpreting, counting, testing, etc.) and output effectors (deciding, reporting, eliminating, etc.). In this manner new possibilities are opened for examining the damaging role of common-sense knowledge and job stereotypes; but of course, the latter suggestion can also be considered as a somewhat malicious payment in kind to all of us who are practitioners or researchers in the field.

REFERENCES

Alexander, R.A., and Barrick, M.R. (1987). Estimating the standard error of projected dollar gains in utility, *Journal of Applied Psychology*, **72**, 475–9.

Algera, J.A., and Greuter, M.A.M. (1989). Job analysis for personnel selection, in M. Smith and I.T. Robertson (Eds.) *Advances in Selection and Assessment*. Wiley, Chichester, pp. 7–30.

Algera, J.A., and Groenendijk, B. (1985). Synthetische validiteit: een vergelijking van benaderingen, *Nederlands Tijdschrift voor de Psychologie*, **40**, 255–69.

Arvey, R.D., Davis, G.A., McGowen, S.L., and Dipboye, R.L. (1982). Potential sources of bias in job analytic processes, *Academy of Management Journal*, **25**, 618–29.

Asher, J.J., and Sciarrino, J.A. (1974). Realistic work sample tests: a review, *Personnel Psychology*, **27**, 519–33.

Balma, M.J. (1959). The development of processes for indirect or synthetic validity (a symposium). 1. The concept of synthetic validity, *Personnel Psychology*, **12**, 395–6.

Barrett, G.V., Caldwell, M.S., and Alexander, R.A. (1985). The concept of dynamic criteria: a critical reanalysis, *Personnel Psychology*, **38**, 41–56.

Brogden, H.E., and Taylor, E.K. (1950a). The dollar-criterion—applying the cost accounting concept to criterion construction, *Personnel Psychology*, **3**, 133–54.

Brogden, H.E., and Taylor, E.K. (1950b). The theory and classification of criterion bias, *Educational Psychological Measurement*, **10**, 159–96.

Campbell, J.P., Dunnette, M.D., Lawler, E.E., and Weick, K.E. (1970). *Managerial Behavior, Performance and Effectiveness*. McGraw-Hill, New York.

Caroll, S.J., and Schneier, C.E. (1982). *Performance Appraisal and Review Systems*. Scott, Foresman, Glenview, Illinois.

Cascio, W.F. (1982). *Costing Human Resources*. Van Nostrand Reinhold, New York.

Cascio, W.F. (1987). *Applied Psychology in Personnel Management*, 3rd edn. Prentice Hall, Englewood Cliffs, New Jersey.

Colbert, G.A., and Taylor, L.R. (1978). Empirically derived job families as a foundation for the study of validity generalization. Study 3: Generalization of selection test validity, *Personnel Psychology*, **31**, 355–64.

Cornelius III, E.T., Carron, Th.J., and Collius, M.N. (1979). Job analysis models and job classification, *Personnel Psychology*, **32**, 693–708.

Cornelius III, E.T., and Lyness, K.S. (1980). A comparison of holistic and decomposed judgment strategies in job analysis by job incumbents, *Journal of Applied Psychology*, **65**(2), 155–63.

Cornelius III, E.T., Schmidt, F.L., and Carron, Th.J. (1984). Job classification approaches and the implementation of validity generalization results, *Personnel Psychology*, **72**(2), 247–61.

Cronbach, L.J., and Gleser, G.C. (1965). *Psychological Tests and Personnel Decisions*, 2nd edn. University of Illinois Press, Urbana, Illinois.

Crowley, A.D. (1981). The content of interest inventories: Job titles or job activities? *Journal of Occupational Psychology*, **54**, 135–40.

Cunningham, J.W., Boese, R.R., Neeb, R.W., and Pass, J.J. (1983). Systematically derived work dimensions: Factor analysis of the Occupation Analysis Inventory, *Journal of Applied Psychology*, **68**, 232–52.

Desmond, R.E., and Weiss, D.J. (1973). Supervisor estimation of abilities required in jobs, *Journal of Vocational Behavior*, **3**, 181–94.

Desmond, R.E., and Weiss, D.J. (1975). Worker estimation of abilities requirements of their jobs, *Journal of Vocational Behavior*, **7**, 13–29.

DeNisi, A.S., Cornelius III, E.T., and Blencoe, A.G. (1987). Further investigation of common knowledge effects on job analysis ratings, *Journal of Applied Psychology*, **72**(2), 161–268.

Dowell, B.E., and Wexley, K.M. (1978). Development of a work behaviour taxonomy for first line supervisors, *Journal of Applied Psychology*, **63**(5), 562–72.

Dunnette, M.D. (1963). A modified model for test validation research, *Journal of Applied Psychology*, **47**, 317–32.

Dunnette, M.D. (1976). Aptitudes, abilities and skills, in M.D. Dunnette (ed.), *Handbook of Industrial and Organizational Psychology*. Rand McNally, Chicago, pp. 473–520.

Fine, S.A. (1963). *A Functional Approach to a Broad Scale Map of Work Behavior*. (HSR-RM-63/2). McLean, VA: Human Sciences Research, Inc.

Fine, S.A. (1974). Functional job analysis: An approach to a technology for manpower planning, *Personnel Journal*, **53**, 813–18.

Flanagan, J.C. (1954). The Critical Incident Technique. *Psychological Bulletin*, **51**, 327–58.

Fleishman, E.A. (1954). Factor structure in relation to task difficulty in psychomotor performance, *Educational and Psychological Measurement*, **17**, 522–32.

Fleishman, E.A., and Quaintance, M.K. (1984). *Taxonomies of Human Performance*. Academic Press, New York.

Forehand, G.A. (1968). On the interaction of persons and organizations, in R. Taguiri and G. Litwin (eds), *Organizational Climate: Explorations of a concept*. Boston, Division of Research, Harvard Business School, pp. 65–82.

Freyd, M. (1923). Measurement in vocational selection: An outline of a research procedure, *Journal of Personnel Psychology*, **2**, 215–49, 377–85.

Ghiselli, E.E. (1956). Dimensional problems of criteria, *Journal of Applied Psychology*, **40**, 1–4.

Ghiselli, E.E. (1960). Differentiation of tests in terms of the accuracy with which they predict for a given individual, *Educational and Psychological Measurement*, **20**, 675–84.

Ghiselli, E.E., and Brown, C.W. (1984). *Personnel and Industrial Psychology*. McGraw-Hill, New York.

Ghiselli, E.E., and Haire, M. (1960). The validation of selection tests in the light of the dynamic character of criteria, *Personnel Psychology*, **13**, 225–31.

Greuter, M.A.M. (1988a). *Personeelsselektie in perspektief*. Uitgeverij Thesis, Amsterdam.

Greuter, M.A.M. (1988b). *Het psychologisch onderzoek bij selektie- en loopbaanadvisering*. Psychologisch Laboratorium, Amsterdam.

Guion, R.M. (1976). Recruiting, selection and job placement, in M.D. Dunnette (ed.), *Handbook of Industrial and Organizational Psychology*. Rand McNally, Chicago, pp. 777–828.

Hahn, D.C., and Dipboye, R.L. (1988). Effects of training and information on the accuracy and reliability of job evaluations, *Journal of Applied Psychology*, **73**(2), 146–53.

Hamilton, J.W., and Dickinson, T.L. (1987). Comparison of several procedures for generating J-coefficients, *Journal of Applied Psychology*, **72**(1), 49–54.

Harvey, R.J., and Hayes, Th.L. (1986). Monte Carlo baselines for interrater reliability correlations using the Position Analysis Questionnaire. *Personnel Psychology*, **39**, 345–57.

Hemphill, J.K. (1960). Dimensions of executive positions, *Research Monograph, Ohio State University*, 98.

Hirsch, H.R., Schmidt, F.L., and Hunter, J.E. (1986). Estimation of employment validities by less experienced judges, *Personnel Psychology*, **39**(2), 337–45.

Hogan, J., and Quigley, A.M. (1986). Physical standards for employment and the courts, *American Psychologist*, **41**(11), 1193–217.

James, L.R. (1973). Criterion models and construct validity for criteria, *Psychological Bulletin*, **80**, 75–83.

Jansen, P.G.W., Roe, R.A., Vijn, P., and Algera, J.A. (1986). *Validity Generalization Revisited*. University Press, Delft.

Jenkins, J.G. (1946). Validity for what? *Journal of Consulting Psychology*, **10**, 93–8.

Jones, A.P., Main, D.S., Butler, M.C., and Johnson, L.A. (1982). Narrative job descriptions as potential sources of job analysis ratings, *Personnel Psychology*, **35**, 813–28.

Kemery, E.R., Mossholder, K.W., and Roth, L. (1987). The power of the Schmidt and Hunter additive model of validity generalization, *Journal of Applied Psychology*, **72**(1), 30–7.

Landy, F.J., and Farr, J.L. (1983). *The Measurement of Work Performance*. Academic Press, Orlando, Florida.

Lawshe, C.H. (1975). A quantitative approach to content validity, *Personnel Psychology*, **28**, 563–75.

Lent, R.H., Aurbach, H.A., and Levin, L.S. (1971a). Predictors, criteria and significant results, *Personnel Psychology*, **24**, 519–33.

Lent, R.H., Aurbach, H.A., and Levin, L.S. (1971b). Research design and validity assessment, *Personnel Psychology*, **24**, 247–74.

Levine, E.L. (1983). *Everything You Always Wanted to Know About Job Analysis and More . . . a Job Analysis Primer*. Marines Publishing Co, Tampa, Florida.

Levine, E.L., Ash, R.A., Hall, H., and Sistrunk, F. (1983). Evaluation of job analysis methods by experienced job analysis, *Academy of Management Journal*, **26**(2), 339–48.

McCormick, E.J. (1976). Job and task analysis, in M.D. Dunnette (ed.), *Handbook of Industrial and Organizational Psychology*. Rand McNally, Chicago, pp. 651–96.

McCormick, E.J. (1979). *Job Analysis: Methods and applications*. Amacom, New York.

McCormick, E.J., DeNisi, A.S., and Shaw, J.B. (1979). Use of the Position Analysis Questionnaire for establishing the job component validity of tests, *Journal of Applied Psychology*, **64**(1), 51–6.

McCormick, E.J., Jeanneret, R.R., and Mecham, R.C. (1972). A study of job characteristics and job dimensions as based on the Position Analysis Questionnaire, *Journal of Applied Psychology*, Monograph, **56**(4), 347–68.

Miller, B.B. (1971). *Development of a Taxonomy of Human Performance: Design of a systems task vocabulary*. Techn. Rep. AIR-72 6/2035-3-7-TRII. American Institute for Research, Silver Spring, Maryland.

Monahan, C.J., and Muchinsky, P.M. (1983). Three decades of personnel selection research: a state-of-the-art analysis and evaluation, *Journal of Occupational Psychology*, **56**, 215–25.

Mount, M.K., and Ellis, R.A. (1987). Investigations of bias in job evaluation ratings of comparable worth study participants, *Personnel Psychology*, **40**, 85–96.

Muchinsky, P.M. (1986). Personnel selection methods, in C.L. Cooper and I. Robertson (eds), *International Review of Industrial and Organizational Psychology*. Wiley, Chichester, pp. 37–70.

Nagle, B.F. (1953). Criterion development, *Personnel Psychology*, **6**, 271–88.

Osburn, H.G., Callender, J.C., Greener, J.M., and Ashworth, S. (1983). Statistical power of tests of the situational specifity hypothesis in validity generalization studies: a cautionary note, *Journal of Applied Psychology*, **68**(1), 115–22.

Pease, P.W., and Switzer III, F.S. (1988). Validity generalization and hypothetical reliability distributions: A test of the Schmidt–Hunter procedure, *Journal of Applied Psychology*, **73**(2), 267–74.

Pannone, R.D. (1984). Predicting test performance: A content valid approach to screening applicants, *Personnel Psychology*, **37**, 507–14.

Pearlman, K. (1980). Job families: A review and discussion of their implications for personnel selection, *Psychological Bulletin*, **87**, 1–28.

Pearlman, K., Schmidt, F.L., and Hunter, J.E. (1980). Validity generalization results for tests used to predict job proficiency and training success in clerical occupations, *Journal of Applied Psychology*, **65**, 373–406.

Peters, L.H., and O'Connor, E.J. (1980). Situational constraints and work outcomes: the influence of a frequently overlooked construct, *Academy of Management Review*, 5(3), 391–7.

Primoff, E.S. (1955). *Test selection of job analysis: The J-coefficient*. Washington DC, US Civil Service Commission, Assembled Test Technical Edition, May.

Roche, W.J. Jr (1961). The Cronbach–Gleser utility function in fixed treatment, *Employee Selection*. Southern Illinois University, Illinois.

Roe, R.A. (1983). *Grondslagen der personeelsselektie*. Van Gorcum, Assen.

Roe, R.A. (1984). Advances in performance modeling: the case of validity generalization. Paper presented at the symposium 'Advances in testing'. Acapulco, Mexico.

Roe, R.A. (1986). A technological view on personnel selection. Invited lecture given at the Colegio de Psycólogos de Madrid. Technische Universiteit Delft, Delft.

Ryan, A.M., and Sackett, P.R. (1987). A survey of individual assessment practices by I/O psychologists, *Personnel Psychology*, **40**, 455–87.

Sackett, P.R. Cornelius, E.T. III, and Carron, Th.K. (1981). A comparison of global judgment vs. task oriented approaches to job classification, *Personnel Psychology*, **34**, 791–804.

Sackett, P.R., Harris, M.M., and Orr, J.M. (1986). On seeking moderator variables in the meta-analysis of correlational data: a Monte Carlo investigation of statistical power and resistance to type I error, *Journal of Applied Psychology*, **71**(2), 302–10.

Schmidt, F.L., and Hunter, J.E. (1977). Development of a general solution to the problem of validity generalization, *Journal of Applied Psychology*, **62**, 529–40.

Schmidt, F.L., and Hunter, J.E. (1981). Old theories and new research findings, *American Psychologist*, **36**(10), 1128–37.

Schmidt, F.L., Hunter, J.E., and Pearlman, K. (1981). Task differences as moderators of aptitude test validity in selection: a red herring, *Journal of Applied Psychology*, **66**(2), 166–85.

Schmidt, F.L., and Kaplan, L.B. (1971). Composite versus multiple criteria: A review and a resolution of the controversy, *Personnel Psychology*, **24**, 419–34.

Schmidt, F.L., Hunter, J.E., McKenzie, R.C., and Muldrow, T.W. (1979). Impact of valid selection procedures on work-force productivity, *Journal of Applied Psychology*, **64**, 609–26.

Schmidt, E.L., Hunter, J.E., Croll, P.R., and McKenzie, R.C. (1983). Estimation of employment test validities by expert judgment, *Journal of Applied Psychology*, **68**, 550–601.

Schmidt, F.L., Hunter, J.E., Pearlman, K., and Shane, G.S. (1985). Forty questions about validity generalization and meta-analysis, *Personnel Psychology*, **35**, 697–798.

Schmitt, N., and Fine, S.A. (1983). Inter-rater reliability of judgements of functional levels and skill requirements of jobs based on written task statements, *Journal of Occupational Psychology*, **56**, 121–7.

Schmitt, N., Gooding, R.Z., and Kirsch, M. (1984). Meta-analysis of validity studies published between 1964 and 1982 and the investigation of study characteristics, *Personnel Psychology*, **37**, 407–22.

Schmitt, N., and Ostroff, C. (1986). Operationalizing the 'Behavioral Consistency' approach: Selection Test Development based on a content-oriented strategy, *Personnel Psychology*, **39**, 91–108.

Smith, J.E., and Hakel, M.D. (1979). Convergence among data sources, response bias, and reliability and validity of a structured job analysis questionnaire, *Personnel Psychology*, **32**, 677–92.

Smith, P.C. (1976). Behavior, results, and organizational effectiveness: the problem of criteria, in M.D. Dunnette (ed.), *Handbook of Industrial and Organisational Psychology*, Rand McNally, Chicago, pp. 745–75.

Sparrow, J., Patrick, J., Spurgeon, P., and Barwell, F. (1982). The use of job component analysis and related aptitudes in personnel selection, *Journal of Occupational Psychology*, **55**, 157–64.

Spector, P.E., and Levine, E.L. (1987). Meta-analysis for integrating study outcomes: A Monte Carlo study of its susceptibility to type I and type II errors, *Journal of Applied Psychology*, **72**(1), 3–9.

Stutzman, T.M. (1983). Within classification job differences, *Personnel Psychology*, **36**, 503–16.

Tenopyr, M.L., and Oeltjen, P.D. (1982). Personnel selection and classification, in M.R. Rosenzweig and L.W. Porter (eds), *Annual Review of Psychology*, **33**, 581–618.

Theologus, G.C., and Fleishman, E.A. (1973). Development of a taxonomy of human performance: Validation study of ability scales for classifying human tasks, *JSAS Catalog of Selected Documents in Psychology*, **3**, 29 (Ms. No. 326).

Thompson, D.E., and Thompson, T.A. (1982). Court standards for job analysis on test validation, *Personnel Psychology*, **35**, 865–74.

Thornton III, G.C., and Byham, W.C. (1982). *Assessment Centers and Managerial Performance*. Academic Press, New York.

Tornow, W.W., and Pinto, P.R. (1976). The development of a managerial job taxonomy: A system for describing, classifying and evaluating executive positions, *Journal of Applied Psychology*, **61**(4), 410–18.

Wernimont, P.F., and Campbell, J.P. (1968). Signs, samples and criteria, *Journal of Applied Psychology*, **52**, 372–6.

Chapter 2.3

Performance Modelling for Personnel Selection

MARTIN A. GREUTER

Adviesbureau Psychotechniek B.V., Drift 10, 3512 BS Utrecht, The Netherlands

INTRODUCTION

As has been shown in Chapter 2.1 of this handbook the selection process can be approached from a technological perspective. Following this approach an appropriate methodology can be found in the design methodology from the engineering sciences. According to the design methodology several steps are to be taken to arrive at a desired product or service (Chapter 2.1, p. 129): (1) definition of required functions, (2) specifying requirements, (3) synthesis, (4) simulation, (5) evaluation and (6) decision making. This design cycle can be applied to each of the basic functions of personnel selection, that is: it can be tied in with information gathering, predictive, decision making and reporting or communicating activities during the selection process. In this chapter we will discuss how the design cycle can be applied to one of these main activities, i.e. to the development of selection-oriented predictive performance models. Other applications of the design cycle to other basic functions are left out of consideration, because they are discussed elsewhere in this handbook (particularly in Chapter 2.4; see also Roe and Greuter, 1989).

Applying the design cycle to predictive performance models

Prediction models can be considered as special cases of performance models. In a performance model the performance criteria under study are explicitly related to a set of exogenous variables. Exogenous variables can be conceived as determinants of the performance behaviour under study. They serve to predict the future

Assessment and Selection in Organizations   Edited by P. Herriot
© 1989 John Wiley & Sons Ltd

outcomes on performance criteria or they may facilitate the understanding of performance behaviours.

Performance modelling has received a growing interest during the last few years (e.g. Campbell, 1983; Naylor, 1983). It should be noted that most of the performance models are of a generic type; they list a large number of variables that influence performance. As an example of such a general model the reader is referred to the well-known management performance model of Campbell *et al.* (1970). In this model the performance of managers is depicted as a function of various individual characteristics (intelligence, aptitudes, knowledge, temperament, preferences, expectations) and environmental variables (e.g. climate and culture conditions). Although such models are informative in the sense that the available literature and research are nicely summarized, they cannot be considered as working models for guiding interventions. Thus, in personnel selection the model should only contain specific variables that (1) are—presumably—relevant for the problem at hand, (2) can be assessed at the moment of application and (3) are stable enough to allow predictions over a longer time period. In

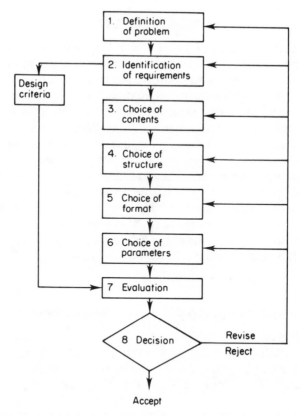

Figure 1   Developing predictive performance models in accordance with the design cycle. (From Roe, 1984.)

addition, (4) the number of variables should be minimized in order to get an acceptable utility–cost ratio.

In the context of personnel selection a prediction model can be defined as a model that transforms information about applicants' past or present behaviour into a forecast of their future behaviour. Prediction models for personnel selection can take many forms, ranging from statistical regression formulae to job simulations.

Figure 1, which has been borrowed from Roe (1984), shows which steps are to be taken to develop predictive performance models. The steps presented can be seen as another elaboration of the general design cycle, but now it has been specialized to the predictive function of personnel selection.

Each of the steps is briefly explained below.

1. *Defining the problem* Performance models serve to predict the future work performance of applicants from a specification of individual characteristics or behavioural styles as measured at the time of selection. Then, the problem to be solved can be stated in general terms by delineating predictive performance models as an aid to transforming information on past or present applicant characteristics into predictions about their future behaviour and the resulting contributions to organizational goals.

2. *Specifying model requirements* An important requirement can be directly derived from the above-stated objective: predictive performance models should allow for accurate predictions of future work performance. Predictive validity constitutes a first model requirement. Furthermore, models should be practical and economical in their use.

3. *Specifying model content* In elaborating performance models, content must be specified in accordance with the problem at hand. In essence, this comes down to specifying relevant criterion variables first. Secondly, predictor variables must be identified that enable one to predict expected performance levels on these criterion variables.

4. *Structure* After relevant model elements (criterion and predictor variables) have been chosen, model relations should be laid down, that is: it is to be specified in what way criterion and predictor variables are related, thereby focusing on relations within and between both sets of variables.

5. *Form* For performance models usually an algebraic function is chosen to depict relationships between criterion and predictor variables, i.e. $Y = f(X)$. Other possibilities are: mock-up systems, simulation models, etc.

6. *Estimating parameters* Relationships between predictor and criterion variables are further specified by estimating model parameters. Parameters contain information about the *strength* or *intensity* of relationships in the model. As such, they relate to the specification of the model's structure (see under 4) by which the *direction* of a relationship is stipulated.

7. *Evaluation of the model* Performance models are evaluated in terms of the model requirements specified at the beginning of the design process. Consequently, evaluation is primarily directed at estimating predictive validity: in

addition, the model can be checked in terms of practical or economical considerations.

As a result of the evaluation phase it may be (deemed) necessary to make several model revisions in which case some or all of the steps as presented in Figure 1 are repeated. As is true for designing in general, adequate performance models are mostly not found at once, but may require several iterations. Model building continues until final results are satisfactory or the designer runs out of time or money.

Structure of this chapter

In subsequent sections of this chapter each of the aforementioned steps will be discussed in more detail. Some major design considerations concerning basic or elemental principles for deriving predictions will be discussed below. The following section concentrates on how the content of prediction models can be specified, that is, how criterion variables can be defined and how predictor variables are derived. Structure and format are treated in the fourth section. This chapter ends with a review of parameter estimation and model evaluation procedures (p. 195), clinical prediction (p. 197) and some final comments regarding the process of performance modelling as a general method in exploring and enhancing the predictive function of the selection process (p. 199).

MAJOR DESIGN CONSIDERATIONS

With respect to designing predictive models there seem to be the following design choices to be made (cf. Roe and Greuter, 1989):

– between the deductive–nomological (or sign) approach and the domain sampling (or sample) approach;
– between clinical and formalized prediction.

In combination there are four options to be chosen from (see Table 1).

Table 1   Basic design choices for selection-oriented prediction models

	Deductive–nomological ('signs')	Domain sampling ('samples')
Formalized methods	measuring capacities and traits; combining scores according to a formalized model	measuring skills, behaviour or performance styles; combining scores according to a formalized model
Clinical methods	measuring capacities and traits ('impressions'); combining scores (impressions) subjectively	measuring skills, behaviour or performance styles; combining scores (impressions) subjectively

Table 2   Basic design choices for selection-oriented prediction models; signs versus samples

Signs	Samples
– Representation by means of an abstract symbolic system (symbolic model)	– Representation by means of a concrete symbolic system (iconic or analogue system)
– Symbols refer to theoretical concepts	– Symbols refer to empirical concepts
– Predictions are based on performance theory	– Predictions are based on point-to-point correspondence between predictor and criterion

The distinction between signs and samples (Wernimont and Campbell, 1968) relates to the way in which predictions are generated. Prediction according to the sign approach is predicated upon a symbolic model, while the sample approach can be addressed in terms of iconic or analogue models (see Table 2).

In symbolic models reality is modelled by means of an abstract or ideal symbolic system, i.e. by abstract concepts which cannot be observed in reality in a direct sense. These concepts are made meaningful in explaining reality by incorporating them in (psychological) theories or hypotheses concerning the phenomena being studied. System characteristics are represented by mathematical and logical symbols and formulae. It will be evident that the existence of adequate theories or hypotheses is a prerequisite for using symbolic models.

With iconic models, performance behaviour is predicted by constructing a concrete or realistic system; in the symbol system the same attributes are used as in reality, a physical mock-up (for example, selecting a pilot by means of an airflight simulator) although differences in scale may exist (a 'maquette'). In principle even the actual system can be used experimentally to study and predict behaviour (a so-called running system). In the context of personnel selection this latter possibility boils down to using an introduction period as a trial and testing phase.*

In the case of analogue models reality and symbolic systems have comparable structures, but in the symbolic system actual circumstances and objects are replaced by symbols. For example, drawing of an electric installation, road maps with divers symbols for main roads, bridges, junctions. In the context of personnel selection an excellent example is provided by Münsterberg who developed a simple work sample device for selecting tram drivers. In his work sample traffic situations were simulated on a map by using figures and letters to represent various traffic participants such as pedestrians, cars and horsed vehicles. By moving the map behind a little window, applicants could be confronted with alternative traffic situations. As is evident in Münsterberg's selection test, analogue models are not anchored in psychological theory; reality is merely encoded

---

* It must be clearly stated that this selection method, although technically feasible, should be prohibited, in our opinion, on moral and legal grounds.

while preserving a one-to-one correspondence between model and system performance to be predicted. Note that this latter point distinguishes analogue models from symbolic models.

To predict future work performance the designer may also opt for an interactional prediction model. The term 'interactional prediction model' refers to a class of models that comprises individual and situational characteristics as well as person–situation interactions. Or, to state it differently, predictions are generated following the paradigm:

Model (task, individual variables, situational variables) → *performance prediction,*

while within the classical individual diagnostic approach predictions are produced by:

Models (task, individual variables) → *performance prediction.*

To our knowledge, interactional prediction models have not been used for personnel selection purposes in any significant way, thus far, although the principle of multiple determination by person and situation factors was already stressed in an early publication of Dunnette (1963), who pointed out that situational factors should be included in prediction models for personnel selection. In a recent study by the author (Greuter, 1988), Dunnette's advice has been put into practice, that is, several person–situation prediction models were formulated and tested for a nursing job in a mentally retarded facility. Also, the interested reader is referred to interactional prediction models as developed by Warr (1987) to understand and predict unemployment and mental health.

DEFINING THE CONTENT OF PREDICTION MODELS

As has been clearly indicated, the process of designing a prediction model always starts with a thorough problem analysis that forms the basis for deriving relevant model requirements and design criteria. Predictive validity will always be an important requirement for predictive models but other objectives may be stated as well; for example, one may wish to raise the recruitment and selection rates for minority members, evade certain kinds of tests (e.g. by using interviews instead of psychological tests because the latter can be heavily attacked in court procedures), prevent unnecessary intrusion of privacy, etc.

Specifying the problem and corresponding requirements first, seems to be a self-evident and obvious matter, but in fact, these important steps that set the stage for further development and evaluation activities, are most of the time not carried out in an explicit fashion or not carried out at all. Therefore, all these requirements should be explicitly laid down, for example by means of a 'program of requirements' as has been illustrated by Roe (1986) (see also Chapter 2.1 of this book). Although important activities, they will not be treated beyond what has been noted thus far: these activities are, in the nature of things, tied in with specific and local circumstances and therefore do not benefit from a general treatment.

We will start with delineating procedures for specifying the content of the prediction model, instead. In the case of a prediction model, content refers to two things, i.e. performance variables that are to be predicted, and predictor variables (also labelled as 'exogenous' or 'structural' variables) that serve as a predictor set. How criterion variables can be specified is reviewed below; it is followed by a discussion of the identification of predictor variables.

Defining the criterion set

The role of criterion development for personnel selection has been amply discussed in Chapter 2.2 of this handbook. To reiterate some of the major points:

- Criteria can be defined in relation to each of a series of hierarchically ordered activities, i.e. they may refer to elementary activities (acts), performance behaviour and/or occupational roles.
- Criterion structure may be multi- or unidimensional. As has been pointed out in Chapter 2.2, a multidimensional criterion is considered to be more informative and productive for predictive purposes.
- Criteria can be classified according to (1) level of specificity (specific behavioural instances v. global estimates), (2) time-span covered and (3) degree of closeness to organizational goals to be approached (actual on-the-job behaviour versus estimated pay-off to organizational goals).
- Criteria can reflect dynamics in underlying behaviour structure; that is, their meaning, both at the construct and measurement level, may change over time.

In this section we will concentrate on how a relevant criterion set can be made available from job content. Before doing this, it should be noted that job analysis techniques do play a very convenient and important role in pointing out relevant criteria. In consequence, the reader may find it instructive to read Chapter 2.2 about job analysis and criterion development first, before reading this section.

In almost every instance conceptual criteria are chosen on the basis of job analysis methods. Especially those job analysis techniques that fall into the category of the behaviour description approach (a term introduced by Fleishman; see Fleishman and Quaintance, 1984) can be useful in stipulating conceptual criteria. Within this category one finds job-/work-oriented methods as well as worker-oriented methods. Job-oriented approaches are best represented by specific, tailor-made job or task inventories. Task inventories comprise a form of structured questionnaires that consist of a listing of the tasks within some occupational field. Some examples can be found in McCormick (1979, pp. 117–35).

Worker-oriented techniques do contain items that are generalizable across a wide variety of jobs. The traditional example is the Position Analysis Questionnaire of McCormick *et al.* (1972).

The Critical Incident Technique of Flanagan (1954) may serve a dual purpose: the incidents of superior, average and inferior behaviours are specifically tied in with the job under study and can be considered as job-oriented descriptions. By grouping incidents into more general behavioural categories, one comes about dimensions that are more or less worker oriented and sufficiently general to be connected to individual characteristics.

Studies that have used the validity generalization approach of Schmidt and Hunter do not rely upon minuscule and detailed analysis of criterion performance. In commenting on the necessity of criterion development and job analysis methods, criticism of Schmidt and Hunter is addressed at two related, but not identical points (see e.g. Schmidt, Hunter, and Pearlman, 1981; Schmidt *et al.*, 1985). First, detailed job analysis procedures are considered unnecessary. Second, criterion fractionation is seen as contributing only to reliability and not to validity of the criterion construct. The former objection has been under discussion in Chapter 2.2 (see pp. 159 and 170 concerning the degree of desired information specificity and the usage of job classification for validity generalization purposes). With respect to the second criticism, it is argued that 'if large between-job differences in tasks do not moderate test validities (or do so to only a small extent), then task dimensions within the same job (e.g. of the kind produced by behaviourally anchored rating scales) are unlikely to do so' (Schmidt *et al.*, 1981, p. 174). Also it has been noted that correlations between criterion dimensions typically approach 1.00 after corrections for attenuation due to unreliability have been made, indicating that criterion dimensions are linearly dependent on each other, on the true score level (Schmidt et al., 1981, p. 174). Thus the only function of this type of linearity in the dataset would be to increase the reliability of the composite criterion measure.

In Chapter 2.2 some counter-arguments were presented. To summarize the major points: the absence of validity differences between different jobs and also within the same job may be seen as an indication of the poor discriminatory power of the Schmidt and Hunter procedure. Job categories are broadly defined and do not seem to tap a homogeneous criterion content. Finally, overall criterion ratings give rise to excessive generalization that would probably not have been demonstrated if criterion measurement had been better controlled.

Choice of predictors

Once the criteria are established the next step is to develop a set of suitable predictors. This involves two steps (cf. Roe, 1983): (1) identification of conceptual predictors, i.e. required traits or critical behaviours, and (2) operationalization into operational predictors, by selecting tests* that are commercially or otherwise available, or by constructing new instruments.

The first (and very obvious) requirement is that predictors should be predictive of future success criteria. This means that one should try to find conceptual predictors with high validities and low intercorrelations. Several other requirements may be of importance as well, especially in choosing operational pre-

---

* The term 'test' is used interchangeably with 'instrument'. It also comprises other (quantitative) selection instruments.

dictors, like intrusion of privacy, duration of administration, costs, personnel implications or other practical aspects.

The prediction principle that has been preferred (signs or samples) determines what type of predictors will be chosen: trait oriented, behaviour oriented (measuring behavioural styles by work samples, etc.) or both. The strategy for identifying predictors at the conceptual level is the same, however. One can choose from the following options (cf. Roe, 1983):

- job analytic and related procedures;
- exploratory validation;
- meta-analysis of published validity data.

Job analytic and related methods

This group of methods can be subdivided into methods that are based on information about the 'job as a whole' versus those that are directed at measuring sub-aspects.

Among others, in Chapter 2.2 of this handbook the following methods are discussed: clinical methods, estimating procedures for rational validities, ability-oriented job analysis, decision trees, attribute ratings (PAQ, OAI), experimental/correlational research of Fleishman (op. cit.) and, finally, theoretically based job analytic procedures as the Task Strategies Approach of Miller (1971).

Exploratory validation

This is in fact the classical way of working (cf. Guion, 1965). The exploration aims at a try-out of criteria and predictors and the generation of hypotheses about possible relationships. In principle this is always a matter of first validation: follow-up research is needed for any validation (Guion, 1965, p. 20).

Due to the rise of validity generalization, exploratory methods have lost much of their significance. However, exploratory validation remains the only viable alternative when a relevant database is lacking or when job and/or situational context are rapidly changing.

Meta-analysis of published validity data

Since the middle of the 1970s there are a number of standardized procedures for meta-analysis (see for a review Bangert-Drowns, 1986). Within the field of industrial and organizational psychology, the validity generalization method of Schmidt and Hunter (1977, 1981) has become the most prevailing method of analysis. It has been applied to personnel selection as well as to several other subjects such as realistic job previews (McEvoy and Cascio, 1985), absenteeism (Terborg, Lee, and Smith, 1982), the leadership model of Fiedler (Peters, Hartke, and Pohlmann, 1985), the job characteristics model of Hackman and Oldham (Fried and Ferris, 1987), etc.

In contrast to the dominant opinion until then (e.g. Ghiselli, 1966), Schmidt and

Hunter have taken the position that differences in observed validity coefficients are not substantial, but can be attributed to sampling errors and other artefacts, such as criterion and predictor unreliability, restriction of range, etc. In order to arrive at a corrected estimate of predictor validities three steps must be taken, according to the validity generalization procedure of Schmidt and Hunter:

1. *Compiling and classifying validity coefficients* Compilation of validity coefficients and classification according to job type, predictor type and criterion type.
2. *Generalizability testing* Examination of the homogeneity of the residual distribution after correction for artefacts such as differences in sample sizes (due to $N \ll \infty$), predictor and criterion unreliability and restriction of range.
3. *Generalization* Making a point estimate of true validity within the population.

The second step also gives information regarding the so-called 'hypothesis of situational specificity': when the remaining variance in the residual distribution does not differ significantly from zero, the hypothesis of 'no situational specificity' is accepted. In practice several decision rules are followed, among others the 75 per cent rule: differences in sample sizes, predictor/criterion unreliability and restriction of range must account for at least 75 per cent of the variance in observed coefficients (see Schmidt and Hunter, 1981).

With regard to the identification and selection of cognitive predictors, Schmidt and Hunter state that it does not seem to be important which predictor test one chooses, because the average ability test (verbal, numerical, spatial reasoning) is a valid predictor for any criterion. 'Any test will do' (Schmidt *et al.*, 1985, p. 712). For the average test the validity lies between 0.34 and 0.56 for 68 per cent of the jobs and between 0.27 and 0.63 for 90 per cent of the jobs (Schmidt, Hunter, and Pearlman, 1981, p. 173). The additional contributions of other types of predictors (content based selection devices, assessment centres, etc.) is seen as only marginal (Hunter and Hunter, 1984).

The validity generalization method of Schmidt–Hunter has not remained undisputed, however (see Algera *et al.*, 1984; Jansen *et al.*, 1986; Sackett *et al.*, 1985; James, Demarree and Mulaik, 1986). Criticism is addressed at the low power of the Schmidt and Hunter 75 per cent rule to test the hypothesis of situational specificity. This may, at least for a part, explain the absence of between and within job differences in validity coefficients and it may also interfere with the detection of situational moderators such as leadership style, organizational climate, etc. Additional work must be undertaken to arrive at unbiased estimates of artefactual and residual variances. This includes better estimating procedures for restriction of range effects and sampling variance of correlations. Also, the practice of making corrections for predictor and criterion unreliability should be reconsidered. Correcting for predictor unreliability is acceptable only when actual reliabilities are available. However, reliabilities are rarely reported in validation studies. This lack of information led Schmidt and Hunter to develop hypothetical distributions for predictor and criterion reliability. A Monte Carlo study of Paese and Switzer (1988) shows that these assumed reliability distributions may result in either an overestimation or an underestimation of artefactual variances. As far as criterion variables are concerned it may be a better strategy not to correct for unreliability at all, even when actual reliabilities are available. In our opinion it is useless to speculate about perfect reliable criterion measures when in reality one has to rely on subjective superior ratings of which reliabilities can probably not be improved beyond a mean value of 0.60. Furthermore, a more stringent rule than the 75 per cent may be warranted, for example a 90 per cent rule, that is: artefactual variance should at least account for 90 per cent of the observed variance of validity coefficients.

Another point of criticism relates to the Schmidt and Hunter procedure for making inferences on the true population validity. True validity is estimated by correcting the mean observed validity coefficient for restriction of range and attenuation (with respect to unreliability of both the predictor and criterion variable). Apart from the above remarks about the appropriateness of these corrections, it has been noted that this procedure is incomplete, that is: it ends with an estimated true validity coefficient ρ but it does not include a procedure for generalizing this value to future selection situations in which the same test is used for predicting a given criterion in a new sample of applicants (see Jansen *et al.*, 1986, pp. 46–7). The estimation of true population validity should be followed by a deductive phase in which an estimate is made of future observed validity thereby taking into account actual test and predictor reliabilities and real sample size. Restriction of range corrections should be omitted because validities must relate to the non-selected group of applicants. For a (Bayesian) elaboration of this deductive phase the interested reader is referred to Jansen *et al.* (1986).

It appears to us that the Schmidt and Hunter procedure can be credited as an important and challenging contribution to the field of personnel selection. At the same time the Schmidt and Hunter model does not permit accurate conclusions as yet. We agree with several other authors (e.g. Algera *et al.*, 1984; Jansen *et al.*, 1986) that a lot of work needs to be done in order to solve some of the dilemmas mentioned above.

STRUCTURE AND FORMAT

Once the criteria and predictor variables have been identified the structure of the model has to be established and format has to be specified.

From the various possibilities that exist for specifying the model's structure (conjunctive, disjunctive and compensatory models) the linear compensatory model is the most well known and seems to be most frequently applied for both sign and sample based prediction models.

Discrete models can be mentioned as well, but their applicability seems limited: critical requirements, that can be considered as 'necessary conditions', do not occur frequently and are at best exemplary exceptions.

Format is usually algebraic, that is: the relationship between predictor and criterion is depicted as an algebraic equation specifying the function $Y = f(X)$. Also graphical or tabular presentations may be chosen. Expectancy charts can be considered as an example of the latter category (i.e. tabular presentation). They specify probabilities of expected criterion performance for each of a series of predictor scores.

A class of models that has been mentioned quite often during the last two decades is the moderator model. Initially these models were proposed as means for a more fair selection. The moderator variable then is an ethnic or other external characteristic. More recently moderator models have been mentioned in the context of validity generalization. In this case the moderator variable is a situational or job characteristic that could serve to increase the homogeneity of a set of predictor validities.

Regarding the first application it can be concluded that efforts to demonstrate moderator effects for racial and group characteristics have generally failed (cf. Schmitt and Noe, 1986). Whenever moderator effects are observed they are caused by differences in regression constants rather than regression weights of separate predictors. In the rare instances that differences are found, criterion scores of minority group members are, surprisingly, not underestimated, but rather overestimated. Although this has been observed several times, a satisfactory explanation is still lacking. On the one hand one could think of statistical explanations: small sample sizes, and little power to detect moderators. This explanation is not completely satisfactory, however: no evidence for systematic underestimation has been found in larger samples.

Regarding the second point (situation and/or job characteristics as moderators for predictor criterion relationships within occupational classes as used for validity generalization purposes) the discussion is still going on. A study by Gutenberg, Arvey, and Osburn (1983) shows that the 'information processing/ decision making' job dimensions of the PAQ moderate the validity coefficients of several GATB dimensions (general ability, verbal and numerical ability). In addition to job characteristics of this type, the situational arrangement of a job, i.e. the work setting, is also a potential source of moderators (Greuter, 1988). This latter aspect has earlier been referred to as illustrative for a special kind of performance models, i.e. interactional prediction models.

In applying the moderator approach, serious statistical problems do arise. A search for moderators is usually carried through by introducing a product or interaction term (predictor × moderator) in ordinary least squares multiple regression analysis, so-called Moderated Regression Analysis. Morris, Sherman, and Mansfield (1986) point to the high correlations between this product term and its constituent predictors, introducing linear dependencies in the set of regression variables (see also Sockloff, 1976). The power of the (traditional) F-test for interaction can be quite low because of the relation among the regression variables. As a consequence moderator effects may have a diminished opportunity for detection, even when sample size is adequate. Morris *et al.* recommend principal regression analysis on the principal components of a predictor set in which the smallest principal has been deleted. However, their remedy may lead to an *over*estimation of the interaction effect as has been suggested by Cronbach (1988).

Dunlap and Kemery (1988) demonstrated in a series of Monte Carlo simulations that detection of moderator effects in regression analysis is hampered by unreliability in either the predictor or the moderator variable. Although (un)reliability can always be acknowledged as a problem in prediction, it has a greater impact on the more complex moderator model: the reliability of the product term is partly determined by the product of the reliabilities of its constituents. More precise and accurate measurement of regression variables is called for, in order to have a reasonable chance of detecting moderating effects.

FURTHER MODEL SPECIFICATION: PARAMETER ESTIMATION AND EVALUATION OF MODELS

The model should be further specified by estimating parameters and by evaluating the model in terms of the *a priori* requirements that have been put forward (among others: predictive validity).

Parameter estimation

Parameters can be estimated with the help of either empirical or rational methods. The empirical methods can only be applied when a complete set of data is available. This poses a problem when validity generalization (or another type of meta-analysis) has been used as an alternative to an empirical validity study. Validity generalization leads to an estimation of true predictor validities but in addition, predictor intercorrelations must be estimated in order to arrive at a set of estimated model parameters. Although validity generalization could in principle be used for estimating intercorrelations as well, the required data are usually lacking, thereby forcing the designer to perform an empirical study after all. The designer may also resort to rational methods, that is: test experts can be called in to make estimates of intercorrelations between tests or other instruments. Until now, there has not been much research into the accuracy of this type of experts' ratings, but it can be expected that these estimates can be made fairly accurately, because they can be backed up by relevant psychological theory concerning individual differences. As a next step, estimated intercorrelations can be combined with validity estimates that are derived from a validity generalization procedure, to yield a set of model parameters that reflect independent contributions of each of a series of predictor variables.

The empirical methods for parameter estimation include the classical (unbiased) multiple regression analysis, and (biased) Stein and ridge regression methods.

Multiple regression according to Stein (1960) differs from classical multiple regression because the regression weights are corrected with a factor that is similar to the shrinkage correction for multiple correlations. As this correction factor is identical for all regression variables, the multiple correlation remains the same. The corrected weights are more reliable estimators of their population counterparts.

Ridge regression is based on the same principle. Again, a correction of regression weights is carried through, but here the correction applies to the principal components and its magnitude is variable, depending on the eigenvalues.

According to Darlington (1978) ridge regression leads to more reliable estimates of parameters than traditional methods, especially when there is a high degree of validity concentration, i.e. large differences in validities between principal components.

Recently, a growing interest in rational methods for assigning weights to predictors can be noted. The simplest rational method is unit weighting, in which all predictors are equally weighted by a factor 1.0. Despite its simplicity unit weighting does an extremely good job in some instances (see also p. 199). Equally weighted prediction models may even out-predict models with optimal weights which are chosen on the basis of regression analysis. The reason for the (unexpected) predictive qualities of unit weighting is that it protects one against a reversal of the relative weighting of the variables on the basis of poor empirical data. Thus, if true weights of predictors X_1 and X_2 are in the proportion of 2 to 1, unit weighting is a safeguard for data showing that the weights for X_2 are larger than that for X_1 (Einhorn, 1986). Instead of an equally weighted set of predictors, one may also opt for differential weighting of predictors. In the latter case weights can be calculated by making use of 'subject matter experts': job incumbents, supervisor and/or psychologist. When using expert judgement, a crucial question is which source is to be consulted for which aspects: job incumbents or supervisors can be expected to be more familiar with work or job samples and how they are related to overall performance, whereas test experts would be expected to provide knowledgeable judgement about test–job performance relationships. Furthermore, there is evidence that accuracy of estimated parameters is highly dependent upon degree of expertness: a study of Hirsch, Schmidt, and Hunter (1986) shows that differences in accuracy can be expected between validity estimates made by a group of top experts on the one hand and those that were made by a group of experts with less experience (although still 'trained professionals in the field of personnel selection') on the other hand.

The Bayesian approach can be seen as a combination of empirical and rational approaches to parameter estimation. It offers a general method to specify *a priori* hypotheses on regression weights and revise these on the basis of empirical data. By applying this method iteratively the estimates converge to their final values when more data are added. General Bayesian methods are described by Lindley and Smith (1972) and Laughlin (1979). The last author starts from a prior distribution of equal regression weights. Also it contains a factor by which the researcher can assign a weight to the importance of the empirical data. A well known application of the Bayesian method concerns the estimation of regression weights in comparable groups (m group regression). Molenaar and Lewis (1979) have improved this method that was originally proposed by Jackson, Novick, and Thayer (1971). It should be noted that the m group method can be used to establish whether validities are generalizable. In a study on the prediction of grades from different curricula Dunbar, Mayekawa, and Novick (1985) have shown with the help of this technique that validities are only generalizable within selected groups of curricula.

Evaluation of models

After model parameters have been estimated empirically or rationally, the model must be evaluated. Evaluation of the prediction model should be done against the requirements and constraints specified in advance. The main requirement is predictive validity. In the case of empirical parameter estimation a validity estimate for the total model is usually obtained simultaneously, i.e. within the same statistical/calculational procedure. The estimated (multiple) correlation coefficient is optimal for the sample used in the validation study. Therefore, it should be statistically corrected for shrinkage effects. Rational models may require an additional analysis to arrive at a validity estimate of the total model. There are few developments here, apart from biased regression methods mentioned above.

One can note a renewed interest in *synthetic validation*. The job is broken down into components for each of which a validity estimate is made. The validity of the overall procedure can be synthesized by rational/empirical methods such as the J-coefficient of Primoff (see for a recent review Hamilton and Dickinson, 1987). The defining component relations of the J-coefficient can be measured with criterion-related validation designs but they can also be estimated rationally, with the help of expert judgement, i.e. job incumbents and supervisors to estimate indicators for job performance (e.g. relations between job elements and total job performance) and test experts to give estimates of relational parameters based on test performance (e.g. validities). As has been already observed in Chapter 2.2, the rationale of the J-coefficient bears great potential for estimating validities when an empirically based validation study is not feasible, or when a relevant database for conducting a form of meta-analysis is lacking.

Evaluational activities can mostly not be conceived as final, concluding activities in the process of building predictive performance models. Rather, evaluation results may indicate that some revisions or refinements need to be made and that some of the earlier design phases must be repeated. In this way model evaluation activities are both evaluative and developmental. The design process stops when model requirements are satisfied or when practical constraints (time, money, etc.) force one to do so.

CLINICAL PREDICTION

Thus far, our consideration of predictive performance modelling has been limited to the more or less structured approach as implied by the design cycle. In doing this we have reviewed the major statistical and rational methods of combining predictor variables, but we have overlooked the most commonly used method, that of making *clinical predictions* to arrive at a forecast of work performance.

Clinical prediction can be subdivided into purely clinical and semi-clinical prediction, depending on the degree of structure that is accomplished with respect to data *collection* and data *combination*. When both data collection and data combination methods are carried out in a judgemental, impressionistic way, the model is referred to as 'purely clinical' prediction. When data are collected objectively or mechanically, but still the various data are combined in a subjective manner, the prediction paradigm can be labelled as 'semi-clinical' (Roe, 1983). Also, some mixed approaches can be distinguished because data collection procedures are commonly both clinical for some parts and mechanical for other parts; for example, interview data are judgementally reviewed while tests are objectively scored (cf. Sawyer, 1966).

In a recent survey of a segment of the Division of Industrial Organizational Psychology of the American Psychological Association (see Ryan and Sackett, 1987), respondents were asked how the information they received from the various assessment techniques was combined. That is, was the approach for combining scores purely judgemental (e.g. an impression based on examining test scores and interview responses), purely statistical (e.g. a combination of numerical scores tests and interviews via a formula), or both judgemental and statistical (e.g. a formula of numerical scores from tests and an impression of interview responses)? The results show that only 2.5 per cent of the respondents used a purely statistical approach. Most used either a purely judgemental (55.7 per cent) or a combination approach (41.8 per cent). Furthermore, only 18.9 per cent combined assessment results to yield an overall rating. Altogether, the Ryan and Sackett survey makes it abundantly clear that in practice, practitioners do not seem to proceed in a fashion analogous or similar to the type of performance modelling processes we have been describing thus far. On the other hand, differences are not very great either. The greatest difference between the formalized procedure described in this chapter on the one hand and semi-clinical prediction on the other hand may manifest itself only in relation to the estimation of model parameters. As we have pointed out above, the classical solution calls for empirical estimates as produced by multiple regression analysis or related techniques. If, however, these estimates are derived rationally, by mobilizing job experts to rate constituent aspects of performance–attribute relations (as is accomplished, for example, by the J-coefficient), the performance modelling approach as suggested here does not differ greatly from semi-clinical prediction. That is, semi-clinical prediction can easily be expanded to accommodate expert judgement in order to arrive at rational or synthetical validity estimates.

Questions as to the relative validity of clinical versus formalized prediction models (comprising statistical as well as rational procedures) have frequently been raised (see, e.g. for a review, Wiggins, 1980). At first, it was generally concluded that statistical prediction methods demonstrated superiority over clinical prediction: in reviewing 50 available studies Meehl (1954) concluded that 33 of them demonstrated the superiority of statistical data combination and the remaining 17 studies indicated that the two methods were approximately equal in predictive accuracy. This early statement most clearly supports the superior qualities of statistical methods, almost without any hesitation ('You cannot beat the formula') but the research of Meehl has been challenged on methodological as well as conceptual grounds. A review of Sawyer (1966) reconsidered 45 of the studies reviewed by Meehl. His resulting comments seem to tone down some of the major conclusions as reported by Meehl. The best prediction method appeared to be that in which both judgemental and mechanical data collection methods were combined. This latter conclusion does in fact coincide with the findings of Ryan and Sackett that show that mixed judgement/mechanical data collection methods are used by upwards of 40 per cent.

With respect to the combining or weighting of scores three types of weighting procedures have been compared in a review of Roe (1983): (1) unit weighting (or equal weighting), (2) differential weighting and (3) optimal weighting procedures as calculating β-weights. Roe concludes that unit weighting will be superior to optimal procedures in most circumstances or, at least, will not be inferior (Roe, 1983, p. 224). This latter conclusion can be understood, at least for some part, in terms of the well known shrinkage effect that hampers statistical procedures, especially if sample size is small. This disadvantage is not incurred by rational procedures (unit or differential weighting) because they constitute non-optimizing procedures. Also, empirical evidence (e.g. Einhorn and Hogarth, 1975; Wainer, 1976; see also Roe, 1983, p. 224) shows that validity of a predictor composite will be higher for unit weighting than for optimizing procedures if predictor validities do not disperse in any significant way. Only when differences in predictor validities are substantial, may statistical procedures be preferred.

Recently, automated clinical prediction (a term introduced by Wiggins, 1980) has become more and more popular. In this method clinical combinations of input data are standardized to such an extent that they may serve as the basis for a computer program which will automatically generate the required interpretations when provided with appropriate input data. In automated clinical prediction (that can be considered as an example of an 'expert system') data can be combined following a simple algorithm, for example unit weighting or a differential weighting scheme that has been made available by job experts. We feel that the growing interest in expert systems in general may, at least for large-scale selection procedures, eventually force a tendency towards extended formalization of prediction models and away from clinical and semi-clinical methods. Thus, the computer may accomplish a change in working methods among psychologists where Meehl and others did not succeed.

FINAL COMMENT

In this chapter we have demonstrated how the general design cycle as presented in Chapter 2.1 of this handbook can be applied to one of four basic functions of selection procedures, i.e. the predictive function of personnel selection.

Applying the design cycle to developing prediction models, offers, in our view, several advantages in comparison with more traditional approaches, i.e. a classical, empirical approach that defines performance within a one-criterion–multiple-predictors frame and proceeds by conducting multiple regression analysis for obtaining parameter estimates.

As a first advantage the design cycle directs attention to activities that are commonly not fully considered, or at least partly neglected, in developing predictive performance models. In this respect we would (again) like to point at the problem-oriented nature of the design process. At the outset, problem and corresponding model requirements must be explicitly stated. Also, the designer is urged to give full recognition of certain assumptions that have to be made to allow predictions of future behaviour. With this latter point we don't mean that mathematical or statistical assumptions underlying statistical operations should be better defined (but of course, they should), because this is commonly already done at a reasonably accurate level. However, assumptions about the stability of the performance system should be laid down: this latter tenet refers explicitly to the prior condition that relevant characteristics of the environment, task to be accomplished and worker characteristics remain stable and unchanged over a certain period of time, at least as long as is necessary for predicted behaviours to occur, normally until two to three years after predictions have been made. Stability with respect to applicant characteristics is self-evident, because it would not be possible to bridge the period between measurements made at the time of selection on the one hand and forthcoming criterion performance evaluation on the other hand. Stability of task and task environment is also assumed though not in a literal sense. Stability is assumed to be relative, that is: it only pertains to a restricted time period and it does not relate to task and environment conditions in all their aspects. Rather, stability is assumed for a selected category of variables that can be taken as potential determinants of performance behaviours, e.g. leadership style, climate conditions, job challenge, stressors, cognitive task complexity.

Another example illustrating the potential usefulness of performance modelling (i.e. directing attention to commonly neglected aspects) relates to the iterative nature of the design cycle. As explained, this means that adequate performance models are mostly not found at once but take shape in several iterations. Viewed from this perspective it may be instructive to have some sort of error recovery method that specifies what parts of the design cycle are to be repeated: should the model's content better be attuned to the problem at hand, meaning that a different criterion or predictor set should be employed? Do poor predictions stem from the wrong parameter values, functional structure and/or format? For this to be accomplished it is necessary that model requirements are being transformed into a set of design criteria for each successive stage (Roe, 1984). This is difficult advice to follow because not much knowledge exists as to what criteria should be formulated for which phase.

The predictive function of performance models can be conceived as primarily evaluative. Given a structure, predict performance. Designing an appropriate performance model is generative however: given performance requirements, design structure. As is clearly evidenced in general design methodology (cf. Card, Moran, and Newell, 1983), this latter statement implies that several solutions can be generated each of which satisfies the model requirements as originally formulated (this principle is referred to as 'indeterminacy of structure'). As a consequence, there are trade-offs to be made in performance prediction. We feel that this latter point is frequently overlooked or simply denied, although it has already long been recognized as is witnessed by such concepts as 'individual dimensionality' of performance behaviour (Ghiselli, 1956). With this latter concept it is meant that two persons may achieve the same overall performance with different performance strategies (behaviour styles).

Also, it is explicitly recognized in what we have been referring to as 'interactional performance modelling'. The goal of interactional performance modelling is to arrive at a set of individual as well as situational conditions that, taken together, help to satisfy model requirements, that is: their combined (conjunctive or compensatory) contributions should optimize predictive qualities. From this perspective it is obligatory to view system performance in its entirety. System performance can be optimized in several ways, meaning that other parts of the system than individual characteristics may be re-designed in order to improve upon predictive accuracy. This makes it possible to interconnet personnel selection with other, situation-oriented interventions. Especially noteworthy are various kinds of interventions addressed at task or environmental conditions that may eventually lead to a situational arrangement that facilitates the expression of task-relevant capacities, traits or behaviour styles. Or to state it more technically: the goal is to find an arrangement of situational conditions that maximizes predictive validities of individual capacities and traits. Under these circumstances personnel selection has a high expected pay-off. On the other hand, one may also try to create a set of environmental conditions that facilitate task performance and make it less dependent upon individual differences (for example by mechanizing or automatizing the production process). Organizations may be forced to this latter strategy when they are confronted with a shortage of labour supply and can therefore not resort to personnel selection. As an illustration of combined person and situation effects on performance behaviours we like to point at a series of studies conducted by (Fiedler *et al.*, (1979) that show validities of a cognitive test battery to be high when stress between workers and their superiors is perceived as low. However, validities are negative or almost zero when perceived stress is high. Another example concerns the effects of payment-by-results systems. With respect to this latter subject some laboratory studies have been reported that can be more easily interpreted in cause–effect terms (see Weinstein and Holzbach, 1973; Dunnette, 1973; Terborg, Richardson, and Pritchard, 1980). These experiments demonstrate either evidence for differential validities (studies of Weinstein/Holzbach and Dunnette) or differential prediction (Terborg *et al.*) as a result of experimental variations in payment conditions.

The above-mentioned points also illustrate some of the practical advantages of performance modelling according to the design cycle. In addition, practitioners may find the design cycle instructive because it explicitly takes into account all sorts of practical constraints that commonly impinge upon the selection process. Time and financial constraints can be formulated as prior conditions for further model building activities. Specific requirements can be put forward with respect to fair employment for different racial, ethnic and sex groups. Finally, the design process does not condemn practitioners to an endless process of empirical validation. Empirical research is seen as an important and valuable tool in building predictions models (especially aggregated research results that can be made available by some sort of meta-analysis), but it does not constitute an indispensable condition for each step of the design process. When relevant empirical data are lacking one may proceed by using such techniques as job analysis, expert opinion, etc., for choosing and weighting predictors. This latter point distinguishes the modelling approach as has been described in this chapter, from the more traditional approach to personnel selection in which selection of relevant predictors can only be accomplished by conducting an empirically based validation study (preferably a predictive validation study).

Although it need not concern the individual designer who is confronted with a here-and-now prediction problem, performance modelling strategy as outlined, can also contribute to a better theoretical understanding of performance behaviour. In the view of James (1973) a general criterion or performance theory should proceed by a process of construct validation wherein several performance behaviours (ratings, objective measures, measurements of capacities, motivation, satisfaction, etc.) are studied in their relationships to one another. Such complex performance structures can be revealed by delineating structure by multivariate latent models in which underlying performance constructs are postulated for explaining correlations at the manifest variables level. In our opinion a performance modelling strategy as conceived here, may serve such a theoretical endeavour because it explicitly furnishes the materials (i.e. criterion and predictor variables; model parameters) for accomplishing this objective.

REFERENCES

Algera, J.A., Jansen, P.G.W., Roe, R.A., and Vijn, P. (1984). Validity generalization: some critical remarks on the Schmidt-Hunter procedure, *Journal of Occupational Psychology*, **57**, 197–210.

Bangert-Drowns, R.L. (1986). Review of developments in meta-analytic method, *Psychological Bulletin*, **99**(3), 388–99.

Campbell, J.P. (1983). Some possible implications of 'Modeling' for the conceptualization of performance measurements, in F. Landy, S. Zedeck and J. Cleveland (eds), *Performance Measurement and Theory*. Erlbaum, Hillsdale, New Jersey, pp. 277–98.

Campbell, J.P., Dunnette, M.D., Lawler, E.E., and Weick, K.E. (1970). *Managerial Behavior, Performance and Effectiveness*. McGraw-Hill, New York.

Card, S.K., Moran, Th.P., and Newell, A. (1983). *The Psychology of Human–Computer Interaction*. Erlbaum, Hillsdale, New Jersey.

Cronbach, L.J. (1988). Statistical tests for moderator variables: Flaws in analyses recently proposed, *Psychological Bulletin*, **102**(3), 414–17.

Darlington, R.B. (1978). Reduced variance regression, *Psychological Bulletin*, **85**, 1238–55.

Dunbar, S.B., Mayekawa, S., and Novick, M.R. (1985). Simultaneous estimation of regression functions for marine corps technical training specialties. ONR Techn. Rep., 85–1. Cada Res. Group, University of Iowa, Iowa City.

Dunlap, W.P., and Kemery, E.R. (1988). Failure to detect moderating effects: is multi-collinearity the problem? *Psychological Bulletin*, **102**(3), 418–20.

Dunnette, M.D. (1963). A modified model for test validation research. *Journal of Applied Psychology*, **47**, 317–332.

Dunnette, M.D. (1963). *Performance equals ability and what?* University of Minnesota, Department of Psychology, Technical Report No. 4009.

Einhorn, H.J. (1986). Accepting error to make less error. *Journal of Personality Assessment*, **50**(3), 387–95

Einhorn, H.J., and Hogarth, R.M. (1975). Unit weighting schemes for organizational decision making, *Organizational Behaviour and Human Performance*, **13**, 171–92.

Fiedler, F.E., Potter, E.H., Zais, M.M., and Knowlton, W.A. (1979). Organizational stress and the use and misuse of managerial intelligence and experience, *Journal of Applied Psychology*, **64**, 635–47.

Flanagan, J.C. (1954). The Critical Incident Technique. *Psychological Bulletin*, **51**, 327–58.

Fleishman, E.A., and Quaintance, M.K. (1984). *Taxonomies of Human Performance*. Academic Press, New York.

Fried, Y., and Ferris, G.R. (1987). The validity of the job characteristics model: a review and meta-analysis, *Personnel Psychology*, **40**, 287–322.

Ghiselli, E.E. (1956). Dimensional problems of criteria, *Journal of Applied Psychology*, **40**, 1–4.

Ghiselli, E.E. (1966). *The Validity of Occupational Aptitude Tests*. Wiley, New York.

Greuter, M.A.M. (1988). Personeelsselektie in perspektief. Thesis, Haarlem.

Guion, R.M. (1965). *Personnel Testing*. McGraw Hill, New York.

Gutenberg, R.L., Arvey, R.D., and Osburn, H.G. (1983). Moderating effects of decision-making/information-processing job dimensions on test validities, *Journal of Applied Psychology*, **68**(4), 602–8.

Hamilton, J.W., and Dickinson, T.L. (1987). Comparison of several procedures for generating J-coefficients, *Journal of Applied Psychology*, **72**(1), 49–54.

Hirsch, H.R., Schmidt, F.L., and Hunter, J.F. (1986). Estimation of employment validities by less experienced judges, *Personnel Psychology*, **30**(2), 337–45.

Hunter, J.E., and Hunter, R.F. (1984). Validity and utility of alternative predictors of job performance, *Psychological Bulletin*, **96**(1), 72–98.

Jackson, P.H., Novick, M.R., and Thayer, D.I. (1971). Estimating regression in m-groups, *British Journal of Mathematical and Statistical Psychology*, **24**, 129–53.

James, L.R. (1973). Criterion models and construct validity for criteria, *Psychological Bulletin*, **80**, 75–83.

James, L.R., Demarree, R.G., and Mulaik, S.A. (1986). A note on validity generalization procedures, *Journal of Applied Psychology*, **71**(3), 440–50.

Jansen, P.G.W., Roe, R.A., Vijn, P., and Algera, J.A. (1986). *Validity Generalization Revisited*. Delft University Press, Delft.

Laughlin, J.E. (1979). A Bayesian alternative to least squares and equal weighting coefficients in regression, *Psychometrika*, **44**(3), 271–88.

Lindley, D.V., and Smith, A.F.M. (1972). Bayesian estimates for the linear model, *Journal of the Royal Statistical Society, Series B*, **33**, 1–41.

McCormick, E.J. (1979). *Job Analysis: Methods and Applications*. Amacon, New York.

McCormick, E.J., Jeanneret, R.R., and Mecham, R.C. (1972). A study of job characteristics and job dimensions as based on the Position Analysis Questionnaire, *Journal of Applied Psychology Monograph*, **56**(4), 347–68.

McEvoy, G.M., and Cascio, W.F. (1985). Strategies for reducing employee turnover, *Journal of Applied Psychology*, **70**, 342–53.

Meehl, P.E. (1954). *Clinical Versus Statistical Prediction: A Theoretical Analysis and a Review of the Evidence*. University of Minnesota Press, Minneapolis.

Miller, B.B. (1971). *Development of a Taxonomy of Human Performance: Design of a Systems Task vocabulary*. Techn. Rep. AIR-72 6/2035-3-7-TRII. American Institute for Research, Silver Spring, Maryland.

Molenaar, I.W., and Lewis, Ch. (1979). Bayesian m-group regression: a survey and an improved model, *Methoden en Data Nieuwsbrief*, SWS/VvS, **4**(1), 62–72.

Morris, J.H., Sherman, J.D., and Mansfield, E.R. (1986). Failures to detect moderating effects with ordinary least squares-moderated multiple regression: some reasons and a remedy, *Psychological Bulletin*, **99**(2), 282–8.

Naylor, J.C. (1983). Modeling performance, in F. Landy, S. Zedeck, and J. Cleveland (eds). *Performance Measurement and Theory*. Erlbaum, Hillsdale, New Jersey, pp. 299–305.

Pease, P.W., and Switzer, F.S. (1988). Validity generalization and hypothetical reliability distributions: a test of the Schmidt–Hunter procedure. *Journal of Applied Psychology*, **73** (2), 267–74.

Peters, L.H., Hartke, D.D., and Pohlmann, J.T. (1985). Fiedler's contingency theory of leadership: an application of the meta-analysis procedure of Schmidt and Hunter, *Psychological Bulletin*, **97**(2), 274–85.

Roe, R.A. (1983). *Grondslagen der personeelsselektie*. Van Gorcum, Assen.

Roe, R.A. (1984). Advances in performance modeling: the case of validity generalization. Paper presented at: the symposium 'Advances in testing'. Acapulco, Mexico.

Roe, R.A. (1986). A technological view on personnel selection. Invited lecture given at the Colegio Official de Psycólogos de Madrid. Techn. University, Delft.

Roe, R.A., and Greuter, M.A.M. (to be published in 1989). Developments in personnel selection methodology, in E.A. Hambleton and J. Zaal (eds), *Advances in Testing*. Kluwer, Deventer.

Ryan, A.M., and Sackett, P.R. (1987). A survey of individual assessment practices by I/O psychologists, *Personnel Psychology*, **40**, 455–87.

Sackett, P.R., Schmidt, N., Tenopyr, M.L., and Kehoe, J. (1985). Commentary on forty questions about validity generalization and meta-analysis, *Personnel Psychology*, **85**.

Sawyer, J. (1966). Measurement and prediction, clinical and statistical, *Psychological Bulletin*, **66**, 178–200.

Schmidt, F.L., and Hunter, J.E. (1977). Development of a general solution to the problem of validity generalization, *Journal of Applied Psychology*, **62**, 529–40.

Schmidt, F.L., and Hunter, J.E. (1981). Old theories and new research findings, *American Psychologist*, **36**(10), 1128–37.

Schmidt, F.L., Hunter, J.E., and Pearlman, K. (1981). Task differences as moderators of aptitude test validity in selection: a red herring. *Journal of Applied Psychology*, **66**(2), 166–85.

Schmidt, F.L., Hunter, J.E., Pearlman, K., and Shane, G.S. (1985). Forty questions about validity generalization and meta-analysis, *Personnel Psychology*, **35**, 697–798.

Schmitt, N., and Noe, R.A. (1986). Personnel selection and equal employment opportunity, in C.L. Cooper and I. Robertson (eds), *International Review of Industrial and Organizational Psychology*. Wiley, Chichester, pp. 71–115.

Sockloff, A.L. (1976). Spurious product correlation, *Educational and Psychological Measurement*, **36**, 33–44.

Stein, C. (1960). Multiple regression, in I. Olkin *et al.* (eds) *Contributions to Probability and Statistics*. Stanford University Press, Stanford.

Terborg, J.R., Lee, Th.W., and Smith, F.J. (1982). Extension of the Schmidt and Hunter validity generalization procedure to the prediction of absenteeism behaviour from knowledge of job satisfaction and organizational commitment, *Journal of Applied Psychology*, **64**(4), 440–9.

Terborg, J.R., Richardson, P., and Pritchard, R.D. (1980). Person–situation effects in the prediction of performance: an investigation of ability, selfesteem and reward contingencies, *Journal of Applied Psychology*, **65**(5), 574–84.

Wainer, H. (1976). Estimating coefficients in linear models: it don't make no nevermind, *Psychological Bulletin*, **83**.

Weinstein, A.G., and Halzbach, R.L. (1973). Impact of individual differences, reward distribution and task structure on productivity in a simulated work environment. *Journal of Applied Psychology*, **58**, 296–301.

Warr, P.B. (1987). *Work, Unemployment and Mental Health*. Oxford University Press, Oxford.

Wernimont, P.F., and Campbell, J.P. (1968). Signs, samples and criteria, *Journal of Applied Psychology*, **52**, 372–6.

Wiggins, J.S. (1980). *Personality and Prediction*. Addison Wesley, Reading, Massachusetts.

Chapter 2.4

Recruiting and Advertising

KAREL DE WITTE

Centre for Organizational and Personnel Psychology, Catholic University of Leuven,
Tiensestraat 102, 3000 Leuven, Belgium

INTRODUCTION

When searching through the literature on personnel policy there are almost no publications on personnel advertising. Notwithstanding the enormous total budget spent on personnel advertisements, no systematic research has been done.

A lot of research about interviewing and psychological testing is available. Theories about how persons choose an organization have been developed. These theories assume the existence of the applicant. The question remains how the organization can influence the potential employee. In many cases the first contact is through a personnel advertisement. The effectiveness of this is, therefore, very important.

How can an organization create a positive image? Is there a different approach necessary for different functions? What is the perception of the reader of personnel advertisements? Does this perception fit the goals of the organization? Is the locus of the advertisement important? Does colour influence the reactions? The personnel manager is confronted with a list of questions when he or she designs a personnel advertisement. The choice is complex and intuition is mostly one's guide.

We try to test these intuitions by more systematic research. First, a conceptual framework will be offered that is based on a review of the literature. The aim of this framework is to understand the interaction between organizations and applicants. An overview of the rare research in this field is integrated within the presentation of the framework.

Assessment and Selection in Organizations   Edited by P. Herriot
© 1989 John Wiley & Sons Ltd

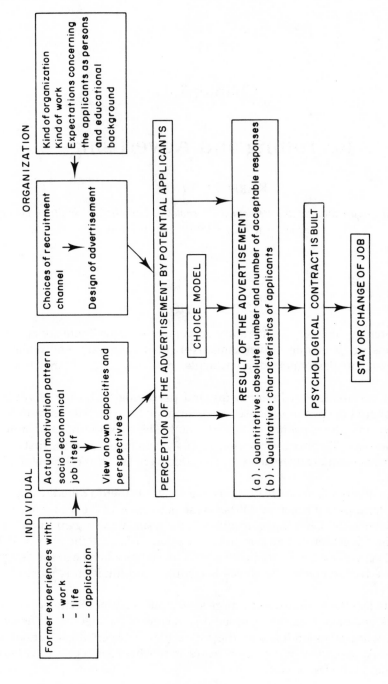

Figure 1   A framework for recruitment through personnel advertisements

Before reporting on our research on personnel advertisements, we situate personnel advertisements within the broader array of recruitment channels.

We conclude with a view on the future, from a practical and from a research perspective.

A FRAMEWORK FOR RECRUITMENT

We need to have a broad theoretical framework within which to consider recruitment and advertising. One such framework is presented in Figure 1.

Viewpoint of the applicant

Several elements influence people's search and application for a job. First of all there is their motivational pattern. Some people are looking for a stable job, others are looking for a job with much challenge. Previous experiences in applying for jobs is a second element, e.g. experiences with anonymous advertisements, with psychological testing, and so on will influence the willingness to apply for certain jobs. Present life situation is a third element: Are they willing to move? How much time are they willing to spend on their job? Which is the remuneration that fits their present life? What are their options for the future? All these elements will play a role in the applicant's behaviour.

Many applicants don't have a clear point of view on these elements. They are unclear about their perspectives. They lack a good insight into their capacities. In recent training programmes and booklets for helping applicants to learn more about the whole selection procedure, we find that one of the first elements in almost every training programme is to help the applicants to clarify their capacities and their perspectives.

Viewpoint of the organization

Past experiences will also play an important role for the organization in the use of recruitment channels. Which recruitment channel will be used? If, for example, the last personnel advertisement elicited only a few responses, one will be tempted to try out another recruitment channel. What is the organization willing to offer to the potential employee, e.g. remuneration, training opportunities, fringe benefits? And how will the organization present this offer to the potential applicants? Some will present only the positive aspects, others prefer to give a realistic view on the job and the organization. Research (Premack and Wanous, 1985) indicates that this difference in presentation has a significant influence on turnover. A realistic job review results in lower turnover but it is not clear if the realistic presentation is less attractive to the potential applicants and will result in a lower response rate to the advertisements. By creating a more realistic and honest relationship the drop out of some candidates may be recovered. This brings us to the kind of relationship that advertising builds between organizations and applicants.

The relationship between organization and applicant

Several assumptions, mostly implicit, determine the kind of encounter between both parties. Some companies strive to build an encounter on an equal basis. Much attention is given to the applicants, all letters are answered, applicants receive feedback on the results of their tests and interviews, and so on. A psychological contract between two parties is negotiated. Other companies look down on the candidates. The company is the powerful party, the applicant is the one who is dependent on the goodwill of the company. Applicants should be grateful that time and attention are being spent on them. As we will see further, this message is given by most personnel advertisements. They give a long list of requirements, but only very vague coverage of what the company offers. In such a perspective it is easy to understand that a lot of managers prefer to be head-hunted. The humiliating kind of relationship that is often implied in personnel advertisements can in our opinion be avoided.

How do applicants make their choices?

Several models have been developed to explain how the choices of jobs are made by applicants. We describe the three main models.

The first model starts from the assumption that there is not enough information available to be really in a position to make a choice. The applicants make an unprogrammed choice. The choice is based on only a few critical factors or contacts. These elements will determine the choice of the applicants (Soelberg, 1967).

The second model postulates that one will choose a job and an organization which corresponds to the self-image (Tom, 1971). Emotional factors play the most important role in this model.

The third model is based on the expectancy theory of Vroom (1966). Applicants take into account different elements. The utility and probability of the elements will determine the choice.

These three models have retained the attention of researchers. However, none seems to be really superior to the others. Maybe the different choice of models fit with different kinds of persons but no research data are available to support this view. This leaves us with an important question unanswered. Depending on the model, different recruitment channels should be chosen. Also the content and the form of personnel advertisements is dependent on the model we assume. Further research of these implicit or explicit assumptions is needed.

Results of the recruitment process

A recruitment process results in a certain quantity and quality of applicants. We may have a large quantity of applicants, but not the required quality. Did we attract the right persons? The result will indicate if we did a proper job. The results of the different recruitment campaigns could teach us a lot about the success of our assumptions and our operationalizations. In a subsequent campaign these results can be taken into account. It is amazing, however, that almost no data are registered or analysed. For the past few years in the Netherlands a prize has been awarded to the most creative personnel advertisement. Some personnel directors questioned the effectiveness of these creative personnel advertisements: their question remained unanswered. We asked newspapers of different European countries for information about research on the effectiveness of personnel advertisement. Not one could give a reference to any systematic research. Although each year several millions are spent in recruitment campaigns, no one seems to bother about the effectiveness and efficiency of the money spent. In a recent research about campus recruitment we were confronted with this same attitude: the companies suppose the campaign results in hiring some people, but there is no search for more information on the impact of the different recruitment channels or on the costs.

We hope that research on this topic may help to change the rigid recruitment procedures that are used in many companies nowadays.

EVALUATION OF RECRUITMENT CHANNELS

Only a few studies have tried to compare the effectiveness (measured as the turnover of the employees) of different recruitment channels. Table 1 presents the results of these studies. As we can see the informal recruitment channels are superior to personnel advertising. There are two possible explanations offered in the literature.

Table 1: Turnover (%) as a function of recruitment channel

Author	Reference of employees	Spontaneous application	Advertising
Breaugh and Mann (1984)	17	13	24
Decker and Cornelius (1979)	22	30	32
Gannon (1971)	26	29	39
Reid (1972)	61	75	84
Ullmann (1966)	28	–	74

The first one is the realistic job preview. People recruited through personnel advertisements have much too high expectations about their job. Those expectations are not countered by the recruiters, in order not to lose candidates. People recruited by the informal channels have a much more realistic idea about what their job will be. Where entering the job will cause a reality shock for the first category, this will not happen for the latter one.

The second explanation is based on individual differences. The recruitment channels have a different effect on different groups. Research (Taylor and Schmidt, 1985) indicates that younger people gather more information through personnel advertisements and that turnover is higher for younger people. The kind of recruitment channel is not responsible for the turnover, but rather the kind of people using that recruitment channel.

The truth may be in between. Realistic job previews fulfil the need of participants to receive honest and adequate information. For one group this information is more important than for the other. For younger people without work experience, honest information is really important to avoid dissatisfaction with the job. Experienced workers have a more accurate image about what they may expect of a new job.

In our research we found that around 30 per cent of the population is searching actively for another job. This percentage is similar to other studies about mobility in Flanders. Personnel advertising is an important medium; family ties and other relations form an even more important way of looking for another job. The least important way is spontaneous application. Nevertheless some large companies rely almost exclusively on this recruitment channel. Other companies on the contrary don't believe in this form of recruitment and prefer personnel advertisements. What is the effectiveness of this form of recruitment? Our research and results will be discussed in the following sections.

THE EFFECTIVENESS OF PERSONNEL ADVERTISEMENTS

Based on the model presented above, research should focus on the applicants as well as on organizations. The first part of the research has its focus on the expectations and the reading behaviour of the applicants. The second part concerns the effectiveness as seen from the organization's point of view.

Questions in the first part are:

– What do applicants expect to find in a personnel advertisement?
– What are their preferences concerning the format of the advertisement?
– What do they remember of the advertisement? Which advertisements do they remember?
– What is the reading behaviour of applicants?
– What are the experiences of applicants with personnel advertisements?

Questions in the second part are:

– What is the response to different personnel advertisements?
– Can the differences be explained by variables such as colour, content, format, . . . ?
– Is there an evolution over time of the characteristics of personnel advertisements?
– Are there important differences between European countries?

The structure of the whole research programme may be summarized in the scheme shown in Figure 2.

We present below, in a systematic way, the results of our research.

The expectations and experiences of the applicants

A representative group of 400 potential applicants were interviewed to reveal

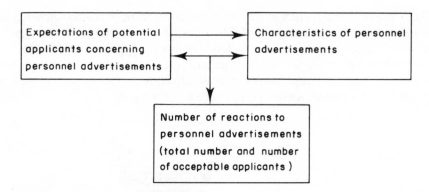

Figure 2   General structure of the research project

their expectations about advertisements and asked for their experiences with personnel advertisements. For the content and form characteristics we used a questionnaire with the possible characteristics. They were asked to indicate the importance of the several characteristics.

Expectations about the content

Figure 3 shows the results of the importance of the several elements. Most importance is attached to the functional requirements, then to the job title and location; followed by the title of the organization. At least in Belgium a lot of personnel advertisements still appear without mentioning the name of the organization. This is clearly not what the applicants want to see.

Figure 3   Expectations about the content of personnel advertisements

Expectations about the form

Figure 4 presents the results of the expectations of form characteristics. It seems that a clear structure is appreciated. The possibility of recognizing the organization quickly also seems important. This confirms what we have stated above about the name of the organization. Further research, based on depth interviews, showed that potential applicants complain strongly about the lack of structure and factual information within personnel advertisements.

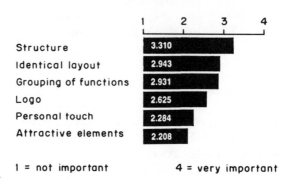

Figure 4   Expectations about the form characteristic of personnel advertisements

Perception of personnel advertisements

We presented four pages of job advertisements in a newspaper to the potential applicants. Afterwards we asked for the elements they could remember. Names of organizations are best remembered, followed by the functional requirements. Form characteristics are mentioned only by half of the persons.

Further research shows other results. In a still ongoing research project we use eye movement measurement to analyse the reading pattern of personnel advertisements. From a first analysis the job title seems to be the element to decide on to move to the next advertisement, and not the organization. Afterwards the persons are asked for which organizations they would like to work or not to work; and which job they would be willing to do or not to do. The respondents had less difficulty in answering the question about the job, than the question about the organization. These results suggest that the importance of the job title in personnel advertisements may be underestimated, while the corporate image may be overestimated.

Experiences with personnel advertisements

We asked also for the experiences in real life with personnel advertising.

Personnel advertisements are accused of sometimes being incomplete and confusing. A small percentage is convinced that personnel advertisements are used sometimes only for marketing purposes. These opinions were confirmed by later research about the perception of personnel advertisements of commercial personnel. They quote the advertisement as the most incomplete channel for communication between organizations and applicants. They expected that personnel advertisements would give much more factual data in a structured way. Nowadays, more attention is given to the phrasing and the design than to the content.

What determines the success of personnel advertisements?

We analysed 800 advertisements of a national newspaper on form and content characteristics. The scoring instrument was similar to the questionnaire presented to the potential applicants, in order to be able to make comparisons between both parts of the research.

From the companies we enquired the number of responses to the advertisement. We also asked what was the number of useful responses, in the sense that the organization replied to them.

On the basis of these two sets of data we were able to investigate the relationship between advertisement characteristics and the number of reactions.

Description of the characteristics of the personnel advertisements

The 800 advertisements were a representative sample for that newspaper; 82 per cent used a logo and a standardized layout. In that period only five used colour; 45 per cent also placed the same advertisement in other newspapers or journals; 80 per cent were advertisements for only one function.

The personnel advertisements contained the following content characteristics:

- 4.81 elements about functional requirements such as age, education, past experiences;
- 3.29 elements about the organization such as size, organizational culture;
- 2.76 elements about the selection procedure such as use of psychological testing, written or oral responses;
- 1.1 elements about what the organization offers as salary, fringe benefits, training possibilities.

As already mentioned above, it is clear that companies ask much but have little to offer. The applicant is put in a subordinate role and is not considered as a future partner.

The number of reactions

We found 34 responses on average for each advertisement: 13 of these are quoted by the companies as useful, which means that 21 responses are not further considered. This is quite a lot, certainly if we think that the potential applicants expect an answer from the company. A lot of work has to be done to ensure good public relations. If one were able to lower the number of unwanted responses, a lot of money would be saved.

The influence of the labour market

The labour market plays an important role in the number of responses. The attractiveness of some functions is much higher than for others. Administrative, staff and service functions score high; the technical functions attract fewer responses. Also the sector has an influence: most responses are found within agriculture, education and distribution. There was no influence of the geographical situation of the company. However, we have to take into account that Flanders is very limited in area. Different response rates are to be expected in other nations.

The AIDA model: a way of explaining our results

The model gives us the possibility of presenting our results in a structured way. First, we consider those features which influence attention to the advertisement. Some characteristics of the media choice have an influence. The more media in which the advertisement is published, the more responses, *but* the number of *acceptable* applicants doesn't follow (Figure 5).

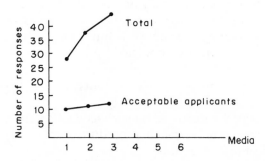

Figure 5   Number of responses as a function of media

However, we have to realize that the companies themselves defined how many responses were acceptable ones. One can argue that at a certain level, around twelve, one stops, because accepting more will cause more work than profit. If there are only a few applicants, one will lower his criterion of acceptability. The criticism that the number of acceptable applicants is artificial may be right, but we didn't see another way around this problem.

The belief that the position of the advertisement (which page and where on that page) is very important is not found to be true. Many persons, certainly those employed in advertising agencies, have a hard time to accept these results. In the follow-up study with the eye-movement camera we try to find an explanation for this result. One possible explanation is that the involvement with the topic is too high; marketing research indicates that a high degree of involvement decreases the influence of attention.

The size of the personnel advertisement has a significant influence on the number of responses.

Also, the use of colour gives more responses. We have to remember that colour was only rarely used. With more use of colour, this relationship may disappear.

Two content characteristics act as repressor variables. The functional requirements have a selective effect; if the selective effect preselects the unacceptable applicants, there is no problem. If, however, persons lose interest in a function because of a wrong description of the functional requirements, one will lose acceptable applicants.

The information about the organization has the same effect, and the same reasoning is valid here.

Information about the selection procedure sometimes has a negative influence. For some more technically oriented professions we found a negative correlation between the information about the selection procedure and the number of responses.

These findings demonstrate the importance of a careful preparation of the advertisements. Nowadays, one sometimes has the impression that the phrasing gets more attention than the content.

An important influence of the nature of the company's offer on the number of responses was found. We mentioned above that these elements are rarely used. In Belgium one will seldom mention the salary; also the fringe benefits are described in a general way. This leaves already working applicants with a problem: they might see a function they would be willing to apply for, but they have almost no information on the conditions the company offers. They may think: 'I will not be better off, so I'll stay with my job'. Thus one loses an acceptable applicant.

Based on these conclusions a consultant in selection tried to convince a client to give more information on the conditions the company offers. The client refused. The advertisement was published, with not one acceptable response. Two weeks later, the same advertisement reappeared, but mentioned, for example that there was a company car (this was not a change in policy, but only a statement of policy) and several acceptable responses came in. It seems logical that if I have a company car in my present job, and I am not certain to have one in my next job, I may decide not to apply for the job.

CONCLUSIONS: WHO CHOOSES WHOM? THE DIFFICULT ENCOUNTER BETWEEN RECRUITER AND APPLICANT

Summarizing the results of the different research projects it seems that several expectations of applicants are realized within the present personnel advertisements. As our research was carried out only in Flanders, one must be careful in generalizing the results. Comparing the pages of personnel advertisements in other European countries taught us that there are important differences. The purpose of the conclusions is to point at the important elements in the mostly unequal and therefore often difficult relation between recruiter and applicant.

Most advertisements are well structured and may quickly be recognized, e.g. through the use of a logo. Content characteristics such as the name of the organization and the job title make it easy for the applicant to make a first choice reading through the large number of personnel advertisements.

Once attention was guided to the advertisement, the following phase of the process starts. Potential applicants expect in the first place extensive information about the functional requirements. Second, they look for information about the organization. The research on effectiveness shows that as long as the information gathered by the applicants is in line with their desires, they will read further. If they meet information different from their desires, they stop the process. The encounter is ended. The interest of the applicant becomes stimulated or depressed by this content information. This stresses the importance of careful preparation of this information. The research on effectiveness of recruitment channels indicates that showing only the good side of these elements will have negative outcomes for the long term.

But attention and even desire is not enough. Action, certainly for persons who have a job, is dependent on what the organization is ready to invest in the applicant. In most cases this information is almost non-existent, although it seems to be crucial. Information about the selection procedure sometimes has a negative influence.

Asking for experience with advertisements taught us that many applicants are sceptical about their first encounter with the organization. Maybe their expectations are too high; on the other hand the implicit power relation with the organization as the strong partner results in applicants being sceptical. Is this a good start for making a psychological contract between future partners? Although these results will be different in other European countries we think that reflection about the assumptions underlying the recruitment process is needed, not only for the good of the applicant, but also for the organization itself.

Our future research will have to confirm or disconfirm the present results. The findings of the present studies do not reveal the psychological processes involved in the encounter between applicant and potential employer. We gave an interpretation which needs to be tested.

The studies point at elements which have an influence on effectiveness. Practitioners may draw their lessons out of these results. Furthermore, we have suggested that the assumptions underlying this encounter and relationship have to be reconsidered. If one advocates partnership and psychological contract, the personnel advertisement in general will need serious changes.

REFERENCES

Breaugh, J.A., and Mann, R.B. (1984). Recruiting sources effects of the alternative explanations, *Journal of Occupational Psychology*, **57**, 261–7.

Decker, J.D., and Cornelius, E.T. (1979). A note on recruiting sources and job survival rates, *Journal of Applied Psychology*, **64**, 463–4.

De Witte, K., and Vermeylen, R. (1986). Effectiviteit van personeelsadvertenties, Vlaamse Uitgeversmaatschappij, Brussel.

Gannon, M.J. (1971). Sources of referral and employee turnover, *Journal of Applied Psychology*, **55**, 226–8.

Premack, S.L., and Wanous, J.P. (1985). A meta-analysis of realistic job preview experiments, *Journal of Applied Psychology*, **70**, 706–19.

Reid, G.L. (1972). Job search and the effectiveness of job-finding methods, *Industrial and Labor Relations Review*, **25**, 479–95.

Soelberg, P.O. (1967). Unprogrammed decision making, *Industrial Management Review*, **8**, 19–29.

Taylor, S., and Schmidt, D.W. (1985). A process-oriented investigation of recruitment source effectiveness, *Personnel Psychology*, **36**, 343–54.

Tom, V.T. (1971). The role of personality and organizational images in the recruiting process, *Organizational Behavior and Human Performance*, **6**, 573–92.

Ulmann, J.C. (1966). Employee referrals: prime tools for recruiting workers, *Personnel*, **43**, 30–5.

Vroom, V.H. (1966). Organizational choice: a study of pre- and post-decision processes, *Organizational Behavior and Human Performance*, **1**, 212–25.

Chapter 2.5

Interactions with Clients in Personnel Selection

PETER HERRIOT

Department of Occupational Psychology, Birkbeck College, University of London, Malet Street, London WC1E 7HX, UK

SELECTION AS A SOCIAL PROCESS

Incautious readers might come to a mistaken conclusion from some of the chapters in this book. They might believe that selection consists of one or more assessment tools producing evidence upon the basis of which the organization takes a decision regarding individual applicants or employees. This is but a small part of the picture. Neither selection nor promotion procedures typically result in single decision points. Rather, they consist of a series of episodes in time, during or at the end of each of which a decision may be made. These episodes may be very impersonal (pre-selection by paper sift) or highly personal (the one-to-one interview). Moreover, these decisions are not taken only by the organization, for there are two parties involved. The individual is also making decisions: whether to apply; to attend for interview, test, or assessment centre; to accept a job offer or a position move (Herriot, 1989).

In sum, assessment cannot be theorized as though it were an instance of information processing and decision making. Rather, it must be considered as part of a social relationship in real time between organization and individual (Lofquist and Dawis, 1969; DeWolff and Van den Bosch, 1984).

Certain conclusions logically follow from this approach. We must not focus narrowly in this chapter upon the impact upon an individual of an organization's rejection of him or her, important though that may be for the applicant. Rather, we must consider the ways in which the applicants' views of themselves and of the organization continuously change as a function of their experiences during

Assessment and Selection in Organizations   Edited by P. Herriot
© 1989 John Wiley & Sons Ltd

the different episodes. It is these perceptions of self and of organization which determine whether the applicant remains in relationship with the organization, and what the quality of that relationship is to be. From this point of view, the assessment procedure, even during the selection process, is not to be seen as a hurdle over which applicants must jump before they can enter into any relationship with the organization. On the contrary, the psychological contract is being formed between the two parties even before an employment contract is offered.

How does this process occur? It is essentially a reciprocal exchange, in which the two parties send messages about what they expect. From the applicants' point of view, the organization gives out indications about how it expects them to act. These expectations may be communicated explicitly and intentionally, for example in an advertisement or a recruitment brochure. Or, they may be inferred by the applicant from the organization's behaviour. For example, the application form might contain intrusive questions, from which the potential applicant might conclude that her private life would not be her own. These expectations which the organization communicates refer to how the applicant should behave during the selection procedure as well as in the job.

As the episodes of the selection procedure unfold one after the other, the applicants receive more and more messages upon which to base their perceptions of how the organization expects them to behave. These messages may well be contradictory ones. For example, the recruitment brochure may give an impression of an almost continuously interesting and responsible job, whereas a subsequent realistic in-tray exercise in the final stage of the procedure indicates that it involves a lot of tedious routine as well. Or the interviewer might say at the beginning of the interview that it is the applicant's chance to find out more about the job, but react impatiently if he or she interrupts the sequence of questions with his or her own. Nevertheless, despite these often contradictory messages, applicants will over time be coming to firmer conclusions about what the organization expects them to do.

However, during the course of the selection procedure, the applicants will have been taking decisions already. The decision to complete an application form, for example, may have been taken solely on the basis of reading a recruitment brochure and the application form itself. It follows that decisions early in the procedure are often taken on the basis of misperceptions of the organization's expectations. Applicants may have an excessively rosy view of the job; or they may mistakenly believe that the purpose of the interview is to see how they react when put under pressure.

How are such decisions taken? Consciously or unconsciously, applicants match what they believe the organization expects of them with their own expectations for themselves. These expectations will concern, for example, the tasks they will be expected to perform; other aspects of their role, for example, how they project the organization's image to clients; the degree of commitment and lifestyle involved; their rewards and career development opportunities; their degree of autonomy and responsibility. There is evidence that applicants prefer those organizations which they believe resemble their view of themselves (Tom, 1971). They may perceive the organization's expectations as congruent with their own, in which case they will have no difficulty in accepting an invitation to proceed further in the selection procedure. Or, they may feel there to be some incongruence. For example, they may not wish to have to be mobile throughout Europe in the first two years of employment, as the organization appears to expect. Or, they may find themselves expected to submit to a lengthy personality test without any explanation or prospect of feedback.

There are alternative ways of dealing with such incongruence. An applicant may regretfully refuse the offer of the European job, or opt not to take the personality test, thereby effectively ruling himself or herself out of contention. In these cases, the applicant has broken off the relationship. Alternatively, the applicant may change his or her own expectations to make them more congruent with those of the organization; he or she may accept the mobility requirement or the personality test as reasonable expectations in the circumstances. Finally, the applicant may try to change the organization's expectations. Only those in a powerful negotiating position in terms of the labour market or having a highly developed degree of self-efficacy are likely to attempt such a strategy. Figure 1 presents a model of this decision process.

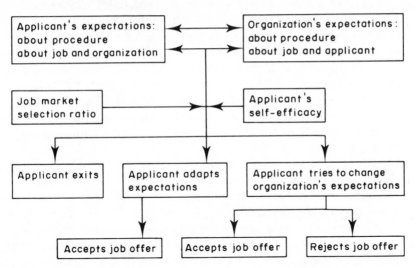

Figure 1   Applicants' decisions

SELF-CONCEPT, SELF-EFFICACY, AND SELF-ESTEEM

Such a decision model implies that applicants use their perceptions of themselves and their own expectations against which to match their perceptions of the organization's expectations. The self-concept fulfils several psychological functions (Markus and Wurf, 1987). It enables us to assess our own aptitudes and abilities in comparison with those of others. In particular, we are good at assessing our own relative strengths and weaknesses, as is demonstrated by the lesser halo effect found in self-ratings than in supervisor ratings. If, therefore, we have a relatively accurate picture of our abilities, we can match organizational expectations of the skills required to our own capacities, and base decisions about our capability for the job on the degree of congruence between the two. Now psychological tests of aptitude and ability are among the most reliable and valid sources of information available about our capacities (Hunter and Hunter, 1984). Organizations which administer such tests during their selection procedures will be helping applicants to take rational decisions if they inform them of the results.

Another function of the self-concept relates more to specific situations. Bandura (1986) suggests that we evaluate our own performance in particular tasks or situations by various criteria. We see what the outcome is, and judge our success by our own standards or by how others respond to our efforts. The result is a sense of self-efficacy, the belief that we are capable of acting in such a way as to achieve desired results. Such 'self-efficacy' may refer to a belief that we can do well in a selection or promotion procedure, or that we are capable of performing the technical function that the organization expects of us. Perhaps a degree of favourable bias towards oneself may be both a requirement for high self-efficacy and self-esteem and the price for achieving it.

Clearly, organizations and their representatives have it in their power to affect the self-efficacy of applicants for selection or candidates for promotion. For example, they can emphasize from the beginning that very few from among the large number of applicants will be selected. They can give off signals during interview that they believe the applicant to be unsuitable. They can so promote an image of organizational excellence that the applicant will believe herself incapable of living up to that image. Obviously, a lowering of the applicant's confidence that she is capable of getting through the selection procedure or of doing the job successfully is likely to affect an applicant's decision whether to stay in the selection procedure or to quit it. It is also likely to affect the number of applicants as the word gets around.

Finally, self-efficacy refers to the belief that we are capable of the actions required to achieve success in particular situations; self-esteem refers to our overall evaluation of ourselves. In the assessment or selection situation, failure on one occasion may merely decrease our belief in our ability to satisfy the requirements of one organization—a matter of specific self-efficacy. Alternatively, we can attribute our failure to the inadequacy of that organization's selection procedure or to the excellence of the competition (Weiner, 1985). This is easy for those with an external locus of control (Rotter, 1966), who prefer to attribute what happens to them to outside events or other people. It is much harder for those with an internal locus, who credit themselves with their 'successes', but, by the same token, blame themselves for their 'failures'. Anyway, repeated failures may be harder to blame on others. And decrease in different specific self-efficacies will lead to lowered general self-esteem. If these failures are to obtain internal promotion, then an employee's motivation and commitment to the organization are likely to be affected, apart from his or her psychological well-being. If they fail to be initially selected into an organization, then applicants may be discouraged from any further applications and feel so worthless as to be unemployable (Warr, 1987).

To sum up, an assessment procedure can affect applicants in several ways. It can give them an idea of what that organization expects of them, both in terms of the selection procedure itself and of the requirements of the job for which they are applying. It can, often inadvertently, give clues as to how well the organization will treat applicants once they become employees. It can indicate an evaluation of applicants, thereby possibly affecting their self-assessment, specifically their self-efficacy and self-esteem. All of these types of influence will affect the applicants' decisions whether to remain in the procedure or quit. They may also in their turn affect the organization's decisions reciprocally. For example, the organization may decrease an applicant's self-efficacy by indicating how hard it is to get into so prestigious a company. This may render the applicant less likely to be selected, since confidence and motivation are often selection criteria, especially at interview. Female applicants are most likely to suffer as a result, since their self-efficacy is likely to be lower on average to start with. Consequences of assessment procedures may reach wider than applicants' or organizations' decisions. They can affect applicants' self-esteem and hence their general well-being. And they can reduce the number of applicants, by being realistic about the jobs they are offering, or by becoming known for unreasonable, intrusive, or unfair assessment procedures. Figure 2 presents a model of effects upon the applicant's self-concept.

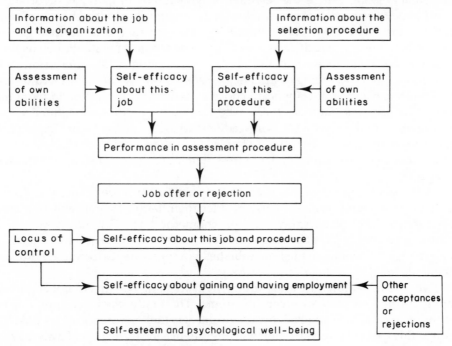

Figure 2　Effects of selection on applicants

THE ELEMENTS OF THE SELECTION PROCEDURE

Now that we have analysed the process overall, we can examine what we know about the effects of particular selection instruments from the research literature.

First, let us consider the recruitment phase: advertisements, brochures, and other sources of information about the job. Premack and Wanous (1985) performed a meta-analysis of 20 studies of the effects of realistic job previews. They found that such information lowered applicants' optimistic expectations of what the job would be like, and as a consequence increased the probability of their leaving the selection procedure voluntarily before employment. However, those that remained and started work demonstrated higher commitment, job satisfaction, and performance, and were *less* likely to leave their jobs than those who had had no such preview. This approach is in marked contrast to attempts to maximize the size of the applicant pool so as to have more chance of selecting 'the best'. The means to attain this latter objective is to paint as attractive a picture of the organization as possible.

Moving on to the selection procedure itself, the way in which the interview is conducted has a major effect upon applicants. In those situations where there are clear differences between the jobs on offer, applicants are likely to accept or reject them on the basis of such characteristics of the job as challenge, opportunities, and variety (Powell, 1984). However, where there is not much to differentiate between jobs, the way the recruiter behaves is of paramount importance (Rynes and Miller, 1983). Where the recruiter is sympathetic in manner, he or she is considered to be a better representative of the organization. However, applicants differ in the extent to which they think interviewers are typical of the organization. When they are perceived as very typical, then their sympathetic behaviour is much more likely to lead to the applicant accepting a job offer (Harn and Thornton, 1985). According to student job-seekers' own reports, the recruiter was the major reason that the applicant chose a particular organization in more that one-third of cases (Glueck, 1973). The applicants particularly influenced by recruiters were those with the best academic records and most work experience. Since the interview is often the first episode in the selection process when the applicant meets an organizational representative face to face, its impact is hard to exaggerate.

As far as job-sample exercises and assessment centres are concerned, applicants for trades and technical jobs consider them fairer, clearer, and of a more appropriate level of difficulty than psychometric tests (Schmidt *et al.*, 1977). Managers certainly pay attention to the outcomes of assessment centre exercises, and change their views of their own abilities as a consequence (Schmitt, Ford, and Stults, 1986).

Two general features are also prominent in affecting whether or not applicants apply in the first place or accept job offers. The first is their perception of the labour market (Liden and Parsons, 1986) and also their perception of how likely it is that this particular organization will offer them a job (Rynes and Lawler, 1983). The second is whether they perceive the organization to have invaded their privacy during the selection procedure (Fusilier and Hoyer, 1980). Only if applicants feel they have some control over personal information and the use to which it is put will they feel secure.

IMPLICATIONS FOR ORGANIZATIONAL PRACTICE

While psychological research has concentrated little upon the impact of selection and assessment procedures on applicants, organizational practice has made some faltering steps in the right direction. However, much more rapid progress will have to be made if the likely decrease in qualified human resources demographically predicted in the early 1990s (at least in the United Kingdom) is to be coped with. Individual organizations are certainly taking worthy initiatives. For example, one major retail organization in the United Kingdom runs an assessment centre procedure for informational rather than selective purposes, reasoning that graduates are likely to have little understanding of retail management.

Such isolated steps are not enough. It is only when organizations accept a different overall perspective to that advocated by many psychologists that significant and pervasive improvements will be made. Individuals will know what is expected of them, and be less likely to leave because their own expectations are disappointed. They will be committed to the organization because it has shared information with them and agreed a psychological contract with them. The organization will run less risk of being rejected by applicants to whom it has made job offers, and of being sued by those who believe they have been treated unfairly or suffered harm. It will enjoy better industrial relations, and it will probably spend less on its selection procedures since more applicants will self-select out at an early stage. If an organization does start to construe the selection process as a mutual exchange of information to facilitate both parties' decision making rather than as an obstacle course which applicants have to negotiate, then certain implications for practice necessarily follow.

- First, organizations have to tell potential applicants right at the beginning what the job is really like; not just its tasks, but the lifestyle involved, the organizational culture, and so forth. This can be done by a variety of methods, including written or filmed case studies, the opportunity to ask questions of a current jobholder, the opportunity to do job-sample exercises, the description of some typical organizational careers.
- Next, they have to explain what it is they are looking for in applicants. They have to describe and justify the leap from job to person specification.
- Then, they have to describe in detail the selection procedure itself. They have to explain why particular methods are necessary and appropriate tools of assessment, relating them back to the person specification. They also need to go through the unspoken rules of the procedures, so as to avoid the danger of rejecting an applicant because he or she is unfamiliar with the rules of the game. Applicants may be rejected, for example, because they fail to fill in the application form as expected rather than as a result of what it contains. Of vital importance is the clarification of the purpose of each episode. If it is to be used to inform the applicants, they need to know this and to feel confident that they are not being assessed at the same time.
- Applicants have to be assured of the confidentiality of the information they

have provided. They need to be informed what will be done with it, and who will have access to it.

- They also should be told of the outcomes of the assessment procedures, and where appropriate have them explained. Applicants benefit from finding out more about themselves as well as about the job, the organization, and the procedure. Tools of assessment differ in terms of the extent to which applicants can tell from their performance alone, in the absence of feedback, how well they are doing. What is certain is that they are anxious to know, and will search for clues in the situation. For example, one of the consequences of a friendly and responsive interviewer is that applicants believe they are more likely to be selected (Rynes and Miller, 1983). Such searching for meaning should be unnecessary. Applicants have been providing information to organizations to enable assessment to be made. If they are told the outcomes of that assessment, they can match these against the personnel requirements for the job, which they should already have been told. A mismatch will enable them to self-select out, thereby avoiding the cost of being rejected by the organization. Moreover, they may incorporate the results of the assessment into their self-concept, so enabling themselves to make more informed decisions.
- The organization should allocate a contact person with whom applicants can get in touch whenever they wish during the course of the selection procedure. This person should not be involved in the assessment itself, and should ensure that applicants are satisfied with the procedure.

Now for some general points:

- It is incumbent upon the organization to supply all of this information rather than upon the applicant to ask for it. Applicants may well feel that asking too many questions will annoy the organization and decrease their chances of selection. Conventionally, the organization is in the more powerful position; its omission or refusal to inform may perhaps result in applicants rejecting it, but the applicant's refusal to provide information for assessment purposes is much more likely to have fatal consequences for the relationship.
- It is also worth noting that the information sought by organizations is usually for assessment purposes. However, from our theoretical analysis it is clear that they would benefit from getting to know what applicants' expectations of the selection procedure are. Some aspects of the selection procedure, for example, may be so contrary to what applicants are prepared to undergo that any increased predictive power may be offset by an increase in job offer rejections. Organizations are beginning to realize that being rejected by applicants whom they have selected can be costly (Murphy, 1986).
- Furthermore, information about what applicants expect of the job can be very useful too. Certainly, there is evidence that campus recruiters are not good judges of what students want from a job (Posner, 1981). If organizations did obtain this information, then they could adapt their initial induction and training procedures so as to move towards an integration of their own and the applicant's expectations. Even if they are not willing to adapt in such a way,

they could at the very least design their informational literature so as to correct the false expectations which they now know are held by applicants. Adaptation of induction procedures or of literature is likely to result in lower turnover.

– However, the implications of the theoretical model for practice do not solely relate to the giving of information. It is the overall design of recruitment and selection systems which is also of concern. If the process is essentially a social and communicative relationship between the parties, then it will proceed most effectively if they take it in turns to provide information. Since decisions are being made as a consequence of each communicative episode, this reciprocal design means that both parties can take more informed decisions throughout the procedure. It means also that more ways of communicating organizational expectations will have to be developed. With the recent developments in forms of distance communication this need not be as difficult or costly as the setting up of face-to-face interaction.

– A broader concept of utility than that currently in fashion is necessary to evaluate recruitment procedures. For example, the costs of particular selection devices should include estimates of the number of applicants who exit as a consequence of being expected to take them. The benefits of reducing turnover should be emphasized as well as the improvements in performance. And some assessment of the benefits of gaining a reputation as a considerate employer should not be omitted.

– The final implication of the theoretical perspective we have outlined is that organizations cannot afford to ignore the context of their assessment and selection procedures. The job market in the light of demographic trends, the changing perceptions of the rights of the individual, the increasing variety in the nature of employment contracts are all having profound effects upon the responses of applicants.

REFERENCES

Bandura, A. (1986). *Social Foundations of Thought and Action*. Prentice-Hall, Englewood Cliffs, New Jersey.

Dodd, W.E. (1977). Attitudes towards assessment centre programs, in J.L. Moses and W. C. Byham (eds), *Applying the Assessment Centre Method*. Pergamon, New York.

Fusilier, M.R., and Hoyer, W.D. (1980). Variables affecting perceptions of invasion of privacy in a personnel selection situation, *Journal of Applied Psychology*, **65**, 623–6.

Glueck, W.F. (1973). Recruiters and executives: How do they affect job choice? *Journal of College Placement*, **33**, 77–8.

Harn, T.J., and Thornton, G.C. (1985). Recruiter counselling behaviours and applicant impressions, *Journal of Occupational Psychology*, **58**, 57–65.

Herriot, P. (1989). Selection as a social process, in M. Smith and I.T. Robertson (eds), *Advances in Personnel Selection and Assessment*. Wiley, Chichester.

Hunter, J.E., and Hunter, R.F. (1984). Validity and utility of alternative predictors of job performance, *Psychological Bulletin*, **96**, 72–98.

Liden, R.C., and Parsons, C.K. (1986). A field-study of job applicant interview perceptions, alternative opportunities, and demographic characteristics, *Personnel Psychology*, **39**, 109–22.

Lofquist, L.H. and Dawis, R.V. (1969). *Adjustment to Work*, Appleton, New York.

Markus, H., and Wurf, E. (1987). The dynamic self-concept: A social psychological perspective, *Annual Review of Psychology*, **38**, 299–337.

Murphy, K.R. (1986). When your top choice turns you down: Effect of rejected offers on the utility of selection tests, *Psychological Bulletin*, **99**, 133–8.

Posner, B.Z. (1981). Comparing recruiter, student, and faculty perceptions of important applicant and job characteristics, *Personnel Psychology*, **34**, 329–40.

Powell, G. (1984). Effects of job attributes and recruiting practices on applicant decisions: A comparison, *Personnel Psychology*, **37**, 721–31.

Premack, S.L., and Wanous, J.P. (1985). A meta-analysis of realistic job preview experiments, *Journal of Applied Psychology*, **70**, 706–19.

Rotter, J. (1966). Generalised expectancies for internal versus external control of reinforcement, *Psychological Monographs*, **80**, 609.

Rynes, S.L., and Lawler, J. (1983). A policy-capturing investigation of the role of expectancies in decisions to pursue job alternatives. *Journal of Applied Psychology*, **68**, 620–31.

Rynes, S.L., and Miller, H.E. (1983). Recruiter and job influences on candidates for employment, *Journal of Applied Psychology*, **68**, 147–54.

Schmidt, F.L., Greenthal, A.L., Hunter, J.E., Berner, J.G., and Seaton, F.W. (1977). Job samples versus paper and pencil trades and technical tests: Adverse impact and examinee attitudes, *Personnel Psychology*, **30**, 187–97.

Schmitt, N., Ford, J.K., and Stults, D.M. (1986). Changes in self-perceived ability as a function of performance in an assessment centre, *Journal of Occupational Psychology*, **59**, 327–35.

Tom, V.R. (1971). The role of personality and organisational images in the recruiting process, *Organisational Behaviour and Human Performance*, **6**, 573–92.

Warr, P.B. (1987). Workers without a job, in P. B. Warr (ed.), *Psychology at Work*, 3rd edn. Penguin, Harmondsworth.

Weiner, B. (1985). 'Spontaneous' causal thinking, *Psychological Bulletin*, **97**, 74–84.

Chapter 2.6

The Organization of a Psychological Consultancy

DAVID ARIS

Adviesbureau Psychotechniek, Drift 10, 3512 BS Utrecht, The Netherlands

INTRODUCTION

This chapter addresses the organization of personnel selection activities as they are developed by a psychological consultancy. These activities are difficult to define. The best approach is typecasting. But then it is difficult to specify the rules for an organizational structure. To overcome this problem it seemed useful to define a psychological consultancy with well specified products. In this way the organizational problems can be made more explicit. Luckily in the end it will turn out that the same principles will apply to a less structured type of consultancy.

As an example of a product-oriented consultancy an existing consultancy in the Netherlands has been chosen. That it is a consultancy to which the writer has been connected is not a complete coincidence. Still it is typical for a group of at least twenty of such consultancies in the Netherlands.

The main activity is psychological testing of candidates for specific functions in organizations (government and private enterprise). That forms two-thirds of the activities. The remaining one-third is a miscellaneous group of activities centred about two focus points: recruitment and general consultancy on psychological problems.

Psychological testing is a well structured type of activity with specific organizational problems which can be described more systematically. In the following description we will mainly focus on these problems.

Assessment and Selection in Organizations   Edited by P. Herriot
© 1989 John Wiley & Sons Ltd

THE START

Anyone setting up a psychological consultancy will quickly discover that the possibilities for putting one's relevant knowledge into practice are largely dependent on one's capacity to attract clients. At the outset, acquisition is crucial. Newcomers in the market will find that opportunism is the only strategy offering any hope of survival. By this we mean that one's own insights and beliefs about how the (potential) client should operate have to be made subordinate to the wishes and insights of the client, and also that no solutions can be presented if the client's confidence has not been won first. This confidence has to be based on the client's feeling that he is understood, and on the adviser's recognizing that reaching a new situation can only take place gradually, in small steps. Common sense and empathy are the major weapons with which the new adviser enters the fray.

The organization of consultants' activities bears all the characteristics of their way of working. There is no semblance of structure in their working hours. The products of their work will also reveal a wide variation. Certainly, in the beginning, many hours will have to be spent in getting work, so that many hours will be unpaid. Office organization, research, investment and other necessary activities will also reveal a pronounced *ad hoc* character.

In the initial years, the consultancy's most important assets will be formed by the confidential relationship it builds up with a more or less stable clientele. The personality of the adviser is crucial for this. The office itself has little value without the adviser who enjoys the confidence of the clients. Gradually, the prestige acquired will make it possible to draw clearer contours around the nature of the problems for which advice is offered, and the manner in which it is offered. The working methods and knowledge of the consultancy will tend to start becoming standardized. There is, however, still a long way to go before the confidence enjoyed by the original adviser among his other clients can be transferred to the quality of the consultancy's advice and way of working. The latter is necessary, though, if the consultancy is to experience further growth. Otherwise, new members of staff would have to follow the same path as the person who originally set up the consultancy.

Due to the working methods and knowledge being standardized, new members of staff can rapidly be trained to reach the same level. It is not, however, their personal reputation which smooths the path in this, but the reputation of the working methods and knowledge of the consultancy. As new staff members join, there will also be an increasing need to regulate activities. Working hours, payment, achievement: i.e. number of hours of advice given at a certain rate, office organization, administration, documentation and research will all gradually gain form. For a fully mature consultancy the way in which these various activities take place will determine what its prestige is on the market. The identity of the consultancy depends on its products and their effectiveness. In the end, the consultancy itself is better known than its staff members or its founder.

There is an enormous distance between the founder/improviser and the established consultancy with a reputation concerning the products it delivers. The two extremes in terms of structure each require their own working methods. In describing the organization of a psychological consultancy, one must realize that neither of these extremes is actually very stable. Dynamism and stability alone are insufficient guarantee for continuity. In the following section, we will give a description of a mature office and deal with a number of organizational characteristics. At the same time, however, one must not forget that within the structure there still has to be room for the consultant full of initiative who manages to cover new ground, working improvisedly, and thus maintains the impetus of development. The consequence is that the consultancy can remain in touch with the market and the developments there, and thus can safeguard its rationale. In giving a description of the administration we will try to keep mentioning these aspects.

CLIENT RELATIONS

In order to give a better idea of the complexity arising in the organization of a psychological consultancy, we will describe one hypothetical such office, together with its associated organizational problems.

The main functional aim of this office is research into the suitability of candidates for posts in firms or organizations. They may be candidates from within the firm or from outside. This task can actually be separated into two important activities. The first is the analysis of the most important distinguishing features of the post to be filled and, on the basis of these, the requirements to be fixed as to the behaviour and qualities of the possible candidate. The second is to give an answer to the question whether or not the candidates are in sufficient possession of the skills required and whether they could, therefore, function satisfactorily in the post.

Reaching an answer to the above double question takes place in two different spheres of operation. In one sphere, there is contact with the client, usually a firm, institute or other organization, with which some kind of contract has to be fixed. In the other, there is some contact with a candidate who has to cooperate in a psychological assessment so that a report can be made on him to the client and the contract with the client can be fulfilled.

At first sight, it seems quite clear that the interests of the psychological consultancy lie with the clients. They are, after all, the ones who are parties to the contract, and in the final instance pay the fee requested, and in future, hopefully, come with new commissions. The contract with candidates, on the other hand, is of another order because there is no commercial contract with them and they merely have to cooperate so that the contract can be met. This kind of reasoning is the first big pitfall into which someone in charge of a psychological consultancy can fall. The consultancy's reputation is actually determined to a great extent by the impression it makes on candidates. The integrity and care taken by the consultancy should, therefore, be beyond doubt for them. We will return to this point when we deal with the treatment of candidates.

The division into two, outlined above, has certain organizational consequences. Let us first look at the relationship with the client. First of all, we should observe that the relation with a client does not in principle need to be a short-term one. When psychological investigations are carried out in relation to staff vacancies, the larger the client the more frequent the consultancy's interventions. It is important to register carefully and keep up to date all the data relating to the client. The relation with the client usually takes place via an adviser. This is a member of the consultancy's staff who is able to assemble the relevant information concerning vacancies and function requirements, to assess it and, possibly, to translate it into questions to which the psychological investigation should provide answers. In addition to this specialist task, the adviser has a clear commercial job. He or she has to win the assignment and settle the items of the agreement. Moreover, he or she has to indicate how many hours' work are spent on the client and how that is to be settled financially. The assignment leads to an amount of work for the consultancy which has to be organized. It is sensible not to leave that to advisers, as they can, in principle, make better use of their time in contact with the clients.

These considerations have as a consequence that as well as an 'in the field' adviser, an office staff has to be formed which takes responsibility for the psychological investigation, and a group which deals with the administrative procedures and handling. As a result, a communication problem arises as information has to be transmitted from one to another. Making the information explicit is beneficial as it allows information to be recorded, which is optimal for the organization. What is more, in this way activities are continually checked.

In principle, four kinds of information can be distinguished:

1. Commercial information.
2. Specialist information.
3. Administrative–organizational information.
4. Management information.

Commercial information concerns all the data indicating what the client gets for what price and at what time. The agreements about a possible division of work between the consultancy and the client, for instance, in approaching candidates, also have to be fixed. In this, it is a good idea to make as much use as possible of procedures which have been standardized by the consultancy. However, some freedom should remain to depart from those for commercial reasons.

As far as *specialist information* is concerned, everything which is important for carrying out the assignment is relevant.

In general, clients will give only that information which they consider to be relevant. What they deem obvious does not come up. The art of the adviser is in getting that information as well, weighing it up and if necessary correcting it. Knowledge of organizational structures and their problems is in principle more relevant in this part of the assignment than psychological insights into candidates.

Administrative–organizational information includes all those things which are concerned with interviews and time limits. On what date is the candidate assessed? What information has the candidate received? Has the candidate been sufficiently informed by the bureau in advance about what will happen on the day of the test? Have candidates' rights been made clear to them? Do the staff members carrying out the psychological test know when they are supposed to report and about what? Are the hours spent on the investigation and contact with the client properly registered, so that it is possible later on to check whether the assignment was profitable? Are the agreements made by the adviser realizable as far as available capacity and office space are concerned? When and how will the client be invoiced? Is the administrative processing of the assignment properly carried out internally? The office has to answer all these questions. The most sensible thing is to set up a sales support department or a customer contacts department to register, manage and check this stream of information.

By *management information* we mean that information which makes it possible to follow the relations with the client over time. When did the client last give a commission? Has the client received the latest information about the bureau's new developments? Is the contact at the client firm still there or has he or she been replaced by someone else in the meantime? What is the client's importance for the bureau? What is the firm's annual turnover? What is its payment behaviour? What is its creditworthiness? All these data can also best be kept track of by the sales support department, and should be regularly supplied to advisers so that they can, in their turn, assemble further information or adjust processes.

CANDIDATE RELATIONS

While the relations with clients are usually strictly businesslike, albeit that a particular confidential relationship plays an important role in them, it is quite different with the equally important relationship with candidates who come for the psychological assessment. The situation is more or less comparable with that of a hospital in many of the nations of Europe. The patients come on their doctor's advice, payment takes place via subsidized health insurance funds or insurance companies, and the monitoring of treatment and prices is carried out by these funds. Nevertheless, the idea is that the patients should get better. Similarly, in the case of a psychological consultancy, the candidates to be assessed are the most important people. Their ideas concerning the day of the test, the contents of the report produced and the recommendations made regarding them, determine the bureau's reputation to a great extent.

There are many reasons which could be listed as to why the bureau should be most careful in its treatment of the candidates. Apart from ethical and public relations arguments, one of the most important reasons is certainly that the psychologists exercise their specialism in relation to these people; the quality of the exercise of that specialism is very closely connected to the attention paid to the candidates and their problems. If the professional expertise is to be exercised at a high level then this is a necessary condition. It is a good idea to have the stream of candidates passing through the office intensively and attentively looked after. This begins from the moment an appointment is made for the day of the assessment. The reception at the office, treatment in the office, contact with the psychologists, attention paid to reporting, the way in which the report is discussed with the candidates, the type of premises, the canteen facilities: they are all equally important. Organizationally it is a good idea to group the whole stream and its associated activities under one management. That means that the receptionist, the test assistants, the psychologists, must all cooperate according to a system which has been well thought out beforehand, in order to put the candidates sufficiently at their ease and to give them that information which will maximize their confidence in the consultancy. Standardized procedures and training are irreplaceable for this.

Here the question immediately arises whether it is possible for the adviser who maintains the relationship with the client, reaches the agreements concerning the report and discusses the results, to be the one who gives the psychological judgement on the candidates. From the point of view of the client, this would be ideal as the adviser could then, if necessary, further illuminate the psychological judgement, and can rapidly adjust to changed circumstances. There are, however, some objections which should be mentioned. Advisers maintain contact with the client, often at the latter's firm. They are therefore often absent. They should organize their work in such a way that they can divide their attention sufficiently between clients and candidates, where both parties have the right to full attention. If the adviser cannot be there for part of the day of the assessment, this can become difficult. A possible solution is that assessments are carried out on a number of fixed days in the week, while the other days are spent on client contacts. This reduces flexibility, though, and can involve limitations for both parties. It may also be beneficial to the objectivity and thus the quality of the judgement if the psychologist does not carry out the (commercial) contact function. Furthermore, problems may arise if a client causes peaks in terms of workload. If advisers serve certain fixed clients and one client temporarily takes up all capacity then the other clients have to be neglected or other compromises have to be made. Giving assessments can take up so much time that the desired visits to, or contacts with, clients are no longer possible. Work has to be handed over to others, with all the problems that that involves. Having a larger number of clients or seeing candidates for a larger group of jobs leads to a more all-round member of staff, which is beneficial to flexibility.

Another problem may be that an adviser has an extremely intensive contact with firms and carries out all the work for them, and therefore a great temptation arises for him or her to leave the consultancy at a certain point, set up his or her own bureau, and take the clients along too. In practice this often turns out to be problematical—as by no means all clients welcome the idea and, also, the consultancy's reputation still commands the loyalty of clients who do not want to take the risk of a new adviser just setting up—but it can be a clear source of disturbance in the relationship.

Another method is for the adviser to maintain contact with the clients and, by means of good written reports, to inform the psychologist of the specification and requirements of the job and the way in which the report should be made. This obviously takes extra time, and there is in addition the danger that information might be insufficiently or incorrectly transmitted, thus impairing the final result; but on the other hand, in this way working methods need to be well standardized which means that procedures go better and quality as a whole can be better monitored. It is also possible to plan better the activities of the psychologists working in the office, as their combined capacity is available for all candidates needing to be tested. This means that peaks and troughs at the various firms can cancel each other out, and the stream of work can take place more continuously so that work can be carried out more efficiently.

Finally, there is also the point that the different activities which psychologists and advisers carry out require a different type of person. Psychologists will need to concern themselves with candidates in a humane and not a commercial manner. assemble facts calmly, and report after careful consideration. Integrity is of great importance because, for the candidate, major interests are at stake. Advisers find themselves in a different situation. The things which are important for them are negotiating skills, rapid insight into organizational problems and having the necessary ability to adapt and adjust to a situation.

It will be clear that the above dilemma can never be solved optimally. There are bound to be advisers who can also carry out good psychological investigations and vice versa, but in general the interests of both the client and the candidate will be served best if the two are looked after separately.

THE OFFICE MANAGEMENT SYSTEM

Budgeting

Of course, as well as procedures regulating contacts with clients and candidates, procedures are also needed which permit the firm itself to function. One of the most important procedures in this context is financial management. However much pleasure may be found in the work itself, however high the quality of the service, continuity is only possible if there is the finance available for it. The finance is well regulated if there is a real certainty that sufficient capital is available to enable the firm to run and, in addition, the receipts are at least equal to necessary expenditure. As in the service sector, it is generally the case that the service is performed before income can be generated. Hence there is a continual need for capital in order to pay salaries and finance the necessary premises and business expenses in the meantime. This requires a certain capital. If this capital is borrowed, the lender will certainly ask for securities. One of the assurances lenders may receive is the justified expectation that with the help of the capital sufficient new money will be earned either to pay back the capital or to be able to guarantee an adequate return on it. The basis for negotiations on this point is provided by a budget estimate. Often, other securities will be requested in addition. In the budget estimate, costs and benefits are set out opposite each other. It is essential that, if benefits are supposed to be equal or higher than costs, one begins with benefits in the budget!

Benefits

In principle these consist of what we charge our clients for our services. This can take place in two different ways: on the basis of a fixed price, or on the basis of a number of hours of work carried out. In practice, it will be better, in the beginning certainly, to take price per hour worked as a basis. It is not too difficult to find out what the going hourly rate is on the market. It will often appear that a number of gradations are to be found in this, depending on the reputation and experience of the adviser. In relation to this it is useful to realize that the price does not only depend on what is performed but also on the confidence felt by the client and the prestige of the adviser. Quality carries a much greater emotional charge in the advice relationship than in the sale of, for example, consumable goods. In the latter case performance is actually easily observable and can be compared with other products. Because the price of advisory work is liable to be so strongly influenced by non-measurable factors, the inverse often also occurs. A high price suggests quality and prestige. A (too) low price does the reverse. Sometimes an order can be won with a high price because only then is the advice credible; sometimes one has to make do with a low price because the type of advice as such has a low priority for the client, or is less important. Certainly in the early stages, it is sensible to tailor the price according to the client's expectations. Here, as well, it is true that as the consultancy gets better known on the market and the provision of services becomes more obvious, gradually the consultancy's own prices will start to function as references in the market.

One problem in calculations based on an hourly rate is that the client often wants to know how many hours are going to be involved in total. In fact, this virtually means that a fixed price is requested for the product. If, though, it is not possible to be entirely clear about the product to be supplied beforehand, it is a good idea to work with estimates. Either a maximum or an expected number of hours is quoted, with the agreement that in the case of changes during the advisory process, the estimate can be adjusted.

In working with an hourly rate, an estimate must be made of the number of productive hours which can be worked in a year. With a normal working week of 40 hours, between 1600 and 1800 hours are available each year. A certain number of these hours will, however, not be able to be included in the estimate of the number of paid hours which can be supplied because they have to be spent on, for instance, acquiring clients, office tasks, lost hours because consecutive contracts do not follow each other exactly, or hours which can only with difficulty be charged to the client because they were not effective enough. Experience teaches that it is difficult to realize more than 1200 paid hours per year in a normal working situation. It is sensible not to count more than 1000 hours per year as productive when making estimated budgets. One advantage is then that if the reality turns out to be disappointing, the budget does not have to be adjusted straight away. Moreover, there is then some reserve for working on product development, study and suchlike, or time to invest in research, quality improvement, or future developments. Newly beginning advisers often face the problem that either they cannot yet achieve enough paid hours' work or they let themselves be tempted into promising to do far too many paid hours. The latter will often be at the cost of health, quality or effectiveness. The often invisible price which you pay for this extra income is high.

When the consultancy's services have taken on a more fixed shape, such as for instance with psychological investigation for the purpose of selection, then fixed prices can be charged. Often, in such a case, the fixed price is worked out on the basis of the number of hours spent. There emerges a kind of cost price, with or without a profit margin. Although this system is now widespread, and is actually a logical consequence of the method of working on the basis of hourly rates which was followed previously, from the point of view of business economics it is often not the best method. The price asked for a product depends on the market and on the value it has for the client. This market price can be higher or lower than the cost price. Of course, there are no problems if it is higher. It is important in that case to ask the higher price, and not the cost price, in order to reach an optimum result in business economics terms. If the market price is lower than the individual cost price, this may be because competitors are able to provide the product for less money or there is a surplus on the supply side in the market and this has a depressive effect on prices. Ways must then be sought to bring the consultancy's own cost price below that price. Re-evaluation of the methods used and the hours spent is necessary. One important cause of a price which is too high can be if one's own (dis)satisfaction with the service performed is not compatible with market expectations. Requirements are being set internally which in some respects go beyond what is necessary. It appears to be very difficult for advisers to change this way of working because confidence in their own quality is thereby damaged. External help is often essential. A good analysis of the work performed often shows that there are indeed pieces of work which are of a very high quality, but in addition there are parts which are considerably lower on the quality scale. The total quality of the product is often determined by those lowest points. Bringing all the component parts on to one quality level in between often gives a better idea of the performance, and in general can make the cost price fall, provided one is prepared to scale down levels which are too high. In any case, it is the only way to get exaggerated time and attention for certain aspects back to normal proportions. Following market indications carefully is a must in order to unearth these kinds of issues.

Costs

In drawing up the estimated budget, on the one hand an estimate has to be made of receipts on the basis of hourly rates or fixed prices and the number of assignments which can be reasonably expected. On the other hand, estimates are needed of the costs, that is to say what has to be done with the money received. The costs can in principle be split into two categories: namely the costs which can be directly influenced, the so-called variable costs; and the fixed costs. The fixed costs are the costs for which one is bound to an obligation over a longer term—at least longer than a year. The variable costs are wages and social security premiums, costs for non-durable materials, costs for rent, heating, lighting, telephone, coffee and tea, in short for living costs, travelling costs, memberships, insurance premiums, subscriptions, post, etc. Fixed costs arise out of borrowing capital, making investments, possible starting losses, etc. In practice, wage and salary costs together with social security premiums and pension provisions take up, in general, 70 per cent of the budget. If the business is run well, certainly initially, these costs will have to form the balancing entry, and of these the salary costs in particular. Only when the firm is developing in a positive way and the prospects and results get better can the salary costs be increased so much that they start satisfying one's personal wishes. Of course, it is difficult to keep the wage or salary costs of staff members who do not share in the profits at too low a level. In that case nobody would be willing to come and work for the firm. As young people often earn less than older people, it is sometimes necessary to set up a consultancy mainly with young people. The lack of experience will then have to be made up for by training and hard work.

FINANCIAL ADMINISTRATION

After the budget has been drawn up, we have to examine how it works in practice. In order to do this, a good financial administration is necessary. First and foremost, the arrangements with clients should be well registered and administered. These form the basis for the invoicing. In addition, it is important to maintain a continuous check on whether the budgeted cost prices agree with the reality. For this, a system for monitoring the time spent by advisers is needed. On the one hand the cost price can thereby be checked, and on the other it is possible to give the client a specification of the bill, so that any discussion about that can be satisfactorily concluded.

The art of administration is to a great extent determined by one's skill in speaking the language of the person using the information. If the adviser wants to know what actual performance of work was compared with expectations, he or she has to get information about the hours spent. The consultancy should get a financial overview about what the costs and receipts have been, what should still be expected and what still needs to be paid. This information should be as up to date as possible. An administration is there to make it possible to check on how things are going, and to clarify the view of developments. This does not always have to take place by means of detailed accounts, but by grouping data in accordance with the major issues. This will have to be tailor-made for each consultancy. However, it turns out that speed and reliability are always top priorities in this. Accounting procedures which force advisers or other members of staff to spend a lot of time in providing information in a way which does not always fit in with their own activities, often overshoot the mark. Moreover, it is often forgotten that staff members cannot be constantly critical of all aspects of their behaviour. It is useful and necessary to set them a number of major points, on which the policy is based, and to give them some leeway as far as other details are concerned. Liberty in one's work is often an important stimulus for good performance, while excessive monitoring is regarded as meddling and is demotivating. On this point, good and clear internal agreements should be made. This is not the place to discuss accounting aspects in any more detail. There exists an abundance of good literature in that field (Arnold and Hope, 1985).

BUSINESS DATA

As well as the important stream of data which reflects the financial situation of the consultancy with which in principle an idea can be given of its continuing progress, it is necessary to record a number of business data to make the functioning of staff members easier and more effective. These may be data concerning the potential market, market developments, the consultancy's own place within that, or data about competitors' behaviour. The possibilities and impossibilities of their own market behaviour can be tested against these. They form an important source of information for the consultancy's own strategy.

Apart from market data, historical data about the consultancy's functioning can often be very useful. It is not clever to go on re-inventing the wheel. If in the past a particular problem has been solved for one client, that solution may be appropriate for a subsequent client. Also, historical data are necessary for verifying the consultancy's quality. Was the service given followed, and did it live up to expectations? Was the selection report which was produced useful for the client, and did the forecasts made in it turn out to be right? The consultancy's methods should be subject to constant critical investigation. Additionally, building up a database with reference to the work activities can raise the quality of the advice. What were the salaries for particular types of employees in various firms? What educational level is generally required for a certain post? What is the response to certain advertisements in some of the media? Can that reveal a preference for a particular medium? How effective is it?

A database has to be built up with care. The pursuit of completeness is often in conflict with the goals set. In this case, the amount of data is often actually so large that it becomes difficult to discover relevant trends in it. Moreover, the data-bank is so big that it is difficult to locate and remove out-of-date information. Within the shortest possible time, the file is polluted. That means that it has become worthless. In data files, it is a good idea to distinguish between hard facts and soft facts. Hard facts are those which will hardly change over time. Somebody's date of birth is a fixed fact. Above a certain age, not much will change as far as educational level is concerned. The specializations chosen by people with respect to certain posts will in general remain the same over a long period. A person's sex can, as a general rule, be considered as unchangeable. Apart from these hard facts, there are also soft facts. By this we mean, for example, the evaluation of someone's performance in a certain post in a certain year. Experience shows, in fact, that a year later this evaluation can be completely different. We could consider this as a soft fact. It is questionable whether hard and soft facts belong in the same data-bank. People's salaries should be verified each year, to see if they are still correct; addresses too. With results of tests it is a good idea to limit the records to age, sex, educational level and score for any particular test. If at a certain point it is necessary to make an itemized analysis of a particular test, that should be done *ad hoc* and the data for this should be assembled and used within a short space of time, and not held on to as a permanent stream of data.

Because often when a data-bank is first being set up it is not entirely clear what should happen eventually, people try to keep future possibilities as open as possible by storing as many facts as possible. This leads to polluted and un-manageable files, and in this way they miss their target. It is a good idea to define carefully beforehand what the data is to be used for, to be certain that this is a useful question, and only then to set up the data-bank. In this manner, it can be kept to a manageable and usable size.

Storing data which are not quite hard, such as reports of discussions, corre-spondence and such things, should also only take place critically. When the facts are still current the decision is taken to keep them, and three months later nobody bothers to take the decision to destroy them on account of their having become out of date. Before you know it, every fact has been stored x times within the firm because each person concerned stored everything. Careful arrangements about this can prevent the current information which rapidly becomes out of date from obstructing the retrieval of even more up-to-date information. Archives whose content is no longer even known to the users themselves are often less useful, as facts are not often looked for in them because it is not known that they are there. Regulations can help to overcome this. One can, for instance, introduce a system whereby data are classified into groups, and the length of time each group is kept depends on certain rules. Financial data have to be kept ten years. Discussion reports can be kept a month, three months, half a year or a year depending on the subject. If they are put into an archive where these storage times are kept to, they are automatically cleared out after the period in question. In general, too little attention is paid to this aspect.

Data should be provided, asked for or unasked for, to maintain an up-to-date view of how things are going. Here as well, the things we have mentioned earlier are relevant. Only produce those facts which are relevant, and in such a form that they can be quickly read. Anything taking up more than a couple of pages is unmanageable for many people. With data that are provided at regular intervals, one should stick to the main points. Any further details can be provided later if they are requested, but only then! People have a psychological need to feel that they have some control of their activities and surroundings. Provision of informa-tion is one of the areas in which that security can be based. The art is to match psychological expectations on that point to realistic possibilities. Uncertainty often leads to a high demand for data. It is better to discuss the uncertainty and indicate ways of reducing it than to fulfil such a demand.

When data are provided it is also a good idea to discuss them. In this way the person receiving them is forced to do something with them and to test his or her thoughts against those of someone else so that effectiveness is increased. By linking provision of data to a discussion, moreover, a kind of balance auto-matically arises in the amount of data requested and the time which can be allocated to them. If that allocation of time is further ruled by the necessity of delivering something productive, then the priorities fall automatically into place.

RESEARCH AND DEVELOPMENT

In the previous sections, we gave an outline of certain aspects which are necessary for guaranteeing the proper functioning of the consultancy. However, that is not enough in itself. A firm which is not continually engaged in improving the quality of its products, on the one hand, and developing new products, on the other, is doomed to vanish in the long run. An important tool for attaining quality improvements is the carrying out of research. The methods used need to be constantly evaluated to see whether the quality strived after is actually being achieved. Experience of certain methods is only valuable if that experience has as a consequence that mistakes are avoided and improvements are brought about. Today's working methods should be better than those of yesterday. Procedural experience should show the way to these improvements.

As far as psychological research is concerned, this means that a data-bank has to be built up containing the results of the investigations which have been carried out. Of course, we are also talking here about so-called hard data, i.e. data which do not alter in value on being processed, and on the basis of which plain and clear statements can be made. Then, using these data, verification can take place regularly to see whether the conclusions drawn from them actually match reality. On the basis of this verification, the procedures according to which the conclusions are drawn can be adjusted or the set of information which is to be assembled for such a conclusion can be altered and improved. For psychological tests, this means that the reliability and validity of the data can be regularly verified, for new groups each time, and where necessary new norms can be set.

Although constant product improvement and adaptation can prolong the life of a product, this does not mean that by doing so a product becomes eternal. In practice it will become obvious that, just like industrial products, immaterial products such as psychological advice can become out of date.

What do we mean by becoming out of date? In fact it means no more than that the consumer group gradually starts to acquire different needs, and the functions fulfilled by the product no longer match those needs. For example, while 50 years ago, determining one intelligence quotient was still a good way of predicting performance at school and, therefore, the level which could be reached by following educational courses, at the moment it appears that this is no longer sufficient, since with the present differentiation of posts, a much greater need has arisen to identify specific aspects of intelligence.

Starting with the existing products, i.e. sorts of psychological advice, which are supplied to existing clients, one has to ask oneself consecutively:

– What functions do our products fulfil and what needs do they satisfy?

– What consumer groups are concerned?

– What alternative solutions are available or possible and what are the different product forms which can be offered per type of solution?

The above set of questions may lead to an analysis of our market (demand–

supply relationships). Schematically, these points could be represented thus:

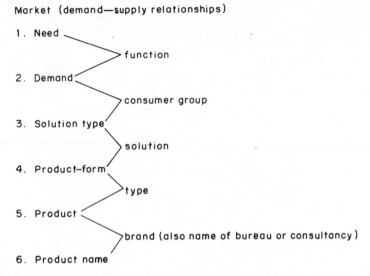

Market (demand—supply relationships)

1. Need
function
2. Demand
consumer group
3. Solution type
solution
4. Product–form
type
5. Product
brand (also name of bureau or consultancy)
6. Product name

Marketing is the technique concerned with type and brand (in our case consultancy name) and which tries to make sure that these remain linked to a particular need, or better still a particular demand. The effectiveness of marketing is determined by the stability of the product form in the market, i.e. that the market share of a product form remains more or less the same. Competition takes place between the various products, i.e. ways of performing the service, or between the attractiveness of the various brands. Price, service, prestige, specification and performance have parts to play in this. The familiarity of the form in which the service is offered, however, brings about protection and stability of the market share.

If new product forms appear, though, as a result of innovation, drastic changes may occur in the market. Competition via the introduction of new forms of providing the service requires a different approach. Apart from a good understanding of the essential points of a particular solution type, one also needs creativity in order to think up and introduce new product forms. It is less feasible to rely on experience and routine; one has to work on a more abstract level. The activities which are aimed at analysing the possibilities within the area between need and product form, with the accent on type of solution, are called strategic planning. The possible consumer group and the solution are the results delivered by this activity. Analytical powers and creativity are the characteristics which determine success, and no longer experience and routine. Strategic planning is concerned with developing a long-term supply position. Marketing concerns above all the saleability of the product. In Figure 1, we give an overview of the main differences between marketing and business strategy.

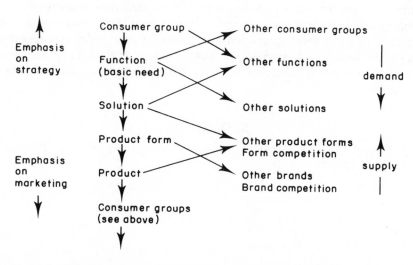

Figure 1 Main differences between marketing and business strategy

Financing and scale

In the estimated budget, an item should be included covering research. In general, an amount of about 5 per cent of turnover will be sufficient for this. With that money, an adequate evaluation can be made of the activities as they are currently carried out by the consultancy, provided sufficient data can be assembled in a standardized manner, and the procedures for carrying out research can be standardized so that the costs involved can be kept to a minimum.

It is a different matter as far as strategic concepts are concerned. Here, not only is the level of abstraction in thinking considerably higher, so that more highly educated and better qualified people will have to handle it, but also the costs are higher. It is necessary in this context to go from abstraction back to reality, that is to say the new solution forms and resulting product forms have to be designed and tested. Because, in general, one cannot rely on an existing routine for this, the chance that mistakes are made is higher and the costs of development thus considerably larger. Also, a longer period of time will be needed for trying out the new product and introducing it on to the market. The more competition that takes place in terms of strategy, the higher the costs. In order to bear these costs, a certain scale is necessary. Small firms will find it hard to compete in this manner. There is, therefore, a continual need to increase turnover in order to free enough resources for further strategic development. This growth target is a bitter necessity. In drawing up an estimate budget and setting the cost price, this has to be thoroughly taken into account.

Personnel

Relations between clients, candidates and consultants are in essence human relations. The quality of the consultant will, in the end, determine the success of the enterprise. Therefore great emphasis should be given to this aspect. Careful selection of staff members is for a start obligatory. Further training and education (even for the senior and experienced staff members) is a condition for survival. But this should not be a major problem for a well organized psychological consultancy!

REFERENCES

Arnold, J., and Hope, T. (1985). *Accounting for Management Decisions*. Prentice-Hall, Englewood Cliffs, NJ.

Chapter 2.7

Selection Procedures in Practice

VIVIAN J. SHACKLETON and SUSAN NEWELL

Aston University Management Centre, The Triangle, Birmingham B4 7ET, UK.

INTRODUCTION

The other chapters in Section 2 have looked at the factors involved in designing a selection procedure in order to maximize the effectiveness of selection decisions. In this respect, they have looked at personnel selection from the point of view of psychological theory and research and have presented what could be termed 'ideal' models of what selection procedures should look like. The authors of these chapters consider both the process (i.e. beginning with a job analysis and ending with an evaluation) and content (i.e. methods used) of selection in an attempt to identify how individuals can be recruited and selected so as to enable the organization to meet its objectives. This chapter is intended to put this into an everyday context, to look at what actually happens in practice. This is not to suggest that the rest of this section is irrelevant, but simply to point out that, in this area of applied psychology at least, theory is still a long way ahead of actual practice.

In terms of attempting to uncover what happens in practice, the first point to note is the sparseness of research on this topic. Most research in the area of selection has involved academics either theorizing about what should happen or attempting to put their theory into practice in what is, therefore, a unique situation. This chapter is thus based at least partly on the authors' knowledge of selection practices as derived from consultancy and other professional contact with companies, academics and consultants. This informal knowledge is reinforced by the small number of surveys which have been done. A second point to note, with regard to these surveys, is that they have focused almost exclusively on selecting for managerial positions. Little work appears to have been carried out on

Assessment and Selection in Organizations   Edited by P. Herriot
© 1989 John Wiley & Sons Ltd

methods in use to select for blue-collar and routine non-manual positions. Furthermore, the surveys have tended to over-represent larger organizations. Both of these factors are likely to lead to an over-representation of the use of more 'rigorous', formal selection procedures. Yet, as will be shown below, even given this bias, methods which are advocated as being more reliable and valid by psychologists are far from being the norm even in the organizations and positions surveyed.

These points are also relevant in focusing on another issue which must be discussed when considering selection procedures in practice: the variability in procedures. Each organization will have its own unique way of making selection decisions. However, there are also likely to be more general variations which can be identified.

This chapter begins by considering the process of selection (the activities involved) and the content of selection (the techniques, tools and methods used). Then it turns to some of the sources of variation in practice. Finally, it will identify various reasons for the mismatch between theory and practice and the implications of this in terms of cost and wasted human resources for the organization.

THE PROCESS OF SELECTION: THE ACTIVITIES INVOLVED

All textbooks on selection emphasize that it involves a sequence of activities which begin with some kind of job analysis to determine 'an accurate job title, the purpose of the job, its position in the organization, the principal duties and responsibilities of the post holder, the limits of his/her authority and the working relationships involved' (IPM, 1978). At the very least this would suggest that a job description would need to be drawn up. In line with this, Gill (1980) found that 76 per cent of the companies surveyed had job descriptions for the executive jobs being considered, although smaller companies were less likely to have had such written job descriptions. However, the fact that this survey concentrated on executives and over-represented larger organizations may exaggerate the use of job descriptions. A study in Britain by Mackay and Torrington (1986) found a much lower use of job analysis and its products for recruitment and selection, with only 50 per cent of personnel departments indicating that they used them. Furthermore, whether these job descriptions are re-analysed on every recruitment occasion, as the literature proposes is necessary, is very doubtful. So many organizations either ignore this first stage of the selection process, or at least short-circuit it.

Similarly, a study in the United States by Ryan and Sackett (1987), which looked at individual assessment (one psychologist making an assessment decision about one individual for a personnel-related purpose) found that formal, standardized job analyses were not the norm. On a more positive note, most of the respondents in this study indicated that they used informal methods to gather information about the individual-job fit. The problem with this, however, is that, as there is no standardization, it is not possible to ensure that all the relevant information is gathered or that subjectivity is minimized.

Following on from this job analysis stage is the recruitment stage. The purpose here is supposed to be to attract potentially suitable candidates, so that a company does not waste time and money examining the credentials of people whose knowledge, qualifications, experience, etc., do not match the job requirements. The recruitment effort needs to find an appropriate source through which to locate those individuals who are potentially suitable and, having done this, to provide the kind of information which will allow them to decide whether they are really 'suitable', i.e. to self-select. For example, Herriot (1984) argues that recruitment should be seen as 'an effort to communicate (the organization's) expectations, norms, values and image to possible applicants', rather than as 'an effort to attract the maximum number of candidates' in order to increase the selection ratio (see also Chapter 2.5). Evidence of what happens at this stage suggests that in practice the recruitment effort fails to meet this objective. For example, Parsons and Hutt (1981) found that one in three graduates who had left a job felt they had received misleading information during the recruitment and selection procedure. It seems that much of the information provided at the recruitment stage is simply presenting glossy images which attempt to market the company, rather than job information which would seriously allow a potential candidate to decide whether the job is suitable for him or her. Thus, Gill (1980) found that in only 36 per cent of companies surveyed was salary information regularly disclosed in job advertisements. At the same time, salary is considered by candidates to be one of the most important factors in deciding whether to apply for a particular job. This has led some to suggest the introduction of realistic job previews (e.g. Wanous, 1977). However, in practice it has been found to be difficult to demonstrate the benefit of such procedures (e.g. Reilly *et al.*, 1981). Given this, companies are going to be very reluctant to disclose realistic information to applicants which could potentially put them at a distinct disadvantage against their competitors who are maintaining the 'glossy image' approach.

Following this recruitment stage, and given that it provides a potential pool of applicants from which a choice is possible, the next stage involves selection itself. The main area of interest here is the type of method used. This is treated under the 'content' heading below. On the basis of these selection tools, information will be gathered about the applicants which can be used in the next stage of the procedure, the decision-making stage.

Textbooks on selection suggest that there are two general ways in which decisions can be made: the actuarial (statistical) and the clinical methods. The actuarial method is generally considered to be more 'scientific', since it is based on an objective, statistical analysis of data about candidates. More importantly, in terms of predictor reliability and validity, most reviews (e.g. Meehl, 1965; Wiggins, 1973) provide evidence which clearly favours statistical over clinical prediction. However, given the methods of selection used by most companies (see below) the use of techniques such as regression analysis would be quite inappropriate. Hence, it is clear that most decisions are made, at the end of the day, on the basis of 'gut feel' or intuition. Where more sophisticated selection tools are used which would permit the use of analytical decision-making techniques, the more usual practice appears to be to use test or exercise scores to eliminate those who score particularly poorly and to maintain clinical judgements, based mainly on interview data, to decide about those who score above the threshold levels (e.g. Gardner and Williams, 1973). Thus, in the study by Ryan and Sackett (1987), only 2.5 per cent of their sample reported using a purely statistical approach, with the majority, 55.7 per cent, relying on their own judgement.

The final stage in the selection process is held to be the evaluation stage, which should involve a systematic analysis to determine whether the selection procedure used is actually selecting candidates who go on to become successful employees. This would involve studying the correlation between the forecasts of selection methods and subsequent job performance. The study carried out by Gill (1980) suggests that this is done very rarely. In fact this survey found that virtually none of the companies had ever conducted a validation study. Similarly, Ryan and Sackett (1987) found that most of those doing individual assessments did not empirically validate the process they used with any regularity.

THE CONTENT OF SELECTION

In order actually to select from a pool of candidates, some kind of selection tool or method must be used. Psychologists have been concerned to develop methods which are more reliable and valid than those traditionally used, especially the interview which has long been the principal tool of selection. Most textbooks on personnel selection, following an overview of the problems of basing decisions on information gathered via interviews, go on to promote more 'objective' methods, such as psychological tests, work samples, assessment centre techniques and more recently biodata. Yet, in practice, it appears that this promotional exercise has not yet reached the ears of practitioners in the field who it seems continue to rely, often exclusively, on interviews and to a lesser extent on references (Anderson and Shackleton, 1986). In order to examine this in more detail, the extent to which a number of different selection methods are used by organizations is described below.

Interviews

All surveys have found that interviews are by far the most widely used selection tool, despite the fact that research has found them to be typically unreliable, invalid and subjective (e.g. Webster, 1964; Ulrich and Trumbo, 1965; Arvey and Campion, 1982). Indeed interviews are used almost universally. For example, Robertson and Makin (1986) found that in only 1 per cent of the companies they surveyed were interviews not used. The use of interviews is not surprising and it is difficult to disagree with Ungerson (1975) that interviews will always be necessary. Yet, what is more important is the fact that surveys reveal that a majority of companies rely *exclusively* on interviews in order to select personnel. For example, Gill (1980) found that 90 per cent of companies surveyed used only interviews to select executives. This might well overestimate the exclusive use of interviews since this survey excluded graduate entry recruits where other types of selection method are more frequently used.

Nevertheless, it is still clear that most selection decisions are based solely on information gathered from interviews. Typically, a candidate will experience two or more interviews, usually with two to three interviewers. Furthermore, Gill (1980) reported that while personnel specialists involved in these interviews had usually undergone some kind of interview training, this was not true of the line representatives involved, despite the fact that it was they who were more likely to have the final say in the decision about whether to proceed with a candidate. Thus, although research has shown that the interview can be improved if interviewers are trained (e.g. Hackett, 1978), in practice many of those who are most crucially involved remain untrained.

The exclusive use of the interview does vary with company size, larger organizations tending to use more varied techniques and to include techniques considered by psychologists to be more reliable and valid.

References

This is the other most widely used selection tool. Robertson and Makin (1986) found that 96.3 per cent of respondents used references on some occasions, although this did vary, with companies recruiting more managers using references less often. Beason and Belt (1976) found 82 per cent of responding organizations used references while Kingston (1971) reported 88 per cent of those surveyed either contacted previous employers or requested reference details. However, as Kingston points out, references are often not used in the actual decision-making process. The majority (61 per cent) in this survey only contacted referees *after* the job offer had been made and accepted, the offer being contingent on satisfactory references.

What evidence there is suggests that in Britain the use of references is as popular as it has always been, despite research which has shown the low reliability and validity of such data (e.g. Muchinsky, 1979; Reilly and Chao, 1982). This is not so in the United States where the law has restricted the scope of personal details that can be included in references.

Psychological tests

In contrast to these two mainstream, but often criticized techniques, psychological tests are used much less often. The most recent survey by Robertson and Makin (1986) found that 64.4 per cent of UK organizations never used personality tests when selecting managers, while 74 per cent never used cognitive tests. This figure does not appear to have changed much since the 1970s. Kingston (1971) found that 67 per cent of companies said they never used tests and Sneath, Thakur, and Medjuck (1976) found that 74 per cent said they never used them. Of those that did use tests only half had tried to estimate the test's validity in their situation and only 5 per cent had used statistical methods to do so.

The Gill survey (1980) did find differences depending on job function. For example, tests were used more often to select for computer staff, but even here the usage was very low. It has also been found that those recruiting more managers tend to make more use of tests (Robertson and Makin, 1986). Tests also appear to be more frequently used by those engaged in individual selection, at least in the United States. Ryan and Sackett (1987) found that 84.7 per cent of those engaged in such selection used ability tests and the same percentage used personality inventories. However, for more general selection procedures, especially in Europe, the conclusion must certainly be that selection tools treated as standard predictors in the classroom are anything but standard in the world of business and commerce.

Assessment centres

Theoreticians are increasingly advocating the use of assessment centres for making selection decisions and one of the more encouraging findings of the surveys is that they are becoming increasingly common. For example, Bridges (1984), looking only at assessment centres, found that 19 per cent of UK companies used such an approach and that 65 per cent of these had only begun to use such techniques within the last five years. The use has been found to be restricted to larger organizations, especially those which recruit a large number of managers each year. For example, Robertson and Makin (1986) found that 36.4 per cent of major recruiters in large organizations used assessment centre techniques. However, even when such techniques are used it appears that assessors insist on exercising their personal judgements when making the final decision even though this reduces the predictive power of the procedure (e.g. Wollowick and McNamara, 1969).

Biodata

Much research has pointed to the reliability and validity of biodata (e.g. Reilly and Chao, 1982; Asher, 1972). However, in the most recent survey by Robertson and Makin (1986) only 5.8 per cent reported that they used biodata. On a more optimistic note, a number of respondents in this survey did indicate that they were currently considering the use of biodata techniques, although all cases were confined to larger organizations employing more than 500.

Graphology

Some surveys have also looked at methods which tend to be written off as 'unscientific' (see Chapter 3.12). Gill (1980) found the use of graphology to be minimal throughout all types of company. Robertson and Makin (1986) found a slightly higher usage with 7.8 per cent reporting use of handwriting analysis on some occasions, although only 2.9 per cent used it all the time. However, all companies which did use it regularly were subsidiaries of continental organizations and Klimoski and Rafaeli (1983) report that the technique is much more common on the Continent. This last finding highlights the idea that cultural factors are likely to be a major influence in variations in selection procedures.

The fact that graphology is used at all points again to the mismatch between the findings and recommendations of empirically based studies and actual practice. Klimoski and Rafaeli (1983) conducted a comparison of the predictions of ten graphologists on over 200 scripts. No statistically significant validity coefficients were found. Yet many employers in Continental Europe seem convinced of the worth of graphology (Richard, 1988).

Overall, therefore, results suggest that traditional methods of selection, interviews and references remain the dominant practice, at least in the UK, despite the fact that theory and research raise considerable doubts about their validity. The more objective methods, especially tests, are still used very sparingly, even at managerial levels and even in larger organizations where we would expect their maximum use. Furthermore, the use of tests does not appear to be increasing, despite the theory and research which continue to show how they can improve selection decisions. On a more optimistic note, the use of assessment centres and biodata does seem to be increasing, although the baseline for this increase is very small. The conclusion must be that the theory and research into personnel selection have so far failed to have any real impact on current practice.

This is especially surprising given the recent work which analyses the utility of selection procedures. For example, Schmidt *et al.* (1986) used the standard deviation of the value of performance to calculate that huge benefits would accrue to employers who used selection methods which make valid predictions. Even though some argue that such utility estimates need to be scaled down (Boudreau, 1983), gains in productivity are easily demonstrated.

VARIATIONS IN SELECTION PRACTICE

While it is difficult enough to find documented evidence of everyday selection practice, with just a few surveys to go on, it is even harder to find firm evidence on the variables which give rise to differences between organizations in their selection processes. Some of the studies mentioned above did highlight sources of variation and an attempt will be made to bring together these variables into a coherent picture.

Size of organization seems to be one such variable. In Britain, the armed forces and the civil service, both very large organizations, have for a number of years adopted many of the methods of best practice laid down in texts of occupational psychology (e.g. Anstey, 1977). Similarly, it was a very large and influential private sector organization, AT & T, which pioneered and published the use of the assessment centre in the United States. The evidence from Robertson and Makin (1986) supports the correlation between the more reliable and valid methods and the frequency of use in larger organizations. Those with more than 500 employees were more likely to use biodata, assessment centres and cognitive tests.

While there may be small public and private organizations whose methods are highly commendable, it seems likely that it is the larger and more prosperous organizations who have the resources and the through-put of candidates to warrant investment in, for example, expensive assessment centres, or the validation of test instruments. Nevertheless, many large organizations still rely exclusively on interviews and references.

Another factor likely to be related to the use of these more objective methods is the numbers actually recruited. Thus, Robertson and Makin (1986) found that, the more managers recruited, the more likely was the organization to use assessment centres, biodata and tests. Although there was a relationship between size of organization and numbers recruited ($r = 0.56$, $P < 0.001$), the overlap was far from perfect, suggesting both factors independently were related to the type of selection methods used.

The use of in-depth psychologically based methods is also likely to be determined by the probable cost of making a mistake (i.e. the level of risk) and the number of candidates to vacancies (i.e. the selection ratio). One can think of a simple 2×2 matrix of these factors (see Table 1).

Table 1   Factors influencing methods of selection

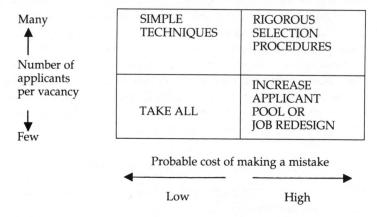

The probable costs of making a mistake might arise from a number of sources including high initial training costs, so that losing a successful candidate after this training would involve wasted resources. Alternatively, human error in operating machinery, or even industrial sabotage or espionage, can result from wrong selection decisions.

It is where there is a favourable selection ratio from the organization's point of view and where the risk is high, that there is most to be gained from the use of rigorous, lengthy and valid methods.

Incidentally, the box representing few applicants and high risk is an interesting, though relatively rare, occurrence. It implies that methods other than purely selection-based ones should be employed. Casting the recruitment net wider, by advertising more extensively, for example, might be one option. Others include training existing employees or, better, redesigning the job to reduce the risk or make it more appealing to applicants.

Another factor which ought to determine the use of different techniques is the validity of the method coupled with the selection ratio. Smith (1986) presents a table showing the utility of different methods in terms of savings per salary where the validity coefficient and the selection ratio can be estimated (see Table 2).

Table 2   Savings per £1000 salary for different validities and ratios (From Smith, 1986)

Validity coefficient	Selection ratio		
	1 in 3	1 in 6	1 in 10
0.1	39	45	61
0.2	77	91	122
0.3	116	137	183
0.4	154	182	245
0.5	192	228	306
0.6	231	273	368
0.7	270	368	429

It can be seen from the table that the highest gains for the organization are obtained with a high selection ratio and high validity. But as we have seen, organizations rarely bother to calculate the validity of their methods, or estimate the selection ratios, and are therefore unlikely to base their decisions on appropriate methods by reference even to the very attractive savings which the table illustrates.

It seems very probable that the level of job vacancy is a factor in determining the sophistication of the selection procedures. A study of individual assessment in the United States (Ryan and Sackett, 1987) found that 73.8 per cent of respondents indicated that the techniques they used varied across positions for which assessments were conducted. Managers and professionals are far more likely to meet psychological tests, work samples or assessment centres than are blue-collar workers, although the latter may be given work sample tests. There is little documented evidence for this, but a number of clues can be found. One is that almost all reviews of selection practices have concerned themselves with managerial selection. If other sections of the workforce were as rigorously selected, we would have expected them to have been covered in reviews. Also, large reputable test publishers, at least in Britain, such as Saville and Holdsworth Ltd, or NFER-Nelson, have a much more extensive and diversified range of instruments available for management selection than for any other sector.

There are exceptions to this concentration of effort on managers and professionals. Young applicants to the very basic grades of the British army, for example, may be subjected to biodata, work samples (such as running around a track or strength exercises in a gym) and cognitive tests, as well as the ubiquitous interview. Clerical workers to banks and other financial service organizations often have biodata forms to complete. Size of organization and favourable selection ratios, particularly in the case of banks, are factors affecting choice of method here.

Finally, at a macro level, the rise in unemployment in most West European countries over the last ten to fifteen years should have offered incentives for the personnel specialist to have investigated, and invested in, more valid methods. As we have shown, an 'employers' market' with its favourable selection ratios makes rigorous methods all the more attractive financially. So has the recession affected methods? A survey by Wood (1982) suggests not. As regards recruitment, Wood reports that the recession has merely encouraged and reinforced the use of the cheapest channel, social networks. For selection there was some suggestion that personnel managers have used more stringent definitions of job stability or age requirements, to select out those older or more job-mobile workers, but little more. Most of the recession's effects had been on working practices or manning levels rather than on recruitment or selection. It looks like the opportunity offered by the recession for those employers has been lost.

Finally, legislation has a part to play in supporting or discouraging certain methods. The legislative climate is fairly benign in Britain and many other European countries, so organizations have a relatively free hand to choose whatever method they prefer. In the United States, by contrast, there are well-documented reductions in the use of tests and references in favour of interviews. This is in response to anti-discrimination legislation and the effects of the 'adverse impact' of tests, in particular, on minority groups.

REASONS FOR THE MISMATCH

This chapter has attempted to show that there are major gaps and mismatches between the recommendations of occupational psychologists, based on theory and empirical findings, and the methods of selection in current use by organizations. We cannot end this chapter without addressing the obvious question of why?

Once again, we have little evidence to go on. The basic fact is that we just do not know why practitioners have not adopted more scientific methods. We can only speculate.

One possibility is that the view held by many psychologists of the nature of selection is not helpful. As Herriot notes in Chapter 2.5, the process may be better conceived as a process of social exchange and negotiation. To use concepts of reliability or validity to understand the selection process is to misread how selection does and should work.

Yet the negotiation view also has certain limitations. It may underestimate the power position which selectors use, whether psychologists approve or not. A recent line of thought within the more general field of organization behaviour has been to highlight the political realities of organization life (e.g. Pfeffer, 1981; Lee and Lawrence, 1985). These authors recognize that within organizations everybody is not always pulling in the same direction and that individuals and groups will have different interests. Those with more power will be able to enforce their particular interests at the expense of the less powerful, even if it is not to the good of the organization as a whole. A limitation of the negotiation view is that it takes little account of the power of the selector in the selection process.

At the present time the organization has administrative power, provided by the fact that in most occupations there are fewer jobs available than there are those willing and able to do them. However, demographic trends in Europe, especially in Britain and West Germany, mean that it will be a sellers' market again by the

1990s. There will be a significant reduction in the number of young people entering the labour market. Figures in Britain are in the region of a 25 per cent reduction by the year 1993. This means that the selection ratio and the power will swing much more in favour of the job seeker.

So the interview, the mainstay of most selection procedures, retains, and almost certainly will retain, its popularity. This may be because it involves a certain amount of give and take, exchange and negotiation. Other methods have less scope for this as presently used. It may be because it gives power to the selector. A cynical point of view is that the interview seems to remain dominant because of the faith of interviewers in their own judgements, coupled with a distrust of other methods such as tests, despite the research to the contrary.

There may be other reasons. Arvey and Campion (1982) have outlined their views on why the interview has retained its popularity despite its poor validity record. They point out that it serves much wider purposes than merely assessment, such as selling the job to the candidate.

Reasons for the slow or negligible take-up of other methods have also been touched on in this chapter. The expense of setting up and maintaining such 'Rolls Royce' methods as assessment centres means that only large organizations with resources, training provisions and candidate numbers can justify the expense. Lack of a legal framework requiring the adoption of job-valid methods, unlike in the United States, may also have played a part.

Other reasons may lie with the human resource specialists. Rarely have they had psychological training. In Britain, many personnel managers have received either very little training or poor quality training (Shackleton and Taylor, 1988). So their receptivity to new ideas, particularly involving statistically based concepts with which they are unfamiliar, may be low.

Whatever the reasons, whether habit, lack of familiarity or resistance, we are likely to see the interview continuing to flourish and more valid methods, or traditional methods used in a more negotiation-based way, taking many years to make inroads into selection practice.

REFERENCES

Anderson, N., and Shackleton, V. (1986). Recruitment and selection: A review of developments in the 1980s, *Personnel Review*, **15**(4), 19–26.

Anstey, E. (1977). A 30 year follow-up of the CSSB procedure with lessons for the future, *Journal of Occupational Psychology*, **50**, 149–59.

Arvey, R.D., and Campion, J.E. (1982). The employment interview: A summary and review of recent literature, *Personnel Psychology*, **35**, 281–322.

Asher, J.J. (1972). The biographical item: can it be improved? *Personnel Psychology*, **25**, 251–69.

Beason, G., and Belt, J.A. (1976). Verifying applicants' backgrounds, *Personnel Journal*, **55**, 345–8.

Boudreau, J.W. (1983). Economic considerations in estimating the utility of human resource productivity improvement programs, *Personnel Psychology*, **36**, 551–76.

Bridges, A. (1984). Assessment Centres: their use in industry in Great Britain. Unpublished MSc dissertation, Dept. of Management Sciences, UMIST.

Gardner, K.E., and Williams, A.P.O. (1973). A twenty-five year follow-up of an extended interview selection procedure in the Royal Navy, *Occupational Psychology*, **47**, 1–13, 149–61.

Gill, D. (1980). *Selecting Managers: How British industry recruits*. IPM, BIM, London.

Hackett, P. (1978). *Interview Skills Training: Role play exercises*. IPM, London.

Herriot, P. (1984). *Down from the Ivory Tower: Graduates and their jobs*. Wiley, Chichester.

Institute of Personnel Management (1978). *Towards Fairer Selection: A code for non-discrimination*. IPM, London.

Kingston, N. (1971). *Selecting Managers: A survey of current practice in 200 companies*. BIM, Management Survey Report, No. 4.

Lee, R., and Lawrence, P. (1985). *Organizational Behaviour: Politics at Work*. Hutchinson, London.

Mackay, L., and Torrington, D. (1986). *The Changing Nature of Personnel Management*. IPM, London.

Meehl, P.E. (1965). Seer over sign: the first good example, *Journal of Experimental Research in Personality*, **1**, 27–32.

Muchinsky, P.M. (1979). The use of reference reports in personnel selection: a review and evaluation, *Journal of Occupational Psychology*, **52**, 287–97.

Parsons, D., and Hutt, R. (1981). *The Mobility of Young Graduates*. Institute of Manpower Studies, Brighton.

Pfeffer, J. (1981). *Power in Organizations*. Pitman, London.

Reilly, R.R., Blood, M.R., Brown, B.M., and Maletsa, C.A. (1981). The effects of realistic job previews: a study and discussion of the literature, *Personnel Psychology*, **34**, 823–34.

Reilly, R.R., and Chao, G.T. (1982). Validity and fairness of some alternative selection procedures, *Personnel Psychology*, **35**, 1–62.

Richard, C. (1988). Personnel Selection Methods in Britain and France. Unpublished MSc dissertation, Aston University Business School.

Robertson, I.T., and Makin, P.J. (1986). Management selection in Britain: a survey and critique, *Journal of Occupational Psychology*, **59**, 45–57.

Ryan, A.M., and Sackett, P.R. (1987). A survey of individual assessment practices by I/O psychologists. *Personnel Psychology*, **40**, 455–88.

Schmidt, F.L., Hunter, J.E., Outerbridge, A.N., and Trattner, M.A. (1986). The economic impact of job selection methods on size, productivity and payroll costs of the federal workforce: An empirically based demonstration. *Personnel Psychology*, **39**, 1–30.

Shackleton, V., and Taylor, P. (1988). What do personnel managers think of their own training? *Personnel Management*, July.

Smith, M. (1986). Selection: Where are the best prophets? *Personnel Management*, December, p. 63.

Sneath, F., Thakur, M., and Medjuck, B. (1976). *Testing People at Work*. IPM, London.

Ulrich, L., and Trumbo, D. (1965). The selection interview since 1949. *Psychological Bulletin*, **63**, 100–16.

Ungerson, B. (ed.) (1975). *Recruitment Handbook*. Gower Press, Epping.

Wanous, J. P. (1977). Organizational entry: newcomers moving from outside to inside, *Psychological Bulletin*, **84**, 601–18.

Webster, E.C. (1964). *Decision Making in the Employment Interview*. Eagle, Montreal.

Wiggins, J.S. (1973). *Personality and Prediction: Principles of personality assessment*. Addison-Wesley, Reading, Mass.

Wollowick, K.A., and McNamara, W.J. (1969). Relationship of the components of an assessment centre to management success, *Journal of Applied Psychology*, **53**, 348–52.

Wood, S. (1982). Has the recession revolutionized recruitment? *Personnel Management*, November, 40–2.

Chapter 2.8

The Impact of Personnel Selection Procedures on Candidates

PAUL A. ILES[1] and IVAN T. ROBERTSON[2]

[1]*School of Management, The Open University, 1 Cofferidge Close, Stony Stratford, Milton Keynes MK11 1BY, UK*
[2]*Department of Management Sciences, UMIST, PO Box 88, Manchester M60 1QD, UK*

The impact of personnel selection procedures on organizations has long been appreciated, in that the quality of selection and assessment decisions has been recognized as having a significant impact on organizational productivity and the achievement of organizational goals. Indeed, recent developments in utility theory have concentrated on assigning monetary values to the benefits selection procedures may confer on organizations under various conditions. Traditionally, the major standard by which to judge a good selection method has been its prediction of future work performance (criterion related predictive validity), with some attention given to other types of validity such as construct and content validity. For validation studies, the development of adequate criteria by which to assess the accuracy of predictions made is of central importance. In practice a rather limited range of criteria has usually been employed, generally representing, in some way, benefit to the organization. This has usually consisted of some assessment of individual job performance, often assessed by supervisors' ratings, though other criteria have sometimes been used, such as peer ratings, productivity, tenure, absenteeism and training success.

INDIVIDUAL BENEFITS

A criterion not often employed is some index of *individual* benefit or well-being, rather than organizational benefit or well-being. Such indices might include job

Handbook of Assessment in Organizations   Edited by P. Herriot

satisfaction or psychological well-being, or an enhanced sense of personal agency or control. Indeed, the whole question of the impact of selection procedures and outcomes on candidates or clients has been greatly under-researched. Individuals who feel unfairly assessed, by invalid techniques, presented in ways which fail to include their active consent, participation or involvement, may feel alienated from the organization, uncommitted to it, think of leaving it, and actively seek another job. Their work performance may also suffer if they feel insensitively treated and their future options closed off. On the other hand, if they are accurately and sensitively assessed and given constructive feedback, individuals may feel a rise in self-esteem, enhanced self-efficacy, a greater sense of personal agency, greater commitment to their organization and greater motivation to undertake further training and work experience. All of this may impact positively on organizational effectiveness. One way of conceptualizing these kinds of effects resulting from candidate experiences with selection procedures and selection outcomes is through the concept of 'impact validity', defined provisionally by Robertson and Smith (1988) as 'the extent to which a measuring instrument has an effect on a subject's psychological characteristics'.

A wide variety of predictors of work performance has been identified and developed and there are various ways of classifying them. One approach adopted by Robertson and Iles (1988) is to use a classification based on whether job performance is to be predicted from the past behaviour of the individual, such as with biodata, supervisor assessments, or references; from the individual's current behaviour, such as with interviews, cognitive, personality and projective tests, work sample tests and assessment centres; or from the individual's future expectancies and intentions, such as with situational interviews or scales measuring self-efficacy perceptions. The published evidence, accumulated over many years (see Muchinsky, 1986), indicates that there are some methods which appear to be good predictors of future work performance. These include tests of cognitive ability, work sample tests, biodata, supervisor and peer ratings, and assessment centres. Other methods, such as references, interviews, personality and interest inventories, and projective tests, provide less accurate but still positive predictions of job performance. Other methods occasionally used, such as graphology and astrology, appear to show little evidence of predictive validity. One or two recently developed methods, such as the situational interview (Latham and Saari, 1984) and the 'accomplishment record' (Hough, 1984), show promising evidence of predictive validity, but the research base is rather limited as yet.

It is the contention of this chapter that such methods need to be evaluated not only in terms of their ability to predict work performance, and in terms of other organizationally based criteria such as cost, utility, applicability and administrative convenience, but also in terms of their impacts on candidates as they experience them and the outcomes they generate. To this end, the evidence on clients' attitudes to selection procedures, such as their perceptions of the method's fairness, validity and accuracy, is reviewed in this chapter. Clients' reactions to the use of various selection procedures, such as their perceptions of the degree to which their personal privacy is justifiably invaded, and their response to various features of their treatment, are also examined. Clients' reactions to selection outcomes are also explored, in particular effects on their continuing involvement in their jobs, commitment to their employing organization, to their careers, and their satisfaction with both job and career.

SOCIAL BENEFITS

Another important characteristic of a selection procedure which needs to be taken into account in any overall evaluation of a method is its social impact, in particular its impact on the selection chances of particular subgroups. The major social groups considered have been racial and ethnic minorities, such as Blacks or Hispanics in US research, and women. Some consideration has been given to other social groups, such as those defined by age or disability. Most research in this area has also been conducted in the United States, but some research has been conducted in the United Kingdom. This research has usually been conceptualized in terms of 'unfair discrimination', 'fairness' and 'bias', especially in terms of whether a predictor makes consistent non-zero errors of prediction, on some criteria such as assessed work performance, for members of a particular subgroup (see Schmitt and Noe, 1986). Another way of conceptualizing this area is in terms of 'adverse impact', the degree to which members of one social group are disproportionately rejected in comparision with the rest of the assessed population when a particular predictor is employed. If a particular subgroup is rejected on grounds which can be shown not to be job relevant, indirect discrimination may be identified as occurring. The issue of the fairness/adverse impact of personnel selection procedures is dealt with in Chapter 1.4. In this chapter the evidence for the adverse impact of various selection procedures is therefore only briefly reviewed.

ADVERSE IMPACT

Some reasonably valid predictors, such as tests of cognitive ability or biodata, seem also to display potential for adverse impact, as do some less valid predictors such as interviews or references. Other valid predictors such as work sample tests and assessment centres, as well as promising but less well studied ones such as the accomplishment record and the situational interview, appear to demonstrate less adverse impact against women or racial and ethnic minorities. These also seem to be methods which applicants regard favourably and see as accurate, fair and valid; in general these methods also appear to generate useful information about the applicant and identify strengths and weaknesses which can be built upon for training, development, self-assessment and self-development purposes.

FAIRNESS, BIAS AND SELECTION PROCEDURES

In the United States in particular, concern over possible discrimination in personnel selection decisions against racial and ethnic minorities grew in the 1960s with increasing participation by black people and others in the movement for Civil

Rights. In the United States the Civil Rights Act of 1965 included references to 'Equal Employment Opportunity' (EEO), and more detailed guidelines and prescriptions followed from the Equal Employment Opportunity Commission and the Office of Federal Contract Compliance. In 1971, the Supreme Court, in the case of *Griggs* v. *Duke Power*, ruled out, as illegal, the use of employment tests not related to the job.

Concerns initially focused on cultural bias, differential validity, and test bias. In some cases this led to an abandonment of psychometric testing altogether; in others a concern with large-scale validation studies. It also led to a renewed interest in job analysis and in content validation strategies, with a concern to devise or identify personnel selection methods with predictive validities equal to or greater than psychometric tests but with much less 'adverse impact' against minorities and women. Thorough job analysis and content validation characterize two of the more successful personnel selection methods in this respect, work sample tests and (to some extent) assessment centres. They also characterize two more recent developments of promise in this area, the 'situational interview' (Latham and Saari, 1984) and the 'accomplishment record' (Hough, 1984). For reviews of such developments in the context of the United States, with its distinctive social, historical and legal background, see Schmitt and Noe (1986).

In the British context, discrimination in personnel selection and in other personnel areas is illegal in terms of the Race Relations Act in 1976 and the Sex Discrimination Act of 1975. Both acts make 'direct discrimination' on race or gender grounds illegal. They also make 'indirect discrimination' illegal. This is defined as applying a requirement or condition which, whether intentional or not, affects adversely a considerably larger proportion of one racial group or one gender than another, and cannot be justified on job-relevant grounds. Examples might include unjustifiable height regulations, clothing regulations, or literacy requirements.

Recent studies conducted since the 1976 Race Relations Act have continued to show evidence of substantial continuing racial discrimination in personnel selection. For example, a study by Brown and Gay (1985) showed that many more black applicants than whites with similar experiences and qualifications were not invited for interview after applying for a range of junior non-manual and skilled manual jobs.

One organizational response to these levels of discrimination, and to the substantial under-representation of women in most professional and managerial jobs (Davidson and Cooper, 1984), has been the development of equal opportunity policies. These have been promoted by interested parties such as the Commission for Racial Equality (CRE) with regard to race and the Equal Opportunities Commission (EOC) with regard to gender, and adopted by many employers in both the public and private sector. One way of evaluating the effectiveness of equal opportunity policies generally is through ethnic or gender monitoring.

With regard to the selection procedures themselves, most attention seems to have been directed at improving shortlisting and interviewing procedures by making selection criteria more job relevant. Often training courses, perhaps incorporating some form of racism or sexism awareness, are used to enable selectors to analyse jobs, devise appropriate job descriptions, and draw up personnel specifications which list job-related attributes, skills and competencies, rather than those merely thought to be job related. Awareness training might be used to enable interviewers to be aware of their own prejudices and assumptions and to ensure that these are not influential in determining selection decisions.

Given that previous studies have shown how discrimination may occur due to interviewers and recruiters often having stereotypes of ethnic minority personality and background (Jenkins, 1986), such an approach seems very relevant. Little attention seems to have been given to the adoption of alternative selection procedures shown to have less adverse impact against women and black people in US research, such as work sample tests and assessment centres.

Pearn (1988) argues that too much effort has been devoted to questions of predictor validity and predictor bias, and too little attention to themes of criterion validity and criterion bias, and to the analysis of social processes involved in selection and assessment decisions. Such a focus lies behind much of the ensuing discussion on candidate attitudes and on the psychological impact of selection procedures and selection outcomes on candidates.

CLIENT RIGHTS: VULNERABILITY AND PRIVACY

In Holland and much of Continental Europe reservations about the 'American model' of personnel selection, with its concern for predictive validity, were initially expressed in concerns over the applicant's vulnerable position *vis-à-vis* the organization. The candidate was seen as unable to engage the organization on equal terms, with his or her labour market position rendering him or her more vulnerable. In addition the organization might claim for itself the right to ask the candidate to divulge various kinds of personal information but retain the right to refuse to disclose to the candidate information it considered 'confidential'. In particular, the applicant was increasingly seen as having rights and interests including a right to 'privacy'. Though the applicant was seen as needing to provide some information about himself or herself in any job application, he or she was also seen as having rights over its possible misuse (de Wolff and Van den Bosch, 1984).

Not much empirical research has addressed the issue of client perceptions of invasion of privacy in personnel selection situations. Some American research suggests that applicants' perceived control over how any personal information disclosed is treated is of prime importance. Individuals perceiving that they had some control over the uses to which the information could be put appear to experience less of a sense of having their privacy invaded. The instrumental value of the selection outcome also seems important. People experiencing a positive outcome decision appear to feel less of an invasion of privacy than those experiencing a negative outcome, such as rejection. In addition, some studies have shown that the type of disclosure has some impact. Disclosure outside the organization such as to another employer seems to be perceived more negatively in this respect. The type of information disclosed seems also to have some impact, with information perceived as 'job relevant', such as productivity data, being less sensitive than information perceived as less job relevant, such as personality data (Fusilier and Hoyer, 1980).

This area has legal as well as psychological implications for organizations and individuals, especially with the growing computerization of personnel information storage. For example, the UK Data Protection Act of 1984 covers the use of computers for applicant screening, regulating the storage of personal information held on computerized information systems. Certain rights are conferred on the applicant, such as the right to demand a copy of the details held on file and knowledge of the assessment criteria used (Anderson and Shackleton, 1986).

Trying to protect one's rights to privacy by omitting to include requested information on an application form, such as details of previous convictions, may not be a very viable strategy. Stone and Stone (1987) found that this resulted in applicants being viewed as less suitable for jobs than those reporting no convictions, and non-response seemed treated as an attempt to conceal.

It might be argued that individuals have a right to see any test scores or assessment ratings and to have feedback on their performance. Some controversy exists about when this feedback should be given, by whom, and in what form. Providing full and detailed feedback on a separate occasion, but relatively close in time to the original assessment, might seem a useful strategy, especially if development plans are to be used and acted on. There is a risk that individuals who have obtained an unfavourable assessment might be further damaged by such a full disclosure, with their self-esteem further affected and their work motivation and commitment further lowered. In some circumstances relatively full oral feedback might be better, with some emphasis on strengths and concentration on only one or two specific, remediable weaknesses (Fletcher, 1986).

CLIENT ATTITUDES AND REACTIONS TO SELECTION PROCEDURES

There has been some research into client perceptions of the assessment and selection process, and client reactions towards selection procedures. Most studies seem to have been of the initial recruitment process, of interview procedures, and of candidates' reactions to assessment centre procedures.

The Recruitment Process

With regard to organizational recruitment practices, most interest has been on the influence of various recruitment practices on applicants' decisions to pursue job applications. Herriot and Rothwell (1981) found that career information issued by organizations had some effect on UK engineering students' intentions to apply for particular jobs. However, Quaglieri (1982) found that US business studies graduates in trainee management and accountancy jobs felt that informal sources of job information and referral, such as word of mouth recruitment, provided more specific and accurate job information than formal organizational sources such as job advertisements. Breaugh and Mann (1984) found that US social service workers, recruited through referrals from existing employees, had more realistic

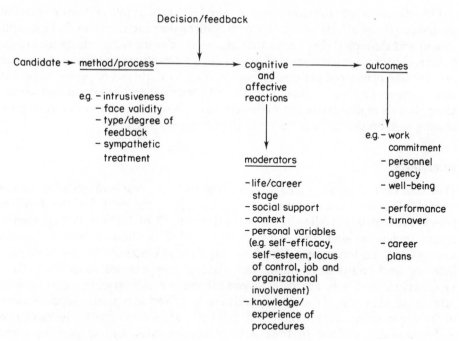

Figure 1 Psychological impact of personnel selection methods on candidates (adapted from Robertson and Smith, 1988)

job expectations and showed longer tenure with the organization than those recruited through direct applications or newspaper advertisements.

This link between realistic expectations and job tenure is also stressed in the realistic job preview literature. Offering potential candidates a 'realistic preview' of the job in question, rather than the over-inflated view of prospects and conditions often offered in glossy recruitment brochures, appears to lower applicant expectations of the rewards a job has to offer to a more 'realistic' level and offers potential candidates more opportunity not to pursue their application further if the position is not perceived as meeting their needs. Those candidates who do pursue their application, if selected, appear to show greater commitment to the organization, greater job satisfaction, better performance and longer tenure (Premack and Wanous, 1985).

One might question, however, how 'realistic' a job preview can be if conducted by means of films or videos, discussions with organizational personnel and recent recruits, and members of the company. One of the advantages of using work sample tests or assessment centre type exercises is that they provide the candidate with an accurate picture of the job, allowing him or her to make a decision as to whether to continue with an application. Non-managerial staff wishing to be considered for a managerial position may, for example, decide that such a career is not for them after sampling various aspects of a management job in a managerial assessment centre. Examples of what the job involves based on realistic job samples may provide much more 'realistic previews' than the oral, visual or written descriptions commonly encountered in 'realistic job previews' and have similar or greater effects on commitment, satisfaction and turnover. For example, Cascio and Phillips (1979) found that introducing work sample tests for US city government employment seemed to reduce significantly the annual turnover rate for new staff compared to those engaged through interviews or paper-and-pencil tests. Downs, Farr and Colbeck (1978) used a trainability test and offered work to all applicants regardless of their performance. They found that far more of those scoring well on the test started work than those scoring badly.

Interviews

There has been increasing recognition of the social processes involved in personnel selection interviews, and increasing interest in the nature of the decisions taken by *candidates* as well as by assessors (Herriot, 1988). Herriot (1987) presents a recent review of such processes. It seems as if candidates form favourable impressions of interviewers who show interest and empathy, demonstrate good listening and counselling skills, and display interpersonal sensitivity. These favourable impressions are likely to lead to a greater willingness to accept any job offer made, especially if the interviewers are perceived as typical or representative of the organization in general. Candidates also appear to expect interviewers to ask technical questions in their area of competence, and to present useful information on the job and the organization. Harris and Fink (1987) have confirmed that candidates' perceptions of such characteristics of the interviewer as personableness, competence and informativeness affect their perceptions of job attributes and their regard for both the company and job. The likelihood that they would take up a job offer was also affected.

Work samples

Candidates appear to have particularly positive reactions to the use of work samples for selection purposes, perceiving them as fair and valid and as presenting them with opportunities to demonstrate their potential in ways that paper-and-pencil tests or interviews do not. Robertson and Kandola (1982) review studies of the reactions of candidates to work samples and to analogous 'trainability tests' or 'miniaturized training tests'. Studies in the United States have shown that black, Hispanic and white applicants all showed equally positive attitudes towards their use, and that their introduction results in a significant decline in the number of complaints received from applicants about selection procedures (Schmidt *et al.*, 1977; Cascio and Phillips, 1979).

Assessment centres

The high face validity and positive endorsement of work sample tests by clients also extends to the use of assessment centres, probably because they often include managerial work samples such as in-basket exercises or group discussions. Early work with IBM managers in various countries reported that, in general, assessment centres were positively regarded by clients as a fair and valid way of measuring managerial potential (Kraut, 1972), while Canadian research also showed that the use of assessment centre technology was positively received, with candidates reporting that they received a realistic view of their strengths and weaknesses and that participation in an assessment centre had a positive effect on morale (Bourgeois *et al.*, 1975). A survey (Nirtaut, 1977) of the use of assessment centres by US organizations also showed that companies uniformly reported positive reactions from clients. The major adverse effects reported were some discouragement from low performers due to perceived harmful career impacts, and some problems caused by high performers perceiving a mismatch between their expectations for promotion and the limited opportunities for such promotion often present in their company.

Dodd (1977) has reviewed many such studies and concludes that assessment centres are in general favourably regarded by candidates and generally perceived as measuring important job-related qualities accurately and fairly. Data collected using a standard questionnaire recommended by him have continued to confirm this generally positive picture, such as the UK study by Dulewicz, Fletcher and Wood (1983). This study found that, in particular, analogous exercises such as in-basket exercises, business decisions simulation execises, and business plan presentation exercises were favourably regarded, presumably because of their high face validity and perceived job relevance.

However, there seem to be differences in how people react to assessment procedures, depending on how well they have performed. A small-scale US study, while reporting similarly favourable endorsements generally, found that assessment centre high scorers had more positive views of the assessment process overall than low scorers (Teel and DuBois, 1983). Low scorers tended to rate the centres as less accurate and less fair, and to report fewer perceived career benefits. They also tended to see their assessment centre behaviour as less like their 'real life' behaviour.

A much larger scale study of assessment centres used in a UK organization by Robertson *et al.* (in preparation) has confirmed this picture of candidates performing well in a centre and selected for further tiering giving more positive endorsements of the use of assessment centre technology for selection purposes than low performers. Such high performers were more likely to perceive it as valid, fair and accurate. All participants, however, tended to see its use in a generally positive light. In this study, low performers not selected for further progress were no more likely to see their assessment centre performance as unlike their real life behaviour. All participants, whether selected or not, tended to be very positive about the use of assessment centres for career development purposes and for identifying training needs. They also saw the feedback they received as valuable and helpful. There were some indications that candidates rejected for progress at senior levels saw their particular centre more negatively than those rejected at lower levels, perhaps because the early career assessment centre appeared better designed to simulate managerial skills appropriate to this level or perhaps because rejection at the more senior centre was more significant in career terms.

Other methods

In contrast to these positive reactions to the use of both work sample tests and assessment centre procedures, some studies have reported less positive reactions to the use of some other selection procedures. For example, Robertson *et al.* (in preparation) report negative views held by internal candidates about the use of biodata to select managerial applicants in their study of selection procedures in a major UK oganization. Candidates rejected by this procedure tended to express doubts about its accuracy, validity and usefulness. However, situational interviews seemed reasonably well regarded, though not as well regarded in terms of accuracy, fairness or validity as most of the assessment centres used in the same management development programme.

Peer assessments, often used in military selection contexts and as a part of an assessment centre process (e.g. Tziner and Dolan, 1982; Schmitt and Hill, 1977; Fletcher and Dulewicz, 1984), also seem less acceptable to candidates than work sample tests or assessment centres. Cederblom and Lounsbury (1980), in a study of peer evaluation schemes in a US university, found them often perceived to suffer from friendship bias and to have a discouraging effect on staff morale. A higher degree of user acceptance of peer appraisal in an industrial setting, especially its use for developmental purposes, has been reported by McEvoy and Buller (1987).

In general, it seems as if applicants prefer some selection procedures to others, seeing work sample tests and analogous devices as more valid and more appropriate than paper-and-pencil tests, biodata, or peer assessment. These techniques, based on a 'sample' approach rather than a 'sign' approach (Wernimont and Campbell, 1968) with predictors used being as close to criterion behaviour as possible, seem to be regarded more favourably and are perceived to be more job relevant.

The evidence also suggests that applicants want to be treated sensitively and sympathetically in the selection procedure, and not to have their privacy unduly invaded. They also seem to want to be presented with realistic job information. Not only will this result in candidates being more favourably disposed to the selection procedure used and more accepting of it, it will also probably generate more realistic expectations of the job and organization. The candidate seems also more likely to accept a job offer and to be more committed to the organization. This may be reflected in longer tenure and perhaps better work performance.

PSYCHOLOGICAL IMPACT; A CONCEPTUAL BASIS

The impacts of selection processes and selection outcomes or decisions on candidates have only recently begun to be considered as an important area needing further study. Selection procedures have tended to be regarded as neutral measuring instruments, assessing various candidate attributes or characteristics with greater or lesser validity but with their impact on these characteristics, or any other candidate characteristics, either not considered at all, or treated as intrusions or 'biases' disturbing otherwise clean psychometric evaluations. The increasing emphasis on selection as a social process (Herriot, 1988), and the increasing evidence that candidates have definite attitudes towards selection procedures and that these affect the decisions they make, indicate the importance of further research in this area.

Experiences with selection outcomes or decisions appear also to have major impacts on candidate and company health and performance. In essence, when selection and assessment methods are utilized, there are three broad classes of outcome: accept, reject, or feedback on strengths and weaknesses. Sometimes feedback may be combined with accept or reject decisions, as is the case of internal assessment centres used to identify candidates for a management development programme. In any true 'selection' situation, at least some of the candidates will be rejected. Some recent speculation has concentrated on possible negative consequences of such decisions, such as immediate stress and later reduced work commitment and lowered job involvement. Reduced career commitment and lower organizational commitment have been shown to lead to thoughts of leaving one's job, organization or career field, to greater absenteeism, reduced work performance, and greater turnover (Griffin and Bateman, 1986). It is possible that negative selection decisions might also lead to damaging psychological consequences for the individual, such as lowered self-esteem, ill-health, and lowered psychological well-being, analogous to the effects of unemployment or downward mobility (Warr, 1987). On the other hand, some candidates receiving a negative decision may develop a more realistic and accurate self-image and a more realistic view of their strengths and weaknesses, with a clearer view of attainable career goals (inside or outside of their present organization). This possibility may be increased if clear feedback is provided, realistic developmental plans are drawn up with input from the participant as well as the organization and immediate line managers, and action taken on such plans. It may also help if the organization makes available realistic career planning and career counselling, training opportunities, and alternative job openings and lateral transfers as well as upward promotions (Hall and Goodale, 1986). Assessment centre exercises or work sample tests, with their opportunities for self-assessment, have an impact on candidates' self-perceived abilities and allow candidates to develop a more accurate picture of their strengths and weaknesses (Schmitt, Ford and Stults, 1986), even in the absence of feedback on performance. Assessments may have an impact on later career behaviour and job attitudes. Individuals' motivation to experiment with managerial skills and seek further work experiences and job- and career-related information seems to be influenced by assessment centre evaluations (Noe and Steffy, 1987). Lower expectations as a result of negative assessment centre evaluations resulted in lower levels of exploratory behaviour, lower job involvement, and less searching for information on managerial jobs and career paths.

Though there has been speculation about the possible impact of selection procedures and outcomes on candidates, little empirical research using valid and reliable psychometric measures has been carried out, beyond a few 'reaction studies' reviewed earlier. Such speculation has particularly focused on the possible 'damaging' effects of negative decisions on morale, commitment and self-esteem, but has not been informed by any theoretical model of likely impacts. Some clues as to possible areas of investigation exist. For example, studies into the psychological impact of unemployment and downward mobility have demonstrated clear effects on psychological well-being, mental health and self-esteem of work-related events (Warr, 1987). Such research has also identified several moderators of this impact, such as age and previous levels of 'employment commitment'. Since a negative personnel selection decision may be analogous in some ways to such life events, one set of 'outcome variables' where selection impacts might be detected is in terms of psychological well-being or mental health. In addition, other evidence shows that a variety of variables normally treated as relatively permanent individual characteristics such as intellectual flexibility, self-directedness, emotional well-being, and orientation to challenges and risks, may change under the impact of job and life events (see Kohn and Schooler, 1982; Brousseau, 1984). For many people, selection and assessment procedures constitute significant life events and changes in these variables might therefore occur.

In addition to effects at an affective level, such as on well-being or anxiety, effects of selection procedures and outcomes might be detected at 'cognitive' levels. In particular, the importance of 'personal agency' variables concerned with an individual's personal efficacy, risk taking and personal responsibility for outcomes (such as self-efficacy, and locus of control) is worth considering.

An important set of variables which also might be affected by personnel selection procedures concerns the employer's 'work commitment'. This includes the candidate's involvement in his or her present job, commitment to the employing organization, involvement in and commitment to his or her general career field, and satisfaction with his or her present job and future career prospects. These variables are likely to be manifested in thoughts about leaving one's job, organization or career, and in taking active steps to look for new jobs or positions.

A preliminary model

Though further research needs to be undertaken before the factors which influence candidates' reactions to selection processes and selection outcomes can be fully identified, it seems likely that these will include the social and organizational context in which the decision is taken, the method used, and the personal characteristics of the candidate. Figure 1 provides an indication of possible key variables and how they are related.

For example, characteristics of the method, such as its perceived intrusiveness, its face validity, its perceived job relevance, and the opportunities it provides for feedback and self-assessment would seem likely to influence candidates' affective and cognitive reactions to the selection process. This seems especially the case if the method is perceived as providing a valid and accurate indication of true strengths or deficiencies of the candidate, or is perceived as being biased, inaccurate or invalid implying no accurate information about the individual. The actual nature of the selection and assessment decision such as accept, reject, accept with feedback, reject with feedback, etc., and the kinds of feedback provided (such as how specific it is, what kinds of training needs are identified, what kinds of career development are recommended and what kinds of developmental action plans are devised and acted upon) also seem likely to be influential in determining applicant reactions. A variety of candidate personal characteristics, such as life and career stage, current level of job and career involvement, strength of self-efficacy with regard to job and career, degree to which an internal locus of control is present, current career plans, current level of self-esteem, and previous knowledge of and experience with the selection procedure, also seem likely to moderate candidate reactions. The degree of organizational or extra-organizational social support candidates receive may influence candidate reactions. Effects on candidates may be in terms of work commitment variables and thoughts about leaving job and career field. In addition, reactions in terms of psychological well-being such as lower or higher mental health may occur, as well as probably also a variety of behaviours related to career planning and exploration, job search, training and development and job/career movements.

CONCLUSION

This chapter has focused on an area of personnel selection research which, in parts, is seriously under-researched—yet is potentially of great significance both to individuals and organizations. Traditional research within the personnel selection domain has focused on establishing which are the best methods for choosing candidates for jobs. If selection is to be useful for individuals and organizations, this traditional line of enquiry is of continuing importance. Nevertheless, as the material contained in this chapter serves to emphasize, to identify selection methods that are valid and predict future job performance accurately is not enough. Care needs to be taken about the effect that selection technology has on individual candidates. With the exception of work on bias/adverse impact, a coherent research programme into these effects is only just beginning.

In the meantime, organizations will need to pay more attention to the impacts that their selection and assessment processes have on job holders and external candidates. As this chapter suggests, some selection techniques, while providing useful predictions of future job performance, may have adverse side effects. Other methods, such as work sample tests and assessment centres, allow relatively full feedback on strengths and weaknesses, provide opportunities for career counselling and the identification of training needs, and enable coherent development plans to be drawn up for individuals or specific cohorts of individuals. Such methods may thus have more beneficial impacts on candidates, regardless of the selection decision.

REFERENCES

Anderson, N., and Shackleton, V. (1986). Recruitment and selection: A review of developments in the 1980s, *Personnel Review*, **15**, 19–26.

Bourgeois, R.P., Leim, M.A., Slivinski, L.W., and Grant, K.W. (1975). Evaluation of an assessment centre in terms of acceptability, *Canadian Personnel and Industrial Relations Journal*, **22**(3), 17–20.

Breaugh, H.A., and Mann, R.B. (1984). Recruiting source effects: a test of two alternative explanations, *Journal of Occupational Psychology*, **57**, 261–7.

Brousseau, K.R. (1984). Job–person dynamics and career development, in K. Rowland and G. Ferris (eds). *Research in Personnel and Human Resources Management*, vol. 2. JAI Press, London.

Brown, E., and Gay, P. (1985). *Racial Discrimination 17 Years after the Act*. Policy Studies Institute, No. 646, London.

Cascio, W.F., and Phillips, N.F. (1979). Performance testing: a rose among thorns? *Personnel Psychology*, **32**, 751–66.

Cederblom, D., and Lounsbury, J.W. (1980). An investigation of user acceptance of peer evaluation, *Personnel Psychology*, **33**, 567–79.

Davidson, M.J., and Cooper, C.L. (1984). *Working Women – An International Survey*. Wiley, Chichester.

Dodd, W.E. (1977). Attitudes towards assessment center programs, in J.L. Moses and W.C. Byham (eds). *Applying the Assessment Center Method*. Pergamon, New York.

Downs, S., Farr, R.M., and Colbeck, L. (1978). Self-appraisal: a convergence of selection and guidance, *Journal of Occupational Psychology*, **51**, 271–8.

Dulewicz, V., Fletcher, C., and Wood, P. (1983). A study of the internal validity of an assessment centre and of participants' background characteristics and attitudes: A comparison of British and American findings, *Journal of Assessment Center Technology*, **6**, 15–24.

Fletcher, C. (1986). Should the test score be kept a secret? *Personnel Management*, April, 44–6.

Fletcher, C., and Dulewicz, V. (1984). An empirical study of a UK based assessment centre, *Journal of Management Studies*, **211**, 83–7.

Fusilier, M.R., and Hoyer, W.D. (1980). Variables affecting perceptions of invasion of privacy in a personel selection situation, *Journal of Applied Psychology*, **65**, 623–6.

Griffin, R.W., and Bateman, T.S. (1986). Job satisfaction and organizational commitment, in C.L. Cooper and I.T. Robertson (eds). *International Review of Industrial and Organizational Psychology*. Wiley, Chichester.

Hall, D.T., and Goodale, J. (1986). *Human Resource Management: Strategy Design and Implementation*. Scott Foresman, Glenview, Ill.

Harris, M.M., and Fink, R.S. (1987). A field study of applicant reactions to employment opportunities: Does the recruiter make a difference? *Personnel Psychology*, **40**, 765–84.

Herriot, P. (1987). The selection interview, in P.B. Warr (ed.). *Psychology at Work*, 3rd edn. Penguin, Harmondsworth.

Herriot, P. (1988). Selection as a social process, in J.M. Smith and I.T. Robertson (eds). *Advances in Selection and Assessment*. Wiley, Chichester.

Herriot, P., and Rothwell, C. (1981). Organisational choice and decision theory: effects of employers' literature and selection interview, *Journal of Occupational Psychology*, **54**, 17–31.

Hough, L.M. (1984). Development and evaluation of the 'accomplishment record' method of selecting and promoting professionals, *Journal of Applied Psychology*, **69**, 135–46.

Jenkins, R. (1986). *Racism and Recruitment: Managers, organisations and equal opportunity in the labour market*. Cambridge University Press, Cambridge.

Kohn, M.L., and Schooler, C. (1982). Job conditions and personality: A longitudinal assessment of their reciprocal effects, *American Journal of Sociology*, **87**, 1257–86.

Kraut, A. (1972). A hard look at assessment centers and their future, *Personnel Journal*, May, 317–62.

Latham, G.P., and Saari, L.M. (1984). Do people do what they say? Further studies on the situational interview, *Journal of Applied Psychology*, **69**, 569–73.

McEvoy, G.M., and Buller, P.F. (1987). User acceptance of peer appraisals in an industrial setting, *Personnel Psychology*, **40**, 785–97.

Muchinsky, P.M. (1986). Personnel selection methods, in C.L. Cooper and I.T. Robertson (eds). *International Review of Industrial and Organizational Psychology 1986*. Wiley, Chichester.

Nirtaut, D.J. (1977). Assessment centers: an examination of participant reaction and adverse effects, *Journal of Assessment Center Technology*, **1**, 18–23.

Noe, R.A., and Steffy, B.D. (1987). The influence of individual characteristics and assessment center evaluation on career exploration behaviour and job involvement, *Journal of Vocational Behavior*, **30**, 187–203.

Pearn, M.A. (1988). Fairness in selection: A comparison of US and UK experiences, in J.M. Smith and I.T. Robertson (eds). *Advances in Selection and Assessment*. Wiley, Chichester.

Premack, S.Z., and Wanous, J.P. (1985). A meta-analysis of realistic job preview experiments, *Journal of Applied Psychology*, **70**, 706–19.

Quaglieri, P.L. (1982). A note on variations in recruiting information obtained through different sources, *Journal of Occupational Psychology*, **55**, 53–5.

Robertson, I.T., and Kandola, R.S. (1982). Work sample tests: validity, adverse impact and applicant reaction. *Journal of Occupational Psychology*, **55**, 171–82.

Robertson, I.T., and Iles, P.A. (1988). Approaches to managerial selection, in C.L. Cooper and I.T. Robertson (eds). *International Review of Industrial and Organizational Psychology*. Wiley, Chichester.

Robertson, I.T., and Smith, J.M. (1988). Personnel selection methods, in J.M. Smith and I.T. Robertson (eds.). *Advances in Selection and Assessment*. Wiley, Chichester.

Robertson, I.T., Iles, P.A., Gratton, L., and Sharpley, D.S. (in preparation). *The Psychological Impact of Personnel Selection Methods on Candidates*.

Schmidt, F.L., Greenthal, A.C., Hunter, J.E., Berner, J.G., and Seaton, F.W. (1977). Job samples vs paper and pencil trades and technical tests: Adverse impact and examinees' attitudes, *Personnel Psychology*, **30**, 187–97.

Schmitt, N., Ford, J.K., and Stults, D. (1986). Changes in self-peceived ability as a function of performance in an assessment center, *Journal of Occupational Psychology*, **59**, 327–36.

Schmitt, N., and Hill, T.E. (1977). Sex and race composition of assessment center groups as a determinant of peer and assessor ratings, *Journal of Applied Psychology*, **62**(3), 261–4.

Schmitt, N., and Noe, R.A. (1986). Personnel selection and equal employment opportunity, in C.L. Cooper and I.T. Robertson (eds). *International Review of Industrial and Organizational Psychology 1986*. Wiley, Chichester.

Stone, D.L., and Stone, E.F. (1987). Effects of missing application-blank information on personnel selection decisions. Do privacy protection strategies bias the outcome? *Journal of Applied Psychology*, **72**, 452–6.

Teel, K.S., and DuBois, H. (1982). Participants' reactions to assessment centers, *Personnel Administrator*, March, 85–91.

Tziner, R.A., and Dolan, S. (1982). Validity of an assessment center for identifying future female officers in the military, *Journal of Applied Psychology*, **67**, 728–63.

Warr, P.B. (1987). Workers without a job, in P.B. Warr (ed.). *Psychology at Work*, 3rd edn. Penguin, Harmondsworth.

Wernimont, P.F., and Campbell, J.P. (1968). Signs, samples and criteria, *Journal of Applied Psychology*, **52**, 372–6.

Wolff, C.J. de, and van den Bosch, G. (1984). Personnel selection, in P.J.D. Drenth, H. Thierry, P.J. Willems and C.J. de Wolff (eds). *Handbook of Work and Organizational Psychology*, vol. 1. Wiley, Chichester.

Section 3: The Tools of Selection

Introduction to Section 3: The Tools of Selection

ALAN JONES

The section's title should itself alert readers to a number of issues which are discussed by the various authors. In many ways these issues are the same as would arise when considering other tools but it is surprising how often they are neglected by potential users:

1. Tools are artificial objects designed with some purpose in mind.
2. Tools vary in how well made they are and how appropriate they are for a specific purpose; for example, a well-made hammer can be used for knocking a nail into a piece of wood but would be of no use in cutting the same piece of wood.
3. We should not assume that any individual or group can immediately make the best use of a tool: training is often required.
4. It would be unwise for a consumer to believe all the claims of the manufacturer or seller of a tool; the sensible consumer likes to try out the tool or check the experience of other users.
5. Buyers of tools may be interested in their legal status, for example whether they meet manufacturing or safety standards. Besides any humanitarian considerations, the buyer will wish to avoid any consequent legal complications and costs.
6. A tool may be well designed, meet safety regulations and so on, but this does not mean that it necessarily confers any overall benefit on a potential user; for example, the purchase of a power tool may not be justified if we have only the occasional need for light work.

These are all straightforward issues and would pass as unremarkable in the world of hammers, saws, pens and typewriters. Sadly, they are often neglected or completely ignored in the world of interviews, psychological tests, reference reports, graphology and other methods of assessing people. Perhaps this tendency is the result of basically simple concepts being given specialist names (reliability, validity, utility, etc.) or of finding their eventual expression as mathematical formulae or statistical calculations. What this section of the handbook sets out to do is to provide the reader with the basic concepts to be used in assessing any selection tool and detailed information about its potential value.

Reading the research literature and textbooks on selection methods and observing day-to-day practice, one quickly becomes aware of the gap between what is recommended and what occurs in many selection settings. The interview continues to be the most popular personnel assessment device despite repeated findings of potential disagreement between interviewers and the poor predictive power of assessments based on interview. Of course, these are general results and it is relatively easy to believe that, as individuals, we are exceptions (just as we may dismiss the relationship between smoking cigarettes and respiratory problems and lung cancer *in our own case*). Although some organizations now include more objective techniques, such as psychometric tests, there still seems a widespread reluctance to withdraw at least some of the influence from the fallible human and transfer it to a more mechanical system. The overwhelming evidence that psychometric tests of aptitude are probably the best off-the-shelf tool of selection available seems to do little to change this reluctance.

Of course, more objective assessment techniques can be criticized for their 'artificiality', a comment which must surely be made without thinking about the setting and dynamics of selection interviews. Some tests do not look anything like typical job content but they may still capture information about a candidate's underlying mental capacity. It may often be the case that tests which more closely resemble job content may be more acceptable to candidates and may offer some increases in predictive power. Trainability tests, work sample tests generally and assessment centre exercises are all intended to embody some of the characteristics of the job or training for it. This increase in realism must, however, be bought at some additional cost (staff time, materials, etc.); there is also an increased emphasis on training assessors and on ensuring consistency across assessors.

Another approach to reducing the artificiality in assessment procedures is to try to make use of the evaluations of others who have been in contact with the candidate; the reference report or check is the most common example of this although organizations sometimes also request peers or fellow candidates to make assessments. Assessors may also try to get the candidate to provide evaluations of his or her abilities and characteristics. All these approaches have attractions but the evidence available tends to point to their limitations rather than revealing them as the answer to the selector's prayers.

Since application forms and interviews place a good deal of emphasis on what the candidate has done in life so far, it is not surprising that attempts have been made to gather and score this information systematically ('biodata'). Although well-constructed biodata instruments can often rival psychometric tests in their predictive power, they typically have to be tailor-made and so more expensive to implement. Their theoretical base is much less strong.

Most of the above techniques have been available for many years, but we now have the possibility of using computer technology for generating, presenting, recording and integrating assessment material. Except for the introduction of optical mark readers (used almost exclusively by large organizations), this will be the first time that improvements in material technology will have a marked impact on the actual practice of assessment. Although electro-mechanical and then electronic calculators, punched cards and computers have been used for research into assessment techniques, the procedures themselves have generally relied on human observation and pieces of paper. Computers now offer the opportunity to present new types of tests and to derive new measures of performance (e.g. speed, accuracy and learning effects over the course of the test). We may also begin to see the breaking down of the distinction between ability and personality measures as computers present candidates with complex job-related problems.

As we have seen, the various tools of selection vary in their intrinsic value. One topic which has been largely ignored is the way in which assessors actually make use of these tools in arriving at a final assessment of the candidate and how they might be helped in making better judgements based on the available evidence. Again there has been something of a gulf between research into the predictive power of assessment techniques and the reality of assessment practice. One outcome of such research is the production of a recommended statistical weighting of a small number of scores; the assessor's everyday experience may be of the need to integrate a large amount of often subjective information. This lack of dialogue is at least in part the result of ignoring how assessors use information and in what practical ways they might be helped to use it more effectively.

Society at large has also begun to take more notice of the tools and processes of selection. Over the last 20 years many countries have passed legislation which focuses on equality of opportunity and fairness of treatment in employment. Unfortunately, some initial reactions to the legislation included the dropping of the more objective assessment procedures since they were more susceptible to external examination. Although this tactic may save some lawyers' fees in the short term, it is very likely that it will ultimately be disadvantageous to the organization since the latter will have to rely on the less effective assessment techniques. In assessment, fairness towards the candidate usually lies in the same direction as ultimate benefit for the organization.

The authors of the twelve chapters in this section discuss the various tools of selection, their value and possible future developments. In Chapter 3.1 Moser and Schuler explore the basic issues of measurement which we use when evaluating assessment procedures. The reader is taken through the various approaches to, and types of, measurement, the techniques used to relate an individual's performance or profile to a relevant standard, and then into the key concepts of reliability and validity. The authors conclude that there is no real alternative to scientific measurement when assessing individuals and that there exists a substantial body of knowledge about how such measurement should be undertaken. Bethell-Fox discusses and explains some of these ideas further in the context of psychological testing (Chapter 3.2). He then reviews the various types of tests and concentrates on how good tests are developed. His aim is not to turn the reader into a test developer but to allow an informed evaluation of tests which may be offered for a given application.

Prieto examines the area of aptitude testing (Chapter 3.3) and draws generally favourable conclusions about its usefulness in the selection of personnel. Tests of general intellectual ability in particular appear to have *some* value in assessing suitability for all jobs and training courses. The extent of their value not surprisingly varies with the intellectual complexity of the job. Prieto's chapter also gives a useful introduction to the estimation of the overall utility (cost–benefit) of selection procedures.

In contrast to the favourable conclusions about aptitude tests, van der Maesen and Hofstee (Chapter 3.4) are more cautious about the benefits to be gained from using personality questionnaires in selection. After explaining the various approaches to inventory development, they examine the practical issues involved in making selection decisions on the basis of such data. They conclude that selectors should think very seriously before using existing paper-and-pencil personality assessment technology; on the brighter side, developments in computer-based personality assessment procedures may help to improve both objectivity and flexibility of use.

Mention of the computer brings us on to Chapter 3.5 where Bartram looks at the impact of this technology on psychological testing. He discusses how the computer enables us not only to automate conventional tests but also to develop new types of tests. The computer can also help us to make better use of available information, for example by the use of expert interpretation packages. The chapter ends with a list of specific points for potential computer-based test buyers to use in evaluating available systems.

An attractive, but more expensive, alternative to the paper-and-pencil aptitude test is the job or work sample test which Downs discusses in Chapter 3.6. The pure job sample test is applicable to candidates who at least claim some proficiency in an occupational area (e.g. word processing). The trainability test, on the other hand, is a form of work sample test which can be applied in order to assess suitability for a particular course of training. It must be tailor-made but research indicates that it has good predictive power and also offers candidates a chance to get some idea of what the job actually involves. The latter benefit is in contrast to the normally unequal distribution of information after an assessment episode: assessors (hopefully) learn a great deal but candidates relatively little.

The assessment centre (AC) method has grown in popularity over recent years. Feltham in Chapter 3.7 draws our attention to the generally good validity and acceptability of well-designed and competently run assessment centres. These benefits must be bought at increased costs but utility analysis indicates that there is almost invariably an overall positive cost–benefit. However, Feltham counsels us against unnecessary duplication in AC procedures and draws attention to the need to improve consistency of assessment across assessors and exercises.

Dobson in two chapters (Chapters 3.8 and 3.11) addresses the question of the value of evaluations solicited from others (teachers, employers, fellow candidates and even the candidate). The reference report may have some value as a check on information supplied by the candidate; under some circumstances it may also provide some useful and perhaps unique information. Peer assessments may also provide valid information but there are serious limitations to their use in selection (as distinct from development, counselling, etc.) Self-assessments have little place in selection because of the problem of self-presentation and the inflation of numerical ratings.

Chapter 3.9 deals with the ever popular interview. As Herriot indicates, research results do not justify this popularity and have been generally depressing to practising interviewers. Herriot argues that we should turn away from the quest to turn the interview into an objective measuring device. The interview is a human encounter and attempts to strip it of its humanity (i.e. subjectivity, lack of system) may be ultimately self-defeating. It would be preferable to accept its faults and to use it as a forum for mutual information exchange and negotiation. This would not mean that interviewers could all revert to being amateur and un-trained: they would need to have a different set of skills.

If the interview does develop along the lines proposed in Chapter 3.9 then other tools will be needed to help supply information for the negotiations. One of them may well be biodata which Drakeley reviews in Chapter 3.10. He first discusses the broad rationale for using biodata and the generally positive research results. However, biodata collection and scoring systems need to be treated with greater caution than aptitude tests since the underpinning theoretical base is not yet available. Biodata systems are also typically tailor-made and so are initially usually more expensive than off-the-shelf tests. Drakeley concludes that the chief value of biodata may lie in pre-selection before the interview or other lengthier selection procedures.

In the final chapter (Chapter 3.12) Ben-Shakhar chooses two non-conventional assessment techniques (graphology and the polygraph) to examine the value of such techniques generally. He concludes that their usefulness in personnel assessment is effectively zero. This conclusion is of course directly opposed to that of practitioners and their clients. Just why this might be the case (leaving aside deliberate charlatanry) is also discussed in this fascinating chapter. Besides the value of his conclusions, Ben-Shakhar's rigorous approach to whether and why techniques may or may not work should be of benefit to readers. He also neatly brings us back to the opening remarks about the straightforward questions we might ask of tools generally.

Chapter 3.1

The Nature of Psychological Measurement

Klaus Moser and Heinz Schuler

Institut für Agrarsoziologie, Landwirtschaftliche Beratung und Angewandte Psychologie, Universität Hohenheim, Postfach 70 05 62 (430), 7000 Stuttgart 70, Federal Republic of Germany

IMPORTANCE OF MEASUREMENT IN THEORETICAL AND APPLIED AREAS

In fundamental research, measuring and measurement methods are *tools* used to scrutinize theories or derived hypotheses. For example, according to critical rationalism it is one of the high quality attributes of theories to possess a high degree of falsifiability (cf. also Moser, Gadenne and Schröder, 1988). One condition is that a theory implies precise explanations and predictions. However, this presupposes *precise* measurement devices. Thus, the development of measurement devices or methods and their technological elaborations support advances in theory. Technological (or applied) research mainly tries to develop and improve methods, for example methods of measurement. New developments in the area of measurement technology can illustrate the interrelations of theory and technology: the use of computers in assessment situations can make it possible to register and control the assessee's behaviour, thus improving the conditions for more accurate measurement (see Chapter 3.5). What about measurement issues in applied areas, for example in personnel psychology?

We assume personnel psychology, including measurement and assessment in organizations, to be primarily technological in nature. This technological research aims at defining, improving and evaluating the quality criteria of measurement and test devices, therefore making available improved methods of measurement and assessment.

Those who want to use the results of psychological research in measurement

Handbook of Assessment in Organizations   Edited by P. Herriot

and assessment can choose between various evaluated testing and measurement devices. They should know how to judge the measurement devices, such as those discussed in this book, by means of the criteria we will introduce in this chapter.

Detailed quality criteria can be found in technical journals, testing manuals or handbooks (e.g. Mitchell, 1985). Choosing between measurement tools according to the criteria we will introduce should result in the use of the best possible method for every practical measurement and assessment problem. Before we have a closer look at various measurement issues we will give a brief historical retrospect to the roots of measurement.

HISTORICAL RETROSPECT

The history of measurement theory teaches us that already in pre-Grecian times there were systematic developments of measurement devices. However, it was only in the late nineteenth century that the fundamental work of Weber and Fechner postulating a law of comparative judgement announced the entrance of measurement theory in physiology and psychology. In psychology, further important steps were the work of L.L. Thurstone on scaling methods in the 1920s and of Stevens in the 1940s.

The beginnings of test theory, which nowadays is called classical test theory (Lord and Novick, 1968), can be traced back to the early work of Spearman in the early twentieth century. The main assumptions of classical test theory will be described below. Measurement theory and test theory developed largely independently of each other until the middle of the twentieth century. Rasch (1960) and others tried to define stricter foundations of testing in measurement theory. With regard to measurement and testing situations in organizations, so far these *probabilistic* models have almost no importance. The classical test theoretical model is still dominant.

Whereas '*measurement*' emphasizes the assignment of numbers to objects (e.g. people, events, jobs), '*testing*' or assessment hints at the consequences or the aims of measurement. Similarly, assessments or judgements are continuations of measurements, but including or adding evaluations, decisions and behavioural consequences.

Measurement, testing and judging can be traced back to early history of mankind. We cannot give a comprehensive account of the history of measurement or testing in general or in personnel selection. However, we will give two historical examples to illustrate some general principles of measurement.

'Now therefore go to, proclaim in the ears of the people, saying, Whosoever is fearful and afraid, let him return and depart early from mount Gilead.' It is in the Old Testament (Judges 7:3) where we find this example of measurement (more precisely: self-assessment). God gave Gideon this advice how to select warriors among an initial 'pool' of 32 000. And there was a further measurement situation or test: Gideon led the remaining warriors to the water. Those who drank water like a dog with their tongue were selected—300 men remained. Another early example of measuring human behaviour is given by Du Bois (1970) who reports that in ancient China 3000 years ago civil servants regularly had to show their knowledge, skills, abilities, and other relevant behaviours (KSAOs), for example music, archery, horsemanship, arithmetic, etc.

These are two illustrations that measurement, testing and judging can be traced back to times long before academic psychology in the nineteenth century was established. The examples demonstrate various principles, strategies, and aims of measurement which are used and relevant until today. The strategy of Gideon is an example of *multi* (two) *stage testing* and the measurement procedure is based on a *combination of measures*. Both examples report procedures to predict (successful) behaviours on the basis of measurement results. Whereas the results in archery can be *objectively* measured, the decisions of the warriors were based on their *self-assessment* or on *observations of behaviour*. Finally, the two examples exemplify various theoretical approaches: (1) In China, measurement and selection were based on *samples* of behaviours which are conceived to be representative of future behaviour. Gideon used self-assessment of attributes. (2) We can assume that the attribute 'fearfulness' can be regarded as relevant for success because of *theoretical reasons*. (He assumed that those who are afraid are not good warriors.) Finally, (3) it might mainly be a (correlational) matter of *empirical experience* that the manner of drinking water can predict bravery. We will see later that these procedures can be taken as examples of what we nowadays call three different aspects of validity, i.e. content validity, construct validity, and criterion-related validity.

TYPES OF MEASUREMENT

Measurement is a rule-governed assignment of numbers to objects or events. More specifically, measurement is the assignment of a numerical relative to an empirical relative, i.e. we do not assign numbers to people or things but to their properties. The simplest case is classification, for example, to assign the number '1' to males and '0' to females. Measurement means decisions about equality or difference between specific attributes. Hence, measurement presupposes comparability, i.e. the possibility of making statements about equality or difference of attributes; measurement is selective.

Measurement: Assigning numerical relatives to empirical relatives

Nowadays we can discern three types of measurement: (1) fundamental measurement; (2) derived measurement; and (3) measurement 'per fiat'. Fundamental measurement is the *direct* assignment of numbers to objects or events. Examples from physics are measurement of length, time or mass; psychological examples are sex, productivity (e.g. sales) or age. Derived measurement presupposes the measurement of other attributes. An example from physics is density as the ratio of mass and volume. A psychological example is 'net hope' as the difference between 'hope for success' and 'fear of failure' in achievement motivation. 'Measuring per fiat' (Pfanzagl, 1968) is the most common procedure. Most scales/tests are grounded on 'per fiat' measurement within the system of classical test theory. Though numbers are assigned according to specific rules, they are derived neither directly from empirical objects nor from other systems of numbers by logical means but are arbitrarily defined. For example, biographical questionnaires contain items of various areas and the sum of scores can be used as a means to predict vocational success. However, it is difficult to find an empirical relative to variations in subjects' test scores. Measuring 'per fiat' often is only pragmatically justified as a provisional arrangement. We will discuss the concepts of reliability and validity mainly because most measurement is 'per fiat'.

Four types of scales can be distinguished: nominal scales, ranking/ordinal scales, interval scales, and ratio scales. The *nominal scale* has the lowest level of measurement. It is only the equality versus diversity of the elements of the numerical in relation to the empirical relative which must be held constant. Examples for a nominal scale are 'sex' or 'education'. We could assign to the empirical relative 'sex' with its attributes 'male' and 'female' any numbers provided that every target of measurement which belongs to one category of 'sex' receives: (*a*) the same number (equality) and (*b*) a different number than members of the other category (diversity). The nominal scale is also called a qualitative scale.

The *ordinal scale* implies equivalence and order. The numbers can be transformed provided the order of numbers is not changed. For example, in the case of a nominal scale we could assign to 'male' the number 1 and to 'female' the number 0 or to 'male' the number 5 and to 'female' the number 6. The only information these numbers yield is the identification of discrete classes of the attribute 'sex'. In contrast to this, ranking of the technical knowledge and skills of workers is an example of an ordinal scale, i.e. the numbers we assign can only be subjected to manipulations with regard to the size of difference but not of direction: instead of assigning a 4 to worker A and a 6 to worker B we could transform these numbers to 2 for worker A and 3 for worker B. The numbers possess meaning in so far as they represent the *direction* of difference (i.e. B is higher than A). One should be cautious about defining the scale type of a variable. For example, 'education' sometimes is interpreted as an ordinal variable though usually it is a nominal variable. Therefore, we see that the assigning of numerical relatives to empirical relatives can be ambiguous.

The *interval scale* implies the properties of the nominal as well as the ordinal scale. In addition, interval scales allow interpretations with regard to equidistance, i.e. whether the differences between numbers are equal or different. Intelligence test scores usually are treated as interval scales, i.e. if worker A has an intelligence test score of 92, worker B has a score of 94 and worker C attained a test result of 98 we could conclude that the difference between C and B is greater than the difference between B and A. The computation of an arithmetic mean is possible for interval scaled variables. The Pearsonian correlation coefficient (see Chapter 3.2) as well as many more complicated statistical procedures assume interval scales. Therefore, it is a crucial point to affirm scales to have the interval level. A typical example with respect to ambiguity of scale level is the area of school grades. Whereas some argue that school grades can only be interpreted as rank scores, others think that they have interval scale characteristics. The same is true for many rating scales. Note that interval scales allow linear transformations, i.e. it is possible to add the same number to all scores. In addition, it is also possible to multiply the scores by the same real numbers.

In contrast to interval scales the *ratio scale* assumes the ratio of scores to be unequivocally determined. This means that there exists an empirically meaningful zero point. An example is age, whereas intelligence scores normally do not possess a natural zero point. Measures of productivity sometimes do belong to this category.

As a general rule one has to keep in mind that the higher scales always allow the interpretations of the lower scales. It is also possible to transform to a lower level. This is important to take into account when deciding which statistics can be used when we have variables of different measurement levels. The distinction between scale types that we use is not the only one possible. Ghiselli, Campbell and Zedeck (1981) distinguish between classification or qualitative descriptions (= nominal scales) and measurement as quantitative descriptions. The quantitative variables are classified in (*a*) ranked variables (= ordinal scale) and (*b*) scalar variables (= interval scales and ratio scales).

We have seen that different scale types allow different interpretations, transformations, and statistical procedures. Though we did not introduce the statististical procedures in detail (see, for example, Nunnally, 1981) we include them in Table 1.

Table 1 includes both descriptive statistics and coefficients of interrelation between at least two variables. Note that the usage of these statistical tools depends on the variable with the lowest measurement level.

Relating and comparing scales: standardizations

In psychology we often face the problem that we have information about different

Table 1   The four most important scale types: admissible statements, admissible transformations, and examples of statistical measures.

Scale	Nominal scale	Ordinal scale	Interval scale	Ratio scale
Admissible statements	determination of equality and difference	additionally: ranking	additionally: equality of intervals	additionally: zeropoint
Admissible transformations	renomination, permutation	only: monotonic augmenting	only: linear transformation	only: similarity transformation
Examples of statistical measures	frequencies, modal score	additionally: median, percentiles, range	additionally: arithmetic mean, standard deviation	additionally: geometric mean, variability coefficient

persons and this information is based on different methods. Provided that the methods measure the same trait/variable one might be interested in comparing the scores. One means could be to compare the absolute or relative scores on this measure. Let us take the example that applicant A received a score of 25 (65 per cent of correct items) in test u and applicant B has one of 46 in test v (65 per cent of correct items). However, this comparison presupposes the existence of ratio scales and we mentioned that this is the exception in psychology. Moreover, we might feel that the really interesting question is how the scores could be compared taking regard of the fact that the measures or tests might be differently 'difficult'. For example, one might ask which score B would receive if assessed by the same means as A. We can achieve this end by standardizations—or one might say 'translations' of scores. The general idea is to compute the deviation of the individual from the mean of the population expressed in units of standard deviations.

The deviation (z_x) score which corresponds to the raw score (x_i) is computed as

$$z_x = \frac{x_i - M_x}{S_x} \tag{1}$$

with M_x = population mean
$\quad\;\; x_i$ = observed individual test score
$\quad\;\; S_x$ = standard deviation within the population

This z-distribution is defined as a normal distribution with 0 as the population mean M and 1 as the standard deviation S. How can we compare the scores of the two applicants A and B? Let us assume that applicant A took a test u which has a population mean of $M_u = 20$ and a standard deviation $S_u = 5$. The z-score of A then is computed as

$$z_A = \frac{x_{u_A} - M_u}{S_u} = \frac{25 - 20}{5} = 1 \tag{2}$$

Applicant B took test v which has a population mean of $M_v = 50$ and a standard deviation of 2. The z-score of B is computed as

$$z_B = \frac{x_{v_B} - M_v}{S_v} = \frac{46 - 50}{2} = -2 \tag{3}$$

We can now see that it would have been erroneous to rely on either the raw scores or the percentages. We can see that applicant A has a much higher z-score than B. As we can see from Figure 1 only about 16 per cent of applicants are expected to be better than A, whereas B exceeds only about 2.5 per cent! How could this happen? A closer look at the descriptive attributes of the tests shows that the raw score of A is one standard deviation (=5) higher than the population mean, whereas the raw score of B is two standard deviations lower than the mean in the population. So we see that z is a measure of distance from the means in standard deviation units.

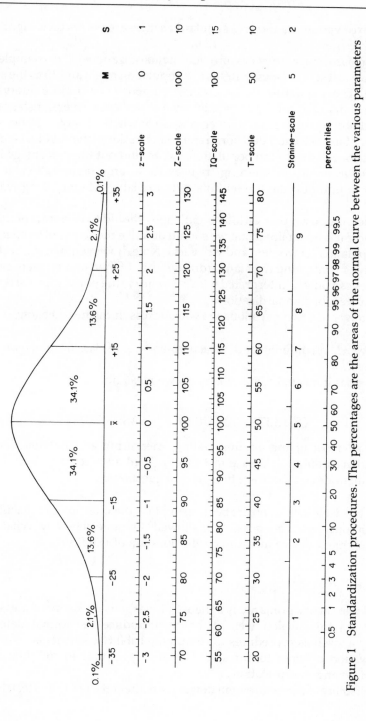

Figure 1 Standardization procedures. The percentages are the areas of the normal curve between the various parameters

There exist various methods to standardize measurement scores. Figure 1 gives a general account.

Many measurement devices provide standardizations. For example, many intelligence test scores assume 100 as the population mean and 15 as the standard deviation. The standardizations summarized above presuppose interval scales and normal distribution of scores. However, there exist several instances when we would not expect to have an interval scale or when it is not even necessary to have one. Many selection decisions refer to the ranking of individuals relative to each other or relative to the population, i.e. to find out the percentage better or worse. For example, in selecting trainees for a large organization, it may be sufficient to find out 'the top ten' instead of reliably differentiating within this group.

It is often proposed that various populations should have norms of their own. For example it is maintained that we should describe the scores of women relative to the population (of women) and vice versa. Note, however, that this restricts the possibility of comparing the standardized scores of men and women. Standardized scores can only be interpreted with reference to the population used to derive the parameters of standardization.

There now arise two questions we will address in the next section:

1. Can we *rely* on differences of measurement, i.e. of classifications, rankings or scalings?
2. What does it mean, or better: *what* do we measure?

QUALITY CRITERIA OF MEASUREMENT

Up to now most of the existing testing, measuring and judging devices are construed according to classical test theory (Lord and Novick, 1968). For every measurement device there are two general questions:

1. How precisely can an object be measured (= the question of reliability)?
2. Which conclusions are possible or allowed? Or more generally: What does the measurement device measure (= the question of validity)?

Reliability

Classical test theory primarily is a theory of reliability, a theory of measurement accuracy. In this section we will briefly introduce the formal definition of reliability as well as procedures to compute reliability coefficients. We will omit the derivation of those formulae and instead give hints to conditions of their applicability and interpretation.

The reliability of a measurement device (hereafter referred to as a test) is derived as

$$r_{tt} = \frac{S_t^2}{S_o^2} \tag{4}$$

with

r_{tt} = reliability of a test t
S_t^2 = true variance of test scores
S_o^2 = observed variance of test scores

Reliability can be defined as the proportion of true variance to observed variance. The 'true score' of a person or an object cannot directly be observed because of errors of measurement. The true score X_t of a person is defined as

$$X_t = X_o - X_e \tag{5}$$

with
X_t = true score of person X
X_o = observed score of person X
X_e = error term

The reliability of a test, r_{tt}, can vary between 0 and 1, when 0 indicates no reliability and 1 indicates perfect reliability.

We can compute the reliability only if we know the true variance, i.e. the true scores of the subjects. This is not possible. However, we can estimate the reliability via computing coefficients of correlations. The correlation we should compute depends on the purpose of our measuring endeavours. In principle, we can distinguish the following four procedures: stability, split-half, homogeneity and parallel forms.

1. *Stability*. When we compute the (correlation) coefficient of stability we assume that the true scores of our subjects are stable over time. We then measure them twice and compute a correlation between the two measurement rows. Note that here we cannot be sure whether low correlations are due to the low reliability of the test or the low stability of the attributes we measured. In addition, there might exist influences on the second measurement because of the first measurement. An example to compute a stability coefficient could be a variant of an assessment centre (Chapter 3.7). The assessment centre could last two days and on both days there might be a group discussion. We could then compute a correlation between the scores in the group discussions and thereby obtain coefficients of stability with regard to the dimensions which have been measured during the discussions.

2. *Split-half reliability*. A second possibility can be to divide the test or measurement in two halves and correlate them with each other. This is especially important when there is no possibility of repeating measurements because of economical or practical reasons. There exist different methods of 'splitting' a measure. The most convenient are to correlate the first half with the second half or the odd with the even items. For example, we could divide an intelligence test into two halves, compute the results of every subject in the 'two sessions' and then correlate them. There are important hints to note: split-

half reliability assumes two comparable halves of a test, i.e. parallel forms. This is especially critical when we have a test of *maximal* performance (e.g. intelligence, concentration) as opposed to typical performance (e.g. personality inventories). Since we expect subjects to respond with less correct answers in the second half of a test both because of difficulty and time pressure, we recommend the computation of split-half reliability by the odd–even procedure (i.e. odd item score versus even item score). In addition, one has to keep in mind that this kind of reliability is a coefficient for one *half* of the test. This warrants a correction by the Spearman–Brown formula which we introduce below.

3. *Inter-item consistency.* Inter-item consistency or internal consistency is a generalization of split-half reliability. Here, we compute the mean correlation between all items of a scale. This is often called a measure of homogeneity, the most common of which is Cronbach's coefficient alpha (cf. Ghiselli, Campbell and Zedeck, 1981, p. 255).

4. *Parallel forms (equivalence).* The fourth way to compute a correlation coefficient as an estimate of reliability is to use two parallel test forms. Parallel tests are defined as possessing equal means, variances and covariances. For example, we could decide to change the topics of the group discussions during an assessment, ensuring, however, that the topics are comparable. (It would be annoying to repeat the discussions. In addition, some subjects might improve because they know the points of views the other participants generated.)

Comparable to parallel tests are parallel raters or judges. For example, we can compute the reliability of assessment centre scores as the correlation between those assessors who observed the same candidates in the same tasks. This interrater reliability is sometimes described as a matter of *objectivity*. Though there still exist some textbooks which treat reliability and objectivity separately, they are difficult to distinguish. Objectivity is also computed by correlations. Generally we can distinguish between objectivity of procedure, scoring, and interpretation. For example, the topic of a group discussion in an assessment centre is a matter of procedural objectivity, the readability of the rating scales for the assessors is a matter of scoring objectivity, and the mode of integration of behavioural observations in the final assessor discussion after an assessment centre can be influenced by the interpretation of scale descriptions. Though most versions of objectivity can be expressed in reliability coefficients there are also differentiations necessary. For example, a certain topic change between two group discussions (with the same members) could lead to a general decrease of performance though the order of performance between the participants would be unchanged. Though we might feel that this could be a matter of lacking objectivity, a shift of mean performance scores is not expressed in the correlation coefficient computed by the scores in the two group discussions. Let us now turn to a few practical applications of the reliability coefficient.

Practical applications

1. *Prolongation of measurement.* It is usually assumed that the repetition of measurement yields more precise estimates of measurement scores. The Spearman–Brown formula gives a formal account of this phenomenon. Under the condition that we add parallel tests or aggregate parallel items we can compute the new expected reliability via

$$r_{kk} = \frac{k \times r_{tt}}{1 + (k - 1) \times r_{tt}} \tag{6}$$

with
r_{tt} = the original reliability of the test
k = factor of prolongation
r_{kk} = expected reliability of a test

We mentioned that the application of the split-half reliability warrants the correction by the Spearman–Brown formula. Let us suppose that we computed a split-half reliability coefficient of $r = 0.40$. We could then compute the reliability of the whole test as

$$r_{kk} = \frac{2 \times 0.40}{1 + (2 - 1) \times 0.40} = 0.57 \tag{7}$$

As a general rule the Spearman–Brown formula tells us that we have the greatest gain of reliability by prolonging measurement when we start with a very low reliability. This is especially important to note with regard to the reliability of single items of the behaviour in one situation. Let us assume (a quite realistic assumption) that an item has a reliability of $r = 0.15$. (This is often assumed to be a very low reliability.) However, let us extend this measurement to a test which consists of 20 items and we will receive the following result:

$$r_{kk} = \frac{20 \times 0.15}{1 + (20 - 1) \times 0.15} = 0.78 \tag{8}$$

2. *Choosing between reliability coefficients.* A test can possess different reliabilities depending on the kind of reliability measure. For example, we can assess a rather stable though heterogeneous variable resulting in high test–retest reliability and low inter-item consistency. However, we often face the problem that we expect a homogeneous scale but changing individual scores (for example because of training or job experience). In this case a homogeneity coefficient would be more appropriate than a stability coefficient to give a reasonable estimate of reliability.

There are important applications of the reliability coefficient. The *standard error of measurement* (SEM) is computed via

$$SEM = S_x \times \sqrt{1 - r_{tt}} \tag{9}$$

SEM can be used to compute a confidence interval of test or measurement scores.

The limits of the confidence interval are computed as

$$t \times \text{SEM} \tag{10}$$

The t-value (see, for example, Guilford, 1956) can be found by reference to tables. Let us look at an example. A vocational consultant wants to report test results to a client. The client (C) received a standardized intelligence test score of 105 ($M = 100$; $S = 10$). The reliability of the test is $r = 0.90$ (This is a quite usual coefficient for intelligence test scores.) The consultant would accept a probability of 5 per cent to be wrong, i.e. to accept that the true score of the client is either above or below the limits. This would lead him or her to the following conclusions: The standard error of measurement for the test is

$$\text{SEM} = S_x \times \sqrt{1 - r_{tt}} = 10 \times \sqrt{1 - 0.90} = 3.2 \tag{11}$$

For '5 per cent' the t-value is 1.96. Hence we can compute

$$t \times \text{SEM} = 1.96 \times 3.2 = 6.3 \tag{12}$$

To compute the limits of the confidence interval we would add and subtract 6 from the score. Therefore we can say that client C has his true intelligence score between 105 +/−6 (between 99 and 111), accepting a probability of 5 per cent of being wrong.

Another practical application is the critical difference between two scores. For example, an employer might receive the test results of two applicants and now wants to know whether there are significant differences between the two applicants. Generally, the critical difference d_{crit} is computed as

$$d_{crit} = t \times S_x \times \sqrt{2 - r_{tt_A} - r_{tt_B}} \tag{13}$$

Let us assume that applicant A has an intelligence test score of 110 and applicant B 95. They worked on the same test ($M = 100$; $S = 10$; $r_{tt} = 0.90$), and so the r_{tt} value is the same. Therefore it follows that

$$d_{crit} = 1.96 \times 10 \times \sqrt{2 - 0.90 - 0.90} = 9 \tag{14}$$

As our observed difference between the two applicants is 15 (110 − 95) it is higher than 9 and so the employer could conclude that there is a real difference between the two applicants. Even under the condition that the observed difference is smaller than 9 the decision would be to offer the job to the applicant with the higher score. However, in this case the employer has to be aware that the decision is subject to chance. We would then recommend that the employer should gather additional valid information about the applicants. Though one could also compute confidence intervals for the two applicants

and then scrutinize whether there is an overlap of the intervals, d_{crit} yields a more efficient tool.
3. The third important application concerns the estimation of the score when we repeat measurement. Let us again have a look at applicant A. Which score would we expect during a second measurement situation? This question can be answered by regression estimations. In our case we would estimate via

$$\hat{z}_{t_2} = z_{t_1} \times r_{tt} \tag{15}$$

with

z_{t_1} = z-score of the first measurement
r_{tt} = reliability of measurement
$\hat{z}_{t_2}$ = estimated z-score of the second measurement

For applicant A we can compute

$$z_{A_1} = \frac{X_{A_1} - M}{S} = \frac{100 - 100}{10} = 1 \rightarrow \hat{z}_{A_2} = 1 \times 0.90 = 0.90 \tag{16}$$

To retransform $\hat{z}_{A_2}$ back to the original standard score system we write:

$$\hat{z}_{A_2} = \frac{\hat{X}_{A_2} - M}{S} \rightarrow 0.90 = \frac{\hat{X}_A - 100}{10} \rightarrow \hat{X}_A = 109 \tag{17}$$

Now we can see that we would expect the applicant to be *closer* to the mean during the next measuring situation. This is generally true and is called the *regression to the mean effect*.

Let us consider another example: Low performing employees might be expected to improve because of training. However, higher performance scores after the training can also be expected because of mere regression to the mean. A means of distinguishing the change scores due to training from the regression to the mean effect is the comparison with the scores of a control group, which is measured twice, but which receives no training. Only under the conditions that the training group outperforms the control group after the training, can the real effectiveness of the training be demonstrated.

Validity

At first glance one might assume that the question of how *accurately* something can be measured (reliability) is independent from the question of *what* is measured. At second glance, however, it is understandable that the decision about which score on a dimension someone or something has precedes the possibility of deciding what this score wants to tell us. At the end of this section we will see that there even exists a formal relationship between reliability and validity. The question of validity is crucial in psychological measurement because most psychological measures deal with constructs that are not directly observable, but only inferred.

Three groups or types of validity are usually distinguished: (1) content validity; (2) construct validity; and (3) criterion-related validity. We will now introduce crude definitions and typical procedures which represent the three types of validity or validation strategies, and then we will briefly discuss their discernibility as well as the relation of reliability and validity.

Usually, measurement consists of more than one item or point of measurement. The reasons are theoretical as well as methodological. First, it is often impossible to represent the target of measurement in one item. Second, single measurements are more prone to errors than repeated measurements. But what is it exactly that explains or justifies the inclusion of an item in our measurement endeavours?

According to Landy (1986; cf. also Wernimont and Campbell, 1968) we can discern three conceptions of meaning or theoretical foundation of test and measurement items: (1) items as samples; (2) items as signs; and (3) items as 'parts'. These three conceptions are closely related to the three 'types' of validity.

Items as samples: Content validation

According to the 'sample' conception of measurement devices, measurement instruments represent reality by sampling representative features. If this kind of representativeness can be relied on, the measurement represents the target defined by the referring population. We would say that the measurement device possesses content validity—and further validation endeavours seem to be renounceable.

The most common procedure of content validation (cf. Moser, 1987) is to have experts rate whether the items are essential to, representative of, or relevant to the target under issue. For example, job samples (cf. Chapter 3.6) are rated whether they 'represent' the job.

Recent criticism of representativeness and content validity concepts leads to the recommendation that content validation should only be a preliminary step in validation. It has even been argued that content validity is at best a part of construct validity—or should better be labelled 'content representativeness'.

Items as 'signs': Criterion-related validation

The classical criterion-related validation strategy dominated personnel selection literature from its beginnings (Guion, 1987). The validity of a measurement device is pragmatically defined as the correlation with a criterion. A criterion-related validation strategy assumes the test items or test scores as mere signs. The decision whether a test is valid is solely to be based on a correlation with a criterion to be predicted.

This empirical item weighting makes the efficiency of a test the principal selection criterion for tests or test items. It implies an instrumental conception of measurement. Dependent on whether the criterion is measured at the same time or in the future the validation strategy is called concurrent validation or predictive validation. Though there exist arguments sharply to discern these two kinds of validity, Schmitt *et al.* (1984) found little evidence of difference in reviewing published validation studies. (In Chapter 3.3 the results of quantitative reviews of validity studies are presented.) Finally, one should keep in mind that there exist as many possible validity coefficients as there are criteria to evaluate.

Though the empirical item weighting procedure mainly is a 'trial and error' procedure, the preselection of items is often, in a way, theoretically motivated. Therefore, it is an over-simplification to label the criterion-related validation strategy as exclusively instrumental.

How should we proceed when we are not able to conduct a criterion-related validation strategy? We propose that we can use the validity coefficients from validity generalization studies as the summary of many single validation studies. However, one has to keep in mind that these studies refer to specific groups of jobs. Though Schmidt, Hunter and colleagues could repeatedly show that validity differences between jobs often are over-estimated (cf. Schmidt *et al.*, 1985) they also hint at the problem that this might not be true for all job families. For example, Funke *et al.* (1987) found validity coefficients for intelligence tests for research and development jobs considerably different from the mean of most other job families.

Items as parts of a construct: Construct validation

The third validation strategy represents a more theoretical approach. First, one should explore the relation between a measurement device and the constructs or variables to be measured. Then, one construes homogeneous scales—in which one *knows* what they measure. If one knows what they measure, computing criterion-related validities seems to be unnecessary. This seems to be the best way to develop a lasting system of theoretically derived relations between predictors and criteria. However, this is an extreme point of view. Actually, construct validation strategies also imply various criterion-related validation procedures. We shall discuss two other strategies of construct validation: factor analysis and multitrait–multimethod approaches.

Factor analysis can be an efficient tool to summarize variables of a big correlation matrix to few general (and 'underlying') factors. However, there do not exist exact solutions for the various possible procedures (cf. Ford, MacCallum and Tait, 1986). To prevent arbitrary factor structures there exist various methods. One of them is to validate the factors with theoretically derived independent external criteria. Another method is to make them the starting point for experimental studies, using the factor scores.

Another example for correlational methods is the multitrait–multimethod approach (MTMM; Campbell and Fiske, 1959). The MTMM is a tool to analyse and separate trait and method effects in various measurement areas. It presupposes at least two methods both assessing (the 'same') two traits. (This approach can also be extended to multimethod–multirater or multirater–multitrait approaches.) Campbell and Fiske (1959) proposed the investigation of the following four questions:

1. *Convergent validity*: The correlation between two methods assessing the *same* dimension should be statistically significant as well as practically meaningful higher than zero.
2. *Discriminant validity*:
   (a) The convergent validity coefficients should be higher than the correlations between different methods. Otherwise, this would be a hint towards one underlying general factor/trait.
   (b) The correlation between different traits with the same method should not be higher than the correlations between the same traits with different methods.
   (c) The *patterns* of the trait intercorrelations should be the same under various conditions, i.e. it should not matter whether a pattern of various traits has been assessed by method (*a*) or method (*b*)—or parts of them by method (*a*) and the other parts by method (*b*).

There exist various informal procedures as well as more or less complicated statistical tools to investigate these four questions (cf. Schmitt, Coyle and Saari, 1977). We refer to a recent discussion on the construct validity of the assessment centre to exemplify some of the questions: are the correlations between the scores of participants in two assessment centre tasks on the same dimension (e.g. delegation) sufficiently high? (=1) Are correlations between different dimensions in different tasks lower than between the same dimensions in different tasks (e.g. do delegation in the in-basket test and activity in the group discussion correlate lower than delegation in the two tasks)? (=2a) Are correlations between different dimensions measured by the same task lower than the correlation between the same dimension in different tasks (e.g. do delegation and planning in the in-basket test correlate lower than delegation in the in-basket test and in the group discussion)? (=2b).

The results are that assessment centres have low construct validity. For example, Sackett and Dreher (1982) found that in one organization correlations of dimension scores across different dimensions in one task were $r = 0.64$. Nevertheless the predictive validity of assessment centres seems to be quite high (cf. Thornton *et al.*, 1987; assessment centres are discussed in more detail in Chapter 3.7). This example has shown that a measurement instrument can be useful although we do not know exactly what it measures.

Application of validity information

One main application of validity information is the estimation of individual performance in the future. We will demonstrate this by means of a fictitious example. A school administrator decides to use an intelligence test to estimate the success of pupils applying for a school. The correlation between test results and school grades is $r = 0.60$. Pupil P gets a test score $Z = 80$ (2 standard deviations below the mean). The estimation of the school grade is computed as follows:

$$\hat{z}_y = r_{tc} \times z_x = 0.60 \times (-2) = -1.2 \rightarrow \hat{y} = 4.2 \tag{18}$$

If we assume that grade 4 is the critical limit to pass the final exam (with a mean = 3 and a standard deviation = 1) the school administrator has to predict the failure of pupil P.

Relation between reliability and validity

From classical test theory it can be shown that reliability defines the maximum of validity as follows:

$$\text{val}_{\max} = \sqrt{r_{tt}} \tag{19}$$

Note that the *absolute* amount of validity coefficients can be higher than the reliability coefficient. Another hint is necessary: validity and reliability must be of the same kind, for example to establish predictive validity, retest reliability would yield the referring upper limit; internal consistency could yield a misleading coefficient for predictive validation but could be used for concurrent validation. We recommend this precaution though recent reviews put in question the distinction between concurrent and predictive validity.

In addition, corrections of attenuations have practical importance. By using the correction of attenuation one can estimate the validity one would achieve if predictor or criterion (or both) were perfectly reliable. Therefore there exist three formulae:

$$r_{t_{**}/c} = \frac{r_{tc}}{\sqrt{r_{tt}}} \tag{20}$$

$$r_{t/c_{**}} = \frac{r_{tc}}{\sqrt{r_{cc}}} \tag{21}$$

$$r_{t_{**}/c_{**}} = \frac{r_{tc}}{\sqrt{r_{tt} \times r_{cc}}} \tag{22}$$

with
r_{tt} = reliability of the test (predictor)
r_{cc} = reliability of the criterion
r_{tc} = correlation between test and criterion (validity)
$r_{t_{**}/c_{**}}$ = estimated validity corrected for lack of both test and criterion reliability
$r_{t_{**}/c}$ = estimated validity corrected for lack of test reliability
$r_{t/c_{**}}$ = estimated validity corrected for lack of criterion reliability

The practical use of these formulae is mainly whether: (*a*) improving the reliability of a test and/or a criterion could yield an important improvement of its validity; and (*b*) whether there could be unrealistic over-estimations of coefficients. The second aspect can be shown by the following hypothetical example. Intelligence test scores are validated by intelligence estimations of teachers resulting in a correlation of $r_{tc} = 0.68$. Reliability of teacher estimations is independently reported to be $r_{cc} = 0.35$. What result would we achieve when we correct for reliability of the criterion?

$$r_{t/c_{**}} = \frac{r_{tc}}{\sqrt{r_{cc}}} = \frac{0.68}{\sqrt{0.35}} = 1.15 \tag{23}$$

This is an impossible result as the theoretical maximum of a correlation coefficient is 1.0. Either over-estimation of the validity coefficient between test scores and teacher rating or under-estimation of the reliability of the teacher ratings can then be deduced.

Relation between the three types of validity

We distinguished above between criterion-related, content and construct validity. To distinguish between three types of validity has been ironically labelled as the *trinitarian* view of validation (Landy, 1986; Guion, 1987). The question is: can we clearly *distinguish* these three kinds of validity or would it be more useful to adhere to a 'unitarian' view?

We said above that measurement in personnel psychology is a mainly *technical* problem and we hinted at the preponderance of 'measurement per fiat', that is acceptance of a certain lack of theoretical foundations. However, there exist several reasons why we want to understand and explain the predictive efficiency of a measure. Our endeavours to analyse measurement devices beyond their predictive efficiency assesses their construct validity. Landy stated that '. . . the concepts of content-oriented and construct validation represented an attempt to correct the past excesses of dust-bowl empiricism and focus attention on understanding rather than on the simpler and less meaningful search for predictability' (Landy, 1986, p. 1183). Note that construct validation *can* mean that we conduct a criterion-related validation study or even compute coefficients of inter-rater agreement which usually is interpreted as an index of reliability. However, our first aim is to know more about our measure. And we have seen that there exists a variety of methods to assess its construct validity.

Construct validity does not necessarily yield information about how well a criterion might be predicted (this is, normally, an empirical question). And because of practical (predictive) success we might rely on a tool though its theoretical foundations are very doubtful (as, for example, in the case of assessment centres).

What about content validity? It is rather doubtful whether a mere 'expert' rating of the appropriateness of a measure can be sufficient. In addition, mostly we cannot 'directly' observe the behaviour in issue and translate it in job sample tests. And, finally, most jobs warrant learning and experiences on the job, whereas content validity only might be sufficient for those who already *possess* the KSAOs when applying for a job (Guion, 1974). An alternative approach could be to assess the degree to which a job contains learning tasks and then to translate them into dynamic job sample tests (i.e. 'show learning'; Chapter 3.6 describes trainability testing). A measure can possess content validity in the sense that it is judged as a measure of the construct under issue—nevertheless yielding no variability in test scores. This is the main reason why content validation 'strategies' are both appropriate and distinguishable from criterion-related validation studies.

Finally, it would be very practical and economically more satisfying to be able to renounce criterion-related measurement both because it is necessary to measure the criteria and because of time-consuming validation procedures in the predictive case.

ASSESSING THE CRITERIA

Our brief historical sketch has illustrated that measurement as well as specific personnel selection and assessment methods have a long history. In our discussion of the three types of validation strategies we got acquainted with various procedures to validate measurement devices. Though we often cited the example of tests which are validated against criteria it is plausible that the criteria themselves should be validated, too. Indeed, in recent discussion we find that the validation criteria, which often are performance criteria, should also be treated as tests or measurement devices: 'Performance appraisers are test developers' (Banks and Roberson, 1985). Therefore, we can apply the three validation strategies to the criteria, too. However, we shall also see that there are several problems with this view.

Content validation of criteria

One possibility to validate a criterion is to assess its content validity. For example, we could ask various supervisors of a job which performance criteria or behavioural dimensions best represent (successful) performance of employees. This presupposes the insight of the 'experts' which can be doubtful and we might therefore propose a 'validation' of the experts. For example, experts should demonstrate their expertness by estimating a performance criterion which can be objectively validated (e.g. absenteeism). Further problems of content validation are dependence on the number of original items to be included, and finally it is difficult to define on which specificity *level* content validity should be assessed (Sackett, 1987).

Construct validation of criteria

The ideal to every expert in personnel assessment is the insight derived from a network of theory and observations about vocational aptitudes and performance. Even if we could be quite sure that we know what our personnel selection devices measure we must ask ourselves what they should predict. This is the question of the construct validity of the validation criteria. As Guion (1987) recently stated, studies of the construct validity of criteria are very parsimonious. A first step can be a look at the intercorrelation of criteria. Schuler and Schmitt (1987) summarize the mean intercorrelations between supervisor, self and peer assessment (cf. Table 2; Chapter 3.8 discusses self and

Table 2   Mean correlations of performance criteria (from Schuler and Schmitt, 1987, p. 267)

	Supervisor	Self-assessment	Peer assessment
Supervisor	1.00		
Self-assessment	0.31	1.00	
Peer assessment	0.22	0.41	1.00

peer assessments more fully, while Chapter 3.11 covers the related area of reference reports).

Correlations between supervisor and peer assessment are lower than between both supervisor/self- and peer/self-assessment. This hints at a need for a more detailed investigation of the question that we measure when we validate. We should also keep in mind that it often is the supervisory assessment which is the most relevant because of practical reasons.

Criterion validation of criteria

There exist a range of possible criteria to evaluate the quality of psychological assessment devices. For example we can discern trait-related criteria, objective criteria and behavioural criteria. The same is true for criteria for predictors: they vary in their theoretical foundations and their intercorrelations are low (however correlations are higher within the objective and within the subjective criteria, respectively). Some have argued for the assessment and combination of various criteria (Schuler and Schmitt, 1987). An alternative is to qualify criterion selection depending on the aim of measurement and state of knowledge:

> If your purpose is to hire generally good people, a global criterion is useful. If you aren't very sure what distinguishes good from better employees, mix up a little of every bit of job behavior . . . in developing a truly global criterion. However, if you need to solve a very specific problem, then more than one specific criterion is called for. But in most situations, a global measure will serve quite well (Guion, 1987, p. 205).

In sum, we have seen that validation criteria warrant validation themselves, too. We must concede that there is some superficiality in both choice and application of performance criteria. Whereas Guion (1987) emphasizes a missing psychometric view in criterion research, Barrett and Kerman (1987) even argue against the comparability of performance criteria and tests: 'A performance appraisal instrument is traditionally considered to be not a test, but a criterion that is correlated with a test. In most organisations, the performance evaluation is the _only_ standard by which an employee's performance can be assessed. Therefore, it is nearly impossible to correlate this standard with any other external measure' (p. 490). We think, however, that in principle it _is_ possible to validate criteria.

JOB ANALYSIS AND MEASUREMENT

To many people it is more common to 'measure' things than people. One of the 'things' we have to deal with is our work duties or jobs. The scientific measurement of jobs is achieved by job analysis methods. Job analysis instruments can be evaluated according to standards of reliability and validity, too (Schuler, 1989). However, we will restrict ourselves to describing the importance of job analysis for measurement and assessment in organizational psychology.

As Donat and Moser (1989) have summarized, job analysis has a number of different application areas. We want to point out four of them as far as they have consequences for assessment problems in organizational psychology.

1. Job analysis can improve the *job relatedness* of both predictors and criteria: it should not be necessary for candidates to answer a large number of questions unless these are really related to the job. Candidates should be judged according to criteria which are relevant to the job under investigation.
2. There might exist a close connection between job analysis and criterion-referenced as opposed to norm-referenced measurement. For example it might be possible that a selection instrument assesses the existence of a certain skill though in the past *every* applicant possessed it (and therefore the criterion-related validity coefficient would be zero).
3. Job analysis could be the starting point for *synthetic validation strategies* (Mossholder and Arvey, 1984). The main idea of synthetic validation is that we start with an investigation of a nomological network of the relations between elements of jobs and elements of behaviour or ability requirements. Afterwards, we only need to analyse a new job, assess its elements, and then we are able to devise the attributes of successful employees. Though there exist some promising attempts towards this end (cf. McCormick, DeNisi and Shaw, 1979), we still lack evidence.
4. Job analysis enables us to derive organization-specific assessment procedures, for example work samples, biographical questionnaires, situational interviews or assessment centres.

In sum, job analysis can contribute to improving measurement in organizations. However, there are also various problems, including the lack of a detailed methodology to translate job requirements into ability requirements.

MEASUREMENT: THE ASSESSEE'S VIEW

Up to this point we have assumed measuring to be the objective assigning of numbers to people (or jobs). Measurement is a relation between measurement device and reality. However, we all know that measuring, especially the measurement of people, can have intended as well as unintended consequences and sometimes it can even be used as a means to guide behaviour. Generally, we can assume artefacts to influence both reliability and validity of measurement. The main sources of artefact are experimenter effects (see Chapter 3.12 for a discussion of this effect in the case of the polygraph), cognitions and motivations of subjects, representativeness of subjects as well as errors of registration, computation or interpretation of measurement data.

Another point is that measurement is more than a one-sided process. Especially, we must assume that subjects, testees or assessees have various hypotheses about the measurement process. For example, there are many endeavours to control social desirability tendencies, i.e. the tendency to answer in a way that subjects assume to be favourable from the perspective of the assessor though it is not their 'true' reaction. There exists another perhaps still more important aspect concerning assessment problems in organizations. Subjects' hypotheses about measurement and the assessment procedures might—e.g. via the image of organizations—influence the probability of applications, to accept an offer or to leave an organization—thus diminishing the validity of measurement (Herriot, 1989). A first step is the assessment of candidates' views of assessment devices. For example, the authors and Donat and Funke asked engineering students to evaluate psychological tests and employment interviews; we found that the employment interview is evaluated as more positive than psychological tests as well as any other selection instrument. Moreover, subjects also believed that they could influence the results during interviewing more than in tests and, finally, thought that their KSAOs have been better assessed in the employment interview. (These beliefs are in fact the reverse of the results of research on the employment interview; see Chapter 3.9.) The experience of assessment or measurement situations might be a decisive variable in various circumstances, the severest of which may be the coping with success and failure. A first step should be to assess various aspects of experiences during the measurement process. As has been argued elsewhere (Schuler and Stehle, 1983), an attempt might be made to take regard of information, participation, communication and transparency as four parts of the 'social validity' of psychological measurement.

SUMMARY AND DISCUSSION

After a brief historical sketch of measurement and assessment we introduced four scale types: nominal, ordinal, interval and ratio. We described their properties as well as the permitted statistical procedures. Then we introduced 'reliability' and 'validity' as the key concepts of psychological measurement. Whereas reliability summarizes the accuracy of measurement, validity informs about what we measure. We showed the practical meaning of both reliability and validity coefficients as well as their mutual interrelations. Then we extended them to criteria as well and stressed the importance of job analysis. Finally, we discussed the effects of measurement on the 'objects' of measurement.

There exist various critical perspectives of psychological measurement as it has been introduced in this chapter. However, we think that every point can be counter-argued:

1. The more philosophical critiques question whether measurability, predictability and freedom of will are compatible; more specifically, we cannot know

what we will know in the future. However, future knowledge influences our behaviour in the future. We think that this is true only when we want to predict behaviour perfectly. And this is neither realistic nor intended.

2. We have seen many ethical concerns in the discussion of psychological measurement (Schuler, 1982). However, we think that there exists no real alternative to scientific measurement—but naive measurement. We do assess people, explain and predict their behaviour. However, research has shown various fallacies of *intuitive* 'measurement' and assessment. Critics of psychological measurement are right to state that psychological measurement can be bothering. We discussed job analysis and investigation of the 'social validity' of assessment as promising perspectives.

3. Classical test theory constitutes the 'hard core' of measurement practice in industrial and organizational psychology. There remains the fact that many measurement instruments lack theoretical foundations in measurement theory. Some critics ironically asked what a 'true score' is (cf. Lumsden, 1976). We think that it is a useful pragmatic decision to maintain that we speak of the real ability or intelligence score of someone.

Our introduction to the nature of psychological measurement primarily is based on what is done in the practical and applied area of personnel psychology. Therefore, we did not include either generalizability theory (Cronbach *et al.*, 1972) or probabilistic latent trait models of measurement. Though generalizability theory implies promising extensions of the classical reliability theory, and probabilistic models of measurement might improve our understanding as well as the theoretical foundation of measurement, their applications in personnel psychology are as yet of little importance.

ACKNOWLEDGEMENTS

Writing of this manuscript has been partially supported by the Volkswagenwerk Foundation AZ II/62 208 and the Land Baden-Württemberg. We thank Michael Donat, Uwe Funke, Peter Herriot and Alan Jones for their helpful comments on earlier versions of this chapter.

REFERENCES

Banks, C.G., and Roberson, L. (1985). Performance appraisers as test developers, *Academy of Management Review*, **10**, 128–42.

Barrett, G.V., and Kerman, M.C. (1987). Performance appraisal and termination: A review of court decisions since Brito v. Zita with implications for personnel practices, *Personnel Psychology*, **40**, 489–503.

Campbell, D.T., and Fiske, D.W. (1959). Convergent and discriminant validation by the multitrait–multimethod matrix, *Psychological Bulletin*, **56**, 81–105.

Cronbach, L.J., Gleser, G.C., Nanda, H., and Rajaratnam, N. (1972). *The Dependability of Behavioral Measurements*. Wiley, New York.

Donat, M., and Moser, K. (1989). Die Arbeits- und Anforderungsanalyse als Grundlage der Gestaltung von Assessment Centers, in Ch. Lattmann (ed.). *Das Assessment Center— Verfahren der Eignungsbensterling*. Physica, Würzburg, pp 155–182.

Du Bois, P.H. (1970). *A History of Psychological Testing*. Allyn & Bacon, Boston.

Ford, J.K., MacCallum, R.C., and Tait, M. (1986). The application of exploratory factor analysis in applied psychology: A critical review and analysis, *Personnel Psychology*, **39**, 291–314.

Funke, U., Krauss, J., Schuler, H., and Stapf, K.H. (1987). Zur Prognostizierbarkeit wissenschaftlich-technischer Leistungen mittels Personvariablen: eine Metaanalyse der Validität diagnostischer Verfahren im Bereich Forschung und Entwicklung, *Gruppendynamik*, **18**, 407–28.

Ghiselli, E.E., Campbell, J.P. and Zedeck, S. (1981). *Measurement Theory for the Behavioral Sciences*. Freeman, San Francisco.

Guilford, J.P. (1956). *Fundamental Statistics in Psychology and Education*. McGraw-Hill, New York.

Guion, R.M. (1974). Open a new window. Validities and values in psychological measurement, *American Psychologist*, **29**, 287–96.

Guion, R.M. (1987). Changing views for personnel selection research, *Personnel Psychology*, **40**, 199–213.

Herriot, P. (1989). Selection as a social process, in M. Smith and I. Robertson (eds). *Advances in Selection and Assessment*. Wiley, New York, pp 171– 88.

Landy, F.L. (1986). Stamp collecting versus science, *American Psychologist*, **41**, 1183–92.

Lord, F.M., and Novick, M.R. (1968). *Statistical Theories of Mental Test Scores*. Addison-Wesley, Reading, Mass.

Lumsden, J. (1976). Test theory, *Annual Review of Psychology*, **27**, 251–79.

McCormick, E.J., DeNisi, A.S., and Shaw, J.B. (1979). Use of the Position Analysis Questionnaire for establishing the job component validity of tests, *Journal of Applied Psychology*, **64**, 51–6.

Mitchell, J.V. (1985). *The Ninth Mental Measurements Yearbook*, University of Nebraska, Lincoln, Nebraska.

Moser, K. (1987). Inhaltsvalidität als Kriterium psychologischer Tests, *Diagnostica*, **33**, 139–51.

Moser, K., Gadenne, V., and Schröder, J. (1988). Under what conditions does confirmation-seeking obstruct scientific progress? *Psychological Review*. **95**, 512–14.

Mossholder, K.W., and Arvey, R.D. (1984). Synthetic validity: A conceptual and comparative review. *Journal of Applied Psychology*, **69**, 322–33.

Nunnally, J.C. (1981). *Psychometric Theory*. McGraw-Hill, New York.

Pfanzagl, J. (1968). *Theory of Measurement*. Physica, Würzburg.

Rasch, G. (1960). *Probabilistic Models for some Intelligence and Attainment Tests*. Nielson & Lydiche, Copenhagen.

Sackett, P.R. (1987). Assessment centers and content validity: Some neglected issues, *Personnel Psychology*, **40**, 13–26.

Sackett, P.R., and Dreher, G.F. (1982). Constructs and assessment center dimensions: Some troubling empirical findings, *Journal of Applied Psychology*, **67**, 401–10.

Schmidt, F.L., Hunter, J.E., Pearlman, K., and Hirsh, H. (1985). Forty questions about validity generalization and meta-analysis, *Personnel Psychology*, **38**, 697–798.

Schmitt, N., Coyle, B., and Saari, B.B. (1977). A review and critique of analysis of multitrait–multimethod matrices, *Multivariate Behavioral Research*, **12**, 447–78.

Schmitt, N., Gooding, R.Z., Noe, R.D., and Kirsch, M. (1984). Metaanalysis of validity studies published between 1964 and 1982 and the investigation of study characteristics, *Personnel Psychology*, **37**, 407–22.

Schuler, H. (1982). *Ethical Problems in Psychological Research*. Academic Press, New York.

Schuler, H. (1989). Some advantages and problems of job analysis, in M. Smith and I. Robertson (eds). *Advances in Selection and Assessment*. Wiley, New York, pp 31–42.

Schuler, H., and Schmitt, N. (1987). Multimodale Messung in der Personalpsychologie, *Diagnostica*, **33**, 259–71.

Schuler, H., and Stehle, W. (1983). Neuere Entwicklungen des Assessment-Center-Ansatzes–beurteilt unter dem Aspekt der sozialen Validität, *Psychologie und Praxis. Zeitschrift für Arbeits- und Organisationspsychologie*, **27**, 33–44.

Thornton, G.C. III, Gaugler, B.B., Rosenthal, D.B., and Bentson, C. (1987). Die prädiktive Validität des Assessment Centers—eine Metaanalyse, in H. Schuler and W. Stehle (eds). *Assessment Center als Methode der Personalentwicklung*. Hogrefe/Verlag für Angewandte Psychologie, Stuttgart, pp. 36–60.

Wernimont, P.R., and Campbell, J.P. (1968). Signs, samples and criteria, *Journal of Applied Psychology*, **52**, 372–6.

Chapter 3.2

Psychological Testing

CHARLES E. BETHELL-FOX

Hay Management Consultants Ltd, 52 Grosvenor Gardens, London SW1W 0AU, UK

INTRODUCTION

Recent research has shown that the sensible use of psychological tests can save organizations large sums of money. This chapter describes how to use and/or develop psychological tests for use in public or private organizations, for purposes such as selection, training, appraisal, or career development. Some of the financial costs and benefits are also outlined.

Psychological testing is concerned with the measurement of mental qualities. Measurement produces numbers, and conclusions about psychological characteristics are typically drawn from these data via the application of mathematical techniques. However, the increasing sophistication of these methods has made the whole area of psychological testing less approachable for many personnel managers and applied psychologists. Consequently, this chapter sets out the basic ideas in plain English and banishes all formulae to appendices. The non-mathematician should, therefore, not be at a disadvantage. The purpose is to equip the reader with the techniques required not only to develop a psychological test but also to appraise critically the qualities of commercially available tests. Thereby, the test user should be in a position to make an informed choice from the myriad tests offered for sale.

Most of the ideas in the chapter are borrowed from classical test theory. Item response theory, which is briefly described in Chapter 3.3, is ignored because it is not required to comprehend the techniques used to construct most published psychological tests.

Handbook of Assessment in Organizations   Edited by P. Herriot
© 1989 John Wiley & Sons Ltd

THREE FUNDAMENTAL CONCEPTS: VALIDITY, RELIABILITY AND NORM TABLES

For a test to be of any practical use it stands to reason that:

1. A test should measure what it is supposed to measure and predict what it is supposed to predict. Consider a selection test designed to predict the performance of accountants under training. If the test gives an estimate of how quickly and accurately a person can perform arithmetic but *fails* to predict how well a trainee will learn more complex skills, such as double entry book-keeping, then the test is of little use to the personnel selector. This quality of measuring something of predictive value is one aspect of the *validity* of the test. The section 'Types of Validity' goes into more detail.

2. No matter what mental characteristic a test purports to measure it should measure this characteristic accurately. If a measurement that one expects to be stable fluctuates the implication is one of imprecise measurement—as when one steps on then off and then back on a pair of bathroom weighing scales and notices that the measurement varies. Similarly, if a person does well when he or she first takes a test he or she ought to do well if the test is taken again. One might expect some improvement with practice but it would be disconcerting if someone who had done very badly suddenly achieved an excellent score—the converse might be even more alarming. The quality of consistent measurement, which implies accuracy, is termed the *reliability* of the test. The section 'Types of Reliability' goes into more detail.

    The concepts of validity and reliability are easily confused but the distinction should become clearer after reading the later sections. For the time being, an analogy may help. Consider trying to estimate a person's weight. Using a tapemeasure, one could probably measure height quite accurately (reliably) to within a couple of centimetres but this measurement would sometimes be a poor predictor of weight (poor validity). The measurement is fairly precise, but it is of the wrong characteristic. On the other hand, good quality weighing scales provide a more valid estimate of a person's weight, in that they measure the appropriate characteristic, but only if the scales have been adjusted properly (i.e. the reading is reliable).

3. When using a test score as an aid to decision making one needs to know how to interpret the score. There are two major ways of interpreting test scores. The first, known as criterion-referenced measurement, equates test score directly with levels of performance in the behaviour to be predicted. For example, breathalyser results are given criterion-referenced interpretations in that results above a certain level are taken to indicate that one is a hazard to others. Different tested levels of typing speed for different kinds of secretarial work are another example.

    The second way of interpreting test scores is known as norm-referenced measurement. Given that a test is known to predict job performance, an individual's score on the test is interpreted by comparing it to other persons' scores rather than directly to the behaviour to be predicted. *Norm tables*, which are described in detail in a later section, facilitate such comparisons. Norm-referenced interpretations lead to statements such as 'Only about one in ten people gets a score as high as this person's'. Thereby, norm-referenced interpretations focus on how well a person matches up against others whereas criterion-referenced scores indicate what a person can do. Because of the strong competitive element in most personnel selection and career development, almost all test score interpretation in personnel work is norm referenced so it is on norm-referenced measurement that this chapter focuses.

THE CORRELATION COEFFICIENT

When investigating whether a test score predicts job performance one can determine whether or not people with high test scores perform well on the job. But this procedure ignores those with low test scores, some of whom may be good at the job. Alternatively, one can construct a complete list composed of test scores and associated job performances for everyone. However, as the list lengthens the amount of information it contains soon overwhelms any attempt to discern how well the test is working as a predictor. Fortunately, the degree to which one measure (e.g. test score) predicts another (e.g. job performance) can be summarized by a single number, the correlation coefficient. Furthermore, the value of the correlation coefficient based on, say, 30 people provides an (albeit rough) estimate of the value that might be obtained with several hundred individuals. A formula for calculating the type of correlation coefficient typically used in developing psychological tests (the Pearson Product–Moment Coefficient of Correlation, to give it its full name) is given in Appendix A. In what follows it is to this particular type of correlation coefficient that we refer when mentioning correlation.

If one measurement does not predict another then the two measurements are said to be uncorrelated with one another. Such a relationship is summarized by a correlation coefficient of value zero. However, if one measurement more or less perfectly predicts another, such as when speed is used to predict distance travelled, then the value of the correlation between the two measures increases up to a maximum of one. Degrees of prediction between these two extremes have correlation coefficients between zero and one. As a rule of thumb, for personnel selection work a test score that weakly predicts job performance has a correlation with job performance of about 0.2 whereas a good predictor has a correlation of about 0.4. A correlation of 0.6 corresponds to a strong level of prediction and correlation coefficients for a test predicting job performance rarely, if ever, exceed 0.7.

Correlations can also have negative values down to a minimum of −1. These negative values correspond to their positive counterparts except that the minus sign indicates that as one measurement increases the other *decreases* in a predictable fashion (such as distance travelled in relation to remaining fuel supply).

TYPES OF VALIDITY

Predictive validity

Whether a test is norm or criterion referenced a major concern must be to what extent a test succeeds in predicting training or job performance for this is one of the factors that influences a test's cost-effectiveness. The degree of relationship between test score and, say, job performance can be summarized by the value of the correlation between the two. This value is known as the predictive validity of the test.

However, in order to maximize predictive validity experience shows that it is worth viewing the validity of a test from a slightly broader perspective. In particular, if *construct validity* is made the central focus predictive validity should follow.

Construct validity

Construct validity is an abstract but important concept. If we claim that a particular mental quality in an employee facilitates good job performance and we put our claim to empirical test (i.e. gather data that can either support or refute our claim) then we are testing theories via scientific methods. For example, our theory might be 'There exists a mental quality called analytical ability which is implicated in the work of accountants. People have differing amounts of this ability, these differences in part explaining why some people make better accountants than others.' Notice that this theory hinges on the supposition that there exists in reality something which corresponds to our invention, the construct 'analytical ability', whatever that might be. Such constructs are abstract. Furthermore, empirical evidence that they correspond to real mental qualities is usually indirect and gathered painstakingly over long time periods. However, to the extent that we can obtain evidence that is consistent with the notion that analytical ability exists, so it seems more valid and reasonable to premise theories such as that above on the construct. In this context, evidence for the construct is referred to as construct validity. Hence, to talk about 'the construct validity of a test' is a slightly imprecise use of language; 'the construct validity of the idea behind the test' might be better.

If we design a test to measure the construct 'analytical ability' and we find that scores on the test correlate with job performance in various fields (e.g. computer programming, market forecasting, scientific research, professional chess), all of which probably require a good deal of analytical ability, then this lends some credibility to the construct validity of the test. Indeed, given this sort of prior evidence one would probably be surprised to go on to find that scores on the test did not predict the job performance of accountants. In other words, knowledge of the construct validity of a test can help one judge the test's likely predictive validity.

Content validity

When designing a test to measure, for example, analytical ability the content of the questions should obviously be such that their solution requires analytical ability rather than, say, an extensively developed vocabulary. Each question should focus on the construct to be measured. In addition, if analytical ability is assumed to be a broad mental faculty that operates in, say, both numerical and verbal contexts then the test should reflect this supposition by posing both numerically and verbally based questions (without making too many demands on vocabulary). To the extent that a test contains questions which, as described above, are both relevant and representative so the test is said to be content valid. Without content validity a test is unlikely to be an effective measure of a construct, in which case studying the predictive validity of the test is most likely wasted effort.

Concurrent validity

Once relevant and representative questions have been selected for use in a test (see later section 'Test Development' for further explanation), establishing the test's predictive validity may involve a substantial time lag while job performance data are collected. On the other hand, using a test executively which has not been shown to predict job performance is a violation of basic testing standards. One practical solution to this dilemma is to administer the test to *current* job incumbents and to correlate performance on the test with job performance. When test and job performance data are gathered at approximately the same time in this way a correlation between the two is referred to as concurrent validation. As with content validation, if the evidence fails to support concurrent validity then a return to the initial design phase of test development is appropriate rather than an attempt at predictive validation.

Convergence and divergence of indicators

Even if one has selected questions carefully and obtained evidence for predictive validity it still might be that the test measures a mental quality other than the one supposed but which is, nevertheless, also important for successful job performance. This is more than a theoretical nicety. It has practical implications for cost-effectiveness.

For example, modern personnel selection systems typically contain several tests or selection instruments as well as several selection stages. If the test under study measures a mental quality also measured to some extent by other aspects of the selection system, then reasonably strong correlations between the measures should appear (i.e. the measurements converge). To the extent that the new test is designed to measure a mental quality not captured by some of the other instruments in the selection system, so scores on the new test should show low correlations with scores on the other instruments (i.e. the measurements diverge). In particular, if a test shows the anticipated pattern of correlations with other instruments (higher correlations with some, lower correlations with others), then one has more reason to believe that the new test does indeed measure the construct. In other words, simultaneous convergence and divergence of indicators are persuasive evidence for construct validation.

If evidence for divergence of indicators cannot be obtained then scores on the new test are probably not adding useful information to the selection system in which case the system's predictive validity is unlikely to increase (sometimes termed lack of incremental validity). Use of such a test is unlikely to be cost-effective.

Face validity

Obviously, test-takers should do their best when taking a test. However, if they think that the knowledge required to answer questions is irrelevant to the workplace they are unlikely to give their best performance. Hence, no matter how ingenious the idea behind a test, questions should give the appearance to test-takers of measuring something relevant to the job even if this perceived relevance, or face validity, is based on superficial judgements by test-takers. For example, in a test designed to measure the analytical ability of trainee accountants it would probably be desirable to have at least some questions set in practical, financial contexts.

TYPES OF RELIABILITY

Reliability limits validity

No matter how much insight a test constructor may have into the mental qualities required to perform a job, for the resulting test to be a good predictor it must not only measure the appropriate mental quality but also measure the quality accurately. Of course, to the extent that a measurement is inaccurate so it is, inevitably, of less predictive value. Hence, the reliability of a test limits its validity. As will be described, the reliability of a test can be expressed as a correlation coefficient and a formula which calculates the ceiling placed by unreliability on the predictive value of a test score is given in Appendix B. So, for example, a test with a reliability of 0.5 limits validity to a possible maximum of 0.7 as opposed to a theoretically possible maximum of 1.0 for a perfectly reliable test.

Test–Retest estimates of reliability

One way to estimate the reliability of a test is by giving the test on two separate occasions to the same group of candidates and correlating the two sets of results. The resulting correlation coefficient (sometimes called a coefficient of stability) is an estimate of the reliability of the test. Clearly, if the test is an accurate measure the two sets of scores should be highly correlated. However, parallel forms reliability (described below) is often a more desirable measure of reliability.

Parallel forms estimates of reliability

To return for a moment to the concept of construct validity, if we have a clear idea of what mental faculty we wish to measure, and some notion of how to write questions whose solution engages that mental faculty, then it should be possible to write enough questions for several versions (known as parallel forms) of the same test. Furthermore, if we have a clear understanding of the construct and of how to write questions to measure it then the performance of the same candidates on different versions of the test should be highly correlated. Such a correlation between parallel forms of the test (sometimes called a coefficient of equivalence) provides an estimate of a test's reliability.

Test–retest reliability, which uses an identical test twice rather than two parallel tests once each, is likely to provide an inflated estimate. This is because factors which are specific to the test, but not relevant to the construct under investigation, will serve to increase test–retest reliability but not parallel forms reliability. For example, if some of the questions are worded ambiguously and the candidate misinterprets them, this is likely to occur on both occasions if the candidate takes exactly the same test twice. Such effects will make a candidate's score appear consistent from one administration of the test to the next yet are not indications of accurate measurement of the construct of interest. Parallel tests, on the other hand, contain questions of similar but not identical content so faults in test design are likely to vary from one version of the test to the next and, thereby, not serve to inflate artificially estimates of reliability.

Internal consistency estimates of reliability

It is possible to estimate the reliability of a test by administering a single version of the test only once. First, think of each question (item) on a test as a separate, one-item test each designed to measure the same mental quality so that all items are parallel test versions of one another. Second, keep in mind that other things being equal the more items appear in a test the more reliable a test becomes. These two notions are developed further below, as a means of conceptualizing internal consistency estimates of reliability.

If each test item measures the same mental quality, such as analytical ability, then a testee's level of performance on any one item should correlate with level of performance on any other item in the same way that performance on parallel tests should be correlated. Furthermore, the average of the inter-item correlations (correlations between performance on each single item with performance on every other single item) should be high. The question now arises how to take this average of the inter-item correlations and express it in such a way that it is numerically comparable to test–retest or parallel forms coefficients (correlations) of reliability.

As a test increases in length (has more items added to it) so it becomes more reliable (other things being equal) because each item is designed to measure the same construct and as more measurements are taken the errors of measurement tend to cancel one another out. For example, when measuring one's weight on bathroom weighing scales one expects some inaccuracy. However, if one uses some different scales (analogous to a different item on a test) and obtains a reasonably similar measurement so one's confidence in the measurement increases. The average across the different measurements is the best estimate of one's 'true' weight, assuming 'true' weight is reasonably constant. And as more measurements on different weighing scales are added to this average the more credible the average becomes. So it is with psychological tests: the more questions the more likely the total score is an accurate reflection of a person's ability. The relationship between reliability and test length can be stated precisely (see Appendix C). Consequently it is possible to estimate how reliable a test would become if one increased its length by a known amount.

Hence, we can take the average of the inter-item correlations as an estimate of the reliability of a single item and then compute the reliability of the whole test by adjusting for the effect on reliability of having more than one item on the test. For example, if the average inter-correlation of performances on single items is 0.2 a test containing 20 such items would have an estimated reliability (using the formula in Appendix C) of about 0.8. This method of computing reliability is known as an internal consistency estimate or internal consistency coefficient. A formula for calculating internal consistency reliability directly, on the basis of all item scores together, is given in Appendix D.

Comparison of different estimates of reliability

As mentioned above, generally speaking, parallel forms estimates of reliability are preferable to test–retest estimates because factors specific to the test but irrelevant to the construct to be measured inflate test–retest reliability estimates. Given the economy of effort required to obtain internal consistency estimates of reliability (administering one test only once) it is perhaps not surprising that such estimates can also be misleading if not interpreted carefully. For example, if a person's level on the mental quality to be measured fluctuates from day to day this inconsistency in performance will not be recorded by a single administration of one test. Parallel tests can be administered with long delays between administrations so such daily fluctuations in performance will, to some extent, be captured by parallel forms estimates of reliability and will serve to decrease the obtained estimate. Given that our concern in prediction is with job performance over long time periods, parallel forms estimates of reliability are typically the most appropriate.

Internal consistency reliability estimates are also prone to inflation if a test is highly speeded, that is when candidates have to solve many test items in a short time. If some candidates do not attempt questions towards the end of the test they will inevitably get no marks for these questions. Hence, performance on later items will appear more consistent than it might if all candidates had time to attempt all questions. However, internal consistency estimates are an economical means of obtaining preliminary indications of reliability and a test that lacks internal consistency is unlikely to prove reliable under more painstaking methods of reliability estimation. But once internal consistency has been demonstrated, then a parallel forms estimate of reliability should be obtained because it best reveals how accurately the test measures general, lasting characteristics of persons.

NORM TABLES

No matter how much effort is devoted to developing a test which is both reliable and valid, test users are still faced with the problem of how to interpret obtained test scores (known as raw scores, i.e. the number of questions answered correctly). Norm tables, described below, can be very helpful in this regard, but their use requires considerable care on at least three counts. First, the values read from norm tables corresponding to particular test scores should be in a form which can be readily linked to other information about the individual concerned so as to facilitate decision making. Second, the test user needs to know how much confidence to place in the score so that the score's likely accuracy can be incorporated into its interpretation. Third, the user must ensure that the norm tables consulted were originally constructed on the basis of data collected from individuals who were in at least some sense comparable to the pool of job applicants currently under consideration. But before addressing these issues an outline follows of what typically constitutes a norm table.

Basic constituents

Essentially, norm tables record the proportions of test-takers who obtain particular scores. So, for a group of 99 persons taking a 20-item test we might find that few persons get less than six items correct and correspondingly few get less than six wrong, with most individuals getting from six to fourteen questions correct, ten out of twenty being the most common mark. Such a distribution of scores is shown in Table 1. Imagine that these are the scores on a test of analytical reasoning from last year's applicants to an organization seeking trainee accountants. If the first applicant in the current year obtains a mark of fourteen we can compare this to the distribution shown in Table 1 and thereby deduce whether this mark constitutes a relatively weak, average or strong performance. In other words the distribution of last year's scores provides norms to which individual scores from the current year can be referred and thereby interpreted.

Hence, the data that constitute a norm table are quite straightforward. But their successful use in test score interpretation requires care for the reasons described in the following discussions of scales, accuracy and relevance.

Normative scales

When comparing an individual's score to the distribution of scores shown in a norm table the immediate, natural temptation is to interpret the score in terms of what percentage of persons get a score equal to or lower than the individual. So, for example, Table 1 shows that a person with a score of 16 scores equal to or better than about 95 per cent of the normative sample, whereas a score of 8 or less is achieved by about 35 per cent. Scores translated in this way into cumula-

Table 1

Score	Number of persons with score	Percentiles	Standard score	Stanine	T-Score
0	0				
1	1	1	−2.25	1	28
2	1	2	−2.00	1	30
3	2	3 to 4	−1.75	2	33
4	4	5 to 8	−1.50	2	35
5	4	9 to 12	−1.25	3	38
6	6	13 to 18	−1.00	3	40
7	8	19 to 26	−0.75	4	43
8	9	27 to 35	−0.50	4	45
9	9	36 to 44	−0.25	5	48
10	11	45 to 55	0.00	5	50
11	9	56 to 64	0.25	6	53
12	9	65 to 73	0.50	6	55
13	8	74 to 81	0.75	7	58
14	6	82 to 87	1.00	7	60
15	4	88 to 91	1.25	8	63
16	4	92 to 95	1.50	8	65
17	2	96 to 97	1.75	9	68
18	1	98	2.00	9	70
19	1	99	2.25	9	73
20	0				

Note: Stanines and T-scores are usually expressed as whole numbers so some rounding error occurs.

tive percentages are called percentiles. Percentiles are useful in test score interpretation because they are readily understood. However, their use can be misleading. Consider a score of 10 versus a score of 11 in the context of Table 1. This corresponds to performing as well as or better than about 55 per cent of the sample versus 64 per cent, a difference of 9 percentage points, i.e. nine percentiles. Now contrast a score of 18 with one of 19. Here, the difference is 98 per cent versus 99 per cent, i.e. only one percentile. Thus, getting one more question correct has marked effects on percentiles in the middle of the score distribution but small effects at the top (or the bottom—see Table 1).

Consequently, there are two pitfalls in the use of percentiles. First, when percentiles are compared, such as when individuals' scores are contrasted or one individual is tested twice, large differences in percentiles may not correspond to marked differences in test performance but merely to the way scores happen to be distributed in the norm table. Second, percentiles should never be averaged because taking the average of two percentiles will normally not lead to the same result as averaging the corresponding number of questions correctly answered.

There are other scales of measurement which are not prone to the above misuses. The three most common are standard scores, stanines and T-scores (see Table 1). All are based on the same principle. First, for each possible total score on the test the difference between this score and the mean raw score in the normative sample is divided by the standard deviation of the raw scores. The standard deviation (see Appendix E for method of calculation) is simply a measure of the variability of the raw scores in the sample. When most obtained scores are bunched in about the middle of the distribution with the remaining scores spread out more or less symmetrically either side of the middle as in Table 1 then one standard deviation either side of the mean typically covers about 68 per cent of the sample whereas two standard deviations cover about 95 per cent. Raw scores transformed in this way are called standard scores. A raw score two standard deviations below the mean has a corresponding standard score value of -2, a raw score equal to the mean has value of 0, and a raw score one standard deviation above the mean has a standard score value of 1. Table 1 shows the complete range of standard scores corresponding to all possible raw scores based on the hypothetical normative sample for our 20-item test.

Stanines and T-scores are nothing more than transformed standard scores. Due to the method of calculation standard scores themselves have a mean of zero and a standard deviation of one. Stanines, which are limited to whole values between 1 and 9, are calculated by multiplying standard scores by two and then adding five (values below one are counted as one and values above nine as nine) as illustrated in Table 1. T-scores are produced by multiplying standard scores by 10 and then adding 50 so T-scores have a mean of 50 and a standard deviation of 10 (see Table 1).

Further examination of Table 1 reveals that unlike percentiles, changes in standard scores, stanines, or T-scores correspond directly (within the limits of rounding error) to changes in raw scores: getting more questions correct results in the same increase in transformed score (within the limits of rounding error) irrespective of whereabouts in the normative distribution the raw scores are located. Also, unlike percentiles, averaging two scores on the same of any one of these three scales gives the same result (again within the limits of rounding error) as averaging the two corresponding raw scores and then transforming the result to the new scale. However, standard scores, stanines or T-scores should not be used when the distribution of scores in the norm table differs strongly from the sort of symmetrical distribution shown in Table 1, as when, for example, most persons obtain scores between 0 and 4 with only a few scoring between 5 and 20. When distributions lack symmetry it is probably best to use percentiles and keep in mind the pitfalls of so doing.

Accuracy and the standard error of measurement

Earlier we described various means for estimating the reliability of a test. Parallel forms estimates of reliability can be used in the derivation of the SEM or standard error of measurement of a test (see Appendix F for formula) which is an indicator of how much confidence to place in a particular individual's score which, in turn, can be incorporated into that score's interpretation. Thus, if one SEM is added to an individual's score and also one SEM subtracted this provides rough upper and lower bounds respectively on what score that person would probably obtain on another sitting of a similar test. To be precise, above-average scores are actually more likely to be over-estimates than under-estimates of the score a person would probably obtain on retesting, and vice versa for below average scores, but this need not detain us. However, roughly speaking, adding and subtracting one SEM provides a score band in which on about 68 per cent of second occasions one would expect an individual's score to appear. Adding and subtracting two SEMs provides a score band covering about 95 per cent of second occasions. So, for example, if a 20-item test has an SEM equal to 1 we can say with about 68 per cent confidence that a person who obtains a score of 15 would on a second occasion obtain a score of 14, 15 or 16, and with 95 per cent confidence a score somewhere between 13 and 17 inclusive.

Knowledge of the standard error of measurement is valuable when using norm tables to interpret test scores. If the SEM is large then a particular individual's relatively low or high score may be nothing more than a consequence of inaccurate measurement. Hence, it is useful to place confidence bands around scores and to identify the corresponding lower and upper bands in the norm table. This helps to prevent placing injudicious weight on test scores which are never perfectly reliable.

Relevance of norms

Many factors such as a candidate's age, sex, ethnicity or educational experience may be related to psychological test performance. Hence, if norm tables have been constructed on the basis of data collected from 21-year-old white male graduates an attempt to interpret the test score of a 35-year-old black female non-graduate via these norms may well be pointless. Consequently, when using a published test one should identify the characteristics of the sample of candidates from whom the norm table was derived. In occupational testing it is unlikely that published norms ever provide more than a rough guide to test score interpretation because any organization's candidate pool is likely to differ in significant ways from the norm table sample. The only practicable solution, given that organizations typically use the same tests over a period of years, is to develop in-house norms. Thus, as soon as sufficient numbers of candidates have taken a test within an organization new norm tables should be derived to replace the published norms. Data from job incumbents can also provide initial pointers.

It is also worth keeping in mind that any changes to the test itself or to the manner in which the test is administered will probably affect normative levels of performance. For example, modifying a test for machine scoring so that candidates shade-in boxes rather than simply tick selected answers may hinder speedy performance. It follows that any changes in test format or administration must be accompanied by the development of new norm tables.

JOB ANALYSIS AND TEST CHOICE

For a test to be an effective predictor of work outcome it must measure mental qualities that influence important aspects of job performance. Thus, part of the process of choosing tests involves job analysis to identify important job components. Careful thought and, sometimes, considerable psychological insight permit deduction of the mental qualities required to execute these components and, thereby, the selection of appropriate tests.

Ideally, we require a comprehensive account of individual differences which is linked to a complete taxonomy of job components but no such tool exists. However, certain broad categories of individual variation have been identified (see, in particular, the next two chapters) and, while job analysis is an incomplete science, it provides techniques of proven value (see, in particular, Chapter 2.2). Consider, for example, choosing tests to select trainee accountants. Accountancy typically requires intellectual ability, interpersonal and communication skills and, eventually, managerial capacity. A careful job analysis would produce a more complete breakdown but even this superficial description shows that exclusive use of a test of analytical ability would be inadequate. For example, good interpersonal skills demand some verbal attainments and a neurotic introvert may prove an ineffective manager. Therefore, while analytical ability is a requirement, tests of verbal ability as well as measures of personality may be needed as part of the selection process.

Recent research suggests that it may be meaningful to group different jobs into families and that the predictive validity of tests for performance on jobs within these families may generalize (see Chapter 3.3). However, the results indicate that the magnitude of the validity varies. At present, especially in times which attach great importance to equal opportunities in employment, the responsibility is on organizations to demonstrate that the particular tests they use are clearly linked to the requirements of the particular jobs concerned. Careful job analysis can achieve this. Furthermore, when jobs are changing rapidly or the number of job incumbents is small, the collection of sufficient data to derive predictive validity coefficients may be impracticable. In these instances job analysis may be the *only* means of establishing the validity of psychological tests.

TYPES OF TESTS

The two main categories of psychological measures used in employment settings are, first, cognitive tests and, second, personality questionnaires. Cognitive tests divide further into tests of achievement and of aptitude. Achievement tests (sometimes called attainment tests) focus on the measurement of particular knowledge and skills, such as knowledge of Newtonian mechanics and its application to the solving of hypothetical, civil engineering problems. Industrial and commercial organizations sometimes make use of such tests to measure training outcomes but achievement tests are, more typically, the province of educational institutions and professional bodies. More recently job sample tests have gained popularity in employment settings but these are discussed elsewhere (see Chapter 3.6).

Aptitude tests, in contrast to achievement tests, measure potential to acquire knowledge or skill rather than levels of prior attainments (see Chapter 3.3). Employers usually use aptitude rather than achievement tests because indications of achievement are usually available from other sources such as educational records; aptitude to acquire new knowledge and skills, rather than past achievement, is typically viewed as more important to the job. However, the principles of psychological testing outlined in this chapter apply equally to tests of either achievement or aptitude except that, for the former, content validity often stands in lieu of predictive validity.

Measures of personality differ from cognitive tests in both method and content (see Chapter 3.4). While cognitive tests seek to assess a candidate's maximum level of performance via questions demanding correct answers, personality questionnaires request information regarding typical behaviour via self-report. Thus, personality questionnaires measure behaviour indirectly. Nevertheless, accuracy of response is crucial and personality questionnaires are of little use in occupational settings if they lack predictive value. However, the present chapter describes methods principally designed for analysing data from cognitive tests demanding correct answers.

TEST ADMINISTRATION AND THE STANDARDIZATION OF CONDITIONS

For responses to a test to reflect only individual differences in the construct under investigation it is essential that any other factors that might influence performance are held constant during test administration. In other words, the conditions of testing should be standardized so that they are the same whenever the test is administered. Because so many extraneous factors can influence outcome, standardizing test conditions depends on the careful training but also the common sense of the administrator. Obviously, the room should always be well lit, quiet and properly ventilated. A stop watch can help to ensure that timing of the test is constant. The directions given to candidates should always be the same: tape recording instructions is one way of achieving this.

It is relatively easy to ensure that the physical conditions of testing are constant across successive administrations. However, different test-takers may interpret the same conditions differently. For example, if the administrator tells candidates simply not to guess on an aptitude test some will take this as meaning that they should not indicate a response unless certain of its correctness, whereas others will respond provided they are not making a wild guess. Furthermore, some candidates will have partial knowledge of the correct answer and if they are inhibited from responding their score will under-estimate their ability. On the other hand, baldly telling candidates to guess whenever they do not know the correct answer may cause large increases in measurement error. Unless the manual states to the contrary, it is probably best to tell candidates to guess if they can rule out at least one of the presented answers. Some candidates will also have a tendency to work more quickly than others. Provided the manual does not say otherwise, candidates should be told to work as quickly as they can without making careless errors and to move on to the next question if they get stuck.

The emotional state of test-takers may also vary. Some, for example, may be highly anxious. This reaction should be treated with sensitivity because the purpose of test administration is to elicit as accurate a measure as possible of the construct under investigation and someone who is upset is unlikely to give of his or her best. If the test is being used in conjunction with other assessments, one possibility is to mention that performance on the test is not the sole criterion. In any event, if a candidate is distraught this should be taken into account in the score's interpretation.

It is often suggested that one of the benefits of computerized testing is that test administration can be more easily standardized. While this may be true, as yet no substitute has been found for a sensitive human observer who ensures that the candidate understands what is expected and is able and willing to produce a performance which is an accurate reflection of the construct under investigation.

TEST DEVELOPMENT

Test development requires care and skill rather than genius. Inspection of most tests with good predictive validity in common use today reveals that their constituent items are not mysterious. On the contrary, it is often obvious why the item writer thought the question might be a good measure of the construct under investigation. Rather than demanding uncanny insight into human nature, test development is much more a question of applying carefully a sequence of logical steps which, if followed, are likely to produce a test of high quality and high predictive validity. The methods which underlie this process are outlined below. Thereby, even if the reader never constructs a test, knowing what should have been done will inform judgement of the quality of commercially available tests.

Test development and construct validation

As described above, the key to predictive validity is construct validation. Consequently, proper representation of the construct to be measured is of central concern in the writing of items. Furthermore, the nature of responses to items depends both on the questions and the particular individuals taking a test. Therefore, test-takers participating in test development should be representative of those persons for whom the test is intended.

Construct validation is also the primary purpose of analysing data from item trials. This is achieved by, first, investigating the relationship between performance on individual items and the test as a whole and, second, exploring how performance on the test relates to other measures of the characteristics of test-takers.

Item writing

Effective item writing demands a clear definition of the construct under investigation. Consider the design of a test to measure the analytical ability of an applicant trainee accountant. Analytical ability could be taken to mean many different things so the definition must be honed. It might be defined as the capacity to infer relationships and deduce conclusions. But given that much of an accountant's analytical ability is directed towards problems set in numerical contexts the definition must incorporate some description of the level of numeracy required. Also, job analysis may reveal that the problems faced by an accountant sometimes lack all the information necessary for precise solution. Job analysis may also indicate that numerical information provided to accountants is often in the form of tables and sometimes charts and graphs. Consequently, the definition of the construct might be sharpened to 'the ability to infer relationships and deduce conclusions in numerical contexts involving tables, charts and graphs where some information is approximate or even missing'. These are only the first steps in honing the definition but already it contains hints as to what sorts of question might appear on the test. Clearly, the sharper the definition, the easier effective item writing becomes.

However, care must be taken to ensure that items on the test demand only numerical and mathematical skills that are necessary to undertake training. Demanding skills at selection that will be taught subsequently is unfair. The skills necessary to pass *selection* should form part of the definition of the construct.

As the definition of the construct evolves its clarity is tested by using it to generate items. So, for example, an item might be constructed for trialling involving a table showing, for a manufacturing organization, the costs of raw materials, wages, distribution, and so on, as well as income from sales. Requesting calculation of the difference between income and costs might require little more than basic numerical skills. More analytical ability might be needed to infer the year in which new equipment was probably bought (perhaps by noticing when output and the use of raw materials increased with no increase in the wages bill). And if some entries in the table were missing such that problem solution necessitated their deduction, this might increase the complexity of the question still further and demand even stronger analytical skills.

The effectiveness of a question also depends, in part, on the form of the answer demanded. For reasons described later, multiple-choice answers are generally preferable to open-ended questions. While multiple-choice questions are open to guessing, the consequent distortion of results is reduced if sufficient incorrect answers (known as distractors) appear. Three or four distractors per question are usually adequate. Consequently, generating distractors is part of writing items. Sometimes, the range of possible distractors is limited by their plausibility (a truck is unlikely to weigh five kilograms) or their possibility (there are no more than seven days in a week). More often than not, however, there is an infinite number of potential distractors. One way to generate distractors in such situations is to trial questions initially in an open-ended format and note common errors in answers generated thereby. Frequent errors may make powerful, multiple-choice distractors.

The number of questions to be written depends on how many are required for final versions of the test. A reliable and valid final version containing fewer than 20 questions is unusual and, typically, many more questions, perhaps three times as many, are written for trialling than the number required for the final versions. This is because even experienced item writers generate many questions which prove unacceptable.

Trialling items

If at all possible, items should be trialled on persons comparable to those for whom the final test is intended as well as under conditions which are as similar as possible to those of formal testing. Overall test scores and patterns of correct answers to particular questions are a result not only of items but of persons taking the test. For example, persons sitting a numerically based test of analytical ability who know little mathematics may focus on questions requiring simple arithmetic only. The mathematically trained, however, may focus their attention on questions requiring more mathematical knowledge and make careless errors on the simpler, arithmetic questions. Thus, the type of test-taker involved in item trials in part determines whether or not the construct under investigation is properly identified. Furthermore, persons of different sexes, ages and ethnic backgrounds should participate so that any biases against individuals with particular characteristics which are not job relevant may be expunged.

Data analysis and retrialling

Once trialling is complete, data analysis is employed to select those items which will produce the best final version of the test. The first step is to compute for each trial version of the test what percentage of test-takers attempted each question, what proportion answered each item correctly (known as the *facility* value of the item) and the correlation of performance on each item with performance on the test as a whole (known as the *discrimination* of the item). Discrimination is calculated by computing for each person whether each item was answered incorrectly or correctly (scored 0 or 1) and, for each person, determining total score on all *other* items on the test. Then, for each item across all persons, the correlation of item with overall performance gives the discrimination of the item.

For each item, the percentage attempted, facility and discrimination are carefully examined. If very few persons have attempted an item which appears towards the beginning of a trial version this may be indicative of a poor question. Perhaps the wording is ambiguous or the solution demands too specialized knowledge, both characteristics of poor questions. Alternatively, deducing the answer may be simply difficult in which case the question may be acceptable. However, if several such items appear towards the end of a test this may result from inadequate time allowances during item trials. In other words, many test-takers may not have even reached these questions, in which case the information yielded is impoverished and ambiguous.

The facility values (once the proportion of persons attempting each item has been considered) measure question difficulty. While questions that are answered correctly by about 50 per cent of the subject pool are also more likely to have higher discrimination values (an inevitable consequence of the way in which correlations are computed), the most desirable range of facility values for final test version items depends upon the purpose for which the test will be used. For example, if 70 per cent of job applicants will be excluded from further consideration on the basis of test score then items which only 30 per cent pass are best suited to the purpose. In general, however, because the use to which a test is put varies from one year to the next (perhaps there are more posts to be filled from a smaller applicant pool) it is as well to have a good spread of facility values in the final test version. Nevertheless, generally speaking, those questions which most candidates answer incorrectly (say 20 per cent or lower correctness) or correctly (say 80 per cent or higher) are of dubious value because taken together they yield so little information on candidates as a whole: if almost everyone answers a question correctly the item indicates little about who are the more able candidates and vice versa for a very difficult question.

Discrimination values indicate how well performance on a single item predicts performance on the test overall. While facility values indicate whether or not an item is of appropriate difficulty, discrimination values indicate the extent to which an item measures the hypothesized construct. If the bulk of items tap the desired construct and performance on an individual item is correlated with overall performance then the item probably also measures the construct. However, no precise value can be predetermined as desirable because discrimination is influenced by facility, the number of items contributing to the total score, and the quality of the other items. As a rule of thumb, a discrimination value of 0.2 or more is a healthy indicator although items with lower values may be considered if, for example, there is a need to include some questions with particularly low facility values.

Discrimination values may be distorted if few persons attempt an item. If such an item appears towards the end of a test in which too little time was allowed it will only have been attempted by those test-takers who were able to get beyond earlier questions and, of course, such test-takers are the most likely to answer questions correctly. Hence, these later questions will inevitably tend to be answered correctly by only high scorers on the test and incorrectly by low scorers resulting in artificially high discrimination values. This effect also results in speeded tests having artificially high internal consistency estimates of reliability, as described earlier.

As also mentioned earlier, distractors affect item quality. The effectiveness of each distractor may be analysed by computing statistics similar to the facility and discrimination values described above. First, the proportion of test-takers selecting each distractor provides a measure of the attractiveness of the distractor. If none selects the distractor then that distractor is serving no useful purpose. Second, for each distractor in turn those selecting the distractor are marked 1 and all other test-takers marked 0 and the result correlated with overall corrrectness on all other items. If a distractor is particularly effective in attracting poor performers then the result should be a negative distractor–total correlation. If the correlation is positive this shows that better performers are selecting the distractor in which case the 'correct' answer should be checked. Alternatively, the distractor may demand too fine a distinction from the correct answer.

Finally, the inter-correlations of performance on each item, one with the other, should be examined. In particular, if performance on an item is unusually highly correlated with an immediately preceding item when both questions draw on the same table, chart or other source of information this suggests that performance on one item is dependent on the other. Such items are to be avoided, given that each item should provide new information about the test-taker.

Once suitable items have been identified final versions of the test are prepared. If possible at least two versions, each containing different questions, should be constructed. Each version should be set at about the same level of difficulty and contain questions requiring comparable skills. Then both of these versions are retrialled on a new group of test-takers and the analyses described above are repeated to check that all items function up to acceptable standards. A parallel forms estimate of reliability is computed to ensure, first, that the construct is reasonably stable over time (given some delay between administrations) and, second, that all versions of the test measure the same construct. Sometimes it is necessary to replace poorly functioning items and to retrial the revised test versions until a satisfactory outcome is achieved.

The effectiveness with which the new test measures the construct can also be assessed by correlating test performance with other known characteristics of the test-takers and conditions such as convergence and divergence of indicators investigated. If job performance data are available the concurrent validity of the test may be computed. Once the test versions appear acceptable preliminary norm tables may be calculated on the basis of the trials before employing the test executively.

SELECTING PUBLISHED TESTS

An appropriate test of the construct derived from a job analysis may already exist in published form. The test and its accompanying manual may be examined to decide whether the test is satisfactory.

The manual should contain a description of the test's design specification which, of course, must be reasonably comparable to the construct identified via the job analysis. Given an adequate match, the question of prime concern must be the predictive validity of the test, and any manual of acceptable quality should report this coefficient. If the predictive validity seems low (say below 0.3) then the test may be of poor quality.

Unreliability may explain low predictive validity and the manual should provide an estimate of the standard error of measurement. An internal consistency coefficient of 0.8 or above (some carefully developed cognitive tests have coefficients in excess of 0.9) is reassuring though 0.7 is acceptable for measures of broader constructs. Low internal consistency may result from some poor questions on the test. The results of item analyses, if reported in the manual, can help to reassure the potential test purchaser.

Other factors can cause low predictive validity. For example, job performance appraisals are often imperfectly reliable so that if these form the test's prediction criteria the validity coefficient is inevitably lowered. Also, if the coefficient is based on a restricted group of candidates, such as only those above a cut score, the coefficient is an under-estimate. If the coefficient is low the manual should offer an explanation and, if possible, an estimate of the predictive validity under more ideal circumstances. However, human behaviour is not always easy to predict and so some well-designed tests have low predictive validity. Given this, and the fact that tests with low predictive validity coefficients can be cost-effective, the acceptability of a test based on its validity requires careful judgement.

On the other hand, if the published validity is very high the careful test purchaser will check on the nature of the prediction criterion. A very high validity coefficient could be due to contamination of the criterion by the test score; for example, the supervisors who rated job performance might have known the employee's test scores.

Some form of norm tables should also appear in the manual. Even though these should be supplemented by data gathered locally, the norm table score distributions may provide some indication of the likely difficulty of the test for the particular candidates concerned. Hence, the more detail the manual provides regarding the characteristics of the norm sample, the better. For example, old norms based on white males may be inappropriate for current use. Indeed, if no data are reported in the manual regarding an examination of sex or culture bias in the test then, in those countries with relevant legislation, use of the test may result in justifiable charges of indirect discrimination.

A published test is an attractive proposition if it is reliable, valid and fair and set at a level of difficulty likely to result in a satisfactory spread of scores in the candidate group. Two or more parallel versions of the test are a useful feature if retesting is anticipated. Generally speaking, practice items should form part of the instructions to candidates. In addition, of course, clear instructions for administration, marking and interpretation should be provided as well as any necessary training: psychological tests should never be administered or interpreted by those who lack the necessary training. Finally, the face validity of the test must be such that it is acceptable to assessors as well as candidates. If not, an otherwise excellent test may suffer only short shrift or be dismissed out of hand.

MAJOR BENEFITS AND COSTS OF PSYCHOLOGICAL TESTING

Major benefits

Psychological tests are sufficiently inexpensive that the financial benefits of improved productivity deriving from their use typically far outweigh the cost. Means of estimating the net benefits are described in Chapter 3.3. Sometimes the introduction of tests can bring immediate savings, e.g. when tests are used in selection systems to screen out candidates who do not meet minimum requirements, thereby saving the expensive time of interviewers. Such utility analyses may prove powerful weapons in the battle to persuade line management that it makes sound financial sense to spend substantial sums on the development and maintenance of selection systems.

However, there is an additional reason why psychological tests are allies to the personnel function. By focusing on construct validation, proper use of tests necessitates the systematic, scientific investigation of the personal qualities required for effective job performance and survival within the organization. This should provide organizations with a clearer understanding of what is required from their personnel. Hence, selection criteria can be more carefully honed, essential skills which require training and development for successful careers can be more clearly identified, and the dimensions of appraisal systems more closely linked to job requirements.

Costs

Typically, the most costly aspect of psychological tests lies in their design and development. These expenses are usually recovered by test publishers over a period of years. The costs incurred by users of tests are relatively small. Test booklets, if accompanied by separate answer sheets, are reusable and answer sheets cost little. Multiple-choice, objectively marked answer sheets can be hand scored both quickly and accurately using templates or, if numbers are large and funds available, via machines such as optical mark readers (OMRs). Open-ended answers are more expensive to mark because each has to be read and interpreted. Scores on open-ended tests also tend to show substantial differences between raters which, of course, diminish test reliability. Therefore, generally speaking, it is probably better to use objectively marked tests wherever possible.

Other costs are incurred from test administration and interpretation. An adequate room must be found in which to administer the test and a trained test administrator must be present. Even tests which are administered by computer usually also require a trained, human administrator (computerized assessment techniques are discussed further in Chapter 3.5). Furthermore, scores on some tests require a trained psychologist for their interpretation. No test should be administered or interpreted by a person lacking appropriate training.

In general, there is little relation between the costs of tests and their quality. Provided a test is properly administered, scored and interpreted the effectiveness of a particular test depends not on its cost but, rather, on the good judgement of the person who selected it.

FURTHER READING

Allen, M.J., and Yen, W.M. (1979). *Introduction to Measurement Theory*. Brooks/Cole, Monterey, CA.

Anastasi, A. (1982). *Psychological Testing*, 5th edn. Macmillan, New York.

Cronbach, L.J. (1984). *Essentials of Psychological Testing*, 4th edn. Harper & Row, New York.

Guilford, J.P. (1956). *Fundamental Statistics in Psychology and Education*, 3rd edn. McGraw-Hill, New York.

Kline, P. (1986). *A Handbook of Test Construction*. Methuen, London.

Nunnally, J.C. (1978). *Psychometric Theory*, 2nd edn. McGraw-Hill, New York.

Thorndike, R.L. (ed.) (1971). *Educational Measurement*, 2nd edn. American Council on Education, Washington, DC.

APPENDICES

A. Pearson product-moment coefficient of correlation (r_{xy}) for calculating the correlation between two variables, x and y.

$$r_{xy} = \frac{\displaystyle\sum_{i=0}^{N} (Xi - M_x)(Yi - M_y)}{N \; S_x \; S_y}$$

where N = number of observations
  i = the ith observation
  Xi = the value of X for the ith observation
  Yi = the value of Y for the ith observation
  M_x = the mean value of X
  M_y = the mean value of Y
  S_x = the standard deviation of X
  S_y = the standard deviation of Y.

Statistics textbooks provide alternative formulae to simplify the calculations involved.

B. The ceiling placed by the reliability of a test $(r_{xx'})$ on the test's predictive validity is given by

$$\sqrt{r_{xx'}}$$

However, this ignores the reliability of the criterion $(r_{yy'})$ against which the test is validated. If the reliabilities of both the test and the criterion are considered then the maximum possible value of the predictive validity coefficient is given by:

$$\sqrt{(r_{xx'} \, r_{yy'})}$$

It follows that the obtained test reliability, criterion reliability and obtained predictive validity coefficient (r_{xy}) can be used to calculate what the predictive validity would be $(r_{x'y'})$ if both test and criterion were perfectly reliable:

$$r_{x'y'} = \frac{r_{xy}}{\sqrt{(r_{xx'} \, r_{yy'})}}$$

C. If a test is lengthened with all else equal its reliability $(r_{xx'})$ will tend to increase. The estimated reliability of the lengthened test $(r_{nn'})$ is given by

$$r_{nn'} = \frac{nr_{xx'}}{1 + (n - 1) \, r_{xx'}}$$

where n = the number of times longer is the lengthened test compared with the original. For example, if the lengthened test contains three times as many items as the original (i.e. a 200 per cent increase) then $n = 3$; if one and a half times as many (i.e. a 50 per cent increase) then $n = 1.5$. The formula can also be used to estimate the reliability of a shortened test. For example, if half the items are removed $n = 0.5$.

D. The reliability of a test based on its internal consistency is given by

$$\frac{n}{n-1} \left[1 - \frac{\sum\limits_{i=0}^{n} p_i q_i}{\sigma_x^2} \right]$$

where n = the number of items
$\quad\quad\;\; p_i$ = the proportion of test-takers passing item i
$\quad\quad\;\; q_i$ = $1 - p_i$
$\quad\quad\;\; \sigma_x^2$ = variance of total scores of persons taking the test.

The above formula is sometimes termed the Kuder–Richardson formula 20, or KR–20 for short.

E. The standard deviation (S_x) of a variable X is given by

$$S_x = \sqrt{\frac{\sum\limits_{i=0}^{n} (Xi - M_x)^2}{n - 1}}$$

where n = the number of observations
$\quad\quad\;\; Xi$ = the value of X on the ith observation
$\quad\quad\;\; M_x$ = the mean value of x.

F. The standard error of measurement (SEM) of a test X is given by

$$\text{SEM} = \sigma_x \sqrt{(1 - r_{xx'})}$$

where σ_x = the standard deviation of total scores on test X
$\quad\quad\;\; r_{xx'}$ = the parallel forms reliability of test X.

Chapter 3.3

Tests of Aptitude

JOSE-MARIO PRIETO

Department de Psicologia Diferencial y Psicologia del Trabajo, Universidad Complutense, Campus de Somosaguas, 28023 Madrid, Spain

PURPOSE

All over Europe, bells play their familiar part in rural and urban landscapes. It is easy to make them out by listening to each clang, since Western bells produce just one clear, characteristic and lingering pitch as soon as they are struck.

More than 50 Chinese bronze bell chimes have been unearthed during the present century and have astonished contemporary acousticians. All the chimes found consist of three tiers of bells and were configured to perform complex, rapidly metered music in the company of ancient and sophisticated orchestras. Each bell sounds two pristine fundamental pitches when played with different kinds of strikers. Each clapperless bell carries inscriptions that indicate the exact striking positions to activate two well-defined percussion tones.

Western bells are found in small numbers in the European belfries because their single tones are combined with temperate parsimony. Chinese chime bells encompass up to five octaves and constitute an entire harmonic ensemble, arranged in tiers to arrive at orchestration.

This comparison between Western and Chinese bells provides a curious and unique analogy to the essential part of this chapter.

Tests of aptitude are often seen as adequate psychological measuring instruments in employment settings. They have been designed and validated by experts to deal with concrete occupational demands like hiring, promoting, training or planning differential job assignments and placement decisions in civilian or military organizations.

Employers and human resource managers view tests of aptitude as valid

Handbook of Assessment in Organizations   Edited by P. Herriot
© 1989 John Wiley & Sons Ltd

psychological aids to make personnel analysis or predictions since they provide a fair technical treatment of all examinees as well as an ascertainable degree of differential validity. Individual scores are understood as a valuable source of information about the individual's average level of performance in distinct and separately appraised aptitudes. Like Western bells, each single test of aptitude produces the fundamental perceived sound and pertinent information.

Psychologists who conduct research on the nature of aptitude and test use, or professionals involved with aptitude testing, know that laypersons' views are insufficient. Like Chinese bells, tests of aptitude maintain the dual-pitch potential. They have been deliberately constructed to supply *process* and *product* psychological information. Besides the scores (product or outcome information through items or tasks attempted successfully or unsuccessfully), test makers and experts have investigated cognitive or sensory–motor strategies involved in attempting the test. Consequently, process, or course of action information is available in addition to the total score obtained. There is also further accumulated information about a wide variety of relevant issues like heritability, race, class, age, sex or cultural differences as well as about job validity and utility generalizability. Since tests of aptitude are usually applied as standardized sets or batteries, there is also enough information about several intercorrelation matrices on similar or different samples, more or less representative of a given occupational population. So, it is possible to link bronze bell chimes and batteries of aptitude, since both reveal a latent sophisticated design that usually remains a mystery for laypersons but alludes to principles and practices actually known by professional psychologists who are acquainted with an elaborate theory of aptitude that specifies the suitable design, scales, instrumentation and psychological meaning and implementation.

Managers ascribe to *aptitude* a diffuse but yet nuanced meaning: sufficient and necessary fitness, natural or acquired occupational talent. This particular sense of the adjective *apt* comes to mind because they are actually searching for a well-suited and a quick-witted applicant. Tests of aptitude become mere examinations that attempt to determine and measure latent attributes, yielding a single score or a profile of scores that are regarded as indices of the required but often ill-defined *aptness*. Their view is confined to the attainment of this fundamental pitch.

By contrast, psychologists ascribe to *aptitude* a theoretical meaning: a set of behavioural characteristics or traits regarded as symptomatic of an individual's capacity or potential ability to perform or to acquire with training some specific task, knowledge, skill or set of responses. Tests of aptitude are understood as assessment procedures to identify the basic abilities which differentiate people and facilitate successful work adjustment and satisfactoriness. So, they contribute to an understanding of human behaviour and to an effective use in administrative actions or decisions. Once again, here is the inner dual-pitch potential.

Laypersons tend to think of tests of aptitude as one or a few batteries which are convenient for a purely pragmatic purpose. Psychologists approach tests of aptitude as different sets of instruments which are in line with a known theoretical and pragmatic frame of reference. The bell's analogy brings to light these entangled aims.

APTITUDE TESTING'S FRAME OF REFERENCE

Psychological tests of aptitude currently administered in an organizational milieu have been constructed by psychologists according to explicit theories conceptually based and empirically tested on data collected from samples of people that performed various tasks or items presumed to measure the focused aptitude. Elsewhere, organizational demands also deal with implicit theories or informal schemata that reside in the minds of top managers, supervisors or workers which are not conceptually based or empirically tested but do reveal common-sense ideas, experiences or expectancies within the culture of organizations.

Separately, Sternberg and collaborators (1981) in the United States and Bohman (1980) in Sweden have asked adult subjects to formulate their beliefs or conceptions of what intelligence is and to specify what they mean or perceive when they talk about bright people or intelligent performances. In both searches, laypersons' answers were compared with those provided by experts (American samples) or by subjects instructed in psychology in the preceding year (Swedish samples). *Correct problem solving* appeared as the main stated dimension. American and Swedish samples made it conditional upon competent knowledge, critical thinking and good decisions. This is the basic feature that allows us to recognize almost any test of aptitude and to judge adequately each testee's own achievement.

Swedish samples pointed to *ease and speed of learning and answering* as another relevant characteristic; it was also mentioned by the American sample but in the context of verbal ability in comprehension and expression.

American laypersons and experts mentioned also a *social and practical competence characteristic of intelligent behaviour* while Swedish samples alluded to it through isolated words and comments. This dimension has played, of course, a salient role in organizational acceptance of the technology and utility of aptitude tests.

There is a good convergence between laypersons and experts' conceptions about the meaning of intelligent behaviour or performance and the way of assessing it. Both seem to share a common point of departure and a system of measurement that can be used to fix individuals' positions. This is something of unusual interest, since academic psychology is full of a great variety of research exhibiting strong internal validity while studying trivial phenomena. Internal, external and ecological validities appear mutually and unavoidably inter-related in tests makers' and practitioners' objectives. They have aimed at solving bottom-up empirical problems and afterwards they have proceeded seriously to consider theoretical or hypothesis-inspired issues in order to attain a psychological understanding of reality. They are used to facing practical and critical questions and to thinking of the people to whom the solution or approach is addressed.

A *test* can be comprehensively considered as 'a standard, portable stimulus situation, containing a defined instruction and mode of response, in which a consenting subject is measured on the response in a predefined way, the measure being designed and used to predict other behavior, elsewhere' (Cattell, 1986). It is, thus, a miniature psychological experiment designed to ensure that individual responses can be compared or matched because items employed are relevant samples of domains that are relatively homogeneous. The cooperation of the subject is of critical importance in order to avoid public criticism and to attain a direct valuation of abilities required for the job.

Aptitudes can be broadly understood here as psychological constructs, with their associated measures, that bear an hypothesized or demonstrated relation to individual differences in learning or correctly performing in the occupational or organizational setting. The 'apt' selected applicant starts to achieve and learn as soon as he or she gets into the job. Both aspects must be considered simultaneously. When it is stated that a worker has, for example, spatial aptitude, that means that this person tends to be able to achieve easily and to learn the spatial tasks involved in a given job.

Finally, *psychological tests of aptitude* are intended to measure cognitive or sensorimotor skills and abilities through psychometrically standardized or functionally structured samples of significant behaviours. Widely available tests cover categories (Fleishman and Quaintance, 1984) such as the following:

1. *General cognitive ability*.
2. *Special aptitudes*, that is, verbal comprehension, verbal expression, fluency of ideas, originality, memorization, mathematical reasoning, spatial orientation, perceptual speed, numerical facility, deductive or inductive reasoning, information ordering, category flexibility, mechanical comprehension, problem sensitivity, speed or flexibility of closure, visualization, perceptual speed.
3. *Physical or sensorimotor abilities*, like multilimb coordination, control precision, response orientation, rate control, reaction time, arm–hand steadiness, manual and finger dexterity, wrist–finger speed, speed of limb movement, selective attention, time sharing, explosive or dynamic strength, trunk strength, extent of dynamic flexibility, gross body coordination or equilibrium, stamina, near or far vision, visual colour discrimination, night or peripheral vision, depth perception, glare sensitivity, general hearing, auditory attention, sound location, speech hearing and clarity.

Present-day aptitude testing and psychological research point towards the following aims:

— To measure operationally and objectively job applicants' suitability in the most valid and least discriminatory way.
— To place on distinct dimensions the defined and empirically validated individual difference constructs.
— To lead efficiently to functional testing procedures through structured psychometrics.
— To advance scientific knowledge about the basis of human differences, the relationships between worker characteristics and occupational requirements, as well as possible changes through training or fair treatment.
— To provide sound support to professional decisions and actions in employment selection, classification or promotion.

Types according to how they are administered

Tests of aptitude can be applied following different modes of presentation, administration and scoring. Users' manuals provide relevant information in order to ascertain that test takers face a standard, portable situation. Seven modalities will be commented on.

1. A great variety of tests of aptitude are administered to applicants in a *group*. Some others are administered to *only one examinee* at a time. All group tests can become individual tests and, with sufficient expertise, individual tests can sometimes be applied as group instruments.
2. Numerous tests of aptitude are based on an uninterrupted succession of *items*, intrinsically ordered to emphasize their difficulty, complexity or homogeneity. A few introduce a *global situation* and deal with a response pattern or with a specific kind of performance expected, like eye–hand coordination, two-hand coordination, pursuitmeter, tracking tests, driving apparatus test or expectancy reaction test.
3. Most aptitude tests are of the *paper and pencil* type since each stimulus and response is presented on a printed page. There are also different modalities of *non-printed* tests requiring visual displays, tactual arrays, mechanical–electronic apparatus, personal computers and monitors.
4. Tests of aptitude that have to be timed become *speed* measures; if they have no time limits they are understood as *power* measures. The time spent by an individual is a mixture of the time consumed in correctly doing some tasks or items, in doing others incorrectly or in inspecting new ones and deciding not to attempt them. Actual differences appear when the same psychological test is administered with or without time constraints. Usually, the faster individual attains new and difficult or complex items that are not attempted by the slower individual. Initial and final items may demand a similar strategy but with some differences in nuances. So, mistake probabilities are higher and the case cannot be reduced to differences in speed of responses between individuals. Faster and more accurate candidates have a lot of advantages in selection procedures, while in many real life circumstances, men or women of average ability seem equally fitted to everyday time pressures and emergencies in jobs and organizations.
5. Aptitude tests usually present *closed items*, i.e. fixed alternative options offering the respondent a choice among different answers available. They have the disadvantage of having a $1/n$ (n = number of options) chance of being right by blind guessing. But on the other hand, a few tests of aptitude use *open-ended* items, supplying a frame of reference for respondents' answers or certain restraints on their content or expression; these can be found, for instance, in oral or written fluency items, alternative uses, decorations, possible jobs, etc., which configure some series of divergent production tests. Such answers can be key-scored if there are lists or external/internal criteria of acceptable and satisfactory alternatives.
6. In practice, raw scores assigned to an individual on a measurement occasion

are compared with the distribution of scores obtained over a population on equivalent occasions. Such a basis of comparison derives from the *normative measurement* model (see Chapter 3.2) that allows a contrast between individual or profile scores. Nevertheless, when it is important to verify the consistency or inconsistency of a single individual in an aptitude or in a series of aptitudes, then the *ipsative measurement* model is taken into consideration (i.e. standardization across successive responses to tests for one and the same person). It is possible to discover how consistent an individual's responses are over time, and to what extent he or she demonstrates different oscillations in performance on given aptitudes.

7. *Machine scoring* and even machine interpretation has become a current practice in the administration of aptitude tests. Now, via screen or computer-assisted presentation (see Chapter 3.5), testees can respond by pressing a button and so feedback and latency measures are available for both right and wrong strategies. The development of probabilistic models, which take individual differences into account (Wright and Stone, 1979), make it possible to fix item difficulties that are independent of the aptitude of persons attempting them and of the difficulties of other items in the test; so person aptitudes become independent of particular items tried out and of other testees taking the test. The Rasch model is specially well suited for item banking use: a common scale represents statistically the single item difficulty and the person aptitude. So a given aptitude can be measured, in each application, with an *ad hoc* untimed tailored test. Machine scoring also allows the production of predictions via regression equations, profile analysis, discriminant analysis, etc., of various job performances or organizational criteria (Prieto, 1982). By contrast, *hand scoring* is still in widespread practice and some of the above-mentioned procedures can also be worked out for this approach.

One or more of the above-mentioned modalities, differently combined, enters into any administration of aptitude tests for selection or classification purposes in organizations.

Types according to how they are constructed

Recently, R.B. Cattell (1986), has proposed a descriptive and operational classification system of tests by internal construction; it is summarized in Table 1. It will be commented on here because it supplies a coherent and practical framework in relation to the plethora of aptitude tests in use.

1. The first category is a general one, since it intrudes on the remaining nine categories. Tests of aptitude are instruments that demand voluntary reactions and do provide voluntary indices as far as they require the fusion of innate and acquired responses. Underlying motivational factors are also involved. Consciously the testee chooses (or receives directions to do so) between reactive or non-reactive modes of behaviour. It is normally expected that the testee reacts to a given stimulus (an item, an auditory or visual signal stated in

Table 1   A taxonomy of tests by internal construction

1.	Reactive	Non-reactive
2.	Restricted	Free response
3.	Inventive	Selected
4.	Single	Extended, repetitive response
5.	Ordered	Unordered sequence
6.	Homogeneous	Patterned
7.	Natural manner of response	Pursuit of a limit
8.	Making a concluding reaction	Reacting to one's own reactions
9.	Immediate meaning	Referent meaning
10.	Itemized	Global structure in presentation and scoring

Adapted with modifications from R.B. Cattell (1986). The psychometric properties of tests: consistency, validity and efficiency, in Cattell and Johnson, *Functional Psychological Testing: Principles and Instruments.* Brunner/Mazel, New York.

advance, a key-word, etc.), but sometimes he or she is ordered to inhibit or omit attentively a given response. This is the unavoidable rule of the game. If a testee does not agree, avoids or misunderstands this rule, present tests of aptitude are valueless.

2. The second category points to the mode of response imposed on the testee. For instance, electromechanical, pen and pencil, auditory or computer-assisted tests restrictively determine the kind of response that is accepted as valid. When a psychologist asks an applicant, during a selection interview, 'Could you introduce yourself and your interests in a five minutes talk?', he or she introduces a free response item situation since it is a part of a structured or semi-structured interviewing plan. Several features are then analysed: how clearly, seriously, friendly, poised or enthusiastically the person speaks; how he or she breaks the ice, selects facts or develops ideas that are relevant to the job; how the candidate provides enough information, introduces personal references or emphasizes detached anecdotes; how he or she pronounces names audibly, distinctly or correctly, phrases properly, keeps eye contact and observes the usual courtesies and so on. So, psychologists can compare self-presentation abilities between applicants when this is something actually important to a job's requirements.

3. The alternate face grouping test (Guilford and Hoepfner, 1971), where subjects group photographs of faces in different ways, each one expressing a common thought, feeling or intention becomes an exemplar of inventive responses in tests of behavioural divergent production and behavioural cognition. Different possible groupings are accepted as valid. The individual answers with anything from his or her personal experience that fits the restricted instruction received. An item like that shown in Figure 1, where the testee is asked to look at the drawing, to read the four sentences provided, to think of the children in this wintry scene and to choose an answer to the main question, is a typical instance of selective item. The available choices to that overt behaviour have been fixed in advance by test makers (Prieto and Seisdedos, 1984).

What are these children talking about?

1. Mommy will be angry with us because the scarf is wet.

2. What a nice snowman we've got!

3. It's really cold; let's go home!

4. We don't know how to build a snowman.

Figure 1: Item exemplar translated from Spanish BPC & BPS aptitude tests (Prieto & Seisdedos, 1984, 1987).

4. A matrix test that requires finding which figure belongs to the vacant spot, is constructed with single response items. A task that requires finding and identifying hidden specified figures or visual elements in a complex scene of camouflage or to find the picture object that is identical to the given one, can be presented as an extended, repetitive response item of a figural adaptive flexibility test.

5. Numerous tests of aptitude theoretically maintain a precise control of empirically estimated difficulties or homogeneities of item and tasks (see Chapter 3.2). Printed or visual materials have been carefully graded and scaled under the assumption that if a testee attempts and passes an item of known difficulty, he or she will correctly answer all items that are less difficult; if he or she fails an item of given difficulty, then his or her response to greater difficulty items will be wrong. So, subjects are requested to answer in the given order fixed by the test maker. However, various recent developments all favour sequential or adaptive tailored items where the probability of a correct response depends simultaneously on the level of ability of the individual (accuracy, speed, persistence, propensity to guess) and on the item parameters (discriminating power, difficulty and probability of a correct answer by chance among less able testees). These approaches are grouped under the heading of Item Response Theory (IRT).

6. Aptitude tests usually present a given number of items, each one similar to the preceding. In such a case, instructions are simple and generic and raw scores are derived from items successfully attempted (with an optional correction formula for blind guessing if the latter is considered organizationally unsound). Nevertheless, some tests involve patterned responses: for instance, apparatus tests such as the Two-Hand Coordinator, Mirror Tracer, Star Discrimeter. In the Two-Hand Coordinator, the testee simultaneously manipulates two handles, one moving the cursor right and left, the other forward and away from the subject. Coordinating these two handles he or she can move the cursor in any resultant direction. The task is to try and keep this cursor in contact with a moving target disc as it moves in an eccentric pattern. Score is time on target. Present developments in computer-based assessment

(see Chapter 3.5) make possible a much greater variety of such tests than is available with classical electromechanical apparatus.

7. There are some tests of aptitude that request the testee to identify at first glance common objects shown in close-up photographs or to write a punch line for each cartoon or to decorate differently, adding lines or colours, two identical outline drawings or vignettes. Usually 'behave at your own will, rate or pleasure' or 'answer as you first see it' is inculcated since it is an important test requirement: natural manner of response is purposely taken into consideration. Many others encourage the testee to 'answer as far as possible', 'look through very attentively', 'press the button as soon and often as the lamp flashes', etc., sometimes even until fatigue appears. Here, the pursuit of a limit has become the goal.

8. In speed anticipation tests each individual reaction finishes the initiated task. The subject has to judge when a cursor, moving with a uniform speed and disappearing from sight, has reached a specified point. This kind of test compels the testee to make a concluding reaction. Elsewhere, the Double Labyrinth Test, the Rotary Pursuitmeter or the Rudder Control Test constrain the operator to react to his or her own reactions while performing the task. The last one, for instance, demands that the subject attempts to coordinate a set of foot pedals inside a cockpit in order to line up the cockpit with one of three target lights as they change in an irregular manner. The score is the total time the cockpit stays precisely lined up.

9. It is almost always the case that verbal comprehension tests, for instance, ask to find the word that means nearly the same (or the opposite) as a given word or analogy. The Spearman 'eduction of relations' law points to an immediate meaning induction, since 'when a person has in mind any two or more ideas he or she has more or less power to bring to mind any relations that essentially hold between them' (inferring the general rule from specific instances). But, the 'eduction of correlates' law is concerned with a referent meaning deduction, i.e. 'when a person has in mind any idea together with a relation, he or she has more or less power to bring into mind the correlative idea (making up or recognizing a specific instance when given one other specific instance and the general rule). A great variety of reasoning items has been constructed in agreement with both mentioned cognitive principles.

10. Classical psychometric theories and methods (as discussed in Chapter 3.2) sponsored the construction of abundant test-centred items. They mainly emphasized binding statistical properties of items that should underlie any acceptable or valuable psychological test. Conventional items statistics are in this way available to determine inner relationships among items, and between them and the test, in a way that does not pay attention to the latent attribute or to the individual difference construct scaled. A plethora of itemized and *ad hoc* tests are now widespread (Buros, 1974; TEA, 1982). Recent innovative approaches view items within a theoretical-concept-centred framework. With the use of statistical and experimental methods they understand intelligence in terms of unitary structures and processes. Items become mere congruent stimuli demanding cognitive strategies from the

testee; aptitude appears as a global structure apprehended through functional testing procedures. Item content is a mere vehicle for presentation and scoring. However, there is a series of techniques, based on correlations among items, between items and the total score, between 'parcels' of a given test or between parallel forms that allows an estimate of the unknown hypothetical true score in the latent attribute (Nunnally, 1981). This method emphasizes the importance of real responses to concrete items.

TENABILITY

Psychological selection procedures without tests of aptitude are rather unusual. Their current inclusion has become a tradition since Munsterberg, in the first decade of this century, thought it was worth dedicating time and attention to the employment of tests for selection and placement of municipal railway employees. Some years afterwards, the notion of the role of aptitude differences in work performance accrued evidence and certain procedures were outlined to promote differential placement and to include differences between and within job performance for encouraging fair personnel decisions. Why do tests of aptitude maintain such a relevant and tenable position? What kind of psychological and organizational criteria or outcomes support this continuous usage (focused on personal characteristics that influence efficiency) against periodical attacks (centred on situational or incidental events) and critical remarks?

Job-relevance validity evidence

Determining the validity of tests of aptitude for predicting job performance has become a repeated and dominant concern of personnel psychologists. There are hundreds of published and unpublished studies where data in the form of criterion-predictor empirical correlations have been amassed to choose a test of aptitude that actually measures the desired and relevant psychological variable which the practitioner or the researcher is proposing as being demanded by a given job, job category or job family. The objective has been to identify existing tests of aptitude yielding standard scores that directly predict standard job-criterion scores. Job performance or productivity of incumbents selected could be maximized by ranking applicants on test scores and selecting them from the top down. Likewise, this means that validating a cut-off score derives from personnel policies in the organization rather than from the decisions of personnel psychologists since, if the test is valid, all cut-off scores are theoretically top-down valid: from a psychological viewpoint there is no genuine dividing threshold between the qualified and the unqualified applicants.

This central concern in the field has a rather curious source. For many years behavioural sciences have inherited the simple experimental paradigm where a dependent variable is a *function* of controlled variation in a presumed independent or causal variable while holding constant other potential factors. Since the eighteenth century, it has been mathematically viable to substitute the *function* concept in the realm of science by the *probability* concept, replacing *determinism* by *probabilism*. So, likelihood and plausibility, measured by the ratio of the favourable cases to the whole number of possible cases, give strength to scientific or technological researches when the number of potential causal factors increases and their fixed representations in measures become rather uncertain or are often interlocked. Psychological assessment in organizations brings into special prominence the concept of probability because it has to deal with valid and reliable predictions rather than stated and unavoidable causalities.

Job-relevance validity researches have been dominated by the multiple regression–correlation general data-analytic system, since attention is directed towards pursuing tests of aptitude which correlate highly with the criterion and at a low level with each other in the battery; so, validity coefficients are generated and accuracy is assessed by means of the standard error of prediction.

Inasmuch as observed Pearson product–moment correlations between tests of aptitude and the job criterion in a sample become validity coefficients, the operational means for differentiating between true and spurious correlations and for learning whether the relationship persists or disappears, have received abstract and practical attention: thousands of such studies have been, and are being, carried out periodically in civil and military organizations to determine the effectiveness of tests already administered for selecting, classifying and placing applicants or incumbents. Moderator variables appear when there is circumstantial evidence showing that a third variable changes systematically and produces an effect on the observed relationship between predictor and criterion variables, which differs consistently depending upon the level of the discovered moderator variable. If there is some concern about the normal theory assumptions underlying predictor–criterion relationship, a new technique is available to attain a more accurate estimate of the variability and actual magnitude of the obtained correlation (Lunneborg, 1985).

Usually tests of aptitude and criteria are introduced and combined on the basis of job analysis (see Chapters 2.1 and 3.2). So, hypothesis testing is approached here as a job-related validation process (Guion, 1976), allowing inferences about performance which have not yet been attempted or which are difficult to obtain directly. In such a way, personnel decisions are made on the basis of already demonstrated relationships or through hypotheses which are progressively supported. The test developer and user also work on the basis that the 'true scores' of an individual are akin but not equal to observed scores.

Since tests of aptitude are readily available psychological instruments, the very first task is to determine critical aspects (not mere casual markers or trivial indices at hand) of performance to be predicted in order to ascertain the degree of generality sought. The development of a conceptual definition or a theory about the criterion performance might take the form of a model of the cognitive or the sensorimotor processes involved, based on some sort of systematic observation, protocol analysis, job or task analysis, incumbent experts' and novices' information processing and decision-making strategies, function analysis, surveys in the organization, etc., mainly to avoid armchair or brain-storming theory building. Organizational questions of relative value attributed to certain aspects of performance are left to personnel policy makers or informed job incumbents and supervisors assembled together in conference, since value systems constitute a purpose-built guide to human resource management priorities. The requirements of criterion development and job analysis have been detailed in Chapter 2.1.

Personnel psychologists tend to show pendulum swings between emphasis on evidenced foundation of firm job-relevance validity and stress laid on the valuable and pragmatic saying 'If it works, use it'. While the former concern is taken into consideration when dealing with submitted papers to congresses or specialized journals, the last informal statement often reappears, on the basis of hunch, when they are talking with managers, job incumbents or supervisors. The first approach underlines correlational, contingency or pattern analysis (with or without sub-grouping and weighting), while the second draws attention to observed average increases in levels or categories of performance as well as broad satisfactoriness attained.

Both frames of reference differentiate between predictive and concurrent validity designs (see Chapter 3.2) on the basis of the time interval. In predictive validation a certain period elapses between assessment predictors obtained from applicants and their current performance appraisal. Methodologically, predictive validation is the accurate model for employment testing when hiring decisions occur without knowledge of test scores. Nevertheless, range restriction is generated each time that predictors are used as the basis for selection. As a matter of fact, concurrent validation is considered a substitute practice since simultaneous data actually produce validity coefficients roughly equivalent but slightly superior to purely predictive selection designs (Schmitt *et al.*, 1984).

Validity generalization

The foundation of the scientific approach of personnel psychology is based on the cumulation of knowledge from the results of a great number of similar studies within the organizational milieu. Nowadays, there is a massive amount of data available as a platform and there has been a certain failure to reject and retain selectively to produce a tenable position in this field. Viewed in isolation and interpreted as showing conflicting tendencies, a proliferation of empirical studies, without critical review and selection, ends in chaos. However, some reviewers have focused on the statistical analysis of accumulated findings and outcomes from many single studies, conducting integrative research reviews that no longer take the stated conclusions of each report at face value. Systematic guidelines, to evaluate the validity of a set of studies and take into account the empirical relationships in theory construction, are already available. Their use has increased exponentially over the past ten years. Such new seminal approaches have been termed *meta-analysis* (Glass, 1976) in psychology or *validity generalization* (Schmidt and Hunter, 1977) in the area of personnel psychology, but their basic ideas were already employed in the 1930s and 1940s by occupational psychologists, based on the use of average correlations and even on some provisory corrections for the effects of sampling error that still remained underestimated.

The effects of four artefactual sources of variance unrelated to the underlying relation between tests of aptitude and job performance have now been identified by Schmidt, Hunter and co-workers:

- Differences between studies in criterion reliability.
- Differences between studies in test reliability.
- Differences between studies in range restriction.
- Sampling error (i.e. variance due to the sample never including the total population).

Such artefacts have been empirically verified in clerical and technical occupations, like computer programmers, health sciences aides, engineering technicians, law enforcement personnel, mechanical repairers, park rangers, petroleum–petrochemical personnel, power plant operators, sales clerks.

Validity generalization analysis must be understood as a method of averaging results across studies to detect, by statistical procedures, that percentage of variance due to artefacts and that attributable to real moderator variables. Nevertheless, some other known artefacts like criterion contamination, computational and typographical errors, differences in the factor structure of tests and criteria, appropriateness of the employed statistical indices, etc., are not systematically faced (Jansen *et al.*, 1986).

Moderator variables, such as sex, age, ethnic origin, are explored via categorization of studies into differentiated clusters within the original entire sample. Since it is possible to assess quantitatively the goodness of the fit, the confirmation of the cross-situational predictive consistency of tests of aptitude implies that a point has been reached at which certainty is more than enough: gathering additional local validity studies would not be a profitable quest.

Recently, Hunter and Hunter (1984), via validity generalization procedures, have reviewed the predictive power of tests of aptitude. Using a huge database of previous studies, they came to the following clear conclusions:

- Most of the variance across studies is due to sampling error.
- Cognitive aptitude has a mean validity of 0.53 for entry-level jobs, where training will follow hiring, and for promotion, where current performance on the job is the basis for selection.
- General cognitive aptitude alone shows a high average validity across all jobs but it differs according to the measure of performance used and it becomes higher as objectivity of the criterion increases.
- Perceptual aptitude mean validities range from 0.26 to 0.53 for training success, and from 0.24 to 0.52 for job performance.
- Psychomotor aptitude average validities range from 0.09 to 0.40 for training success, and from 0.21 to 0.48 for job performance.
- Validity of cognitive aptitude declines as job complexity and information processing demands decrease, while the validity of psychomotor aptitudes increases as job complexity lessens.
- If cognitive, perceptual and psychomotor aptitude tests are combined the average validity is 0.53, with little variability across job families.

- Combination of aptitude tests does not entail an automatic increase in validities; it requires the assignment of the corresponding weight that each aptitude deserves in accordance with actual estimates.
- Estimated true validities of aptitude tests are lower when the criterion measures are supervisory ratings than when job sample indices are introduced as criterion estimates.
- Selection procedures, other than tests, do not show substantially higher validities and are typically poorer as predictors across job training or performance criteria.

This review has become a milestone since it involves the use of a great variety of published and unpublished studies of criterion-orientated measures of cognitive, perceptual and motor aptitudes and it points out that there are no current jobs for which reliable tests of aptitude do not have some relevant degree of validity. There become visible, however, reliable differences among jobs, since tests are not equally valid for all jobs.

The above-mentioned results indicate that aptitudes are significantly related to current job performance. Recently, the relationships among aptitudes, job knowledge and experience as well as performance have been investigated (Schmidt, Hunter and Outerbridge, 1986) through validity generalization and subsequent path analysis. Such researches consistently show that:

- The validities of aptitude tests are larger when the effects of individual differences in job experience are partialled out.
- High aptitude individuals maintain their job performance advantage right through their tenure of the job.
- Time spent in the job does not reduce or increase the standard deviation of aptitudes.
- There appears a high correlation between aptitudes and job knowledge that shapes job performance, because higher ability leads to increased acquisition of job knowledge by speeding up the process.
- The correlation between aptitudes and work sample performance is somewhat lower and it derives in part from a direct causal impact and from the indirect effect of aptitude on job knowledge.
- Supervisors are rather sensitive to differences in job knowledge when rating workers with up to five years of experience; afterwards, they tend to overrate job experience.

Finally, Hunter and Hirsch (1987) have reviewed studies which have introduced meta-analysis to current relationships in personnel psychology. Table 2 summarizes their main findings concerning tests of aptitude in predictive and concurrent designs.

Five short comments can be made:

1. The validity of general cognitive aptitude becomes steadily higher as objec-

Table 2   The validity generalization of aptitudes for different occupational criteria as stated in Hunter and Hirsh (1987)

	GENERAL COGNITIVE ABILITY	
	HH	SGNK
Criteria	VALIDITY	VALIDITY
Performance ratings by supervisors	0.53	0.41
Training success	0.63	0.63
Promotion or status change	—	0.40
Work sample performance	0.75	0.71
Job knowledge	0.80	—
Job tenure	0.26	—

SPECIAL APTITUDE	
	SGNK
	VALIDITY
Performance ratings by supervisors	0.21
Training success	0.31
Work sample performance	0.31

PHYSICAL ABILITY	
	SGNK
	VALIDITY
Training success	0.31
Promotion or status change	0.61
Work sample performance	0.47
Job tenure	0.15

Source: HH = Hunter and Hunter's (1984) data mainly. SGNK = Schmitt *et al.* (1984). All values have been corrected for attenuation due to error of measurement and for range restriction.

tivity becomes higher in criterion measures: from 0.40 for promotion to 0.53 for ratings to 0.63 for training success to 0.75 for work sample performance to 0.80 for job knowledge.

2. There is a positive correlation between general cognitive aptitude and tenure: it seems that the brighter incumbents stay longer.
3. Much of the high validity for general cognitive aptitude may be due to the fact that it predicts job knowledge.
4. Physical or sensorimotor abilities show more relevance than special aptitude for several occupational criteria.
5. Hunter and Hunter proceeded to look back on published and unpublished validity studies, while Schmitt and colleagues have reviewed only available researches from two relevant journals in this field.

It can be argued that this validity generalizability is based almost entirely on the pervasive influence of general intelligence. Actual indicators suggest that cognitive aptitude predicts job performance because the major cognitive abilities are involved in everyday learning and achieving while working in the post.

Nevertheless, in the strictest sense, the validity generalization model merely asserts that the observed variation in job-relevant validities is mainly due to statistical and methodological artefacts and implies the acceptance of the null hypothesis of no differences in validity coefficients between jobs across situations.

The situational specificity hypothesis

The alternative explanation holds that true validities markedly vary as a function of a host of contextual factors like jobs, organizations, criteria, applicant or incumbent pool, working milieu, geographical location, etc. It implies also that if a stated occupational setting remains unchanged, observed test validities do not vary. As a matter of fact, it postulates that tests of aptitude can be valid for some jobs but become useless for others.

This hypothesis is rooted in the empirical fact that the raw observed validity coefficients have varied from study to study, even when the jobs and tests studied appeared to coincide in almost every detail. In the past, most personnel psychologists accepted this belief: empirical validation acquired meaning or practical use for only the particular situation for which the test of aptitude–criterion relationships was set up.

This view was challenged in the 1970s by the introduction of validity generalization methods and the subsequent research findings and conclusions stating that all aptitude tests appear valid at relevant and pertinent levels for all jobs. That is, there is no situational variance in true criterion-predictor coefficients. It has also been demonstrated that the statistical artefacts operating within a single setting are the same that appear across entirely different settings; they account for a conservative 75 per cent of the variance in both kinds of validity distributions. This is something that ultimately challenges and refutes the situational prediction that when the occupational milieu is held constant, true estimated validities will not vary (Schmidt and Hunter, 1985).

Local validation studies address important makeshift issues like setting cut-off scores, predicting specific criteria, improving prediction through composites or providing new aptitude–job combinations, because mere occupational differences stand right in the middle of organizational settings and exist independently of job-relevant measurement methods and procedures. But such high visibility studies are unlikely to replicate; their troublesome variation is artefactual, mainly because sampling error or small sample size cannot be reliably interpreted in isolation. The overall pattern of findings is best seen through validity generalization approaches based on cumulated individual studies conducted over a long period of time.

That means that both frames of reference are not mutually exclusive and may coexist. It leads to more careful thinking about situational variables and moderators that are inherent in single studies and organizational settings which cannot be ignored by personnel practitioners. While there is sufficient evidence to conclude that tests of aptitude validities generalize across a variety of jobs, there are enough reasons to realize that they are more valid for some jobs than for others. Job-relevant components like motivation, interests, values, styles of supervision, organizational climate and structure, etc., do not apparently influence true validity coefficients between aptitudes and job performance.

A reasonable alternative view argues that the basis of some variance attributed to 'artefacts' is grounded in the situation itself. This provides an explanation for the situational specificity of such behavioural, cognitive and organizational variables that have not fallen by the wayside through validity generalization studies and may often involve the existence of potentially important known differences between and within organizations. This percentage variance unaccounted for has no direct impact on the practical and predictive purpose of selection procedures, but it enables personnel psychologists to understand some of the reasons why employees have to behave as they do and to anticipate the consequences of organizational programmes or, even, of their own acts. It is an aid for identifying *which* aptitudes and competencies the workers show and *what structures* have evolved through their tenure and experience in the post.

Estimates of utility

Personnel psychologists have often stayed aloof from cost–benefits evaluation regarding the degree of fitness and effectiveness obtained from selection devices. However, several approaches have been advanced and attempted over the years. They produce estimates that are no more arbitrary than those which are currently introduced in traditional cost-accounting procedures.

Utility gain or loss has become the operational aim in mind when bringing together validity coefficients, selection ratio, tenured posts, rejected offers, monetary value ascribed to stated performance, probability of success for applicants or incumbents selected or promoted, cost of the personnel system in use, cost–benefit rise and fall variations with productivity, tax liabilities, investments in human or technical resources, etc.

The problem of determining the estimated usefulness of tests of aptitude in selection procedures has received considerable attention. Practical methods of evaluating their impact on workforce productivity are available and their respective equations can be ordered around their own inherent assumptions:

- A personnel programme has been undertaken, one group of applicants or employees enters or modifies the existing workforce and the group becomes a marked cohort within the organization.
- A personnel programme encompasses, likewise, the flow of employees into and out of the workforce, including the additive cohort effects over time.
- A personnel programme achieves little benefit when some of the applicants with the highest test scores either will not receive offers or will reject them.

Such formulae intend to link the answer to two classical questions assuming that there is a low probability of randomly hiring a successful worker:

1. Do tests of aptitude as predictors move the mean of the performance distribution up towards the high end of the occupational execution scale? This point is clearly related to validity studies already discussed.

2. If the more able and higher test scorers are selected, does the mean value of the performance distribution gain an apposite profit or an estimated benefit? This point becomes central to utility analysis.

Two aspects have become critical for this target approach:

(a) The possibility of securing real comparisons in output level between successful and unsuccessful groups of employees.
(b) The possibility of converting into accurate monetary terms the indexed worth of job performance.

While the first point is a matter of performance appraisal, the second can be calculated through standard cost-accounting methods. However, it is a fact that current outcomes of many jobs cannot be directly set forth in economic figures. Until recently, both techniques had been only sporadically put to practical use at the same time.

The main method makes use of experienced supervisors as judges. They have to estimate the yearly value of the products and services brought at various levels of stated proficiency. The cost of hiring an outsider or using another firm may be contemplated mentally as a plausible referent. The difference between employees at the 15th, 50th and 85th percentiles in performance allows the verification of whether the judged distribution appears, in fact, normal or not.

The basic formula introduces available data about the following aspects:

– The tenure of the average incumbent in the post.
– The number of applicants selected in a given year.
– The validity coefficient of the administered test.
– The above-estimated standard deviation in monetary terms.
– The selection ratio (vacant positions divided by the number of applicants).
– The average aptitude test score among selected applicants.
– The per applicant cost of the testing procedure under consideration.

Boudreau's (1983) formula assumes, further, variable costs, taxes, discount rates as well as how long the personnel programme remains. Murphy's (1986) formula takes into account the known fact that high-scoring applicants are most likely to decline an offer because they get a greater number of competitive proposals. Both formulae thus take account of realistic circumstances.

Empirical research evidence supports the hypothesis that productivity in monetary terms does appear, approximately, normally distributed. Findings support the use of 40–60 per cent of annual wage as a conservative estimate of such standard deviation in economic figures. They also point out payroll savings since it is expected that a 10 per cent reduction of new hires can be achieved with no decline in output for organizations mainly concerned with the increase of efficiency as a goal when the amount of production is essentially fixed. Top-down selection via aptitude tests produces an increase in average performance of about 10–20 per cent, generates very large savings in monetary values, eliminates adverse impact for minorities and preserves 80–90 per cent of the productivity. Hunter and Hunter (1984) showed that using aptitude tests composites (including the use of quotas fair to minority group members) allows employees to attain the greatest economic benefit compared with any alternative available predictor (like job tryout, biographical inventory, reference check, experience, interview, training and experience rating, academic achievement, education, interest, age). Actual gains are maybe two or more times higher when different cohorts are introduced in the utility analysis. However, under some realistic circumstances current formulae may overestimate utility gains by 30–80 per cent if 10–70 per cent of high-scoring applicants decline the initial offer.

For the purpose of decision making in personnel selection, this means, broadly speaking, that applicants selected by an aptitude test will be more productive than a workforce selected randomly or by a less valid approach. Schmidt *et al.*'s (1986) empirical results from improved personnel selection using aptitude tests show a utility gain of:

- US$ 1758 to 15 839 per year per person selected for eighteen job levels of new white-collar hires in the US Federal Government agencies.
- US$ 600 million per year as the total value accrued if new employees stay an average of only one year; such figures increase when aptitude tests are used for a period of 5–10 years.
- 9.7 per cent increase in output among new hires.
- 9 per cent yearly decrease in the number of new full-time hires resulting in payroll cost savings of US$ 272 million for every year the new incumbents remain in the post.
- A factor of 2.59 reduction in the percentage of new hires who are considered as unsatisfactory performers (i.e. the bottom decile in performance would be decreased, in fact, to 3.86 per cent).

The publication of such results is beneficial because:

1. They promote a new kind of dialogue between personnel psychologists and their budget analyst colleagues in projecting benefits as well as costs.
2. They connect psychometric and econometric approaches under the heading of cost–benefit implications applied inside the boundaries of selection and classification decisions.
3. They relate practical to theoretical frameworks in the research of personnel psychology because job validity and organizational effectiveness studies attain a genuine conceptual redefinition.
4. They convey the aim of optimizing the economic usefulness of a personnel strategy for an organization, while simultaneously assessing the legitimacy and tenability of aptitude testing.

Once again it can be stated that this long-standing and recurrent effort to review and back up aptitude test tenability has no equivalent in alternative theoretical or applied frameworks in this field.

FINAL REMARKS

Tests of aptitude have been under criticism throughout most of the last two decades. Seen in perspective, they still retain high visibility in selection procedures and may provide personally unpleasant and unflattering information. For years, personnel psychologists have been concerned with convincing managers and workers in organizations as well as judges in courtrooms or congressmen in legislative halls that something new was evolving around test security and accuracy. Tests are psychological instruments that arrive at evaluations quickly. This is their known Achilles heel. Managers, workers, judges or congressmen are expected to produce frequent and ready statements, judgements or decisions about people they meet, know or are acquainted with that are almost never empirically verified or replicated. 'This is a matter of opinion', they pronounce without feeling responsible. For instance, there is no judge subject to examination because he or she passed false positive or negative judicial decisions. He or she only tries to avoid such mistakes. This is not a strong accusation to anybody who knows common facts and practices.

This chapter has supplied enough information about the variety of types of aptitude tests available as well as on the subject of their substantive tenability. It sums up successive researches repeatedly accepted by, and published in, the major journals in the field. This acceptance constitutes a high level of scientific and professional favourable reception. The past failure to reject or retain selectively highlighted an almost devastating panorama. However, the ability to generalize validities and utilities clearly puts down a marker that aptitude testing is moving beyond a mere technology to the status of a science.

As is often the case in social sciences (Heller, 1986) three different types of implementation avoidance can be expected from certain clients or users:

1. To ignore the research, at least for a while and turn one's attention to other organizational concerns.
2. To criticize the research or some part of it, raising doubts about some methodological issues. So, it becomes unwise to take the matter further until subsequent nuances are satisfactorily solved.
3. To accept and praise the findings but to question whether they apply in all occupational settings, especially in those that the user perceives as prevailing at the time in an organization.

Nevertheless, if clients or users are receptive to the results of psychological research, this chapter introduces tests of aptitude as forecasting psychological aids that provide the decision maker with a means whereby the future may be deprived of some of its surprises. This is clearly the case in personnel psychology as far as tests of aptitude are concerned.

REFERENCES AND FURTHER READING

American Psychological Association, American Educational Research Association and National Council for Measurement in Psychology (1985). *Standards for Educational & Psychological Tests*. American Psychological Association, Washington.

Bohman, S. (1980). *What is Intelligence?* Almqvist/Wiksell, Stockholm.

Boudreau, J.W. (1983). Economic considerations in estimating the utility of human resource productivity improvement programs, *Personnel Psychology*, **36**, 551–76.

Buros, O.K. (1974). *Eighth Mental Measurements Yearbook*, Gryphon, Highland Park, NJ.

Cascio, W.F. (1982). *Costing Human Resources: The Financial Impact of Behavior in Organizations*. Kent, Boston.

Cattell, R.B. (1986). The psychometric properties of tests: consistency, validity and efficiency, in R.B. Cattell and R.C. Johnson (eds). *Functional Psychological Testing: Principles and Instruments*. Brunner/Mazel, New York.

Cattell, R.B. (1987). *Intelligence: its structure, growth and action*. North-Holland, Amsterdam.

Ekstrom, R.B., French, J.W., and Harman, H.H. (1979). Cognitive factors: their identification and replication. *Multivariate Behavioral Research Monographs* (No. 79–2), 1–84.

Embretson, S.E. (1985). *Test Design: Developments in Psychology and Psychometrics*. Academic Press, London.

Fleishman, E.A., and Quaintance, M.K. (1984). *Taxonomies of Human Performance: the description of human tasks*. Academic Press, New York.

Ghiselli, E.E. (1966). *The Validity of Occupational Aptitude Tests*. Wiley, New York.

Glass, G.V. (1976). Primary, secondary and meta-analysis of research, *Educational Research*, 5(9), 3–8.

Guilford, J.P., and Hoepfner, R. (1971). *The Analysis of Intelligence*. McGraw-Hill, New York.

Guion, R.M. (1976). Recruiting, selection and job placement, in M.D. Dunnette (ed.). *Handbook of Industrial and Organizational Psychology*. Rand McNally, Chicago.

Heller, F. (1986). Conclusions, in F. Heller (ed.). *The Use and Abuse of Social Science*. Sage, London.

Hunter, J.E., and Hirsh, H.R. (1978). Applications of meta-analysis, in C.L. Cooper and I.T. Robertson (eds). *International Review of Industrial and Organizational Psychology 1987*. Wiley, Chichester.

Hunter, J.E., and Hunter, R.F. (1984). Validity and utility alternative predictors of job performance, *Psychological Bulletin*, **96**, 72–98.

Hunter, J.E., and Schmidt, F.L. (1982). Fitting people to jobs: the impact of personnel selection on national productivity, in M.D. Dunnette and E.A. Fleishman (eds). *Human Performance and Productivity: human capability assessment*, vol. 1. Erlbaum, Hillsdale.

Hunter, J.E., Schmidt, F.L., and Jackson, G.B. (1982). *Meta-Analysis: cumulative research findings across studies*. Sage, London.

Jansen, P.G.W., Roe, R.A., Vijn, P. and Algera, J.A. (1986). *Validity Generalization Revisited*. Delft University Press, Delft.

Jensen, A.R. (1980). *Bias in Mental Testing*, Methuen, London.

Lunneborg, C.E. (1985). Estimating the correlation coefficient: the bootstrap approach, *Psychological Bulletin*, **98**, 209–15.

Murphy, K.R. (1986). When your top choice turns you down: effect of rejected offers on the utility of selection tests, *Psychological Bulletin*, **99**(1), 133–8.

Nunnally, J.C. (1981). *Psychometric Theory*. McGraw-Hill, New York.

Prieto, J.M. (1982). Multivariate techniques in work psychology (Técnicas multivariadas en Psicología del Trabajo), *Estudios de Psicología*, **11**, 99–124.

Prieto, J.M. (1985a). Psychological tests' homologation (La homologación de pruebas psicológicas), *Papeles del Colegio*, **4**(21), 4–31.

Prieto, J.M. (1985b). Psychological intervention in selection and classification processes (La intervención psicológica en procesos de selección y clasificación), *Encuentros de Psicología*, **(7)**, 37–51.

Prieto, J.M., and Seisdedos, N. (1984). *BPC-1 & 2* (Collective Aptitude Test Battery). TEA Ediciones, Madrid.

Prieto, J.M., and Seisdedos, N. (1987). *BPS* (Selective Aptitude Test Battery). TEA Ediciones, Madrid.

Reilly, R.R., and Chao, G.T. (1982). Validity and fairness of some alternative employee selection procedures, *Personnel Psychology*, **35**, 1–62.

Sackett, P.R., Schmitt, N., Tenopyr, M.L., Kehoe, J., and Zedeck, S. (1985). Commentary on forty questions about validity generalizations and meta-analysis, *Personnel Psychology*, **38**, 697–798.

Schmidt, F.L., and Hunter, J.E. (1977). Development of a general solution to the problem of validity generalization, *Journal of Applied Psychology*, **62**, 529–40.

Schmidt, F.L., and Hunter, J.E. (1985). A within setting empirical test of the situational specificity hypothesis in personnel selection, *Personnel Psychology*, **37**, 317–25.

Schmidt, F.L., Hunter, J.E., and Outerbridge, A.N. (1986). Impact of job experience and ability on job knowledge, work samples performance and supervisory ratings of job performance, *Journal of Applied Psychology*, **71**(3), 432–9.

Schmidt, F.L., Hunter, J.E., Outerbridge, A.N., and Trattner, M.H. (1986). The economic impact of job selection methods on size, productivity and payroll costs of the federal work force: an empirically based demonstration, *Personnel Psychology*, **39**, 1–29.

Schmidt, F.L., Hunter, J.E., Pearlman, K., and Hirsh, H.R. (1985). Forty questions about validity generalization and meta-analysis, *Personnel Psychology*, **38**, 697–798.

Schmitt, N., and Noe, R.A. (1986). Personnel selection and equal employment opportunity, in C.L. Cooper and I.T. Robertson (eds). *International Review of Industrial and Organizational Psychology 1986*, Wiley, Chichester.

Schmitt, N., Gooding, R.Z., Noe, R.A., and Kirsch, M. (1984). Meta-analyses of validity studies published between 1964 and 1982 and the investigation of study characteristics, *Personnel Psychology*, **37**, 407–22.

Sternberg, R.J., Conway, B.E., Ketron, J.L., and Berstein, M. (1981). People's conceptions of intelligence, *Journal of Personality and Social Psychology*, **41**, 37–55.

TEA Seccion de Estudios (1982). *Tests y Documentos Psicológicos* (Tests and Psychological Documents). TEA Ediciones, Madrid.

Thorndike, R.L. (1982). *Applied Psychometrics*. Houghton Mifflin, Boston.

Wright, B.D., and Stone, M.H. (1979). *Best Test Design: A Handbook for Rasch Measurement*. Mesa, Chicago.

Yela, M. (1987). Studies on intelligence and language (*Estudios sobre inteligencia y lenguaje*). Pirámide, Madrid.

Zurfluh, J. (1976). *Les tests mentaux*. Delarge, Paris.

Chapter 3.4

Personality Questionnaires and Inventories

PAUL VAN DER MAESEN DE SOMBREFF[1] and WILLEM K.B. HOFSTEE[2]

[1]*Rijks Psychologische Dienst, Postbus 20013, 2500 EA 's-Gravenhage, The Netherlands*
[2]*Department of Psychology, University of Groningen, Grote Markt 31–32, NL 9712 HV Groningen, The Netherlands*

INTRODUCTION

Personality questionnaires and inventories are among the most frequently used tools of selection. Managers, personnel officers and psychologists acknowledge the critical importance of personal attributes such as emotional stability, achievement motivation and leadership style for success of employees in their jobs. At the organizational level, too, excellence and malfunctioning have been linked to the personality of managers and, projected on to the level of collectivity, to the personality of the organization: its culture and its set of values when interacting with clients and with its own employees. Kets de Vries has applied personalistic labels (such as 'neurotic') to organizations; in the Michigan theory of organizational achievement of Likert and co-workers, output variables such as productivity, absenteeism and turnover have been related to participative versus authoritarian style of leadership. Peters and Waterman (1982), in their inductive search for attributes that may distinguish excellent companies from their not so excellent counterparts, have found several factors leading to success that seem related to personality traits such as personal trust versus distrust, risk taking, practical attitude versus reflective behaviour and analytical attitude. Schneider (1987) recently proclaimed his professional credo that important organizational variables are strongly influenced by the personalities of important people in service, and that one has to take into account this organizational personality in

Handbook of Assessment in Organizations   Edited by P. Herriot
© 1989 John Wiley & Sons Ltd

recruiting and selecting new employees. This view on personality reminds one of the 'personality of situations' theory of Bem and Funder (1978); these authors provided a method to construct a 'template' of organizational personality with which the personalities of applicants have to fit. Sternberg (1985), in his triarchic theory of human intelligence, regards successful adaptation to the culture of the organization as an important aspect of intelligent behaviour.

In the face of this strong interest in personality variables for organizational success, what has psychology to offer with respect to theoretical insights that are applicable in organizational contexts? Can one measure relevant personality constructs? How much can scores on personality questionnaires and inventories be trusted? What is the incremental value of information resulting from personality tests with respect to other information that can be assessed with commonly used selection methods such as interviews and intelligence tests? How much is the return on investment of personality tests?

This chapter is devoted to answers to these questions. For a better understanding of several of these answers, the reader is offered some background information about the history of personality assessment, the content of personality constructs, the use of questionnaire formats, the major modes of construction of personality scales, and the big 'personality dispute' of recent date in which many psychologists have invested their abilities and efforts and on whose battlefield many new insights have been born. We will give these general issues priority over discussions about the relative merits of specific commercially available measurement instruments.

Sometimes, answers on these general questions are only partial since our knowledge about the benefits from personality assessment displays many gaps, in particular where empirical relations of personality scores with organizational output variables are concerned. Nevertheless, we hope that this chapter can contribute in generating a frame of reference for our readers that enables them to judge present and future claims about personality assessment.

A SHORT OVERVIEW OF CONCEPTS, METHODS AND HISTORY OF PERSONALITY ASSESSMENT

The daily use of personality constructs

Concern and theorizing about personality traits and temperaments, and the interests and values of the people with whom we interact and of ourselves is an inherent inclination of humans. Differences between people in their behaviours have always drawn attention and have led to attempts at classification, because of the practical relevance of insight into these differences, if not for other reasons. Knowing how an individual will react to situations in the future can be favourable for one's own adaptation in society. We have built a large vocabulary of trait names and propositions to convey events, states and patterns of behaviour that are meaningful to us. We readily perceive certain consistencies in the behaviour of other people; we describe other people with personality labels on the basis of perceived patterns of behaviour; and we predict how those people will react in other similar (but sometimes very *dis*similar) situations on the basis of personality traits that they are assumed to possess. People seem to be more inclined to describe other people in abstract terms than in terms of concrete reactions in specific situations; economy of labels seems to be a value in itself.

Personality is also a culturally interesting phenomenon. Writers have been honoured for their capability to portray the characters in their books in a psychologically meaningful and consistent manner despite the phenomenologically very diverse behavioural manifestations of those characters.

Types of personality theories; what makes a trait theoretically interesting?

Theories about the structure of personality and about the underlying causes of a certain personality pattern, syndrome or type have been postulated since the remotest ages. The four-fold typology of the Greek physician Galen—the choleric, phlegmatic, sanguine and melancholic types of personality—is an example of an old theory that has survived centuries in our language of personality—both lay and scientific—as an applicable scheme for describing differences between people.

Theories about personality often have included postulates about the mechanisms and processes behind manifestations of personality constructs. Hyland (1985) distinguished three modes of account: (1) physiological accounts, for instance by Galen who postulated that each type was caused by a dominant volume of one of four liquors in one's body, and Eysenck's account of extroversion–introversion based on cortical arousal mechanisms; (2) mentalistic accounts; for example, the process of cognitive attribution of aversive events to the internal and stable factor of one's own inability is invoked by authors such as Seligman and Dweck (for instance, Dweck and Leggett, 1988) as an explanation of the symptoms of 'learned helplessness' exhibited by an individual; (3) mechanistic accounts; for example, the need reduction theory of Freud and the drive theory of Thorndike, both inspired by the reflex model which proposes that the energy accumulated in the organism is discharged in behaviour by a stimulus that presents itself.

Hampson (1982) mentions four major criteria for admitting a personality variable as an object of theoretical interest: (1) internality—the behaviours which, in the theory of the construct, form the manifestations of the personality variable, can be ascribed to the person and not to situational characteristics; (2) cross-situational consistency—a personality variable is theoretically relevant only when the situational domain in which it is manifested is not restricted to very specific situations; (3) temporal stability—traits must be relatively stable over time, that is, individuals must have relatively unchanging positions on the trait; (4) inter-individual differences—the range of differences displayed by individuals on the trait is broad.

In a multi-trait theory one must add one more criterion: (5) minimal overlap—when two traits strongly go together in the sense that across individuals the level of one trait can be predicted with a great amount of certainty from the level of the other trait, it makes economical sense to join the two traits into one.

Measuring personality and interest variables

Three ways of measuring personality and interest variables can be discerned. In the first place, one can observe individuals in daily activities and rate their behaviours on one or more personality scales. Heymans's typology, for instance, has been construed on such 'L(ife) data'. Secondly, one can ask the individuals to rate themselves on a personality scale, collecting so-called 'Q(uestionnaire) data'. Because of its low costs of administration, Q ratings are the most frequently used form of rating, both for theoretical and for applied purposes. The third possibility, providing so-called 'T(est) data', is to observe and to rate individuals in specially designed situations, such as tests and laboratory situations. For example, how do applicants cope with a very frustrating situation; how is their aspiration level with respect to achievement in a task influenced by a series of successes or failures?

In personnel selection we meet these three sources of personality assessment in the methods used. L-data are assessed, for instance, in the interview where the applicant is asked to give evidence of possessing a trait (for example 'initiative') by describing how he or she acted in a past situation that, ideally, resembles situations to be encountered on the job. (It should be noted that the example is problematic since the 'observation' is vicarious, and may well be biased; however, direct observation is seldom possible.) Q-data are gathered through questions in paper-and-pencil personality tests and inventories in which applicants rate themselves on broad dispositions (how optimistic, how interested in abstract ideas versus concrete things are you?), and on behaviours in situations, both in the past (when I travel by train, I am fond of talking with other travellers) and in the future (in a management position, I would devote much time to the needs of my colleagues). Work samples, for instance assessment centre exercises (see Chapter 3.7), are miniature simulations of critical job elements whose purpose is to provide T-data. Other tests, such as projective techniques, also belong to this class of T-data.

A short history of personality measurement

Personality measurement started in the beginning of the twentieth century with Binet who tried to classify people into types (for example theoretical–practical, literary–scientific) based on the production of 20 words that came into their memories. Free word association tasks of Jung were the predecessors of projective tests such as the Rorschach ink blots, the Thematic Apperception Test and the Szondi Test. These open answer tests were supposed to disclose all that is interesting (dominant) in a given personality.

Heymans and Wiersma were among the first who made use of Life and Questionnaire data, on which they based their typology with three dimensions (activity, emotionality and secondary function). Later on, in the First World War, administration of questionnaires was used as a quick and inexpensive device to keep the extremely unstable individuals out of military service.

The desire to classify psychiatric patients into one of the main clinical syndromes such as hypochondria, paranoia and schizophrenia was the point of departure for the most researched and used personality inventory in the world, the Minnesota Multiphasic Personality Inventory of Hathaway and McKinley. The MMPI has 550 items in 13 scales, of which three are intended to check the validity of scores on the other ten scales. With the Strong–Campbell Interest scales, the MMPI belonged to the first inventories for which computerized interpretation of score profiles was provided.

The California Personality Inventory, another influential personality test, was mainly constructed with those MMPI items on which normal people could be differentiated from one another. Therefore, it is also called the 'sane man's MMPI'. The CPI, 480 items long and responded to with 'true' or 'false', has eighteen subscales, for instance, dominance, sociability, responsibility and self-control. Three of the eighteen scales are designed to diagnose test-taking attitudes, the inclination to 'fake bad' or 'fake good', and the propensity for popular answers. The inventory did produce many offspring, for instance the Management Potential Scale, validated and cross-validated by Gough in dozens of studies with ratings of managerial effectiveness as criteria.

The hundreds of items developed by Strong and Campbell examine the preference of persons for a great variety of activities, objects, or persons, encountered in everyday life. Items are grouped in scales (for instance, adventure, medical service, teaching, sales); these scales in their turn can be classified under certain themes, for instance, realistic, scientific and social. Computerized interpretation of individual answers is done by means of matching an individual profile with occupational profiles; the assumption is that members of an occupation are characterized by a common and unique profile of interest, and that future success of an individual in an occupation is a function of the similarity of his profile with the job profile.

Besides MMPI, CPI and the Interest Scales of Strong and Campbell, being instruments that are devised mainly with items on which persons belonging to contrasting groups gave different answers (for example, the group of males and that of females for the scale femininity), inventories have been developed as a by-product of systematic research into the internal structure of self-ratings. The most frequently used personality scales based on theoretical research with factor analysis as a favoured method are those of Cattell, Guilford, Eysenck and Comrey. We refer to Hampson (1982) for more information about these scales.

Many scales have been constructed deductively, on the basis of already formulated theories. One can distinguish between multi-trait and single-trait theories. Known examples of the first type are the Edwards Personal Preference Schedule and the Jackson Personality Inventory, both based on the personality theory of Murray, and the Study of Values of Allport *et al.*, based on the values taxonomy of Spranger. Examples of inventories based on one-trait theories are the Rotter Locus of Control Scale, the Machiavellianism scales, and the scales for measuring the achievement motive.

THE CONSTRUCTION OF PERSONALITY AND INTEREST INVENTORIES

Three approaches to inventory construction

Three ways of constructing a personality questionnaire may be distinguished . We will follow Burisch's (1984) terminology. The first one Burisch calls the *external* (empirical, actuarial) approach. Persons can be characterized as being personalities of a certain kind by means of methods independent of the inventory itself. For example, some people are judged by their psychiatrist as 'neurotic' and others as 'psychotic', or supervisors rate their co-workers on the dimension of 'participative leadership'. The purpose of the external approach, after having administered a set of the items that might be of interest for the construct(s) to be measured, is to select the items that discriminate best between members of the groups or do a good task in predicting the level on that external construct. Selection of items is carried out with help of statistical techniques such as discriminant analysis or multiple regression analysis.

Examples of tests construed with an external procedure are the MMPI and CPI, the Strong Vocational Interest Blank, biographical inventories or biodata (see Chapter 3.10) and, recently, the Tacit Knowledge Scales for measuring managerial success of Sternberg. The external approach is apt to be afflicted by certain risks: (1) small size of the sample on which research and development of criterion keyed scales is done is the rule rather than the exception. Due to these small numbers the selection process leads to unstable results in the sense that in another sample different items are selected; (2) people are inclined to seek an explanation as to why the particular subset of items is successful in predicting the criteria. With externally keyed items, explanation is often difficult and false inferences are quickly made. When multiple regression analysis is applied to reduce the set of items, typically a very heterogeneous subset is the end result. In the case of so-called suppressor variables (variables that suppress irrelevant redundancy with other predictors) one may also become confused about the direction of the weight that one has to attach to an item to achieve optimal prediction.

The second approach is called by Burisch the *inductive* (internal) approach. This approach assumes that there exist coherent clusters of behaviour, subsumable under trait (or momentary state) categories, and that one can detect those categories by techniques such as factor analysis. Factor analysis is a method to reduce the variables (items) in a test to a smaller number of underlying dimensions or factors. Items that elicit responses that covary highly with one another will typically belong to one factor. A factor is usually interpreted by inspection of the content of items that represent that factor most clearly and that do not represent other factors. The factor analytic method, too, can have its difficulties (although, used sensibly, it can be a highly valuable method): (1) which factors will result is critically dependent on the content of the items included in one's research; (2) because scale homogeneity is the target of factor analysis, there is a risk that a factor composed of highly redundant items and (thus) of limited theoretical and practical value will emerge; (3) modes of conducting a factor analysis and interpreting its results depend to a certain degree on the theoretical and methodological preferences of the researcher. For example, Guilford and

Eysenck have quarrelled about the question whether the results of their factor analyses indicate that sociability and impulsiveness belong to one factor (Eysenck's extroversion) or are the constituents of two separate factors (Guilford's social activity and introversion–extroversion). In studying the subsequent handbooks of the Sixteen Personality Factors (16PF), an extensively researched and used personality questionnaire by Cattell, it can be discovered that several items have been 'reshuffled' under factors or reinterpreted as new items were added to the set of variables being studied; (4) the last disadvantage of the inductive approach is that traits that do not covary with other traits, but that are nevertheless very important in human society, will not survive the analysis.

The third approach is labelled by Burisch the *deductive* (rational, common-sense) approach. The deductive approach is favoured by Burisch because of the proven possibility of constructing shorter personality scales in less time and with equal (or even higher) validity with this method than with the two other methods. The premise of the deductive approach is that 'one can construct a scale for each trait for which there is a name', as Burisch contends. An implication of this premise is that, in constructing a personality questionnaire for specific purposes, it makes sense to select only those constructs that seem to have *a priori* relevance for the task of prediction at hand. It is not evident at all in advance that questionnaires developed according to the *inductive* tradition—as is primarily the case with the much used personality tests of Guilford, Cattell and Eysenck—are entirely relevant for a specific application. The purpose of these questionnaires was to represent the structure of personality without restriction to specific applications. Taking practical utility as the point of departure for the construction of personality scales can lead to the following differences compared to the other two methods: (1) some scales found in the inductive tradition are omitted because of their irrelevance for the problem at hand; (2) some scales can be broken up into subscales, for example, 'gregariousness' into 'social anxiety' and 'need for social contacts'; (3) new scales can be devised, for example, 'experimental attitude in work/readiness to change work methods', a more precise form of the dimension 'flexibility versus rigidity'.

Buss and Craik (1985) have offered a methodological basis to the deductive approach of scale construction by means of their 'prototype analysis'. The common-sense knowledge of personality stored in our languages serves as the starting point in considering a trait as potentially relevant. Their research procedure stipulates several other, methodological criteria for inclusion of that trait for measurement purposes, to which the criteria of Hampson mentioned earlier in this chapter must be added. Such criteria are for instance: (1) the trait name can be 'substantiated' by judges with a significant volume of acts. For example, the trait of 'dominance' is exemplified with diverse acts such as 'used the authority of his (her) position' and 'persuaded him to do something he didn't want to do'; (2) judges agree as to which acts are central (prototypical) members of the trait. For example, the two acts above have been rated as very good manifestations of dominance, whereas 'flattered her in order to get his (her) way' is rated low in this respect; (3) judges agree that acts rated as highly prototypical for one trait cannot be regarded as good examples of other distinct relevant traits. This is the criterion of 'low overlap' mentioned earlier.

Buss and Craik have accumulated evidence that the frequency of multiple acts pertaining to one trait is stable in time. Act frequency is predictable with a moderate degree of accuracy with scores on personality scales measuring the same trait.

Commenting upon the three approaches, it seems to us that ideally one approach is combined with (one of) the other(s). Clearly one should start by using a rational approach, making a conscientious effort to cover the concept to be operationalzied in a systematic manner. Facet analysis (Roskam, 1987) is an appropriate tool for constructing a representative set of items for a concept. It is wise to check the dimensionality (internal approach) of deductively constructed scales afterwards, for the reason that common-sense ideas sometimes do not coincide with empirical relationships between traits. It is also possible that a set of items that increased the (internal) homogeneity of a scale has to be removed from that scale when it becomes evident that, in comparison with the rest of the scale, this set of items is reversely related with a relevant (external) criterion. In our own research with a self-rating scale for 'dominance', for example, it appeared that items that had to do with 'authoritative' behaviour ('when I supervise others performing a task, I am impatient of any argument') go along with items as mentioned above. However, the set of 'authoritative' items appeared to be *negatively* related with supervisory ratings of management effectiveness on the job, and the other items positively.

Finally, to avoid an endless proliferation of scales by the common-sense approach, any newly constructed scale should be compared with existing, established scales to see whether it has incremental value.

Answer formats for personality tests

A main distinction between answer formats for personality tests is that between *open* and *closed* answer formats. Projective techniques for personality assessment such as graphology (Chapter 3.12) and Rorschach test are well-known examples of the open format that is preferred by some psychologists for the reason that these methods induce persons to express their 'deeper, unconscious layers of personality', as Allport says. This is a property with which the closed ('reaction') type of test is not thought to be endowed. Because of scientific doubt about the validity of projection (it is highly unlikely that people show their personalities through their expressions such as handwriting and non-autobiographical story telling), because of the unreliability of interpretation—although there are exceptions such as Thematic Apperception Test for measuring the achievement motive—and because of the inefficiency of administering and scoring them, projective techniques are not recommended methods for personnel selection.

The most frequently used open-ended method for measuring personality traits is, of course, the interview (Chapter 3.9). The 'psychological', unstructured interview that is directed towards impressions of someone's character has been shown to be inferior in predictive accuracy to the 'behavioural', structured interview that asks information about someone's past behaviours in situations that are relevant for the job.

The *closed* answer self-rating questionnaire is the most used form of personality test. The *multiple-choice* questionnaire can be administered very easily, for instance, on answer forms processable by optical mark readers or through computerized testing, and the response process does not take much time; the estimated minimal response rate per hour is about 200 items.

The most frequently applied answer scale in personality inventories is the so-called Likert scale. In this answer format, subjects rate themselves (or are rated by another person) on several categories of frequency or applicability of a behavioural description. Research has demonstrated that the number of choices on the rating scale of an item is ideally about five. In offering fewer alternatives than five, one loses information about valid inter-individual differences; in offering more, one introduces informational overload which leads subjects to anchoring strategies (one starts responding to personality test items with a particular scale value, and one sticks to the neighbourhood of that initial value in responding to the other items) and other invalidating responses.

Another important closed answer multiple-choice personality test type is the '*ipsative*' or '*forced choice*' test. In items of this test type subjects are asked to choose one of two (or more) descriptions that applies most or least to themselves. The test does not give direct information about the position of a subject on a trait relative to other subjects (for example, other applicants for the same job), but diagnoses to what extent someone exhibits a trait relative to other traits within the subject. Inter-individual comparability of traits is sacrificed in order to eliminate a serious problem of 'free choice' items: the individual may respond to personality items based on the characteristics of the situation in which the test is administered, notably the effect of *social desirability* of responses on items. Social desirability means that it is, *a priori*, clear to the average individual how responses on a specific item will be interpreted by the selector in terms of suitability for a particular job. For example, most applicants for a management position who are asked to indicate how much the proposition 'I like to motivate other people in their work' applies to themselves know that the negative answer will be interpreted as a negative indication of management potential. This knowledge of what is and what is not desired can have a distorting influence on the response process so that the information on some scales becomes untrustworthy. Forced-choice formats circumvent such distortions.

Nevertheless, the construction of an ipsative test is an endeavour with many pitfalls. The requirements that have to be met to obtain a scientifically valid instrument generally appear high enough to reach the decision that investment in its construction is unwise. Moreover, many applicants object to being forced to choose one alternative, when all alternatives fit them equally well.

THE PERSONALITY DEBATE

During the last twenty years a very lively debate has raged about the question whether it is meaningful at all to hypothesize 'personality traits' to explain and predict human behaviour. The attack on the trait construct has been vigorously opened by Mischel in his book *Personality and Assessment* (1968). The point of departure of Mischel's criticism was a review of empirical data which revealed that measures of personality traits are unable to predict external criterion measures (for instance, the counted frequency of dishonest behaviours) with an accuracy higher than 0.20 and 0.30. This means, says Mischel, that those traits predict only up to 10 per cent of differences in real behaviours. This criticism, together with other objections against personality tests such as their liability to distortion and their invasion into privacy, has probably been responsible for the reduction in the use of these tests in the United States.

According to Mischel, personality traits are invalid because behaviours that these traits pretend to explain are not *consistent* over situations but highly *specific*. Thus, it seems not possible to meet one of the criteria for using traits, as mentioned by Hampson (1982). That a person manifested, for instance, honest behaviour in situation A appeared to correlate only 0.20 with honest behaviour in situation B. The honesty of persons is highly dependent on the specific situation, and 'personalists' were reproached by Mischel for being guilty of the 'fundamental attribution error', the human tendency to attribute behaviour to personal dispositions where instead this behaviour is caused primarily by the situation.

Much research has been devoted to demonstrating that humans discover a structure in their own behaviours and those of others that in reality does not exist and is thus illusory. Some have argued that the 'conceptual similarity' between propositions such as 'frequently visits a pub with friends', 'always has a lot to say' and 'has an optimistic view of his future' unjustifiably leads (self-) ratings of these behaviours to go in the same direction. Our ('theory-driven') language about personality, and thus the personality factors found in inductive research, are invalid.

There have been several, not so successful, attempts to reconcile situationism and personalism, for example by Bem and Allen (1974) who postulated that certain traits are not relevant for everybody. Further research into 'moderator variables' of person consistency and predictability has been reported by Angleitner and Wiggins (1986). When moderator variables exist, there is no ground to be optimistic about the incremental validity of questionnaires where these variables have been accounted for in the scoring of answers (Hofstee and Smid, 1986).

We think that authors such as Epstein (Epstein and O'Brien, 1985), Block, Weiss and Thorne (1979), Moskowitz (1982), Rushton, Brainerd and Pressley (1983), and Amelang and Borkenau (1986) have demonstrated convincingly that most of the arguments of Mischel and followers that have for a long time fastened suspicion on personality measurement are flawed. The main counter-arguments are:

1. Mischel's arguments have been wrongly concentrated on single all-or-none behavioural criteria. Since Spearman at the beginning of this century it is a known statistical law that those single criteria contain a large proportion of error. Psychometrics takes this law into account by aggregating single parts of behaviour (responses on items) into one global score. (The much more appealing counterpart of this law, to which Mischel seems to have fallen

victim, has been called the 'law of the small numbers' in psychology of judgement.) In a personality scale, a high reliability is achieved by taking the *sum* of diverse behavioural referents, manifested on diverse situations, of the trait one wants to measure, although the *single* behavioural elements are unreliable and manifest low correlations with other elements. Epstein and others have shown that aggregate ratings of the behavioural referents of traits are highly stable in time and predictable to a greater degree than single referents.

2. It seems proven that the 'systematic distortion' results of the studies by Shweder and D'Andrade (1980) can be explained for a large part by an artefact in their rating procedure (Amelang and Borkenau, 1986). Recent research of Borkenau reveals that the 'implicit personality theories' of persons are of great help to them in rating others accurately in retrospect, a condition which is, by the way, quite common in personnel appraisal situations.

3. Mischel has wrongly used the so-called 'determination coefficient' (90 per cent unexplained variance in the criterion) to prove the futility of prediction with traits. However, the practical utility of a predictor is a linear, not a quadratic, function of the validity coefficient (see Chapter 3.3). In addition, an uncorrected validity of 0.30 must be valued as a quite desirable coefficient in personnel psychology. This point is substantiated further in the following section on (incremental) validity and utility.

For a recent view on lessons from the person–situation debate, one is recommended to read Kenrick and Funder (1988).

VALIDITY AND UTILITY OF PERSONALITY TESTS

A good way to evaluate the economic value of a personality test in a selection procedure is to compute the incremental validity and utility of that test with respect to a selection procedure without that test.

We will concentrate here on a one-phased selection procedure that consists of one aptitude test. The question is then: how much is validity and utility increased when one adds a personality questionnaire to this procedure?

To determine incremental validity one needs information about three parameters: (1) the validity of the aptitude test; (2) the validity of the personality questionnaire; and (3) the redundancy of aptitude and personality test, expressed as the correlation coefficient between them.

When the aptitude test at hand is sufficiently reliable and when it covers a broad enough range of tasks, one may generalize recent meta-analytic validity (see Chapter 3.3) results to one's own situation. Hunter and Hunter (1984) found an average true validity of 0.53 for test of general mental ability, with 90 per cent of the coefficients of individual studies lying above 0.34.

To our knowledge, meta-analytic research on the validity of personality tests, let alone on their generalizability, has been scarce or completely absent. The depressingly low validities of personality tests in selection reported from 1965 to 1985 stem from a few studies. That of Ghiselli (1973) is the most important, but the mean coefficients that it reports cannot be regarded as true validities (as is also acknowledged by the author himself). Fairly soon, however, results of a large-scale meta-analytic study (over 1000 validities, 26 inventories) will be published in the United States by Shannon (in press). Preliminary results of Shannon (personal communication) do not give rise to much optimism about the utility of personality test scales. The majority of the scales under investigation failed to reach the criterion for validity generalization: a 90 per cent credibility interval lower bound value greater than 0.10.

Hereafter, we will present some utility calculations based upon an expected, a pessimistic and an optimistic validity coefficient of an overall score on a personality test with respect to an employee's overall value to the organization (with the term 'overall score' is meant here the sum of standardized scale scores, where scores on desirable traits get a weight of +1 and undesirable traits a weight of −1). The expected value is set to 0.20, the pessimistic and optimistic values to 0.10 and 0.30, respectively.

Research into the redundancy of overall scores on personality tests and aptitude scores is also scarce. In the Netherlands, research with the RPDV, a twelve-scale personality questionnaire developed for personnel selection (Van der Maesen and Zaal, 1987), correlations between between 0.00 and +0.15 have been found consistently.

The composite validities of the unweighted scores of two instruments, the first one with validity 0.53 and the second with validity 0.30, 0.20 or 0.10, and with a correlation of 0.15 between both predictors, are 0.575, 0.544 and 0.5304. To answer the question how much the economic value of the procedure is increased per selected applicant due to the gain of 0.045, 0.014 and 0.004 in validity, one needs information about several other parameters: (*a*) the selection ratio (the proportion of applicants selected); (*b*) the standard deviation of performance expressed in financial units (this parameter indicates how much employees, on the job on which the vacancies exist, differ from each other in their worth to the organization—40 per cent of annual salary is typically taken as a conservative estimate of standard deviation of performance); and (*c*) the extra costs per applicant of the additional instrument.

As an example we take a prototypical selection situation, one with a selection ratio of 0.10, a standard deviation of performance of £16 000 (corresponding to an annual salary of £40 000), and additional costs of the personality test of £50 per applicant (£1 sterling is about 3.0 Deutschmarks, 10.5 French francs and 3.7 Dutch guilders).

The organization invests an added £500 per accepted applicant in the new procedure. Added returns on these investments total up to an average of £765 per selected applicant per year, when the optimistic validity value of 0.30 is the true one. When validity is 0.20, one loses £107 per selected employee, and the loss will be £388 when validity is only 0.10. These amounts have to be multiplied by the number of persons hired and by the expected service life in years of these employees. As one can see, it depends very much on the size of the validity coefficient whether it will be a wise decision to invest in an extra personality test in the selection procedure.

EPILOGUE: THE FUTURE OF PERSONALITY TESTS

Recent reviews of personality tests, for instance, by Hogan *et al.* (1985) and by Muchinsky (1986) are optimistic about their future. Hogan *et al.* regard the mean personality test validity of 0.23 with respect to job proficiency in the study of Ghiselli (1973) as high, when one takes the great variety of tests and of their quality into consideration. Both authors have noticed a revival of the interest in personality tests in recent years. They believe that in selection it is worthwhile to replace personality tests that once were constructed to diagnose psychopathological disorders with tests that are relevant in *working situations* and for *normal* individuals. Close inspection of the work of Shannon will reveal whether the expectations of Hogan and Muchinsky are too optimistic or not.

A further point that merits consideration is the lack of intersubjective consistency in interpreting sentences and words used in personality items. Research in this area can deliver linguistic principles to be used in formulating questions that have minimal ambiguity (Helfrich, 1986).

It seems very useful to conduct research into the predictive validity of personality tests with respect to occupational variables such as success in training and on the job, absenteeism and turnover. Also important is research on overlap of personality test scores with scores on aptitude tests and on other selection methods. Results of individual studies must be accumulated and meta-analysed.

A topic of special concern is the interpretation of a social desirability (SD) score. Has SD to be interpreted as a validity check or as a style variable, connected with a pattern of traits, as authors such as Wiggins and Jackson suggest? If SD does not 'moderate' the interpretation of other scales, how has SD to be weighted in predicting success? Does a high score on SD mean 'faking' or 'unreliable' or, on the contrary, 'adaptive' and 'flexible'? Our own research yields *positive* correlations of SD with job success, thus suggesting the latter interpretation.

Computerized administration of personality tests will perhaps give rise to new response formats. A method of testing that is hardly exploited at present is the 'ideographic' method in which persons formulate themselves the personality adjectives that are salient in their own self-peceptions. Claeys *et al.* (1985) have recently constructed a personality test based on this principle. These open answers, which are typed in on the computer keyboard, are subsequently matched with items stored in a computer database, and connected with a smaller set of categories. These categories stem from lexical analysis (for example the SPEL categories found by Hofstee, Brokken and Land, 1981) or from prototypicality analysis (Buss and Craik, 1985). The rated level of prototypicality of the adjective for each of the higher order categories, and its weight, are also stored in the database. By summing the scores on the categories for each of the generated adjectives, and by averaging, one gets scores on the category scales. For example, an applicant types the attribute 'outgoing' on the PC-keyboard. In previous research, this attribute is judged as highly prototypical for the personality dimension of 'extroversion', for example, with plus eight on a scale of -10 to $+10$. Possibly, this same attribute has received a score of -2 on the category of 'studious'.

Generally speaking, computerization offers a perspective of reconciling two central requirements in personality testing: the requirement of objectivity and the need for flexibility. Personality questionnaires have their origins in the oral interview. Whereas the interview is highly flexible, it is insufficiently systematic and objective for the purpose of comparing applicants. Personality questionnaires, on the other hand, with their fixed items and multiple-choice answering formats, have almost completely sacrificed flexibility in favour of objectivity. Sophisticated computer programs that can learn from respondents—in the sense of accumulating information with each new respondent—are an exciting and nonetheless realistic prospect.

REFERENCES AND FURTHER READING

Amelang, M., and Borkenau, P. (1986). The trait concept: current theoretical considerations, empirical facts, the implications for personality inventory construction, in A. Angleitner and J.S. Wiggins (eds). *Personality Assessment via Questionnaires: Current issues in theory and measurement*. Springer Verlag, Berlin.

Angleitner, A., and Wiggins, J.S. (eds) (1986). *Personality Assessment via Questionnaires: Current issues in theory and measurement*. Springer Verlag, Berlin.

Bem, D.J., and Allen, A. (1974). On predicting some of the people some of the time: The search for cross-situational consistencies in behaviour, *Psychological Review*, **81**, 506–20.

Bem, D.J., and Funder, D.C. (1978). Predicting more of the people more of the time: assessing the personality of situations, *Psychological Review*, **85**, 485–501.

Block, J., Weiss, D.S., and Thorne, A. (1979). How relevant is a semantic similarity interpretation of personality ratings? *Journal of Personality and Social Psychology*, **37**, 1055–74.

Burisch, M. (1984). Approaches to personality inventory construction, *American Psychologist*, **39**, 214–27.

Buss, D.M., and Craik, K.H. (1985). Why not measure that trait? Alternative criteria for identifying important dimensions, *Journal of Personality and Social Psychology*, **48**, 934–46.

Claeys, W., De Boeck, P., Böhrer, A., Van den Bosch, W., and Biesmans, R. (1985). A comparison of one free-format and two fixed-format self-report personality assessment methods, *Journal of Personality and Social Psychology*, **49**, 1028–39.

Dweck, C.S., and Leggett, E.L. (1988). A social–cognitive approach to motivation and personality, *Psychological Review*, **95**, 256–73.

Epstein, S., and O'Brien, E.J. (1985). The person–situation debate in historical and current perspective, *Psychological Bulletin*, **98**, 513–37.

Ghiselli, E.E. (1973). The validity of aptitude tests in personnel selection, *Personnel Psychology*, **26**, 461–77.

Hampson, S.E. (1982). *The Construction of Personality*. Routledge & Kegan Paul, London.

Helfrich, H. (1986). On linguistic variables influencing the understanding of questionnaire items, in A. Angleitner and J.S. Wiggins (eds). *Personality Assessment via Questionnaires: Current issues in theory and measurement*. Springer Verlag, Berlin.

Hofstee, W.K.B., Brokken, F.B., and Land, H. (1981). Constructie van een standaard-persoonlijkheids-eigenschappen-lijst (SPEL), *Nederlands Tijdschrift voor de Psychologie*, **36**, 443–52.

Hofstee, W.K.B., and Smid, N.G. (1986). Psychometric models for analysis of data from personality questionnaires, in A. Angleitner and J.S. Wiggins (eds). *Personality Assessment via Questionnaires: Current issues in theory and measurement*. Springer Verlag, Berlin, pp. 166–77.

Hogan, R., Carpenter, B.N., Briggs, S.R., and Hansson, R.O. (1985), Personality assessment and personnel selection, in J. Bernardin and D. Bownass (eds). *Personality Assessment in Organizations.* Praeger, New York.

Hunter, J.E. and Hunter, R.F. (1984). Validity and utility of alternative predictors of job performance, *Psychological Bulletin, 96,* 72–98.

Hyland, M.E. (1985). Do person variables exist in different ways? *American Psychologist, 40,* 1003–10.

Kenrick, D.T., and Funder, D.C. (1988). Profiting from controversy: lessons from the person–situation debate, *American Psychologist, 43,* 23–34.

Maesen de Sombreff, P.E.A.M. van der and Zaal, J.N. (1987). Incremental utility of personality questionnaires in selection by the Dutch government. *Proceedings of the Conference on Benefits of Psychology,* Lausanne.

Mischel, W. (1968). *Personality and Assessment.* Wiley, New York.

Moskovitz, D.S. (1982). Coherence and cross-situational generality in personality: a new analysis of old problems, *Journal of Personality and Social Psychology, 43*(4), 754–68.

Muchinsky, P.M. (1986), Personnel selection methods, in C.L. Cooper and I.T. Robertson (eds). *International Review of Industrial and Organizational Psychology 1986.* Wiley, Chichester, pp. 37–70.

Peters, T.T., and Waterman, R.H. (1982). *In Search of Excellence.* Harper & Row, New York.

Roskam, E.E. (1987). Methodische aspecten van de vragenlijst, in J. de Jong-Gierveld and J. van der Zouwen (eds). *De vragenlijst in het sociaal onderzoek; een confrontatie van onderzoekspraktijk en-methodiek.* Van Loghum-Slaterus, Deventer, pp. 85–105.

Rushton, J.P., Brainerd, C.J., and Pressley, M. (1983). Behavioral development and construct validity: The principle of aggregation, *Psychological Bulletin, 94,* 18–38.

Schneider, B. (1987). The people make the place, *Personnel Psychology, 40,* 437–53.

Shannon, P. (in press). Meta-analysis of personality and biographical inventories. Doctoral Dissertation, University of Minnesota, Wells Fargo Bank, San Francisco.

Shweder, R.A., and D'Andrade, R.G. (1980). The systematic distortion hypotheses, in R.A. Shweder and D.W. Fiske (eds). *Fallible Judgement in Behavioural Research. New directions for methodology of social and behavioural science,* No. 4. Jossey-Bass, San Francisco.

Sternberg, R.J. (1985). *Beyond IQ: A Triarchic Theory of Human Intelligence.* Cambridge University Press, Cambridge.

Chapter 3.5

Computer-based Assessment

DAVID BARTRAM

Ergonomics Research Unit, The University of Hull, 26 Newland Park, Hull HU5 2DW, UK

INTRODUCTION

Throughout history, the initial impact of any new technology tends to have been constrained by the difficulty people have divorcing themselves from ways of thinking related to the old technology. This has been apparent in the area of office automation where the introduction of word processors is often looked on as a process of upgrading secretaries' typewriters. The possibilities provided for completely reorganizing the whole management of the office, staff duties and responsibilities, communications with other departments and so on are frequently missed.

The main argument underlying this chapter is that not only does computerization provide an alternative assessment 'product' to paper-and-pencil technology; it also provides a medium which will allow us to develop radically and expand both the process of human assessment and the range and type of products we can use in that process. To take real advantage of this new technology, we must be willing to reconsider established procedures. For example, one oft-quoted argument against the use of computer-based assessment (CBA) is that it is not practical for group testing. But why do we carry out group testing in the first place? It is a function of logistic constraints and cost–benefit analyses predicated on the old technology: the need to provide expensive manpower for test supervision and administration, the recurrent cost of paper-and-pencil materials and so on. We will see that new technology provides real alternatives to these procedures.

Over the past 20 or so years, computers have played an increasingly vital 'backroom' role in test development and the analysis of test data for research

Handbook of Assessment in Organizations   Edited by P. Herriot
© 1989 John Wiley & Sons Ltd

purposes. However, what we are now seeing is the automation of a range of components of the assessment procedure itself. Since the early 1980s interest in the potential occupational applications of CBA has grown.

1. Within the United States, CBA software is available for a great variety of instruments. A good indication of the proliferation of software within the United States can be obtained by looking through Krug's (1987) *Psychware Sourcebook*. The first edition of this was published in 1984. The new edition published only three years later lists nearly twice as many products available from more than twice as many suppliers.
2. Within Europe we have seen a growing number of articles on CBA directed at professionals in the occupational field (e.g. Bartram and Bayliss, 1984; Grant, 1987). In addition, the major test publishers in Europe (e.g. NFER–Nelson and Saville and Holdsworth in the United Kingdom) have now begun to publish CBA software which has been specifically designed and developed for the 'occupational market'.

While the commercial exploitation of CBA software has been largely confined to the United States, there has been a major input to research and development within Europe: in terms of test theory, test development and special-purpose CBA applications. Most of this large-scale occupational work has been sponsored by government bodies for their own use in selection and evaluation. As a result, many people in industry and commerce may be unaware of the revolution in assessment methods which is just around the corner!

The remainder of this chapter is divided into three sections.

– Components of the assessment procedure.
– Present practice and future directions.
– Advice to would-be users.

The first section shows how the assessment procedure can be broken down into a number of functional components, each of which may be more or less automated.

The second section opens up the question of 'what is being automated', and shows that there is a whole range of options available between the paper-and-pencil test and the fully automated assessment system. In addition, it discusses and illustrates some of the new possibilities which CBA has opened up.

Finally, some general pointers are presented for those considering the use of CBA.

COMPONENTS OF THE ASSESSMENT PROCEDURE

The assessment procedure can be considered to consist of seven main components which are discussed below.

1. The selection of a test (or sequence of tests) for presentation to a specific client or group of clients

Choosing which test (or tests) to use for a given purpose requires a high level of knowledge about the nature of available tests, their psychometric properties and their usefulness for a particular client population. In addition, it requires the selector to make judgements about the relative appropriateness of each test.

Test selection need not simply be a process which occurs as the first step in assessment. There are many situations where it is desirable to 'tailor' a battery of tests to an individual's needs or abilities, with this tailoring being dependent partly on the individual's performance during the testing procedure. With CBA, the immediate availability of scores enables the computer to select the next most appropriate test in a branching sequence, assuming that it has been given suitable rules. Such rules may concern a variety of criteria.

Optimizing incremental and differential validity

If you are selecting tests from an available battery in order to obtain the best predictive validity with the least amount of testing, then you are trying to optimize the incremental validity. In effect incremental validity is concerned with how much you can improve your level of prediction of success by using a specific test.

If you are trying to decide into which of two jobs you should place someone, you need to use a battery of tests which has good differential validity (i.e. given the person's overall level of suitability, which of the jobs he or she is likely to be better at).

Suitably programmed, computers can easily handle these sorts of decisions. If the system has information about the predictive validities of a set of tests for each of the jobs, then it is possible to define rules which select the minimum number of tests required to discriminate best between the two jobs. These may not necessarily be the same sequence of tests for each person.

Rapid estimation of specific ability levels

A second function of 'tailoring' is the provision of precise estimates of ability levels when the ability range of the population being tested is very broad. Broad-bandwidth tests are designed to provide rough 'ball-park' estimates of ability levels across a broad range of abilities and tend to discriminate best around the mid-range. Narrow-bandwidth tests on the other hand provide much finer discrimination but only within a narrow range of ability.

With CBA one can present and score a short broad-bandwidth test to obtain a rough estimate of ability and then let the computer select the appropriate narrow-bandwidth test to improve the accuracy of the estimate.

2. Administration of tests

Test administration can be broken down into a number of sub-stages.

(a) Presentation of instructions.
(b) Administration of example and test items.
(c) Collection and recording of response information.

The level of expertise required for test administration varies considerably from one test to another. However, in all those cases where test administration can be separated from interpretation, the expertise required is essentially 'technical': that is, people may need training in how to administer a test, but they do not need to be psychologists.

When compared directly with traditional paper-and-pencil assessment procedures, automation provides the following advantages.

– Administration becomes a clerical rather than psychological task.
– Each candidate has identical conditions of administration.
– Scoring is more reliable and accurate than hand-key scoring.
– Scores are immediately available for further analysis or interpretation.
– Scores may be automatically stored without the need for error-prone human data-entry operations.

In short, the procedure is faster, more reliable and less costly in human resources than traditional testing. In addition, people tend to prefer being assessed by computer and tend to be more open in the answers they give to items which ask for 'personal' information.

The main disadvantage is the initial capital investment in hardware. This is becoming less and less of a problem as (a) the hardware becomes cheaper and (b) in many cases, people who might use tests only on an occasional basis will have the hardware already on site.

The capital cost issue tends to be confounded with the issue of group versus individual testing. Many paper-and-pencil tests are ideally suited to group administration procedures. Most computer-based tests on the other hand require one computer per person. Hence group testing would entail having a large number of machines available. For large organizations with a high volume of people to be assessed this will be cost-effective. For the smaller organization, wanting to assess, say, 20 people on one occasion per year, it clearly would not! However, one computer could be used to assess 20 people, one at a time over a one-week period with minimal disruption to the normal routine of a small company. Setting aside a half-day to carry out a group assessment, on the other hand, may be more costly.

The important point is that computer-based assessment should not be compared directly for cost with paper-and-pencil testing. What one has to do is compare optimized implementations of each technology in a given setting in order to see which provides the better alternative.

3. Scoring

Computers carry out scoring both more quickly and more reliably than people. The fact that the computer can carry out scoring in parallel with item presentation has made possible the development not only of the tailored batteries mentioned earlier, but also of adaptive tests—that is, tests where the selection of an item is some function of the respondent's performance on the previous items. We will look more closely at adaptive testing when we consider some of the new types of test made possible by CBA.

4. Analysis of test measures

Analysis can be distinguished from interpretation as follows: analysis involves the derivation of measures from raw scale scores; interpretation involves saying what those measures mean.

Analysis can range from simple procedures like looking up standardized scores, to more complex ones like computing specification equations. There can be no doubt that one of the major advantages of automation lies in this area. Analyses which might take a person a few days to carry out by hand can be carried out far more reliably in seconds. The availability of this sort of facility on one's own microcomputer provides quick and accurate computations, it also opens up the possibility of making test analysis a highly interactive process. Because users do not have to expend large amounts of time and energy in carrying out the computations, they can afford to carry out much more detailed analyses (e.g. comparing individuals against a range of different norm groups).

However, while analysis software reduces the need for the user to have both computational skills and a lot of free time, it does not reduce the need for a good knowledge of the test and what the computed measures mean.

5. Interpretation of test measures

As defined above, interpretation involves going beyond the analysis and saying what the measures mean. In order to interpret a test, a good knowledge of the test itself is required, plus the knowledge and experience necessary to draw psychologically valid conclusions from the results.

The growing use of personality assessment in pre-selection screening, assessment centres and career guidance has led to a growing demand for computer-based test interpretation (CBTI) within occupational psychology. CBTI offers considerable potential advantages over traditional methods of interpretation.

– To write a detailed report on a 16PF or Occupational Personality Questionnaire profile would take an experienced expert one or two hours. A computer can do it far more rapidly, and less expensively.
– The human report writer will find it difficult to maintain a uniform standard across a number of reports and will have difficulty giving the same weight to particular profile patterns every time they occur.

In short, the best human report writer cannot match the speed, degree of standardization, accuracy and repeatability obtainable with a computer. However, can the computer produce a report which is as 'good' as the human expert? The answer to this depends very much on the nature of the system used.

Most of the current systems fall into one of three categories (see Wiggins, 1980): descriptive; expert-modelled; mixed expert–actuarial.

(a) *Descriptive* These simply contain a list of statements related to different score values on each scale. They do not attempt to deal with scale profile patterns or interactions between scales. Systems such as these can be refined to produce what looks like very coherent and well-structured text. However, the interpretations they produce tend to be very simplistic and are no match for the human expert.

(b) *Expert-modelled* These systems are built around a set of rules which attempt to model the judgements made by expert interpreters. The rules themselves are obtained in one of two ways: either by getting one or more experts to elucidate the rules they use when writing their own interpretations, or by developing a predictive statistical model or 'paramorph' of the experts' judgements (using, for example, multiple regression techniques). While systems using the former approach are about as reliable as the experts themselves, those using the latter tend to be more reliable and accurate than the people on whose behaviour they were based.

(c) *Mixed expert–actuarial* For a pure actuarial approach, all narrative statements used by the system would be based on actual empirical findings about the relationships between scale scores or patterns and behaviour. In practice, this approach tends to be combined with the expert-modelling approach. As an example, the Minnesota Multiphasic Personality Inventory (MMPI) report developed at Assessment Systems Corporation in 1982 for National Computer Systems was based on one expert who used both his clinical judgement and actuarial data. Ideally, the judgements of several experts should be pooled.

Within the UK, narrative report generators are available for a number of instruments. While most of these are 'imports' from the United States, Saville and Holdsworth Ltd have recently developed a report generator for their Occupational Personality Questionnaire and NFER–Nelson are preparing to publish one for the 16PF.

CBTI is not, though, without its problems. Matarazzo (1983) has pointed out the potential damaging effects of CBTI in the hands of those not qualified to understand it. He recommends restricting its use to qualified users until it develops to the point where understanding does not depend on training and experience in the use of the relevant instrument; in other words, until it provides the sort of client feedback we would currently expect from a well-qualified counsellor. We are a long way from this at present.

Another problem with CBTI, is that while you can ask human experts to justify the conclusions they reach, or to explain the reasoning behind them, so far as the present author knows there are no CBTI systems which provide this facility. Ideally, expert systems should contain an interrogation facility whereby the user can ask the system why a particular judgement has been reached. Such facilities are quite 'standard' in most other areas of expert systems application.

6. Feedback of information to clients

The ability to provide feedback to clients requires more than just skill in test interpretation. It also requires the ability to communicate a valid interpretation of the test results in terms comprehensible to and appropriate for the 'lay' client, and, depending upon the situation, some degree of counselling skill.

Some people tend to assume that clearly written expert test interpretations produced by a computer could simply be handed to the client. For most assessment instruments this would be most unwise. The 'consumer' of the report needs to:

- be aware of the product's limitations;
- appreciate that the output is only as good—or bad—as the data underlying the rules and the rules themselves;
- have access to information about the rationale and validity of the program;
- have access to other sources of information about the candidate.

Clearly, while suitably qualified professionals can meet these requirements, their clients cannot.

7. Decision making

Assessment data are frequently used to aid the making of decisions. Should we hire this person? Should he or she be offered job A or job B? Should Mr X or Ms Y be promoted? What advice might we offer Ms Z about her career change? And so on.

A fully integrated assessment system would employ a means–ends analysis approach whereby knowledge of what information is required to make the final decision would 'drive' the first stage (test selection). Systems with this sort of expertise can provide a support role in those situations where decisions depend, at least in part, on information about human characteristics and behaviour: selection, appraisal, clinical diagnosis, educational placement and so on.

An example of this sort of decision support system is PARYS (Business Information Techniques Ltd) which consists of four inter-related modules:

- Jobs manager—job analysis and personnel specification and job data collection.
- Screen-based testing suite—test administration scoring and results analysis.
- Personnel selector—general selection management, interview prompting and candidate ratings, etc.
- Performance monitor—in-post appraisal, training needs assessment and training plans.

Systems like PARYS satisfy many of the criteria for an integrated personnel decision-support system. However, the computer technology is still ahead of psychological and psychometric theory: at present we only have a relatively crude idea of what knowledge such a system needs to possess and what rules it would use to relate selection data to job analysis and person specification data.

PRESENT PRACTICE AND FUTURE DIRECTIONS

Degree of automation in CBA

The above outline of components of the assessment process, while not exhaustive, should suffice to illustrate the wide range of potential areas for automation: from the automation of scoring through to the fully self-contained computer-based assessment system.

We can regard a component as being 'automated' when all those activities normally carried out by a human operator are carried out by the machine. A fully automated assessment system would, therefore, require all the above components to be carried out by computer. Such a system could properly be called an 'intelligent assessment system' (IAS). The possibility of achieving this level of automation will depend crucially upon the tests chosen and the use to which they will be put. In general, given the above definitions of components, it should be rather easier to produce an IAS for situations where criteria are well defined (e.g. personnel selection) than for those where they are ill-defined (e.g. career guidance).

A useful approach to considering the value of various levels of automation is based on the seven 'components of the assessment procedure' discussed above. Each of the components performs a function which requires an input (which may come from another component) and generates an output (which may form the input for other components). These 'inputs' and 'outputs' may be either computer generated or person generated.

The relative importance of each component and the value of automating it (either wholly or partially) will vary from application to application. In practice, it

Component	Input	Output
1. Test selection	Test information	Test selection
2. Test administration	Test specification	Item response
3. Scoring	Item responses	Scale scores
4. Analysis	Scale scores (and item responses)	Analysis report
5. Interpretation	Scale scores (and item responses)	Narrative report
6. Feedback	Scale scores and other client data	Interactive counselling
7. Decision support	Test and other relevant data	Recommendations

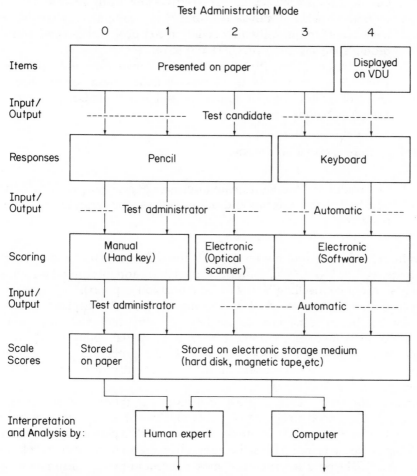

Figure 1   Various degrees of automation involved in the different modes of test administration and scoring

is necessary to break down this simple input/output model further to take account of the various alternative ways in which test administration can be automated. We can define four main alternative 'modes' of automation as follows (see Figure 1).

Mode 4   Fully automated test administration and scoring. The items are presented by the computer; responses are entered directly into the computer which calculates scale scores and maintains a database sufficient to provide access to other software dealing with the analysis and interpretation of results.

Mode 3   This is similar to Mode 4, but the test items are presented in their 'traditional' paper format, while the responses are entered directly into the computer.

Mode 2   Here the complete test is administered 'off-line' using paper and pencil, but the response sheet is scored electronically (using an optical scanner) with the data being transferred directly to a computer. These data then have access to the software needed to compute scale scores, carry out profile analyses, perform CBTI and so on.

Mode 1 As for Mode 2, but with the scoring done by hand, using scoring keys. The scale scores and clients' details are hand entered on to a computer and can access the same analysis and interpretation packages (see below) as Modes 2 to 4.

By default, there is also a fifth mode:

Mode 0 The traditional 'non-automated' form of paper-and-pencil administration with hand scoring and all analysis and interpretation done 'by hand'.

Apart from Mode 0, all four modes generate the scale scores required as inputs to Components 4, 5, 6 and 7 (computer-based analysis and interpretation software packages, 'client-counselling' software, and decision support).

Given the present standard of microcomputer graphics displays, Mode 4 is ideal for text-based tests, but should be used very cautiously for computer versions of tests involving graphical items (e.g. spatial ability tests). Mode 3 implementation provides an ideal solution to the problem of ensuring equivalence of items while still benefiting from direct entry of responses into the computer.

However, for both these modes (especially Mode 4), there could be problems of equivalence for 'speed' tests. Most paper-and-pencil 'speed' tests have time constraints which are based not simply on how quickly a person can think, but on how long it takes to respond (find the right cell on the answer sheet and black it in with a pencil). The poor ergonomics of most paper-and-pencil instruments makes the response process both slow and error prone (e.g. Hodgkinson, 1986). For a speed test, changes to the design of the interface could well influence the scores obtained. For this reason the issue of test equivalence is especially important here.

Mode 2 provides the solution for those who need to retain group testing, but still want the advantages of computerized data handling: e.g. the development of a client database, the use of sophisticated analysis and interpretation software.

Mode 1 provides the same final result as Mode 2 but via a more time-consuming and error-prone route.

For Modes 1 to 4, the computer involved may be local (i.e. 'on-site'), remote, or there may be both a local and a remote device. If remote, it may be accessed in one of two ways: directly through a network link or via a telephone modem connection; or, in the cases of Modes 1 and 2 only, access may be by posting clients' answer sheets.

Figure 2 shows various configurations of local and remote devices: each having certain advantages and disadvantages. As yet, genuine networked systems have not appeared, though such systems have been proposed as providing paperless application forms (e.g. US forces CENSUS system) and for graduate recruitment and selection use (see below).

The equivalence of computer-based and traditional methods of assessment

In effect, we have three categories of equivalence to consider.

1. *Inter-mode equivalence* The relationship between the traditional form of an instrument and an automated version of it.
2. *Intra-mode inter-system equivalence* The relationship between versions of the same instrument implemented on different computer systems.
3. *Intra-mode intra-system equivalence* The relationship between different versions of the same instrument implemented on the same computer system.

The problem of inter-mode equivalence arises when automated tests are developed as parallel forms to existing paper-and-pencil tests. The British Psychological Society's Test Standards Committee has already commented (1984) on the need to ensure that data are obtained to assess the reliability (both test–retest and inter-mode) and—where appropriate—the validity of the computer version of a test. In many cases, however, this is insufficient.

It is quite feasible to produce a test, which is highly correlated with its alternate form and has an equivalent level of predictive validity for some common criterion, and yet find that the norms for the two tests are quite different. This is particularly likely to be a problem with speed as opposed to power tests.

Intra-mode equivalence concerns the parallelism between different automations of the same test. One must beware of talking about *the* computerized version

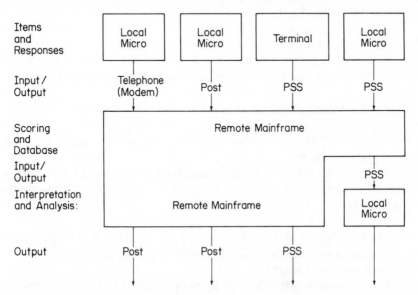

Figure 2 Some example configurations of remote and local devices. (PSS = Packet Switched System)

of a test. Each implementation of a test on a specific computer system should be regarded as a new form of the test until proved otherwise. I would stress again that the main differences in such forms (especially for ability tests involving 'speed' rather than 'power' measures) are likely to be found in the norms rather than measures of reliability or validity coefficients.

Achieving equivalence of forms may be particularly difficult for tests involving graphical items (e.g. the AH series of tests, or the Bennett Mechanical Comprehension Test). As yet there are few widely available microcomputers capable of presenting graphical items with the degree of resolution necessary for such items. The developments of cheap very high resolution graphics and interactive video are likely to change this situation in the near future. While interesting research and development work on special purpose video-disc assessment systems is being carried out, interactive video techniques still represent a rather expensive solution for the problem of producing parallel versions of current tests.

Despite the above cautions, most inventories and 'power' tests containing text-only items are unlikely to be affected by automation *per se* if it is done well. The majority of studies carried out to compare traditional and automated versions of such tests have only found minor differences between the two modes (see for example, Bartram and Bayliss, 1984; Lukin *et al.*, 1985).

The developing of novel methods of assessment

So far this chapter has concentrated largely on the automation of paper-and-pencil tests. For such tests, the existing literature and test materials provide baselines for comparison. However, the use of computers in assessment has opened up possibilities for radically new forms of testing.

Traditional tests tend to be:

1. Pre-defined—in that they consist of a set of fixed items.
2. Static—in that each item remains constant over time.
3. Non-adaptive—in that the selection of items follows a fixed sequence.

Computer-based tests on the other hand can be:

1. Generative—in that items are produced by an algorithm rather than selected from a pre-defined set.
2. Dynamic—in that the test materials can change and transform with time.
3. Adaptive—in that the sequencing of events can be a function of the test-taker's performance.

Some traditional tests fall into the category of dynamic tests (e.g. continuous tracking tasks). However, there are few instances of generative or adaptive tests prior to the advent of computers.

Such tests cannot be administered by people, and can have no parallel non-computerized forms. A further complication is that aspects of traditional test theory are often inapplicable to some of these forms of assessment. For example, the notion of a scale score, being an estimate of some 'true' trait based upon responses to a sample of parallel items, cannot be applied when a test contains no identifiable 'items', nor, strictly speaking, can classical notions of reliability be used when talking about such tests (see Chapters 3.1 and 3.2).

The following sections discuss some of the novel ways in which CBA can be used with examples from the present author's own work on the Micropat system. This system, which has been undergoing development and validation since the late 1970s, contains a range of novel 'task-based' tests designed to assess both psychomotor coordination and information management skills (the system and the tests are more fully described in Telfer, 1985; Bartram, 1987a). The Micropat candidate interface has a set of two keypads, a joystick and slide controller with a set of pedals. In addition, Micropat is unusual in using two visual displays: one shows instructions while the other is used to present the 'active' part of the test.

Dynamic adaptive tasks

The Micropat battery includes a number of 'adaptive tracking' tasks. Performance on pursuit tracking is assessed using a task which varies in difficulty as a function of the candidate's level of skill. The better the candidate, the more difficult the task becomes (and vice versa). During the first few seconds of each task the system 'finds' the optimal difficulty level for the candidate. From then on, in effect, the person is presented with a task whose difficulty is ideally matched to ability. As discussed earlier, when talking about 'tailored' testing, this approach produces much better discrimination over a wide range of abilities.

Measurement of error-tolerance

The above type of adaptive tracking task allows us to assess the optimal difficulty level a person can handle when the limits of 'acceptable error' are defined by the computer. Having assessed this, one can then give control of the adaptation to the candidate (i.e. as the task proceeds he or she can choose whether to make the task more or less difficult). In this way one can obtain a measure of relative tolerance for error: does the candidate prefer to perform more accurately at an easier level, or would he or she rather sacrifice accuracy for difficulty?

Using rules to generate test items

For most of the tasks developed for Micropat, there are no pre-written sets of items. Each test or task contains a set of rules and constraints from which items are generated. These rules can specify either that the same set of items be generated every time, or that different (but equivalent) sets be generated for each candidate.

A simple instance of this is an adaptive digit-span test in which strings of digits are defined in terms of: the number of digits in the string; the set of digits from which they are sampled; constraints on the frequency and proximity of repeated digits. Random number generators are then used to produce items which conform to these constraints.

A more complex use of item generation can be seen in a test of navigational orientation. In this, candidates are presented with a sequence of commands defining legs of a flight from their homebase. For example: 'Fly 12 miles East (90 degrees).'

After receiving these instructions, they are then asked to indicate the heading and distance of their 'homebase'. The sequence of commands is generated by the computer for each trial using rules which define:

- The number of outward legs.
- The range of different headings which may be used.
- The maximum and minimum homeward journey distances.
- The maximum changes of heading between each outward leg.

Analysis of performance on this test shows that items generated by these rules are equivalent in difficulty and discrimination.

On-line rule-based item generation has a number of advantages over the use of pre-defined test items.

1. It does away with the need for many hours of work in designing items.
2. One only needs to assess the psychometric properties of the rules (through assessment of sample items from the domain defined by those rules) rather than do so for each specific set of items.
3. One can develop parallel versions of a test almost *ad infinitum*.
4. It provides a solution to the problem of test characteristics being highly item dependent, as the rules used to create the item provide a *de facto* definition of the relevant domain of behaviour from which they have been drawn.

Scoring performance on complex tasks

One problem with using complex tasks as psychometric test instruments is that of scoring. For item-based tests, scores are usually simple to define (e.g. the sum of the correct items). A number of the Micropat tests are not item based: they present continuous tasks with which the candidate interacts to try to achieve some pre-defined goal. Two main methods have been developed to 'score' performance on such tasks.

Continuous comparison against an optimal system

One of the dynamic Micropat tests (Schedule) presents the candidate with a continually changing array of five boxes (one in each of five columns). These boxes contain numbers (their 'values') and have 'lives' (boxes with a double outline have a value of twice the number they contain, but only last, on average, for half the time of single boxes). These boxes appear at different distances from the top of each column. The candidate's task is to choose columns: in the most recently chosen column a line moves down from the top towards the box. If the line reaches the box before the box's 'life' expires, the candidate's score is incremented by the value of the box. Whenever a box's life expires or whenever it is reached by a line, everything in its column is erased and a new box is generated.

Even if one starts off this task with the same display for everyone, by its interactive nature, each trial will present a different set of possibilities for each candidate. Unlike the rule-based item generation discussed above, the rules underlying this task do not generate a discrete sequence of items but rather define the constraints on how the display is updated. This entails the possibility that some candidates could have 'bad luck' (i.e. a run of difficult-to-reach low-scoring boxes) while others could have 'good luck'. The nature of the task is such that to average out these variations would require a very long set of trials. Thus, instead of using the candidate's actual score (number of points gained by catching boxes) as the test measure, performance is measured against a simulation of an 'optimal operator' which is run in parallel with the candidate. Every 200 milliseconds, the 'optimal operator' carries out a cost–benefit analysis—looking at the likely outcome of choosing each of the five columns—and then looks to see if the real candidate is performing optimally or not.

Assessment by scoring rules which model expert judgements For many tasks it is difficult, if not impossible, to specify the sort of rules needed to define 'optimal operators' (as in the Schedule task). One of the Micropat tests (Landing) requires the candidate to perform a complex time-dependent tracking and monitoring task leading to a final goal (obtaining a display which shows an aircraft symbol correctly aligned for landing). While a large range of measures are generated by the program (speed of approach, various alignment measures, rate of descent and so on), it is not obvious how one should combine these measures into a score which represents how well the candidate has met the task criteria.

One solution to this problem is to ask experts to provide ratings of a range of 'landings'. One can then statistically model these judgements using the measures available from the test. The resultant equations are then built into the test and used to generate the measures of test performance. (A more complete description of this approach is provided in Bartram, 1987a.)

Item-based adaptive testing

The example of adaptive tracking given earlier illustrated the general principle of adaptive testing: that the goal of the test is to obtain an estimate of the candidate's ability by modifying the test (i.e. making it easier or harder) until some criterion is reached. The way in which this is achieved varies considerably from test to test.

The technique described for adaptive tracking is analogous to what has been called 'stradaptive' (stratified adaptive) testing. For this, items are grouped into a sequence of 'strata' according to their difficulty. Subjects then branch up or down through the strata (i.e. difficulty levels) until a fixed number of items have been responded to, or a fixed time has been reached.

While adaptive tests can embody one of a number of item-selection strategies, the term 'adaptive test' has tended to be identified with one particular class of strategies: those based on Item Response Theory (IRT). While it would not be appropriate to go into a discussion of IRT in the present chapter (see Chapters 3.2 and 3.3), the essential feature of IRT-based systems is that they contain a large 'bank' of items. Linked to each item are a number of parameter estimates. Typically, these will be estimates of the item's difficulty, discrimination and guessing rate. This information forms the database for a system which then selects items for presentation to the candidate. The system typically selects items on the basis of its current 'hypothesis' about the candidate's ability. Each response to an item is regarded as being probabilistically related to an underlying 'latent trait' and becomes incorporated into the system's current estimate of the candidate's trait level. The system continues to select items which will optimally improve its estimate of the candidate's ability until some criterion is reached: this may be a fixed number of items, a fixed time, or a minimal level of confidence associated with the trait estimate.

Given the need for large amounts of data for parameter estimation, it is not surprising that the main developments in this area have tended to occur where large-scale testing is employed. One of the first adaptive batteries in operational use is CAST (Computerized Adaptive Screening Test) developed for the US forces (Hakel, 1986). Trials of the computerized adaptive testing (CAT) version of the US Armed Services Vocational Aptitude Battery (ASVAB) suggest that candidates feel less pressured by the CAT version and do not perceive any differences in either difficulty or fairness compared to the paper-and-pencil ASVAB. Furthermore, testing is completed more quickly.

In general, positive results have been obtained for IRT-based tests, both for reliability and comparability with their paper-and-pencil equivalents. The main advantages of CAT are seen as being better psychometric properties; better differentiation between candidates; a wider range of difficulty levels within one instrument and a general increase in the quality and efficiency with which ability can be measured.

The above examples should suffice to give the 'flavour' of developments in adaptive, rule-based, dynamic tests and, more particularly, make clear how they are dependent on the new technology. In practice, item generation and adaptive testing are likely to represent the main application area for CBA in the immediate future.

Changes in the logistics of assessment

We have so far described the ways in which the new technology can be used to automate the use of existing test materials, and looked at some new forms of test which the technology has made possible. What we have so far said very little about is the issue of how computer technology may affect the logistics of assessment.

The issue of group versus individual testing was raised earlier. It was argued that this is something of a false issue, as for any technology one should consider how it may best be used—not whether it can be used in the same way as the old technology. With CBA there is in fact a range of options which greatly increase the possibilities open to the user. Two relatively recent developments have opened up new possibilities (included new forms of group testing) for CBA. These developments represent two extremes, in terms of size:

- The advent of the truly portable lap-top microcomputer.
- The growth of national and international networks.

The lap-top portable

Within the US forces, serious consideration is being given to the use of CBA on small portable computers, as much of their testing is done by travelling recruiters. The Essex Corporation has developed a system called APTS (originally developed on the NEC PC 8201A and now being developed for IBM compatible portables), with software for over 30 different ability tests and inventories. The low cost of systems such as this, together with their networking capability, makes group assessment a real possibility. Their portability also makes them ideal for use in awkward or 'hostile' environments, making it possible for assessment to be carried out under conditions where only CBA is practical.

The nation-wide network

The potential uses of networked systems for the development of large item-banks has already been mentioned. However, one can go further and envisage a situation where tests are 'published' only in electronic format with access through a national network. This would provide a means of publishers controlling the use of their test materials and provide control over the use of personal data on test results. Essentially, the advent of 'electronic tests' would lead to a complete change in the way tests are sold. Apart from training courses and test manuals, there would be no 'materials' to sell. Instead, people would purchase test results: i.e. they would pay for information.

For example, the old style 'graduate-milk-round' (where potential employers travel around the UK universities and polytechnics looking for new recruits) could be transformed into a situation where a standard range of ability tests and biodata forms were 'published' on the network. Undergraduates would have access to these through terminals and be able (under appropriate supervision) to complete a range of the available tests during their final year. They would also be able to specify which potential employers they would want to have access to their information. In turn, these employers would be able to put their own specialized tests or 'application forms' on to the system and be notified of any 'applicants'. They would then have the option of purchasing information about them. The advantages of such a system are described below.

Test publishers and developers would benefit as follows:

- The security of their products—assuming they were only available in electronic format—and the resultant increase in test revenue and royalties.
- The possibility of developing new more powerful assessment instruments as

item-data would be automatically accumulated and would be obtained at much greater rates than is now possible.

Those being assessed would gain in the following ways:

- They would have the freedom to take the tests at a time and place which suited them.
- They would be able to exercise total control over who should, and who should not, have access to their results.

However, probably the greatest gains would be for employers, especially those of small- to medium-sized companies.

- The costs of handling and sifting application form data would be massively reduced, as all the data would arrive already on computer.
- They would have access to highly sophisticated assessment procedures with minimal overhead and capital investment costs.
- They would be able to carry out a more effective pre-screening of candidates before the first interview.
- They would know the 'assessment history' of each candidate: which tests had been taken and when; in cases where the system permitted repeated administrations, whether the data were from the first or fifth administration of a test; and so on.

ADVICE TO WOULD-BE USERS

General guidelines on the design of CBA systems have been prepared for the British Psychological Society (Bartram *et al.*, 1987) which make recommendations about 'good' ergonomic practice in the design of systems and also stress the need for users and producers of CBA to be aware of the potential problems of test equivalence. 'Good' design is taken to encompass the following issues.

Ease and flexibility of use

The level of administrative skill required to use an automated system clearly depends on the degree to which components of the testing procedure have been automated, and how well these have been supported by general system management software. It is this level of system support which distinguishes the 'automated test' from the CBA system. The use of psychological tests, especially in large numbers, involves a considerable amount of information management and basic clerical skills. CBA system software should be designed to deal with all the general management aspects of testing (client logging, data collection and recording, printing of assessment audit trials and so on). To provide these facilities while being simple and safe to operate means that the software must be robustly designed and sufficiently sophisticated to deal with possible system failures and human error.

Reliability and 'robustness'

In terms of technology, there is little that can go wrong in a paper-and-pencil testing session. This is not the case for CBA. Badly designed software and unreliable equipment can lead to interrupted test sessions and loss of data. For most computer applications such problems are merely annoying. For psychological testing they are far more serious: in many cases it would be inappropriate to get people to re-take tests if there had been a system failure during their first attempt.

CBA system software should contain procedures to check the operation of all relevant pieces of hardware (e.g. reaction timers, keyboards, joysticks, etc.) and software (e.g. ensuring there is space available for storage of results, that the current test taker has not already been tested). Where information is required from the test administrator (e.g. the client's name, date of birth, etc.), the data entry procedures should be simple to use and contain checks on the accuracy of the information entered.

Instructions

In traditional testing conditions, it is possible to ask people if they have 'any questions' about the instructions. This is not so easy with automated testing. For this reason it is essential that test instructions are developed and refined through empirical testing.

Test instructions must be simple and unambiguous. Wherever possible, the software should check on the comprehension of instructions by monitoring responses to sample items.

Special hardware requirements

Most of the widely available software for CBA makes use of the 'traditional' computer interface: alpha-numeric QWERTY keyboard and a single visual display unit. For many forms of test, this interface is ergonomically unacceptable. For this reason most of the specially designed batteries of 'novel' tests (of which few are generally available) have incorporated specially designed interfaces for the test candidate. However, in addition to the QWERTY keyboard, there is a wide range of 'standard' input devices now available (for example, 'mouses', light-pens, tracker balls, touch-screens, concept-keyboards, digitizer pads). In addition, 'non-standard' devices are available from companies like the Austrian G. Schuhfried Gmbh, which markets a range of input and output devices (keypads, pedals, buttons, arrays of lights, etc.) for use with their CBA software.

A checklist for the would-be user

The level of human experience and expertise required for each of the seven assessment components, varies considerably as a function of the type of tests being used and purpose of the assessment. In looking at a CBA system for any particular application one needs to ask the following questions.

1. Can the system decide on the appropriateness of each of a number of tests for a particular application?
2. Can it administer them?
3. Can it score them?
4. Can it derive the necessary measures?
5. Can it interpret what these measures mean?
6. Can it be used to provide client feedback?
7. Can it assist in making relevant decisions (e.g. selection, allocation, promotion)?

One also needs to consider what the hardware requirements are and what support facilities are provided.

8. What sort of computer will it run on?
9. Are any special peripheral devices needed?
10. What software support and upgrade facilities are provided by the supplier?
11. What training is required and where is it available?

Finally, one needs to know what additional data handling facilities the software provides.

12. Can it store test data in a secure but accessible form?
13. Can it be integrated with other applications packages such as word processors, spreadsheets, databases, statistical analysis programs?
14. Can it be used to develop local test norms?

When considering the use of automated versions of existing paper-and-pencil tests potential users should satisfy themselves on the following points.

1. During development, the software has been field-tested to ensure that:
   (a) the instructions are clear and unambiguous;
   (b) the mode of presentation is 'acceptable' to users and facilitates the development of an appropriate 'rapport';
   (c) the software is sufficiently 'robust'.
2. Data have been obtained to assess the equivalence of the two modes. Ideally, this should have been done using a complete four-group test–retest design (comparing all possible combinations of the two modes—see Bartram, 1987b, for an example). The minimum design should involve at least two groups— one presented with the traditional form followed by the automated one, the other receiving the tests in reverse order.
3. The software is distributed with a supplement to the standard test manual which both describes how to use the software and presents the results of any inter-mode equivalence studies (e.g. Bartram, 1987b, 1987c).

4. Where necessary, norms for the automated version have been obtained and are presented with the test manual supplement.

CONCLUSIONS

It is likely to become standard practice to use some form of adaptive technique in the design of CBA instruments. Some stand-alone microcomputer CAT materials based on Item Response Theory are already available (e.g. the Psychological Corporation's Apple IIe version of the Differential Aptitude Tests). However, the main future for instruments based on IRT probably lies with networked systems where large item-banks can be developed and supported. We are likely to see an increasing use of CAT based on such item-banks in selection and placement (initially within the military and Civil Service and subsequently spreading out into industry and commerce through the graduate selection process).

In certain highly specialized selection areas (such as pilot selection) and in the areas such as management development and appraisal, however, we will see the development of another type of CBA. While computers are ideal for presenting real-time dynamic tasks, the problems of assessing performance on these tasks has only recently begun to be addressed. The use of expert judgement modelling embodied within assessment instruments provides one means of using more complex tasks as assessment instruments: for example, work samples and job simulations such as in-basket tests and 'business games' (Elgood, 1981).

It seems clear that while specific advances in CBA will continue on the research and development front, in practice we will see a trend towards CBA becoming more integrated into other systems, forming a part of a larger whole which will combine selection, training and assessment functions and playing a general decision-support role in the personnel office of the future.

REFERENCES AND FURTHER READING

Bartram, D. (1987a). The development of an automated testing system for pilot selection: the Micropat project, *International Review of Applied Psychology*, **36**, 279–98.

Bartram, D. (1987b). *Lewis Counselling Inventory Software Documentation*. NFER–Nelson, Windsor, Berkshire.

Bartram, D. (1987c). *Vocational Preference Inventory Software Documentation*. NFER–Nelson, Windsor, Berkshire.

Bartram, D., and Bayliss, R. (1984). Automated testing: Past, present and future, *Journal of Occupational Psychology*, **57**, 221–37.

Bartram, D., Beaumont, J.G., Cornford, T., Dann, P.L., and Wilson, S.L. (1987). Recommendations for the design of software for computer-based assessment—summary statement, *Bulletin of the British Psychological Society*, **40**, 86–7.

Elgood, C. (1981). *Handbook of Management Games*, Gower, Aldershot.

Grant, D. (1987). Automating the selection procedure, *Personnel Management*, July.

Hakel, M.D. (1986). Personnel selection and placement, *Annual Review of Psychology*, **37**, 351–80.

Hodgkinson, G.P. (1986). An evaluation of the Vocational Preference Inventory answer sheet in the light of population stereotypes, *Ergonomics*, **29**, 925–7.

Krug, S.E. (1987). *Psychware Sourcebook 1987–1988*, 2nd edn. Test Corporation of America, Kansas City.

Lukin, M.E., Dowd, E.T., Plake, B.S., and Kraft, R.G. (1985). Comparing computerized versus traditional psychological assessment, *Computers in Human Behavior*, **1**, 49–58.

Matarazzo, J.D. (1983). Editorial on computerized psychological testing, *Science*, **221**(4608), (22 July), 323.

Standing Committee on Test Standards (1984). Note on the computerization of printed psychological tests and questionnaires, *Bulletin of the British Psychological Society*, **37**, 416–17.

Telfer, R. (1985). Microcomputer based psychological testing and record-keeping, *Defence Forces Journal*, **54**, 57–61.

Wiggins, S.J. (1980). *Personality and Prediction: Principles of Personality Assessment*. Addison Wesley, Reading, Massachusetts.

Chapter 3.6

Job Sample and Trainability Tests

SYLVIA DOWNS

*Pearn Kandola Downs, Windsor House, 12 High Street, Kidlington,
Oxford OX5 2DH, UK*

JOB SAMPLES—WHAT ARE THEY?

Any definition of job samples must include, first, that there is a careful analysis of
the crucial elements of a job and, second, that these elements are put together to
give a fair representation of the whole job.

The job may consist of a few movements made repeatedly, such as assembly
line work. In such circumstances, there is no need to analyse crucial elements
because the whole job can be used as the sample. At the other end of the scale, a
jobbing carpenter may be faced with a wide variety of carpentry tasks and it is
necessary to select a sample which most accurately reflects this variety.

When talking about job sampling, confusion sometimes arises from the ter-
minologies which are used. One such difficulty is over job sampling and job
simulation. It is always best to base a job sample in the actual working environs
and conditions, so that, for example, the materials and tools are those used in the
job itself. Sometimes, however, machinery used in the job is so large, or breakages
and wastage could be so costly, or the possible damages or dangers are of such
magnitude that using the actual equipment or environs is out of the question. The
next best thing in such circumstances is to design a simulation of the job.
Although simulation loses the veracity of the real working environment, it is
sometimes necessary and this loss can be minimized by careful design such as can
be seen in a flight simulator.

Another confusion occurs over job titles. It is tempting to think that the job, say,
of cook is the same for any cook and one job sample could therefore represent the
job of all cooks.

Handbook of Assessment in Organizations   Edited by P. Herriot

However, many jobs have been divided into specializations with little common ground between them. It is therefore vital to analyse the crucial elements of each job and only when there is a match between jobs can one say that not only are the job titles the same, but also the jobs. The same point can occur in reverse, where jobs with very different titles turn out to consist of the same crucial elements.

Another semantic problem lies in the number of different names by which a job sample is known. There are two main categories of description, one of which describes either the content or the way the job sample has been arrived at. Examples of this category are work samples, job replicas, motor work samples and verbal work samples. The second category describes the end use to which the job sample will be put, such as performance test and trainability test.

Whatever the description, all job samples consist of a careful analysis of crucial elements put together to give a fair representation of the whole job.

THE USES OF A JOB SAMPLE

Tests form the major use of job samples. Familiar among these are the driving test, craft tests, and typing and shorthand examinations. All of these are typical of job samples used to test the acquisition of certain skills involved in carrying out the respective jobs or tasks. Their additional characteristic is that they lead to certification, either, as in the driving test, as a simple pass or, as in the typing and shorthand examination, by grade.

A great number of training courses involve the same process of 'passing out' by means of achievement tests, whether or not certificates are given, while also using job or skill sample tests at intervals during the training programme to provide feedback both to the trainees and trainers. Because this feedback is in objective terms, it is of great help to the trainees for them to assess their own development of the necessary job skills and is also a valuable aid to the trainer in evaluating the progress of each trainee. Job sample tests have been used to assess the effectiveness of training methods and the suitability of training content; to determine training needs; to assess suitability for a particular job or salary grade; to predict success in training; and to validate certain other selection methods.

A job sample test, therefore, is one of a range of selection methods available to selectors. On the basis that the more evidence collected the better the chance of making reasonable selection decisions, the appropriate job sample test joins all other valid selection instruments to enable better selection choices.

TRAINABILITY TESTS

A trainability test is, as its name implies, a test to predict the ability of applicants to succeed in training. It involves giving applicants a highly structured period of training in the skill they will have to learn if their application is successful, and then seeing how well they have absorbed the instruction and can carry out the test they have been taught. Trainability is assessed by careful observations of errors of technique and, where appropriate, an assessment of any workpiece produced. It is designed so that applicants are always given uniform instruction and demonstration before they attempt the tasks.

A trainability test is used to predict future training performance, while the majority of other job sample tests are used to assess present levels of skill. Combining both these elements, we can define a work sample test as a performance test based on work- or job-related elements, the design of which allows for measurement or objective assessment of the skills involved in all, or crucial, aspects of the job. The measurement may be used to measure past learning or predict potential to learn in the future. Hence trainability tests are a subset of work sample tests.

The first research on trainability tests was carried out in UK government training centres. It focused on the problem of selecting older applicants for training as welders and carpenters and showed that this practical approach was both acceptable to older recruits and predictive of their likelihood of passing the course (Downs, 1968). The first studies in industry were carried out in clothing companies to help in the selection of sewing machinists, electronic assemblers and apprentices in the ship-building and constructional industries (Robertson and Downs, 1979).

Apart from these studies, validated tests were also produced in engineering, forestry, catering, dentistry and for naval helicopter navigator/tactical controllers. In each case skilled movements formed a crucial element of the job, but it is interesting to note that trainability tests have also been developed for certain supervisory and management jobs (Downs, 1985).

In the validation studies trainees were followed up at periods ranging from one week to six months. The periods were governed by the length of each training programme. The criterion measures used in the validation included workpieces, phase tests, training results and on-the-job ratings of performance. The number of trainees involved in separate studies ranged from 11 to 228. Using error scores in the tests as predictors, statistically significant correlations ranged from 0.31 to 0.70, and, using ratings as predictors, from 0.37 to 0.89.

The validity coefficients were predictive rather than concurrent (see Chapters 3.1 and 3.2). In most cases the tests were given after the selection decision had been taken and before training began. This method of validation is obviously the most satisfactory but is not always possible. In some cases the number of entrants is so small that validation would take far too long. In other cases, the problems of selection were considered so urgent that management was not prepared to wait the necessary time for validated research results. This is a practical problem which can be tackled by using a carefully monitored trainability test, and comparing subsequent training results with those of previous training groups. For example, an electronics company introduced a board wiring trainability test which resulted in raising the training pass rate from 27 per cent of a group of 21 trainees, to 83 per cent of a group of 62. The dangers of rejection based on an unvalidated test are always pointed out to companies, together with the need to accept a broader range of applicants than might otherwise be recruited, and to monitor carefully early results.

The design of trainability tests is based on the classic model of test development (see Chapter 3.2). The job analysis concentrated on the specific difficulties in learning which occur in training and on the job. Information is gathered from training instructors and work supervisors, who are asked to describe actual pieces of behaviour of recent poor trainees. Further, it has been found that if the instructor or supervisor is thinking of poor trainees or performers in general, then the comments are general. The informant is guided to think in terms of a specific poor trainee. This process is repeated, until information is built up from a number of instructors and supervisors, each of whom describes a number of individuals rated as poor trainees. The whole process can be repeated, but in terms of good trainees, so that a comparison can be made between the two. The descriptions must be job specific, for example, phrases such as 'poor coordination' or 'very inaccurate' are inadmissible because they are generalized statements common to a number of jobs, whereas 'not squaring off face' and 'not sawing on waste side' are both specific to carpentry faults.

Having identified the behavioural aspects which distinguish good from bad trainees, these should be discussed with all the instructors and supervisors interviewed, in order to get agreement of the list, and clear up any misunderstandings.

The test is compiled by incorporating the specific work behaviours which distinguish between good and bad trainees into a single task. This task represents the job as closely as practicable, contains a range of opportunities for error derived from the critical incident job analysis, and contains areas of difficulty both in the job and training for the job. It must practically be a task which can be taught to inexperienced recruits in a reasonable length of time. In practice it has been found that the more complex the task the better it discriminates between applicants and the better it predicts. Trainability tests designed for British Airways apprentices and apprentice electricians were too simple and failed to be predictive. Later a more complex trainability test for electricians gave statistically significant results over two years (Robertson and Downs, 1979).

Having selected the task, an error checklist is produced which contains, in the order in which they would be made, all the errors in procedure which a trainee could make, and any errors in the finished workpiece, if one is produced. The checklist is written in negative rather than in positive terms, in order to concentrate on errors made, and their frequency, and to minimize recording time.

At the end of the error checklist, an opportunity is provided for the instructor to make an overall rating of the recruit's training potential, normally on a five-point scale. Descriptions of the ratings, for example, for sewing machinists are as follows:

A. Extremely good. The assessor would expect her to become a very good machinist in a short time.
B. Fairly good without being outstanding. The assessor would expect her to reach 100 per cent performance in a reasonable time.
C. Good enough for simple work. The assessor would expect her to become a steady worker on a simple machine, or task. (This is based on the fact that the sewing machinist test was designed to cover both the simpler overlock machines and more complicated lockstitch machines.)

D. Would have difficulty in training. The assessor would expect her to take longer in training, and to perform a simple task.
E. Would not be trainable. Even with a great deal of attention she would not make the grade, even on an easy operation.

The last stage in design is to construct a detailed script for use by the instructors, with the aim that the test should be uniformly given. The script should reflect the style and method of instruction used in the training school or programme, and should be couched in simple, clear, unambiguous words and phrases. It must, of course, contain all the information necessary for the recruit to be able to perform the task for himself or herself.

The test itself consists of an instructional stage, when the instructor demonstrates the task, and during which the applicants are encouraged to ask questions, followed by a performance stage, when they duplicate as near as they can the demonstration task. This is assessed by the instructor using the error checklist and rating form.

Once the script has been written, therefore, it is necessary to carry out experimental trials to make sure that the entire test can be operated; that the instructional period is clear; and that the script corresponds to the error checklist. For example, every time a recruit is told to do something, or not to do it, then there should be a corresponding item in the error checklist.

These experimental trials, which are not conducted with applicants, are also used to ensure that the test discriminates, that some people will make few errors and some many.

The next stage is the validation of the test for predictiveness and an assessment of its reliability. While the reliability of a psychometric test can be assessed by giving the test twice over a period of time, this is not the case for any work sample test because of the influence of intervening training or experience. This problem was overcome in the clothing industry by designing separate tests for overlock and lockstitch machines, which resulted in the same workpiece and involved the same crucial skills of cloth handling and hand–eye–foot coordination. The two tests were given to 91 applicants and the results were compared. The error scores gave a correlation of $r = 0.64$ and the ratings $r = 0.89$, both significant at beyond the 0.001 probability level.

While all the trainability tests have been validated with applicants who claimed no previous experience, an obvious criticism of the tests concerns the effect of experience. In the Scottish bricklaying apprentice research (Downs and Gowan, 1972), the group was divided into those with no experience, up to six months' experience, and over six months. Total error scores in the trainability test were compared with scores on a practical test one year after training started. There was a highly significant difference in both the trainability and criterion tests between those with no previous experience and those with more than six months. A short period of experience did not appear to affect the trainability test results, although it did affect the criterion test, while a longer period of experience resulted in better performance both in the trainability test and criterion test one year later. It is obviously sensible to give work sample tests to experienced applicants, but if trainability tests only are available, these have proved useful indicators of the competence, work methods and adherence to safety procedures of experienced people.

Whereas in most psychometric tests standard scores based on normal distributions are statistically produced (see Chapter 3.2), this is not the case with trainability tests. Indeed, it is argued that the trainability test population may not be distributed normally, either in its ability to learn the skill or in applying for the job.

There are, therefore, no standard scores with recommended cut-off points for trainability tests, and instead expectancy charts, based on predictive validity coefficients, are produced which indicate the likelihood of an applicant successfully completing training. An example of such a chart for fork lift truck operators is shown in Figure 1.

Where the personnel staff apply their cut-off depends on a number of facts such as availability of labour, length of training, material costs and the quality of the eventual product.

Having carried out the job analysis, designed the trainability test and validated it, there are certain requirements which must always be met, regardless of whether the test is for sewing machinists, dentists, fork lift truck operators or naval helicopter navigator/tactical controllers.

1. It must be given by an instructor who is both an experienced trainer in the particular job, and has been trained in the use of the test.
2. It must be given in an environment as similar as possible to the one in which the applicant will train and work.
3. The instructor must first explain carefully the procedure to the applicants;

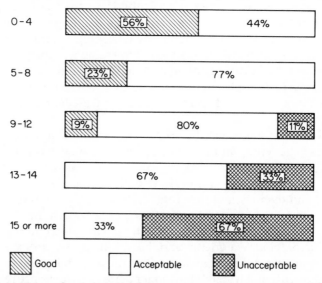

Figure 1   Expectancy chart showing how to gauge the expected performance of a trainee fork truck operator from the trainability test total error score (based on 263 results)

beginning with the fact that they will be taught a task which is part of the training for the job. During this training period they will be encouraged to ask questions and receive help, following which they will be expected to perform the task unaided.

4. The teaching content and method must be closely defined and adhered to so that each applicant has equal opportunity to learn and subsequently perform the task. This involves the options of the instructor memorizing a script, demonstrating to a tape recording, or where instruction is lengthy, highlighting key facts based on a good procedural job breakdown.

5. Applicants are asked to perform the task without help, and interference only occurs if they are putting themselves or others into danger.

6. The instructor observes carefully and marks down any errors made by the applicant on the standardized error checklist, either as the errors are made, or, if that is not possible, as soon afterwards as practicable.

7. Immediately after the test, the instructor rates the applicant. This subjective assessment is, and should be, strongly influenced by the errors noted, as it includes memory of procedures, ability to see errors and correct them and evidence of relevant manual and perceptual skills. Instructors are encouraged to use their expertise to take into account such factors as nervousness, speed of work, confidence and interest.

DISADVANTAGES AND ADVANTAGES OF WORK SAMPLE TESTS, INCLUDING TRAINABILITY TESTS

A major problem of job samples is that each job has to be the subject of a different job sample. Furthermore, as jobs change, job samples may again have to be amended. If, for example, a job changed from assembling mechanical switchgear to assembling electronic switchgear, a job sample test for the former may or may not continue to give good predictive validity. If it did not do so, then it points to the fact that the job sample no longer relates to the skills involved in the changed jobs.

Where the job sample is based on motor ability, it can be costly in terms of materials, machinery and the time of the tester or assessor. Job samples for some occupations, such as management, may not involve materials and machinery, but can be complex in order to include crucial aspects of the job: therefore, they are costly to design and administer.

People undertaking trainability forms of a job sample test are best evaluated singly, or at most in groups of two or three, because the assessors are equally interested in the way a person goes about the task as they are in any final workpiece or end result. By comparison, large numbers can be tested at the same time using psychometric tests of aptitude.

A trainability test can be developed only for jobs or parts of jobs that can be behaviourally described. Job sample tests can, however, be developed for some jobs where the crucial element is the end product. In typing, for example, the crucial aspects are speed, accuracy and appearance of the typing and not how these were achieved. How some other jobs are carried out often determines the end product and in these circumstances a job sample test would have to be based on behavioural descriptions. Delegation, for example, is often cited as a crucial ingredient of management, but what, when and how managers delegate would have to be described behaviourally before any job sample test could be designed.

Another disadvantage is that predictive validity coefficients of these sorts of tests tend to attenuate over time. A number of reasons for this can be suggested, such as the fact that the work may change; organizational and environmental factors may inhibit the better performer and the best and worst performers may leave the job. Whatever the reasons, users of job sample tests should bear in mind that the longer the period in between giving the test and the follow-up, the less predictive the test will be.

Finally, trainability tests are particularly vulnerable to distortion by the tester, owing to the fact that he or she is involved in explaining, demonstrating, answering questions and assessing usually one person at a time. Each test is therefore unique, while at the same time the procedures, script, demonstration and test have to be carried out in the manner that the test was validated. It is important, therefore, that the tester should be both well trained to give the test and monitored from time to time.

Balancing these drawbacks, the advantages of work sample tests include the fact that they are work specific and verify the acquisition of a skill. As Anastasi (1972) said, 'surpassing all other types of standardised tests in sheer numbers, achievement tests are designed to measure the effects of a specific programme of instruction or training'. A paper-and-pencil test may, for instance, establish how much theoretical knowledge an applicant for the job of welder has, but a work sample test would be needed to see if the person was a proficient welder.

Work sample tests have more face validity than interviews or aptitude tests. Robertson and Mindel (1980) found that both trainees and instructors were much more at ease with a trainability assessment and Schmidt *et al.* (1977) pointed out that a work sample test had considerably less adverse impact on minority/ protected groups than other forms of testing (see Chapter 1.4).

Trainability tests allow an element of self-selection which applies equally to applicants for specific jobs and where several tests are used as tasters to a range of jobs. Such comments as 'If that is what the job is like I would not want it' and 'I was worried if I would be able to weld and now I know I can' are equally valuable. Job sample tests may therefore act as a realistic job preview (see Chapter 3.8).

Because work sample tests are derived from crucial elements of the job, the only criterion of the test is whether or not a person could do, or, in a trainability test could learn, the job. Work sample tests are therefore relatively free from sex or culture bias and a Joint Working Party of the Runnymede Trust and British Psychological Society (1980) in discussing culture fair techniques, said 'The trainability assessment is likely to have minimal disproportionate impact'. No work sample test can be guaranteed to be entirely free of sex or culture bias because such tests require assessors who may wittingly or unwittingly distort the results. However, the tests do not suffer from the problems of some psychometric tests where these have been developed and validated in one culture or for a single sex and are being used in different cultures and for both sexes.

Wernimont and Campbell (1968), in describing the advantages of work sample tests, say that 'a number of old or persistent problems fortunately appear to dissipate, or at least become significantly diminished'. They list faking and response sets, since behaviour samples demonstrate what one can do; discrimination in testing related to lack of relevance and unfairness of content; and invasion of privacy.

THE PLACE OF WORK SAMPLE TESTS

There is always a danger that in describing one thing it may appear to be at the expense of others. Work sampling should not be seen as an alternative, but as an additional method of assessment available to selectors and appraisers. In selection, biographical details, psychometric tests and interviews provide a great deal of information. Work samples supplement this by identifying an achieved level of skill or, in the case of trainability tests, by predicting the likely success rate of training. Despite the problems and difficulties associated with work sampling, it remains the most effective way of establishing levels of skill or the likelihood of achieving such levels.

REFERENCES AND FURTHER READING

Anastasi, A. (1972). *Psychological Testing*, 3rd edn. Macmillan, London.

Downs, S. (1968). Selecting the older trainee: A pilot study of trainability tests, *National Institute of Industrial Psychology Bulletin*, 19–26.

Downs, S. (1985). *Testing Trainability*. NFER–Nelson Personnel Library, Windsor.

Downs, S., and Gowan, C. (1972). The use of trainability assessments for apprentices; carpenters and bricklayers. Industrial Training Research Unit, Cambridge. Unpublished report.

Industrial Training Research Unit (1977). *Trainability Tests: A practitioners' guide*. Industrial Training Research Unit, Cambridge.

Joint Working Party (1980). *Discriminating Fairly: A guide to fair selection*. Runnymede Trust and British Psychological Society.

Jones, A., and Whittaker, P. (1975). *Testing Industrial Skills*. Gower Press, Epping.

Robertson, I., and Downs, S. (1979). Learning and the prediction of performance: the development of trainability testing in the United Kingdom, *Journal of Applied Psychology*, **64**(1), 42–50.

Robertson, I., and Mindel, R.M. (1980). A study of trainability testing, *Journal of Occupational Psychology*, **53**(2), 131–8.

Schmidt, F.L., Greenthal, A.L., Hunter, J.E., Berner, J.G., and Seaton, F.W. (1977). Job sample vs paper-and-pencil trades and technical tests: Adverse impact and examinee atttitudes, *Personnel Psychology*, **30**, 197.

Wernimont, P.F., and Campbell, J.P. (1968). Signs, samples and criteria, *Journal of Applied Psychology*, **52**(5), 372–6.

Chapter 3.7

Assessment Centres

ROB T. FELTHAM

NFER–Nelson, Darville House, 2 Oxford Road East, Windsor, Berkshire SL4 1DF, UK

The term 'assessment centre' (AC) has nothing to do with a 'centre' or fixed geographical location. It is used to describe a process by which an individual, or group of individuals, is assessed by a team of judges using a comprehensive and integrated series of techniques (Fletcher, 1982). At least one of these techniques should be a 'work sample test' or 'simulation'—in other words an exercise which more or less directly represents or simulates important elements of real job tasks (see Chapter 3.6). Other techniques frequently include interviews and standardized pencil-and-paper tests of mental abilities, aptitudes and personality characteristics. An AC generally results in a written report which combines quantitative information—for example, scores on tests and exercises, ratings on dimensions of performance—with a more qualitative, descriptive account of the individual's apparent strengths and weaknesses. ACs result in decisions—to select or not, to promote or not—and/or recommendations for individual development which may consist of feedback and career counselling, career planning, training and so on. Most frequently organizations use ACs to identify managerial potential, but ACs are equally effective in assessing for non-managerial roles.

Good ACs tend to be expensive. Among the costs to be considered are those of analysing jobs, developing and/or purchasing tests and exercises, training assessors, hiring accommodation and paying for travel. There is also likely to be considerable investment of staff time in setting up and operating the AC. The AC itself typically lasts between half a day and three days. Where candidates are existing employees, there may be further costs associated with feedback, counselling and career development.

Given the costs, the rationale for using ACs as opposed to cheaper methods may seem questionable. Many organizations get by with interviews alone, possibly aided by one or two standardized pencil-and-paper tests. The fact is, however, that most kinds of interview-based assessment give little indication of subsequent job performance (see Chapter 3.9).

Good quality ACs have a number of advantages over traditional assessment methods. Chief among these is their greater accuracy in forecasting job performance, which is demonstrated by the steady accumulation of validity evidence since AC methods were introduced around the time of the Second World War. With the aid of recently developed techniques it is possible to put monetary value on the benefits of improved selection. As a result, the expense of ACs can generally be justified in cost–benefit terms. Other benefits of ACs are that they facilitate candidates' ability to self-select; they are generally perceived to be fair; and they provide a good basis for identifying individuals' development needs. However, to obtain these benefits, attention needs to be given to the process of AC design and to factors which contribute to the quality and consistency of assessments.

This chapter will look at all of these areas in more detail. But to start with, the AC approach is illustrated with a modern example taken from the European oil industry.

ASSESSMENT AT SHELL

Shell International Petroleum Company has recently introduced ACs in the recruitment of graduates, with the particular aim of identifying those with senior managerial potential.[1] The company operates a number of broadly similar ACs, each directed towards specific areas within which graduates work, for example commerce, finance, engineering and so on. The specific AC to be described here is one which was used to select graduates for employment in the finance function.

One of the factors leading to the introduction of ACs was an investigation into the ability and personality profiles of 299 graduate applicants, of whom a proportion were selected following interview. This research indicated that selectors were generally using somewhat limited sets of criteria. Some personality characteristics, for example those associated with creativity, were found to be associated with poor performance in interview but potentially useful contributions to the work of the organization. It was felt that the introduction of ACs would provide selectors with information from which to make more comprehensive judgements about candidates.

A job analysis exercise was conducted with senior executives in the company in order to identify ways in which successful executives differed from less successful executives, and also to pinpoint behaviours associated with competent handling of critical situations. A list of twelve dimensions of performance was derived, each one carefully defined. Examples are 'analysis and judgement', 'divergent thinking', 'business awareness', 'persuasiveness', 'communication skills' and 'sensitivity'.

---

[1] Information supplied by Richard Scriven of Shell International Petroleum Company Ltd.

Next a set of assessment procedures was put together, designed to simulate executive work and to provide opportunities for observing and measuring relevant behaviour within each of the twelve dimensions. The range of exercises was such that each dimension was covered at least twice. In designing simulations, efforts were made to bridge the gap between candidates' experience and the types of competency required by the organization. Where simulations were set in a specific organizational context, care was taken to ensure that no specific prior knowledge was required to meet the demands of the task.

There were three simulations, each observed by three assessors:

1. *Case study*   Candidates were each given the role of an assistant to the Finance Manager in an oilfield construction project. They were required to stand in for the Finance Manager in a critical meeting with the Chief Engineer. The Chief Engineer, who was project manager, was mainly concerned to get the oil flowing; work was slightly behind schedule. The Finance Department had a lot of responsibility and was accountable to the highest levels in the company, but had very little power over the course of the construction work. Candidates were given one hour in which to prepare for the meeting from a file of relevant papers. The papers included a proposal from the Chief Engineer to speed up the construction work. However, there were big financial risks inherent in this proposal. By the end of the hour, candidates were expected to have produced some written conclusions. They then went straight into a half-hour one-to-one meeting with the Chief Engineer (role-played by an assessor). In this meeting candidates had to defend their position and ensure that correct financial procedures were adhered to.
2. *Discussion*   Six candidates participated in a role-play group exercise. In one version, the candidates made up an editorial committee of a newspaper. Six news items had been identified as contenders for main headline status the following day. As a group, the candidates were instructed to find the most appropriate news item. However, each individual was required to try as hard as possible to get one particular item selected. Candidates had 10 minutes to prepare, and then the committee met for 50 minutes. Which candidate should advocate which news item was a matter for the group to decide at the beginning of the meeting. Then there was an unconstrained discussion before the group made a choice.
3. *Presentation*   Each candidate was asked to make an oral presentation, and given a list of topics from which to choose. Topics were sufficiently general to be familiar to candidates, but also of relevance to the organization, for example, a topic to do with the role of the trade unions. Candidates had one hour in which to prepare, and 5–10 minutes in which to present. Afterwards they were questioned by the assessors.

Performance of participants in each of the simulations was carefully observed and noted, and then assessed on an appropriate subset of the overall list of twelve dimensions. In the case study, for example, dimensions such as analysis and judgement, business awareness and persuasiveness are clearly relevant, and were rated on 6-point scales. As well as the dimension ratings, there was an overall rating for performance in each exercise.

In addition to the simulations, each candidate was interviewed by a panel of two assessors. There were also computer-administered tests of creativity, work values and personality preferences.

Twelve participants and six assessors attended each AC. Assessors were all senior executives within finance divisions of Shell. Beforehand they had attended a two-day training session which included guidance on assessment and interview techniques, observation of 'guinea-pig' candidates undergoing the simulations, interview practice and discussion of criteria to be applied during the AC. The AC itself lasted one and a half days, finishing up with an assessors' conference at which all the information on candidates was brought together and conclusions reached. The assessors, who had observed different participants in different exercises, agreed final ratings for each candidate on each of the twelve perform-ance dimensions, then rank ordered the candidates in terms of career potential, and finally arrived at an overall assessment rating (OAR) for each candidate which indicated the organizational level he or she might be expected to reach if selected. Selection decisions were made on the basis of OAR.

The Shell assessment procedure is a good example of a modern AC, and it illustrates the amount of detailed work and resources that need to go into design and operation. The next issue to address is the justification for using elaborate and costly assessment procedures of this kind. One way to understand the growth in the use of ACs is by looking at the historical development of the method and the build-up of evidence in its favour.

HISTORY OF ASSESSMENT CENTRES AND THE ACCUMULATION OF VALIDITY EVIDENCE

Perusal of many North American texts would lead one to believe that ACs are a US invention. In fact their origins are European; the approach can be traced back to multiple assessment procedures developed for officer selection in pre-war Ger-many (Vernon and Parry, 1949). The general pattern of these procedures was that candidates were assessed over three days by a board consisting of a colonel, a medical officer and psychological examiners. There was a wide range of assess-ment techniques, including the following:

- 'Leadership sample' tests which consisted of instructing a group of soldiers in a practical task, e.g. making a coat hanger out of a piece of wire.
- 'Expression analysis', a type of personality assessment which included obser-vation of facial expression in reaction to distractions or painful stimuli such as electric shock.
- A detailed biographical interview.
- To round off the procedure, a group discussion of some general topic by all the candidates, designed to show up their competitiveness and other social reactions.

These officer selection programmes were discontinued around 1941–2 due to a number of political and practical difficulties, and their legacy is in the originality of the approach rather than any proven merit.

The German procedures were instrumental in inspiring the next stage of AC development—the British War Office Selection Board (WOSB) (Harris, 1949; Vernon and Parry, 1949). The development of WOSB was motivated by widespread dissatisfaction with the system of short interviews used to select army officers in the first two years of war. In early 1941 there were experiments in multiple assessment encouraged by an ex-military attaché in Berlin who had observed some of the German procedures. Within a year the first WOSB was in operation, and the method quickly spread throughout the army. By the end of the war some 140 000 candidates had been assessed, of whom about 60 000 passed.

Boards were made up of a mixture of military and psychiatric personnel, with psychologists in a research/advisory role. An officer of major/captain rank would take charge of a group of seven to twelve candidates for three days, mess with them, observe their social behaviour, and put them through a variety of practical/situational tests. These consisted of such things as lecturettes, obstacle courses, command situations, in which the candidate was placed in charge of a group and assigned a practical task, and leaderless group tests. In addition to situational tests there were standardized pencil-and-paper ability tests, projective tests, biographical questionnaires, peer assessments and interviews with the senior military personnel. At the end there would be a final conference after which the most senior military officer would make a decision.

In 1942 some selection boards were using the new multiple assessment procedures, while others continued to rely on interviews alone. Large-scale comparisons were undertaken of performance in training of those selected by the two methods. Of those selected by the new methods 35 per cent were graded above average, compared with 22 per cent selected by the old methods. Similarly 25 per cent of those selected by the new methods were below average, compared with 37 per cent of those selected by the old methods. Later, assessments of performance in the field confirmed the finding that the new methods were moderately valid as predictors of performance.

However, as important as WOSB's ability to predict was the fact that the method won wide acceptance in the army and stimulated recruitment. According to Vernon and Parry (1949), the 'combination of slightly more valid selection procedures with greater attractiveness to candidates resulted in the sending of two-and-a-half times as many above-average cadets to . . . [training units] as the old boards would have done, within five months after the establishment of new boards' (p. 124). There was also a general boost to morale as, despite methodological shortcomings, the 'Army was led to believe that it was . . . getting the best possible officers' (p. 66).

The WOSB process continued in operation for many years, and is the direct forerunner of today's Regular Commissions Board which takes responsibility for army officer appointments. Many other ACs in the British and Commonwealth public sector also have a direct historical link with WOSB: the most notable British descendants are the Civil Service Selection Board, the

Admiralty Interview Board and the Royal Air Force Officers and Aircrew Selection Centre.

The first AC in the United States was also military and a direct WOSB-descendant. This was at the US Office of Strategic Services (OSS), set up in 1942 to deal with such things as secret intelligence, operations behind enemy lines and disinformation campaigns. Following some disastrous recruitment policies in the early years of war, the most notorious of which was the deliberate recruitment of known criminals on the assumption that it takes dirty men to do dirty work, WOSB methods were borrowed and adapted, and brought into use in 1944. For a succinct account, the reader is referred to MacKinnon (1977). Some follow-up studies of successful candidates (OSS Assessment Staff, 1948; Wiggins, 1973) produced evidence of the procedure's validity which overall is consistent with that coming from WOSB, i.e. moderate but significant improvements in the accuracy of selection.

Probably the next important step in AC development occurred after the war with the creation of the British Civil Service Selection Board (CSSB) (Vernon, 1950). Prior to the war, academic examinations had been used in making fast-stream Civil Service appointments. However, this was clearly inappropriate for candidates whose studies had been disrupted by war. It was decided instead to adopt the WOSB approach. But there was more emphasis at CSSB on intellectual capacity, and on paperwork to test it, and tests of physical aptitude were eliminated. CSSB's design was based on a detailed analysis of the work of over 500 senior civil servants, carried out in 1945. Candidates seen at CSSB were later assessed by a Final Selection Board—a high level interview panel. Although the Final Selection Board had final responsibility for selections, ultimate decisions were strongly CSSB determined.

In the early CSSB procedure, candidates were assessed in groups of seven at a residential centre over 48 hours. The assessors were two administrative civil servants and a psychologist. Techniques used consisted of a battery of mental ability and aptitude tests, questionnaires on interests and leisure pursuits, projective tests, peer assessments, interviews of each candidate by each assessor and situational tests about which Vernon writes:

> All three [board] members listened to the first session—a Group Discussion—and gave a preliminary grading on a five-point scale . . . Subsequent exercises were designed to resemble the work of a higher Civil Servant. They included sitting on a Committee, writing an Appreciation of a dossier, and the exposition and handling of a Problem in Committee. Each candidate also gave a Short Talk on a subject of his own choice, and there was a Second Group Discussion.

Finally, following consultation, each assessor awarded a grade based on judgement of all the evidence. The overall CSSB mark was normally an average of these three grades.

CSSB has operated continuously from 1945 until the present day. Though there have been many developments to, and refinements of, CSSB since the early days, the interviews and simulations which formed the heart of the process bear strong resemblance to the CSSB procedures used today.

Table 1   Ranks obtained by Civil Service fast-stream entrants after 30 years—grouped according to Board mark

Rank attained	Board mark		
	Acceptable pass (n = 108) (%)	Good pass (n = 119) (%)	Very good pass (n = 74) (%)
Permanent Secretary[a] and Deputy Secretary	12	24	39
Under Secretary	33	39	42
Assistant Secretary and Senior Principal	45	33	15
Principal[b] and Assistant Principal	10	4	4

Note Figures adapted from Anstey (1977).
[a] – Top of the Civil Service.
[b] – Bottom of senior management.

CSSB is probably the first AC for which convincing evidence of high predictive validity was found. Vernon (1950) reported follow-ups of up to two years, and found very strong relationships between CSSB overall grade and performance in training and on the job. Anstey (1977) continued Vernon's follow-up of immediate post-war recruits to 30 years' service, when the administrators 'were nearing the end of their careers; it could reasonably be assumed that their rank reached constituted a fair criterion of the progress made by the individual' (p. 152). Again, very strong relationships were observed between final selection marks and rank attained. This can be seen in Table 1. Nearly 40 per cent of those given the highest marks reached the topmost ranks in the Civil Service, compared with 12 per cent of those given borderline acceptable marks.

The 1940s and 1950s saw several small-scale commercial/industrial applications of WOSB- and CSSB-type methods. In one of these an AC procedure, which included intelligence tests, interviews and group discussions, was used to select for promotion to supervisory positions in a Scottish engineering works (Handyside and Duncan, 1954). A follow-up of 44 successful candidates over four years showed the procedure to be an extraordinarily good predictor of later promotions and job performance ratings.

However, a procedure which has had far more influence on the longer term development of ACs was one developed at the US company American Telephone and Telegraph (AT&T). This AC was inspired by the wartime procedure used at the OSS, and was developed experimentally as part of AT&T's Management Progress Study—a longitudinal research investigation into the development of young men in a business environment which began in the late 1950s (Bray and Grant, 1966). Of 422 men assessed, approximately two-thirds were college graduates recently recruited by interview methods; the remainder were internal promotees who had reached management relatively early in their careers.

On the basis of a literature review and the judgements of personnel staff within the company, a list of 25 characteristics or dimensions was derived which informed the choice of assessment techniques and was used for rating candidate's performance.

Participants spent 3½ days at the AC and underwent: a 2-hour interview; an 'in-basket' exercise in which three hours was allowed to deal with the contents of a fictitious telephone manager's in-tray, after which candidates were interviewed about their performance; a manufacturing problem which was a group simulation of a small-business enterprise; a group discussion in which candidates were assigned roles and had to argue out a promotion decision; and a variety of objective tests, projective tests and questionnaires.

Groups of twelve participants were assessed by teams of about nine staff, who were mostly psychologists (Thornton and Byham, 1982). In group exercises subjects were split into teams of six and assessed by two staff. Written reports were prepared for each assessment technique, and at the end of the procedure all staff assembled to review results. Following presentation of the reports, each staff member independently rated each participant on all of the 25 dimensions. Each dimension was then reviewed, and judgements about managerial potential were made.

The accuracy of these judgements was periodically checked, with quite impressive results. Bray and Grant (1966) reported that for those remaining with AT&T in 1965, 42 per cent of the 103 predicted to 'make middle management' had done so, compared with 7 per cent of the 166 not predicted to do so. Bray, Campbell and Grant (1974) continued the follow-up for the college graduates only, using the criterion of management level eight years after initial assessment. At this point in their careers, 64 per cent of those predicted to reach middle management had done so, compared with 32 per cent of those not predicted to do so.

These results are of particular interest since all the information collected on the participants was held in strict confidence; it was a pure research study. 'Thus the judgments of the assessment staff have had no influence on the careers of the men being studied' (Bray and Grant, 1966, p. 1).

The AT&T research had considerable impact on the subsequent shape of ACs in the US. The process by which this occurred is described by Crooks (1977):

> After AT&T published favorable research results, visitors from other companies flocked to AT&T to observe their assessment centers and to ask for copies of their exercises, rating forms, manuals, and whatever else was available. Even today in observing programs from company to company, the basic AT&T format . . . is readily discernible (p. 71).

In particular, it is simulations which give ACs their individual characters—these are what people seem to remember—and those used by AT&T still predominate in US ACs. US-style ACs have also made a considerable impact in British industry and commerce. Dulewicz, Fletcher and Wood (1983) point out that many British users of ACs are in fact UK subsidiaries of US multinationals such as IBM and Rank Xerox, which may in part explain the trend. The AT&T pattern is also evident in ACs in other countries.

VALIDITY UP TO DATE

Evidence about the accuracy of AC predictions has continued to accumulate, and the method is now commonly believed to be one of the most valid approaches to selection and identification of long-term potential. Recent large-scale reviews of validity studies confirm this (Schmitt *et al.*, 1984; Gaugler *et al.*, 1987). However, it is necessary to sound a note of caution. It is reasonable to expect ACs which have been professionally designed and operated to result in good quality decisions about people assessed. But there are very many ACs which do not come into this category—procedures where insufficient attention has been paid to such things as job analysis, exercise design and assessor training. Generally speaking, ACs which have been reported on in the professional literature, and have therefore been covered by validity reviews, represent the quality end of the spectrum. Even for these ACs, a wide range of levels of validity has been found. Generalizing from this, it is likely that many low quality ACs—cheap and hastily assembled with little or no professional input—have negligible validity. There is a large number of such ACs.

HOW SHOULD ONE DESIGN AN ASSESSMENT CENTRE?

There are some basic principles of AC design which increase the likelihood that the assessment procedure will result in good predictions of future job performance. These principles also apply to other selection procedures — see Chapters 2.1 and 2.2. In brief what is needed is:

1. A *systematic analysis of the job*(s) for which one is selecting, with the aim of identifying the most important or critical elements. Job analysis frequently results in some systematic categorization of work tasks and relationshps, together with the identification of the types of knowledge, skill and basic ability needed to carry out the job satisfactorily. However, where ACs are concerned, it is particularly important for the job analysis also to give a good descriptive account of situations and tasks typically encountered in the job. This provides the basic material for the development of simulations.
2. A set of *carefully designed* and chosen *assessment techniques* which are as far as possible representative of the more important job tasks and of the competencies needed to perform those tasks. Simulation design requires particular attention. Simulations should ideally represent real job situations, but the content should not be such as to give unfair advantage to candidates with detailed specialized knowledge. Where possible, simulations should be standardized situations, i.e. situations which are the same for all candidates. This is particularly difficult with group exercises, where the situation will vary greatly according to group composition. Preferably exercises of this type should be supplemented by simulations of more standardized kinds, for example using written materials. In addition, rating methods need to be developed which provide a systematic basis for observing critical behaviours displayed during exercises. Simulations and rating methods should be tried out prior to use in

order to ensure that they are practicable for candidates and assessors, and to bring to light any flaws in exercise design.
3. *Assessor training* to ensure that assessors are competent in behaviour observation and are working to a common standard.

In the next two sections a more detailed look is taken at the results of the design process, i.e. the variety of simulations used in modern ACs and the methods by which performance is rated and assessed.

TYPES OF ASSESSMENT CENTRE SIMULATION

The simulation is clearly the key AC technique. In theory, any relevant work situation which can be translated into a structured assessment context can form the basis for a simulation. Nevertheless particular types of simulation commonly recur.

Probably the most popular single type of simulation is the *in-tray* or *in-basket* exercise. This directly simulates a manager's in-tray, frequently using real items from real in-trays—memos, letters, reports, etc.—with suitable amendments for confidentiality. Participants are required to stand in for the manager at short notice, and cope with the in-tray as best they can, working against the clock. They attach notes to each item indicating the actions they are taking, or record actions on a separate sheet. Frequently the exercise is followed up by an interview with an assessor who explores thinking behind actions. In-tray exercises are useful for simulating pressure of decision making in busy office environments.

A wide variety of *group exercises* are used in ACs. These exercises are often leaderless. Sometimes participants are given roles and required in some way to compete with one another. The discussion exercise in the Shell AC provides one illustration of this approach. At other times there are no roles; the group is given a task, and the emphasis is on individual participants to make an effective contribution to the work of the team. An example of this is the business game approach where participants typically make a series of decisions about such things as advertising volume, prices to be charged, capital investment and production levels. Results of their actions are fed back to them, creating a constantly changing situation.

In other group exercises a leader is assigned, and leadership rotates as the exercise progresses so that each participant has a turn. An example is the type of command exercise used by the British Royal Navy (the Admiralty Interview Board) in officer-level recruitment. Here each candidate is given some practical problem, e.g. building a bridge over water, and required to take command of other candidates to achieve the objective. This leadership model is also seen in sedentary group exercises where each candidate chairs a committee of his fellow candidates in order to obtain agreement on how to tackle a managerial problem of some kind.

In the United States, two-person role-play exercises are very common. These involve one candidate, and one assessor trained to play a standardized role. Often the role-play is of an interview situation. For example, the candidate, in the role of manager, interviews a capable but troublesome employee.

Most ACs are designed to identify managerial potential, and the popularity of the simulations described so far is probably due to the fact that they provide a basis for assessing managerial skills. Where ACs are used for other purposes, some very different types of simulations are found. Often these are very specific, and targeted on fairly tightly defined jobs. A good example comes from Schmitt and Ostroff (1986) where the AC was designed to select for the job of emergency telephone operator in a police support capacity. One of the simulations required applicants to take the role of an operator receiving a call from a member of the public—in reality, a trained role-player working from a script. One practice call was given for applicants to acquaint themselves with the procedure. After that the applicant 'talked with the caller, who was occasionally emotional or hysterical, and obtained the information necessary to send help to the caller. A variety of questions needed to be asked by the candidate in order to elicit the appropriate information. Candidates recorded information on a standardized form' (Schmitt and Ostroff, 1986, p. 102).

But whatever types of simulations are used, it has to be remembered that they provide only a structure within which to observe job-related behaviour. Equally as important as simulation design are the processes by which that performance is rated and evaluated.

HOW SHOULD PERFORMANCE BE RATED?

Methods by which assessors process information and evaluate performance vary considerably in different ACs. Nowadays most ACs, though not all, make use of some overall list of dimensions on which performance of candidates is evaluated. However, ACs differ in the point at which dimensional assessment is applied. In some ACs candidates are rated on dimensions after each exercise, and also at the end of the AC as a whole. In other ACs, rating of dimensions is left until the end of the AC, after all information has been collected.

There is no convincing research evidence to suggest that either of these two approaches is superior. However, it is critical that dimensions are job related, clearly defined, and preferably illustrated with examples of relevant behaviour that might be observed during the AC. Well-designed dimensions of this kind give assessors a framework which guides their attention to important points of evidence and provides a common basis for discussion. Without dimensions, or some other clear guidance on the criteria to be applied, assessors may find themselves disagreeing not about assessees' performance but about the aspects of performance which they think are important. As far as possible, criteria should be determined at the job analysis stage, leaving assessors free to concentrate on gathering evidence.

Where dimensions are not applied at the end of each exercise, some other systematic framework needs to be employed. While a variety of approaches is possible, a common method is to break down the exercise into its component objectives and indicate the sorts of behaviour which are associated with meeting those objectives. For example, if in an analysis and presentation exercise a candidate was instructed to read a policy report, write down the salient points, summarize and present the main arguments including a personal recommendation in front of an audience, and then deal with questions and criticisms, assessment could focus on how satisfactorily each of the elements of the task had been dealt with. As with dimensions, the important thing is that assessors know what is expected and have a common framework for evaluating performance.

POTENTIAL PROBLEMS WITH DIMENSIONS

While dimensions can be useful, there are potential pitfalls. These can generally be avoided if dimensions are viewed as means of examining candidates' performance rather than as ends in themselves. The main mistake is to interpret AC dimensions as measures of stable and enduring personality-type traits. Two conclusions from recent research indicate that such interpretations are likely to be invalid.

The first of these conclusions is that ratings of the same dimensions can vary considerably in different exercises (Sackett and Dreher, 1982; Robertson, Gratton and Sharpley, 1987). For example, the 'persuasiveness' of a particular individual might appear much higher in a group problem-solving task than in a presentation exercise. Moreover, correlations between ratings of different dimensions in the same exercise have been found to be higher than correlations between ratings of the same dimension in different exercises. So, to continue the example, ratings of 'persuasiveness' in the group problem-solving task might correlate more highly with ratings of 'analytical ability' in the same task than with ratings of 'persuasiveness' in the presentation exercise. One explanation for this is that skilled performance tends to be specific to particular kinds of tasks and situations. For example, one cannot assume that interpersonal skills demonstrated in a team task will necessarily translate into the interpersonal skills required for effective one-to-one counselling.

As a consequence, conclusions about individuals are likely to be more valid if related to tasks and situations than if related only to dimensions. For example, a final report on an individual could include a statement like: 'This candidate responded well to the intellectual demands of the written exercises, and reached well-balanced conclusions. The candidate also showed considerable sensitivity in the one-to-one counselling situation, but made little effective contribution to the group exercises due to . . . , etc.' A conclusion in this form is likely both to be more valid and of more practical value than a conclusion like: 'This candidate was above average on intellectual skills and sensitivity, slightly below average on interpersonal skills, and well below average on persuasiveness'.

A second important conclusion is that the numerous dimensions on which candidates are normally rated create an impression of complex multi-faceted decision making which is somewhat misleading. When one gets below the surface, the reality is that a much smaller number of 'source' dimensions underlie assessors' judgements. For example Russell (1985) showed (through use of the statistical technique known as 'factor analysis') that ten assessors who each rated large numbers of candidates on sixteen dimensions of AC performance were all in reality making use of much smaller numbers of source dimensions—between two and four. This ties in with research done by Sackett and Hakel (1979) which showed that, although assessors were instructed to use all dimensions, OAR could be predicted accurately from a subset of only three (leadership, organization and planning, and decision making).

The above arguments are not against the use of dimensions. Dimensions can provide useful frameworks within which to examine the detail of candidate performance. The message is simply that dimensions should be seen as aids to assessment rather than as objectives in themselves. In the final analysis, ACs provide information about skills in particular kinds of situations. The validity of any given AC is strongly related to the degree to which the situations in the AC make demands comparable with those found in the job. The primary objective of the AC should be to match the individual to a job or set of tasks rather than to a set of dimensions.

PROBLEMS WITH DISCUSSION AND JUDGEMENT

When exercise performance has been rated and individual assessors have formed some opinions about candidates, there are issues about the best way to decide final dimensions ratings and OARs. The almost universal approach is to hold a discussion where assessors pool their judgements and reach consensus. This discussion is generally seen as useful by organizations who use ACs, and also by assessors themselves. However, there is little real evidence in favour of it. For example Sackett and Wilson (1982) showed that a simple decision rule could predict final post-discussion dimension ratings from assessors' pre-discussion ratings with about 95 per cent accuracy. Moreover Wingrove, Jones and Herriot (1985) found that in those cases where pre- and post-discussion ratings did differ, their overall accuracy, in terms of predicting later performance in training, was the same. The implication is that simple mechanical pooling of ratings would not only save time, but should have no detrimental effect on AC validity.

There is, in fact, quite a lot of evidence that mechanical combination of AC information is at least as valid and probably more valid than judgemental combination (Feltham, 1988a). If one were to run an AC in which the assessors confined themslves to evaluating performance, and their ratings were put into a formula to arrive at OAR, the result should be decisions of as good or better quality than those produced by the consensus process. Unfortunately this conclusion is counter-intuitive, and likely to be rejected by many of those involved with ACs. In practical organizational terms, the only feasible way to implement a mechanical approach may be by means of some kind of compromise. For example, mechanical 'recommendations' could be briefly reviewed by assessors in discussion.

Those who are interested in maximizing the validity of the AC process should give some thought to this type of approach.

STANDARDIZATION AND RELIABILITY OF ASSESSMENT CENTRE METHODS

Standardization and care in the design of exercises and rating procedures should result in assessments which have good *reliability*. In crude terms reliability, which can be measured statistically, is the degree to which different assessments of the same thing agree. For example, reliability might be examined by looking at the degree of agreement between two assessors who have co-observed a candidate's performance in a simulation.

It is clearly desirable to have reliable standards of assessment. And most texts on the subject assert that ACs are highly reliable. However, there are a number of problems with the way most of the reliability research has been conducted. The only definitive way to assess an AC's reliability would be to have some candidates go through two ACs with a short time gap in between. The two ACs would be similar in structure, but employ different assessors; the specific content of the tests and exercises would also be different. Reliability could then be judged in terms of the degree of agreement in the OARs obtained from the two ACs. In fact, there are only three published research studies in which anything like this has been done (Vernon and Parry, 1949; McConnell and Parker, 1972; Moses, 1973). The results obtained suggest that the reliability of a full AC is probably no higher than the equivalent reliability which might be expected from a reputable pencil-and-paper aptitude test lasting half an hour or so.

However, this comparison is misleading for at least two reasons. First, it reflects more on the high reliability of aptitude tests than on any lack of reliability of ACs. Secondly, ACs capture some of the complexity of real world situations—for example, group interactions—but by so doing inevitably elicit behaviour which is difficult to assess in a rigorous and reliable way (Bedford, 1987). So the strength of ACs—their job-relatedness—is also a weakness. In the final analysis, ACs appear to provide a reasonable balance between reliability and job-relatedness. The most important point is that ACs work for the purpose intended—predicting performance on the job.

COSTS AND BENEFITS OF ASSESSMENT CENTRES

Though ACs have been shown to be good predictors of job performance, they are also, as has been mentioned, expensive relative to many other kinds of selection procedure. There is no getting away from this fact, but it should be emphasized that spending on selection is an investment. When looked at in relation to the potential (dis)benefits of recruitment decisions, a few hundred or even a few thousand pounds per selected candidate may not be excessive. This is particularly true of critical management positions, where headhunters typically charge around one-third of annual starting salary to find someone.

The claim that money invested in selection procedures is money well spent has been given empirical support by recent developments in a technique known as 'utility analysis' (see Chapter 3.3). Utility analysis is an investment appraisal technique by which the benefits of alternative selection procedures (or other types of personnel programme, for example, training) can be estimated in monetary terms. Utility analysis can be characterized by three basic attributes (Boudreau, 1989): *quantity*, reflecting the number of employees and period of time affected by a particular selection programme; *quality*, reflecting the consequences (per person, per time period) associated with the programme; and *cost*, reflecting the resources the programme requires. The payoff from a personnel programme is measured by multiplying quantity by quality and then subtracting cost.

The mathematics of this are well established; in fact, the basic equations have been known for nearly 40 years. However, early attempts to apply the approach in the personnel field foundered because of the difficulty of quantifying some of the elements involved, particularly those relating to the monetary value of an individual's contribution to the work of an organization. Recently, useful progress has been made by means of some simplifying assumptions. These assumptions necessarily result in a certain amount of imprecision. But research indicates that the assumptions are generally conservative and that, more often than not, true benefit is underestimated.

Evidence steadily accumulating from studies in a range of private and public sector organizations suggest that any professionally designed assessment procedure should more than pay for itself in terms of the subsequent performance of selected personnel (Boudreau, 1989). Usually the investment in selection is returned several times over. Furthermore, an analysis by Cascio and Silbey (1979) of the potential benefits of ACs demonstrated that AC cost has a relatively small impact on the overall balance between costs and benefits. In effect, where one has a job with reasonable scope for above-average and below-average performance, and where one has an AC which produces moderately good predictions of job performance, the monetary benefits of using the AC as opposed to some unsophisticated method like interviews are likely to be very great. Typically these benefits will be so large that AC cost is almost insignificant in relative terms.

CREDIBILITY AND PERCEIVED FAIRNESS OF ASSESSMENT CENTRES

Another benefit of professionally designed ACs is that they tend to be rated highly by both candidates (Thornton and Byham, 1982) and assessors (Dodd, 1977). This is particularly important where an organization uses an AC to make selections from among existing staff. A well-designed AC can increase morale and confidence in the selection system. A good example is wartime WOSBs where, as described earlier, the AC was successful in winning confidence at all levels within the army, with beneficial effects on application rates and recruitment. A similar process probably occurs in modern in-company ACs: well-run and well-designed ACs can improve confidence, morale and turnover, though poorly conceived ACs can have negative effects.

Not only are ACs rated favourably by those involved, but evidence from the US suggests that, compared with other selection methods, the courts are more likely to accept ACs as fair in the face of allegations of unfair discrimination (on the basis of sex, ethnic origin, etc.). Probably because properly designed simulations resemble, to some degree, job tasks, those observing ACs are more likely to regard them as fair. Another selection procedure which may be equally predictive but does not bear such resemblance to the job (e.g. pencil-and-paper ability testing) may be regarded as less fair. The United States is as yet the only country where ACs have been the subject of detailed legal scrutiny. But the underlying lesson is relevant elsewhere.

REALISTIC JOB PREVIEWS AND REDUCTIONS IN WASTAGE

The job-relatedness of ACs has a further advantage. When candidates are given the opportunity, via simulations, to find out how well they might fare in a job, they are more likely to self-select before joining the organization, and less likely to resign after joining (Robertson and Kandola, 1982). Technically this process is known as 'realistic job preview' (RJP).

Not all kinds of RJP have an effect on self-selection (Guzzo, Jette and Katzell, 1985). Makin and Robertson (1983) draw a distinction between the RJP which requires active participation—e.g. a simulation of an actual try-out on the job—and the RJP which is more passive—e.g. a video, a booklet, or a job visit. Technically, active RJPs are termed 'experiential' and passive RJPs 'vicarious'. An advantage of experiential RJPs is that the individuals learn not only about the job, but also about their ability to perform in job-like situations; this appears effective in helping them make balanced decisions about whether or not they are suited to an organization. However, vicarious RJPs assume that individuals already have some realistic understanding of their own abilities, and that the main purpose is to provide knowledge about the nature of the job. This assumption appears to be mistaken in many cases, and the evidence is that vicarious RJPs have little effect on self-selection. Further discussion of RJPs and self-assessment may be found in Chapters 3.6 and 3.8.

CAREER DEVELOPMENT AND FEEDBACK OF ASSESSMENT RESULTS

In recent years there has been a considerable growth of interest in the use of ACs for career development as well as for selection. This is logical since ACs enable rich and detailed descriptions of individual strengths and weaknesses, which can be used to identify development needs. Moreover, since many ACs are used to select from among existing employees, it makes sense for organizations to maximize use of the information obtained. There seems to be a move away from using ACs to make formal pass/fail decisions towards identifying career paths appropriate to individuals' abilities and needs. Sometimes ACs are used completely outside the context of selection, for example, to set learning objectives prior to a course of training. The term 'development centre' is used occasionally instead of 'assessment centre' to reflect the different emphasis.

For self-development to take place, good quality feedback is required from the AC. A wide variety of approaches to feedback have been developed by different organizations (Slivinski and Bourgeois, 1977). However, experience of those involved in this area suggests some basic ground-rules. Points which I would highlight are:

1. Good quality feedback consumes considerable time and resources. But hastily or ineptly given feedback can be counter-productive, and possibly worse than no feedback at all.

2. Feedback needs to be a team effort. Though the feedback itself may be one to one, those responsible for the candidate's future development, including the line manager and personnel manager, should be closely involved in outlining options and implementing decisions.

3. Giving constructive feedback requires particular kinds of interpersonal skills, and those doing this job should be trained and/or carefully selected.

4. The person giving the feedback should have observed at least some of the candidate's performance. This could either be by observing the AC directly or by studying performance second hand, through written materials, videos and so on.

5. Feedback should ideally be face to face, with the full involvement of the candidate, and it should focus directly on behaviour observed in the AC. A general comment such as 'your communication skills were weak' is of less use than drawing the candidate's attention to an instance where impact was marred by poor communication, and working out some alternative approaches.

6. Behavioural feedback should be linked to some plan of action which will allow the candidate scope for new learning and development, or for capitalizing on existing strengths. This could mean, for example, a course of training, a contract with the line manager, or a change of job within the organization.

CONCLUSIONS AND SCOPE FOR FURTHER DEVELOPMENT

The main thrust of this chapter has been to show that ACs, when properly designed and operated, can be highly accurate as methods of assessment and selection, with many useful spin-offs for perceived fairness, self-selection, career development and so on. However, it would be wrong to leave the impression that all is right with AC technology. In some areas scope remains for refinement and improvement. For example, though utility calculations show that the benefits of using ACs almost always outweigh the costs, there is also evidence that duplication of what is measured can result in inefficiency (Feltham, 1988b). The only accurate way to establish whether this is the case for any particular AC is by detailed research into the validity of the component parts of the procedure—research which is rarely done. Similarly, more attention should be given to methods for improving the consistency of assessments resulting from individual simulations. Some research has found marked differences in the assessments made of the same individuals in different but similarly structured simulations (e.g. Bycio, Alvares and Hahn, 1987). One way to counter this may be more rigour in the standardization of simulation content and assessment procedures (e.g. Schmitt and Ostroff, 1986).

None of this alters the main overall conclusion—that ACs are currently among the best of the methods of assessment and selection available to personnel managers. Scope still remains for research and development to increase the validity and value of the approach.

REFERENCES AND FURTHER READING

Anstey, E. (1977). A 30-year follow-up of the CSSB procedure, with lessons for the future, *Journal of Occupational Psychology*, **50**, 149–59.

Bedford, T. (1987). New developments in assessment centre design, *Guidance and Assessment Review*, **3**(3), 2–3.

Boudreau, J.W. (1989). Selection utility analysis: a review and agenda for future research, in M. Smith and I.T. Robertson (eds). *Advances in Selection and Assessment*. John Wiley, New York.

Bray, D.W., Campbell, R.J., and Grant, D.L. (1974). *Formative Years in Business: A long-term AT&T study of managerial lives*. Wiley, New York.

Bray, D.W., and Grant, D.L. (1966). The assessment center in the measurement of potential for business management, *Psychological Monographs*, **80**, 1–27.

Bycio, P., Alvares, K.M., and Hahn, J. (1987). Situational specificity in assessment center ratings: A confirmatory factor analysis, *Journal of Applied Psychology*, **72**, 463–74.

Cascio, W.F., and Silbey, V. (1979). Utility of the assessment center as a selection device, *Journal of Applied Psychology*, **64**, 107–18.

Crooks, L.A. (1977). The selection and development of assessment center techniques, in J.L. Moses and W.C. Byham (eds). *Applying the Assessment Center Method*. Pergamon Press, New York, pp. 69–87.

Dodd, W.E. (1977). Attitudes toward assessment center programs, in J.L. Moses and W.C. Byham (eds). *Applying the Assessment Center Method*. Pergamon Press, New York, pp. 161–83.

Dulewicz, V., Fletcher, C., and Wood, P. (1983). A study of the internal validity of an assessment centre and of participants' background characteristics and attitudes: a comparison between British and American findings, *Journal of Assessment Center Technology*, **6**, 15–24.

Feltham, R. (1988a). Assessment center decision making: judgemental versus mechanical, *Journal of Occupational Psychology*, **61**, 237–41.

Feltham, R. (1988b). Validity of a police assessment center: A 1–19 year follow-up, *Journal of Occupational Psychology*, **61**, 129–44.

Fletcher, C. (1982). Assessment Centres, in D. Mackenzie-Davey and M. Harris (eds), *Judging People: a guide to orthodox and unorthodox methods of assessment*. McGraw-Hill, London, pp. 42–54.

Gaugler, B.B., Rosenthal, D.B., Thornton, G.C., and Bentson, C. (1987). Meta-analysis of assessment center validity, *Journal of Applied Psychology*, **72**, 493–511.

Guzzo, R.A., Jette, R.D., and Katzell, R.A. (1985). The effects of psychologically based intervention programs on worker productivity: A meta-analysis, *Personnel Psychology*, **38**, 275–91.

Handyside, J., and Duncan, C. (1954). Four years later: a follow-up of an experiment in selecting supervisors, *Occupational Psychology*, **28**, 9–23.

Harris, H. (1949). *The Group Approach to Leadership Testing*. Routledge and Kegan Paul, London.

McConnell, J.J., and Parker, T.C. (1972). An assessment center program for multi-organizational use, *Training and Development Journal*, March, 6–14.

MacKinnon, D.W. (1977). From selecting spies to selecting managers, in J.L. Moses and W.C. Byham (eds). *Applying the Assessment Center Method*. Pergamon Press, New York, pp. 13–30.

Makin, P.J., and Robertson, I.T. (1983). Self-assessment, realistic job previews and occupational decisions, *Personnel Review*, **12**(3), 21–5.

Moses, J.L. (1973). The development of an assessment center for the early identification of supervisory potential, *Personnel Psychology*, **26**, 569–80.

Office of Strategic Services Assessment Staff (1948). *Assessment of Men: Selection of Personnel for the Office of Strategic Services*. Rinehart, New York.

Robertson, I.T., and Kandola, R.S. (1982). Work sample tests: validity, adverse impact and applicant reaction, *Journal of Occupational Psychology*, **55**, 171–83.

Robertson, I., Gratton, L., and Sharpley, D. (1987). The psychometric properties and design of managerial assessment centres: dimensions into exercises won't go, *Journal of Occupational Psychology*, **60**, 187–95.

Russell, C.J. (1985). Individual decision processes in an assessment center, *Journal of Applied Psychology*, **70**, 737–46.

Sackett, P.R., and Dreher, G.F. (1982). Constructs and assessment center dimensions: some troubling empirical findings, *Journal of Applied Psychology*, **67**, 401–10.

Sackett, P.R., and Hakel, M.D. (1979). Temporal stability and individual differences in using assessment information to form overall ratings, *Organizational Behaviour and Human Performance*, **23**, 120–37.

Sackett, P.R., and Wilson, M.A. (1982). Factors affecting the consensus judgment process in managerial assessment centers, *Journal of Applied Psychology*, **67**, 10–17.

Schmitt, N., and Ostroff, C. (1986). Operationalizing the 'behavioral consistency' approach: selection test development based on a content-oriented strategy, *Personnel Psychology*, **39**, 91–108.

Schmitt, N., Gooding, R.Z., Noe, R.A., and Kirsch, M. (1984). Meta-analyses of validity studies published between 1964 and 1982 and the investigation of study characteristics, *Personnel Psychology*, **37**, 408–22.

Slivinski, L.W., and Bourgeois, R.P. (1977). Feedback of assessment center results, in J.L. Moses and W.C. Byham (eds). *Applying the Assessment Center Method*. Pergamon Press, New York, pp. 143–59.

Thornton, G.C., and Byham, W.C. (1982). *Assessment Centers and Managerial Performance*. Academic Press, London.

Vernon, P.E. (1950). The validation of Civil Sevice Selection Board procedures, *Occupational Psychology*, **24**, 75–95.

Vernon, P.E., and Parry, J.B. (1949). *Personnel Selection in the British Forces*. University of London Press, London.

Wiggins, J.S. (1973). *Personality and Prediction: Principles of Personality Assessment*, Addison-Wesley, Reading, Mass.

Wingrove, J., Jones, A., and Herriot, P. (1985). The predictive validity of pre- and post-discussion assessment centre ratings, *Journal of Occupational Psychology*, **58**, 189–92.

Chapter 3.8

Self and Peer Assessment

PAUL DOBSON

Centre for Personnel Research and Enterprise Development, The City University Business School, Northampton Square, London EC1V 0HB, UK

This chapter outlines the nature and psychological basis, reviews psychometric evidence, and makes recommendations for the use of both self- and peer assessment methods in selection.

SELF-ASSESSMENT

For many years self-reports have been used to measure an individual's personality, interests, attitudes and values. More recently, they have been used to assess an individual's abilities, skills, knowledge and performance. The same process underlies the measurement of these differing characteristics, and therefore some of the research reviewed here is relevant to all self-report measures. However, as personality, interest, attitude and value self-report measures have been reviewed in Chapter 3.4, we will concentrate on the use of self-assessments of ability, skills, knowledge and performance in selection.

The nature of self-assessment

The method of self-assessment is self-explanatory. The individual is asked to disclose his or her own assessment of his or her own competence at some specified ability, skill or knowledge. Typically, this is done relative to a standard, for example, 'How accurate are you at typing when compared with other typists that you know. Above average, average, or below average?'

Self-assessments are easy to obtain, relatively inexpensive and unlikely to be challenged by applicants as being an unfair selection practice.

Handbook of Assessment in Organizations   Edited by P. Herriot

The validity of self-assessment

Very few studies have been undertaken which investigate the validity of self-assessment as a selection method. Reilly and Chao (1982) review ten studies that they consider are directly relevant to the use of self-assessment in selection. While a number of these studies report positive results, only three studies include validity coefficients with overall criteria. Reilly and Chao calculate an average weighted validity coefficient of 0.15 (total sample size (N) = 545). They conclude that based on the research evidence available, self-assessment cannot be recommended as a promising alternative selection method.

Mabe and West (1982) review the use of self-assessment in the measurement of skills, abilities and knowledge. Fifty-five studies are included in their review, and an average validity coefficient of 0.29 is reported. Their analysis reveals that four conditions improve the accuracy of self-assessments: the expectation that the self-assessment will be validated; instructions using social comparison terminology; experience of self-assessment; and instructions of anonymity. In addition, high intelligence, high achievement status and internal locus of control were associated with more accurate evaluations. However, while the research is moderately encouraging, it must be noted that few of the studies actually used self-assessment for selection. Given the impact of subject motivation on the likely accuracy of self-assessment (see section below on psychological basis), these studies almost certainly overestimate the validity that would have been obtained had the self-assessments been undertaken in a selection context. Hunter and Hunter (1984) consider four studies that actually used self-assessments in validation research. They find that the average validity of self-assessments across these four studies is zero and conclude, 'Self-assessment appears to have no validity in operational settings' (p. 83).

The leniency and fakability of self-assessment

Thornton (1980) states 'When used for gathering information at the time of selection, self-appraisals are likely to lead to inflated statements of qualification' (p. 269). Leniency may result either because individuals possess overly favourable perceptions of their competence, or because they fake a favourable response.

Meyer (1980) found that when individuals are asked to make self-assessments by comparing their own performance with the performance of others in a comparable job, at least 40 per cent of the respondents rated themselves in the top 10 per cent, and usually only 1 or 2 per cent rated themselves below average. Meyer considers that these findings reflect 'self-delusions' due to the need to maintain a positively valued self. Wesman (1952) compared the responses of a group of students who completed a personality questionnaire on two occasions a week apart. On one occasion the students were instructed to complete the questionnaire as though they were applying for the job of a salesman, and on the other occasion they were instructed to report as though they were applying for the job of a librarian. Wesman found conspicuous differences between the two administrations. Green (1951) found that job applicants do fake personality test responses. The scores obtained from a group of job applicants were compared with the scores of a comparable group of job holders who were tested for research purposes only. Under these contrasting motivating conditions, the score for the two groups differed in the expected direction.

Self-assessments may reflect an accurate or inflated self-perception, or a response bias. As these are difficult to distinguish, the interpretation of all self-report measures is problematical. Anderson, Warner and Spencer (1984) have developed devices to increase the probability of detecting the faker in self-report measures. They report that their procedures were effective in reducing inflation bias and have the potential for enhancing test validity. However, given the low base for the validity of self-assessment in selection, one wonders whether there are many situations in which the adoption of such complex procedures is worth while.

The psychological basis for self-assessment

In order to understand the difficulties associated with the use of self-assessment in selection, it is important to distinguish between self-knowledge and self-disclosure: for what we say about ourselves is not necessarily what we believe to be true. The factors which underlie the development of self-knowledge and those which influence self-disclosure, determine the accuracy of self-assessments and thus their likely validity. A simplified model of the basis of self-assessment is given in Figure 1.

Our beliefs regarding our competencies, or self-efficacy (Bandura, 1977), are largely gained from observing and evaluating our own behaviour and its effects. In order to learn and adapt effectively to our environment, we need knowledge about our own capabilities and characteristics which is essentially accurate. We also have a need to maintain a positive self-image, self-esteem or feelings of self-worth. For example, Mischel (1979) found that a clinically depressed group of subjects had more accurate but less positive perceptions of their social competence than a normal control group. The latter reported unrealistic self-enhanced self-assessments. Thus, the potential conflict between the need for accurate self-knowledge and the need for positive self-knowledge appears to be resolved, by the majority, by slightly distorting or inflating one's self-evaluations. This is particularly likely to be the case with regard to one's physical attractiveness, intelligence, sexual competence, social status, etc. That is, with regard to issues which the individual considers to be important or finds ego-involving. It

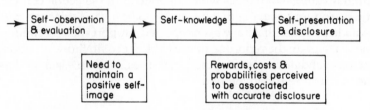

Figure 1   A simplified model of the basis of self-assessment

would seem likely therefore that most people possess a fairly accurate, if at times slightly inflated, view of their capabilities and characteristics (see Meyer, 1980, above).

When self-assessment is used in selection the important question would not appear to be whether or not an individual has accurate self-knowledge, but rather the circumstances under which he or she will disclose this information or deliberately distort it. Consequently, the most appropriate model for understanding self-assessment used in selection would appear to be a motivational one, where the choice between accurate or inflated self-disclosure is governed by the individual's perception of the expected rewards and costs associated with the alternative courses of action. On the basis of such a model it can be inferred that the probability of an inflated self-assessment increases when: honesty is not valued; it is believed that an inflated self-assessment increases the probability of being selected; the job concerned is highly valued; or there are no alternative jobs available. Similarly, the probability of an accurate self-assessment increases when: honesty is valued; it is believed that an inflated self-assessment does not increase the probability of selection; the self-assessment is likely to be validated; penalties are incurred for deception; the job is not highly valued; or alternative employment is available.

As far as the validity of self-assessment as a selection device is concerned, it is of no consequence whether all respondents make accurate, or all make inflated, self-assessments: the rank-ordering is not altered. What is of consequence, however, is when different individuals are motivated to respond with varying degrees of accuracy. The work of Mabe and West (1982) suggests that there are significant individual differences operating which are likely to invalidate the method and discriminate against those who are intelligent, of high achievement status and self-esteem, just as it may work against those who value honesty. In such situations the validity of the method will suffer and, unless steps are taken to validate the self-reports, unfair discrimination seems inevitable.

Conclusion

Previous authors who have included validities obtained outside the realities of the selection context in their reviews of self-assessment, have most certainly missed the crucial point regarding its nature. While self-assessment can make a valuable contribution to decisions in the context of placement, identification of training needs, management development, training and counselling, it is prey to the poignant motivational dynamics which operate in the selection context. There is very little reason for believing that it is likely to be a valid selection method, and the few validity studies that have been reported support such reasoning. With the exception of its use in the reporting of verifiable fact or in those situations where it can be cross-validated against other measures, self-assessment has little to recommend it as a selection method.

Realistic job previews

The previous section concludes that self-assessment is unlikely to provide useful information on which the organization can base selection decisions. However, self-assessment may allow applicants to make a better selection of organizations.

Our decision to apply for a job and, if it is offered, whether or not to accept it, involves some self-assessment and a comparison of our abilities with job requirements. Organizational entry is a mutual choice process. This fact has led a few researchers to investigate the value of the Realistic Job Preview (RJP) in selection. The RJP assumes that the individual has a realistic view of his or her own abilities, interests, etc., and it therefore seeks to promote a good fit by providing the individual with a realistic view of the nature of the job. RJPs are carried out at an early stage in selection, typically as part of the screening procedure. They are most suited to situations where the employer is faced with large numbers of acceptable applicants.

Most studies of RJPs have used vicarious methods to preview the job, for example, booklets, an audio-visual presentation, a job visit or talk with a current employee. A few studies have used more experiential RJPs where the applicant undertakes a work sample or spends a period of time actually doing the job. For example, Downs, Farr and Colbeck (1978) used a trainability test for sewing machinists, and most potential officers in the British Army spend a period on attachment to a regiment. Williams (1984) has suggested that assessment centres have a potential role in facilitating self-selection. When experiential methods are used the organization can make assessments of the individual's performance, while the individual can make assessments of his or her capability to do the job and whether it will satisfy his or her needs. Clearly the experiential RJPs involve the use of considerable resources and in many situations would be impracticable as a screening mechanism.

Little attention has been paid to whether self-selection results in employees with more suitable skills. Instead, the discussion in favour of RJPs has concentrated on whether they result in increased commitment and job satisfaction, and reduced labour turnover.

Premack and Wanous (1985) report a meta-analysis of 21 RJP studies. They conclude that overall the influence of RJPs on new employee perceptions, attitudes and job behaviour is modest. More specifically, they found that RJPs tended to lower the initial expectations of individuals about the job and the organization; increased the drop-out rate prior to selection; slightly increased level of organizational commitment and job satisfaction; reduced labour turnover; and, when audio-visual methods were used in the RJP, resulted in improved job performance. They note that RJPs are likely to have utility for organizations when labour turnover is high. This is true, but most likely when unrealistic preconceptions of the nature of the job or organization are a significant determinant of the labour turnover.

While the logic behind the use of RJPs is attractive, there is a need for some purpose-designed research on an operating system. Such research needs to determine not only the potential benefits of RJPs, but also their potential costs to employers. For example, what happens to the better candidates who typically have higher aspirations and more employment opportunities? Are RJPs appropriate in highly competitive labour markets? Under what circumstances are alternative strategies such as job re-design or 'key-man' bonuses more effective in promoting commitment?

PEER ASSESSMENT

Peer assessment has been used to identify the potential, promotability and team membership of, and—but less frequently—to select external candidates for, bomber and tank crews, scientists and technicians, pharmacists, insurance agents, supervisors, middle and senior managers, secretaries, chemical, steel and factory workers, police and army officers, army cadets, candidates and trainees, naval recruits and ratings, schoolchildren and civil servants. A considerable amount of research has been undertaken into the psychometric properties, use and acceptability of peer assessment, and major reviews are given by Mouton, Blake and Fruchter (1955), and Kane and Lawler (1978), and meta-analyses by Hunter and Hunter (1984) and Schmitt *et al.* (1984).

The nature of peer assessment

Peer assessment is characterized by the existence of an identifiable group of individuals of equal formal status who have had the opportunity to observe each other's behaviour, and who make separate judgements of, or choices between, one another, on an explicit criterion.

The fact that peer assessment requires the existence of a group of individuals who know each other is the reason why peer assessment is rarely appropriate for the selection of external applicants. The major exception is their use in assessment centres used for such a purpose. It should be noted that peer assessment involves pooled individual judgements; not judgements which are arrived at through a process of group discussion. Given the apparent superiority of statistical over clinical combination of information (as found in the literature on impression formation and assessment centre decision making), it is likely that the statistical combination of judgements is a significant contributor to the validity of peer assessment methods.

Three different peer assessment methods have been used:

1. Peer nomination — each member of the group nominates and ranks a specified number or proportion of group members as being high or low on some characteristic or capability. For example:

   'Choose the three group members whom you would most prefer as your co-pilot.' 1st _____ 2nd _____ 3rd _____

   'Least-prefer' or negative nominations are generally inadvisable for they may reflect intra-group rivalry or may elicit hostile reactions. They can also result in a less valid measure and lower inter-rater agreement.

2. Peer ranking — each member of the group ranks all the other members, from highest to lowest, on some characteristic or capability. For example, for a group of eight:

'Rank order (from 1 to 8, where 1 = greatest and 8 = lowest) all the members of your group in terms of their contribution to the solution of the group problem. (Do not include yourself, and ties are not allowed.)'

Peer rankings are the most discriminating of the alternative peer assessment methods.

3. Peer ratings — each member of the group rates all the other members on some characteristic or capability. For example:

'Rate all the other members of your group on the following scales (exclude yourself).'

Peer ratings' use of rating scales makes them susceptible to the response biases of level, spread and correlation as outlined by Cronbach (1955).

Normally, the assessors are not allowed to nominate, rank or rate themselves. Consequently individual scores are given by summing the $N - 1$ assessments and then dividing by $N - 1$ (Where N = number of persons in the group being rated). If peer nominations have been used, this procedure is unsatisfactory when individuals from groups of differing size are to be compared. In such cases, it is preferable to request nominations as a fixed proportion of group size. Alternatively, statistical corrections for variation in group size can be applied (see Amir, Kovarsky and Sharon, 1970; Willingham, 1959). When choosing between the alternative peer assessment methods it is worth while to bear in mind the fact that peer nominations present a number of statistical problems not shared by ratings and rankings. Further, they are likely to result in a very skewed distribution with only a small number of group members receiving nominations. However, rankings and ratings are not suitable for use with large groups.

Reliability

If one subjects a peer assessment method to a re-test design and finds considerable change in the assessments over a period of a few weeks, should one conclude that the method is unreliable or that it is unstable? Has the change resulted from the differing opportunities of assessors to observe? Has the change resulted from changes in the behaviour of the assessees? Or, has the change resulted from no identifiable cause and thus it can be assumed to be a random effect? Only in this last situation is reliability—as an entity that limits validity—being measured.

In order for the reliability of peer assessment methods to be estimated, an experimental design is required that enables these various effects to be partitioned; the analysis of variance can then be used to estimate the reliability of the method (see Winer, 1962). Although it was pointed out many years ago that the reliability designs and statistics developed by the capacity testers (see Chapter 3.2) were inappropriate when applied to peer assessment (see, for example,

Pepinsky, 1949), researchers have continued to use them. The 'reliability' coefficients reported in the literature are most sensibly interpreted literally as measures which either reflect the amount of agreement between the raters, or reflect the amount of change in assessments over time. In neither case do the coefficients indicate necessarily any limit to the attainable validity of the measure.

Given the above observations the interpretation of the literature on the 'reliability' of peer assessment is quite difficult. However, the level of inter-rater agreement and stability found appears to vary with: the length of time the group has been together—older groups showing more agreement and stability than new groups; the dimension being assessed—there being more agreement and stability with assessments of, for example, numerical ability than with leadership or friendship choices; the peer assessment method used—peer nominations showing higher levels of agreement and stability earlier in the group's history than rankings or ratings.

Validity

Studies of the validity of peer assessment published over the last 40 years have repeatedly reported impressive validity coefficients obtained in a wide variety of settings and across a range of different criteria. The results of three recent reviews are given in Table 1.

An analysis of the 39 separate studies known to the present author produced average sample-weighted validity coefficients of 0.50 for peer nominations (N = 13 169); 0.43 for peer ranking (N = 608); and 0.39 for peer ratings (N = 2263). Considerable variation was found with different criteria. Analysis of the peer nomination sample revealed validity coefficients of: 0.60 for promotional criteria (N = 5647); 0.45 for supervisor ratings (N = 3700); 0.42 for performance criteria (N = 3098). The analysis suggests that nominations and rankings are typically more

Table 1   The validity of peer assessment

Author	Peer method	N	Criterion	Validity
Reilly and Chao (1982)	All combined	3 774	Performance ratings	0.37
		4 742	Promotion	0.51
		3 682	Training	0.31
		12 749	Overall average =	0.41
Hunter and Hunter (1984)	All combined	8 202	Supervisor ratings	0.49
		6 909	Promotion	0.49
		1 409	Training	0.36
		16 520	Overall average =	0.48
Schmitt *et al.* (1984)	All combined	1 389	Performance ratings	0.32
		4 224	Promotion	0.51
		301	Wages	0.21
		6 620	Overall average =	0.43

valid than peer ratings, a conclusion supported by those studies that have compared the different methods directly (see, for example, Love, 1981).

Of practical concern is the stage in the group's life at which assessments should be made. Hollander (1965) found that peer nominations made in the third week of military officer training correlated 0.40 with ratings of success as an officer three years later. Assessments made much earlier are feasible if the group members have had adequate opportunity to observe the relevant behaviour. Thus peer assessments can be made during a one-day assessment centre as long as the appropriate behaviours have been elicited by the group exercises.

Finally, the research suggests quite clearly that validity is likely to be enhanced if there is a good correspondence between the nature of the peer assessments made and that of the criterion. If one wants to predict who is going to be the top salesperson in three years' time, ask the peers that question; not who they think is most likeable or charismatic. Because peers assess each other rather than themselves, questions with high face validity can be asked directly with relatively little fear of faked responses.

Psychological basis of peer assessment

Peer assessment is the application of the sociometric methods of Jacob Moreno to human resource management. The key to the validity of peer assessment is the role of the group members as participating and evaluating actors. As a consequence, assessors are able to make attributional judgements which take situational factors into account; assessors are part of the social milieu and possess a greater empathy and understanding of the group dynamics than outside observers; and they are likely to observe more open and candid behaviour than that presented to superiors.

The validity of individual judgements is dependent upon the opportunities that the assessors have had to observe relevant behaviours. Validity is likely to be enhanced if the dimensions of assessment are relevant to the group experience, and if group experiences are structured to ensure relevance to assessments. There are a number of difficulties associated with the use of individual subjective judgements as the basis of assessment. Firstly, individual judges are prone to stereotyped responses and individual bias. However, peer assessments use averaged scores which are likely to moderate individual bias and error. Secondly, individual choices and assessments are correlated with friendships. This would appear to be inevitable as knowledge, interaction and friendship are causally related. Nevertheless, Love (1981) found that validity was not adversely affected when friendship was held constant. As Hollander (1956) has pointed out, friendship may frequently be the result of high status on attributes, rather than the determinant of ratings of high status. Further, given that social and interpersonal skills are invariably implicated as determinants of occupational success, it would seem likely that popularity is a valid dimension in its own right. The crucial question for peer assessment is whether it is anything more than a popularity contest. The answer would appear to be that it is, for while there is every evidence that assessments are related to friendship, there is little evidence that this invalidates the procedure. It is probably a related fact that peer choices tend to be made within race, sex and socio-economic subgroups. Lewin and Zwany (1976) state that racial bias is generally to be expected in peer evaluations. Where practicable, homogeneous groups should be used.

Acceptability

The major problem associated with the use of peer assessment is that, in some situations, participants do not like evaluating each other. Nominations, rankings and ratings have been found to create quite strong adverse reactions, when used in selection or placement, among such groups as college faculty, military and police officers. As Kane and Lawler (1978) state 'Peer evaluations seem more prone to failing to obtain the cooperation of their users than most other methods . . . Peer assessments can easily infringe on areas that will either raise havoc with the group or cause resistance to making the assessments' (p. 583). In contrast, Roadman (1964) found that 98 per cent of a management sample considered peer feedback to be of value when used in career counselling. It would seem likely that the acceptability of peer assessment is dependent upon the situation in which it is used and the use to which it is put. It is acceptable as feedback given in a supportive climate but unacceptable as an evaluation used for the identification of potential or for selection.

A number of hypotheses have been put forward to explain the adverse reactions of participants to peer assessment used in personnel administration. Namely, that peer assessment is perceived to be no more than a popularity contest; that the procedure involves 'cutting one's buddy's throat'; that it represents a shift in political power contrary to the organizational culture; that it has a negative impact upon personal relationships and group morale; and that peer evaluation is inherently more threatening than other forms of assessment.

The avoidance of the use of negative nominations and friendship evaluations may moderate some of the objections to the procedure, as may its use in cultures that are compatible and supportive. However, the adverse reactions generated by peer assessment are unlikely to be totally overcome and thus severely limit its use as a selection method.

Finally, although it should be obvious, it is worth pointing out that it is extremely difficult for individuals to withdraw from a peer assessment procedure. Evaluations of the individual's characteristics are made by the peers not by the individual. Thus, while the individual can refuse to make assessments, this does not prevent the individual being assessed. Therefore, peer assessment methods should include a procedure whereby participants can withdraw entirely from the assessment should they choose to do so.

Conclusion

Although peer assessment is a very valid method of assessment with a valuable role to play in management development centres and in identifying team composition of, for example, tank and aircrews, it is of limited use in selection.

Because group members have to observe each other on relevant dimensions the method is, with the exception of its inclusion in an assessment centre, not appropriate for the selection of external job applicants. Further, because the method can be racially and sexually biased, it is only appropriate for use with homogeneous groups. Finally, because the method, when used in selection, frequently elicits strong adverse reactions from participants, it is likely to be suitable in relatively few political and cultural settings.

REFERENCES AND FURTHER READING

Amir, Y., Kovarsky, Y., and Sharon, S. (1970). Peer nominations as a predictor of multistage promotions in a ramified organisation, *Journal of Applied Psychology*, **54**, 462–9.

Anderson, C.D., Warner, J.L., and Spencer, C.C. (1984). Inflation bias in self-assessment examinations: implications for valid employee selection, *Journal of Applied Psychology*, **69**, 574–80.

Bandura, A. (1977). Self-efficacy: towards a unifying theory of behavioural change, *Psychological Review*, **84**(2), 191–215.

Cronbach, L.J. (1955). Processes affecting scores on 'understanding of others' and 'assumed similarity', *Psychological Bulletin*, **52**, 177–93.

Downs, S., Farr, R.M., and Colbeck, L. (1978). Self-appraisal: a convergence of selection and guidance, *Journal of Occupational Psychology*, **51**, 271–8.

Green, R.F. (1951). Does a selection situation induce testees to bias their answers on interest and temperament tests? *Educational and Psychological Measurement*, **11**, 503–15.

Hollander, E.P. (1956). The friendship factor in peer nominations, *Personnel Psychology*, **9**, 435–47.

Hollander, E.P. (1965). Validity of peer nominations in predicting a distant performance criterion, *Journal of Applied Psychology*, **49**, 434–8.

Hunter, J.E., and Hunter, R.F. (1984). Validity and utility of alternative predictors of job performance, *Psychological Bulletin*, **96**, 72–98.

Kane, J.S., and Lawler, E.E. (1978). Methods of peer assessment, *Psychological Bulletin*, **85**, 555–86.

Lewin, A.Y., and Zwany, A. (1976). Peer nominations: a model, literature critique and a paradigm for research, *Personnel Psychology*, **29**, 423–47.

Love, K.G. (1981). Comparison of peer assessment methods: reliability, validity, friendship bias and user reactions, *Journal of Applied Psychology*, **66**, 451–7.

Mabe, P.A. III and West, S.G. (1982). Validity of self-evaluation of ability: a review and meta-analysis, *Journal of Applied Psychology*, **67**, 280–96.

Meyer, H.H. (1980). Self-appraisal of job performance, *Personnel Psychology*, **33**, 291–5.

Mischel, W. (1979). On the interface of cognition and personality: beyond the person–situation debate, *American Psychologist*, **34**(9), 740–54.

Mouton, J.S., Blake, R.R., and Fruchter, B. (1955). The validity of sociometric responses, *Sociometry*, **18**, 181–206.

Pepinsky, P.N. (1949). The meaning of 'validity' and 'reliability' as applied to sociometric tests. *Journal of Educational and Psychological Measurement*, **9**, 39–49.

Premack, S.L., and Wanous, J.P. (1985). A meta-analysis of realistic job preview experiments, *Personnel Psychology*, **38**, 706–21.

Reilly, R.R., and Chao, G.T. (1982). Validity and fairness of some alternative employee-selection procedures, *Personnel Psychology*, **35**, 1–62.

Roadman, H.E. (1964). An industrial use of peer ratings, *Journal of Applied Psychology*, **48**, 211–14.

Schmitt, N., Gooding, R.Z., Noe, R.A., and Kirsch, M. (1984). Meta-analysis of validity studies published between 1964 and 1982 and the investigation of study characteristics. *Personnel Psychology*, **37**, 407–22.

Thornton, G.C. III (1980). Psychometric properties of self appraisals of job performance, *Personnel Psychology*, **33**, 263–71.

Wesman, A.G. (1952). Faking personality test scores in a simulated employment situation, *Journal of Applied Psychology*, **36**, 112–13.

Williams, A.P.O. (1984). The neglected process of self-selection. Paper given to the 26th Conference of the Military Testing Association, Munich.

Willingham, W.W. (1959). On deriving standard scores for peer nominations with subgroups of unequal size, *Psychological Reports*, **5**, 397–403.

Winer, B.J. (1962). *Statistical Principles in Experimental Design*. McGraw-Hill, New York.

Chapter 3.9

The Selection Interview

PETER HERRIOT

*Department of Occupational Psychology, Birkbeck College, University of London,
Malet Street, London WC1E 7HX, UK.*

MOST INTERVIEWS ARE POOR SELECTION TOOLS

The focus of this section of the book is on the tools of selection. I will start by
evaluating the interview as a selection instrument, but will not restrict the scope of
this chapter within these confines. Rather, I will look at the potential functions the
interview might have in the design of recruitment procedures as a whole.

First, then, how good as a selection tool is the interview? Using traditional
psychometric criteria, this question can be rephrased as:

– How reliable are interviews?
– How valid are they?
– How fair are they?

Before we can answer these questions, however, we have to clarify what it is we
are talking about. Elsewhere (Herriot, 1987), I have proposed that the term
'interview' is really a generic word which covers a wide variety of procedures. At
the very least, we need to distinguish two forms. First, we have the typical two-
way interchange which is dynamic in nature. The interviewer may have an overall
agenda of areas he or she wishes to cover, but the order in which they are covered
and the questions which are framed depend upon the responses of the interviewee. The second form of interview consists of a set of questions which the
interviewer asks of all interviewees. These questions are often based on a job
analysis, and ask the interviewees what they would do in certain job-related
situations. Alternatively, they ask about details of the interviewees' present or

Assessment and Selection in Organizations.   Edited by P. Herriot.
© 1989 John Wiley & Sons Ltd

previous experience and circumstances (biodata) which have been shown to relate to subsequent job performance.

These two forms of interview differ markedly in their psychometric properties. The dynamic form has a very poor record indeed. Meta-analyses demonstrate that validity seldom rises above 0.20 (Hunter and Hunter, 1984; Schmitt *et al.*, 1984), while reliability is in general far lower than is usually considered necessary for a psychometric instrument (Reilly and Chao, 1982). As far as fairness is concerned, Arvey (1979), and Reilly and Chao (1982) demonstrate clear evidence of bias. Women tend to be discriminated against, with a great deal of evidence that women with exactly the same credentials as men come off worse. However, this effect is moderated by the nature of the job for which they are being selected. It is only for jobs which are considered masculine that women are likely to be unfairly rejected. Since, however, managerial work and many professions are supposed to require masculine characteristics, women are grossly disadvantaged overall.

We should not be surprised at these findings. The unstructured interview lacks those features which typically result in reliable and valid instruments. And it contains features which make it almost inevitable that it will result in bias:

– It has no standardized format, so reliability is likely to be low.
– It is rarely based on a job analysis, so validity is likely to be low.
– It is a social encounter, so it encourages the use of stereotypes and preferences in interpersonal judgements.

Evidence to support the first two of these explanations is obtainable from the use of the second form of interview. When questions *are* predetermined and job related, reliability is much improved (Latham *et al.*, 1980). When selecting foremen, Latham and Saari (1984) obtained a validity of 0.41, while Weekley and Gier (1987) achieved a 0.45 coefficient for sales positions. These results are a vast improvement on the unstructured interview validities (see p. 498, this volume).

As for fairness, the evidence is clear that decisions derive from the impressions the interviewer forms on the basis of the interviewee's social behaviour. For example, Kinicki and Lockwood (1985) found that judged suitability of the interviewee was predicted by three factors:

– The applicant's attraction for the interviewer.
– Whether the parties were of the same or different gender.
– Interview impression.

'Interview impression' consisted of perceived ability to express ideas, job knowledge, appearance, and drive. Applicant attractiveness and interview impression were more powerful predictors than gender. Thus immediate perceptions of and attraction to the applicant determine interview outcomes. Since we tend to like those who are like ourselves, attraction to the interviewee is likely to result in organizational cloning as well as in unfair selection decisions.

WHY IS THE INTERVIEW SO POPULAR?

In a recent review of the usage of various tools of selection, Robertson and Makin (1986) found that the interview was easily the most popular and frequently used tool for managerial selection in the United Kingdom. Indeed, excluding such fringe methods as astrology and graphology, the frequency of use of various methods was in approximate inverse relationship to their validity. This is a very interesting finding indeed, which we need to explain. Why is it that organizations consistently prefer the interview to more reliable and valid instruments?

One possible answer is that they use the interview because it is a face-to-face encounter. They believe that only by these means can they discover whether the applicant is likely to fit into the organization—whether others will like him or her and will work well together. Only by these means, they believe, can they assess 'what the person is really like'. Perhaps this desired fit also explains the relative popularity of personality inventories despite their low validity.

Now this expressed need to select people who will 'fit in' is exactly what we would predict on the basis of a recent theory about organizational identity and culture. Schneider (1987) has published an article entitled 'People make the place'. What he suggests is that members of any organization resemble each other in terms of their personal characteristics. They will differ in terms of their aptitudes, with people in different functions demonstrating different aptitude profiles. But they will be similar in personality, to the extent that, for example, accountants working in the YMCA will be more like social workers in the YMCA than like accountants working in commercial organizations. Organizations keep their 'personality' by attracting people like them, by selecting them, and by attrition (those who jump the selection hoop but find they don't fit in and leave).

A second possible reason for the continued popularity of interviews is that they offer the opportunity for other things to be achieved than selection only. In particular, organizations may assume that the interview offers the opportunity for applicants to ask questions to find out more about the job. The evidence available suggests that this hope is likely to be disappointed. Herriot and Rothwell (1983) found that the applicant expects the interviewer to talk more about the organization than the interviewer expects to; and the interviewer expects the applicants to talk more about themselves than the applicants expect to. Both parties were disappointed by the reality. On the other hand, applicants may be getting other sorts of evidence. Harn and Thornton (1985) found that applicants decided whether or not to accept a job offer partly on the basis of how the interviewer behaved towards them. Specifically, the better listener the interviewer turned out to be in the interview, the more favourably his or her organization was regarded, especially if the interviewer was taken to be typical of the organization. In other words, applicants judge the organization and take their own decisions on the basis of how they are treated as much as on the basis of what they are told about it.

Informing the applicant is not the only additional function the interview may serve. It may also be used to sell the organization. In the United Kingdom many organizations are unwilling to stop sending recruiters to interview students on the so-called 'milk round' of universities. If they are not seen to be conducting interviews, they believe they will lose prestige and suffer a decrease in applications. In addition to such general promotion of the organization, the interview may also be used to *negotiate* with or persuade specific applicants whom the organization is eager to recruit.

So the interview is popular probably because it serves a variety of purposes. Its use as a tool of selection is only one of the purposes. The fact that it is really a very poor selection tool in its usual form is outweighed by its versatility. Why is such a chameleon-like procedure so attractive? Perhaps because recruiters face rapidly changing and varied recruitment needs. We can only understand the use of the interview in the light of the entire recruitment situation; and we can only understand the recruitment situation in the light of the job market.

Consider the recruitment of graduates in the United Kingdom. An organization might have a target number of graduates to recruit. Visiting universities in a sequential order, recruiters find that they are falling far short of their target in terms of the number of graduates in the earlier universities which they visit who accept job offers. They therefore move rapidly into a different mode—one of seduction rather than selection. Alternatively, the organization might be recruiting in two different graduate labour markets: for engineers and for personnel managers. There is a shortfall of engineers, whereas there are large numbers of arts and social science graduates wishing to become personnel managers. The consequence will be that the interview is used for a different purpose for these two groups of graduates.

There is some evidence for the profound effect of the labour market on the interview. Liden and Parsons (1986) found that applicants for seasonal work in an amusement park were, naturally enough, more likely to accept the job if they liked the sound of it as described by the recruiter. However, this relationship was moderated by the extent to which they believed they could get alternative work. Only when they thought alternative work was available were these applicants strongly affected by the job description. When you have no alternative, you take what you can get.

A NEW CONTEXT FOR THE SELECTION INTERVIEW

Instead of bemoaning the continued use of the unstructured interview by organizations, we should place the interview into the context of the recruitment process of which it is a part. The recruitment process cannot be construed as a selection process. Selection by the organization is a one-sided view of recruitment. As is clear from the research on the selection interview, both parties are taking decisions throughout the recruitment process. At any point in the sequence of events from the organization's initial advertisement to the applicant's turning up for work on the first day of employment, either party may take a decision to leave the process. The organization may reject the applicant, or the applicant may reject the organization. Hence the model is one of a developing relationship, in which information is exchanged and mutual trust increases (Herriot, 1989). The psychological contract between organization and individual does not start being made once the employment contract has been signed. It starts during the recruitment process itself. The recruitment process is not a series of hurdles over which the applicant has to leap before he or she can enter the heavenly gates; it is the clarification by both parties of what each expects of the other, and a negotiated agreement of compromise.

Current research tells us that this is a more appropriate model of recruitment, since it forces us to accept that applicants as well as interviewers make choices. But the descriptive accuracy of this account is reinforced by its prescriptive power for the 1990s. Throughout Europe there will be a shortfall of skilled professional, technical, and managerial human resources as a result of increased demand and demographic trends. It is rapidly becoming a sellers' rather than a buyers' market. Selection by the organization will give way to negotiation between organization and applicant as the prime recruitment mode.

The main challenge to organizations is to surrender the *administrative* power they hold over the recruitment process so as to recognize the *market* power wielded by the applicant. They will have to redesign their recruitment procedures so as to give applicants the information they need, and they will have to negotiate with them about their future relationship with them. Then the interview will come into its own. Interviews with existing employees will enable applicants to discover more about the job; final interviews before the employment contract is signed will permit negotiation and consequent mutual commitment; and structured situational interviews will enable the organization to select and the applicant to learn more about the job. Different forms of interview will serve different purposes in the next decade. One thing we can be sure of, its use will continue unabated whatever psychologists advise!

REFERENCES

Arvey, R.D. (1979). Unfair discrimination in the employment interview: legal and psychological aspects, *Psychological Bulletin*, **86**, 736–65.

Harn, T.J., and Thornton, G.C. (1985). Recruiter counselling behaviors and applicant impressions, *Journal of Occupational Psychology*, **54**, 165–73.

Herriot, P. (1987). The selection interview, in P.B. Warr (ed.), *Psychology at Work*, 3rd edn. Penguin, Harmondsworth.

Herriot, P. (1989). Selection as a social process, in M. Smith and I.T. Robertson (eds), *Advances in Assessment and Selection*. Wiley, New York.

Herriot, P., and Rothwell, C. (1983). Expectations and impressions in the graduate selection interview, *Journal of Occupational Psychology*, **56**, 303–14.

Hunter, J.E., and Hunter, R.F. (1984). Validity and utility of alternative predictors of job performance, *Psychological Bulletin*, **96**, 72–98.

Kinicki, A.J., and Lockwood, C.A. (1985). The interview process: an examination of factors recruiters use in evaluating job applicants, *Journal of Vocational Behavior*, **26**, 117–25.

Latham, G.P., and Saari, L.M. (1984). Do people do what they say? Further studies on the situational interview, *Journal of Applied Psychology*, **69**, 569–73.

Latham, G.P., Saari, L.M., Pursell, E.D., and Campion, M.A. (1980). The situational interview, *Journal of Applied Psychology*, **65**, 422–7.

Liden, R.C., and Parsons, C.K. (1986). A field-study of job applicant interview perceptions, alternative opportunities, and demographic characteristics, *Personnel Psychology*, **39**, 109–22.

Reilly, R.R., and Chao, G.T. (1982). Validity and fairness of some alternative employee selection procedures, *Personnel Psychology*, **35**, 1–62.

Robertson, I.T., and Makin, P. (1986). Managerial selection in Britain: A survey and critique, *Journal of Occupational Psychology*, **59**, 45–57.

Schmitt, N., Gooding, R.Z., Noe, R.A., and Kirsch, M. (1984). Meta-analyses of validity studies published between 1964 and 1982 and the investigation of study characteristics, *Personnel Psychology*, **37**, 407–22.

Schneider, B. (1987). The people make the place, *Personnel Psychology*, **40**, 437–53.

Weekley, J.A., and Gier, J.A. (1987). Reliability and validity of the situational interview for a sales position, *Journal of Applied Psychology*, **72**, 484–7.

Chapter 3.10

Biographical Data

RUSSELL J. DRAKELEY

Craig, Gregg and Drakeley Associates, 14 Grange Gardens, Pinner,
Middlesex HA5 5YE, UK

Imagine that you are the new recruitment manager of a large multinational
company. It is your first day back in the office after a week spent on the road
talking to your regional personnel managers about vacancies on next year's
graduate training scheme. This scheme was advertised in the national press last
week and already applications from final year undergraduates are starting to
arrive. Your morning post appears and with it a handful of application forms from
job hopefuls. Not bad, you think, it should not take long to read this lot: but this is
the tip of the iceberg. Tomorrow will bring a few more, the next day a few
hundred more, and so on until in two months' time you will have received over
3000 application forms. You cannot possibly interview everyone and there are
only 50 places on the training scheme anyway. How on earth are you going to
decide whom to interview?

Your problem is further compounded when you start to read the forms and
after a while they all begin to look the same. Slowly your strategy begins to
change. Instead of reading each form to pick out only the best candidates, you
start to look for reasons not to read the majority of the forms at all; this one failed
his maths examinations, hardly wrote anything about his spare time interests,
and used blue ink when the instructions on the form require black . . . on to the
reject pile I'm afraid!

This problem will be familiar to some extent to a great many personnel
professionals and line managers alike. Its solution, though common (Wingrove,
Glendinning and Herriot, 1984) and perhaps understandable, leads to the rejection of candidates on the basis of information which may not be demonstrably
related to job performance. Indeed, the traditional 'paper sift' approach to pre-

Handbook of Assessment in Organizations   Edited by P. Herriot
© 1989 John Wiley & Sons Ltd

selection is a highly subjective and haphazard process. There is, however, an alternative: objectively scored biographical data, or 'biodata'.

The use of biodata is by no means confined to large multinationals, graduate applicants, or even pre-selection. This chapter is concerned with the use of biodata in the widest sense, but firstly, what exactly do we mean by the term?

WHAT ARE BIODATA?

There is such a wide range of biodata that definitions tend to be circular; biodata are the sort of items that might be found on a biographical questionnaire. These include age, marital status, educational attainments, job history, hobbies, and other items typically found on job application forms, together with items such as:

When people in front of you talked through the beginning of a film at the cinema did you

1. Ignore them?
2. Get up and move?
3. Ask them to be quiet?
4. Call the manager?
5. None of the above?

Which of the following has most often caused you to settle for less than you had hoped for?

1. Your upbringing.
2. Other people.
3. Bad luck.
4. Your qualifications.
5. Something else.

The above two items would appear to be more at home in a personality or self-concept inventory than in an application form, but are consistent with Owens's (1976) definition of biodata as permitting 'the respondent to describe himself in terms of demographic, experiential, or attitudinal variables presumed or demonstrated to be related to personality structure, personal adjustment or success in social, educational or occupational pursuits'.

A distinction can, however, be drawn between 'hard' items and 'soft' items. The former represent historical and verifiable information about an individual, whereas the latter are of a more abstract nature and cover value judgements, aspirations, motivations, attitudes and expectations. While soft biodata may be open to distortion and could lead individuals to 'fictionalize' their past lives (Asher, 1972), they may be useful to tap into success-related constructs not readily measured by hard items (such as 'assertiveness' in the first of the above examples).

Whatever the nature of the individual items within the questionnaire, there is one fundamental difference between biodata and conventional application forms:

with biodata the respondent's answers are combined to produce a score analogous to that produced from a test. It is this score, rather than the value judgements of individuals reading the questionnaire, that is used for selection purposes. The mechanics of producing a scored biographical questionnaire are outlined below. However, it is first necessary to consider why such a device is desirable, other than to relieve managers of the burden of reading conventional forms.

REASONS FOR USING BIODATA

It is often said that what a person will do in the future is best predicted by what he or she has done in the past. Biodata represent one objective and systematic way of making use of information about past events to predict future job success. This objectivity brings certain advantages. The same questions are asked of everyone who completes the form, and the answers given are assessed in a consistent way. In this sense a biodata questionnaire is probably a fairer means of selection than more conventional procedures. It is also possible to monitor candidates' responses to individual questions and eliminate items that show evidence of discrimination against some social groups. This is a far more difficult proposition with the traditional interview, for example, where the overall decision can be monitored quite easily, but not the questions that led to the decision.

When developed properly, biodata devices are demonstrably related to job performance because this is the basis upon which items are selected for inclusion in the questionnaire. This is important in terms of most countries' equal employment opportunities legislation, since job relatedness is usually regarded as the acid test of the appropriateness of a selection procedure.

Biodata forms can be developed in multiple-choice formats which are amenable to machine scoring or direct entry to a computer terminal. Thus, processing large numbers of applicants can become a routine clerical activity, freeing-up valuable personnel professionals' or line-managers' time. Finally, and perhaps most importantly, there is ample evidence to attest to the criterion-related validity of biodata in an applied setting, as can be shown by a brief review of the literature.

THE VALIDITY OF BIODATA

While many individual biodata validation studies could be cited, their message is summarized in three recent reviews. Reilly and Chao (1982) reviewed various alternatives to ability tests for predicting a variety of criteria, and found that the mean validities for biodata ranged from 0.32 against job tenure to 0.46 against productivity. All validities listed are from cross-validation studies since, as will be discussed, development sample validities will tend to capitalize on chance. Validities for clerical or sales occupations were also higher than those for military or non-specific non-management occupations. Their overall conclusion was that '. . . of the alternatives reviewed, only biodata and peer evaluation have evidence of validity equal to that of tests'.

Hunter and Hunter (1984) used 'meta-analysis', a set of techniques for accumulating independent validity coefficients that statistically account for sampling error, restriction of range in the predictor and lack of criterion reliability (see Chapter 3.1), to re-analyse Reilly and Chao's results. They confirmed the relative superiority of biodata among the alternatives to tests (a mean validity of 0.38 versus the next best alternative re-analysed, the interview, at 0.23) but questioned whether *any* alternative was the equal of tests of cognitive ability. In a series of new analyses, they reported that the three best predictors of entry level job performance (as assessed by supervisors' ratings) were ability tests (average validity 0.53), job tryouts (0.44) and biodata (0.37). However, since empirical data on restriction of range were available only for measures of cognitive ability, corrections for this artefact were made to the validities of the tests, but not to the validities for the other predictors.

Schmitt *et al*. (1984) also used meta-analysis but did not attempt to correct for range restriction or any other artefact except sampling error. Their best predictors of performance ratings were assessment centres (0.43), and work samples and biodata (both 0.32). In this case, the validity of general mental ability tests for predicting performance ratings was only 0.22.

The *mean* validity of biodata across a range of criteria was 0.24 (from a total of 99 studies). This estimate is lower than that obtained by Hunter and Hunter, and only personality tests, of the other seven predictors considered, yielded a lower average validity. However, biodata were used to predict turnover more frequently than any other predictor, and validities for this outcome were generally low. When the mean validities for different predictor–criterion combinations were calculated, biodata were nevertheless the best predictors of turnover (0.21) and of wages (0.53). They were also the second best predictors of performance ratings (as noted above) and the only predictor with published validities against productivity (0.20). Only in the case of more objective measures of achievement (e.g. examination grades) was the superiority of aptitude tests apparent. Here the mean validity for tests of general mental ability was 0.44, whereas for biodata it was 0.23; again, only personality tests had lower validities.

The overall conclusion appears to be that biodata are among the best, if not the best, predictors of turnover. Where no range restriction corrections are applied in the analysis, they predict performance ratings at least as well as tests, but not as well as assessment centres or work samples, and they are poor predictors of objective measures of achievement (but see Drakeley, Herriot and Jones, 1988).

METHODS OF OBTAINING AND USING BIODATA

While Owens's definition of biodata seems to imply that biodata are obtained from *auto*-biographical accounts, they can be obtained from other than self-report forms. Employers' references, for example, can provide a good source of work-history-related items, and educational biodata can often be obtained from school or university reports (see Chapter 3.11). There is no reason why biodata cannot be obtained from a suitably structured interview so long as candidates' responses can be recorded without too much interpretation by the interviewer.

Interviews are, of course, time consuming and expensive, and employers do

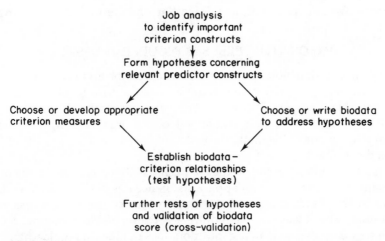

Figure 1　The rational approach to the development of biodata questionnaires

not usually take up references until the later stages of recruitment. The aforementioned methods are probably only suitable when biodata are used as a part of a longer selection procedure. For pre-selection, there is really no substitute for a purpose designed self-report questionnaire.

DEVELOPMENT OF BIODATA QUESTIONNAIRES

The development of a biodata questionnaire should follow the same principles governing the development of any good selection procedure. Ideally, it is a rational 'deductive' sequence of stages which begins with a thorough analysis of the target job, as shown in Figure 1.

Job analysis and criterion development are discussed at length elsewhere in this book and the processes involved will not be elaborated here. Suffice to say that some form of job analysis is necessary to ensure that biodata devices are job related, and that biodata can be developed to predict virtually all the commonly used criteria, as long as 'good' versus 'bad' employees can be identified.

The selection of biodata items then follows directly from the job analysis. If 'leadership potential' is identified as a requirement of the job, for example, it might be reasonable to hypothesize that evidence of prior acceptance of responsibility for others would be an appropriate predictor construct, assuming this to be one component of leadership. Items can then be written to probe respondents' experience of, or attitudes to, taking responsibility. Such items might be selected from established item banks or published catalogues. Unfortunately, the latter tend to be North American in origin, and are difficult to obtain. Even then, they require considerable translation before they can be used successfully in other countries and some items may be extremely culturally specific (cf. Glennon, Albright and Owens, 1966).

Once the criterion has been decided and the biodata have been selected, the developer has then to make two decisions, one concerning which design to use, predictive or concurrent, and the other, the method of combining items.

PREDICTIVE VERSUS CONCURRENT DESIGNS

In a predictive design biodata are obtained from all job applicants prior to hiring. Selection decisions are then made on the basis of the *existing* selection procedure. After a suitable time period, criterion data are collected on the successful applicants, i.e. those that are now employees of the organization, the biodata are combined using one of the methods described below, and the validity of the total score is determined.

The main advantage of the predictive design is that it is realistic; the questionnaire is intended to be used for applicants, hence it is developed using data *from* applicants. The disadvantage is that it is a very time-consuming process. It might, for example, take at least twelve months to obtain reliable, meaningful criterion data on new employees. If an organization does not have a regular intake of new staff, there could be a two- or three-year delay between sending the draft biodata form to applicants and obtaining a large enough sample of employees to warrant further development work.

Thus the alternative, a concurrent design, is often used in practice. Here the biodata are collected from existing employees and criterion data are collected at the same time. The biodata are then combined and validated as for predictive designs. While this approach cuts down drastically on development time, it has its disadvantages.

To improve the realism of the responses, the participating employees are usually asked to complete the biodata form as if they were applying to the organization for the first time, and to recall their own situation immediately prior to hiring. This may place an unrealistic burden on the respondents' memories unless the developer of the device chooses recent employees; then there is a trade-off against obtaining reliable criterion data. More importantly, the responses of typical applicants (even those who go on to be selected) may be different from those of typical employees. This may be due to applicants' natural desire to look good on paper, although a potentially more serious problem is criterion contamination, whereby the biodata responses of current employees become, perhaps unconsciously, distorted through contact with the organization. If an assertive, competitive work style is part of the culture of an organization, for example, employees' responses to items which appear to measure these characteristics might be biased towards the cultural norm. The use of relatively hard biodata can reduce this problem, but there is ultimately no substitute for a final check of a concurrent scoring key using actual job applicants. In this way a compromise can be reached between obtaining a usable biodata device quickly and a truly predictive design.

METHODS OF COMBINING ITEMS

The individual biodata must next be combined to produce a total score which can be validated and used for selection purposes. This is normally achieved by the development of a system of 'weights'. These can be determined intuitively, objectively, or by a combination of the two. The solely intuitive method relies on expert judgements concerning likely predictor–criterion relationships. The choice of items and the size of the weights are based purely on theoretical considerations. While this approach is undoubtedly simple, it does not appear to be particularly effective (Mitchell and Klimoski, 1986).

There are two principal approaches to combining biodata objectively. In the first of these items are weighted with respect to their ability to predict an external criterion. This can be achieved in several ways, although the 'per cent' methods (Guion, 1965) are certainly the most popular.

For these methods, it is necessary to use a dichotomous criterion and hence to define 'good' versus 'bad' employees. The *horizontal* per cent method weights each response according to the probability of success with which it is associated. To take the item 'degree subject' as an example, if 50 per cent of the successful applicants with English degrees turn out to be 'good' employees then this percentage can be converted to a basic weight by simply moving the decimal point. The weight for 'English' would thus be five. If 70 per cent of the employees with mathematics degrees are good, the weight for 'mathematics' would be seven, and so on for psychology, business studies, etc. Guion outlines various modifications to this system, for example, the basic weight can be converted to an ascribed weight which takes into account the numbers of successful, versus unsuccessful, employees in the organization (the 'base rate' of success). Alternatively, unit weights can be used, whereby responses are only weighted (plus or minus one) if their associated probability of success either substantially exceeds, or is less than, the base rate.

The *vertical* per cent method weights an item proportional to the discriminating power of the response. In the aforementioned example, if 60 per cent of the good group were English graduates, whereas only 40 per cent of the bad group were, the vertical difference in percentages would be $60 - 40 = 20$ per cent. This difference in percentages can then be transformed into a weight for 'English' by reference to published tables, or a zero range can be defined (say, plus or minus 10 per cent) and unit directional weights can be developed as for the horizontal method. This method lies at the heart of the weighted application blank (WAB) approach to biodata described by England (1971). While some authors use the terms WAB and biodata interchangeably, the former has become synonymous with English's methods, hence the use of the all-inclusive term 'biodata' to mean all such devices throughout this chapter.

The second objective method of combining items relies on the relationships within the biodata, rather than between the biodata and an external criterion. This approach, which could be described as 'inductive', is usually accomplished through the use of techniques that maximize the homogeneity of a set of items. Chapter 3.4 discusses this approach in developing personality inventories. An example in the context of biodata is known as 'keying by patterns of response' (Levine and Zachert, 1951). Levine and Zachert first grouped their biodata items into subjectively homogeneous sets (for example, all of the items concerned with hobbies). Validity coefficients were then calculated for each of the individual items within a set. Where the number of significant validity coefficients exceeded that expected by chance, and the coefficients for all items within a set revealed a consistent pattern, weights were ascribed to the whole set of items. Where these criteria were not met, the entire set was rejected.

A well-established statistical method for combining variables into composite scores is factor analysis. This is perhaps the most popular inductive method as far as biodata are concerned, and the resultant 'personal history constructs' can often be used to build a theory for the validity of the items (cf. Owens and Schoenfeldt, 1979). However, the cost of ignoring specific item–criterion relationships in the development of the scoring key (i.e. validating the biodata *after* they have been combined) seems to be a slightly lower criterion-related validity compared to strictly empirical methods (Mitchell and Klimoski, 1982; Drakeley, 1988).

CROSS-VALIDATION

All methods of combining biodata capitalize on chance relationships to some extent. The effect of capitalization on chance is to inflate the validity of the scoring key in the sample upon which it was developed. It is therefore necessary to check out, or 'cross-validate', the scoring key on a second sample. This can be achieved by splitting the original sample into development and 'hold-out' groups at random, and using the second group as a cross-validation sample. This has the disadvantage of reducing the size of the sample used to develop the scoring key, so increasing sampling error and capitalization on chance; the solution exacerbates the problem!

A better alternative is to develop the scoring key on as large a sample as possible, and then to regard the results as provisional until data can be obtained from a subsequent independent sample. This 'two-sample' approach to cross-validation not only mirrors the introduction of selection procedures in real life, but also is statistically superior to the use of hold-out groups (see Murphy, 1983).

As a final note, a meta-analysis of unpublished technical reports conducted by the present author showed that shrinkage on cross-validation for empirically keyed biodata is probably in the region of 25 per cent (Drakeley, 1988). Where soft items are used exclusively, the criterion is subjective (e.g. performance ratings) and keys are developed concurrently (i.e. developed on job holders and used on job applicants) shrinkage may well be considerably greater than this, and little confidence can be placed in the results of studies where no cross-validation results are quoted.

WHY DO BIODATA PREDICT?

Although the criterion-related validity of biodata has often been demonstrated, it is perhaps still in search of an entirely satisfactory explanation. Some authors have suggested that biodata predict where there is a high overlap or 'point-to-point' correspondence between the predictor space and criterion space (Asher, 1972). This approach is based on the behavioural consistency model of Wernimont and Campbell (1968) who suggested that good predictors should be 'samples' of future job-relevant behaviours. This implies that individuals succeed to the extent that they already perform some of the behaviours required for successful job performance, and that this is indicated by their biodata. While this is certainly true of some items, such as previous work experience or educational attainment, this explanation copes less well with soft biodata (which could be regarded as 'signs' rather than 'samples'—see Chapter 3.1) and not at all for some items cited in the literature. Why, for example, should eldest sons make the best scuba divers (Helmreich, Bakemen and Radloff, 1973), or attendance at a show or circus predict success as a door-to-door salesman (Appel and Feinberg, 1969)?

Individual explanations for these kinds of items could be found. There is, for example, an extensive literature on birth order effect, but a more integrated theory is needed. This has been attempted by Owens and Schoenfeldt (Owens, 1976; Owens and Schoenfeldt, 1979), who proposed two classes of biodata: 'inputs' to the organism which reflect environmental influences, and 'prior experiences' which comprise the aforementioned samples of, and signs for, future behaviour. They went on to suggest that individuals with similar patterns of input and prior experience variables will behave in a similar way, and can be subgrouped on this basis. Moreover, different subgroups will behave in ways that are broadly distinct. Individual prediction is achieved by identifying subgroup membership and ascribing the modal subgroup behaviour to the individual.

While Owens and Schoenfeldt have produced a compelling 'classification of persons' (or, more correctly, a classification of North American university students) their approach is perhaps too general to account adequately for the relationship *between* biodata predictors and *specific* job criteria.

Both of the above explanations invoke the principle of behavioural consistency. While this is useful, it can focus excessive attention on the individual. For example, should we wish to predict voluntary turnover, we ought not to employ individuals who have resigned from similar jobs in the past. This is clearly an over-simplification, because factors external to the individual play a part in the turnover process. McCormick and Ilgen (1980) suggested that there are two kinds of biodata; items that are 'job related' and those that are 'labour market related'. Examples of the former should by now be familiar; an example of the latter would be possession of a home address in an area of high unemployment. Such individuals would, presumably, be reluctant to give up a job without good reason, and this would be reflected in a below average turnover rate. A satisfactory theory of biodata would therefore take into account both the individual and the situation.

It is possible to suggest a three-fold classification of biodata. There is ample evidence that situational constraints, such as parents' social class, ethnic origin, type of school attended, etc., serve to limit access to, and success in, certain occupations (e.g. Roberts, 1981). Some types of biodata can reflect these influences and would be expected to predict job performance. These might be termed 'background' biodata. Then there are 'commitment' biodata. These reflect an individual's inclinations, needs and values, and might also be related to performance in work roles. Such commitments may find expression in biodata items that cover, for example, affiliations to societies, leisure pursuits, or stated work preferences. A further class of commitment biodata would reflect an individual's expectations about the world of work, since unrealistic expectations might lessen subsequent commitment (Wanous, 1977). Evidence of success in similar pursuits would comprise the third class of items, 'achievement' biodata, such as scholastic performance, work record and achieved positions of responsibility.

This classification implies that recent achievements and commitments are in turn related to more distant background. This poses a problem for the practitioner because while it may be legitimate to select on the basis of achievement or commitment, selection on the basis of background would be discriminatory. Unfortunately, even legitimate achievement and commitment items may be correlated with background. The only appropriate use of background biodata might thus be to help *control* for, or at the very least to monitor the impact of, these kinds of influences.

Another perspective on the validity of biodata has been provided by Winter (1988). He suggests that previous experiences and past interactions in the social world act as some of the origins of an individual's beliefs in his or her own ability to achieve important goals. This is the notion of 'self-efficacy' as expounded by Bandura (1986). Biodata, being measures of such experiences and interactions, reflect self-efficacy beliefs and are thus indirect predictors of organizational criteria such as job performance. Winter further suggested that the experience of success or failure in the social world only affects self-efficacy beliefs in individuals with an internal locus of control. This has the implication that biodata might work best in occupations where employees believe that it is their own personal effort that brings success (e.g. salesmen) but not as well in businesses where the dominant belief is 'it's just a question of being in the right place at the right time'.

IMPRESSION MANAGEMENT

A common objection to biodata is that the items are 'transparent' and that it is easy to see which is the best response to give. The same thing could be said about interviews and personality inventories, but biodata seem to attract more than a fair share of criticism in this respect. To what extent do job applicants 'fake good', and if they do, does it matter?

Some studies have compared self-reported biodata with information obtained from other sources. Keating, Paterson and Stone (1950) investigated the accuracy of three work history items (wages, length of previous employment and job duties) and found that the lowest correlation between self-reported and previous employers' data was 0.90. Mosel and Cozan (1952) similarly compared application blanks from sales and office staff with work histories supplied by their previous employers. Correlations of 0.93 and 0.99 between applicants' and employers' accounts of previous earnings and duration of employment were obtained, confirming the results of Keating *et al.* (1950).

Although the correlations in these two studies are impressive, the range of items was rather limited. More recently, Cascio (1975) obtained a median correlation of 0.94 between reported and verified responses to seventeen wide ranging 'historical and verifiable' application blank items. There is, therefore, some evidence that self-reported biodata can be very reliable.

This view has been challenged by Goldstein (1971). Goldstein also constrasted self-reports with previous employers' data, but found marked discrepancies between the two sources (up to 57 per cent disagreement). Unfortunately Goldstein did not report the *size* of the difference that constituted a 'disagreement' for his most discrepant items. These items were measured on a continuum (e.g. previous salary) so it is hard to judge the practical significance of these results, because continuous biodata are often reduced to a small number of response categories before they are weighted. Small disagreements may not be particularly important.

Moreover, a situation could be imagined in which all respondents exaggerated by exactly 10 per cent. In this instance there would be *complete disagreement* (0 per cent) between applicants' reports and employers' records, but a *perfect correlation* (a coefficient of 1.0) between the two. This hypothetical situation would be highly unlikely. However, Goldstein stated '. . . the average over-estimation was not raised substantially by a few applicants but, rather, occurred across most of the applicants'. Where there is some consensus about the appropriate direction in which to fake, response distortion might be largely absorbed by correlational methods of combining biodata. The scrupulously honest applicant would nevertheless be penalized unless attempts are made to control for response distortion. This presupposes that biodata blank scores (as opposed to individual item responses) can be, and are, distorted to fake good.

Research has shown that volunteers can fake high scores on empirically keyed biodata blanks. Walker (1985), for example, administered a 112 item questionnaire to 1788 US Army enlistees who were instructed to play the role of a civilian applying for military service. The subjects were then instructed either to fake unrestrainedly good, fake discreetly good, fake discreetly bad, or were given no special instructions. All three faking conditions produced total scores that were different from those of the control group. Interestingly, the effect was only large and consistent in the fake discreetly *bad* condition, suggesting that it is easier to fake the characteristics of bad applicants than those of good ones.

Of course, showing that experimental subjects *can* fake is not to say that job applicants *do*. Means and Lawrence (1984) compared the biographical blank responses of US army enlistees with the responses they had previously made to the same blank as applicants. The mean percentage agreement for the 121 multiple-choice items was a reassuring 85 per cent. The agreement rate was particularly high for items where response verification was expected; not surprisingly applicants are less likely to fake if they think this will be discovered.

In summary, the difficulty posed by response distortion by job applicants has probably been over-stated. The problems that response distortion does present can be minimized if biodata devices are developed using historical and verifiable items with small numbers of response categories, if the questionnaire carries a warning that deliberate falsification carries a penalty, and where items with responses of varing social desirability are avoided.

APPLICANTS' REACTIONS TO BIODATA

For some occupations the number of vacancies outstrips the supply of suitably qualified applicants. In these circumstances employers are concerned not to put off suitable people by using unpopular selection procedures. Procedures which invade the privacy of job applicants are viewed particularly unfavourably (Fusilier and Hoyer, 1980). Undoubtedly biodata will be seen as intrusive, impersonal and mechanistic by some job applicants, whereas others will see biodata as a refreshing change from the usual type of application form—something which relieves them from the burden of trying to think up new answers for the same old questions. Some will even be intrigued and attracted by biodata. Unfortunately, the meagre research evidence suggests that some initial *adverse* candidate reaction is more likely. While interviews and conventional application forms are readily acceptable to candidates, biodata and aptitude tests tend not to be because they are more unfamiliar and therefore somewhat threatening. As biodata become more widely used this will cease to be such a problem, but what can be done in the short term?

Firstly, it is important to check that the biodata questionnaire does not contain items that are excessively personal, potentially discriminatory against some groups, or likely to offend particular sensibilities. It may even be sensible to pilot the questionnaire on a small group of applicants in order to canvass their reaction to the items.

Next, the instructions of the form should attempt to explain the purpose of biodata to the applicant. The biodata questionnaire is valid because it is systematic, the same questions are asked of everyone, it is objective, and it is related to job performance. These same attributes make it considerably *fairer* to all applicants than a conventional form, and this can be stated quite simply in the instructions. Skilful wording of the introduction to the questionnaire can thus allay some of the fears candidates might have while promoting the organization as fair and progressive.

Lastly, the final section of the form could contain a few well-chosen open-ended questions that permit the respondent to write something in support of his or her application. These questions should not be scored, but they can provide useful background information for any subsequent interview while giving the applicants an opportunity to get things off their chests.

VALIDITY GENERALIZATION

While there is much compelling evidence that mental ability tests show considerable generality across jobs and organizations (e.g. Hunter and Hunter, 1984), the same cannot be said of biodata. Reilly and Chao (1982), for example, noted that biodata devices appear not to 'transport' from one organizational setting to another. This is probably most true of empirically keyed biodata which are developed within a single organization. Here there is not only the problem of capitalization on chance, but also that of capturing situational elements of job performance which may have no relevance elsewhere. Biodata also appear to be specific to the criterion used in development. Drakeley, Herriot and Jones (1988), for example, found that items which predicted voluntary turnover were different from those which predicted training performance in the same sample. Moreover, some responses were a 'good' sign for one criterion and a 'bad' sign for the other (Drakeley, 1988). This lack of generality perhaps reflects the largely atheoretical approach that is traditionally associated with biodata. Where items are chosen rationally and inductive methods of combination are used, the resulting personal history constructs do appear to generalize to different groups and organizations (Owens and Schoenfeldt, 1979). The lesson for practitioners is that the validity of a key developed in one setting cannot be *assumed* in another, and it may be necessary to develop new keys whenever the job, the criterion or the applicant group changes from that used in development.

SHRINKAGE OVER TIME

Biodata scoring keys do not appear to hold up indefinitely. There is evidence that the validity of biodata shrinks over time, and periodic re-validation and re-weighting may be necessary. How often should biodata keys be re-validated? Wernimont (1962) noted that the validity of a weighted application blank developed to predict turnover of women office staff shrank from 0.61 to virtually nothing over a five-year period. Roach (1971) reported shrinkage for a similar key of 0.46 to 0.29 within two years, and suggested that the loss could have been due to changes in the company hiring policies and labour market conditions. Similarly, changes in attitudes, the opportunity structure of society and the education system could all contribute to this shrinkage in validity over time.

In general, the evidence suggests that the 'shelf-life' of biodata is between three and five years. It should be noted, however, that the majority of the studies that have reported large amounts of shrinkage have used turnover as the criterion. Turnover is more readily affected by labour-market conditions than performance measures and where the latter are used the outlook may not be as bleak.

CONCLUSION: IS BIODATA FOR YOU?

A properly developed biodata scoring key can provide an effective and fair means of increasing the validity of any multiple stage selection procedure. Some of the strengths and weaknesses of biodata have been highlighted in this chapter but there are also some practical points to consider before an organization should embark on a development programme.

Biodata are most cost-effective when they are used for pre-selection, particularly for organizations that have a routine requirement to select from a large pool of applicants. Where the total number of applicants is small, organizations may not be able to recover the costs of investing in biodata within the shelf-life of the scoring key. These costs include not only the time and money spent developing the biodata, but also the costs of printing biodata questionnaires, having them scored, or developing scoring systems (for example, writing computer software to permit direct entry of biodata responses or the purchase of optical scanners for processing large numbers of forms), and the time spent training clerical or other staff in the ways of biodata. Having said this, biodata may still be a good option even in small organizations if the utility gains of using them are high and there is no equally valid but cheaper alternative.

To ensure that biodata keys are reliable it is necessary to use large development and cross-validation samples (say, 500 and 250 individuals respectively). If criterion data cannot be obtained from a sufficiently large sample within a five-year period it is probably not worth developing a scoring key; it will most likely be out of date by the time it is implemented.

Biodata are most valid when the target job is relatively homogeneous, e.g. clerical work, insurance sales, apprentice electrical engineering. They are less effective when placement decisions are made after hiring, or where the job requirements are very general, e.g. 'management trainee'. If, on the other hand, the organization is *extremely* selective in choosing from its applicants and appoints only those with first class honours degrees from certain universities, for example, there can be the problem of range restriction (in this case, a restricted range of degree results and anything correlated with high academic attainment). This can at best obscure possible biodata–criterion relationships and at worst perpetuate irrelevant selection criteria. In the above example, were the organization to drop its 'firsts only' rule, the implicit assumption that firsts do better could be tested; with it in place any new biodata device would merely preserve the *status quo*.

Finally, from development to implementation, biodata resemble psychometric testing more closely than any other type of procedure. Organizations that are reluctant to use tests should think twice before using biodata. Those that are prepared to use tests would certainly feel at home with this versatile selection tool.

REFERENCES AND FURTHER READING

Appel, V., and Feinberg, M.R. (1969). Recruiting door-to-door salesmen by mail, *Journal of Applied Psychology*, **53**, 362–6.

Asher, J.J. (1972). The biographical item: can it be improved? *Personnel Psychology*, **25**, 251–69.

Bandura, A. (1986). *Social Foundations of Thought and Action*. Prentice-Hall, Englewood Cliffs, NJ.

Cascio, W.F. (1975). Accuracy of verifiable biographical information blank responses, *Journal of Applied Psychology*, **60**, 767–9.

Drakeley, R.J. (1988). Achievement, Background and Commitment: Classifications of biographical data in personnel selection. Unpublished Ph.D. thesis, University of London.

Drakeley, R.J., Herriot, P., and Jones, A. (1988). Biographical data, training success and turnover, *Journal of Occupational Psychology*, **61**, 145–52.

England, G.W. (1971). *Development and Use of Weighted Application Blanks*. University of Minnesota Industrial Relations Center, Minnesota.

Fusilier, M.R., and Hoyer, W.D. (1980). Variables affecting perceptions of invasion of privacy in a personnel selection situation, *Journal of Applied Psychology*, **65**, 623–6.

Glennon, J.R., Albright, L.E., and Owens, W.A. (1966). *A Catalog of Life History Items*. Richardson Foundation, Greensboro, NC.

Goldstein, I.L. (1971). The application of blank: how honest are the responses? *Journal of Applied Psychology*, **55**, 491–2.

Guion, R.M. (1965). *Personnel Testing*. McGraw-Hill, New York.

Helmreich, R., Bakemen, R., and Radloff, R. (1973). The life history questionnaire as a predictor of performance in Navy diver training, *Journal of Applied Psychology*, **57**, 148–53.

Hunter, J.E., and Hunter, R.F. (1984). Validity and utility of alternative predictors of job performance, *Psychological Bulletin*, **96**, 72–98.

Keating, E., Paterson, D.C., and Stone, H.C. (1950). Validity of work histories obtained by interview, *Journal of Applied Psychology*, **36**, 365–9.

Levine, A.S., and Zachert, V. (1951). Use of biographical inventory in the Air Force classification program, *Journal of Applied Psychology*, **35**, 241–4.

McCormick, E.J., and Ilgen, D. (1985). *Industrial Psychology*, 7th edn. Prentice-Hall, NJ.

Means, B., and Laurence, J.H. (1984). Improving the prediction of military suitability through educational and biographical information, in B. Means, (chair). *Recent Developments in Military Suitability Research*. Symposium 26th Annual Conference of the Military Testing Association. Munich.

Mitchell, T.W., and Klimoski, P.M. (1982). Is it rational to be empirical? A test of methods of scoring biographical data, *Journal of Applied Psychology*, **67**, 215–25.

Mitchell, T.W., and Klimoski, P.M. (1986). Estimating the validity of cross-validity estimation, *Journal of Applied Psychology*, **71**, 311–17

Mosel, J.N., and Cozan, L.W. (1952). The accuracy of application blank work histories, *Journal of Applied Psychology*, **36**, 365–9.

Murphy, K.R. (1983). Fooling yourself with cross-validation: single sample designs, *Personnel Psychology*, **36**, 11–118.

Owens, W.A. (1976). Background data, in M.D. Dunnette (ed.). *Handbook of Industrial and Organizational Psychology*, Rand McNally, Chicago.

Owens, W.A., and Schoenfeldt, L.F. (1979). Towards a classification of persons, *Journal of Applied Psychology*, **64**, 569–607.

Reilly, R.R., and Chao, G.T. (1982). Validity and fairness of some alternative employee selection procedures, *Personnel Psychology*, **35**, 1–62.

Roach, D.R. (1971). Double cross-validation of a weighted application blank over time, *Journal of Applied Psychology*, **55**, 157–60.

Roberts, K. (1981). The sociology of work entry and occupational choice, in A.G. Watts, D.E. Super, and J.M. Kidd (eds). *Career Development in Britain*. Hobsons Press, Cambridge.

Schmitt, N., Gooding, R.Z., Noe, R.A., and Kirsch, M. (1984). Meta-analyses of validity studies published between 1964 and 1982 and the investigation of study characteristics, *Personnel Pschology*, **37**, 407–22.

Walker, C.B. (1985). *The Fakability of the Army's Military Applicant Profile (MAP)*. Annual Conference of the Association of Human Resources Management and Organizational Behaviour, Denver.

Wanous, J.P. (1977). Organisational entry: newcomers moving from outside to inside, *Psychological Bulletin*, **84**, 601–818.

Wernimont, P.F. (1962). Re-evaluation of a weighted application blank for office personnel, *Journal of Applied Psychology*, **46**, 417–19.

Wernimont, P.F., and Campbell, J.P. (1968). Signs, samples and criteria, *Journal of Applied Psychology*, **52**, 372–876.

Wingrove, J., Glendinning, R., and Herriot, P. (1984). Graduate pre-selection: A research note, *Journal of Occupational Psychology*, **57**, 169–71.

Winter, B.C. (1988). An Interactionist Model of Early Performance and Voluntary Turnover in the British Army: The antecedents and consequences of self-efficacy beliefs. Unpublished Ph.D. thesis, University of London.

Chapter 3.11

Reference Reports

PAUL DOBSON

Centre for Personnel Research and Enterprise Development, The City University Business School, Northampton Square, London EC1V 0HB, UK

This chapter outlines the nature, use and psychological basis of reference reports, reviews the research that has been undertaken into their psychometric properties, discusses the factors likely to influence their validity, and in conclusion makes recommendations for their use in practice.

THE NATURE OF REFERENCE REPORTS

Reference reports are known by a number of different terms, for example, letter of reference or recommendation, reference check, referee report, employer's reference, testimonial, etc. What they have in common is that they all ask for the assessment of an individual by a third party. While testimonials have traditionally been used as testimony only to good character, the underlying process is the same and they are included here as an example of a reference report.

Although all reference reports share a common process, they vary quite widely in other respects, namely:

1. In the format of the report.
2. In the type of information requested.
3. In whether this information is gained orally or in writing.

These differences are important for they appear to impinge upon the likely validity of the instrument.

Examples of reference reports are shown in Figures 1 and 2. The reader may

Assessment and Selection in Organizations   Edited by P. Herriot
© 1989 John Wiley & Sons Ltd

EMPLOYEE REFERENCE FORM

Date of commencement of employment . . . .

Capacity in which employed, and/or job title. . . . .

Main duties. . . . .

. . . .

Full-time or part-time. . . . .

If part-time, number of hours per week for which employed . . . .

Assessment of performance . . . .

Attendance record: number of days absent in last full year, if employed for less than one

year, during the period of employment . . . .

Salary (or wage rate) . . . .

If no longer in the employment:

      Date of leaving. . . . .

      Reason for leaving . . . .

      Would you re-employ him/her?. . . . .

Are you aware of any convictions (other than spent convictions) recorded against him/her?

If so, please specify these . . . .

Do you know of any reason why we should not employ him/her? If so, please specify

these . . . .

. . . .

Did you find him/her: Honest. . . . .

                           Punctual . . . .

                           Reliable. . . . .

Do you have any further information or comments which you wish to offer about him/her, bearing in mind the post for which he/she has applied, as described in the accompanying letter?

. . . .

. . . .

Signature: . . . .

Name: . . . .

Date: . . . .

Position: . . . .

Telephone number and extension . . . .

Name and address of company/organisation. . . . .

From Walton (1985), reproduced by permission of the *Industrial Relations Digest*.

Figure 1   Example of a reference report used for selection for employment

London Business School

THE MBA PROGRAMME

Reference Form

CONFIDENTIAL

Full-time ☐ please

OR

Part-time ☐ tick

Applicant's Name: ....

To the referee: The person whose name appears above has applied to the MBA (Master's in Business Administration) Programme at London Business School, and has nominated you as his/her referee. We would be very grateful for your comments on his/her suitability for the Programme. Any information you can supply us with will be of great assistance, and will be confidential to the Admissions Committee.

The MBA Programme is a general management programme offered on either a full-time (21 months) or part-time (36 months) basis. The Programme is designed to broaden perspectives, enhance career potential and equip participants with the general management and specialist skills required for senior management positions in both the private and public sectors. Participants are deliberately selected from a wide range of academic, cultural and professional backgrounds and management interests. A university degree or equivalent professional qualification is required for admission, and in addition participants will typically have several years' work experience before being accepted. A few candidates with less experience, but who can demonstrate exceptional maturity, academic performance, managerial potential and the ability to contribute to the Programme, are accepted as full-time students.

The Programme relies heavily on the active participation of all members and involves substantial interaction between participants and teachers. A considerable amount of work is done in small groups, and personal qualities are therefore as important as academic ability and previous work experience and expertise.

REFERENCE:

1. How long have you known the applicant and in what connection?

2. What do you consider to be his/her major talents and strengths?

3. What do you consider to be his/her major weaknesses?

4. In what ways might he/she benefit from an MBA Programme?

5. Are you aware of any personal circumstances that might affect his/her performance in the Programme?

6. Please rate the applicant on the qualities listed below. The applicant should be rated by marking the scale in the appropriate place (1 d low and 5 d high; 0 d Not observed). Please compare the applicant with other members of his or her peer group (typically this would mean graduates with several years' work experience)

	Low 1	2	Average 3	4	High 5	Not observed 0
Ability to work hard	1	2	3	4	5	0
Maturity	1	2	3	4	5	0
Warmth and social skills	1	2	3	4	5	0
Leadership	1	2	3	4	5	0
Capacity to reason and present him/herself logically and fluently	1	2	3	4	5	0
Intellectual or Academic ability	1	2	3	4	5	0
Perseverance	1	2	3	4	5	0

7. Please feel free, either in the following space, or in a separate letter, to elaborate on the ratings you have assigned in question 6 or to comment on how the applicant might contribute to the Programme, or to make any further points which you feel will be helpful.

Signature of referee: .... Date ....

Name and Position ....

Address ....

.... Telephone ....

Thank you for supplying this information. Please could you return the completed reference form to the applicant in the self-addressed envelope and sign across the envelope seal. The applicant should forward the sealed envelope to us together with his/her application form. If you would prefer to return the completed form directly to the School please address it to either the Full-time or Part-time MBA Registry, London Business School, Sussex Place, Regent's Park, London NW1 4SA. Telephone: (01) 262 5050; Telex 27461; Facsimile (01) 724 7875. Applications will not be processed unless references are received

Figure 2   Example of a reference report used for selection to an MBA programme

Reproduced by permission of the London Business School.

find it an interesting exercise to form an impression of these now, and then to review them again on completing this chapter.

Format of the report

Reference reports vary in the amount of structure provided for the referee. Thus, the reference:

- may simply request a letter on whatever the referee considers to be of value;
- may request a semi-structured pen-picture on identified attributes, behaviours or job experiences;
- may utilize an open-ended question/answer format;
- may include closed questions, rating scales, or a forced-choice design to measure quite specific attributes.

Obviously, the more structured the reference the more care has to be taken to ensure all relevant areas are concerned. Thus, typically, structured references include an open-ended section where the referee can add anything that is considered to be important.

Other things being equal, structured references are to be preferred to unstructured ones. Structured references guide the referee as to what is relevant, and, when examples of specific behaviours are requested, they can cause the referee to re-evaluate his or her judgements. Such references give the requesting organization more control over the kind of information that is going to be provided, make omissions more apparent, and make references provided by different referees on the same or on different applicants more comparable.

Cronbach (1955) found that when rating scales are used to measure impressions of personality, the results are subject to a number of different forms of inaccuracy. Judges were found to differ in how they used the scales. Some judges were found to be more lenient than others; some judges were found to make greater use of the extremes of the scales; and some judges had a tendency not to discriminate between different traits, but rather to rate them similarly. These biases of differential leniency, spread and halo, while first observed and measured using rating scales, may be reasoned to influence all human judgement. The fact that referees differ in their leniency, use of extremes and halo makes it difficult to compare references given by different referees.

There are a number of ways in which these biases can be overcome or their effects reduced so that comparisons can be made between different applicants on a more sound footing. These methods are:

1. The use of forced-choice items, for example, 'Which of the following is most characteristic of the individual? A. Has boundless energy. B. Is calm and self-assured. C. Is a good conversationalist.'
2. The use of ranking methods, where, for example, the referee is asked to select the individual's five main strengths and weaknesses from a stimulus list of relevant and equally desirable characteristics.

3. The use of behaviourally anchored rating scales, where each part of the scale is behaviourally defined.
4. The use of relative comparisons, where the referee is asked to make judgements 'relative to the individual's peers', or 'compared with those of similar age and experience'.

Content of the report

Reference reports vary in the type of information they request and include. This may be:

1. Facts, for example, degree class, salary, absence and sickness records, etc.
2. Behaviours, for example, 'introduced new accounting system', 'organized school field trip', etc.
3. Evaluations, for example, 'one of the best head pupils the school has had', 'a very trustworthy individual', etc.

Although there is no empirical research that directly supports the conclusion, it may be reasoned that reports requesting objective information are less prone to error than those that request only subjective evaluations of the individual's personality or experience. The reasons for this conclusion will be discussed in the section on the psychological basis of reference reports. Restricting the references to objective facts, such as the individual's age, examination results, etc., does exclude referee assessments which, while prone to inaccuracy, are potentially of considerable value. The accuracy of subjective evaluations is likely to be enhanced by requesting instances of behaviour which exemplify the assessment.

One of the fundamental tenets of selection practice is that the dimensions or characteristics on which selection decisions are based should be relevant to effective job performance. The use of job analysis in order to identify the critical behaviours provides a rationale for the content of referee requests. Schmitt (1976), among others, has suggested that the careful linking of job analysis to question content can have beneficial effects on reliability and validity.

Written and verbal reports

Not all reference reports are made by way of questionnaire or letter. Some, particularly in the case of senior executive appointments or positions involving a security risk, are made by telephone or face-to-face interview. Once again there is little empirical evidence to support the conclusion that oral reports are less prone to error than written ones, but it can be reasoned that this is indeed the case. Firstly, referees are likely to be more candid when their judgements are not committed to paper. And, secondly, the exchange allows the interviewer the opportunity to assess the weight that should be given to the report, by probing for evidence in support of judgements, by determining what opportunity the referee has had to observe relevant behaviours, and by assessing the referee's motives in providing the information.

Presumably, one may apply many of the same conclusions as those drawn from the selection interview (see Chapter 3.9) regarding the factors likely to enhance the accuracy of oral reports. Thus, reports gained by trained interviewers soliciting information on relevant dimensions, are likely to be more accurate.

While oral reports can be reasoned to be preferable to written ones, they are considerably more time and resource consuming and as a consequence they are probably only cost-effective in the case of senior or security-sensitive appointments. One variant that is used by executive search and security vetting agencies, is the use of 'throw-off' references. That is, those obtained from referees named by other referees rather than by the job applicant. Thus referees are asked to name others who know the applicant well or who could provide additional information on some matter of interest. Obviously, such secondary references provide an opportunity to cross-validate information gained from primary sources, and in doing so are likely to add to the validity of the exercise.

THE USE OF REFERENCE REPORTS

Legislation has affected the use of reference reports in the United States (see Von der Embse and Wyse, 1985). There has been a decline in the use of references in selection, with more organizations restricting their use to the checking of personal details or using reference checking agencies to obtain the report. The majority of empirical work on references has been undertaken in the United States and therefore care needs to be taken when extrapolating this research to Europe.

Frequency of use

Reference reports are widely used. Mosel and Goheen (1958) in a survey of 325 American companies found that 83 per cent used some form of reference report. Kingston (1971) reported that 88 per cent of those surveyed in the United Kingdom either contacted previous employers or requested reference details. Beason and Belt (1976), in a study of 150 public sector and 100 private sector American employers, found that 82 per cent of responding organizations used references, and Robertson and Makin (1986) found that references were used on some occasion by 96 per cent of the 108 British organizations surveyed when selecting management level employees.

The stage in the recruitment process at which references are used varies across organizations. Beason and Belt (1976) found that 13 per cent of their sample obtained references prior to selection, 69 per cent after selection but before hiring took place, and 18 per cent after the individual had been appointed. Apparently, only 13 per cent of the sample used reference reports in selection.

Purpose of use

Organizations use references for a number of different purposes. Beason and Belt (1976) found that of those who used reference reports, 48 per cent indicated that they used them simply to verify information provided by the applicant, 52 per cent using references to obtain additional information about the candidate. Nash and Carroll (1970) have stated that reference reports have two purposes: serving as a check on the information provided by the applicant; and serving as a means to predict success in the new job. Hyde (1982) points out that people already in employment who are seeking a change of job do not normally want their employers to know that they are on the move. He suggests that the general practice in the United Kingdom is to make such people an offer of employment that is conditional on satisfactory references. The purpose of the reference is largely to check personal details and whether there are reasons, such as alcoholism, or theft, for not hiring the individual. Thus, references frequently include the question, 'Do you know of any reason why we should not employ him/her?'

The use of reference reports in the recruitment of school leavers and graduates would appear to be slightly different given the reluctance of teachers and lecturers to give references when a job offer has already been made: the UK National Association of Head Teachers advises its members to refuse to give references in such cases. It would seem likely that in the United Kingdom, it is the practice of employers to obtain reference reports on college and school leavers prior to making an offer of employment. It is primarily the larger recruiters of school leavers and graduates, for example, the armed forces, higher education and the Civil Service, which obtain the reference reports prior to selection and use the information as a component in the selection procedure.

References are also likely to be used in selection at junior clerical and secretarial levels where it is considered not to be cost-effective to use more sophisticated selection methods. In these cases the interview and reference are likely to be the main inputs to the selection decision.

In summary, it would appear likely that despite their widespread use, reference reports are used as part of the formal selection process in the minority of cases. The main exceptions are in the recruitment of graduates and school leavers, in the selection of clerical and secretarial staff, senior executives and appointments with a security element. Regardless of whether the references are used in the selection decision, or afterwards as conditions for confirmation of the employment offer, they are being used as part of the hiring decision and should be reliable, valid and fair.

PSYCHOMETRIC PROPERTIES OF REFERENCE REPORTS

As a number of authors have previously commented (e.g. Mosel and Goheen, 1958; Browning, 1968; Muchinsky, 1979; Jones and Harrison, 1982), relatively little empirical research has been carried out on the psychometric properties of reference reports.

Reliability

Only four studies have reported on the reliability of reference reports. Mosel and Goheen (1982) investigated the amount of agreement between referees for an applicant: 2800 mailed recommendations were obtained on 904 applicants for nine different jobs. Using the intra-class correlation as a measure of reliability, the obtained coefficients ranged from 0.01 to 0.98 with 80 per cent being less than 0.40. They concluded that reliability was in part influenced by the nature of the target job. Mosel and Goheen (1959) investigated the agreement among referees for references submitted on 116 printers. References given by supervisors correlated −0.12 with those given by acquaintances, while those given by co-workers and supervisors correlated 0.24 with acquaintances. Bartlett and Goldstein (1976) found good agreement between two independent interpretations of the same reference. Sharon (1980), in a study of reference ratings for administrative law judge candidates, estimated a reliability of 0.17. The results of these studies are disappointing but perhaps not surprising. One would expect different referees to observe different aspects of the applicant's behaviour.

Validity

In their review article, Reilly and Chao (1982) find average correlations of 0.18 with rating criteria (N = 3696), and 0.08 with turnover (N = 2022). The average of all the coefficients was found to be 0.14 (N = 5718). In their meta-analysis, Hunter and Hunter (1984) find average correlations of 0.26 with supervisor ratings (N = 5389), 0.16 with promotion (N = 415), 0.23 with training success (N = 1553), and 0.27 with tenure as the criterion (N = 2018). The overall sample weighted average of the Hunter and Hunter study is 0.25 (N = 9375). While the results suggest that reference reports are capable of being predictively valid, it would appear that typically they are not. Reilly and Chao (1982) conclude from their review that 'the low levels of validity typically obtained do not recommend reference checks as an alternative selection procedure'. Similar conclusions have been made by Cascio (1978) and McCormick and Ilgen (1980).

Poor validity may in part result from low reliability or leniency and restriction of range in the scales which are used. Muchinsky (1979) has suggested that validity may be improved if steps are taken to counteract leniency and restriction problems. The reported validities for the studies using forced-choice report forms support this conclusion.

The research of Jones and Harrison (1982) also provides some pointers as to how validity may be improved. Jones and Harrison considered that the basis of the good validity that they found was derived from the references providing, within a carefully constructed format, samples of characteristic behaviour similar to the criterion. This conclusion is supported by the advocacy of Wernimont and Campbell (1968) of the use of samples rather than signs of behaviour, and by the wisdom that the best indicator of future performance is similar past performance. There is one other characteristic of the Jones and Harrison study that is worthy of note. The referees, who were head teachers, were aware that the applicants would be subjected to a two-day assessment centre where one of the assessors would be a head teacher. A similar situation is found in the selection of British Army officers where an assessment centre is used and considerable efforts are made to familiarize referees, primarily by inviting them to observe the procedure, with the competencies required in the applicants. Williams and Dobson (1987) found a correlation of 0.26 between reference reports and performance during officer training.

Carroll and Nash (1972) have suggested that the predictability of reference reports is increased when: (a) the referee has adequate time and different situations in which to observe the worker; (b) the applicant is the same sex, race and nationality as the referee; and (c) the old job and the new job are similar in content.

Research by Tucker and Rowe (1979) serves to illustrate the potential dangers of using invalid reference reports. They had subjects read interview transcripts and make a recommendation as to whether to accept or reject the applicant. However, prior to reading the transcripts the subjects read a reference report which was either favourable, unfavourable or neutral. The research found that prior exposure to the references created an expectancy which influenced the interpretation of the interview transcript and the accept or reject decision. The implication is not that references should not influence what goes on at interview, but rather that, since they do, they should be as valid as possible.

Utility

Even in those situations where high validities are obtained, the value of the procedure may be mitigated by a poor response rate for mailed reports. Mosel and Goheen (1959) reported a 56 per cent return rate, and although Carroll and Nash (1972) report an 85 per cent return, this was the result of a second attempt, the first resulting in a return rate of 35 per cent. Nash and Carroll (1970) point out that many employers, particularly in the United States, decline to complete reference forms for fear of litigation. Face-to-face or telephone reference interviews are the only solution to this problem.

The value of the reference information may also be negated because it does not provide unique predictor information. That is, it adds little to the information already existing on the applicant. The studies by Rhea, Rimland and Githens (1965) and Rhea (1966) found this to be the case, while the more recent study by Jones and Harrison (1982) found that the reference reports provided some incremental validity to the final selection decision.

THE PSYCHOLOGICAL BASIS OF REFERENCE REPORTS

A theoretical analysis of the processes underlying reference reports provides insight into the factors likely to influence their validity. Appropriately, much of the social psychological research into the processes of person perception and social cognition has used reference-like stimulus materials. There is, as a consequence, a vast body of literature relevant to understanding the way referees, and recipients of reference requests, form impressions of applicants, and the factors likely to impinge upon the accuracy of these impressions. It is intended to draw upon this research in order to sketch a simple framework which can be used to identify the major variables involved in the generation and interpretation of references. Those who wish to investigate the research in greater detail are referred to recent texts in the areas of person perception, social cognition and attribution theory, for example, Cook (1984).

Figure 3 shows a suitable model for the analysis of reference reports. On receipt of the reference request the referee has to identify correctly the information that is required. Then, the referee assembles the relevant information, gained either from memory or from written records such as performance appraisal or examination reports. Next, the referee evaluates the information and writes the reference report in terms of the information requested. Finally, the assessor interprets the report, decides its significance and the weight that should be given to it. Even this simple analysis clarifies one characteristic of references, that is, that they are highly subjective and complex procedures. In fact, it is difficult to envisage a measuring device that is more open to error and abuse. A reference is characterized by the passage of information between two people who will never meet, on an applicant who will never know what was written. The arguments in favour of references gained from interviews appear very strong from this viewpoint, and even the idea of open reference reporting has some attractions.

Figure 3 suggests that the characteristics of the reference request and report, of the information available on the applicant, and of the referee and assessor, are all factors likely to moderate the accuracy and validity of reference reports.

Accuracy of referee and assessor impressions

Referees and assessors can differentiate between individuals and can form accurate impressions of the characteristics of other people. The more important issue is under what circumstances are accurate impressions of other people made.

Our perception of other people is active and organized. We do not simply reflect the behaviours and information that are presented, but analyse our perceptual world and infer dispositions, abilities, aptitudes, motives, attitudes and enduring personality characteristics (traits) in others. This active organization of our perceptions reflects our need to regularize, conceptualize and evaluate our social world. It results in implicit theories of personality (Bruner and Tagiuri, 1954) and social schemata (Kelley, 1972), which are our own developed theories of the causes of behaviour and the nature of personality. Referees utilize such

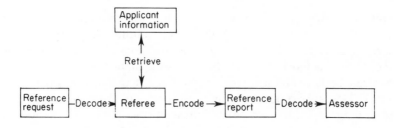

Figure 3   The generation and interpretation of reference reports

theories in inferring the personality and characteristics of job applicants, and assessors use theirs in interpreting the reference, and in inferring the motives and dispositions of the referee. When the referee has little information on the candidate, he or she is likely to rely heavily on these implicit theories of personality. For example, cold people are likely to be seen as hostile; quiet individuals as timid; those wearing glasses as intelligent, etc. People can, and do, make—generally inaccurate—judgements of other people's personality on the basis of relatively little information (Asch, 1946). First impressions of others do tend to be given more weight than later impressions (Luchins, 1957). And information about an individual that is inconsistent with formed impressions does tend to be discounted (Pepitone and Hayden, 1955). As a result, references gained from referees who possess little information on the applicant, or where the information is ambiguous, inconsistent or based upon observations made in the distant past, are likely to reveal more about the referee's personality than that of the applicant (Mischel, 1968).

The use of structured referee reports, where the referee is asked to support observations with specific instances of behaviour, are likely, in part, to counteract these effects and result in a more accurate assessment. The inclusion of an item designed to discover what opportunities the referee has had to observe relevant behaviours, and when and in what situations these opportunities arose, is likely to help the requesting body to determine the weight that should be given to the reference.

Motives of the referee

Thus far we have assumed that referees intend to give accurate references. In many cases this assumption appears worthy of question. While it is known that references suffer from errors of leniency (Muchinsky, 1979), there is no research which bears directly upon the motives of referees. It would appear that the majority of referees, out of a sense of fair play or perhaps because they doubt their own ability to make accurate assessments, within limits, deliberately write the most favourable assessment of the individual possible. The values and attitudes of the referee will clearly have an effect here, and one suspects that the attitude of the referee towards the employing organization is particularly significant from this perspective. It is perhaps not surprising that Jones and Harrison (1982) in the Navy, and Williams and Dobson (1987) in the Army, found referee reports to be of value. In both cases the applicants accepted would be responsible for the welfare of other people. Is it likely that a similar motivation will apply when the job in question is a computer operator, secretary or retail manager or when the reference is requested by a competitor?

Unlike other selection instruments, there is little control exercised over the accuracy of reference reports. The referee and assessor are unlikely to meet, and it is possible that reports are occasionally complete fabrication. Telephoning or interviewing referees provides a partial control over this problem, as does obtaining references on an applicant from different referees, or interpreting the reference in the light of information gained from other selection methods.

CONCLUSIONS AND RECOMMENDATIONS

Reference reports are used by organizations in three different ways: to check credentials and information given on the application blank; to check whether there is any reason why the individual should not be hired; and to provide information on the individual's competencies, experience and personality. Regardless of whether references are used as part of the formal selection process, or as a condition of confirmation of employment, they should be both fair and valid.

This review leads one to conclude, as others have done, that typically reference reports are not valid as predictors of future job success. Further, because employing organizations do not expect references to be entirely accurate, the majority of reference requests compromise the referee, who in many cases may feel obliged to be economical with the truth. Consequently, one cannot recommend the use of the typical reference report in selection. In practice, many organizations appear to recognize the weaknesses of reference reports, and as a consequence, restrict their use to providing a check on personal details and whether there are any reasons why the individual should not be hired.

This disappointing conclusion reflects the present state of the art. Given their widespread use, reference reports are grossly under-researched and, as a consequence, under-developed measures. In theory they have a very sound basis. That is, the use of past samples of behaviour to predict future performance. The majority of referees will have had the opportunity to observe the applicant over a quite long period of time, in a natural setting, undertaking tasks of direct relevance to the target position. Thus, the majority of referees do possess information about the applicant that is likely to be valid to the prediction of job success and that is difficult to obtain in any other way. There is little doubt that, potentially, reference reports are an extremely valuable selection method. Of course, the problem is how to obtain the information from the referee in a reliable and error-free manner, and how to ensure that it is valid to the prediction of job success. This review has identified some of the answers:

1. If possible interview the referee.
2. Base questions on job analysis.
3. Provide as much structure as possible.
4. Solicit facts and behaviours rather than evaluations.
5. Avoid rating scales, and use methods to counteract leniency, spread and halo biases.
6. When personality traits have to be measured, define them, and ask for specific examples.
7. Identify the opportunities that the referee has had to observe relevant behaviours.
8. Provide the referee with some relevant background information about the target job.
9. Obtain a number of references on each applicant.
10. Assess the reference in the light of other information available on the applicant.

REFERENCES AND FURTHER READING

Asch, S.E. (1946). Forming impressions of personality, *Journal of Abnormal and Social Psychology*, **41**, 258–90.

Bartlett, C.J., and Goldstein, I.L. (1976). A Validity Study of the Reference Check for Support Personnel of the National Academy of Sciences. Unpublished paper, University of Maryland.

Beason, G., and Belt, J.A. (1976). Verifying applicants' backgrounds, *Personnel Journal*, **55**, 345–8.

Browning, R.C. (1968). Validity of reference ratings from previous employers, *Personnel Psychology*, **21**, 389–93.

Bruner, J.S., and Tagiuri, R. (1954). Person perception, in G. Lindzey (ed.). *Handbook of Social Psychology*, vol. 2. Addison-Wesley, Reading, Mass.

Carroll, S.J., and Nash, A.N. (1972). Effectiveness of a forced-choice reference check, *Personnel Administration*, **35**, 42–6.

Cascio, W.F. (1978). *Applied Psychology in Personnel Management*. Reston Publishing Company, Reston, VA.

Cook, M. (1984). *Issues in Person Perception*. Methuen, London.

Cronbach, L.J. (1955). Processes affecting scores on understanding others and assumed similarity, *Psychological Bulletin*, **52**, 177–93.

Hunter, J.E., and Hunter, R.F. (1984). Validity and utility of alternative predictors of job performance, *Psychological Bulletin*, **96**, 72–98.

Hyde, B. (1982). First job references—a different ballgame, *Personnel Management*, **14**, 5.

Jones, A., and Harrison, E. (1982). Prediction of performance in initial officer training using reference reports, *Journal of Occupational Psychology*, **55**, 35–42.

Kelley, H.H. (1972). Attribution in social interaction, in E.E. Jones, D.E. Kanouse, H.H. Kelley, R.E. Nisbett, S. Valins, and B. Weiner (eds). *Attribution: perceiving the causes of behaviour*. General Learning Press, Morristown, NJ.

Kingston, N. (1971). *Selecting Managers: a survey of current practice in 200 companies*. British Institute of Management, London.

Luchins, A.S. (1957). Primacy-recency in impression formation, in C. Hovland (ed.). *The Order of Presentation in Persuasion*. Yale University Press, New Haven, Conn.

McCormick, E.J., and Ilgen, D. (1980). *Industrial Psychology*, 7th edn. Prentice-Hall, Englewood Cliffs, NJ.

Mischel, W. (1968). *Personality and Assessment*. Wiley, New York.

Mosel, J.N., and Goheen, H.W. (1958). The validity of the employment recommendation questionnaire in personnel selection: I. The skilled trades, *Personnel Psychology*, **11**, 481–90.

Mosel, J.N., and Goheen, H.W. (1959). The employment recommendation questionnaire: III. Validity of different types of references, *Personnel Psychology*, **12**, 469–77.

Mosel, J.N., and Goheen, H.W. (1982). Agreement amongst replies to an employment recommendation questionnaire, *American Psychologist*, **7**, 365–6.

Muchinsky, P.M. (1979). The use of reference reports in personnel selection. A review and evaluation, *Journal of Occupational Psychology*, **52**, 287–97.

Nash, A.N., and Carroll, S.J. (1970). A hard look at the reference check, *Business Horizons*, **13**, 43–9.

Pepitone, A., and Hayden, R. (1955). Some evidence for conflict resolution in impression formation, *Journal of Abnormal and Social Psychology*, **51**, 302–7.

Reilly, R.R., and Chao, G.T. (1982). Validity and fairness of some alternative employee selection procedures, *Personnel Psychology*, **33**, 1–62.

Rhea, B.D. (1966). Validation of OCS Selection Instruments: the relationship of OCS selection measures to OCS performance. US Naval Activity, Technical Bulletin STB 66–18 San Diego, California.

Rhea, B.D., Rimland, B., and Githens, W.H. (1965). The Development and Evaluation of a Forced Choice Letter of Reference Form for Selecting Officer Candidates. US Naval Personnel Research Activity, Technical Bulletin STB 66–10 San Diego, California.

Robertson, I.T., and Makin, P.J. (1986). Management selection in Britain: a survey and critique. *Journal of Occupational Psychology*, **59**, 45–57.

Schmitt, N. (1976). Social and situational determinants of interview decisions: implications for the employment interview, *Personnel Psychology*, **29**, 79–101.

Sharon, A.T. (1980). An Investigation of Reference Rating for Applicants for Administrative Law Judge. Personnel Research Report 80–6 US Office of Personnel Management, Washington, D.C.

Tucker, D.H., and Rowe, P.M. (1979). Relationships between expectancy, causal attributions, and final hiring decisions in the employment interview, *Journal of Applied Psychology*, **64**, 27–34.

Von der Embse, T.J., and Wyse, R.E. (1985). Those reference letters: how useful are they? *Personnel*, **62**, 42–6.

Walton, F. (1985). Good references, *Industrial Relations Digest*, **12**, 12–14.

Wernimont, P.F., and Campbell, J.P. (1968). Signs, samples and criteria, *Journal of Applied Psychology*, **52**, 372–6.

Williams, A.P.O., and Dobson, P.M. (1987). *The Validation of the Regular Commissions Board*. Army Personnel Research Establishment, January 1987.

Chapter 3.12

Non-conventional Methods in Personnel Selection

GERSHON BEN-SHAKHAR

Department of Psychology, The Hebrew University of Jerusalem, Jerusalem 91905, Israel

This chapter focuses on the use of non-conventional methods for personnel decisions. The term 'non-conventional' is used in reference to tools that are not typically
used by psychologists either for research purposes or in the applied sphere.

The line between conventional and non-conventional psychological tests is not
easy to draw. For one, the term 'psychological test' itself is not precisely defined,
and it is used to describe a very broad set of tools that focus on different aspects of
human behaviour (e.g. personality, scholastic achievements, special abilities),
and rely upon different measurement techniques (e.g. projective techniques,
multiple choice items). Moreover, non-conventional methods are sometimes
used by conventional psychologists for various purposes. For example, in a large
psychological clinic in Israel palmistry is used in combination with conventional
psychological tests for psychodiagnostic purposes. Graphology too has been
advocated by some psychologists. For example, Drory (1986, p. 171) concluded
that 'job performance can be predicted on the basis of handwriting analysis'.
Nevo and Halevi (1986, p. 241) claimed that 'there is a strong case for the
statement that handwriting does contain some information with regard to the
personality of the writer'.

In this chapter the following loose criterion is used to differentiate conventional
from non-conventional methods: conventional tools are tests developed by
psychologists to predict behaviour or to classify individuals into specified categories. These tests include inference rules (i.e. rules by which the response
pattern to the test items is translated into predictions) that are derived either from
a psychological theory or from data accumulated through research. Usually
conventional tools are standardized, and data pertaining to their reliability and

Assessment and Selection in Organizations   Edited by P. Herriot
© 1989 John Wiley & Sons Ltd

validity are available (see Chapter 3.2). Non-conventional tools either lack explicit inference rules or include rules lacking theoretical or empirical justification. For example palmistry, which is based on a set of assertions and predictions relating certain patterns of the palm to personality, is non-conventional, because this set of assertions does not constitute a testable theory, and because empirical evidence supporting such predictions is unavailable. This does not mean that conventional tests are necessarily valid, or that non-conventional ones are necessarily invalid. The validity of many conventional tools (e.g. Rorschach) is questionable; and the present lack of a theoretical basis for some of the other methods does not imply that such a theory cannot be formulated and tested.

The goal of this chapter is to examine more closely some of the more promising non-conventional methods, and to evaluate their potential contribution to making better personnel decisions.

Conventional psychological tests can be loosely divided into tests of ability (Chapter 3.3) and tests of personality (Chapter 3.4). Various types of ability tests (e.g. intelligence tests, general aptitude tests, tests of special abilities) have been used quite successfully in educational settings as well as for personnel selection. Tests that were designed to measure personality dimensions (e.g. objective personality questionnaires, projective techniques, personal interviews) were generally much less successful in predicting the future behaviour of individuals. Validity coefficients for ability tests typically range from around 0.4 to 0.6; whereas personality measures seldom enjoy validities of over 0.2 to 0.3 (e.g. Hunter and Hunter, 1984).

Unfortunately, for many personnel selection purposes it is not sufficient to estimate and predict abilities, and employers often feel that without some knowledge of certain personality characteristics of the applicants it would be impossible to reach satisfactory personnel decisions. An interesting example of a personality characteristic that is considered to be crucial in many personnel selection contexts is honesty (e.g. McDaniel and Jones, 1986). Psychologists have long attempted without much success to develop instruments for measuring honesty.[1] Mischel and Peake (1982), among others, have argued that the major reason for our failure in measuring honesty, as well as many other personality

---

[1] Recently, several paper-and-pencil tests were developed to identify dishonest job applicants (Sackett and Harris, 1984). McDaniel and Jones (1986) demonstrated that the theft scales of the Employee Attitude Inventory produced useful levels of validities for identifying theft among current employees. This demonstration must be treated with some caution, since the validation criterion used in most studies analysed by McDaniel and Jones (self-report of theft) was very close to the test items (e.g. 'How often do you actually take merchandise home from work without paying for it?'; McDaniel and Jones, 1986, p. 33). In addition, it is possible that the high level of validity obtained for paper-and-pencil tests is mediated by social desirability and response bias. Sackett and Harris (1984, p. 239) raise the possibility that 'validity findings using admissions as the criterion may at least in part be artefactual: both the honesty test predictor and the admissions criterion are correlated with social desirability score. The inclusion in a study of a group of people who fake good on the honesty test and conceal actual theft when asked for admissions of past theft can create a spurious relationship between honesty scores and admissions.'

traits (e.g. aggressiveness, conscientiousness), is the lack of cross-situational consistency in these traits. Recently, Epstein (e.g. 1986), and Rushton and his colleagues (e.g. Rushton, Murray and Erdle, 1987) argued against Mischel, claiming greater consistency in personality traits than previously believed. They attribute the small correlations usually obtained between different measures of the same trait mainly to the use of unreliable measures (e.g. single items or events), rather than to a real lack of consistency in the measured traits.

This is an ongoing and interesting debate, but the fact remains that thus far standardized valid tests for measuring many important personality traits are scarce. This unfortunate state of affairs has led many employers to search for other, non-conventional, methods. The following is a non-exclusive set of various examples of non-conventional methods: (a) tests based on time and place of birth (astrology and numerology); (b) tests based on line patterns on the palm (palmistry); (c) patterns of bumps on the skull (phrenology); (d) body characteristics (somatotype theory); (e) patterns in externally produced configurations of cards (tarot readings). These methods have different rationales, and different historical and cultural backgrounds. Since their only common feature is that they produce individual differences among people, it seems that almost any instrument that produces such differences may be regarded as a potential personality test (Bar-Hillel and Ben-Shakhar, 1986).

I shall not attempt to discuss all the non-conventional methods that are used or might be used for personnel decision making. Instead I shall focus on two examples—graphology and polygraphy. These two tools were chosen because unlike all the other examples mentioned above they are based on a sample of behaviour. In addition, they have some *a priori* rationale, which makes them more promising candidates for personnel selection. Graphology and polygraphy seem to differ in many respects: they have different rationales and objectives and they are based on entirely different samples of behaviour (handwriting versus physiological reactions to a set of questions). Handwriting analysis is typically used as a general and very broad personality test, and its output is usually a detailed description of one's personality. Polygraphy, on the other hand, when used as a personnel selection device attempts to reflect upon the candidates' honesty, and to verify statements regarding their work history.

In spite of those obvious differences I shall try to lay out some of the common features of these two methods, and the similar conceptual and methodological difficulties that underlie them. Then I will suggest a model describing how such tests are utilized and how decisions based on them are reached. It is believed that the model is valid for any other non-conventional technique, as well as for some of the more conventional methods.

GRAPHOLOGY

Initially, handwriting analysis was used as a forensic tool to establish the identity of a certain document's writer. It had additional purposes, such as to diagnose drug effects or intoxication. Handwriting analysis may also provide a very interesting example of an acquired complex motor skill, that can be used by scientists interested in processes underlying the acquisition of such skills. However, fairly early it attracted people who were interested in personality assessment and who attempted to derive personality descriptions or behaviour predictions from samples of handwriting. In time this became the major application of graphology in many countries and it seems to be on the increase (Ben-Shakhar *et al.*, 1986; Rafaeli and Klimoski, 1983).

The attraction of people to handwriting analysis as a potential source for making personality inferences should not come as a surprise. Bar-Hillel and Ben-Shakhar (1986) laid out some of the features of handwriting that make it an appealing candidate for a personality assessment device. They argue that unlike palmistry, astrology, etc., handwriting analysis relies on an actual sample of individual behaviour. Indeed, the behaviour is self-generated and therefore potentially expressive of its producer. Handwriting is also very rich in features and attributes, which afford it the requisite scope for expressing the richness of personalities. Indeed, handwriting is as unique as personalities. Moreover, people can be more or less similar on various dimensions of handwriting, just as they can be more or less similar on various dimensions of personality. Like personality, handwriting exhibits both individual differences and shared structure.

Furthermore, handwriting is a stable characteristic of the individual (Fluckinger, Tripp and Weinberg, 1961) which nevertheless shows development over time. It more or less retains its recognizable identity across writing media (i.e. pen versus pencil). Similarly, changes in writing circumstances (e.g. taking a dictation, copying a text, writing a complex essay, jotting down a shopping list), and in moods of the writer, seldom hinder us from recognizing a familiar handwriting, even if it undergoes some changes due to these changing circumstances. This allows handwriting to reflect persisting cross-situational components of personality as well as those that are more occasional and transient. From a pragmatic point of view, just about anyone who is likely to undergo a personality test can write. A sample of handwriting is obtainable cheaply and quickly. Finally, graphology seems not to be limited in terms of what it can divulge about the inner person. It claims to be able to detect attributes for which no other tests exist—most notably, honesty. Indeed, handwriting allegedly divulges the whole personality (Bar-Hillel and Ben-Shakhar, 1986, pp. 28–9).

Obviously, these considerations are not sufficient to establish handwriting analysis as a tool for personality assessment, or as a basis for personnel decisions. Two requirements need to be fulfilled: (a) a theory relating personality characteristics to features of handwriting ought to be formulated; and (b) this theory should be supported by appropriate data, or at least some data pertaining to the predictive validity of the inferences made on the basis of handwritten analysis should be provided. In the following sections both aspects will be discussed, and it will be argued that neither holds for graphology.

The theoretical basis for graphology

In examining the literature on graphology, one can find many assertions about the relationships between specific signs of handwriting and personality traits. For example, it has been claimed that sadism is allegedly expressed by strongly pointed end strokes; angular writers are expected to be firm, strong-minded and uncompromising persons who lack the ability to 'feel'. However, such assertions do not constitute a theory, and it would be a major challenge to formulate a model accounting for these alleged relationships.

Inferences made by graphologists are of two general classes. The first is based on a strong version of the cross-situational consistency assumption. Of course, other methods, such as biographical data (Chapter 3.10), assessment centre exercises (Chapter 3.7), and job sample tests (Chapter 3.6) are often based on this assumption, and since writing is clearly a behaviour, one can make inferences from it to similar behaviours. According to this very general assumption, sloppy handwriting suggests a sloppy person, artistic handwriting reflects an artistic personality, and bold energetic writing characterizes energetic personalities. These types of inference, although requiring empirical support, are commonsensical. They are interesting because they may shed some light on the limits of the cross-situational hypothesis. But as demonstrated above, graphology claims to derive from handwriting a much broader set of personality traits, including many traits that could by no means be claimed to be an extension of handwriting behaviour, or some motor activity in general. This brings us to the second category of inferences, inferences for which no logical or psychological explanation has been offered thus far. What reason is there to believe that traits such as honesty, leadership, responsibility, intelligence, loyalty, and the like would be expressed in features of handwriting?

The empirical basis for graphology: methodological considerations

Two classes of relationships between handwriting and personality were listed in the previous section. The weak class of relationships claims that writing is a behaviour and as such can tell us about 'similar' behaviours. The other class constitutes a list of alleged relationships between various features of handwriting and personality characteristics without specifying their logical or psychological basis. Clearly, both classes need to be tested empirically before any of the inferences based on handwriting analysis can be used for personnel decisions. At first glance it may seem that the design of an empirical test for these graphological assertions would be a simple straightforward task. As it turns out this is not the case, and there are many conceptual and methodological obstacles. A proper study of the relationships between graphological features and personality requires the following necessary conditions:

1. *An independent measurement of the criteria (i.e. various personality traits and characteristics).* This condition is difficult to fulfil, because most personality traits are not directly observable, and can seldom be independently ascertained with sufficient certitude. Clearly, a validation criterion must be based on some observed behaviour, but behaviours and personality traits do not correspond one to one. Indeed, the same trait can cause a whole range of different

behaviours and even apparently opposing ones (e.g. some aggressive people may display their aggression physically and even hurt other people, while others may be very quiet and display their aggression in a subtle verbal manner); and many different traits, even contrasting ones, can result in the same behaviour (e.g. some of those who display polite and quiet behaviour in a social context may be genuinely polite and non-aggressive individuals, while others may display the same behaviour only because they have a need to conform to a certain norm and to the behaviour of others). Moreover, two people, though possessing the same trait, may display different behaviours even in the same situation, if the situation assumes a different subjective meaning for them. Some traits are applicable to a person without there even being much of an expectation of cross-situational consistency. For example, it is sufficient that a person be occasionally dishonest, or occasionally creative, to deserve the trait name. Some traits may designate latent dispositions that are not realized in behaviour because of lack of opportunity, incentive, etc. Thus, 'inability to withstand temptation' would only manifest itself in the presence of temptation of sufficient magnitude.

The traditional way of overcoming these problems is to use as criteria either more conventional and standard personality tests, or the subjective evaluations of people who are well acquainted with the writers. The problem with these criteria is that personality tests have notoriously low validities themselves, and subjective evaluations are often unreliable. This makes it hard to identify the culprit if a mismatch is found between the graphologists' predictions and the criteria.

An interesting method to bypass the difficulties of defining and measuring a proper criterion was developed by Crumbaugh and Stockholm (1977). Their method, labelled 'The Holistic Technique', is based on judges who are well acquainted with all the writers in a given sample. The judges match the graphologists' free-style personality descriptions, based on their analysis of handwritten scripts, with the names of the writers. Correct matches in excess of chance expectation are taken as evidence that the descriptions carry at least some valid information about the writers. This method, however, has only limited applicability because it cannot be used to corroborate specific relationships between handwritten features and personality traits, and it cannot indicate which traits can be predicted from handwriting analysis.

2. *An unconfounded measurement of the handwriting parameters that constitute the basis for inferences about personality.* Unfortunately, the standard practice of most graphologists does not allow for a direct and unconfounded measurement of handwriting features. First, the typical graphological output is a free-style overall qualitative personality description. This kind of material is hard to correlate with any independent criterion. More importantly, very often the outcome of the graphological analysis is confounded with non-graphological information because contaminated texts are typically used for that analysis. Contamination is most apparent when the handwritten text is a brief autobiography of the writer, as it typically is in personnel screening contexts. Clearly, such texts contain a great deal of information about the writer that is

relevant for predicting job performance criteria (e.g. education, previous work record). Moreover, non-biographical but spontaneous text is also contaminated, most notably by the writer's verbal abilities, such as vocabulary, fluency and clarity of expression. These are correlated with successful performance in many jobs. Because graphological validity refers to the form, rather than the content, of written material, the confounding of the two makes it difficult to assign the appropriate weight to the one versus the other (Ben-Shakhar *et al.*, 1986).

Contamination is hard to eliminate, because many graphologists insist on analysing only spontaneously produced text, claiming that copying a text changes the graphological characteristics of the written material. Graphologists insist that they attend only to the graphological features of the text, ignoring its contents. However, besides the *a priori* implausibility of this claim, studies typically find that non-graphologists who read the same scripts achieve the same (low) validities as do graphologists (e.g. Jansen, 1973), or even outperform them (Frederick, 1965).

The empirical basis for graphology: summary of the available research

Despite the methodological difficulties mentioned in the previous section, there exists a body of research which attempts to estimate the validity of graphological predictions in the context of personnel selection. Instead of reviewing this literature, I shall summarize the results and conclusions of a recent meta-analytic study conducted by Efrath Neter and the present author, based on this research body. This meta-analysis was based on seventeen studies dealing with the validity of graphological inferences in a personnel selection context. Two types of criteria were used in these studies: (a) job proficiency appraisal, usually done by supervisors; and (b) training success. In order to control for possible confoundings as a result of the use of contaminated scripts (e.g. short biographies) most studies used non-graphologists as an additional control group that made judgements on the basis of the scripts' content. Non-graphologists were supplied with information identical to that given to the graphologists, and they were asked to assess the writers on the same scales used by the graphologists. We examined data separately for two kinds of non-graphologists—psychologists and lay persons. Both groups consisted of individuals with no knowledge and no training in graphology. Only a few studies controlled against confounding variables by using neutral scripts that did not include information other than the handwriting itself.

The results of this meta-analysis showed that the average correlations between inferences based on content-laden scripts and the criteria ranged between 0.14 and 0.19 for all judges. The most surprising result was that graphologists did not do better than the other types of judges, and in fact they did consistently worse than the psychologists. In the few cases where neutral scripts were used the validities of graphologists were near zero.

Clearly the small validities obtained by graphologists can be accounted for simply by the possibility that biographical and other information contained in the scripts is used, or at least influences the graphological assessment. There is nothing new or surprising in the fact that biographical data can be utilized for making valid predictions, and these can be regarded as a conventional tool for personnel selection (see Chapter 3.10). This conclusion is strengthened by the lack of a sound theory for the relationship between handwriting features and personality. Clearly, the influence of the script's content is a more parsimonious explanation of the results. A similar conclusion was drawn by Ben-Shakhar *et al.* (1986), based on two studies. In one of their studies, which was not included in the meta-analysis, five graphologists tried to guess the profession (out of eight possibilities) of 40 successful professionals on the basis of uniform scripts. None of the graphologists performed significantly better than a chance model. In Ben-Shakhar *et al.*'s (1986) other study, contaminated scripts were used. None of three graphologists predicted supervisors' evaluations any better than a clinical psychologist with no knowledge of graphology. In order to examine more closely the possibility that the results might be attributable to the script's content, Ben-Shakhar *et al.* (1986) systematically extracted several variables (e.g. education, writing quality) from the texts. An *a priori* simple linear combination of those variables outperformed all the human judges.

THE CASE OF POLYGRAPHY

The historical background as well as the nature of 'lie detection' are very different from those of graphology. Detection of deception through psychophysiological measures (polygraphy) is based upon a different sample of behaviour—physiological responses to a set of questions, usually pertaining to some specified event. Originally it was designed and developed with a rather restricted goal in mind (as compared with the very broad scope of graphology as a general personality test) to find out whether a given person is deceptive regarding a *specific event* (e.g. whether a suspect took part in a criminal act despite the suspect's claim of being innocent). This type of polygraph test has been typically utilized by police departments as an aid in interrogating suspects.

During the past two decades a different application of the polygraph has emerged mainly in the United States, and psychophysiological techniques have been used quite extensively for personnel selection and for screening of employees. Clearly, when the goal of a given test is to select among a group of applicants for a certain job, no specific event is being investigated. The test is then used as a personality test (e.g. a test attempting to describe behaviour tendencies).

This distinction between the event-related use of the polygraph and its event-free usage is crucial for two reasons: (a) the event-related usage does not rely on the assumption of cross-situational consistency, because the inferences made on the basis of the test results relate to a single situation; (b) the known features of the event can be utilized to establish empirically sound inferences based on the test results (e.g. certain aspects of the crime are known only to person(s) who took part in it), as in the Guilty Knowledge Test (GKT)—a method of polygraph interrogation based on the idea that knowledge of certain information leads to enhanced physiological reactions to this information (Lykken, 1974).

All polygraph techniques are based on comparing several physiological responses evoked by two classes of items—relevant and control. The relevant items focus on the central issue under investigation; whereas the control items must be *a priori* equivalent in terms of their arousal value, but with no relationship to the investigated matters.

In the event-related usage the relevant questions may relate to a specific crime, either directly (e.g. 'Did you steal the diamond ring from Mr Smith last Friday?') as in the Control Question Technique (Ben-Shakhar, Bar-Hillel and Lieblich, 1986); or indirectly (e.g. 'Was the colour of the stolen car red, white, etc.?') as in the GKT. An enhanced physiological reaction to the relevant item is taken as an indication of a deception regarding that question, or of a guilty knowledge that could tie the suspect to the event. However, absolute criteria for 'an enhanced physiological reaction' are unavailable, and the evaluation of responses is relative and based on an ipsative measurement. In other words, in order to assess the suspect's reaction to the relevant item one must construct proper control items. The nature of these control items is the centre of a very heated debate surrounding polygraph assessment and usage.

When the GKT is being used, the problem of choosing proper control items is easily resolved by the indirect nature of the questions, and by the choice of neutral features of the event such as the colour of a stolen car. The different colours are equivalent in their arousal value for an individual who does not have any guilty knowledge (i.e. knowledge about the event in question). The Control Questions Test (CQT) utilizes different types of control questions—general honesty questions pertaining to universal sins to which, presumably, very few people can truthfully and confidently answer 'No' (e.g. 'Did you ever take something that did not belong to you?'). The main criticism of CQT polygraphy relates to the nature of those control questions. Specifically, it was noted that they are not equivalent to the relevant questions, and that even an innocent suspect could perceive those differences and be more concerned with and anxious about the relevant questions. Typically, this aspect of the CQT is related to high rates of false positive errors (i.e. classifying innocent suspects as guilty).

In the event-free applications all these problems become even more serious. The GKT cannot be utilized, because, when the test does not revolve around a specific event, it is not possible to extract proper items for this indirect method. Even the more controversial method of the CQT cannot be applied to the event-free situation in a straightforward way. Recall that the relevant questions used in the CQT pertain to a specific event (crime). In order to use it for detecting hypothetical crimes, control questions (which relate to general misdeeds) must play the role of the relevant questions. In other words, enhanced physiological reactions to the control questions (e.g. 'Did you ever steal from your employer?') are now taken as an indication of deception and a consistent responding to those questions might mean that an applicant for a certain job will be rejected on the grounds of failing the polygraph test. But in order to make such inferences one must compare the responses to those critical items with responses to equivalent items. Unfortunately, it is not possible to construct such items, because equivalent items must relate to other hypothetical crimes of similar importance, and naturally a consistent responding to those items is not going to make a job applicant more attractive as a future employee.

In practice the common usage of polygraph for screening job candidates is done by the 'Relevant–Irrelevant Questions' method (US Congress, 1983). This method is based on comparing the responses to the relevant items (e.g. 'Did you steal from your employer in the past?') with the responses to completely neutral items (e.g. 'Do you wear a green shirt?'). Clearly, such a procedure poses even greater concerns about the logic of the inference rules for deriving conclusions from the test, and in particular it means that the risks of false positives could be even greater than for the CQT in its event-related application.

Methodological problems in polygraph validity research

In the previous section the basic rationale of the polygraph test inference rules was explained. It seems that in this respect polygraphy stands on somewhat stronger foundations than does graphology. While it is totally unclear why dishonesty, for example, would be displayed by specific ways of writing, it is not unreasonable to assume that deception is accompanied by emotionality and increased arousal, which in turn are followed by certain physiological reactions. The major problem raised regarding the polygraph test's inference rules was that of choosing proper control questions. On the other hand, graphology and polygraphy share many methodological problems, problems that make the task of assessing the validity of those tools very difficult.

Two crucial factors in any attempt to assess validity are the definition and measurement of a proper criterion, and the unconfounding of the specific test information from all other information. In the case of polygraphy it is very seldom possible to establish a criterion of truth. One method to overcome this difficulty is to use studies in which a crime is simulated in laboratory conditions. In these studies, subjects are instructed to 'commit a crime' (e.g. to take an envelope containing a $20 bill out of an office). The subjects are aware of the unrealistic nature of this test which has no real consequences for them. These features of the mock crime studies severely restrict their external validity, and accuracy estimates derived from them cannot be generalized even to the specific event applications of the polygraph test. An attempt to generalize the results of such studies to event-free usages of polygraphy is even more far-fetched and risky.

Some studies have attempted to assess the polygraph test in real life settings. These studies commonly used two types of criteria: (a) the consensual judgement of a panel of legal experts who are privy to all the information gathered about the case, except for the polygraph results; (b) confession of guilt. Both these criteria suffer from major drawbacks. Panel decisions are not necessarily accurate and may be even less valid than the polygraphers' evaluations. Confessions, on the other hand, might constitute a biased sample of the entire population of poly-graph investigations—one characterized perhaps by exceptionally clear psycho-physiological indications of guilt. Obviously, innocent suspects cannot prove their innocence by confessing. Hence, they can only find their way into a confessions criterion study through the confession of someone else, presumably the true perpetrator of the crime. Guilty suspects, on the other hand, will usually be included in such studies through their own confessions. Confessions are particularly likely to be elicited from suspects whose polygraph results are particularly damaging. If so, suspects whose charts are less clear and harder to evaluate are also less likely to be included in such studies, thus raising the observed accuracy beyond its actual value, and lowering the reported miss rate (Ben-Shakhar, Lieblich and Bar-Hillel, 1982). Recently, Iacono (in press) provided a very clear numerical demonstration of how a polygraph examiner operating at an overall chance level of accuracy would appear to be of almost perfect validity, if his or her validity is estimated on the basis of confessions.

Another methodological problem concerns the possible contamination of the information at the interrogator's disposal. The physiological data typically come in the company of other information, such as the intelligence gathered about the suspect, the impressions of former interrogators, records of previous convictions, and observations of the suspect's behaviour during the pre-test interview and during the actual polygraph test. Indeed, Barland (1975) has found a high rate of agreement between polygraph examiners' final evaluations and those solicited just prior to the actual polygraph test. This factor must be borne in mind whenever interpreting the results of a polygraph validation study, since it implies that the observed validity may not be due exclusively to the physiological data.

A more subtle source of contamination is the 'experimenter expectancy effect' (Rosenthal and Rubin, 1978). The expectations that the polygraph examiner forms, based on any of the above-mentioned cues, might affect the suspect in ways that will manifest themselves later in his or her physiological records. This source of contamination is inherent to the CQT, since the CQT is essentially a clinical method that calls for an intense interaction between the interrogator and the suspect.

Validity of the polygraph test for personnel selection

It is somewhat surprising that in spite of the widespread use of the polygraph test for the selection and screening of employees (see Sackett and Decker, 1979; US Congress, 1983), there is practically no research bearing on its validity in these situations. Sackett and Decker (1979) claim that the published evidence relating to the value of polygraph tests deals exclusively with the criminal investigation context. In a more recent review (US Congress, 1983), only two studies attempted to assess the validity of the polygraph for pre-employment screening. Both were mock crime studies with very limited external validity. In the Correa and Adams (1981) study, 75 per cent of the deceptive responses were correctly detected against a chance expectancy of 50 per cent. In the second study described in the US Congress (1983) report Barland conducted a question-by-question analysis of different methods of chart interpretation. This analysis yielded between 77 and 88 per cent correct identification of truthful responses, but only between 43 and 67 per cent of the deceptive questions were correctly identified, against a chance expectancy of 50 per cent.

There is a vast literature pertaining to the validity of the polygraph test for its event-related usage (e.g. detecting criminals) (see Saxe, Dougherty and Cross, 1985). The methodological problems mentioned in the previous section made it difficult to reach an overall estimate of the polygraph validity based on this research body. Saxe *et al.* (1985) summarized ten field studies conducted to evaluate the CQT. They reported a false negative rate ranging between 0 and 29.4 per cent and a false positive rate ranging rom 0 to 75 per cent (against a chance expectation of 50 per cent). Any attempt to generalize from these studies conducted under specific event settings to the event-free situation typical of the personnel selection application will be very limited.

Sackett and Decker (1979) make the important distinction between identification and prediction. In the event-related application the goal of the polygraph test is to identify the individual(s) involved in the event. In pre-employment screening on the other hand, the goal is to predict whether a candidate will steal from the organization (or will use drugs, be frequently absent, etc.). According to Sackett and Decker (1979, p. 497):

> The generalization of an accuracy figure from a criminal investigation to a pre-employment context assumes that past behaviour is a perfectly valid predictor of future on-the-job behaviour. The accuracy figure for identification should be multiplied by the best estimate one has of the strength of the past behaviour–future behaviour relationship to obtain a more realistic picture of the value of the polygraph in pre-employment screening.

Another factor that ought to be considered if polygraph tests are to be used for pre-employment screening is the base rate. The screening set-up is typically characterized by a low base rate of the event of interest (i.e. lying). Hence, the evidence for the test validity must be particularly strong in order to justify its use. Lykken (1978) estimated the base rate of deception in a pre-employment screening context to be around 5 per cent. In an analysis of the different polygraph usages from a decision–theoretical perspective, Ben-Shakhar *et al.* (1982) concluded that polygraph tests are unlikely to be of positive expected utility when the base rates are that low, even if false positive errors (unwittingly accepting a candidate with a bad past working record) are considered to be much more harmful than false negative errors (rejecting an honest candidate). This conclusion was based on validity estimates derived from field studies using specific events. Most of these studies based their criterion upon confessions introducing a positive bias. In all likelihood the real validities of the polygraph test for pre-employment screening purposes will be much lower, further decreasing its expected utility, and the range of situations to which it could be successfully applied.

A COMPARISON OF GRAPHOLOGY AND POLYGRAPHY AS TOOLS FOR PERSONNEL SELECTION

Evidently, graphology and polygraphy are quite different tools for personnel selection. The obvious differences are in their content as well as in the inference rules for drawing conclusions from them. Despite those basic differences there are many similarities, which will be laid out and discussed in this section.

Both graphology and polygraphy are impressionistic tools which lack well-defined rules for making inferences from the test results to behaviour predictions or personality classifications. One exception may be the recent attempt by Raskin and his colleagues (e.g. Kircher and Raskin, 1983) to define quantitative rules for measuring the physiological responses extracted during a polygraph test and to make inferences based on them. The general practice of CQT-based polygraphy is subjective and impressionistic.

Another, related, common feature of those tests is the contaminated way in which the tests are administered and used. Contamination refers to the fact that both the polygrapher and the graphologist know much more than what the tests reveal. This factor was mentioned as a methodological problem that makes the validation task more difficult. It seems that contamination is an inherent feature of those tests. Graphologists insist upon using spontaneous and expressive scripts rather than copied material, and often refuse to rely upon text written down from memory. Polygraphers, too, have access to a great deal of information before they ever subject their suspects to a polygraph test. They have access to background information about the suspect and about the case, information that is needed to construct the questions. Moreover, they conduct a pre-test interview with the suspect, an interview which is an inherent part of all CQT-based polygraph tests. This pre-test interview is an indispensable component of the CQT test, because it serves to convince the subject that the polygraph is an extremely accurate device for detecting deception, that any deception will be detected, and that any deception might be harmful to the subject's cause. Obviously this pre-test interview provides the polygrapher with additional information, and additional impressions about the subject. Those additional impressions and information might influence both the way the test will be administered (the tone of voice in which different questions are presented to the subject), and the interpretation of the charts. The combination of impressionistic methods of data interpretation and a great deal of *a priori* knowledge may increase the likelihood that conclusions derived from the test are based on the prior knowledge and not on the test-specific information.

This type of contamination is potentially more serious in the case of polygraphy than of graphology. While the non-graphological information contained in the scripts might influence the graphologist's interpretation and assessment, in the polygraph test it might also affect the physiological reactions themselves. This could occur if the prior knowledge and impressions of the polygraph investigator influence the way that he or she administers the test to the subject. Such influences may occur without the conscious awareness of the investigator. There are no direct data available to support this hypothesis, but the vast literature on the 'experimenter expectancy effect' (Rosenthal and Rubin, 1978) is sufficient to make it a serious possibility. If this is indeed the case, it means that it is more difficult to decontaminate the CQT polygraph test, and that it is not sufficient to assess this technique by simply using 'blind' chart interpretations.

Another common feature of graphology and CQT-based polygraphy is the absence of an underlying theory for the inference rules of those tests. The previous sections revealed that except for some general principles (i.e. deception is associated with increased arousal, which leads to enhanced physiological reactions; neat handwriting may be associated with neatness in other areas), there are no explicit theories accounting for the alleged relationships between the test content and behaviour or personality traits for both tools. In both instances the case for the use of the tests is made almost exclusively on alleged empirical grounds. But, as the previous discussions revealed, the empirical basis for those tests is either non-existent or at best very weak and questionable. In this regard the case of polygraphy is somewhat better than that of graphology. Even the critics of CQT polygraphy admit that it is capable of discriminating between guilty and innocent subjects at better than chance rates (e.g. Lykken, 1979). This claim applies, of course, only to the event-related usages of polygraphy, and cannot be generalized to the screening and personnel selection applications. The empirical status of graphology is very weak however, and our review of all the available studies suggests that the small positive validities obtained by graphologists can be completely accounted for by the non-graphological information contained in the scripts. In other words, graphologists do no better than anyone else on the basis of handwritten material.

Judgement based on non-conventional tools: a hypothetical model

In this section I shall try to lay out and discuss a hypothetical model for the decision processes underlying the use of graphology and polygraphy. This model is potentially applicable to many other non-conventional tests, and perhaps to some of the conventional psychological tests as well. The model rests on several assumptions:

1. A great deal of complex information is available to the judge. In the case of CQT polygraphy the test-specific information consists of at least three physiological indices, and at least three sequences of about ten questions each. In each sequence there are at least three pairs of relevant and control questions. Thus, the decision maker's task is to compare each pair on the basis of each physiological measure and to repeat these comparisons at least nine times. This is an extremely difficult task, because each physiological measure is complex and contains several relevant parameters, and because no *a priori* measurement rules are available to the polygrapher. In the case of graphology there is perhaps an even larger amount of test-specific information, because the shape of each and every letter may be indicative of some feature of the writer's personality, in addition to combinations of letters and words and the general pattern of the script. As a result of this complexity it is extremely difficult to combine all the different information in order to draw conclusions and to make judgements and predictions strictly on the basis of the test.

2. The judge starts with an *a priori* hypothesis. The hypothesis may be derived from some background information usually available to the judge, from a prior interaction with the subject (e.g. the pre-test interview in the case of

CQT polygraphy), or from the script's content in the case of graphology.
3. The test-specific information is used to test the *a priori* hypothesis, but the hypothesis-testing process is influenced by the confirmation bias (Wason, 1968). In other words, instead of looking for evidence that will disconfirm the *a priori* hypothesis, the judge is looking for evidence that will support it. The richness and vagueness of the information contained in those tests increase the likelihood of finding some confirmatory evidence. Indeed, it is most likely that both polygraph charts and handwritten scripts contain some confirmatory information for almost any possible hypothesis.

This model means that whatever *a priori* hypothesis serves as the starting point for making judgements and predictions, chances are it will be confirmed on the basis of the test. Since this hypothesis-testing process is not carried out with conscious intention to confirm the original hypothesis, it usually results in an impression that the test is indeed valid and accurate. This can explain the fact that users of such tests often have a sense of personal validation that far transcends the empirical evidence. The important implication of this model is that the validity of tests used in the manner described by the model cannot be greater than the validity of the *a priori* information on the basis of which the *a priori* hypothesis is formed.

This accounts for the fact that graphologists do no better than laypersons on the basis of handwritten scripts. It also explains why both graphologists and polygraphers are not willing to work under decontaminated set-ups, and are reluctant to give up background information, pre-test interviews, or authentic and spontaneous scripts in the case of graphology. They prefer to rely upon vague inference rules that enable them to choose whatever criteria they see fit in any given case. Practising polygraphers, for example, usually prefer to rely upon the respiration index despite the fact that research results indicate again and again that the skin conductance measure is more reliable (e.g. Podlesny and Raskin, 1977). This practice is also in line with the present model, because respiration is much more complex than the skin conductance. It contains richer information and is less ready for quantification and for being used in a mechanical and objective way.

The model presented in this section is based on the common characteristics of polygraphy and graphology as very rich information sources on the one hand, and as based upon impressionistic and subjective inference rules on the other. These characteristics may also characterize other non-conventional tests, as well as some of the conventional tests used routinely by psychologists (e.g. projective techniques). The model was suggested here as an hypothesis. So far there is no evidence in support, and it ought to be empirically tested before it can be seriously considered as a description of judgemental processes on the basis of certain types of tests (conventional or non-conventional). The purpose of this discussion is to argue that there is a sufficient *a priori* reason to offer the model, and that it has important enough implications to justify more thorough investigation.

This chapter focused upon two examples of what were labelled 'non-conventional' tools for personnel selection. As earlier stated, it is believed that polygraphy and graphology are the most promising candidates among the set of non-conventional tools that were mentioned. The main reason for this assertion is that both these tools enjoy a stronger *a priori* rationale as compared with other non-conventional tests. Graphology (in contrast, e.g. to astrology, palmistry) is a sample of expressive behaviour, and as such has at least a potential of generalizability to other behaviours. Unfortunately, as the present discussion demonstrated, this potential is not supported by the data. Thus it must be concluded in the spirit of Mischel and Peake (1982) that though there might be a great deal of temporal stability in handwriting behaviour, there is no evidence for cross-situational consistency or for drawing inference from handwriting to other behaviours. Polygraphy may be an even more promising candidate as a personnel selection tool. It is also based upon a behaviour sample, it has an *a priori* sound rationale (i.e. deception is accompanied by arousal which is reflected by physiological responses). In addition, there are data showing that polygraph tests have a positive validity in the event-related application. Unfortunately, the present chapter revealed that results based on the event-related application of polygraphy cannot be generalized to the event-free context that characterizes the personnel selection application. Furthermore, a closer look at the *a priori* rationale of the CQT polygraphy reveals that it is very shaky, because the control and the relevant questions used are not equivalent in terms of their arousal value. The present chapter argues that the case for both graphology and polygraphy as tools for personnel selection is very weak. It is believed that the case for other non-conventional tools is no better.

Finally, the theory presented to explain the decision processes involved in the use of non-conventional tools has a very practical lesson for all involved in choosing or rejecting them. It is to beware of the feeling of subjective validity. A graphologist may give us interpretations of our personality which accord with our own self-concept, but this is no reason to suppose that graphology has criterion validity.

ACKNOWLEDGEMENT

I wish to thank Maya Bar-Hillel for her helpful comments on an earlier draft.

REFERENCES AND FURTHER READING

Bar-Hillel, M., and Ben-Shakhar, G. (1986). The a priori case against graphology, in B. Nevo (ed.), *Scientific Aspects of Graphology*. Charles C. Thomas, Ill.

Barland, G.H. (1975). Detection of Deception in Criminal Suspects: a field validation study. Ph.D. dissertation, University of Utah.

Ben-Shakhar, G., Bar-Hillel, M. and Lieblich, I. (1986). Trial by polygraph: scientific and juridical issues in lie detection, *Behavioural Sciences and the Law*, **4**, 459–79.

Ben-Shakhar, G., Lieblich, I., and Bar-Hillel, M. (1982). An evaluation of polygrapher's judgements: a review from a decision theoretic perspective. *Journal of Applied Psychology*, **67**, 701–13.

Ben-Shakhar, G., Bar-Hillel, M., Bilu, Y., Ben-Abba, E., and Flug, A. (1986). Can graphology predict occupational success? Two empirical studies and some methodological ruminations, *Journal of Applied Psychology*, **71**, 645–53.

Correa, E.I., and Adams, H.E. (1981). The validity of the pre-employment polygraph examination and the effects of motivation, *Polygraph*, **10**, 143–56.

Crumbaugh, J.C., and Stockholm, E. (1977). Validation of graphoanalysis by 'global' or 'holistic' method, *Perceptual and Motor Skills*, **44**, 403–10.

Drory, A. (1986). Graphology and job performance: a validation study, in B. Nevo, (ed.). *Scientific Aspects of Graphology*, Charles C. Thomas, Ill.

Epstein, S. (1986). Does aggregation produce spuriously high estimates of behaviour stability? *Journal of Personality and Social Psychology*, **50**, 1199–210.

Fluckinger, F.A., Tripp, C.A., and Weinberg, G.H. (1961). A review of experimental research in graphology, 1933–1960, *Perceptual and Motor Skills*, **12**, 67–90.

Frederick, C.J. (1965). Some phenomena affecting handwriting analysis, *Perceptual and Motor Skills*, **20**, 211–18.

Hunter, J.E., and Hunter, R.F. (1984). Validity and utility of alternative predictors of job performance, *Psychological Bulletin*, **96**, 72–98.

Iacono, W.G. (in press). Can we determine the accuracy of polygraph tests? In J.R. Jennings, P.K. Ackles, and M.G.H. Coles (eds). *Advances in Psychophysiology*, vol. 4, JAI Press, Greenwich, CT.

Jansen, A. (1973). *Validation of Graphological Judgements: an experimental study*, Mouton, The Hague, Netherlands.

Kircher, J.C., and Raskin, D.C. (1983). Clinical versus statistical lie detection revisited: through a lens sharply, *Psychophysiology*, **20**, 452 (abstract).

Lykken, D.T. (1974). Psychology and the lie detection industry, *American Psychologist*, **29**, 725–39.

Lykken, D.T. (1978). Uses and abuses of the polygraph, in H.L. Pick (ed.). *Psychology: from research to practice*, Plenum Press, New York.

Lykken, D.T. (1979). The detection of deception, *Psychological Bulletin*, **86**, 47–53.

McDaniel, M.A., and Jones, J.W. (1986). A meta-analysis of the validity of the employee attitude inventory theft scales, *Journal of Business and Psychology*, **1**, 31–50.

Mischel, W., and Peake, P.K. (1982). Beyond deja vu in the search for cross-situational consistency, *Psychological Review*, **89**, 730–55.

Nevo, B., and Halevi, H. (1986). Validation of graphology through the use of a matching method based on ranking, in B. Nevo (ed.). *Scientific Aspects of Graphology*. Charles C. Thomas, Ill.

Podlesny, J.A., and Raskin, D.C. (1977). Physiological measures and the detection of deception, *Psychological Bulletin*, **84**, 782–99.

Rafaeli, A., and Klimoski, R.J. (1983). Predicting sales success through handwriting analysis: an evaluation of the effects of training and handwriting sample context, *Journal of Applied Psychology*, **68**, 212–17.

Rosenthal, R.R., and Rubin, D.B. (1978). Interpersonal expectancy effects: the first 345 studies, *The Behavioural and Brain Sciences*, **3**, 37–415.

Rushton, P.J., Murray, H.G., and Erdle, S. (1987). Combining trait consistency and learning specificity approaches to personality, with illustrative data on faculty teaching performance, *Personality and Individual Differences*, **8**, 59–66.

Sackett, P.R., and Decker, P.J. (1979). Detection of deception in the employment context: a review and critical analysis, *Personnel Psychology*, **32**, 487–506.

Sackett, P.R., and Harris, M.M. (1984). Honesty testing for personnel selection: a review and critique, *Personnel Psychology*, **37**, 221–45.

Saxe, L., Dougherty, D., and Cross, T. (1985). The validity of polygraph testing: scientific analysis and public controversy, *American Psychologist*, **40**, 355–66.

US Congress, Office of Technology Assessment (1983). Scientific validity of Polygraph Testing: a research review and evaluation. UIA-TM-H0-15. Washington, DC.

Wason, P.C. (1968). On the failure to eliminate hypotheses—a second look, in P.C. Wason and P.N. Johnson-Laird (eds). *Thinking and Reasoning*, Penguin, Harmondsworth, Middlesex.

Section 4: Selection in Specific Occupational Areas

Introduction to Section 4:
Selection in Specific Occupational Areas

Ivan T. Robertson

In many areas of occupational psychology there is a notable gap between ongoing research and contemporary organizational practices. Personnel selection is one area where the gap is relatively small. Although there is often a clear separation between the current concerns and activities of researchers (at least as they are reported in the scientific journals) and the everyday activities of practitioners there are also, on many issues, areas of shared interest. Examples of common interests concern work on utility analysis and validity generalization (see Muchinsky, 1986 for a brief review). Utility analysis provides a mathematical basis for calculating the monetary benefits of selection decision procedures. Validity generalization work is designed to investigate the extent to which specific selection methods (e.g. psychometric tests) produce similar results (in terms of their accuracy in predicting subsequent work performance) across a range of jobs and situations. Validity generalization work and the associated technique of meta-analysis have led to some revolutionary and important conclusions of particular relevance to this section of the book.

In a series of publications Hunter and Schmidt (e.g. Hunter, Schmidt, and Jackson, 1982) have focused researchers' attention on the inadequate sample sizes and low statistical power in much previous research on the validity of personnel selection techniques. They have been able to show that much of the variation in validity observed from one situation to another is due to statistical artefacts (principally sampling error due to the small size of sample) rather than differences in true validity coefficients. The work on meta-analysis and validity generalization is rather esoteric in parts and requires some mathematical/statistical sophistication. The conclusions drawn by researchers in this field, however, are neither esoteric nor difficult to grasp. The two major conclusions are: (i) that many selection methods are more valid than we had previously believed; and (ii) that the validity of a method is not limited to one job or to one single situation—in other words validity will generalize across jobs and situations.

The first of these conclusions is being pressed home with some force by meta-analysis researchers and has certainly had an impact on the views of many psychologists causing them to reconsider their views on the validity of most major selection methods. Some specific techniques such as cognitive (general mental ability) tests, work-sample tests and assessment centres have been shown to have particularly good validities. Recently, however, even the *bête noire* of personnel researchers, the unstructured employment interview, has emerged from meta-analysis with some credit and low but positive validity coefficients have been reported after meta-analysis (Weisner and Cronshaw, 1988).

On the validity generalization front several studies have produced results supporting the proposition that selection methods have validity which is not limited to specific jobs and situations. Acceptance of these studies leads to the view expressed succinctly by Tenopyr (1981) that, 'The results of the validity generalization studies done to date suggest that almost any test is valid for any job' (p. 1122). Taken together, in their most extreme form, the two conclusions expressed above suggest, with Tenopyr (1981), that any method is useful for selection decision making and can be used for taking selection decisions regardless of the specific job involved. This section of the book, concerned as it is with the problems of which method to use in which circumstances, seems to be rendered irrelevant by such conclusions. To understand why this is not so it is important to consider three issues concerning the meaning of the conclusions, their scientific status and the likely impact of such conclusions on practitioners.

Viewed in perspective the initially striking conclusion that selection method validities will generalize becomes easier to interpret. Meta-analysis results have shown, for example, that as far as psychometric ability tests are concerned, general mental ability predicts performance well across a wide range of jobs (Hunter and Hirsch, 1987) and that as job complexity increases so does the predictive power of such tests. It seems unsurprising that cognitive ability is linked with performance in most jobs, particularly if they are complex. It seems equally likely that in some jobs certain sub-components (e.g. verbal, numerical) of cognitive ability are more important than others—thus suggesting some job-specific requirements. It is important to qualify the results of validity generalization work with the comments that broad validity generalization across all job families is restricted to psychometric tests of general mental ability and that relatively few studies have employed multiple ability measures, making it impossible to draw conclusions about the advantages or otherwise of multiple/specific versus general mental ability tests. In addition to this it is also likely that in many practical selection situations the applicant pool will have a limited range of cognitive ability, thus restricting the discriminatory power of cognitive ability tests.

Graduate recruitment is a good example here—where most applicants will have relatively high levels of cognitive ability. A cognitive ability test will be of less value in actual selection decision-making situations where candidates' scores have very restricted range; thus other qualities (e.g. a personality or motivation) will need to be assessed in order to take selection decisions. Similarly, although job-related interviews have been shown to produce better validities than unstructured, psychological interviews, application of this approach to different jobs requires the use of a job-specific range of questions. Thus, in practical terms validity generalization does not imply that the same selection procedures should be used for all jobs and sets of circumstances.

In addition to placing the results of recent research in perspective, it is also wise to acknowledge that the techniques of meta-analysis have not escaped without criticism and debate (see Schmidt *et al.*, 1985; Sackett *et al.*, 1985). Detailed coverage of the debate is beyond the scope of this section. It is clear, however, that neither meta-analysis nor validity generalization has been accepted unreservedly by the scientific community—although most of its members do acknowledge that the techniques and associated research have made a major contribution to selection theory and research. Whether the influence of this work on practice will be equally profound is uncertain as yet. Although the connection between theory, research and practice is stronger in selection than in some other areas of occupational psychology, there is still a gap between discovery and application. It seems clear that most practitioners, at least in Europe, have not yet been influenced by the outcomes of validity generalization work. Taken overall then, while there is a clear trend towards generalization, there is still a clear need for an understanding of how selection technology may be applied to specific occupational areas.

SELECTION IN SPECIFIC OCCUPATIONAL AREAS

Jobs may be organized into collections of different categories based on various indicators of similarity or difference. Very few specific job categories have coherent research programmes on selection methods associated with them. Furthermore, although selection research has been extensive it is not so voluminous that extensive and coherent research evidence can be identified for more than a very limited number of fairly general job categories (e.g. sales, managerial, professional). The problems involved in identifying a reasonably small but fairly comprehensive set of job groupings are significant. For the purposes of this section of the book these problems were resolved by a careful search of the literature to identify major groupings, discussions with colleagues and the availability of willing and competent authors. The nine chapters which follow cover a range of occupational groupings based on both functional (e.g. sales) and non-functional (e.g. high stress/risk occupations) features. Coverage is clearly not comprehensive but the contents of one or more chapters should help to provide at least some insight into selection decision-making procedures for most applications.

In many cases the chapter authors have had the difficult job of providing the first review of its kind for the occupational field in question. Some groupings of jobs have proved more amenable to definition than others. Peter Makin, for example, in Chapter 4.3, gives a clear definition of professional jobs as they are dealt with in his chapter. By contrast and for good reason, Paul Thorne (Chapter 4.7) resists the temptation to place a clear boundary on what is meant by creative occupations.

All of the chapters attempt to provide a view of the occupational area involved, the personal qualities linked with successful job performance, current procedures for selection, evidence on the validity of specific methods for the occupational area in question and a critical review of the current situation. Despite these common themes, differences in the availability of material, coherence of the jobs involved and authors' preferences have led to an interesting and unique contribution in each chapter.

REFERENCES

Hunter, J.E., and Hirsch, H.R. (1987). Applications of meta-analysis, in C.L. Cooper and I.T. Robertson (eds), *International Review of Industrial and Organizational Psychology 1987*. Wiley, Chichester.

Hunter, J.E., Schmidt, F.L., and Jackson, G.B. (1982). *Meta-analysis: Cumulating research findings across studies*. Sage, Beverly-Hills, California.

Muchinsky, P.M. (1986). Personnel selection methods, in C.L. Cooper and I. T. Robertson (eds), *International Review of Industrial and Organizational Psychology 1986*. Wiley, Chichester.

Sackett, P.R., Schmitt, N., Tenopyr, M.L., Kehoe, J., and Zedeck, S. (1985). Commentary on forty questions about validity generalization and meta-analysis, *Personnel Psychology*, **38**, 697–798.

Schmidt, F.L., Hunter, J.E., Pearlman, K., and Hirsch, H.R. (1985). Forty questions about validity generalization and meta-analysis. *Personnel Psychology*, **38**, 697–798.

Tenopyr, M.L. (1981). The realities of employment testing, *American Psychologist*, **36**, 1120–7.

Weisner, W.H., and Cronshaw, S.F. (1988). A meta-analytic investigation of the impact of interview format and degree of structure on the validity of the employment interview, *Journal of Occupational Psychology*, **84**, 275–90.

Chapter 4.1

Selection of Operatives, Manual, Casual and Seasonal Workers

MARK COOK

Centre for Occupational Research Ltd, 14 Devonshire Place, London W1N 1PB, UK

SCOPE OF THIS CHAPTER

Table 1 cross-classifies jobs by responsibility and skill, and general area. It also outlines jobs covered by the heading 'operatives' and 'casual workers'. At first glance operatives and casual workers aren't a major element in the workforce, but surveys show skilled, semi-skilled and unskilled workers account for 56 per cent of the American working population (Roe, 1956).

The boxes Level 4 = Technology and Level 5 = Technology in Roe's classification contain a great number of occupations, from blacksmith to wood-carver, and from annealer to wheelwright. The boxes Level 4 = Outdoors and Level 5 = Outdoors contain jobs in agriculture, oil and mining, and forestry. Level 6 jobs in these two areas are unskilled 'handling' and labouring jobs: longshoremen (dockers), packers, helpers (mates), ditch diggers, lumberjacks, farm labourers, etc. (Table 2).

More recently Goldthorpe (Goldthorpe and Hope, 1974) has categorized occupations, using official British census data, and ratings of prestige. Table 1 shows that 50 per cent of British workers are 'operatives'; the most numerous groups are Semi-skilled manual (bus and truck drivers, postal workers, etc.), Semi-skilled manual—manufacturing (machine tool operators, assemblers, etc.), Unskilled manual (labourers), and Skilled manual—higher grade (fitters, tool makers, etc.). Table 1 also gives the occupation's average prestige ranking. Goldthorpe's prestige scale has 36 categories, and 'operatives' all fall in the bottom half; they evidently aren't held in great esteem by the man in the street. Wright (1985) confirms the class structure of occupations is much the same in Sweden (a socialist

Handbook of Assessment in Organizations   Edited by P. Herriot
© 1989 John Wiley & Sons Ltd

Table 1 Proportion of British workforce in twelve broad categories of 'operative', with grading on Goldthorpe–Hope scale, from least prestigious (36) to most prestigious (1) **NB** The highest grading for operatives is 18.

	Workforce (%)	Grading
Unskilled manual	6.11	35
Semi-skilled manual		
— transport	10.40	33
— construction/extractive	1.38	32
— manufacturing	6.33	27
Skilled manual		
— higher grade	5.89	18
— intermediate grade	3.55	22
— lower grade	4.97	30
— construction	4.04	23
— transport/extractive	2.84	27
Service workers	1.71	34
— intermediate	1.39	28
— higher grade	0.50	25

country for many years) as in the United States; some 40 per cent of the workforce in both populations are 'proletarians'.

Between 1910 and 1950 the proportion of unskilled workers in the American workforce had declined steadily (from 36 to 19.8 per cent) while the proportion of semi-skilled workers had increased from 14.7 to 22.4 per cent. The proportion of skilled workers had remained roughly constant (Roe, 1956). These trends are likely to continue, and the demand for unskilled workers will continue to decline.

ANALYSING THE JOB AND THE WORKER

In Britain, jobs are often still very vaguely defined, and training is often still at the 'Sit next to Nellie and watch how she does it' level. In the United States, the official *Dictionary of Occupational Titles* lists every job, with ratings of its complexity, training needs, working conditions, and of the interests, aptitudes and temperaments needed by workers.

In the United States very detailed *job analysis* systems have been devised to describe work, and identify attributes needed by effective workers. The *Position Analysis Questionnaire* (PAQ) provides information for 1000 jobs, including many in the 'blue-collar' area. PAQ analyses what workers do, in fairly general terms— e.g. assembling/disassembling, use of keyboard devices—then lists the attributes workers need (McCormick *et al.*, 1979). Sparrow *et al.* (1982) used PAQ to identify seven attributes needed by plastics injection-moulding setters in a UK plant: long-term memory, intelligence, short-term memory, good near-visual acuity, perceptual speed, convergent thinking, and mechanical ability. PAQ has one feature which limits its usefulness for operatives and casual workers; it requires a high (almost college) level of literacy, which respondents might not always possess.

Table 2   Two-way classification of occupations—by 'domain' and responsibility level (Roe, 1956)

Level	Group							
	I. Service	II. Business Contact	III. Organization	IV. Technology	V. Outdoor	VII. Science	VII. General Cultural	VIII. Arts and Entertainment
1	Personal therapists Social work supervisors Counsellors	Promoters	United States President and Cabinet officers Industrial tycoons International bankers	Inventive geniuses Consulting or chief engineers Ships' commanders	Consulting specialists	Research scientists University, college faculties Medical specialists Museum curators	Supreme Court Justices University, college faculties Prophets Scholars	Creative artists Performers, great Teachers, university equivalent Museum curators
2	Social workers Occupational therapists Probation, truant officers (with training)	Promoters Public relations counsellors	Certified public accountants Business and government executives Union officials, average Brokers, average	Applied scientists Factory managers Ships' officers Engineers	Applied scientists Landowners and operators, large Landscape architects	Scientists, semi-independent Nurses Pharmacists Veterinarians	Editors Teachers, high school and elementary	Athletes Art critics Designers Music arrangers
3	YMCA officials Detectives, police sergeants Welfare workers City inspectors	Salesmen: auto, bond, insurance, etc. Dealers, retail and wholesale Confidence men	Accountants, average Employment managers Owners, catering, dry-cleaning, etc.	Aviators Contractors Foremen (DOT I) Radio operators	County agents Farm owners Forest rangers Fish, game wardens	Technicians, medical, X-ray, museum Weather observers Chiropractors	Justices of the Peace Radio announcers Reporters Librarians	Ad writers Designers Interior decorators Showmen
4	Barbers Chefs Practical nurses Policemen	Auctioneers Buyers (DOT I) House canvassers Interviewers, poll	Cashiers Clerks, credit, express, etc. Foremen, warehouse Salesclerks	Blacksmiths Electricians Foremen (DOT II) Mechanics, average	Laboratory testers, dairy products, etc. Miners Oil well drillers	Technical assistants	Law clerks	Advertising artists Decorators, window, etc. Photographers Racing car drivers
5	Taxi drivers General houseworkers Waiters City firemen	Pedlars	Clerks, file, stock, etc. Notaries Runners Typists	Bulldozer operators Deliverymen Smelter workers Truck drivers	Gardeners Farm tenants Teamsters, cowpunchers Miner's helpers	Veterinary hospital attendants		Illustrators, greeting cards Showcard writers Stagehands
6	Chambermaids Hospital attendants Elevator operators Watchmen		Messenger boys	Helpers Laborers Wrappers Yardmen	Dairy hands Farm laborers Lumberjacks	Non-technical helpers in scientific organizations		

PAQ's main rival, the *Occupational Analysis Inventory*, is very long; it lists 602 elements, because it is *job oriented*, concentrating on the tasks done (whereas PAQ is *content oriented*, concentrating on the worker). The OAI analyses job elements into 28 factors. Examples of factors involving operatives' work are:

1. *Building/repairing structures*—carpenter, bricklayer, shopfitter.
2. *Food preparation*—short order cook, chef, school lunch supervisor.

OAI's analysis of over 1000 jobs found the 28 factors left a lot of variation unaccounted for, implying a lot of tasks are too specific to be grouped (Cunningham *et al.*, 1983).

The *Job Components Inventory* (JCI) was developed in Britain (Banks *et al.*, 1983) specifically for jobs requiring limited skill; it has five principal sections: tools and equipment, perceptual and physical requirements, maths, communication, decision making and responsibility. JCI ratings distinguish clerical jobs from engineering jobs, proving JCI finds a difference where there ought to be a difference. JCI profiles for the four engineering jobs differ in minor respects; grinding machines require more complex skills than milling and drilling machines and lathes, implying possibly different selection and training requirements.

Another specialized job analysis system is Fleishman's (1979) *Physical Abilities Analysis* (Table 3). Detailed *physical* job analysis is especially useful, and may be legally necessary, when women and the handicapped are assessed for jobs with physique requirements, and which are traditionally done by men.

Job analysis serves many purposes (Cook, 1988), including guiding choice of assessment methods. It can be used in conjunction with aptitude batteries.

Table 3   The nine factors underlying human physical ability, according to Fleishman 1979

Dynamic strength—ability to exert muscular force repeatedly or continuously. Useful for doing push-ups, climbing a rope.

Trunk strength—ability to exert muscular force repeatedly or continuously using trunk or abdominal muscles. Useful for leg-lifts or sit-ups.

Static strength—the force the individual can exert against external objects, for a brief period. Useful for lifting heavy objects, pulling heavy equipment.

Explosive strength—ability to expand a maximum of energy in one act or a series of acts. Useful for long jump, high jump, 50-metre race.

Extent flexibility—ability to flex or extend trunk and back muscles as far as possible in any direction. Useful for reaching, stretching, bending.

Dynamic flexibility—ability to flex or extend trunk and back repeatedly. Useful for continual bending, reaching, stretching.

Gross body coordination—also known as agility.

Balance—ability to stand or walk on narrow ledges.

Stamina—or cardio-vascular endurance, the ability to make prolonged, maximum exertion. Useful for long distance running.

Mecham (see McCormick *et al.*, 1979) analysed 163 jobs, and found a job's PAQ ratings predicted moderately well the average aptitude profile of people doing it, showing that people who have 'gravitated' to a particular job and 'survived' there have a particular profile of abilities. This implies each job needs a particular set of attributes, that can be identified by PAQ, and then assessed by an aptitude battery.

ASSESSMENT OF OPERATIVES, MANUAL, CASUAL AND SEASONAL WORKERS

Selection procedures for operatives and casual workers divide into *traditional methods*, *psychological tests*, and *physical tests*.
   Traditional methods include:

- CV/application form
- interview
- letter of reference
- qualifications and trade tests
- present employee referral
- union nomination/seniority

Psychological tests divide into:

- mental ability
- personality/interests
- biographical data

Physical tests include:

- manual dexterity
- physique/strength
- work sample/trainability

   In Britain operatives are generally selected by interview; Ungerson's *Recruitment Handbook* (1983) says nothing about any other way of assessing shop floor staff. Investigations of the Commission for Racial Equality (CRE), e.g. CRE (1984), confirm this, and show workers are often recruited by word of mouth, through the present workforce, a practice CRE frown on because it tends to perpetuate the existing—generally all white—composition of the workforce.
   In Britain surveys by the British Psychological Society (1985) and Income Data Services (1985) show aptitude tests are sometimes used to select apprentices, whereas personality tests are never used for selecting apprentices or shop floor workers.
   Generally, information about selection of operatives in Britain remains very sketchy, while information about selecting casual and seasonal workers is non-existent.

In the United States testing has gone into a sharp decline; the 1975 American Society for Personnel Administration survey found three-quarters of employers had cut back their testing programmes, and 14 per cent intended to drop testing altogether. A recent survey of published research showed skilled and unskilled workers were assessed by psychological tests, including personality tests, by biodata, work sample, and physical test, but not by assessment centre or peer ratings (Schmitt *et al.*, 1984).

VALIDITY AND FAIRNESS OF SPECIFIC PREDICTORS

Interviews

The interview's poor validity has been documented by numerous reviews, none of which suggests it does any better (or any worse) selecting operatives and casual staff, as compared with other grades. Surprisingly, the interview has largely escaped accusations of 'unfairness', even though it is the easiest way of all to discriminate, consciously or unconsciously, as Arvey's (1979) review shows. Many ways of improving the interview have been suggested; the most promising is the 'structured interview', in which the interviewer is told both what questions to ask, and what weight to attach to the answers.

The recently devised 'situational interview' uses 'critical incidents' of particularly effective or ineffective behaviour to develop a standard list of questions, e.g:

> Your spouse and two teenage children are sick in bed with a cold. There are no friends or relatives available to look in on them. Your shift starts in three hours. What would you do in this situation?

Interviewers are also given 'benchmark' answers for good, average and poor workers:

> I'd stay home—my spouse and family come first. (poor)
> I'd phone my supervisor and explain my situation. (average)
> Since they only have colds, I'd come to work. (good)

Research with sawmill workers finds the 'situational' interview is very reliable, and predicts supervisor ratings of effectiveness very well (Latham *et al.*, 1980). The 'situational' interview is 'fair' because it deals with very specific behaviour, of proven direct relevance, and because it avoids mention of legally risky abstractions like abilities or dispositions.

References

In Britain the completely unstructured reference—'tell me what you think of John Smith'—is still widely used, whereas American employers prefer specific questions and simple ratings. Research on the reliability and validity of letters of reference by and large shows both to be disappointingly low, but little research has been reported specifically on operatives and casual workers.

Qualifications and trade tests

Employers often specify educational qualifications, such as OND, HND, or 'O levels' in Britain, and high school graduation in the United States. General educational requirements have been repeatedly challenged in the United States, usually successfully, because they exclude ethnic minorities who do less well at school. It is also claimed that educational requirements often are not 'job related': 'O level' English is required, even though workers don't have to read or write anything more complex than orders for components. Critics argue this takes too narrow a view of educational qualifications, which reflect more generally desirable characteristics, such as motivation, persistence, and willingness to fit in. Reviews (Hunter and Hunter, 1984; Reilly and Chao, 1982) unfortunately do not confirm this hypothesis, and show educational achievement has limited predictive validity.

In the United States 'trade tests' are available for car mechanics, carpenters, plumbers, truck drivers, welders, etc. These show a would-be bricklayer *knows* about bricklaying, but not necessarily that he or she can actually lay bricks. Trade tests presuppose literacy, which not all trades absolutely require. 'Fair' employment agencies may object to paper-and-pencil tests being used to select for manual jobs.

Mental ability tests

This is a broad category including general intelligence (IQ) tests, various aptitude tests, aptitude batteries, mechanical comprehension tests and short 'screening' tests. All mental ability tests inter-correlate to some extent, suggesting,

Table 4 Average validities reported by Ghiselli (1966) for four classes of skilled and unskilled worker, for three types of mental ability, against two criteria. Int—general intelligence; S & M—spatial and mechanical ability: Perc acc—perceptual accuracy

		Int	S & M	Perc acc
Vehicle operation				
	training	0.15	0.30	0.08
	proficiency	0.14	0.20	0.36
Trades and crafts				
	training	0.41	0.41	0.31
	proficiency	0.19	0.23	0.22
Industrial occupations				
	training	0.40	0.39	0.22
	proficiency	0.19	0.16	0.18
Unskilled workers				
	training	−0.03	–	–
	proficiency	0.22	0.35	–

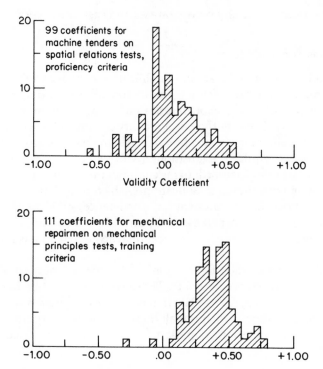

Figure 1   Distribution of validity coefficients for two pairs of predictor and criterion measures (Ghiselli, 1966)

very crudely speaking, they are measuring the same general thing.

Data from the Second World War conscripts (Harrell and Harrell, 1945) show the less skilled the occupation, the lower the average level of general intelligence of people doing it, although there is great variation about the mean, between and within occupations. Classic early studies found mental ability predicted success in a range of occupations, skilled, semi-skilled, and unskilled, such as machinists, bus maintenance crews, and packers and wrappers.

Ghiselli's (1966) review of test validity appeared to prove two very important points: firstly, that mental ability tests were generally *rather poor* predictors; and, secondly, that they were *very inconsistent* predictors. Table 4 summarizes the average predictive validity of three classes of ability test, for four classes of operative and casual worker, against 'training' criteria, and supervisor ratings. The averages are all low—so low that critics argued the tests were not worth using. Training criteria were more accurately predicted; otherwise it is hard to detect any pattern in the data of Table 4.

Figure 1 shows the data for two of Ghiselli's averages; 111 separate correlations between mechanical principles tests and training grades in repairmen ranged from 0.75 through a median of 0.39 to a low of −0.30 (where high scores on the test 'predict' poor training grades). Similarly 99 correlations between tests of spatial relations and proficiency as a machine tender ranged from 0.55 to −0.60, with a median of 0.11.

Ghiselli's second conclusion—variable validity—led many occupational psychologists to argue that predictive validity of tests for operatives and casual workers depends on other factors, like organizational climate, the precise nature of the job, plant location, etc. The employer could not be sure the test would have any predictive validity in a particular plant, without testing it locally—an expensive procedure. It certainly would not be safe to use ability tests 'off the shelf'.

More recently opinion has swung against these pessimistic conclusions. New analyses of validity data attribute their variability to limitations in validation research, especially varying, but usually too small, sample sizes, and attribute the low overall average validity to unreliable measures, unreliable criteria, not having any information about applicants who were rejected, etc. Schmidt and Hunter (1981) argue that the predictive validity of ability tests for operatives is really much more consistent, and much greater, than Ghiselli's analysis indicated.

For example, the 'true' validity of tests of mechanical principles for repairmen is $r = 0.78$, twice the uncorrected average Ghiselli quotes, and the variation about the mean in Figure 1 is entirely illusory. This implies employers can use tests of mechanical comprehension 'off the shelf' to select repairmen. (Whereas tests of spatial relations genuinely are quite unable to predict proficiency in machine minders, the estimated 'true' validity being $r = 0.05$.)

More recently the US Office of Personnel Management has re-analysed its ability test data, calculating 'true' validities. Table 5 shows Northrop's (1984) re-analysis of data for over 1 million apprentices, divided into four main classes, and tested with seven aptitudes. All but reasoning and clerical ability achieve 'true' validities around $r = 0.50$. Perhaps apprentices leave clerical work to clerks, and reasoning to management.

'League tables' of validity of assessment methods usually place ability tests near the top, for both selection and promotion. Despite this, ability tests have lost favour in the United States, especially for operatives, where American employers once used short 'screening' tests such as the Wonderlic Personnel Test. 'Fair' employment laws, and their interpretation in key cases, caused this. It is particularly difficult to persuade courts that paper-and-pencil tests are 'relevant' to

Table 5 Estimated mean 'true' validities of seven ability tests for four categories of apprentice: Category 6—Machine Trades; 7—Benchwork; 8—Structural Work; 9—Miscellaneous. Northrop (1984)

Category	6	7	8	9	All
Reasoning	0.16	–	0.31	0.31	0.30
Verbal	0.34	0.42	0.55	0.54	0.56
Quantitative	0.31	0.56	0.54	0.57	0.54
Space visualization	0.30	0.63	0.43	0.43	0.48
Clerical	0.24	0.31	0.24	0.23	0.24
Mechanical	0.53	0.57	0.50	0.40	0.50
Information	0.58	0.51	0.59	0.46	0.58

manual jobs, so use of ability tests for operatives has been particularly restricted.
Mental ability tests have not yet fallen foul of the law in Britain.

Personality tests

Ghiselli's (1966) review found personality tests had very modest predictive
validities (around r = 0.25) for operatives. He also found a relative dearth of
research, and none at all for unskilled labourers, so it has not been possible to re-
analyse the data in the way ability test data were re-analysed. A later review of
research in the American petroleum industry found interest and personality
inventories achieved near-zero median validity (Dunnette, 1972); however, the
best 25 per cent of coefficients for personality tests exceeded r = 0.37, suggesting
perhaps tests can predict productivity if used properly.

Personality inventories like 16PF and California Psychological Inventory can be
difficult for unskilled workers, so shorter inventories with lower reading levels
may be needed. The Work Opinion Questionnaire has 35 items, all fairly short—
'Supervisors are too bossy', 'If something goes wrong on the job, I get blamed'—
and correlate moderately well with supervisor ratings (Johnson, Messe and
Crano, 1984). Saville and Holdsworth are currently producing a new form
(FMX-5) of the Occupational Personality Questionnaire aimed at shop floor
workers.

Biodata

Biographical methods take two forms: the *weighted application blank* (WAB) which
uses routine application forms information-keyed to productivity or turnover,
and the *biographical inventory* which uses a questionnaire format.

WABs have proved useful for casual and seasonal workers. The Green Giant
Co. used one to reduce turnover in seasonal pea- and corn-canners:

> The typically stable Green Giant production worker lives [locally], has a telephone, is
> married and has no children, is not a veteran [not an ex-serviceman], is either young
> (under 25) or old (over 55), weighs more than 150 pounds but less than 175, has
> obtained more than ten years' education, has worked for Green Giant, will be available
> for work until the end of summer, and prefers field work to inside work (Dunnette and
> Maetzold, 1955).

This profile retained validity over time, and in three other canning plants, but
could not be used for non-seasonal cannery workers. *Permanent* cannery workers
who did not leave had family and domestic responsibilities (and tended to be
women), whereas the profile for *seasonal* workers identified people who wanted a
short-term job—either young college students, or semi-retired people (Scott and
Johnson, 1967).

Biodata have been used to predict success as a bus driver (Baehr, unpublished,
cited by Reilly and Chao, 1982), and in the oil industry. Oil company employees
could be classified biographically into eighteen subgroups: unskilled employees

in one 'bio-group' were much more successful than those in another (Brush and Owens, 1979).

WABs and biodata inventories *as a whole* do not seem to create much adverse impact on protected minorities. This is a little odd, for many of their individual component items will reflect race or sex differences. Many WAB and biodata questions directly or indirectly measure social class: owns an automobile, owns own home, lives in suburbs, parental occupation, etc. It is not illegal, even in the United States, to discriminate on grounds of social class; it is risky however, because measures of class are often also measures of race, and because a selection method that *looks* arbitrary or biased is more likely to attract criticism.

Physical assessments

Workers assembling small components need manual dexterity: workers shifting large ones need physical strength. Skilled workers often need both. Managers, clerks and sales staff by contrast can, with relative impunity, be unfit, overweight, physically weak, or poorly coordinated. Physical tests are rarely used except to select for skilled or unskilled manual jobs (Schmitt *et al.*, 1984).

Two broad approaches may be distinguished: *part* and *whole*. The *part* approach argues the job needs a particular ability, so candidates are assessed with standardized tests. The *whole* approach makes the candidate do the job, or a simulation, and assesses how well he or she does. Presently the *whole* approach seems more popular.

Manual dexterity

Manual dexterity tests typify the *part* approach. They are standardized, so a particular applicant can be compared with people in general, with other applicants, and with the job's requirements if these have been measured.

There are commercially available dexterity tests. The Minnesota Manual Dexterity Test assesses *arm and hand* dexterity, as the subject moves coin-sized counters in and out of circular slots. The O'Connor Finger and Tweezer Dexterity Tests and the Purdue Pegboard are *finger and wrist* tests, in which very small components are placed in slots or over pegs. Some aptitude batteries include dexterity tests, notably the (US) General Aptitude Test Battery (GATB); official ratings estimate how important dexterity is for different occupations, and what GATB dexterity scores to aim for. In Britain Saville and Holdsworth have recently produced two new dexterity tests: FINDEX, a test of finger dexterity, and MANDEX, a test of manual dexterity and spatial ability.

Ghiselli reports moderate validities for dexterity tests against training grades, and supervisory ratings, for vehicle operation, trades and crafts, and industrial occupations. Ghiselli's low averages are probably underestimates; the average (r = 0.25) for finger dexterity in bench workers increases to r = 0.39 when 'corrected' for various sources of error.

Physique/strength

British employers often include tests of physique or strength, in an arbitrary, haphazard way. By contrast, some North American employers use physical tests very systematically. Armco Inc. has devised a battery of physical work sample tests for steel works labourers, and has extensive data on norms, correlations and sex differences (Arnold *et al.*, 1982). American Telephone and Telegraph has devised a battery of pole-climbing tests for linemen (Reilly, Zedeck and Tenopyr, 1979); applicants with good balance, adequate 'static strength' (ability to pull on a rope), and higher 'body density' (less fat, more muscle) performed better in training, and were more likely to 'survive' at least six months.

Measures of physique and physical performance often inter-correlate highly; AT&T initially used fourteen measures, and found only three necessary. Fleishman (1979) analysed 'physical proficiency' into nine basic physical abilities (Table 3). Some US organizations take a different approach to the problem; they employ work physiologists who measure the *oxygen uptake* each job demands. The employer then selects people whose 'aerobic' (oxygen uptake) capacity, measured by treadmill, step test, or exercise bicycle, is adequate (Campion, 1983).

Physique tests achieve moderate validity (Schmitt *et al.*, 1984). Chaffin's research (Campion, 1983) suggests the relation is continuous and linear, and does not have a threshold; the greater the discrepancy between a worker's strength and the physical demands of the job, the more likely the worker is to suffer a back injury. Hence an employer who wants to minimize the risk of back injury—a notorious cause of absence and lost output—should choose the strongest applicant, other things being equal.

Most physical tests create substantial 'adverse impact' on women, who are generally lighter and less strong than men. Despite this, carefully devised physical tests have survived legal scrutiny in the United States. AT&T's pole-climbing tests for linemen reject five times as many women as men, but were not ruled 'unfair', because AT&T had proved conclusively that strength is essential in linemen. Cruder physical tests, such as minimum height, have generally not survived legal scrutiny in the United States.

Work sample and trainability tests

The work sample test uses the 'whole' approach. Campion (1972) describes a typical work sample for maintenance mechanics. After a thorough job analysis, Campion selected four tasks: installing pulleys and belts, disassembling and repairing a gear box, installing and aligning a motor, pressing a bush into a sprocket and reaming it to fit a shaft. Campion compared the work sample with paper-and-pencil tests: Bennett, Wonderlic, Short Employment Tests (Verbal, Numerical and Clerical Aptitude). The work samples predicted supervisor ratings fairly well, whereas the paper-and-pencil tests predicted poorly.

Reviews have consistently shown that work samples have good predictive validity, for selection and promotion (Dunnette, 1972; Robertson and Kandola, 1982; Schmitt *et al.*, 1984). One review concluded work samples achieve better validity than intelligence and personality tests (Asher and Sciarrino, 1974). Another concluded work samples were the best test for promotion decisions (Hunter and Hunter, 1984).

Work samples have other advantages. They are very plausible to applicants; Cascio and Phillips (1979) used some for Miami Beach municipal employees, including sewer mechanics, and electricians' mates. If would-be electricians had completed the wiring correctly, lights lit up; if the wiring was not correct, the bulbs did not light, and the applicant could not deny he or she had made a mistake. Some Miami Beach tests doubled as 'realistic job previews'; applicants for sewer mechanic vacancies sometimes withdrew after being tested in an underground sewage chamber.

True work samples presuppose the person has already learned the job's underlying skills; there is no point giving a typing test to someone who cannot type. *Trainability tests* assess how well the applicant can *learn* a new skill; they are widely used in the (UK) Training Agency's 'Skillcentres' (Robertson and Downs, 1979). First an instructor gives standardized instructions and a demonstration. Then the applicant's efforts are rated, using a simple checklist. Robertson and Downs report good results for bricklaying, carpentry, welding, machine sewing, forklift truck driving, fitting and machining. In America trainability tests are called 'miniature training and evaluations'; Siegel (1983) describes nine tests, including ones for Dual Tasking and Social Interaction, as well as for Computation and Record Keeping. The Social Interaction Test is essentially a lower level of the 'command tasks' used in UK War Office Selection Boards; subjects cooperate in folding a large heavy tarpaulin. Siegel (1978) found the tests popular with subjects: 'Gave me a chance to prove that I could do some things with my hands, not just my head'.

Work samples look 'fairer' than other tests. They create less 'adverse impact' on protected ethnic minorities, compared with aptitude or intelligence tests (Gordon and Kleiman, 1976). As many blacks and Hispanics as whites 'passed' the Miami Beach work samples. Mental ability tests assess the applicant's *general* suitability, and make an intermediate inference—this person is intelligent so he or she will be a productive flange-bracketer. Testing the employee with a real or simulated flange-bracket press makes no intermediate inferences. Asher and Sciarrino (1974) argue that 'point-to-point correspondence between predictor and criterion' ensures a higher validity and—perhaps more important these days—gives less scope for legal challenge. Work samples also avoid inappropriate overemphasis of the ability to read and write.

THE WAY FORWARD

Selecting operatives

The selection of managers and salesmen has preoccupied psychologists since the earliest days, and has generated a vast literature; research on the selection of operatives, by contrast, has been very patchy.

We know mental ability tests can predict productivity in operatives: what we don't know is why or how. Several hypotheses need testing. Herrnstein (1973) argues that a given level of intelligence is 'necessary but not sufficient' for most occupations. A dull person is unlikely to succeed as an accountant, but a bright person is not assured of success in a prestigious and well-paid job; he or she may only succeed in becoming a lumberjack, if poorly adjusted, idle, unambitious, or just unlucky. This implies operatives and casual staff will be recruited from the ranks of those not bright enough to get 'good' jobs, and of those too poorly adjusted to progress in them—a disturbing prospect for the personnel department.

The 'threshold' hypothesis is popular with personnel managers and psychologists alike. It says anyone of 'normal' intelligence can do most blue-collar jobs; there is no need to select especially bright people (who might indeed become easily bored and disruptive). The employer needs only to avoid employing the small minority of the especially dull. Critics of the threshold hypothesis (Schmidt and Hunter, 1981) argue that ability is normally distributed, that productivity is normally distributed, and that the correlation between them implies the brighter the worker, the more productive he or she is, through the whole range of ability. Therefore, the employer should always, other things being equal, go for the brightest applicants whatever the job.

Only one study throws any light on *why* ability tests predict productivity. Hunter (1983) found mental ability does not correlate *directly* with supervisor ratings, but does correlate with job knowledge and work sample performance, which *in turn* correlate with supervisor ratings. More intelligent people make better workers because they learn quicker what the job is about. In skilled work, learning takes months or years; in unskilled and casual work the employee needs to learn only where to find the raw materials, what to do with them, and where to put the finished product. Hunter's findings suggest less able people may make successful operatives, if the employer has the time, patience and money to wait for them to learn the job (and if there is not too much re-learning involved).

Unskilled, casual and seasonal workers

The most obvious area in need of more research is the selection of unskilled, casual and seasonal workers, where we know next to nothing. There is virtually no information about how such workers *are* selected, nor about how they *should* be selected. In the far-off days of full employment, there was no need to investigate either question, because there was no *selection* problem, but a *recruitment* problem. Employers can now *select*, but need confirmation that methods that are effective for higher level employees are also effective for casual and seasonal workers.

The recent work of Schmidt and Hunter has shown mental ability predicts productivity, from park ranger to manager—but their analyses do not include any unskilled or casual workers. There is no reason to suppose mental ability is not a good predictor for such workers, but empirical evidence is clearly needed. The shrinking labour force, and the increasingly widespread use of ability tests, are likely to 'shake out' the intellectually ungifted more and more, so an investigation of their potential value as employees is urgently needed. Cattell (1936) argued that persons with IQs below 85 have limited scope for employment in an industrialized society; 16 per cent of the population have IQs below 85.

Off-the-shelf tests

Occupational psychologists traditionally assumed every job differed, so a thorough job analysis was essential before selecting tests for operatives. Re-analyses of validity data have challenged this assumption. The (US) Army Classification Battery's (ACB) nine sub-tests have been validated for 35 very different army trades, ranging from radar repairman, through welder and dental laboratory technician, to army cook. There are reliable differences between jobs in ACB sub-test validities—but the differences are *too small to have any practical use* (Schmidt and Hunter, 1978); in effect the ACB predicts productivity equally well for all 35 trades. Other research shows the same aptitude battery can be used to select 74 different types of apprentice, without losing information (Northrop, 1984), and that the same aptitude battery can be used to select for all 24 varieties of technician employed by the US government and armed services (Lilienthal and Pearlman, 1983).

'Will' v. 'can'

Ability tests and work samples have good validity, but they only tell us what the operative *can* do, not what he or she *will* do. They provide little or no information about likely future turnover, time keeping, absence, or sickness. They do not identify applicants likely to prove idle, dishonest or disruptive. Only assessments of personality, motivation, interests and attitudes can provide this information. (Of course poor morale and low productivity are not necessarily the employee's fault and cannot necessarily be solved by better selection.) Yet assessing how employees *will* behave is difficult, partly because assessors do not usually feel able to be more open about the information they want.

Projective tests, like the Rorschach 'inkblot', or graphology (see Chapter 3.12), have been convincingly shown to be useless. Psychophysiological methods too have proved disappointing, and are not likely to be acceptable. Assessment centres have good validity for selecting managers, military officers and civil servants, but have not been tried for operatives. Assessment centres are fairly expensive—although arguably still cost-effective. The way forward seems to lie in developing improved inventories, and in biographical methods, especially where the information does not come from the person being assessed.

Past behaviour is the best predictor of future behaviour

The employer's problem has always been how to get a large and unbiased sample of 'past behaviour'. The interview is ludicrously short and easily doctored; even the three full days of an assessment centre are not really very long. Lately, government training schemes, in Britain, have given employers six-month samples of school leavers' behaviour by which to judge them. An unknown, but increasingly large, number of operatives are being recruited this way—presently rather casually. Employers could use the six months of the training period to collect detailed records of output, attendance, sickness, etc., using both supervisory ratings, and standard 'personnel' criteria.

Which methods?

Cook (1988) lists five criteria for selection and promotion assessments:

1. *Validity* is the single most important criterion. Unless a test predicts perform-ance, there is no point using it.
2. *Cost* too often preoccupies selectors. It is rarely a major consideration, so long as the test is *valid*. It is always worth spending money to get and keep the right staff, except perhaps for the most transient casual and seasonal workers.
3. *(Im)practicality* is a reason for *not* using a test.
4. *Generality* means how many types of employees the test can be used for. Constraints on generality include availability of information, and problems in getting and using it. The armed services will accept peer ratings, but it is much less likely that a tightly unionized manual workforce would do so.
5. *(Il)legality* is another reason for *not* using a method. It is hard to evaluate, because the legal position on many tests is obscure or confused.

Taking *validity* as the over-riding consideration, there are six classes of test with *generally* high validity: peer ratings, biodata, ability tests, assessment centres, work sample tests, and job knowledge tests. Peer ratings and assessment centres are not used for operatives: peer ratings probably would not be acceptable, while assessment centres are generally thought too expensive.

Biodata achieve fairly good validity, although not quite as good as ability tests. Biodata are not as 'transportable' as ability tests, which makes them more expensive. WABS and biodata also 'decay' over time, faster than other selection methods. It is very unlikely Dunnette and Maetzold's WAB for cannery workers would still work, because American patterns of home ownership, phone owner-ship, military service, and family size have all changed so much since 1955. Biodata methods also create a 'security' problem; when the scoring rules of the US insurance industry's biodata leaked, it rapidly lost all predictive power.

Ability tests have excellent validity, are 'transportable', can be used 'off the shelf' and are cheap. They create 'adverse impact' on certain minorities, which makes them unpopular and legally problematic. Ability tests may eventually encounter similar difficulties in Britain and Europe.

Work samples have excellent *validity*, are easy to use and are generally quite 'safe' legally. However, they are expensive, because they are necessarily specific to each job. Much the same applies to *job knowledge tests*, except that they are cheaper because they are commercially available. On the debit side, they are also more likely to cause legal problems because they are usually paper-and-pencil tests.

Of the four, ability tests are probably best, and certainly the cheapest—so long as 'fair' employment agencies do not object. (Complaints of 'unfairness' about tests usually concern ethnic minorities; most tests do not create any major sex discrimination problems.) American psychologists currently argue that ability tests are entirely 'fair', in the technical sense of 'fairness'; ability tests predict productivity equally accurately for male and female, white and non-white.

Traditional methods—*interview* and *reference*—have only very 'moderate' validity, but are cheap, easy and fairly 'safe' to use. Conventional 'unstructured' interviews are virtually useless, but 'structured' interviews require considerable development work, which means extra cost. References can be improved, up to a point, by re-wording and the use of rating scales.

Large employers can employ biographical methods, and construct their own work samples, giving them legally safe and fairly valid assessments of both ability and habitual performance. Small employers are not so well placed, lacking the numbers to make either method feasible or cost-effective. The small employer tends to be pushed in the direction of 'ready made' methods. Trade tests and mental ability tests are cheap and effective but slightly risky. Personality tests are more of an *unknown* quantity. Perhaps the best advice to the small employer is, for the purposes of selection, to become a *large* employer by joining forces with other small employers to develop biographical methods and work samples.

REFERENCES

Arnold, J.D., Rauschenberger, J.M., Soubel, W.G., and Guion, R.G. (1982). Validation and utility of strength test for selecting steelworkers, *Journal of Applied Psychology*, **67**, 588–604.

Arvey, R.D. (1979). Unfair discrimination in the employment interview: a summary and review of recent literature, *Psychological Bulletin*, **86**, 736–65.

Asher, J.J., and Sciarrino, J.A. (1974). Realistic work sample tests: a review, *Personnel Psychology*, **27**, 519–33.

Banks, M.H., Jackson, P.R., Stafford, E.M., and Warr, P.B. (1983). The Job Components Inventory and the analysis of jobs requiring limited skill, *Personnel Psychology*, **36**, 57–66.

British Psychological Society (1985). The Use of Tests by Psychologists: report on a survey of the members of the British Psychological Society. BPS, Leicester.

Brush, D.H., and Owens, W.A. (1979). Implementation and evaluation of an assessment classification model for manpower utilisation, *Personnel Psychology*, **32**, 369–83.

Campion, J.E. (1972). Work sampling for personnel selection, *Journal of Applied Psychology*, **56**, 40–4.

Campion, M.A. (1983). Personnel selection for physically demanding jobs: review and recommendations, *Personnel Psychology*, **36**, 527–50.

Cascio, W., and Phillips, N.F. (1979). Performance testing: a rose among thorns? *Personnel Psychology*, **32**, 751–66.

Cattell, R.B. (1936). *The Fight For Our National Intelligence*, P.S. King, London.

Commission for Racial Equality (1984). St Chad's Hospital: report of a formal investigation. CRE, London.

Cook, M. (1988). *Personnel Selection and Productivity*. Wiley, Chichester.

Cunningham, J.W., Boese, R.R., Neeb, R.W., and Pass, J.J. (1983). Systematically derived work dimensions: factor analyses of the Occupation Analysis Inventory, *Journal of Applied Psychology*, **68**, 232–52.

Dunnette, M.D. (1972). Validity Study Results for Jobs Relevant to the Petroleum Refining Industry. American Petroleum Institute.

Dunnette, M.D., and Maetzold, J. (1955). Use of a weighted application blank in hiring seasonal employees, *Journal of Applied Psychology*, **39**, 308–10.

Fleishman, E.A. (1979). Evaluating physical abilities required by jobs, *The Personnel Administrator*, **24**, 82–92.

Ghiselli, E.E. (1966). *The Validity of Occupational Aptitude Tests.* Wiley, New York.

Goldthorpe, J., and Hope, K. (1974). *The Social Grading of Occupations.* Clarendon Press, Oxford.

Gordon, M.E., and Kleiman, L.S. (1976). The prediction of trainability using a work-sample test and an aptitude test: a direct comparison, *Personnel Psychology*, **29**, 243–53.

Harrell, T.W., and Harrell, M.S. (1945). Army General Classification Test score for civilian occupations, *Educational and Psychological Measurement*, **5**, 229–39.

Herrnstein, R.J. (1973). *IQ in the Meritocracy.* Allen Lane, London.

Hunter, J.E. (1983). A causal analysis of cognitive ability, job knowledge, and supervisory ratings, in F. Landy, S. Zedeck, and J. Cleveland (eds). *Performance Measurement and Theory.* Erlbaum, Hillsdale.

Hunter, J.E., and Hunter, R.F. (1984). Validity and utility of alternate predictors of job performance, *Psychological Bulletin*, **96**, 72–98.

Income Data Services Ltd (1985). Psychological assessment. Report No 341, IDS Ltd, London.

Johnson, C.D., Messe, L.A., and Crano, W.D. (1984). Predicting job performance of low income workers: the Work Opinion Questionnaire, *Personnel Psychology*, **37**, 291–9.

Latham, G.P., Saari, L.M., Pursell, E.D., and Campion, M.A. (1980). The situational interview, *Journal of Applied Psychology*, **65**, 422–7.

Lilienthal, R.A., and Pearlman, K. (1983). *The Validity of Federal Selection Tests for Aid/Technicians in the Health, Science, and Engineering Fields.* US Office of Personnel Management, Washington, DC.

McCormick, E.J., DeNisi, A.S., and Shaw, J.B. (1979). Use of the Position Analysis Questionnaire, *Journal of Applied Psychology*, **64**, 51–6.

Northrop, L.C. (1986). *Validity Generalization Results: items types, types types, and job groupings.* US Office of Personnel Management, Washington, DC.

Reilly, R.R., and Chao, G.T. (1982). Validity and fairness of some alternative employee selection procedures, *Personnel Psychology*, **35**, 1–62.

Reilly, R.R., Zedeck, S., and Tenopyr, M.L. (1979). Validity and fairness of physical ability tests for predicting performance in craft jobs, *Journal of Applied Psychology*, **64**, 262–74.

Robertson, I., and Downs, S. (1979). Learning and the prediction of performance: development of trainability testing in the United Kingdom, *Journal of Applied Psychology*, **64**, 42–50.

Robertson, I.T., and Kandola, R.S. (1982). Work sample tests: validity, adverse impact and applicant reaction, *Journal of Occupational Psychology*, **55**, 171–83.

Roe, A. (1956). *The Psychology of Occupations.* Wiley, New York.

Schmidt, F.L., and Hunter, J.E. (1978). Moderator research and the law of small numbers, *Personnel Psychology*, **31**, 215–32.

Schmidt, F.L., and Hunter, J.E. (1981). Employment testing: old theories and new research findings, *American Psychologist*, **36**, 1128–37.

Schmitt, N., Gooding, R.Z., Noe, R.A., and Kirsch, M. (1984). Metaanalyses of validity studies published between 1964 and 1982 and the investigation of study characteristics, *Personnel Psychology*, **37**, 407–22.

Scott, R.D., and Johnson, R.W. (1967). Use of the weighted application blank in selecting unskilled employees, *Journal of Applied Psychology*, **51**, 393–5.

Siegel, A.I. (1978). Miniature job training and evaluation as a selection/classification device, *Human Factors*, **20**, 189–200.

Siegel, A.I. (1983). The miniature job training and evaluation approach: additional findings, *Personnel Psychology*, **36**, 41–56.

Sparrow, J., Patrick, J., Spurgeon, P., and Barwell, F. (1982). The use of job component analysis and related aptitudes in personnel selection, *Journal of Occupational Psychology*, **55**, 157–64.

Ungerson, B. (1983). *Recruitment Handbook.* Gower Press, Aldershot.

Wright, E.O. (1985). *Classes.* Verso, London.

Chapter 4.2

Work of the Manager

LYNDA GRATTON

London Business School, Sussex Place, Regents Park, London NW1, UK

The word 'manager' is applied in industry to a wide variety of people and jobs. In some companies managerial levels are clearly defined and benefits such as cars make the status of the holder apparent to all. Generally the title 'manager' refers to an individual responsible for the management of a number of subordinates and/or responsibility for a part of the business. However, the title can be confusing. For example, at Ford Motor Company the manager of an assembly line, with responsibility for up to 100 workers, is termed a 'supervisor'.

Companies often distinguish between managers and general managers. Typically, a general manager is responsible for a group of functional managers. For example, a district general manager in the National Health Service will be responsible for managers of acute hospitals, community health managers and financial managers.

When using the word 'manager' here we will be referring to an individual who has subordinates, but remember that these jobs can differ markedly across companies as the following case studies illustrate:

1. *A large manufacturing company: the works manager*   In manufacturing functions the production manager, supported by a hierarchical reporting structure, is typically responsible for the manufacturing of a product line. The job is one of management control, delegation, quality assurance and planning. The focus is primarily inwards to the workforce although time is also spent with key customers and suppliers.
2. *A pharmaceutical company: the research manager*   In contrast, a research manager at the research group of one of the large pharmaceutical companies has fewer people reporting to him or her and operates within a complex matrix organiza-

Assessment and Selection in Organizations   Edited by P. Herriot
© 1989 John Wiley & Sons Ltd

tional structure. This matrix involves a structure which is both functionally based, within the research group, and business based. Here, reporting lines are to the research director with a dotted reporting line to the business head who is responsible for the business area within which the manager works. The job is about supporting the technology of the business area, liaison with customers to enhance products, and working with a team of researchers on long-term 'blue sky' research.

3. *A major clearing bank: the strategic manager*   At this bank the strategic manager works within a small, professional team providing strategic support and information to the general managers responsible for the long-term profitability of the bank. Involvement is primarily with large projects and liaisons with other parts of the bank. Key competencies are planning and organizing, taking a longer term strategic view and monitoring the implementation of policy.

In summary, managerial jobs differ in many ways. Some of the most important variables against which they differ are:

– Type of organization structure.
– Numbers of subordinates.
– Type of subordinates.
– Time horizon of the job.
– Primary focus of the job (inward, outward).
– Amount of business control and responsibility.

For example, the research manager works within a matrix organization, with a medium size work group which is primarily professional. The time horizon of the job varies from short-term production improvements to very long-term 'blue sky' research projects. The focus of the job is primarily to peers and subordinates, both in the business area and other research managers. With regard to business controls, while they are responsible for their own research function, they are not autonomous profit and cost centres.

In contrast, the works manager works within a hierarchy with large numbers of subordinates who are skilled and semi-skilled. Time horizons are generally short-term production (though an increasing emphasis is currently being placed on longer time scales). Much time is spent with subordinates and peers and the plant is run as a profit centre.

Current managerial jobs are complex and differ across situations, yet when companies identify people with managerial potential they are making assumptions about senior management jobs in five to ten years. What sorts of jobs will these people be doing?

Managerial jobs in the future

When predicting future managerial work particular emphasis has been placed on three trends: the increasing importance of the strategic manager; the entrepreneurial manager; and the integrated manager.

Trend One: the strategic manager

A number of people have viewed the business place of the future as requiring increasing strategic orientation. For example, Ansoff (1970) argues that managerial jobs have moved from focusing on production to marketing, and for the future he believes increased importance will be placed on the strategic manager. Since the environment within which such managers operate is increasingly competitive, global and unpredictable they must be able to call upon strategic and visionary abilities which will allow a clear view of where the organization is going. Furthermore, the manager must communicate that vision in a compelling manner to people both within and outside the company.

Trend Two: the entrepreneurial manager

An increasing trend in industry is the decentralization of larger companies and the creation of businesses which are autonomous profit centres. These demand managers who are capable of behaving like entrepreneurs or intrapreneurs. Much has been discussed about this elusive breed who are becoming of increasing value as bureaucracies, fettered by their own procedures and inertia, seek people capable of bucking the system, taking risks, and living with ambiguity.

As Drucker (1985) has argued this will involve increasing emphasis on the creative individual, who can develop new ways of solving old problems and can use innovation to gain competitive advantage in the market place.

Trend Three: the integrated manager

Traditionally, in the United Kingdom, organizations are structured as hierarchical functions which are separate and distinct. Consequently, manufacturing and R & D functions have on occasions suffered from technical myopia, producing products which may have been technically innovative but which the customer does not want: Sinclair's C5 is an example of such a product. Alternatively, marketing promised products which manufacturing could not produce, the sales function sold them at the wrong price, under the wrong conditions.

To remain competitive companies can no longer afford this functional autonomy. Instead, functions are becoming more closely integrated to deliver products or services which meet customer needs. This process of integration will make new demands on the manager. Already organizations are calling for research people who are interested in, and who can talk to, customers, and for marketers who have an empathy with production opportunities.

This need for integration will necessitate cross-functional development and a broadening of the factors against which managers are selected and developed.

REVIEW OF MANAGERIAL JOB TASKS/FUNCTIONS

We have briefly discussed the role of the manager and likely future trends. The basis of any assessment and development process must be a clear understanding of the tasks the manager performs and the competencies which support these tasks and which are associated with effective performance. This section examines commonalities between these tasks and looks particularly at two aspects:

- The business sector in which the manager works.
- The business situation of the organization.

Business Sector: Culture of the sector

The demands that an industry sector makes on the managers who work within it are in part reflected in the tasks and roles those managers perform. For example, managers in the public health sector have particular demands placed upon them to manage in a consultative way with health authority committees who represent the views of the general public. Thus, their roles and tasks reflect this by involving a larger proportion of committee work and representational tasks than found in other sectors.

Similarly, within the manufacturing sector managers are now increasingly concerned with using and exploiting technology and changing the focus of their strategy from production to manufacturing. These issues place particular demands on them and intimately affect the tasks they perform.

Similarly, a major concern of managers in the financial sector is to develop a flexible workforce that is increasingly capable of providing sales and service to the customer and reshaping the culture to one where customers and their needs come first.

Thus, in attempting to understand the role of managers and the tasks performed, the sector in which they operate will make particular demands.

Business situation of the organization

The business strategy the company is operating makes particular demands on its managers. This has been illustrated in a model described by Gerstein and Reisman (1983) who relate the business strategy to managerial tasks. Table 1 shows two of the strategic situations they identified with the key managerial tasks they believe to be related to these situations.

Thus, for example, the manager who is involved in a start-up situation must be

Table 1. Strategic situations and related managerial tasks

Strategic Situation	Key Managerial Tasks
I. Start-up of company	Creating vision of business Establishing core technical and marketing expertise Building management teams
II. Turnaround of a company	Rapid, accurate problem diagnosis Fixing short-term and ultimately long-term vision

concerned with the task of building management teams with its selection, development and role clarification implications. The manager who is turning around a company must be very competent at collecting data to diagnose, analyse and solve problems in both the short term and ultimately the longer term.

Thus, managers in different sectors and business situations have differing demands placed upon them. In the following section we discuss the profiling of these tasks and their supporting competencies in more detail and review the methods available to identify these dimensions.

RESOURCING MANAGERIAL REQUIREMENTS

Organizations have used a number of strategies to identify and develop their managers. These range from the complex planned approach to one which is primarily reactive to short-term needs. Differences reflect the culture of the organization, its size, structure, patterns of growth, history and market-place characteristics.

This is illustrated by analysis of the ways two organizations seek to resource their managerial requirements:

1. *A large clearing bank* This bank has a complex and integrated approach to resourcing managerial requirements. The bank has developed this approach on the basis of a number of axioms for identifying and developing managers. These can be described in the following four ways:

   (a) Managerial resource needs are best met by a large recruitment programme focused on O levels, A levels and graduate entrants.
   (b) The possibility of attaining a management position should be open to as wide a group as possible. Therefore, large-scale systematic assessment processes are required across the bank to identify those young people who are likely to have potential to become managers.
   (c) Managers should be flexible, capable of performing a wide variety of tasks. Thus, narrow horizontal career paths are not the norm except for the most specialized posts.
   (d) The process of identifying potential can be best performed in a centralized manner, by a trained personnel function.

   Thus, there is a large, sophisticated assessment process in place which uses a variety of methods to identify potential at a number of stages in an individual's career. These processes are developed, executed and monitored on a central basis by the personnel function.

2. *A computer software house* Contrast this with the practices of a rapidly expanding computer software house. Their practices appear to be based on four axioms for resourcing their managerial requirements:

   (a) Managerial requirements are best met by specific recruitment of managers and senior people when the need arises.

(b) Contracts are short; wastage rate is high; skill and experience requirements change rapidly.

(c) Managerial tasks are specialist, cross-function moves do not typically occur.

(d) Responsibility for identifying potential and succession planning rests with individual managers, not with a centralized personnel function.

Thus, managers are recruited by a variety of methods by individual managers at points of need. Responsibility is highly devolved from the centre.

In summary, the demands an organization makes upon its managers are many and various. We know that these demands are likely to change in the future particularly around the increasing importance placed on strategic and entrepreneurial aspects. In meeting their requirements for managerial talent, organizations have developed different strategies. We have contrasted here the highly structured, planned approach adopted by a retail bank with the more reactive approach of the software house. Both strategies are designed to meet their differing needs.

In the following sections we shall discuss how organizations go about selecting people who can perform effectively as managers. However, before analysing the selection processes it is necessary to bridge the gap between managerial tasks and managerial effectiveness by concentrating on those skills, abilities and values which render one manager effective and another less so. These are the dimensions against which assessments of likely effectiveness are made.

UNDERSTANDING THE DIMENSIONS OF MANAGERIAL EFFECTIVENESS

We discussed earlier the range of objectives and tasks that managers face. These reflect such aspects as the type of organization the manager is working in and the current strategy of the company.

Therefore, it is hardly surprising that many competencies and abilities have been used to describe managerial effectiveness. With regard to their operationalization it is possible to categorize the methods into three broad categories: the checklist, the framework, and the observation approach to competencies.

The checklist approach

This suggests there are a finite number of competencies or dimensions against which managerial jobs can be profiled. An example of this approach is the work of 'Development Dimensions Incorporated'. They propose a list of 25 competencies, examples of which are:

1. *Impact*   Creating a good first impression commanding attention and respect, showing an air of confidence.
2. *Written communication skill*   Clear expression of ideas in writing.
3. *Work standards*   Setting high goals or standards for performance for self,

subordinates, others, and the organization. Dissatisfaction with average performance.

4. *Tenacity* Staying with a plan of action until the desired objective is achieved or is no longer reasonably attainable.
5. *Independence* Taking actions in which the dominant influence is one's own convictions rather than the influence of others' opinions.
6. *Analysis* Relating and comparing data from different sources, identifying issues, securing relevant information, and identifying relationships.

The advantage of such an approach is its simplicity and ease of use. It ensures that when describing managerial jobs some common yardstick of measurement applies.

The most obvious disadvantage of the model is this simplicity. It does not provide for sector-specific, level-specific or function-specific competencies and fails to cover some dimensions.

The conceptual framework approach

From his extensive research, Boyatzis (1982) has developed a generic model of management which isolates five major management functions (planning, organizing, controlling, motivating, coordinating). These are clusters of managerial tasks, for example the function of planning can be seen in the tasks of determining organizational goals, establishing plans of action, and communicating to others.

Effective managers are differentiated from less effective managers by the way in which they perform these tasks. This behaviour is determined in a process of dynamic interaction by competencies, characteristics, motives, and traits. For example, Boyatzis's research suggests that those who were effective in functions related to leadership demonstrated conceptualizing skills, self-confidence, and effective oral communication.

In summary, Boyatzis has developed an all-embracing model of managerial effectiveness which clearly specifies the interaction between the aspects of effectiveness and presents a detailed profile of its elements.

The observation approach to managerial competencies

The first model discussed presents a finite number of dimensions against which managerial effectiveness can be assessed. The second provides an underlying theory of managerial effectiveness which relates to a range of levels. This final model takes a situational approach and simply focuses on the behaviours of effective managers without recourse necessarily to the interpretation of these behaviours or the hypothesis of an underlying structure.

Mintzberg (1973) placed particular emphasis on the observation of managers and discovered that rather than behaving in a clearly defined, planned way, their work was more likely to be fragmented and verbal.

More recently, Kotter (1982), by closely observing general managers, found a large gap between the conventional wisdom on management functions and actual management practice. Boyatzis's model describes management in terms of concepts such as staffing, controlling, and organizing. Instead, Kotter found actual observed behaviour was less systematic, more informal, and more reactive. He believed that two central concepts of general management effectiveness are agenda setting and networking. Agenda setting describes a number of visions or agendas made up of loosely connected goals and responsibilities. These agendas address a broad range of issues and provide the framework towards which the general manager is working in the short, medium, and long term.

Kotter observed that effective general managers spend significant amounts of their time and effort developing a network of cooperative relationships among people they feel are needed to satisfy their agendas. These networks are aimed at a wide range of people both within and outside the organization, and the relationships vary significantly in intensity and type. They are developed using a wide variety of face-to-face methods and a number of skills.

IDENTIFYING THE DIMENSIONS OF MANAGERIAL EFFECTIVENESS

As we discussed earlier, the cornerstone of effective managerial selection is an understanding of the key objectives of the job, the tasks the manager performs to meet these objectives effectively, and the competencies which support these tasks.

In the last section three possible models for operationalizing the dimensions of effectiveness were presented. This section considers how organizations go about discovering the dimensions required for managerial effectiveness. Classically, they have focused on the job as viewed by the job holder, the boss, and other key players. These will be looked at in more detail below.

The current job holder

He or she can provide a great deal of information about the job. This information typically focuses on a number of aspects, for example:

- Key objectives—what is the aim of the job as seen by the incumbent?
- Key tasks—what are the day-to-day tasks performed by the incumbent to achieve these objectives?
- Key competencies—what are the competencies believed to be important in performing the tasks?

This information can be collected by observation (as Kotter did in the General Manager Study), by analysis of the results of the job (for example diaries, reports produced) or by discussion with the job holder. Discussions with job holders can be structured around a set of predetermined questions [as in the Job Analysis Checklist (Lewis, 1985)] and/or involve repertory grid methodology.

To illustrate the type of information collected by structured discussions with job holders, below is an example of a structured discussion with the regional sales manager of a large retail organization about how she saw her job.

Key objectives

- Achievement of sales targets.
- Improvement of sales effectiveness.
- Development of a sales environment in retail outlets.

Key tasks

- Weekly monitoring of sales figures to identify key trends.
- Weekly meetings with sales managers to discuss and agree action plan.
- Monitoring salespeople's action plans to ensure targets are met.
- Visiting retail outlets to present strategy to sales managers and staff.
- Presenting sales strategy to salespeople at the annual sales conference.
- Developing and communicating a national campaign sales package by delegating to her team and working closely with it.

Key competencies

Some of the key competencies she thought were critical are:

- Communicating to others in an enthusiastic manner.
- Leading a team and delegating.
- Planning and organizing tasks.

However, current job holders can only provide one view of the job. This is particularly important if they are ineffective job holders. As Rosemary Stewart (1982) has suggested, there are many ways of performing managerial jobs, people interpret them and mould them to meet their own values and needs. Therefore, simply talking to job holders gives a very parochial view.

The boss of the job holder

He or she can talk about a number of job holders and may be able to place a historical perspective on the job, particularly with regard to future orientation.

Simply asking what effective people do tends to elicit a range of stereotypic and non-behavioural descriptions; for example, most often the job has to be performed by someone who is 'charismatic' and a 'leader'.

The repertory grid provides a useful method of highlighting those behaviours associated with effectiveness. The Stewarts (1981) have described the approach in some detail. Briefly the topics of discussion (elements) are most often two effective job holders, two less effective and two average. The elements are discussed and contrasted 'in terms of the way they do their job'. Discussions are often followed with the questions: 'Can you tell me exactly what that means?', 'What would I see someone actually doing?'

The analysis of a repertory grid with the head of research in a multinational

Table 2.   Analysis of a repertory grid

Effective	Less effective
He has business awareness. He visits the competition and customers.	He is not aware of the business context. He spends all the time in the laboratory.
He integrates with other groups, argues, debates; for example he has just commissioned work from MIT.	He prefers his group to work on its own, he is defensive if people argue with him.
He works well with his team, he communicates to them and they seem to communicate with him a great deal.	He appears isolated from his team, for example he closes the door to his office all the time, he doesn't hold formalized meetings.
He strives for excellence, he spends time encouraging his people, travels, has links with the universities.	He works in an ivory tower, he is technically excellent and is seen to be so by many people.

chemical company, is shown in Table 2. He is contrasting effective and less effective research managers.

The short description in Table 2 demonstrates the boss trying to explain how he sees effective and less effective behaviour. Note that his less effective research manager is technically competent but is not aware of the business context of his work and is isolated. Contrasting other research managers he focused later in the discussion on the manager's ability to sell his ideas to the business areas, to pull resources together from a number of areas and spot new business initiatives.

Other key players

Typically a managerial job has other people around it who can comment on effectiveness. For example, a personnel manager's job can be discussed with line managers, and the personnel officers. In other major jobs, this can encompass customers or suppliers. Lewis (1985) has described a group process to elicit information on effectiveness.

THE ASSESSMENT OF MANAGERIAL POTENTIAL AND SKILLS

We have discussed the tasks managers perform and the various ways these tasks relate to the dimensions of effectiveness. There are a number of ways to assess managerial potential and the various tools are reviewed in Sections 2 and 3 of this book. Two appear to be particularly appropriate to managerial work primarily because they are acceptable to potential managers and focus on the actual managerial tasks: these two processes are situational interviews and assessment centres.

Situational interviews

Most attempts to identify managerial potential involve interviewing (Robertson and Makin, 1986, report 81 per cent of companies in their survey sample use them as the major process). Yet as repeated research has shown (e.g. Reilly and Chao, 1982), they have poor predictive power. Recently a number of approaches to structuring interviews have met with some success. These structured interviews are based on the premise that managerial performance can in part be predicted by how applicants say they will tackle various sample problems or tasks taken from the job itself.

The approach was developed initially by Latham and Saari (1984) and may have considerable potential in the selection process because such interviews are less time consuming than assessment centres and can be administered on an individual basis. They may also prove to meet the negotiational/expectational needs of organizations while increasing the validity of the selection process.

There are currently a number of organizations using situational interviews in the United Kingdom. A detailed description of the process is provided by Robertson, Gratton, and Rout (1989).

The following case study describes the development of the situational interviews for a large retail bank. The interviews were designed to identify managerial potential in people presently engaged in customer service and administration work. From this was developed a set of behavioural observation scales along each of the dimensions. Next, critical incidents were collected from current managers, who were asked to describe some of the difficult situations they faced in their job. These covered a range of subjects from the management of staff to the provision of service. This part of the process highlighted those situations commonly faced by managers in the bank. Next, a measure of effective response to each situation was developed initially by asking effective and less effective managers to respond to the situations. Their responses were noted, collated and later checked. For example, one of the key dimensions in the managerial job is 'motivating others' which covers such aspects as listening to others and taking an interest in them. One of the critical incidents developed for the situational interview was:

'Following reorganization, a member of your staff must be offered a job which is lower in status but which will allow him to retain the same salary level. You have looked at all alternative opportunities for redeployment and this is the only option open.

You anticipate a negative reaction to the job offered.

What approach would you take to present the new job to your member of staff?'

Effective people gave a range of responses which covered one or more of the following aspects:

1. Talk to the member of staff in private and diplomatically.
2. Be completely honest and acknowledge that the new job does represent a drop in status.
3. Indicate that the job is the only option—alternatives have been sought but to no avail.
4. Emphasize that salary will not be affected.

5. Point out particular talents/experience of the member of staff that make him or her valued by the bank and particularly suited to this job.
6. Look at longer term career possibilities.

Assessment centres

Assessment centres are being increasingly used to identify managerial potential, particularly where this represents promotion, for example from chief cashier to bank manager or research scientist to project manager. In the latter case, the characteristics which make for high performing research scientists, for example a theoretical, detailed approach, may be the very opposite of those which make for high performing managers where delegation skills may be important (Gratton, 1987b).

The use of assessment centre methodology is illustrated here by a case study of a large British manufacturing company which used the methodology, in this case called 'Career Development Workshops', to identify potential for senior management jobs.

This large, traditional British company has manufacturing plants spread throughout the United Kingdom and is a nationalized industry working in heavy engineering. One of the issues facing the company was the identification and training of potential plant managers. This required a system which identified those people with senior management potential early in their career, which created a clear plan of action and elicited commitment both from the individual and the organization.

The assessment centre process uses simulated job-related exercises to provide a range of objective information about an individual's skills and abilities. It had a number of advantages which were seen to be particularly pertinent to the organization. The exercises are job related and seen as fair and valid by participants. Since the assessors are line managers, the centre was seen as part of the normal managerial activity. Furthermore, line managers become skilled in systematic observation of behaviour and aware of the behaviours distinguishing effective performance.

An initial job analysis highlighted the nine dimensions associated with effective managerial performance. While there are a number of ways of designing assessment centres, this particular process used tailor-made exercises rather than off-the-shelf exercises.

There has been some debate about the merits of off-the-shelf simulations and exercises versus those tailor-made to fit the individual company's culture and needs. Some companies have believed packages are sufficient. Thus, we have seen a preponderance of Lego block and paper towers. However, as Cohen (1980) has argued, these have limited value.

The exercises were designed to simulate typical situations in the life of a plant manager. Simulations were developed through careful job observation and sampling. Here are two examples:

1. *Intray* This simulated the type and quantity of information that passed

through a plant manager's office. This information was synthesized and grouped, some information being vital to the smooth running of the plant, other information being inconsequential. Participants synthesize the information, then prioritize it, deciding how each item would be actioned. This provided an opportunity to observe management style, for example managers' propensity to delegate.

The intray was followed by a discussion with an assessor during which the individuals explained their reasoning behind the administration task and talked about a number of significant decisions.

2. *Counselling*   Plant managers spend some part of every day talking to their subordinates on an individual basis. For example, the foreman might report a particular problem to the manager or a charge hand may have a personal problem which is adversely affecting the quality of his work. This exercise simulated such an occasion when a subordinate had a problem which adversely affected his performance.

Having talked through the issues, the participants then spent some time writing up the results in a form which could be placed on a personnel file.

The assessment centre centred upon a range of job simulations but it also contained a number of other predictors: the PAPI, locus of control, and self-appraisal.

1. *The PAPI*   This workstyle inventory examines both primary work roles and sources of motivation across a range of work-related factors. As part of a discussion with a trained assessor it highlights primarily sources of motivation and the major structure of values (Coules and Kostick, 1976).
2. *Locus of control*   This questionnaire places the participant on the internal to external control dimension. Effective plant managers tended to have internal control. That is, they perceived they had some control over the situations and incidents arising in their working life.
3. *Self-appraisal*   Following each simulation, participants had an opportunity to review and describe their performance. This information served two clear purposes. First, the congruence between the participants' and assessors' description of the behaviours within the simulation provided some measure of accurate self-assessment. Successful plant managers were described as being able to see their strengths and weaknesses and know their limitations, a characteristic that Bray, Campbell, and Grant (1974) called self-objectivity. The self-assessment also played a useful role at the feedback session when the participants' description of the simulation helped them 'anchor' their memories of the situation.

The synthesis of information

There has been some discussion about the role of dimensions and simulations in the synthesis of information. Sackett and Dreher (1984), particularly, have argued that utilizing a set of global dimensions and producing assessments on these dimensions, based on an aggregate over a number of different exercises, may be inappropriate. They suggest an alternative where '. . . critical managerial roles are identified and exercises designed to simulate these roles. Effectiveness in each exercise, or role, is evaluated.' Effectiveness of behaviour is assessed on each exercise—*not* on a set of global dimensions.

In the final synthesis data were collected for both dimensions and simulations. About one hour was spent talking through each participant examining performance across both dimensions and simulations. Later, information from inventories was added to isolate any underlying trends of strengths or development needs. For example, it may be that a participant was skilled in one-to-one simulations but performed less well in a group situation. Alternatively, there may be dimension trends where participants were disorganized or socially skilled across the range of simulations.

Following this discussion it was the chairperson's role to synthesize performance across each of the clusters and finally agree with assessors key areas of strengths and development needs. From this information was gained an understanding of the individual's ability to gain from rapid promotion and development.

The training of assessors

The training of assessors is a key determinant to the validity of the Workshop and to the professionalism with which information is fed back to participants. The training of assessors was divided into three distinct stages:

Stage 1 Familiarization with simulations and design of behavioural framework.
Stage 2 Training in observation, recording and rating.
Stage 3 Training in chairing and feedback.

The first stage familiarized assessors with those behaviours associated with effective performance in the simulations.

Following this, the second phase of the feedback session concentrated on assessors using counselling skills to achieve a framework within which participants talked about their feelings about their performance and discussed their careers in general.

The feedback process and outcomes

Discussions with participants about their skills, abilities, aspirations and motivations formed an integral part of the Career Development Workshop. These occurred within three weeks of the Workshop and represented an opportunity for participants and assessors to talk through the Workshop and together draw up a joint action plan.

Feedback of information to participants must be seen as critical to the process, particularly from the individual's point of view, and should be performed by someone who knows the job (though not necessarily the individual's boss), is empathic, has credibility, but most importantly, is trained (Gratton, 1984).

Participants generally react positively to the Workshop. A follow-up by Fletcher and Dulewicz (1984) at Standard Telephones and Cables has shown that most participants found the experience rewarding, and an American study (Teel and Dubois, 1983) reported similar results. Participants generally feel positive about the experience and see the results as an accurate reflection of what they could do regardless of whether they were high or low scorers (Robertson *et al.*, 1988).

AN INTEGRATED APPROACH TO ASSESSMENT

We have so far described in isolation those methodologies available to identify competencies and potential. However, increasingly, organizations are using a 'boutique' approach to these methods, choosing the method most appropriate to the situation. Their choice of methodology typically takes account of:

- the importance of the job in the organization;
- the number of times selection is required for the job;
- the number of people to be considered;
- whether candidates are from internal or external sources.

These types of decisions underpinned the decisions made by the two organizations discussed earlier. Let us now review the selection processes they employ in more detail.

The use of an integrated approach

As we described earlier a large retail bank meets most of its requirements for managers by internal development. This implies a system which identifies potential from within a large group of people at various times in their career.

The system it is currently using is described in Table 3.

The process is used to tier people within the bank by identifying those with potential to attain executive, middle and junior management levels. It uses cost-effective methods initially (biodata, criteria-based interview) and increasingly

Table 3.   A bank's system for identifying potential

Time/age	Methodology	Dimensions
30+	Structured interview	Executive management competencies
	Week long assessment centre including self-development programme	Middle manager competencies
24+	One day assessment centre	Junior management competencies
Entry point (16+)	Situational interviews Biodata	Basic competencies Historical perspective

reliable yet time-consuming methods (a one-day and five-day assessment centre) as the numbers are reduced. This demonstrates a highly integrated, systematic approach to identifying future managers. A cornerstone is the provision of behaviourally based feedback to the individual to ensure that self-management development plays as important a role as company-managed development.

The use of an *ad-hoc* approach

The small computer company discussed earlier does not have the central resources available to attempt such a programme. What is more, its competency and experience needs are changing so rapidly that such an approach would not be appropriate. The company recruits externally as and when the need arises. Assessment centres are not an option, the jobs are highly specific so the development costs associated with assessment centres cannot be justified. The best attempt the company makes to increase the validity of the selection is to profile the competencies of effectiveness and use a criterion-based structured interview together with a verbal and numerical ability test.

However, the validity of the interview rests on it being related to the job and performed by a trained interviewer who can remain professional and accurate in the collection of data.

In this section we have discussed some of the more commonly used selection processes. The following section examines a number of issues in rather more detail, in particular focusing on the impact of selection methods and the role of the feedback process.

IMPACT AND THE ROLE OF FEEDBACK

Organizations have long been aware that selection processes are themselves an intervention. They communicate to the individuals something about how the organization makes decisions and the way in which they are viewed. Thus, for example, many organizations report resistance to the use of testing as part of the senior manager selection process, and very few search consultants use any form of psychological measurement. This may in part account for the increasingly sophisticated selection processes used for graduate recruitment, for many organizations may not have the opportunity to develop this type of psychological measurement later in the individual's career.

This question of impact is receiving increasing attention. For example Herriot (1987) has argued that the selection process is two way, with the participant judging the organization in part, on the way the selection process is conducted.

There may be two issues here: first, the perceived fairness of the selection; and, secondly, the impact it has on the individual's career. Research by Robertson *et al.* (1988) has suggested that the more participants can draw a link between the selection process they are going through and the job for which they are being considered, the more satisfied they feel with the outcome. Therefore, for example, people are more satisfied with situational interviews and assessment centres, less satisfied with biodata and cognitive tests. This is an aspect organizations have to take into consideration and balance against cost and reliability factors.

The second issue is one of careers and the process of tiering or streaming people with potential. It may well be that organizations are faced with a dilemma between making explicit tiering decisions, and therefore focusing development resources, and providing a system which is flexible. Inflexible, highly structured selection processes can suffer from a number of problems. First they have very well defined 'windows of opportunity' for people with management potential to be spotted. This may mean that late developers peak too late to receive development attention. Many large-scale management selection processes make the implicit assumption that high potential people can be spotted early in their twenties. As Hirsh (1985) has argued, this can result in increased expectations and the 'crown prince' syndrome. Elsewhere, Gratton (1989) has suggested that people in their twenties may have the potential to be managers but may later decide that this is not for them.

Evans and Bartolome's (1980) follow-up study of INSEAD participants suggests that many subsequent successful managers go through a period of exploration and unfocused activities before they become focused.

These arguments do not invalidate the use of large-scale systems to identify management potential but they do point to the necessity of flexibility both in terms of what is measured and when it is measured.

Finally, a word about impact and feedback. Psychologists have tended to focus on the reliability and validity of selection processes and clearly this is a primary source of consideration. If these processes do not work, then organizations should be aware of this. Less importance however has been placed on selection as a social process. Our work with many organizations has suggested that while the collection of selection information has been handled professionally, the subsequent dissemination of this information has not. This has resulted in the 'walking wounded' (Gratton, 1984) scared by inaccurate, non-behavioural feedback or the lack of feedback. As Evans and Bartolome's (1980) work has demonstrated, most successful managers have received in their career unambiguous, helpful feedback. Too often this is not the case for managerial selection. This aspect of managerial selection as organizational and individual processes requires further research and debate.

REFERENCES

Ansoff, I.H. (1970). *Corporate Strategy: An analytical approach to business policy for growth and expansion*. McGraw-Hill, New York.

Boyatzis, R.E. (1982). *The Competent Manager: A model for effective performance*. Wiley, New York.

Bray, D.W., Campbell, R.J., and Grant, D.L. (1974). *Formative Years in Business: A long term AT and T study of managerial lives*. Wiley, New York.

Cohen, S. (1980). Pre-packaged vs tailor-made: The assessment centre debate, *Personnel Journal*, **12**, 989–91.

Coules, J., and Kostick, M.M. (1976). Breakthrough in the use of self-perception in management development, *Applied Psychology Associates*.

Drucker, P. (1980). The discipline of innovation, *Harvard Business Review*, May–June.

Evans, P., and Bartolome, F. (1980). *Must Success Cost So Much?* Grant McIntyre, London.

Fletcher, C., and Dulewicz, V. (1984). An empirical study of a UK based assessment centre, *Journal of Management Studies*, **21**, 83–97.

Gerstein, M., and Reisman, H. (1983). Strategic selection: Matching executives to business conditions, *Sloan Management Review*, Winter.

Gratton, L.C. (1984). Assessment Centres, The Promises and Pitfalls? Paper presented to the CRAC Conference, Cambridge.

Gratton, L. (1987a). General managers: Universal or firm specific? *Manpower Policy and Planning*, Spring.

Gratton, L. (1987b). How can we predict managerial potential in research scientists? *Research and Development Management*, **17**(2), April.

Herriot, P. (1987). The selection interview, in P.B. Warr (ed.), *Psychology at Work*, 3rd edn. Penguin, Harmondsworth.

Hirsh, W. (1985). Flying too high for comfort, *Manpower Policy and Planning*, Summer.

Kotter, J.P. (1982). What effective general managers really do, *Harvard Business Review*, **60**, 156–67.

Latham, G.P., and Saari, L.M. (1984). Do people do what they say? Further studies on the situational interview, *Journal of Applied Psychology*, **69**, 569–73.

Lewis, C. (1985). *Employee Selection*. Hutchinson, London.

Mintzberg, H. (1973). *The Nature Of Managerial Work*. Harper and Row, New York.

Reilly, R.R., and Chao, G.T. (1982). Validity and fairness of some alternative employee selection procedures, *Personnel Psychology*, **35**, 1–62.

Robertson, I.T., Gratton, L., and Rout, J. (1989). The validity of situation interviews, *Journal of Organizational Behavior* (in press).

Robertson, I.T., Iles, P., Gratton, L., and Sharpley, D. (1989). The psychological impact of personnel selection methods on candidates (in preparation).

Robertson, I.T., and Makin, P.J. (1986). Management selection in Britain: A survey and critique, *Journal of Occupational Psychology*, **59**, 45–57.

Sackett, P.R., and Dreher, G.F. (1984). Situation specificity of behaviour and assessment centre validation strategies: A rejoinder to Neidig and Neidig, *Journal of Applied Psychology*, **69**, 187–90.

Schmitt, N., Gooding, R.Z., Noe, R.A., and Kirsch, M. (1984). Meta-analyses of validity studies published between 1964 and 1982 and the investigation of study characteristics, *Personnel Psychology*, **37**, 407–22.

Stewart, A., and Stewart, V. (1981). *Tomorrow's Managers Today*. Institute of Personnel Management, London.

Stewart, R. (1982). A model for understanding managerial jobs and behaviour, *Academy of Management Review*, **7**, 7–13.

Teel, K.S., and Dubois, H. (1983). Participants' reactions to assessment centres, *Personnel Administrator*, March, 85–91.

Chapter 4.3

Selection of Professional Groups

PETER J. MAKIN

School of Management, UMIST, PO Box 88, Sackville Street, Manchester M60 1QD, UK

It will be necessary, before considering what literature exists on the subject, to define what is meant by the term 'professional' in the present context. Wilensky (1964) has suggested that we will eventually see the 'professionalization of everyone', from surgeons to hairdressers. Indeed, it would not be surprising to find that the number of 'professional bodies' has grown apace since Wilensky's article.

For the purposes of the present chapter however, the definition of professional that will be used is closest to what most would consider to be the 'traditional' view. Briefly, in order to qualify for such a title, the following are required:

1. A period of formal training, to the equivalent of a university degree, the content of which is monitored by a professional body, and which is required for membership of that body. (In Britain the professional body would normally be one that is incorporated by Royal Charter.)
2. A period of structured professional experience, after graduation, which is required for full professional recognition.
3. A commitment to client service, often formalized in professional codes of conduct.
4. A system of professional discipline linked to the code of conduct.

Using this definition, the following discussion is limited to such occupations as lawyers, doctors, dentists, pharmacists, accountants, psychologists, engineers and teachers. The main occupations that are excluded are those of 'manager', and various other occupations whose formal qualifications either fall slightly below that of a first degree, or where there is such variety that professional certification is not possible. The exclusion is also required because the selection of managers and some others in this category is dealt with elsewhere in the book.

Obviously, it has to be recognized that many professionals, during the course of their career, move into positions that are increasingly 'managerial' rather than 'technical' in nature. Thus it is often the case that such professionals may be subjected to selection techniques designed to assess their managerial abilities and/ or potential. Once again, however, this aspect will not be considered here. The focus of the present chapter is upon the selection of professionals *qua* professionals, not as managers.

Professionals receive some of their practical training within their first employing organization but, with a few exceptions, the formal training is usually undertaken, full time, at a university or similar institution. With the professions, therefore, there are often two points at which selection decisions are made. First, the decision to admit the individual to the training required in order to gain admission to the profession, and, secondly, the decision to employ a particular individual within the organization. Each of these will be considered, although the emphasis will be on the latter.

SELECTION FOR THE PROFESSION

As mentioned above, most professionals receive their initial training at university or other institutions of higher education. It is these institutions, therefore, that inevitably make the initial selection decision. Their criteria for selection may not be, and perhaps should not be, whether the individuals they select are likely to be successful practitioners, but whether they will successfully complete the study period. The monitoring of future job performance is usually left to the employer or professional body. (There is one, perhaps unique, exception to this—selection for training for the ministry. This will be considered later.)

Two requirements are generally assessed. First, the ability to cope with the intellectual demands of the course, together with the requisite technical knowledge upon which the course will build. Second, the motivation, or commitment, of the individual to the chosen profession.

The obvious method of assessment of the first of these is by formal examination performance. Indeed this is inevitable. The largest part of the formal training period concerns itself with the 'technical' aspects of the profession, and will be largely 'academic' in nature. Examinations, in this context, tap three aspects. First, they are a measure of general cognitive ability. Secondly, most courses use formal examinations as the main assessor of performance. Previous examinations are, therefore, work samples. Finally, in those subjects which require specific preentry knowledge, they are job knowledge tests. In a recent survey, meta-analysis has shown all of these to be valid predictors of job performance (Hunter and Hirsh, 1987).

Other aspects of the ultimate job, such as interpersonal skills and other, rolerelated rather than technical, skills are often considered late in formal training, if at all.

The second consideration, that of motivation, is more difficult to assess. It is suspected that a large number of institutes do not attempt to assess this directly, since admission is purely on the basis of academic grades achieved in previous examinations. It might be argued that grades are themselves a measure of motivation. This may be true if *all* the steps in the equation hold. Thus, if motivation is reflected in effort, and effort is directly related to performance, then examination performance will indirectly measure motivation. This may not always be the case.

The direct assessment of motivation is more difficult to achieve. London (1983) has suggested that career motivation consists of career insight, career identity and career resilience. It could be argued that, of these the most important, at this stage, is career insight—the extent to which the individual can accurately assess his or her own career interests and needs. This assessment, at the point of entry to training, seems to be largely by references and interview.

References, at this stage, are usually obtained from the head of the candidate's current school or college. While not strictly concerned with the selection of professionals, as defined above, the study by Jones and Harrison (1982) showed that some aspects of references supplied by head teachers were predictive of examination performance and 'leadership and general conduct' ratings in military training.

Herriot (1984), in his book on the selection of graduates, has suggested that the role of the interview should change. It is, he argues, an inaccurate means of assessing what are assumed to be stable personal characteristics. Instead, it should be used to explore the nature and range of the individual's occupational self-concept, in order to assess the extent to which it matches organizational procedures. It should not, he concludes, be used as a psychometric device at all. Having 'debriefed' my own children after interviews at a number of universities it does appear that, while there is some attempt to assess their interest in the subject, the interview is often used to assess 'technical' ability. This is not perhaps surprising. Keenan and Wedderburn (1980) have shown that interviewers on the graduate 'milk round' tend to prefer those subject areas in which they have expertise. While it is not surprising, it is inefficient. Technical knowledge is far more reliably assessed by examinations taken over a period of a few years.

In Britain a very small percentage of school leavers are admitted to university or polytechnic, and the demand for admission to courses leading to 'professional' qualifications is particularly high. The principal method of selection is by examination grades and, with large numbers applying, it is inevitable that the requirements will be set even higher. This practice is likely to spread to other areas. As the formal training required by quasi-professionals rises, the pressure to select on academic criteria will, if past experience is repeated, grow. With large selection ratios the utility of these predictors will, of course, be high because cut-off points can be increased. Such increases in the predictor cut-off point do lead to fewer Type I errors (i.e. wrongly accepting those who have high scores on the predictor but fail to perform adequately). They also lead, inevitably, to a proportionately larger number of Type II errors (i.e. wrongly rejecting those who have lower scores on the predictor but who would have performed adequately). This, of course, raises the secondary issue of to whom is the selector responsible: the client, the profession, the institution, or society? If the answer is any but the client, then perhaps no great harm is done in wrongly rejecting those who would have proved capable.

Another distinction arises here between those professional courses, such as full-time degrees, that operate high selection hurdles, but where almost all will successfully complete the course as in the United Kingdom, and those that operate 'minimum entry' but have high failure rates, e.g. French and Italian universities. From the individual's point of view, the latter is perhaps fairer, if riskier, as long as the pass rate is not adjusted in order to limit admission to the profession on other grounds, e.g. to limit supply. It also depends on how valid previous examinations are as a predictor of degree result. In the United Kingdom the best prediction is 0.2 to 0.3, probably partly because the quality of teaching varies so much across schools.

So far the only emphasis has been upon the intellectual aspect of the job. The other, role-related, aspects of working in the profession have been ignored. For the part-time routes there is, of course, the additional element of job experience. This, it might be expected, would lead a few individuals to withdraw if their expectations proved wildly inaccurate. This may be one reason for the high 'drop-out' rate in accountancy. For those going straight to full-time study the same source of experience does not exist. How then can career perceptions be checked?

Some professional training institutions, especially medical schools, have a reputation for preferring those candidates who have fathers or mothers in the profession. Presumably it is assumed that these candidates will have a clearer impression of the 'real' tasks that the job entails. This has been demonstrated in other areas, e.g. Breaugh and Mann (1984). However, given the very limited experience of most of the candidates there may be little of what Makin and Robertson (1983) have called realistic job knowledge (RJK), to measure. A possible alternative that suggests itself is that of vocational guidance tests, but these again suffer from the lack of RJK. As Kline (1982) points out, the effectiveness of such tests is modest and 'little better than the correlation between job success and the subject's answer to the question of whether the job would be enjoyed or not'. Basically, there is little appropriate behaviour to sample! What then are the alternatives? 'Signs' such as personality tests might also be suggested, but the relationship between personality and various professions has yet to be demonstrated. The other alternative, which many selectors may adopt, albeit in an unstructured way, is an assessment of the amount of RJK in the particular field. This is on the assumption that more job-related information will be sought, retained, and used in decision making by those who are suited and motivated to the profession. While the problem of Type II errors still exists, properly constructed questions may reveal the depth of RJK for an individual.

Personal experience, together with anecdotal evidence from other staff in higher education, lead the author to conclude that 'mature' students differ from others. Such 'mature' students, while not being more intellectually capable than their younger fellow students, are often more informed about the nature of the profession they intend to enter. This reflects itself in increased RJK. There is another aspect, however, that may often be overlooked by selectors. As well as having more RJK about the specific profession they wish to enter, they have more RJK about other, often related, professions that they have, for whatever reason, decided against pursuing. Career theorists (e.g. Super, 1957) have demonstrated that the career decision-making process goes through a characteristic developmental pattern as fantasies are replaced with, it is hoped, realism. Perhaps a more accurate assessment of career motivation and self-concept is required. This will be considered later.

There are, however, a small number of subjects where motor skills are required. For surgeons and dentists, in particular, the level of manual dexterity will be important. However, surgery is a specialism and selection will be made within the profession. In dentistry, on the other hand, the majority are practitioners. The scope for tests, such as those of manual dexterity, is therefore greater. Deubert *et al.* (1975) demonstrated the potential of such tests, but it is not known how widely they are currently applied.

SELECTION FOR THE ORGANIZATION

Selection for what criteria? Level of performance is the most obvious but, as Gouldner (1957) has pointed out, professionals are more likely to be 'cosmopolitans' rather than 'locals'. According to Gouldner, this means that their allegiance, rather than being to the employer, is to their profession. This is likely to manifest itself in high turnover rates and reduced levels of organizational commitment. Virtually all the studies that will be considered have used performance or other ratings as criteria. The appropriateness of each criterion will, of course, vary from situation to situation, depending upon the difficulties the organization is encountering. The emphasis of the following review, therefore, will be on the predictors.

One of the problems associated with developing valid selection procedures for professionals is the relatively small number of individuals who are selected. Even when large enough numbers are recruited, they are often to very diverse jobs. In such a situation even large organizations become 'small' employers for the purposes of validation. This may be one of the reasons why the number of relevant reported studies is small.

Cognitive tests

The use of cognitive tests is not, judged by the number of research reports, widespread in the selection of professionals. Given that they are not widely used in other areas (e.g. managers; Robertson and Makin, 1986), this is not perhaps surprising. Some studies have, however, been reported. A report by ERIC (1987) on the recruitment and selection of teachers quotes only one study that used cognitive tests as selection devices. It is reported, however, that these were not as accurate predictors as were the opinions of the teachers' supervisors.

In their recent meta-analysis, Hunter and Hirsh (1987) have shown that general cognitive ability is a 'far higher predictor than any known alternative predictor'. Its main contribution to performance is indirect, through the learning of job knowledge. It has, however, a smaller but direct effect on performance. Such evidence would suggest that cognitive tests might be useful in the selection of professionals. This may not be so, for two reasons. First, the figures given by Hunter and Hirsh (1987) are corrected for restriction of range, i.e. by comparing the standard deviation of the test scores of incumbents with those of applicants. This may not be appropriate for professionals who have already been highly selected on the basis of formal examinations. The assumption that the applicant population has the same distribution of general cognitive ability as the general population needs justification. Secondly, Howard (1986) has shown that college grades are modestly, but significantly, related to intellectual ability. Thus there is little to be added by supplementing information concerning grades with tests of general cognitive ability.

Personality tests

A well-documented example of the use of 'traditional' psychological tests is by Keller (Keller and Holland, 1979; Keller, 1984) who studied R & D professionals. In two studies he used seven 'personality' variables: need for clarity; innovative orientation; self-esteem; existence need desire; relatedness need desire; growth need desire; and locus of control. These were validated against performance ratings, nominations for innovativeness, job level, number of patents granted, and number of publications. In the first study subjects were 256 professionals employed in three American organizations. In the second study subjects were 51 Mexican employees in a Mexican company. Of the 70 possible correlations (7 measures, 5 criteria, 2 groups), slightly over half (37) reached statistical significance. The highest single correlation was -0.48 between 'need for clarity' and number of patents, for the American sample. Overall, the number of significant correlations for each variable (maximum possible 10) was: 'innovative orientation', 8; 'need for clarity', 7; 'growth needs', 6; 'self-esteem' and 'related-ness needs', 5; 'locus of control', 4; 'existence needs', 2. Level of education was also included in the battery and multiple Rs for all the criteria were all significant, with a range of 0.24 to 0.58 and a mean of 0.43.

Follow-up data were available for the American group only but, of the 21 correlations that reached significance for concurrent validity purposes, 12 were also still significant one year later.

On the surface these figures appear rather encouraging. However, as the authors note, the data were collected with a promise of individual confidentiality. Many of the measures, they suggest, would need modification if 'faking' were to be avoided. In addition there is the problem, not raised by the authors, but considered later in this chapter, of the degree of acceptability of the battery to 'real' candidates.

Perhaps the most widely used personality test in personnel selection is the 16PF (Cattell, Eber, and Tatsuoka; 1970). Recently, especially in the United Kingdom, other test batteries have been developed (e.g. Saville and Holds-worth, 1984). While considerable data exist which compare the profiles of different occupational groups, there is little work which directly relates profiles to any performance criteria for any group, let alone professionals.

Some studies suggest that 'professional' employment interviewers have inferential trait structures for diverse occupational groups, including some professional groups (e.g. Jackson, Peacock and Holden, 1982). A total of 132 employment interviewers judged the degree to which 20 personality traits (drawn from Jackson's Personality Research Form, 1974) were characteristic of a number of occupations, including veterinary surgeons, accountants, teachers and engineers. Eight factors were identified, but only 7 of the 20 traits did *not* load at 0.4 or above on the first factor (Impulse expression versus Impulse control). While authors such as Fear (1978) have argued that the purpose of the interview is to appraise personality, many more recent writers would disagree with this (e.g. Latham *et al.*, 1980). While Jackson and his co-workers acknowledge that their findings are explicable in terms of occupational stereotypes, they argue that their results demonstrate that interviewers discriminate rather than simplify, as stereotyping would suggest.

Education and related issues

Educational level has sometimes been found to relate to job performance but the evidence is mixed. Overall, Dalessio (1986) found no relationship between grade point averages (GPA) and various performance criteria for engineering and scientific professionals. He did, however, report small but significant relationships between promotion and supervisor skill ratings for employees from 'less prestigious universities'. This, he suggests, may be due to restriction of range of ability at the more prestigious universities.

Keller and Holland (1979) and Keller (1984) found some relationships between educational level and various measures of job performance for R & D personnel. Level was related to performance on four out of five criteria. Follow-up data one year later, however, showed that none of these relationships was maintained. Given that R & D is perhaps *the* area where technical expertise is a continuing necessity, this lack of relationship is significant.

Perhaps the best example of the collection of biographical data directly related to professional experience is that of Hough, Keyes and Dunnette (1983). The subjects were attorneys in a large federal agency in the United States. Two of the inventories developed were related to previous experiences and interests. The 'background inventory' was developed to tap personal experiences related to preparation for, and experience of, the law as a profession. Items were developed and grouped to form scales, e.g. publications, honours earned at law school, etc. The 'Interest and Opinion Inventory' consisted of items designed to tap the individual's academic pursuits and extra-curricular activities during high school and college. With a total overall performance criterion, the former yielded a median cross-validity estimate of 0.37, the latter 0.25. In addition, there was little evidence of adverse impact.

Once again the evidence is initially encouraging. Once again, however, the same criticisms may be made. First, the study is based upon concurrent performance data. Secondly, there is no indication as to the acceptability of the inventories as selection devices. As Hough *et al.* (1983) point out, both are 'static' measures. There is no way in which an individual can alter his or her 'scores'. Some alternatives to these static measures will be considered later.

Work sample tests

Work sample tests have become increasingly popular recently in personnel selection, especially at managerial levels (Robertson and Makin, 1986). The main reason for their popularity may be the high levels of validity (Hunter and Hirsh, 1987), but an additional factor may be their face validity, and hence acceptability, to both candidates and decision makers. Makin and Robertson (1983) have suggested that, as well as their usefulness in assessing skill levels, their value is enhanced by giving the candidates real job knowledge (RJK) rather than being just a realistic job preview (RJP). The latter are often in the form of videos or booklets which describe the job. Occasionally, job visits or talks with job incumbents are used. Realistic job knowledge, on the other hand, is only acquired through doing the job, a process which involves self-appraisal as well as appraisal of the job.

Can such work sample tests be meaningfully created for professional jobs? In terms of knowledge required, there is no reason to suppose that they cannot. The exercise of *practical* professional skills, however, may be more difficult and less acceptable to candidates.

Once again, the most comprehensive study found comes from Hough *et al.* (1983). Two approaches were used: a Situational Judgement Inventory; and a Task Importance Inventory. The former was based upon behaviour examples, developed from a job analysis. Items were generated which described realistic situations with which an attorney might be faced, followed by four possible responses, the correctness of which was judged by experts. The Task Importance Inventory was also developed from the job analysis. Activities which over 60 per cent of attorneys reported as being part of their job responsibilities were rated according to their importance. These were used to generate three groupings of fourteen activities, differing widely in reported overall importance. Scoring of the inventory for each attorney was based upon the extent to which their assessments of importance agreed with the mean, or 'correct', rating.

Despite the care of construction, the Situational Judgement Inventory showed correlations no greater than 0.18 with performance criteria. While correlations of the Task Importance Inventory with performance were higher, at around 0.30, the authors conclude that its reliability is no higher than 0.60. As the authors later point out, these 'pencil-and-paper' tests are far less predictive than the data gathered from biographical and interest data in the same study.

CONCLUSIONS

The results of this review may be interpreted as somewhat depressing. Little work, it would appear, has been done on the systematic selection of professionals, either for training or employment. The experience of reviewing it has, however, led the author to question seriously, for the first time in a comprehensive manner, the nature of current selection theory, especially as applied to professionals. Some of the criticisms that follow are along the line suggested by Herriot (1984); others arise directly from the review and personal experience of recruiting professionals. First, the evidence from personal experience.

The current author and his colleagues have recently had experience of the difficulty of devising a selection procedure for a professional when a vacancy for an occupational psychologist arose in their own department. In doing so we felt beholden to practise what we had long been preaching. The criteria for selection were, it was decided, an ability to teach effectively, to undertake research, and to supervise postgraduate researchers. To this end a number of selection techniques were considered. Teaching ability, it was decided, would be best assessed by a 'work sample'. It was here, of course, that practicalities, and in particular the nature of demands made upon the candidates, came into play. To use existing courses as 'testing grounds' was obviously unfair, both to candidates and students. Therefore, the final decision was the presentation to all postgraduate students and members of academic staff, of a research topic of the candidate's choice. Research activity it was decided, would be assessed by asking the candidates to submit two articles which they thought best reflected their own research. This topic was, in all cases, the same as that chosen for presentation. Thus the presentation enabled staff to assess both content and process.

The final part of the criteria, the ability to supervise research, proved more difficult to assess. Consideration was given to role-play work samples using current Ph.D students. This idea was, however, abandoned for two main reasons. The first reflected a concern about standardization for all candidates. The second, and it is suspected the most important, reason was a feeling that the use of this method may not have been seen as valid by the candidates, with the anticipation that some promising candidates might withdraw their applications. As Hough (1984) has pointed out 'professionals seem especially adamant about being tested in the employment setting'. This is because they feel that their record 'speaks for itself'.

In the light of this decision two of the members considered the alternative of a situational interview (Latham *et al.*, 1980) in an attempt to assess this attribute. As Latham *et al.* have shown, such a technique may have validities comparable with assessment centres. After some discussion this idea too was abandoned, for a particularly interesting reason. It was felt that, while the replies to such a technique would be heavily weighted in decision making by the two members who had used it, there would be no such recognition from the other members of staff involved in making the decision.

Two issues therefore arose which, it is suspected, arise in many selection procedures for professionals.

1. The anticipated unacceptability to candidates of selection techniques which attempt to assess anything other than particular areas of their technical expertise (e.g. knowledge of the 'latest' techniques).
2. The apparent unwillingness of selectors who are not themselves selection

specialists, to weight differentially information that has been shown to be more predictive of future performance in similar situations.

This latter point is likely to be more of a problem the more individuals are involved in the process. As Hobbs (1985) has shown, for hospital doctors the selection panel increases as the job level increases. The same is often true of local authorities. Despite the evidence showing that 'actuarial' judgements are superior to 'clinical' judgements, it is suspected that the latter predominate.

The second criticism, that of Herriot, is more fundamental. He argues that recent findings in social psychology, particularly attribution theory, throw considerable doubt on the ability of some standard selection devices to measure individual characteristics. Further, the basic assumption that stable individual characteristics 'cause' behaviour is open to doubt. Measures of 'signs' (e.g. personality tests) are therefore open to the criticism that behaviour is more determined by the situation than had previously been accepted. Behavioural 'samples' (e.g. leaderless group discussions), on the other hand, are criticized because they often assess behaviour in 'out of role' situations and attempt to extrapolate to 'in role' situations. For these and other reasons Herriot suggests that the selection process should be a 'matching' process between the individual's occupational self-concept, and the organization's purposes.

Putting the two parts of the criticism together, the following appear to be the way in which professional selection, and perhaps selection strategies in general, should be developed.

1. There need to be developed techniques, that are acceptable to candidates, that accurately assess a candidate's 'track record'.
2. These techniques need to be acceptable to the decision makers.
3. The crucial criterion for selection is an adequate match between the individual's self-concept and the role required by the organization.

Surprisingly, the answer to all of these may lie in one area—biodata. The first two in traditional biodata, the last by collecting, as Herriot (1984) suggests, biodata about the future. To this might be given the title 'future-oriented' biodata.

First, what of the backward-looking biodata? Given the small number of professionals selected, together with the need for large numbers of subjects for 'shotgun' biodata validity, a useful approach might be in terms of previous professional accomplishments. Such an approach has indeed been tried by Hough and her colleagues (Hough, Keyes and Dunnette, 1983; Hough, 1984). A critical incidents method of job analysis yielded a number of job dimensions, of which eight finally formed the basis for an 'Accomplishment Record' (AR). On each of these dimensions attorneys were asked to write descriptions of major accomplishments illustrative of their performance on each dimension. This description included a general description of what was achieved, a precise description of what was actually done, any formal recognition received, plus the name and address of a person who could independently verify the facts.

'Expert' attorneys were then used as the basis for scoring. Initial results showed a strong relationship between the AR score and length of time in practice. Regressions were carried out against length of time since graduation. Residual scores, expressed as Z scores, were then used in the validation against performance data. All relationships between the eight dimensions and three performance ratings were significant, with a range from 0.16 to 0.27. In addition, there was no apparent adverse impact. Since correlations between the AR and professional tests such as the Bar examinations were essentially zero, the AR would appear to be tapping an additional area not tapped by these formal tests of professional expertise. Unlike other biodata measures the AR has the advantage that it is not static—individual scores can change over time. As Hough (1984) points out, this means that, in addition to its perceived fairness, it can be used for performance development.

What then of 'forward-looking' biodata? Herriot (1984) suggests that the most useful predictors for graduates are their self-identity and self-esteem. In this he is perhaps reflecting the re-emergence in social psychology of the 'self-concept'. Previous studies have often failed to find strong relationships between global self-concepts and work-related behaviour. More recently Cantor *et al.* (1986) have suggested that there are two main conceptual elements: 'life tasks', and 'possible selves'. Life tasks are 'what people see themselves as working on'. They are the basic units into which people lump daily activities, and give meaning to goals. According to Adler (1929) there are three global life tasks: cooperation with others, marriage, and occupation. In each area of life tasks, it is argued, there is a self-concept that is specific and dynamic, incorporating both views about what one presently *is*, and the 'possible selves' in the future. These 'possible selves' will obviously reflect the perceived opportunities but will also have desired 'limits'. What one would 'like to be' has to be modified to what one 'could become', or even what one would 'fear to become'. These perceived selves depict both expectancies and efficacies, both of which are important determinants of behaviour (Bandura, 1977). As Cantor *et al.* (1986) have shown, even college students have diverse sets of these possible selves.

In the face of career decisions the 'working self-concept' appropriate to the individual's career will be activated, leading to the emergence of 'possible selves' and the selection of appropriate behavioural strategies. This, albeit using slightly different terminology, is what Herriot is suggesting interviews, assessment centres, and other techniques should be trying to tap, rather than 'personal characteristics'.

An example may be useful at this stage in order to indicate why such techniques may be useful in selecting professionals. As has been mentioned previously, there is one organization where selection for training and for employment are synonymous, and where the degree of personal commitment required to the organization's underlying values is essential—the ministry in the Christian Church. Pollock (1986) has reviewed the methods of selection for training for the ministry and has, like others before him, come to the conclusion that 'traditional' psychological approaches based upon traits are inadequate for this purpose. Instead, he suggests, interviews should be used to 'map' the limits of the candidate's 'understanding and acceptance of self, vocation, and God'. In order for this to be possible, as Herriot points out, there has to be a strong future orientation before social exchange can take place with the selectors. In self-concept theory terms what is required is that the appropriate 'working self-concept' has to be recruited from memory. This perhaps is where the pre-selection procedure can be influential. Often, especially in newly qualified candidates, these self-concepts have not been fully explored, nor tested against expectations and past performance. These should perhaps be 'primed' in advance by indicating to the candidate the nature of the selection process. This would also have the advantage of indicating to the candidate that he or she is an integral part of that process (Herriot, 1984).

What is needed, perhaps, are not 'new' techniques but 'old' techniques applied in new ways. Of all groups it is perhaps professionals to whom their self-concept, both now and in the future, is important. But how, practically, can these be applied?

In terms of historical biodata, Hough's (1984) application of job analysis, together with behavioural rating techniques, to the generation of the Accomplishment Record is a development that will be well worth pursuing, as it clearly addresses the criticisms previously mentioned. The collection of 'forward-looking' biodata is less obvious. The assessment of the candidate's occupational self-concept, and its matching to organizational purposes may not be easy. Herriot (1984) has suggested ways in which assessment centres and interviews might be used to accomplish this task. Perhaps another possible method is that used by Smith, Hartley and Stewart (1978). Their study showed that the Repertory Grid technique has potential value in making explicit an individual's occupational perceptions.

To conclude, it is apparent to the author that, when selecting professionals *qua* professionals, the existing 'standard' selection techniques, as presently used, are often inappropriate. Consideration of the possible alternatives has, *inter alia*, led to broader conclusions about the nature of current selection practice. It is apparent that the area of occupational psychology that deals with selection is somewhat insular. It has not yet absorbed the developments elsewhere in psychology, in particular attribution theory and self-concept theory. The former has shown the extent to which the process of evaluation is 'contaminated' by attributional biases, the latter the extent to which individuals' behaviour is affected by their self-concepts. The selection process will gain much from incorporating these advances.

REFERENCES

Adler, A. (1929). *The Science of Living*. Greenberg, New York.

Bandura, A. (1977). *Social Learning Theory*. Prentice-Hall, Englewood Cliffs, NJ.

Breaugh, J.A., and Mann, R.B. (1984). Recruiting source effects: A test of two alternative explanations, *Journal of Occupational Psychology*, **57**, 261–7.

Cantor, N., Markus, H., Niedenthal, P., and Nurius, P. (1986). On motivation and the self-concept, in R.M. Sorrentino and E.T. Higgins (eds). *Handbook of Motivation and Cognition*. Wiley, Chichester.

Cattell, R.B., Eber, H.W., and Tatsuoka, M.M. (1970). *Handbook for the Sixteen Personality Factor Questionnaire*. Institute for Personality and Ability Testing, Champaign.

Dalessio, A. (1986). Academic success and job performance of engineering and scientific personnel, *IEEE Transactions on Engineering Management*, **EM-33**, 67–71.

Deubert, L.W., Smith, M.C., Jenkins, L.C.B., and Berry, D.C. (1975). The selection of dental students: A pilot study of an assessment of manual ability by practical tests, *British Dental Journal*, **139**, 357–61.

ERIC (1987). *Recruiting and Selecting Teachers. The Best of ERIC on Educational Management, Number 88*. ERIC Clearing House on Educational Management, Eugene, Oreg.

Fear, R.A. (1978). *The Evaluation Interview*. McGraw-Hill, New York.

Gouldner, A.W. (1957). Cosmopolitans and locals: Towards an analysis of latent social roles, *Administrative Science Quarterly*, **3**, 281–92.

Herriot, P. (1984). *Down from the Ivory Tower: Graduates and their jobs*. Wiley, Chichester.

Hobbs, K.E.F. (1985). Getting a job: The interview, *British Journal of Hospital Medicine*, **33**, 220–2.

Hough, L.M. (1984). Development and evaluation of the 'accomplishment record' method of selecting and promoting professionals, *Journal of Applied Psychology*, **69**, 135–46.

Hough, L.M., Keyes, M.A., and Dunnette, M.D. (1983). An evaluation of three 'alternative' selection procedures, *Personnel Psychology*, **36**, 261–76.

Howard, A. (1986). College experiences and managerial performance, *Journal of Applied Psychology*, **71**, 530–52.

Hunter, J.E., and Hirsh, H.R. (1987). Applications of meta-analysis, in C.L. Cooper and I.T. Robertson (eds). *International Review of Industrial and Organizational Psychology*. Wiley, Chichester.

Jackson, D.N., Peacock, A.C., and Holden, R.R. (1982). Professional interviewers' trait inferential structures for diverse occupational groups, *Organizational Behaviour and Human Performance*, **29**, 1–20.

Jones, A., and Harrison, E. (1982). Prediction of performance in initial officer training using reference reports, *Journal of Occupational Psychology*, **55**, 35–42.

Keenan, A., and Wedderburn, A.A.I. (1980). Putting the boot on the other foot: Candidates' descriptions of interviewers, *Journal of Occupational Psychology*, **53**, 81–9.

Keller, R.T. (1984). A cross-national validation study toward the development of a selection battery for research and development professional employees, *IEEE Transactions on Engineering Management*, **EM-31**, 162–5.

Keller, R.T., and Holland, W.E. (1979). Toward the development of a selection battery for research and development professional employees, *IEEE Transactions on Engineering Management*, **EM-26**, 90–3.

Kline, P. (1982). Personality and individual assessment, in R. Holdsworth (ed.). *Psychology for Careers Counselling*. British Psychological Society & Macmillan, London.

Latham, G.P., Saari, L.M., Pursell, E.D., and Campion, M.A. (1980). The situational interview, *Journal of Applied Psychology*, **65**, 422–7.

London, M. (1983). Toward a theory of career motivation, *Academy of Management Review*, **4**, 620–30.

Makin, P.J. and Robertson, I.T. (1983). Self-assessment, realistic job previews and occupational decisions, *Personnel Review*, **12**, 21–5.

Pollock, W. (1986). A theoretical consideration of selection for training for ministry, *Journal of Psychology and Theology*, **14**, 125–34.

Robertson, I.T., and Makin, P.J. (1986). Management selection in Britain: A survey and critique, *Journal of Occupational Psychology*, **59**, 45–57.

Saville, P., and Holdsworth, R. (1984). *OPQ Manual*. Saville & Holdsworth, Esher.

Smith, M., Hartley, J., and Stewart, B. (1978). A case study of repertory grids used in vocational guidance, *Journal of Occupational Psychology*, **51**, 97–104.

Super, D.E. (1957). *Psychology of Careers*. Harper & Row, New York.

Wilensky, H.L. (1964). The professionalization of everyone? *American Journal of Sociology*, September, 137–58.

Chapter 4.4

Service Occupations

STEVE E. POPPLETON

Psychology Department, Wolverhampton Polytechnic, Wilfruna Street,
Wolverhampton WV1 1LY, UK

INTRODUCTION

The key feature of service occupations is the servicing of customer or client needs by someone who is therefore in a sales/public relations role. In an increasingly competitive business environment, the emphasis in such occupations is upon selling a service or product to a customer, often on a recurring basis.

Such occupations include not only direct sales roles, but also a range of jobs within retailing, the hotel industry and the related licensed house trade, banking and the financial services sector in general. Although the job title may not include the term 'sales', nevertheless almost all occupations within this area possess a significant sales element.

Within sales jobs themselves, it is possible to distinguish between different types of job. Traditionally, a distinction has been made between those jobs requiring a 'hard sell' and those requiring a 'soft sell' (Poppleton, 1981). More recently, it has been suggested that four different types of sales role can be distinguished: consultative, closing, relationship and retail display (Moine, Friedenreich and Stevens, 1987).

Research conducted by the Chally Consulting Group (Moine *et al.*, 1987) suggests that sales jobs can be categorized in terms of the value of the product or service to the customer. The value of a product in turn is hypothesized to be a function of: (a) technical and application support requirements, i.e. product sophistication; and (b) purchase and delivery support requirements, i.e. need for an ongoing relationship. They suggest, and cite evidence to support the notion, that each combination of these two customer requirements characterizes a kind of

---

Handbook of Assessment in Organizations   Edited by P. Herriot
© 1989 John Wiley & Sons Ltd

sales situation which in turn has implications for the kind of salesperson who is likely to succeed.

Specifically, they suggest that high technical support and low purchase and delivery support requirements can be characterized as a 'closing' sales situation; high technical and purchase support requirements as 'consultative'; low technical and high purchase support as 'relationship'; low technical and purchase support as 'display'. 'Consultative' sales are likely to fall into Rackham's (1987) category of high value sale, whereas 'display' sales will generally be of low value.

There is clearly a significant difference psychologically to both the salesperson and the customer between a retail sales situation in which the potential customer approaches the salesperson and that when the first approach is made by the salesperson. In the former case, the customer is likely to buy and hence the likelihood of perceived rejection on the part of the salesperson is relatively low.

However, with increasing competition in the retailing trade, salespeople are expected increasingly to 'sell' to the customer. For example, when buying a pair of shoes, it is quite likely that the customer will be asked if he or she requires shoe polish and possibly other accessories. It is also increasingly likely that the salesperson may receive a bonus/commission element for items sold. The result is a more aggressive form of selling than used to be the case, with the salesperson being exposed in such cases to a higher degree of rejection than formerly.

Job holders in different kinds of sales role are likely to exhibit different kinds of attributes. In doing closing sales jobs, the salesperson has a limited amount of time and number of contacts with each potential customer. Compensation is typically results based (i.e. via commission on sales made) and the risk of failure is high. Typical examples are demonstration sales and trade show promotions. Moine *et al.* (1987) suggest that such job holders tend to be extravert, energetic, optimistic, competitive, self-confident and possess a strong work ethic. On the other hand, consultative selling occurs for high technology sales, professional sales and in various kinds of consulting role. Such roles require both patient interpersonal contact and aggressiveness. Job holders are typically career orientated, status and image conscious, more academic, patient, self-confident, independent and self-developmental, team orientated and not impulsive.

There are clearly overlapping areas between the personal contact occupations referred to. For example, within the hotel and licensed trades, retailing is the essential element. This is perhaps the main reason why several senior managerial staff concerned with retail shoe shops were recently recruited by a large brewery company to run a catering operation.

Similarly, it is becoming increasingly difficult to distinguish between banks and other financial services organizations such as insurance companies and building societies. In many cases, very similar products are being marketed.

Because of the increasingly competitive environments in all the sectors to which I have referred, the sales function has assumed an increasing significance in the jobs of people not thought of as being salespeople. For example, one of the large banks is currently training senior management personnel who lend to the corporate sector, in sales techniques. These personnel include branch bank managers who are not generally perceived to be salespeople, at least by the general public. The changes which are currently taking place in banking reflect a trend which is taking place in the whole of the service sector. Thus, whereas, some years ago, the bank manager was seen as someone who decided whether or not a customer seeking finance could be given a loan, the current job involves the bank manager, to an increasing degree, in trying to sell his or her services to a potentially 'good' (i.e. creditworthy) customer.

Furthermore, in many sales jobs correspondingly increasing demands are being made by the employer. The salesperson is set more and more demanding targets. Along with this goes an increased emphasis on selling skills. For example, in one brewery company, representatives who had been with the company for many years in a growing market were not able to succeed in the more recent, more competitive and 'cut-throat' markets. They were not able to cope with aggressive competitors, nor were they able to capture new business from competitors. The good relationships they had built up with their customers were no longer sufficient to meet business targets.

The opportunities for financial reward in selling are extremely good for those jobs which are remunerated on a commission-only basis. For example, in such jobs in the fields of computer sales and the selling of life assurance, it is not unusual for the highest earners in the organization to come from the salesforce. In such industries, it is quite common for sales personnel to undergo a reduction in income when taking a sales management post. Similarly, over recent years, stories about the very high income of those who sell (and buy) stocks, shares and currencies are legion, although this may be done with a minimum of personal contact.

Along with the opportunity for high reward, however, is the corollary that sales personnel of the highest calibre are scarce. Turnover of staff is typically high, and in some commission-only salesforces (e.g. in the life assurance industry) may reach 50 per cent within a few months (Poppleton and Lubbock, 1977). Furthermore, it is frequently the case that a small proportion of the salesforce produces a large proportion of the business.

Unusually, for occupations with such a potentially high level of earnings, employers are often not very concerned with academic attainments, at least for types of selling other than consultative. They are typically much more concerned with past work experience (particularly with sales success) and with personal qualities (e.g. temperament and motivation) than with academic achievement.

Given the increasing importance of sales skills over a whole range of occupations, the selection and recruitment of salespersons are likely to receive increasing attention in future employment.

In order to deal comprehensively with issues of selection for personal contact occupations, this chapter is subdivided into sections comprising: a review of job functions; an analysis of the attributes required; current selection practices; validity, fairness and impact of specific predictors; factors influencing choice of selection methods.

REVIEW OF JOB FUNCTIONS

In this section I shall focus on two specific jobs which represent the two main kinds of jobs within the area of service occupations. These are (a) a sales position and (b) a managerial job with a significant selling function. I shall then use these illustrative examples as a basis for a broader discussion of the job tasks and functions involved over the range of service occupations.

The sales position on which I shall focus is that of a life assurance salesperson. It is an area of selection which has received a considerable amount of attention from psychologists. As early as 1965, Guion stated that 'one area of sales selection where systematic and competent research has followed a long history is the selection of insurance salesmen'. Most of this research, however, focused on validation studies of particular selection instruments, particularly psychological tests. Little systematic job analysis was carried out in relation to this work. Some change came about with the development of Flanagan's (1954) critical incident technique which stimulated the analysis of Kirchner and Dunnette (1957).

Their study in the United States revealed 135 different critical incidents (i.e. incidents critical to success or failure in job performance). These incidents were grouped into fifteen broader and more meaningful categories, namely: following up complaints, requests, orders and leads; planning ahead; communicating all necessary information to sales managers; communicating truthful information to managers and customers; carrying out promises; persisting on tough accounts; pointing out uses for other company products besides the salesman's own line; using new sales techniques and methods; preventing price cutting by dealers and customers; initiating new selling ideas; knowing customer requirements; defending company policies; calling on all accounts; helping customers with equipment and displays; showing a non-passive attitude.

These categories compare with the following eleven based on a UK study (Poppleton. 1981; Poppleton, Allen and Garland, 1984): showing and generating enthusiasm for the product; paying attention to the customer's needs, feelings and requirements; showing integrity and professionalism; planning and organizing; persuading and overcoming objections in the sales interview; working steadily with relatively little supervision; responding positively to the incentives of a commission-only payment system; devoting time and energy to work activities; making effective contacts with prospective customers; coping with 'rejection'; showing mood control.

It can be seen that there is a considerable degree of agreement between the two sets of categories, although some of the categories in the UK study encompass more than one of the Kirchner and Dunnette categories.

Allen (1987) has pointed out that the life assurance salesperson has a very high degree of autonomy as to how he or she can typically perform the job. A consequence of this is that some salespeople focus on different markets and products according to their preferences. In this way, their typical situation may be 'closing', 'consultative' or 'relationship' according to the above categorization. As the salesperson becomes more experienced, there is a tendency to move to a very high predominance of closing sales stemming from the need to find customers and generate new business, towards a higher proportion of relationship and consultative sales. The importance of the 'relationship' sales situation is indicated by a typically high proportion of sales which are done with existing clients. The 'consultative' situation is often the operative one for very successful sales personnel who often have business arrangements with other professional people and generally operate via 'referred leads', i.e. where a customer is asked to provide names of potential customers from their customers and contacts (Poppleton, 1974).

Job analyses over a broad range of sales roles have been carried out not only by the Chally Group in the United States and Australia, but also by the Huthwaite group under Rackham (see Poppleton, 1981) in the United Kingdom. Both groups have analysed thousands of sales interactions in order to arrive at those behaviours which distinguish effective from less effective sales personnel.

The Huthwaite group collected data by observers trained in a behaviour analysis technique and arrived at a 32 category system. This has been reduced to nine for practical purposes. Seven of these are concerned with salesperson behaviours and two with customer behaviours. The seven salesperson behaviours include four which refer to types of questioning corresponding to what they term the 'SPIN' model. Thus, one category refers to 'situation' questions which are about the background to the current situation. They typically refer to the customer's company, its size, market and other features. Another category refers to 'problem' questions, which probe for the customer's feelings of dissatisfaction with the current situation. A third category comprises 'implication' questions, which are intended to highlight the importance of a need implied by the customer. For example, if the customer says that the main problem is one of unreliability, the salesperson might ask an implication question such as 'How much down-time on the line is caused by unreliability?'

The fourth category is that of 'need-payoff questions', in which the salesperson shifts attention from the problem to the solution and so obtains a statement of 'explicit need' from a customer. For example, a need-payoff question might be 'How much would you save if . . .?' A customer's statement of explicit need might then be 'I need a way to solve this particular problem—I'm going to get a new supplier'.

The customer behaviours included in the category system are statements of dissatisfaction or of the nature of the problem. Thus the above-mentioned research suggests that successful salespeople are more likely to show the behaviours encompassed in the 'SPIN' model. This work has consequently led to behavioural training programmes in order to increase the frequency of those effective behaviours outlined in the model.

The Chally group has similarly carried out detailed micro analyses of effective salesperson behaviours and designed training programmes to increase the occurrence of such effective behaviours. In spite of their emphasis on the four different types of sales situation, they nevertheless highlight the area of 'rapport building' as being a key to sales effectiveness over a wide range of sales jobs.

This work is consistent with the finding that customers who made purchases perceived themselves as more similar to the salesperson than did customers not purchasing the product (Davis and Silk, 1972). It is known as neurolinguistic programming (NLP), and was developed initially to help therapists develop more trust, rapport and understanding with clients.

Buzzota, Lefton and Sherberg (1972) and Buzzota and Lefton (1982) studied the interaction among different sales personality types and various customer types and concluded that the effective salesperson is better able to adapt to all personality types. Similarly, Grinder and Bandler (1976) developed a 'NLP' model linking behavioural manifestations (macro and micro) and verbal cues to thought processes (ways of thinking or strategies for problem solving). Their research suggested that people process information primarily via one of three modes: visual, auditory or 'kinaesthetic' (concerned with feelings). Nickels, Everett and Klein (1983) suggest that effective salespeople attend to both verbal cues and eye movements and so better understand a customer's internal thought processes. Specifically, they suggest that effective salespeople are aware (perhaps only intuitively) that eye movements are similar in most people and usually indicate the following: when people look up and left, they are visualizing something from the past, they are picturing it in their minds; when people look up and right, they are constructing an image, visualizing what it would eventually look like; when people look down and right, they are either recalling or imagining feelings; when people look sideways to the left, they are hearing sounds from the past; when people look sideways to the right, they are constructing a future conversation, thinking of the right words; when people look down and to the left, they are talking with themselves in a kind of internal dialogue. They argue that the effective salesman is more likely to use words corresponding to the customer's thought processes, which he assesses via non-verbal cues. Moine (1982) cites evidence in support of this. However, these suggestions must be considered highly speculative in view of the paucity of research evidence.

Moine (1982) cites evidence that, more generally, effective salespeople use 'hypnotic pacing', by which he means the use of statements and gestures that play back a customer's observations, experience or behaviour. Pacing is thus a kind of mirror-like matching which leads to perceived similarity and trust.

Although the above discussion has been related specifically to selling, it is clear that those behaviours involved in building up rapport will make for effectiveness generally in personal contact occupations. In fact, it is likely to be the essence of effectiveness in such occupations in so far as relationship building is a key to success.

This is illustrated in the following job analysis which was recently carried out by the author on a group of middle managers in a brewery company. They were essentially sales managers, being responsible for a number of sales representatives. A critical incidents analysis revealed fifteen categories of effective behaviour: communicates with people indirectly affected by a decision or event; knowledge of the customer and job; makes difficult and/or unpopular decisions; makes sound, realistic business decisions; understands subordinates and shows sensitivity to them; generally establishes good relationships with others; helps others and shows consideration; takes the responsibility for decisions and actions; effective in sales situations; enthuses and motivates others; shows integrity and honesty and carries out promises; tolerates stress well and shows mood control; delegates effectively; plans and organizes; institutes and monitors effective control systems.

Within the brewery industry, such jobs are frequently characterized as 'people jobs', and the critical incident analysis supports this characterization.

We have looked in some detail at 'people jobs'. We turn next to the implications for selection for such jobs, i.e. what attributes are required for successful job performance.

ATTRIBUTES REQUIRED FOR PERSONAL CONTACT OCCUPATIONS

In line with the focus in the previous section, I shall focus upon the attributes for the two illustrative jobs outlined (i.e. life assurance salesperson and sales management trainee in a brewery/retailing company).

The UK life assurance job analysis (Poppleton, 1981) gave rise to the Poppleton–Allen Sales Aptitude Test (PASAT) (Poppleton, Allen and Garland, 1984), a factor analytically based test. It measures fifteen attributes, each of which may be relevant to a particular sales job. Although based on life-assurance selling, there is evidence that it has relevance to a range of sales jobs covering what the Chally group terms closing sales, consultative sales and relationship sales. There is some limited evidence that it may also have relevance to display sales.

The fifteen factors measured are: administrative effectiveness; a social skill factor labelled social sophistication; emotional resilience; dynamism; economic motivation; empathy; competitiveness; the ability to organize others; work commitment; emotional stability; self-sufficiency; verbal fluency; determination; self-confidence; and entertaining. These factors give rise to four higher order factors, the one accounting for most of the variance not surprisingly being a social effectiveness factor. It is likely that this factor is relevant to a broad range of personal contact occupations.

The other higher order factors comprise: an organizational efficiency factor, incorporating elements of administrative effectiveness, work commitment and self-sufficiency (conscientiousness seems to play a significant part in this factor); an emotional strength factor on which the factors of emotional resilience, emotional stability and self-confidence load most highly; a motivational factor concerned with economic motivation, competitiveness and determination.

Although at a general level, such attributes as social effectiveness and organizational efficiency might be desirable for a broad range of sales positions, it is nevertheless likely that the specific factors of importance for social effectiveness in a particular job may vary.

The Chally group (Moine *et al.*, 1987) presents some evidence to support this contention. The data suggest that applicants most suited to consultative sales are likely to be: career orientated (especially into management), status and image conscious, more academic, patient, self-confident, independent and self-developmental, team orientated and not impulsive or extreme risk-takers. Those most suited to closing sales tend to be: extravert, energetic, optimistic, strong in the work ethic, competitive, positive in their self-image of success, less likely to save frugally and highly self-confident. Effective relationship sales personnel tend to show: a strong work ethic (and feel guilty when doing nothing), self-sufficiency, independence, cooperation, patience and strong traditional value systems. Effective display sales personnel tend to show: low career ambition, boredom easily, enjoyment of people, a high physical energy level, impulsiveness and a tendency for work to revolve around home and other goals.

The management trainee personnel specification, which stems from the job analysis described in the preceding section, has a number of similarities to the attributes required of sales applicants referred to above. It also includes a number of non-psychological attributes such as age, appearance and health.

Typically, service occupations place considerable stress on job incumbents through long working hours and the stress of coping with rejection, failure and unpleasantness in their frequent dealings with others who are often not well known to them. This can lead to a 'burn-out' effect. These stresses can be particularly traumatic for older people and the tendency is to aim such jobs at young people. This 'burn-out' fear can be seen in the common preference of individuals for less stressful personal contact demands even when their incomes may be considerably reduced as a result (e.g. a very successful salesperson taking on a significantly less well paid job as a sales manager).

The increasing pressures on those in service occupations (e.g. increasing sales targets and work schedules) highlight a significant area of health, namely, stress-related illness. A number of unpublished studies have found past incidence of stress-related illness in salespersons to be negatively related to job performance.

Many service jobs require long hours of work, working unsocial hours, job mobility and the requirement to socialize which can pose particular difficulties for the spouse of the job holder. Consequently, supportive domestic circumstances may often be incorporated into the personnel specification. Another facet required on the management trainee specification is a valid driving licence, which is often a necessary requirement for service occupations, Another requirement is for the applicant to have no financial over-commitments. In such occupations, there is often scope for dishonesty.

Psychological requirements include average minimum levels of the following attributes compared with applicants: intelligence; judgement; creativity; the ability to communicate in speech and writing; persuasiveness; leadership (an above-average minimum requirement); numeracy; the ability to work effectively in a team (above average); an interest in people as individuals and in influencing them; a lack of extreme attitudes of a religious or political kind; maturity; emotional stability; extraversion; the need for achievement (above average) and self-confidence. Additionally, a minimum level of academic attainment is required, normally a degree.

CURRENT SELECTION PRACTICES

Most selection procedures for service occupations are probably still restricted to the use of application form and interview. Frequently, such interviews are carried out by untrained interviewers. The use of the recently developed situational interview is extremely rare. As in the brewery selection procedure referred to above, a panel interview, usually of two panel members, is sometimes used.

For managerial selection, assessment centres are increasingly used, although their use outside large organizations is limited. For sales selection, however, the use of assessment centres is uncommon, although this use is probably increasing. This is somewhat surprising as the effective use of group methods of selection for sales personnel was reported by Higham (1951) at Rowntrees.

In the brewery company referred to, assessment centres are sometimes used for the selection of sales representatives and always for management trainee selection. Such assessment centres typically involve about twelve applicants and four assessors. The procedure comprises psychological testing, including tests of sales aptitude, personality, interests and abilities. This is followed by various group exercises, some chaired and some unchaired. Exercises include presentation, unchaired group discussion centred around a business problem and an exercise in which candidates have to advocate a position in competition with one another. The exercises are followed by a final interview. All applicants have previously been screened via application form and then a screening interview.

In a major UK clearing bank selection procedures vary widely in different areas. Assessment centres are not as yet used, although they are under consideration. However, testing has started to become widely used for entry to higher grades within the organization. This normally includes ability and personality measures.

My major criticism of current practices for selection in service occupations is that they do not make sufficient use of group and interpersonal exercises when assessment centre research typically shows these to be particularly good predictors of performance. This is particularly likely to be the case for service occupations for such exercises are primarily aimed at assessing interpersonal effectiveness which is likely to be a key attribute for such occupations. There is also clearly more scope for interviewer training and the use of validated psychological tests. More generally, too little concern is shown for establishing the validity of selection procedures. It is to this issue I now turn.

THE VALIDITY OF CURRENT SELECTION PRACTICES

Too few validity studies are published or carried out in the area of service occupations. This has particularly been the case over the past twenty years or so, due to the editorial policies of journals, the reluctance of organizations to allow data to be published which might benefit competitors and a reluctance on the part of organizations to invest in selection research.

Reviews of validation studies for sales occupations can be found in Poppleton (1975) and Poppleton, Allen and Garland (1984). Essentially they show that although certain attributes often appear to be related to sales success, there are sufficient exceptions to indicate that validation studies on the specific population of interest are highly desirable. For example, Poppleton *et al.* (1984) report that different factors as measured by PASAT are important for sales jobs in life assurance, selling advertising space and selling speciality chemicals.

Most studies of sales personnel have been carried out on salesmen of the predominant ethnic group in Western, industrialized countries. Few studies are available on large samples of saleswomen, and fewer on ethnic minorities. Consequently, it cannot be assumed that an instrument such as PASAT is a valid and fair tool for the selection of ethnic minority groups or women. Validation studies need to be carried out separately for such groups to establish the validity of such an instrument. Poppleton *et al.* (1984) cite evidence to suggest that for sales personnel of advertising space, different relationships between test attributes and performance may exist for men and women.

An unpublished study by the author on the predictive validity of the brewery management trainee assessment centre provides some illustrative data for such service occupations with a sales orientation. Those who left within a year were compared with a group of stayers. The leavers had lower interests in people as individuals ($p < 0.05$) and lower interests in activities involving the use of words ($p < 0.05$) as measured by the Connolly Interests Questionnaire.

On PASAT, the leavers were higher on economic motivation ($p < 0.001$), lower in the ability to organize others ($p < 0.01$) and lower in self-sufficiency ($p < 0.05$).

On the Cattell 16PF Questionnaire, leavers obtained a lower score in imagination ($p < 0.05$), while they also obtained poorer effectiveness ratings in chaired discussion ($p < 0.05$).

When performance was measured by superiors' ratings, then a positive correlation was found with an interest in people as individuals ($r = 0.29$, $p < 0.05$). On PASAT, there were significant relationships with the ability to organize others ($r = 0.42$, $p < 0.05$), and with economic motivation ($r = -0.53$, $p < 0.01$), although the sample size was small for PASAT relationships.

There were highly significant relationships between performance and group discussion ratings. In a non-chaired group discussion there was a correlation between an overall rating and job performance of 0.41 ($p < 0.01$). In chaired discussions there were significant correlations of 0.58 between performance as chairman and job performance and of 0.55 between job performance and overall rating as a group member when not in the chair.

Interestingly, there were no significant relationships between measures of intellectual ability and job performance, although there was a positive correlation with number of examination passes at Ordinary Level ($r = 0.29$, $p < 0.05$).

There was a significant positive correlation between an average interview rating (averaged over two or three separate one-to-one interviews) and job performance of 0.28 ($p < 0.05$), which is better than generally found in the research literature where the average is about 0.15 (Schmitt *et al.*, 1984). This is probably due to two factors: (a) interviewers had all been trained in biographical interview techniques; and (b) the interview may well act as a kind of situational exercise with a higher degree of validity for personal contact occupations than for occupations in which personal contact is less critical.

On the Cattell 16PF, there were significant correlations at the $p < 0.05$ level for dominance ($r = -0.25$) and shrewdness ($r = 0.26$). There was also a tendency for those educated privately to be rated higher in job performance.

THE CURRENT SITUATION

The use of psychological testing for sales selection and other service occupations has increased considerably over the past decade in the United Kingdom. This is particularly the case for personality measures, where a recent development has been the advent of occupationally orientated questionnaires such as PASAT and the Occupational Personality Questionnaire published by Saville and Holdsworth.

Unfortunately, some tests are used where there are insufficient data on basic attributes such as reliability and validity to justify their use.

Not enough attention is being paid to exercises of the assessment centre type. Some of the few studies which have been published (e.g. that referred to above for brewery management trainees with particular reference to sales positions), show that such an approach can be very fruitful. What are required here are exercises which simulate important aspects of sales behaviour. It is likely that role-play and other exercises in which persuasion plays a key role will be particularly effective.

DIFFERENT SELECTION METHODS AND APPROACHES

All methods should be based on validated procedures, even if organizational size and the number of vacancies mean that sample sizes are small. In this case, it is at least possible to estimate the synthetic validity of a procedure (see Ribeaux and Poppleton, 1978).

An important issue is whether decisions should be made via statistical means (i.e. cut-off points and/or regression equations) or via the judgement of an assessor or group of assessors. The answer to this question should be empirically based, depending on which method is most effective. There is evidence from both clinical and occupational studies that actuarial (statistically based) decisions are often superior.

However, a clinical judgement by an assessor may have the added bonus of the commitment of the assessor to the decision, with the consequent effort on the part of the assessor (who may be the future superior of the applicant) to justify the selection he or she has made.

An overall evaluation of selection procedures should attempt to take account of such factors, and more generally should attempt some kind of cost–benefit analysis of alternative procedures.

Service occupations often place a particular strain on family relationships because of the often long unsocial hours of work. Furthermore, their nature often makes it easy for job incumbents to develop relationships through their work contacts which may be perceived as domestically threatening. The consequence of this is that spouses of job holders often need to be emotionally well adjusted to avoid undue stress which can ultimately affect the job holder's performance.

A particular difficulty in some personal contact jobs such as retailing is that husband and wife often must work together for much of the time. A common example of this is the situation of publican and spouse. In such a situation marked stresses may be put upon a relationship. Consequently, this relationship needs to be taken into consideration in selection.

Poppleton (1975) notes that previous research of sales personnel suggests that psychological tests give better job performance predictions for younger less experienced job applicants. Conversely, job experience information from application form and reference data should be weighted more heavily for more experienced applicants. This latter finding also points to the value of performance review and appraisal data in helping to make selection decisions.

REFERENCES

Allen, E. (1987). A Multi-Variate Analysis of the Determinants of Effectiveness in Life Assurance Salesmen. Unpublished Ph.D. thesis (CNAA), The Polytechnic, Wolverhampton.

Buzzota, V.R., and Lefton, R.E. (1982). Is there a preferred style of sales management? *Journal of Personal Selling and Sales Management* (November), 1–7.

Buzzota, V.R., Lefton, R.E., and Sherberg, M. (1972). *Effective Selling through Psychology: dimensional sales and sales management strategies*. Wiley Interscience, New York.

Davis, H.L., and Silk, A. (1972). Interaction and influence processes in personal selling, *Sloan Management Review*, **13**, (Winter), 56–76.

Flanagan, J.C. (1954). The Critical Incident Technique, *Psychological Bulletin*, **51**, 327–58.

Grinder, J., and Bandler, R. (1976). *The Structure of Magic II*. Meta Publications, Palo Alto, CA.

Guion, R.M. (1965). *Personnel Testing*. McGraw-Hill, New York.

Higham, T. (1951). In National Institute of Industrial Psychology Paper, 'Group methods of selection'.

Kirchner, W.K., and Dunnette, M.D. (1957). Identifying the critical factors in successful salesmanship, *Personnel* (September–October), 54–9).

Moine, D.J. (1982). Use of hypnotic language by ultra-successful salespeople. Part II: Examples and exegis, *Hypnosis Quarterly*, **XXV**(1), March 1982.

Moine, D.J., Friedenreich, K., and Stevens, H. (1987). *Hiring Effective High-Tech. Salespeople*. The H.R. Chally Group, 900 Artesia Boulevard, 104 Redondo Beach, California 90278, USA.

Nickels, W.G., Everett, R.F., and Klein, R. (1983). Rapport building for salespeople: a neuro-linguistic approach, *Journal of Personal Selling and Sales Management*, **III**(2), November, 1–7.

Poppleton, S.E. (1974). A Study of Referred Leads. Unpublished paper for the Sun Life of Canada Assurance Company.

Poppleton, S.E. (1975). Biographical and Personality Characteristics Associated with Success in Life Assurance Salesmen. Unpublished M.Phil. thesis, Birkbeck College, University of London.

Poppleton, S.E. (1981). The social skills of selling, in M. Argyle (ed.). *Social Skills and Work*. Methuen, London.

Poppleton, S.E., Allen, E., and Garland, D. (1984). *The Poppleton–Allen Sales Aptitude Test Technical Manual. The Test Agency*. Cournswood House, North Dean, High Wycombe, Buckinghamshire.

Poppleton, S.E., and Lubbock, J. (1977). Marketing aspects of life assurance selling, *European Journal of Marketing*, **11**, 418–31.

Rackham, N. (1987). *Making Major Sales*. Gower, London.

Ribeaux, P., and Poppleton, S.E. (1978). *Psychology and Work: an introduction*. Macmillan, London.

Schmitt, N., Gooding, R.Z., Noe, P.A., and Kirsch, M. (1984). Metaanalyses of validity studies published between 1964 and 1982 and the investigation of study characteristics, *Personnel Psychology*, **37**, 407–22.

Chapter 4.5

Selection in High-risk and Stressful Occupations

MIKE SMITH

Manchester School of Management, UMIST, PO Box 88, Sackville Street, Manchester M60 1QD, UK

Selection in high-risk or high-stress occupations is a grey area which is attracting less attention from occupational physiologists. The difficulties are manifold. First, outside the armed and security forces, the numbers employed in these occupations by any single organization are usually quite small and consequently validity studies are rare. Second, many of the occupations are militarily or politically 'sensitive' and publication and publicity are often avoided. Third, the occupations do not form a neat group but instead cut across many categories of job because risk and stress can arise in many different ways.

DEFINITION OF HIGH-RISK AND STRESSFUL OCCUPATIONS

One approach to the definition of high-risk and stressful occupations is to rely upon mortality statistics such as those given in Table 1.

Unfortunately, using mortality statistics to define high-risk and stressful occupations presents three conceptual difficulties. First, occupational statistics are only meaningful when they are based upon fairly large numbers and these aggregates often conceal important subgroup differences. For example, most people would agree that circus lion tamers face an above-average occupational risk. However, occupational statistics subsume lion tamers under the heading of recreational and service workers. Thus, at an official level, their occupational risks are below average. Second, accident statistics do not provide a direct index of the risks inherent in a job: accidents may be low simply because the selection system has done its work and has chosen employees who are able to negate the risk.

Handbook of Assessment in Organizations   Edited by P. Herriot

Table 1   Standard mortality rates from external causes of injury and poisoning (E800–E999)

	Deaths per 10 000
Miscellaneous occupations	330
Farming and fishing	144
Catering and cleaning	136
Construction and mining	113
Machine tool operations, metal workers, fitters	102
Transport	111
Assembly, packing and inspecting	98
Security and protective services	97
Metal making, processing and repairing	93
Materials storing and handling	92
Selling	92
Electrical and electronic workers	90
Materials processing and making	83
Professional in education welfare and health	76
Managerial	74
Clerical	69
Professional in science, engineering and technology	65

Third, accident statistics represent blind empiricism: they do not give much help to giving an understanding of the nature of risky and stressful work.

Regrettably, few empirical job analyses of dangerous work are published. Probably some of this omission is because much of the work is confidential or sensitive, but it is also clear that the importance of job analysis as a first step in the selection procedure is not appreciated. Much of the literature seems to be characterized by trial and error where an investigator will try out many methods of prediction in the hope that one of them will be successful. Exceptions to this generalization are given by Naylor (1954), who gave details of the work of air traffic controllers, and Slovic (1969) who analysed the requirements of the stockbroker's decision-making process. Perhaps the only avenue open is to analyse the characteristics of stressful and high-risks jobs within a logical framework. Figure 1 gives a classification of high-risk, high-stress occupations.

DIMENSIONS OF RISK AND STRESS

The characteristic common to all these jobs lies in the possibility of severe damage if the job is not performed adequately. Inadequate performance in many jobs can result in damage but to qualify in this context, the damage must be severe, and be difficult to reverse. In general, the damage will be important enough to alter, irrevocably, the course of at least one person's life for the worse. However, even within this definition, the damage can be very diverse and range from damage to an individual on an operating table to the damage to a whole continent as a result of a Chernobyl-type disaster. Consequently, the first dimension of a high-risk occupation is the *scale of damage* which might result in poor performance of the job.

The concept of damage generally implies energy and so there tends to be a

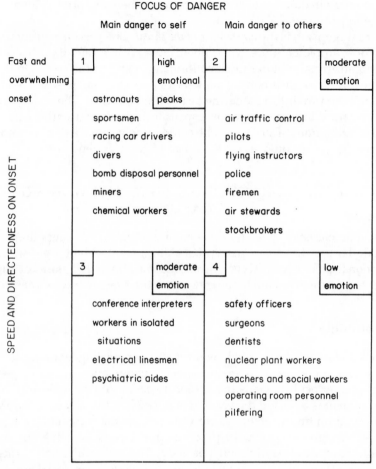

Figure 1   Classification of high-risk, high-stress occupations

concentration of high-risk jobs where energy is released—possibly without proper control (i.e. explosives, armaments, transport). Damage can also be caused by the collapse of support systems, and so another concentration of high-risk jobs is found in hostile environments where artificial support systems are of paramount importance.

Another dimension concerns the *entity likely to suffer* the damage. At least three types of entity are worthy of distinction. First, there is damage to the person performing the job and his or her immediate team. For example personal safety is a vital aspect of undersea divers as well as most of the jobs which head a league table of occupations according to accident statistics. Second, there is damage to other people: for example a mistake by an air traffic controller or a surgeon will alter the lives of others rather than their own. In many risky occupations, such as an airline pilot or policeman, poor performance can result in damage to both the job incumbent *and* others. Finally, there is damage to property.

The third dimension is the *appearance of the threat*. The presence of some threats is clear. For example an underwater diver must always safeguard his or her air supply and an Arctic explorer must continually keep out the cold. On the other hand some threats, in the financial markets for example, have a sudden onset and a benign bull can turn into a menacing bear within minutes. The ambiguity of the stimuli also varies. In some situations, especially in medical situations, symptoms can be very ambiguous: a stomach ache could merely signal a diet containing too much green fruit or it could signal the onset of acute appendicitis.

PERSONAL CHARACTERISTICS NEEDED TO COPE WITH HIGH-RISK SITUATIONS

Personal characteristics which are needed in high-risk occupations can be grouped under four headings: perceptual ability, mental ability, physical ability, and emotional stability. However, it should be noted that none of these are universal requirements—much depends upon the exact nature of the threats.

Perceptual ability

Perceptual ability is an essential requirement for dealing with most difficult situations and there are two main aspects: acuity and vigilance. Generally speaking, greater acuity means the earlier detection of problems and often the earlier a problem is detected the easier it is to resolve. In risky occupations there will be a premium on the ability to scan the environment frequently and detect signs of events going wrong. In practice, this means that in most high-risk occupations vision and hearing must be good. The main exception to this rule is when the precursors of threat are vague and nebulous, as in social and financial situations, or where the onset of the threat is either very fast so that no one can react in time or so slow that everyone can react in time. High-risk jobs where perceptual abilities are particularly important focus upon monitoring equipment and situations such as air traffic control or control of high speed machines such as express trains or even dentists' drills!

Vigilance is a slightly different aspect of perceptual ability. It involves the capacity to identify the precursors of danger even when they are infrequent and embedded in a field which is boring. In some respects, the need for vigilance may increase during the next decade as more processes are automated, and where control devices take over routine operations so that the employee's task is merely to be on hand to detect and cope with 'exceptional' situations (e.g. sea captain of an oil tanker). However, the second generation of automation is usually ergonomically designed to enhance the detection and cueing of abnormal occurrences.

Mental ability

Mental ability is also a key requirement for most high-risk jobs. The incumbent needs to interpret correctly the signals he or she receives from the environment and then choose among the available responses. However, intelligence may contribute to effective performance in high-risk jobs in another way: it may enable people to gain the maximum benefit from the training and experience they receive so that they are better able to diagnose the cause of faults or problems. Provided that the nature of the threat and the situation does not change, experience and intelligence may be largely interchangeable and in many situations experience will be the more important of the two. Typical high-risk jobs where mental ability is important are those such as an aircraft pilot, where a great deal of information needs to be integrated quickly and accurately.

Physical ability

Many high-risk occupations take place in hostile environments where workers need to operate in the face of abnormal conditions of heat, cold, gravity and vibration. Often, working positions are unnatural and the manipulation of heavy equipment can make demands upon stamina, strength and suppleness. For example, firemen need to be able to carry loads which may exceed their own weight in hot, slippery conditions and where the air is filled with smoke. To perform adequately in these environments requires at least average physical fitness and it is highly desirable to have an extra margin of physical capacity in reserve. Fleishman and Hogan (1968) isolated factors of skill. Fleishman's factors can be grouped under three headings: steadiness, coordination and speed, as shown in Table 2.

Steadiness and coordination seem to be relevant to many high-risk jobs and

Table 2   An adaptation of Fleishman's psychomotor factors

STEADINESS

1. *Control precision:* fine control, rapid and precise actions
2. *Aiming*
3. *Arm/hand steadiness*
4. *Response orientation:* making directional and speedy movements in response to a stimulus
5. *Rate control:* making continuous adjustments to a moving target

COORDINATION

6. *Finger dexterity:* the manipulation of tiny objects
7. *Manual dexterity:* the manipulation of fairly large objects
8. *Multi-limb coordination*

SPEED

9. *Reaction time:* speed of making simple, discrete, responses to a stimulus
10. *Wrist and finger speed*
11. *Arm speed*

speed of reaction is an extra requirement when the onset of threat is fast.

Unfortunately, the measurement of physical abilities is complicated by the fact that physical abilities may change in extreme environments. For example, Kiessling and Maag (1962) found that manual dexterity was reduced by about 8 per cent in a pressure chamber which simulated the pressure of 100 ft of water and Baddeley (1966) showed that, in open-sea conditions, dexterity declined by 28 per cent at a depth of 10 ft and by 48 per cent at 100 ft.

Fleishman (1960) specifically analysed the physical requirements of aircraft pilots and identified six factors:

1. *Control precision* involving highly controlled, but not over-controlled, movements, e.g. rudder adjustments.
2. *Spatial orientation* involving judgements about location in three-dimensional space.
3. *Multi-limb coordination* emphasizing the movement and placement of several links.
4. *Response orientation* involving the need to make rapid responses under rapidly changing circumstances.
5. *Rate control* anticipating changes in velocity and rate—usually with visual feedback from the environment rather than instruments.
6. *Kinaesthetic discrimination* emphasizing the ability to 'feel' the control characteristics.

Emotional and temperamental stability

There appear to be quite clear requirements in terms of the personality of people in high-risk occupations. On the one hand they need to be sufficiently sensitive to appreciate the dangers they face. On the other hand, they should not be so sensitive that they are overwhelmed by the emotional onslaught they may experience in a crisis. Factor analytic theorists divide temperament into four main factors: extraversion–introversion; emotional stability; realism; and independence. The first three of these factors seem to have direct relevance to suitability for hazardous and stressful work.

In many ways introverts seem suited to hazardous occupations where the onset of danger is insidious, since they will have a greater tendency to pay close attention to detail and maintain high standards of precision over long periods. Eysenck (1967) suggests that in introverts the mechanisms which block the passage of messages in some nerves are weak. With extraverts, these blocking mechanisms are strong and a smaller proportion of messages is received. It would follow that introverts should be better at detecting the first, tentative indications that all is not well and consequently they would be best in hazardous occupations where the onset of threat is insidious (sectors 3 and 4 in Figure 1). Paradoxically, an extravert would seem to be suited to hazardous occupations where the threat is obvious and the danger bells are ringing loud and shrill. The very intensity of these signals could produce inaction in others which either prevents escape or enables the situation to deteriorate. But, the blocking mechanisms in the neurones of an extravert act as a filter and produce an intensity level which is not immobilizing (sectors 1 and 2 in Figure 1).

For present purposes, emotional stability may be considered as the ability to withstand and recover from 'short, sharp shocks' and it may be viewed as the inverse of neuroticism. A stable person is able to cope wth distractions, is rarely lethargic and lacking in energy. Interestingly, there is some evidence that stable people tend to have better perceptual abilities—especially night vision. According to one factor analytic personality theorist (Cattell, 1957), emotional stability has three main components: emotional detachment, self-assurance, and the absence of tension. In most circumstances emotional detachment would be an asset in hazardous situations since it implies a resistance to pressure and a mature, calm, resilient approach. Self-assurance and the absence of tension could be a two-edged sword. On the one hand, it could imply a complacent, laid-back mien ignoring or encouraging hazardous situations to develop. On the other hand, it could indicate someone who is resilient and who does not over-react or get disorganized. The deciding factors will be other aspects of personality such as conscientiousness and self-control.

Realism reflects the degree to which the individual's thought processes are anchored in reality. An imaginative person who is preoccupied with his or her own thoughts may be oblivious to, or may shy away from, facing the facts of a difficult situation. In contrast, a tough minded, practical and perhaps conven-

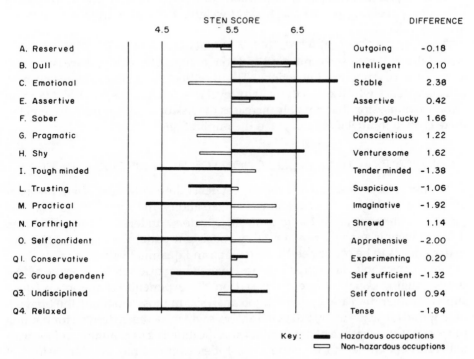

Figure 2 Comparison of composite profiles for hazardous and non-hazardous occupations

tional person will have a capacity for tolerating routine periods of non-excitement which are encountered in some hazardous jobs such as monitoring armament production.

These conclusions have partial support from the data collected for different occupations (Cattell, Eber and Tasuoka, 1970). Figure 2 compares the composite profiles for five hazardous occupations (airline pilots, airline hostesses, firemen, electrical engineers, policemen) with the composite profile of five non-hazardous occupations (janitors, nuns, foremen, Roman Catholic brothers and artists). It can be seen that people employed in hazardous occupations tend to be emotionally stable, less apprehensive and less tense. It is also interesting to note that they are less imaginative. The higher scores on venturesomeness and enthusiasm (happy-go-lucky), which are two of the main components of extraversion, suggest that hazardous occupations require the ability to filter out some of the environment's stimulation. It is also possible to speculate that extravert traits are only useful in hazardous occupations when they are also combined with conscientiousness and self-control. Using Krug's (1981) terminology the composite profile would represent a 2132 pattern (i.e. moderate extraversion, low anxiety, high tough poise and moderate independence) which is found in about 1 per cent of the population. He comments, 'This kind of person represents a reasonably good risk for placement in stressful occupations, particularly if he or she can work alone.'

Additional evidence concerning the personality of individuals for placement in hazardous jobs is given by a regression formula to predict the likelihood of individuals avoiding accidents. The beta weights for *freedom* from accidents are given in Table 3.

The profile of a person who avoids accidents seems to be intuitively correct. Above all else the person is practical and conventional. Secondly, there is stability and control of emotions and actions. Thirdly, there is a kind of submissiveness and desurgency which keeps the activity level low and reduces the risk of random error of commission (but possibly increases the risk of error of omission). Finally, there is enough intelligence to grasp the implications of events.

CURRENT PRACTICES IN SELECTION FOR HIGH-RISK OCCUPATIONS

At an anecdotal or descriptive level, a great deal is known about current practices in selection for high-risk occupations. Conversations with specialists responsible for the recruitment of air traffic controllers, pilots, undersea divers and bomb disposal technicians will reveal a fairly consistent pattern. Unfortunately, this pattern needs to be confirmed by systematic and quantitative research.

Almost invariably the occupations are covered by job descriptions of one or two pages' length. Usually these are based on the experience of the job holder's superior rather than any systematic job analysis. In most situations the brief job description is backed up by a detailed analysis which has been derived for training purposes. The existence of a personnel specification is less common and individual recruiters are left to translate the job descriptions into the dimensions of human abilities they should seek. This emphasizes the point made elsewhere (Smith and Robertson, 1986) that the link between job descriptions and personnel

Table 3 Regression weights for freedom from accidents

Weight	Scale	Interpretation
0.30	−M	*Practical and conventional*: anxious to do the right thing, conformist, not eccentric, over-sensitive or imaginative; ready to do the job expected, capacity for boredom.
0.18	+C	*Stable*: mature, calm, realistic about life, able to tolerate frustration, absence of neurotic symptoms such as phobias, sleep disturbances, fatigue, psychosomatic complaints.
0.18	−O	*Self-confident*: placid and calm with unshakeable nerve; unanxious confidence in self and capacity to deal with things. Absence of worrying, brooding and suspiciousness.
0.18	+Q_3	*Self-controlled*: self-respect and control over own emotions and behaviour; considerate and careful but sometimes obstinate and possibly status seeking.
0.18	−Q_4	*Relaxed*: composed and satisfied; not easily excitable or fretful; patient.
0.14	−E	*Submissive*: takes action which follows the opinions of others; avoids railroading people or pushing through own ideas.
0.12	+B	*Intelligent*: quick to grasp ideas and identify the key components of a problem and the relationship between them and the consequences.
0.12	+F	*Desurgent*: taciturn, reticent, languid or slow; a dour view of life; reliable and serious.

characteristics is often the weakest link in the selection process. Often, as in the fire service, there will be strict physical specifications such as a minimum height of 5ft 6 inches, a chest measurement of 36 inches with a 2-inch expansion, no aids to vision and no marked degree of colour blindness.

High-risk jobs are rarely directly advertised in the press. There seem to be two routes by which a field of applicants emerges. First, as in, say, bomb disposal technicians they make a general application for employment in a larger organization. An applicant's eventual placement in a high-risk occupation is made on the basis of the individual's preferences or the organization's judgements of his or her suitability. The second route, common in underwater divers and airline pilots, is for the applicants to make a personal approach to employers. Often, the applicants have considerable knowledge and some experience of the occupation which has been gained either from a pastime grouping (e.g. scuba diving club or flying club) or from family connections and experience (e.g. lion tamers). Thus in most high risk occupations there is an avoidance of formal methods of recruitment and considerable pre-selection by the applicants themselves. Consequently, at the start of the selection process the suitability of the pool of applicants is likely to be high.

The actual mechanisms of selection are varied and depend greatly upon the sophistication of the organization involved, with the armed forces and the airlines adopting the most sophisticated approach. There are three recurrent components: subjective interviews; objective tests; and oι -the-job observation or work samples.

Typically, candidates will be invited to visit the organization for a day where they will be given a short battery of objective tests such as the AH2, the Minnesota Form Board and a test of mechanical reasoning such as the Bennett Mechanical Reasoning Test. Personality testing is far from universal but it is reasonably widespread and its use in this field is increasing. The 16PF test is the most widely used questionnaire. Several clinically based tests (Minnesota Multiphasic Personality Inventory (MMPI) and the California Personality Inventory (CPI)) are also employed but their use is declining. Applicants may also be asked to write a short essay on a relevant topic. During the course of the day applicants may be asked to perform a number of physical tests. These may be crude adaptations of PE drill (e.g. 20 press-ups in one minute, or a long distance run) or they may be more standardized measures such as the fire service's requirement that a recruit should be able to carry a 12-stone load over a distance of 100 yards in 60 seconds. There are also likely to be a number of work samples. An applicant for underwater diver training may be asked to assemble a piece of breathing apparatus and his or her performance at diving under controlled conditions in a water tank will be observed. An applicant to the fire services will usually be asked to assemble a piece of equipment from a diagram and he or she may be observed for a short period in a small smoke filled room.

Almost inevitably, candidates will then be subjected to two interviews: an informal interview (of 30 minutes) with, say, two or three interviewers and then a formal interview of similar duration where the interviewing board may involve six or more interviewers. Usually these interviews will be unstructured and only one or two of the interviewers will have received interviewer training. In some organizations, applicants will undergo an in-depth interview with an occupational psychologist. Slightly surprisingly, some organizations continue to use interviews by clinical psychologists or psychiatrists. Candidates who are not eliminated by these procedures will be asked to undergo an often stringent medical examination where attention will be paid to perceptual fitness—vision testing, colour blindness testing and, sometimes, hearing tests. Motion sickness testing is used in rare situations such as astronaut selection.

Selection procedures for high-risk occupations rarely result in an offer of 'permanent' employment. There is usually a probationary period of several years. For example, a bomb disposal technician will have been assessed by tests and interviews prior to his or her joining the army. Further assessment takes place during basic army training and during the next two years while the individual pursues normal army work. At the point of placement as an ordnance disposal technician there will be further tests, interviews, scrutiny of past appraisals and assessment by a superior officer. The individual's suitability will be under close scrutiny during a fairly lengthy training course in general ordnance disposal. In addition, the 'apprentice' ordnance disposal technician will attend several 'specialist' courses listing four or five days and suitability will be assessed during each of these. Only after a period of perhaps five or more years will the final selection decision be made whether to allow the individual to dispose of a real bomb in operational conditions. It is a tribute to the rigour of this system that the 'accident' rate is very low indeed.

EQUAL OPPORTUNITIES

Approximately 40 per cent of the working population are women yet only a tiny proportion, probably less than 1 per cent, of incumbents in high-risk occupations are women. At a philosophical level, it is possible to muse upon exactly who is suffering from bias: the women who may be excluded from these jobs or the men who are exposed to risk. Much of the imbalance in the proportions of men and women in these occupations arises from the imposition of physical requirements such as height and strength. Women tend to be smaller and less strong than men and consequently a higher proportion of women are excluded. Such requirements should only be permitted when they are a direct requirement of the job. Minimum heights should only be stipulated if it is inordinately difficult to operate equipment (e.g. fire-turntable ladders) or perform key activities (e.g. retrieve a body from a burning building) if these requirements are not met.

It is also important to recognize that even in areas where men, on average, exceed women, there is a considerable spread about the average performance of the sexes. Consequently, even though the *proportion* of women who can fulfil the physical requirements may be lower in absolute *numbers*, there may be a considerable number of women who would be eligible. Furthermore, women may be superior in other characteristics which give them an advantage. For example, there is some evidence that women are more 'durable' than their male counterparts.

The unequal proportions of men and women in high-risk occupations could arise in a different and less acceptable way. Earlier it was noted that much of the recruitment into these occupations was by word of mouth and other informal means. Unfortunately these methods of attracting a field of candidates tend to perpetuate the status quo which, in this case, means a preponderance of male incumbents.

Other aspects of equal opportunities, age and racial bias may be even more complex. At a prima facie level, age 'bias' may seem justified in high-risk occupations since physical prowess may be at a premium and may be believed to decline with age. Unfortunately, this decline has not been demonstrated in a convincing way. The decline shown in early studies may be due to statistical artefact (comparing cohorts having different life chances and therefore confusing generational and ageing effects). Research suggests that physical decline occurs much later than is commonly believed and Belbin (1955) suggests that older workers actually gravitate towards heavy work. Indeed, the main limitation concerning age would appear to be difficulties with pacing and time pressures. It is interesting to note that the preferred age for astronauts seems to be about 42.

SELECTION IN SPECIFIC GROUPS OF HIGH-RISK OCCUPATIONS

The preceding sections have given a generalized view of selection in high-risk occupations. However, it is also necessary to examine specific groups of occupations, e.g. underwater divers, aviation occupations, security occupations, operative occupations and occupations involving isolation.

Underwater divers

The selection of undersea divers is probably the best researched area of selection for high-risk occupations. Even here, there are few classic studies which use performance data as criteria but most of the studies have used training success to measure the effectiveness of selection method. Probably the best study is Gunderson, Rae and Arthur's (1972) investigation of 293 navy divers in which they found that *physical fitness tests* (squat-jumps, sit-ups and pull-ups) were the most important predictors of training success (median correlation 0.34). This suggestion has received support from a study of 46 divers by Hogan (1985) which provided information that the specific physical attributes of cardiovascular fitness, muscle endurance and flexibility were most highly related to finishing a training programme.

Biersner and Ryman (1974) examined the possibility of using a variety of physical and non-physical characteristics as predictors of diver training performance. They found that visual ability was a significant predictor and, lke Gunderson *et al.* they obtained a correlation of about 0.24 between *psychological attributes* such as mental health and training performance. Ryman and Biersner (1975) considered *attitudes*, as predictors of diving training success. Starting from Stouffer's (1949) observation that attitudes towards combat and physical injury were related to performance ratings and that soldiers who were not apprehensive about combat effectiveness had the highest ratings, they constructed an attitude scale with three factors: leadership; training concern; and conformity. Leadership was positively related with success while training concern was negatively related with success. Knapp, Capel and Youngblood (1976) administered a scale to measure anxiety at five different times before, during and after involvement in dangerous diving situations. Their results again indicated that the treatment of anxiety is a key variable. Divers seemed to be able to control or reduce their anxiety at the early stages of a dive and then allow their anxiety to rise after the dive was finished. A more recent paper by Biersner and Larocco (1983) outlines a simple descriptive study of the scores of divers on a battery of personality tests. They suggest that divers have an internal locus of control, are less anxious and tend to be poorly socialized, uninhibited, experience seeking and adventure seeking. It is possible that these traits are not independent but reflect the underlying source trait of extraversion. This explanation would also be consistent with findings that divers have a higher interest in risks that involve physical dangers which are consistent with the male role but avoid activities which are novel or unconventional. Consequently, the lower level of socialization is indicative of social autonomy and independence rather than sociopathology.

Aviation occupations

A great deal has been written about the selection of pilots. Some of the research is descriptive. Some research has focused on specific predictors. Bair, Lockman and Martoccia (1956), for example, examined the predictive validity of a battery of thirteen measures including spatial/perceptual measures, verbal reasoning, mathematical skills, English expression, mechanical reasoning and general intelligence. Most of the correlations with final training performance were tiny (less than 0.1) but the highest correlations were obtained with the Minnesota Paper Form Board and the L (language) score of the ACE Physical Examination Test. In parenthesis, it should be noted that the low correlations could be caused by the inadequacies in the trainers' evaluations which were used as criteria. For example, Want (1959) demonstrated that trainers' evaluations tended to be relative and vary with the ability of the groups they were training. Vernon and Parry (1949) describe a battery of 23 tests (2 sensorimotor, 3 coordination tests and 18 pencil-and-paper tests) which together with a board interview were used to select pilots for the UK Royal Air Force. Initial corrected correlations of 0.47 were obtained but over the years the validities fell. More recent work suggests that general intelligence is important in pilot suitability and that most pilots obtain an intelligence score which is at least one standard deviation above the mean (i.e. 115+).

Personality is also a key variable. Cattell *et al.* (1970) indicate that pilots tend not to be anxious (i.e. they are stable, self-confident and relaxed). They also tend to be toughminded yet trusting. Jessup and Jessup (1971) examined the validity of the Eysenck Personality Inventory (EPI) in predicting pass or failure in initial pilot training. Using quadrant analysis they found that both the extraversion scale and the neuroticism scale of the EPI were valid predictors: the failure rate was highest among neurotic introverts and lowest among stable introverts. Jessup and Jessup explain these findings in terms of the introvert's greater ability to learn and the dysfunctional effects of anxiety in a high-stress situation. However, they note that while the introvert may be superior in a training situation, an extravert may be superior in an actual job situation. Bartram and Dale (1982) also examined the validity of the EPI using a sample of men from the Army Air Corps. They again found that successful trainees tended to be stable but, contrary to Jessup and Jessup, they also found a positive relationship with extraversion. Upon a re-analysis of Jessup and Jessup's data they concluded that the relationship between introversion and success was not significant. Using the combined forms of the EPI, Bartram and Dale found a correlation of 0.37 between extraversion and training success and a correlation of 0.11 between stability and success.

Pilots are not the only aviation occupations to be characterized by high risk and stress. Indeed it may be that the instructors of the pilots face higher risks than the pilots themselves. Swanson and Johnson (1975) indicate that successful pilot instructors adopt a supervisory style which is characterized by both consideration to the trainee and a structuring of his or her activities. Airline stewardesses face lower risks than either pilots or their instructors but it could be argued that their job involves higher stress. Lipe (1970) obtained the scores of tests of the motives and abilities which 121 stewardesses had completed during their school years. He was then able to correlate these scores with their performance as airline stewardesses as rated by their superiors. He found that useful correlations (above 0.3) were obtained for both motives and abilities.

Air traffic controllers represent a slightly different genre of aviation occupations involving high risk. Like other aviation occupations the onset of the danger is acute but the threat affects the lives of other people while the air traffic controller remains in relative safety. This could mean that the selector should look for a rather different blend of characteristics. For example, it could be hypothesized that an introverted personality which emphasized precision and accuracy would be most suitable in these situations where 'stimulus' overload is unlikely. Naylor (1955) investigated 93 Australian air traffic controllers and found that a battery of ability tests produced correlations of 0.58 with training performance and 0.43 with supervisor's evaluation of actual work. The abilities measured were spatial, general intelligence, memory, map reading (with interruptions) and arithmetical ability: general ability, memory and map reading obtained the highest correlations.

Security occupations

Security occupations are typified by police work and firemen but they also include less researched occupations such as prison and parole officers. The risks in these occupations generally have a sudden onset with danger largely to the incumbent.

Typically, selection for these occupations involves written examinations, medical examinations, checks for criminal records and interviews, usually in the form of board interviews. Landy (1976) investigated the effectiveness of board interviews of 57 officers. The study involved many correlations, none of which was significant unless corrected for attenuation of range. A recent study in the United Kingdom (Brier, 1987) suggests that the interview component of police selection procedure is just as invalid as most other interviews: he obtained a correlation of 0.19 between interview performance and subsequent on-the-job performance. James, Campbell and Lovegrove (1984) investigated interviews in the Victoria Police Department, Australia and suggested that interviewers tended to focus upon two factors: social conformity and educational achievements.

A substantial number of investigators have examined the validity of personality tests such as the 16PF in the prediction of police performance. Generally, correlations between individual scales and police performance are low (0.2–0.3) but multiple correlations of 0.4–0.5 are frequently obtained, e.g. Dunnette and Motowidlo (1976). British policemen tend to be stable, enthusiastic, venturesome, self-confident and group dependent (Gibson, 1981). Sterne (1960) contrasted the scores of police and protective occupations with the general norms on the Kuder Personal Preference Record. Police officers were less likely to avoid conflict and more likely to give *directions to others*. The other protective occupations showed similar, but not significant, trends. Spielberger *et al.* (1979) used the California Personality Inventory as a predictor of police performance. Hogan (1971) produced a scale of police effectiveness based upon four CPI scales: social presence, self-acceptance, achievement via independence and intellectual efficiency. Johnson and Hogan (1981) investigated the interests of effective policemen. They found that policemen tend to have high interests in social, realistic and enterprising activities. However, effective policemen were less artistic and more conventional in their interests. Roe and Roe (1982) provide a technical summary of validity studies in police selection.

A special topic of importance in the United Kingdom, where police officers do not routinely carry guns, is the selection from within the police force of a cadre who are fully trained to carry firearms. Early work concentrated upon the psychomotor aspects of marksmanship and suggested that this was best predicted by measures of steadiness. MacCaslin and McGuigan (1956) examined marksmanship and six predictors: rifle steadiness, firing experience, education level, intelligence, mechanical aptitude and mechanical information. They found that marksmanship was predicted best by measures of intelligence and firing experience. Much more recently Cooper, Robertson and Sharman (1986) examined the differences between fourteen British police officers who were authorized to carry firearms and 30 officers who were not trained to carry firearms. They produced results which run counter to intuition and found that police officers who carry firearms tend to be more reserved, but more trusting.

Probably the best study of policemen and firemen applicants is Matarazzo *et al.*'s (1964) investigation. They subjected 243 applicants for the positions of policemen and firemen to an eight-hour battery of measures. Their results suggest that successful police and fireman applicants have an average IQ of 113 (80th percentile) and report few problems of emotional and personality adjustment. These results also suggest that these applicants had a low need for autonomy but high needs for intraception (ability to analyse the feelings and behaviour of others) and exhibition. Johnson (1965) used Matarazzo *et al.*'s results to examine trends in firemen and police applicants by comparing them with the results obtained by Terman in 1917. It would appear that a policeman and fireman in the 1960s was better educated and more intelligent than his counterparts earlier this century.

Occupations involving isolation

Some occupations impose stress or high risk because of the isolation of the incumbents. This isolation can be *physical, cultural, psychological* or combinations of the three. Personal physical isolation is a characteristic of some of the occupations, such as undersea divers, which were discussed in an earlier section. Longer term physical isolation is, perhaps, typified by personnel who serve on isolated island bases or on isolated northern bases. Cooper and Green (1976) attempted to predict the conduct and performance of Royal Air Force airmen and corporals on remote islands of Masirah and Gan which were both characterized by day temperatures above 80 °F. Conduct and social interaction were best predicted by youth together with an accommodating, relaxed and self-assured personality (as measured by the 16PF). Performance in the job was predicted by an enthusiastic and adventurous personality.

Morgan, Sisler and Chylinski (1963) investigated the personality characteristics associated with favourable adjustment of electronic technicians who had volunteered for a one-year tour of isolation duty on the Bell Telephone Company's Mid-Canada Line. Previous military research had suggested that the best predictor was an individual's previous history of adjustment to his job and social history. Wright *et al.* found low, but useful correlations, between the supervisor's evaluation of the individual's adjustment and low scores on the schizoid, psychopathic deviate and psychasthenic scales of the MMPI. There was also a similar relationship with low scores on the aggression scale of the Edwards Personal Preference Schedule. Not surprisingly, they also found that adjustment was best for subjects who had grown up and spent most of their lives in a small community.

Cultural isolation is typified by occupations in the foreign service and by members of the peace corps. Selection of peace corps volunteers is generally by means of an intensive system involving preliminary screening on the basis of references, questionnaires and aptitude tests as a first stage. The second stage consists of a selection board which considers many facets of a volunteer's performance over a two- to four-month training period. Goldberg (1966) studied the reliability of those boards and found very high correlations in the range of 0.8 and 0.9. He also found that these boards tended to produce lower ratings and greater differentiation between trainees. Although direct evidence of validity is absent, greater differentiation is an important precursor to validity. Uhes and Shybut (1971) examined the use of a Personal Orientation Inventory for prediction of success in peace corps training. They found that successful trainees were more inner directed in the sense that they had greater autonomy, self-support and freedom from rigid adherence to social pressures and expectations. They were also more existential in the sense that they were flexible in applying self-actualizing values and principles. It was interesting that high 'time competence' was positively associated with success in female peace corps volunteers but negatively associated with success in males. They write, 'a transplanted American male who prides himself on being efficient in the use of time may be perceived by the Micronesians as an impatient individual and rated poorly on his adjustment to a relatively easy going, non-scheduled daily approach to living'. Walther (1961) developed a self-description questionnaire which showed strong resemblance to a biodata inventory and developed 'keys' for secretaries, code clerks and mail clerks in the US foreign service. The results were used to predict performance and turnover of each of these groups and produced correlations which indicate that the biodata approach would be a useful screening instrument. The correlations were: secretaries 0.6 and 0.4; code clerks 0.4 and 0.3; record clerks 0.3 and 0.4 for performance and turnover, respectively.

He noted that various lie scales such as the L scale on the EPI, the K and L scales on the MMPI and the Edwards Social Desirability scales are all measures of social desirability rather than a proclivity for dissimulation.

RISK OF EMPLOYEE THEFT

It seems appropriate to end this chapter with a brief mention of an unusual aspect of risk: the risk of employee theft. In many situations the main risk associated with an occupation is that the employee will prove untrustworthy. Concern is particularly acute in settings where employees have access to cash or merchandise such as retail stores, financial institutions and warehousing. Considerable attention has been devoted to reducing this risk by employing four main types of selection device: polygraph, lie scales, honesty questionnaires and weighted application blanks, but success is limited.

FUTURE HORIZONS IN SELECTION FOR HIGH-RISK SITUATIONS

There are probably two major conclusions to be drawn from the preceding account of the literature on high-risk and stressful occupations. *First*, we need to develop and test a taxonomy of the appropriate occupations. It is hoped that the early parts of this chapter have started this process but the taxonomy needs to be tested and extended. The benefits of having such a taxonomy are huge because we could then begin to check the generalizability of various selection techniques within different categories of high-risk jobs. If validity generalization proved appropriate a great deal of time and effort could be saved in creating and validating systems *'de nouveau'*.

Second, we urgently need to devise practical criteria of performance in high-risk jobs. The absence of such criteria is probably the cause of our present, rather unsatisfactory, reliance upon studies using training data as their criteria. Since it is often held that a selection system can only be as good as the criteria which define it, and since it is highly probable that training performance and job performance differ in significant ways, we must regard our present knowledge with care.

It is, of course, difficult to predict the future emphasis which will be placed on selection for high-risk occupations. It is possible to argue that the emphasis will rise during the next decade in response to the development of more powerful and explosive systems and the extension of human endeavour into environments of even greater hostility. However, this is probably more than counterbalanced in the improvement in systems and ergonomics which will more than mitigate the increased psychological and physical demands. Despite these improvements, many jobs will retain their high risks and stress. While it seems likely that the problem of selection of people for these occupations will diminish, it will certainly not go away!

REFERENCES

Baddeley, A.D. (1966). Influence of depth of the manual dexterity of free divers: a comparison between open sea and pressure chamber testing, *Journal of Applied Psychology*, **50**(1), 81–5.

Bair, J.T., Lockman, R.F., and Martoccia, C.I. (1956). Validity and factor analyses of naval air training predictor and criterion measures, *Journal of Applied Psychology*, **40**(4), 213–19.

Bartram, D., and Dale, H. (1982). The Eysenck Personality Inventory as a selection test for military pilots, *Journal of Occupational Psychology*, **55**, 287–96.

Belbin, R.M. (1956). Older people and heavy work. *British Journal of Industrial Medicine*, **12**, 309–319.

Biersner, R.J., and Larocco, J.M. (1983). Personality characteristics of US Navy divers, *Journal of Occupational Psychology*, **56**, 329–34.

Biersner, R.J., and Ryman, D.H. (1974). Prediction of scuba training performance, *Journal of Applied Psychology*, **59**(4), 519–21.

Brier, P. (1987). Can Psychological Testing Improve the Validity of the Police Selection Process? Unpublished B.Sc. Dissertation, Department of Management Sciences, UMIST.

Cattell, R.B. (1957). *The Scientific Analysis of Personality*. Penguin, Harmondsworth.

Cattell, R.B., Eber, H.W., and Tasuoka, H.M. (1970). *Handbook for the Sixteen Personality Factor Questionnaire*. National Foundation for Educational Research, Windsor, Berkshire.

Cooper, C.L., and Green, M.D. (1976). Coping with occupational stress among Royal Air Force personnel on isolated island bases, *Psychological Reports*, **39**, 731–4.

Cooper. C.L., Robertson, I.T., and Sharman, P. (1986). A psychometric profile of British police officers authorised to carry firearms: a pilot study, *International Review of Applied Psychology*, **35**, 537–46.

Dunnette, M.D., and Motowidlo, S.J. (1976). *Development of a Personal Selection and Career Assessment System for Police Officers*. Dept of Justice, Washington, DC.

Eysenck, H.J. (1967). *The Biological Basis of Personality*. Thomas, Springfield, Illinois.

Fleishman, E.A. (1960). An analysis of pilot flying performance in terms of component abilities, *Journal of Applied Psychology*, **44**(3), 146–55.

Fleishman, E.A., and Hogan, J.C. (1978). *A Taxonomic Method for Assessing the Physical Requirements of Jobs: the physical abilities analysis approach*. Naval Personnel Research and Development Laboratory, Washington, DC.

Gibson, J. (1981). An Exploratory Study of Psychological Tests in Recruitment of Police Constables, Unpublished B.Sc. Dissertation, Department of Management Studies, UMIST.

Goldberg, L.R. (1966). Reliability of peace corps selection boards, *Journal of Applied Psychology*, **50**(5), 400–8.

Gunderson, E.E.K., Rae, R.H., and Arthur, R.J. (1972). Prediction of performance in stressful underwater demolition training, *Journal of Applied Psychology*, **56**(5), 430–2.

Guskinos, U., and Brennan, T.F. (1971). Selection and evaluation procedure for operating room personnel, *Journal of Applied Psychology*, **55**(2), 1645–9.

Hogan, I. (1985). Tests for success in diver training, *Journal of Applied Psychology*, **70**(1), 219–24.

Hogan, R. (1971). Personality characteristics of highly rated policemen, *Personnel Psychology*, **24**, 679–84.

James, S.P., Campbell, I.M., and Lovegrove, S.A. (1984). Personality differentiation in a police-selection interview, *Journal of Applied Psychology*, **69**(1), 129–34.

Jessup, G., and Jessup, H. (1971). Validity of the Eysenck Personality Inventory in pilot selection, *Occupational Psychology*, **45**, 111–23.

Johnson, R.W. (1965). Successful policemen and firemen applications, *Journal of Applied Psychology*, **49**(4), 299–301.

Johnson, J.A., and Hogan, R. (1981). Vocational interests, personality, and effective police performance, *Personnel Psychology*, **34**, 49–53.

Kiessling, J.R., and Magg, C.H. (1962). Performance impairment as a function of nitrogen narcosis, *Journal of Applied Psychology*, **46**, 91–5.

Knapp, R.J., Capel, W.C., and Youngblood (1976). Stress in the deep: a study of undersea divers in controlled dangerous situations, *Journal of Applied Psychology*, **61**(4), 507–12.

Krug, S.E. (1981). *Interpreting 16PF profiles*. Institute for Personality and Ability Testing, Champaign, Ill.

Landy, F.J. (1976). The validity of the interview in police officer selection, *Journal of Applied Psychology*, **61**(2), 192–8.

Lipe, D. (1970). Trait validity of airline stewardess performance ratings. *Journal of Applied Psychology*, **54**(4), 347–352.

MacCaslin, E.F. and McGuigan, F.J. (1956). The prediction of rifle marksmanship, *Journal of Applied Psychology*, **40**(5), 341–2.

Matarazzo, J.D., Allen, B.V., Saslow, G., and Wiens, A.N. (1964). Characteristics of successful policemen and firemen applicants, *Journal of Applied Psychology*, **48**(2), 123–33.

Naylor, G.F.K. (1954). Aptitude tests for air traffic control officers, *Occupational Psychology*, **25**, 28–9.

Naylor, G.F.K. (1955). Aptitude tests for air traffic control officers, *Occupational Psychology*, **29**, 209–18.

Roe, A.V., and Roe, N. (1982). *Police Selection: a technical summary of validity studies*. Diagnostic Specialists, Inc., Orem, Utah.

Ryman, D.H., and Biersner, R.J. (1975). Attitudes predictive of diving success. *Personnel Psychology*, **28**, 181–188.

Slovic, P. (1969). Analysing the expert judge: a descriptive study of a stockbroker's decision process, *Journal of Applied Psychology*, **53**(4), 255–63.

Smith, J.M., and Robertson, I.T. (1986). *The Theory and Practice of Systematic Staff Selection*. Macmillan, London.

Spielberger, C., Spaulding, H., Jolley, M., and Ward, J. (1979). Selection of effective law enforcement officers. In C. Spielberger (ed.). *Police Selection and Evaluation: issues and techniques*. Hemisphere, Washington DC.

Sterne, R. (1960). Use of the Kuder Preference Record, personal, with police officers, *Journal of Applied Psychology*, **4**(5), 323–4.

Stouffer, S.A. (1949). *Studies in Social Psychology in World War II*, vol. 1. Princeton University Press, Princeton, NJ.

Swanson, R.G., and Johnson, D.A. (1975). Relation between peer perception of leader behaviour and instructor–pilot performance, *Journal of Applied Behaviour*, **60**(2), 198–200.

Terman, L.M.A. (1917). A trial of mental and pedagogical tests in a Civil Service examination for policemen and firemen, *Journal of Applied Psychology*, **1**, 17–29.

Uhes, M.J., and Shybut, J. (1971). Personal Orientation Inventory as a predictor of success in peace corps training, *Journal of Applied Psychology*, **55**(5), 498–9.

Vernon, P.E., and Parry, J.B. (1949). *Personnel Selection in the British Forces*. University of London Press, London.

Walther, R.H. (1962). Self description as a predictor of rate of promotion of junior foreign service officers, *Journal of Applied Psychology*, **46**(5), 314–316.

Want, R. (1959). Frames of reference of flying instructors, *Journal of Applied Psychology*, **43**(2), 86–8.

Wright, M.W., Sisler, G.C., and Chylinski, J. (1963). Personality factors in the selection of civilians for isolated northern stations, *Journal of Applied Psychology* **47**(1), 24–29.

Chapter 4.6

Caring Occupations

P. Spurgeon and F. Barwell

Health Service Management Centre, University of Birmingham, Park House,
40 Edgbaston Park Road, Birmingham B15 2RT, UK

CARING—AN OPERATIONAL PERSPECTIVE

In attempting to provide an operational definition for the 'caring occupations' one is struck by the considerable difficulty in achieving what initially appears to be a straightforward task. Inclusion or exclusion from the category seems equally likely to provoke resentment and dispute. Some of the likely members of 'caring occupations' may be offended by associations, however unfair and stereotypic, with 'do-gooders'. Similarly, groups excluded may quite reasonably feel that they are equally capable of offering 'care' to their clients.

The dilemma lies primarily in a rather loose and very wide-ranging use of the concept of personal need. Surely if care means anything, then it involves attempts to meet the needs of others. This is well expressed by Henderson (1966), describing the essential function of the nurse as 'to assist the individual, sick or well, in the performance of those activities contributing to health or its recovery (or to peaceful death) that he or she would perform unaided had he or she the necessary strength, will or knowledge'.

Clearly, nurses unequivocally form a core group of 'carers', but then by similar criteria so do paramedic groups (physiotherapy, occupational therapy, etc.) and indeed medicine, although this is treated separately as a professional group in a later chapter. However, would we quite so readily assign radiographers and pharmacists to this group, or does their more apparent technical expertise suggest other categories?

Perhaps then it is the greater degree of sustained personal contact with the patient or client that is the defining characteristic. But here again we need to be

Handbook of Assessment in Organizations   Edited by P. Herriot
© 1989 John Wiley & Sons Ltd

careful because there is a range of occupations in service industries where the prime goal is to meet the needs of the client and where interpersonal client-oriented behaviour is essential. The airline steward/stewardess, waiter and shop assistant all aim to meet the individual's requirements, albeit in less critical contexts.

Similarly, it is over-restrictive to see need as exclusively physical. There are many ways in which physical and psychological needs present themselves to the caring professional. People experiencing divorce, bereavement or serious illness, such as cancer or AIDS, may well need both medical care and the care of a skilled counsellor. Once we acknowledge the huge range of physical, psychological and also social needs people may have, it is apparent that social workers, probation officers, and others dealing with clients in the community also offer some form of care.

This brief discussion illustrates that no single occupation has a monopoly on care, or indeed a specific context in which care is given. The fundamental feature linking the caring professions together is where an individual requires help and where the provision of the necessary care seems to be the focus, rather than the technical or professional skills, often considerable, possessed by the provider. Although many possible groups provide care, it is not possible in the space provided to detail each profession separately. Rather, accepting the nature of care as discussed above, we will draw from a range of these groups to illustrate some of the tasks and skills involved in the caring professions. Subsequent sections will focus upon the personal attributes required for these tasks and how selection procedures may contribute in identifying those with the appropriate prerequisites for effective on-the-job performance.

TASKS AND SKILLS

The classical route to developing selection techniques is initially to undertake a detailed job analysis, although there is a great deal of debate concerning the best way of describing jobs, tasks and skills. This has often resulted in definitional confusion and a plethora of analysis methods and techniques. To some extent much of the resultant confusion is largely semantic. However, in order to avoid becoming ensnared in this issue, the simple premise taken here is that by examining what people do (tasks) it is possible to infer the types of psychological attributes or qualities (temperament and skills) necessary to carry out the required tasks effectively. On this basis, rational approaches to selection can be developed which can help to identify these required characteristics.

Moreover, a secondary outcome of this analysis of tasks is required here, since we are not dealing with a single occupation. We are concerned with a number of job groups whose common theme is 'caring'. By examining tasks of such groups we may come closer to understanding the particular nature of this link. Our selected occupations are by no means exhaustive and reflect more the degree of previous analytic work that has been undertaken. In each example discussed here, attention has been given to those tasks which may be described as direct and client oriented. It is acknowledged that in virtually all cases there is a substantial and increasing set of secondary tasks involving administration and management.

Social workers

A recent government enquiry (Social Workers: their role and tasks, 1982) has examined in some detail the diverse roles and tasks of social workers. It is clear that as a group, social workers deal with a wide range of clients, including those with family problems, the elderly, the physically handicapped and emotionally distressed. Despite this diversity, the report suggests that the tasks undertaken remain broadly similar, although the emphasis and involvement vary considerably across contexts.

Important 'direct' social work tasks include:

1. Diagnosis and assessment of client need. Typically this occurs by collecting sufficient information to establish the nature of the problem, forming a judgement about the client's capacity to address these problems, identifying possible causes of action and communicating these to the client.
2. Giving practical assistance or advice. This can involve taking action, promoting action in the client, maintaining surveillance of a fraught situation or simply offering advice.
3. Acting as an intermediary. Often this requires reference to a host of contacts with other agencies as appropriate.
4. Providing support to clients. This may involve sustained personal counselling, emotional support through crisis or monitoring development and progress.

It is important to note that many of the client groups represented here are in considerable distress and may present many aspects of human inadequacy. Often clients are hostile and negative to the care offered. Such a working environment places great demands upon the values, attitudes, prejudices and personal stability of the social worker. However, Bedford and Bedford (1985) in a study of personality traits of social workers found no evidence of greater personal disturbance than any other group in the population. Nevertheless, they did comment that the high indicators of initial 'warmth, submissiveness and acceptance' might create a group vulnerable to long-term pressure and subsequent drop-out.

The particular skills involved in social work are, firstly, an understanding of, and sensitivity to, human relationships (the ability to listen, to respect others, to assess critical cues and to maintain personal dignity). Secondly, skill in assessing interpersonal behaviours is vital (the ability to gather information in difficult settings, to interpret often contradicting information, and to assess the impact of intervention). Finally, effective social workers need to possess the skills of effective action (liaison with other bodies, negotiation and advocacy skills, resilience and stamina).

Current entry/selection requirements

The primary qualification in the United Kingdom is the CQSW (Certificate of

Qualification in Social Work), which is offered in a variety of formats by many colleges, polytechnics and universities. Each institution offers a particular qualification and has specific entry requirements. However, in general a 20–25-year-old needs five passes at the appropriate level of GCSE although two 'Advanced' level passes are also sought by many bodies. GCSE examinations are taken by 40 per cent (approximately) of UK school students at age 16, Advanced levels by some 15 per cent at age 18. Candidates over 25 do not need the formal requirements but evidence is sought in terms of ability to succeed in the course based on relevant personal experience.

The Certificate in Social Service is offered by many further education colleges on a day-release basis. It is primarily oriented to residential/day care staff and is generally considered to be a slightly lower level of qualification.

Additionally, there are a number of undergraduate (typically four-year) and post-graduate courses at universities and polytechnics.

Existing selection practice has tended to look for substantial experience of volunteer work or other kind of 'relevant' work (Shaw, 1977). However, as funding sources become scarce it is increasingly difficult for more mature candidates to accept the financial hardship of a student grant. Recent evidence from Shaw (1985) suggests that this may be restricting the entrance of non-graduates to the profession. Current selection methods are not particularly innovative, relying largely on the interview alongside background information. The stress and responsibilities inherent in many aspects of the occupation would appear to warrant more sophisticated approaches to selection in the United Kingdom.

Occupational therapists

Occupational therapy (OT) is one of the groups of 'paramedic' occupations defined as those professions supplementary to medicine. The basic aim is 'the treatment of physical and psychiatric conditions through specific selected activities in order to help people reach their maximum level of function and independence in all aspects of daily life' (College of Occupational Therapists, 1986). The work takes place typically in hospitals, in day care centres and, increasingly, in the patient's home. Facilitating independent functioning at home is a fundamental goal, but this is often supplemented by a range of other activities such as communication techniques, 'industrial' training, social and sporting involvement as well as educational programmes. The client group may range from very small children to adults, typically treated on a one-to-one basis, although families or groups may become involved.

There are some interesting parallels between the tasks of the OT and those of the social worker. In general terms the tasks of the OT are:

1. Diagnose and assess client needs. Although with a greater medical orientation, the occupational therapist, like the social worker, will be involved in identifying the nature and degree of the client's limitations, assessing the client's motivational state, and identifying possible courses of treatment.
2. Devising and providing developmental activities to enhance the individual's

independence. This will involve a great deal of direct contact with the patient to practise physical body movements, as well as promoting self-help and subsequent coping capacity.
3. Liaison with a number of other support groups (nurses, volunteer groups, community-based agencies). Typically, this involves the provision of information on client capabilities, and advice on aids to specialists, such as ergonomists designing equipment.

Once again the working context and client group can be far from easy. Many patients may be suffering from distressing conditions both for themselves and their relatives. Many who require treatment are extremely bitter and resentful and this can be directed towards the OT who may have to force them through tasks which can be painful and difficult to achieve.

Coping with this stress and distress is one of the personal skills that must be acquired. Perhaps, as with social workers, a form of emotional detachment is essential. Among the other qualities required are those of being a good listener, being perceptive and sensitive to the needs of others, and of accepting the weaknesses and vulnerabilities of people in need of help.

OTs will also need to be innovative and creative in devising activities to promote client recovery. This flexibility in approach must be linked with a good practical understanding of human movement and its interaction with remedial equipment.

As with social workers, the necessary knowledge and technical skills must be allied with the core interpersonal and counselling skills in dealing with individuals needing help and sustained care.

Current entry/selection requirements

The basic qualification in the United Kingdom is the Diploma in Occupational Therapy in which the main topics covered are anatomy, physiology and psychology. This is usually a three-year course, but can be four in some institutions. Colleges, polytechnics and hospitals provide courses where entry requirements are a minimum of five/six GCSE passes, including English and a science subject, plus one 'Advanced' level pass, although again, increasingly, two 'Advanced' level passes are demanded. The basic qualification is seen as a general training. After gaining experience for a year or two, OTs specialize in particular areas of work such as paediatrics, the elderly or mentally handicapped.

In selection, evidence of having gained relevant voluntary experience is very desirable. Formal plus informal interviews are typically used, but increasingly some institutions are using some form of psychometric (ability) measure, coupled with some form of written assessment. There are parallels here with physiotherapy schools where the demand for places is very high and academic standards are becoming increasingly rigorous. One might question, however, whether academic qualifications are the most relevant selection criteria in these highly interpersonal work areas.

Nursing

Of the selective group of occupations examined here, nurses are by far the largest. Training provision is well developed and consequently many attempts exist to describe nursing tasks. Many of these operate at a very detailed descriptive level, literally observing the nature and frequency of specific ward-based activities. A recent study by Gott (1983) lists tasks such as 'take and record blood pressure, make empty bed, chart fluid level, feed patient, etc.'. At a more abstracted level the influential text edited by Kratz (1979) describing the 'nursing process' has characterized nursing as:

1. Assessing the patient's needs (physical, emotional and social).
2. Planning how the nursing provision can attempt to meet these goals by identifying specific objectives for the individual nurse or nursing team.
3. Direct intervention to carry out the nursing procedures recommended.
4. Evaluation of the nursing care provided with a view to modification and improvement.

This holistic approach, which requires treating each patient as an individual with a set of integrated needs, is an increasingly widespread practice, although it would be wrong to assume that more functional, mechanistic perceptions of nursing do not exist. None the less, by examining what is involved in the four main aspects of nursing, it is possible to locate many of the necessary skills.

Assessment involves seeking information from the patient by integrating medical history and the current situation. Sensitive interviewing skills provide a first descriptive account, from which inferences and decisions about what treatment the patient may need can be made. Following this stage, planning requires an empathetic awareness to set goals which are both appropriate and compatible with the patient's perspective coupled with a knowledge of nursing care to assign relevant procedures to these goals.

The final task of evaluation requires many of the skills needed in the assessment stage. The provision of nursing care obviously depends upon sound technical expertise, but also involves considerable liaison with colleagues (other nurses, doctors, paramedics, etc.). It is essential that nurses are sensitive to the patient's response to treatment so that adaptation and tuning of the care programme can take place as appropriate.

Gott (1983) reports a study concerned with nurse training and discusses the adequacy or otherwise of clinically based experiences. She points in particular to the fact that as a caring profession, nurses are expected to emerge from their training as 'socially skilled'. Unfortunately since training in interpersonal areas is poor and contact is perceived as threatening, nurses often learn to deal with patients in ways which actively prevent close and intimate relationships developing. It is interesting to note that patients have repeatedly described such interpersonal skills as the ones they felt above all that the nurse should acquire.

Many other writers have reinforced the crucial role of interpersonal skills in nursing (Tait, 1985; Davis, 1985). Maguire (1985) highlights the vital role of communication using as examples difficult situations; e.g. the angry patient, the withdrawn patient, the dying patient and the distressed or bereaved patient. In these situations good interpersonal communication can be crucial in avoiding further problems. He argues that a major difficulty is that nurses are either assumed to possess such skills 'naturally' or will somehow acquire them during their training.

Current entry/selection requirement

Training in the UK Health authorities is via their own nursing schools. The obvious close links with practising nurses provide good opportunities for work experience. However, there is considerable debate fuelled by economic pressures on health authorities that trainee nurses are being used as cover for full-time staff.

The basic five or six GCSE passes still exists as an entry requirement, although many nursing schools now look for additional 'Advanced' level passes. For a number of years the available places have been oversubscribed, but recently the situation has reversed as the population of 18-year-olds declines, and salaries and conditions are seen as relatively unattractive.

Degree courses in nursing exist and require normal university entrance requirements. However, these furnish a relatively small population of the number of trained nurses coming on to the job market.

Wastage rates in nurse training have long been an issue of concern and a number of reasons have been proposed, including personal factors, poor integration of training, and conditions of service. Although intelligence is related to success, it would seem that above a certain level, ability does not further enhance the likelihood of success. Personality factors appear to be more predictive, although the numerous studies involving personal qualities have not been conclusive. Recently Lewis (1983) tested a large sample of trainee nurses using Cattell's 16PF, and found that successful trainees were better at dealing with people and gruelling emotional situations without becoming fatigued, and 'rattled'.

Once again it is perhaps surprising that current selection relies heavily on academic attainment and formal interview. The traditional approach and alternative strategies are discussed later in the chapter.

ATTRIBUTES OF CARING PROFESSIONS

The previous sections have discussed the nature of selected groups representing the caring profession. Amalgamating these ideas leads us to a critical set of attributes of the caring professional. In this section these are discussed and problems inherent in assessing them pinpointed.

Competence and trust

The credibility and effectiveness of any professional group ultimately rests on the client's belief that the professional who is dealing with him or her is competent in providing the appropriate intervention. Engendering the trust of the client or patient is particularly important for the caring professions since they are all people-oriented occupations and those requiring help are, at the time of intervention, often not in a physical or mental condition to evaluate either what treatment they need or the appropriateness of actual treatment they receive. Patients and clients are often dependent, distressed and vulnerable and this heightens the emotionality of the transactions and can lead to stress for both those giving and those receiving care.

The assessment of professional competence is critical not only in maintaining the integrity of professional standards but also in ensuring that those who require care are able to place their trust and confidence in those who provide it.

Competence and performance

In addition to maintaining professional standards and client confidence, the assessment of competence is essential in order to monitor the progress and performance of care professionals not only during training and post-training, but also throughout the course of their subsequent professional career. Understanding the deficiencies between what is required for effective performance and current work behaviour provides the necessary feedback on which individual future performance can be improved. This is of prime importance at all stages throughout an individual's career, although it is reasonable to expect higher standards of performance from those with longer experience since some aspects of performance should improve throughout the professional's working life. For example, in many occupations one key difference between the novice and the fully experienced practitioner is often the increase in speed of performance which comes with practice. Speed-related features of tasks have the advantage of being relatively easy to assess, but increase of speed *per se* may prove to be an inappropriate means of assessment for those occupations with a large interpersonal content. The evidence suggests that good interpersonal transactions require frequent communication which needs to be maintained for as long as necessary rather than being curtailed prematurely (Burton, 1985). Macleod-Clark (1984) concludes from a review of nursing activities in a variety of care contexts that the pattern of one-to-one verbal communication is often infrequent, perfunctory and typically occurs within the performance of specific nursing tasks. The establishment of a good caring relationship stems from frequent, sustained and appropriate communication. Ley (1977) suggests that a good caring relationship can shorten the time required for recovery and discharge for patients who have undergone surgery. Of course, opportunities for interaction and duration of these transactions vary both within and between professional contexts. In hospital settings it has often been found that interactions between nurses and patients are often infrequent, cursory and related to the performance of ward duties.

The ability to relate to patients and clients by establishing and maintaining good communication and interpersonal skills has been identified as critical within all caring professions, although the relative emphasis placed upon the philosophy of individualized care to meet personal needs varies. Many social workers regard direct interpersonal counselling as the core skill, indeed the hallmark of their profession whereas in the nursing field, the recognition of the importance of the interpersonal factors is only more recently becoming established. For paramedical professions such as physiotherapy and occupational therapy, the opportunities for therapeutic interactions may in actuality occur more frequently than for the regular ward staff.

Job skills

The development of competence in the caring professional is not related to speed of performance, particularly for the core interpersonal aspects of their work. More complex and subtle measures than speed are needed to assess proficiency, but the twin monitoring and feedback benefits of assessment will not ensue unless relevant and realistic job skills, and their associated performance criteria, have been initially accurately identified through some form of job analysis. The specific job skills which underpin competence vary according to the caring profession in question, but at a broad level competence demands the demonstration of good practical skills supported by an understanding of relevant theoretical knowledge. Exactly what theoretical background is relevant and should be included in training and post-training courses is more contentious. This uncertainty stems from two sources—firstly, from disagreement about the nature of the jobs themselves and, secondly, from disagreement about how skilled performance itself is supported and guided by theoretical understanding. It is clear that knowledge itself does not guarantee good job skills, although appropriate knowledge can have other positive effects like reducing anxiety and increasing self-esteem. In a study of anxiety, conflict and stress in student and pupil nurses, Birch (1983) provides evidence that the pattern of general nurse education fails to prepare the student nurse adequately for his or her role in dealing with the patients' psychological needs. He recommends that schools of nursing should stress the psychological core to the curriculum laying particular emphasis on conflict, anxiety, the nature of pain, bereavement, and sexual aspects of illness and patient care. Enhancing sensitivity to the psychological needs of patients appears to be a potentially beneficial area for improving the education and training of nurses. Similarly, Dickson and Maxwell (1985) have argued that more systematic training in interpersonal skills is required for physiotherapists because of the job demands discussed earlier.

The integration of skills

The relative emphases on the theoretical and practical content of training courses for caring professionals highlight the difficulties of adequately conceptualizing these occupations in ways which facilitate assessment. However, at a general level competence is often characterized as three broad skill areas, which although not completely independent, are discrete enough to provide a practical foundation for developing assessment schemes. These three areas of skilled behaviour have been variously described but can be summarized as:

1. Technical–practical skills. This refers to skill in effectively carrying out required job behaviours.
2. Cognitive–intellectual skills. This refers to skills in analysing and appraising people, situations and the results of actions taken.
3. Social–interpersonal skills. This refers to skills in human relationships and communication.

Clearly all three aspects of effective performance are of importance but it is by integrating these three skill groupings that competence is achieved (Caney, 1983). The extent to which this integration takes place is influenced to a large extent by the individual's reactions to the process of coping with the pressures of becoming a caring professional. Assuming responsibility for others is an emotionally demanding and stressful role that requires individuals who have the stamina and resilience to cope with the emotional conflict inherent in sustained close contact with those in need.

Stress and vulnerability

Caring professionals are often forced to confront the dilemma of dealing with apparently unlimited human needs in the context of inadequate resources. The consistent pressure to relate directly to those in need can prove extremely stressful, particularly when the requirement of fulfilling job duties often necessitates reconciling moral and practical considerations. The Briggs Report (DHSS, 1972) commented on the pressures and demands of nursing and noted the profound and often unpredictable stresses inherent in the job. Similarly, social workers in their day-to-day contact with human inadequacy and distress face many dilemmas and conflicts.

The particular pattern of psychological factors inherent in these professions presents a similar pattern of stressors on the job incumbents, but the relationship between work stress and physical and psychological health is an issue which is complicated by a diverse range of individual and subjective factors.

Stress may result from a conflict between job demands and an individual's abilities and aspirations. People perform best under moderate levels of stress, too little or too much hinders effective performance. At one extreme, monotonous undemanding tasks result in boredom and frustration, while at the other end of the spectrum, excessive job demands can result in a reduced effectiveness and psychological and physical exhaustion. Squires and Livesley (1984) have discussed the physiotherapist's vulnerability to stress and the onset and process of the 'burnout' syndrome. These authors make the point that it is those very individuals who have been selected on the basis of characteristics associated with a 'good' caring approach (e.g. enthusiasm, idealism and energy) who are particularly vulnerable to 'burnout'. Perlman and Hartman (1982) have defined the condition as: 'a response to chronic emotional stress with three components:

1. Emotional, and/or physical exhaustion;
2. Lowered job productivity;

3. Overdepersonalisation'.

Other writers have included a variety of additional symptoms including cynicism, depression, negative attitudes towards patients and clients, exaggerated confidence in own competence, and a tendency to escapist behaviour through drink, drugs, absenteeism or frequent job changes. Niehouse (1981) has contrasted the symptoms of job stress with 'burnout', which would appear to be a more extreme reaction than stress-induced physical or mental exhaustion. Squires and Livesley (1984) define burnout as: '. . . a total loss of purpose, idealism and enthusiasm experienced by the helping professions when conditions at work produce an inability to function because of loss of will'.

The breadth and generality of definitions such as the above suggest that 'burnout' may be a multidimensional syndrome which requires further research to elucidate its structure. 'Burnout' has become a popular expression in professions with a high degree of personal contact and may be a syndrome specific to interpersonal occupations, although there is little hard evidence to support this view.

Individual differences in patterns of appraising potentially harmful events at work, coping strategies and adaptation to chronic and repeated stressful job demands are not fully understood. Birch (1975) identified anxiety as an important influence in student wastage from nurse training schools and suggests (Birch, 1983) that stress-prone candidates could be psychometrically identified as part of an improved selection regime. Lewis and Cooper (1976) have reviewed personality measurement among nurses and found a great deal of variation among the methodology and objectives in reported studies. Despite this variability, the review suggests there is some limited evidence that personality measurements are able to predict completion of a nurse training programme. Lewis (1983) assessed and compared a large sample of completing and non-completing student nurses on a number of intellectual and personality measures. The results showed that intellectual capacity is only a partial predictor of success and completing pupils were less anxious, more confident and better able to face emotional wear and tear than non-completing pupils.

Cognition and the self-concept

The caring professions can be characterized as sharing certain ideals, values and beliefs which appear to be more influential in these sorts of professions and which serve to distinguish them as a distinct cluster from the professions in general. Combs, Avila and Purkey (1974) identified common beliefs across a range of 'helping' professions and found a high degree of similarity between effective practitioners. The belief structures related to the professional's self-concept and perception of clients were central to their approach to their work. These studies highlight the role of the healthy self-concept with its feelings of worth, competence, adequacy and confidence in effective interventions and demonstrate that the self-concept can become its own architect in the ongoing transaction of life and work events. In a similar vein, the Barclay Report (1980) has discussed the value of social workers understanding their own personalities, prejudices and attitudes in determining how these critical factors influence their reactions to clients and events.

Dealing with the chronically sick, the terminally ill, the socially inadequate, the physically or mentally distressed, in a genuine empathic manner which is at once both effective yet enables the individual to retain his or her dignity requires a healthy self-concept and a great deal of interpersonal skill.

Unfortunately, patients and clients often express criticism about poor communication with the caring professionals they meet, and the early assumption that interpersonal skills are a matter of common sense which can occur as a natural by-product of job experience has been shown to be over-optimistic.

Current views on interpersonal communication suggest that it is a learned behaviour resulting from a complex interaction between emotional and cognitive factors. Anxiety and negative self-appraisal can both act as constraints to the expression of skilled interpersonal behaviour. These emotional and cognitive constraints are often engendered by organizational processes and conflict, including the stress of sustained interpersonal contact itself.

APPROACHES TO SELECTION

From the relatively small sample of 'caring professions' discussed here, similar themes and conclusions emerge which should influence selection practice. Although some degree of intellectual ability is essential for each job area, it is a necessary but not sufficient characteristic. Beyond a certain level, increased intellectual ability does not necessarily produce enhanced job performance. The nature of the work contexts described here (stressful, severe emotional, physical or social distress, client group hostility, etc.) serve to emphasize the demand for good interpersonal skills, a high degree of personal commitment and motivation as well as valued individual qualities such as empathetic awareness, resilience, patience and warmth.

The extending influence of the 'nursing process' is increasing this emphasis upon interpersonal skills. There is also a major policy change of eliminating institutional care and replacing it with more community-based care which may change the working situation of many caring groups. Inevitably, meeting people in their home environment is less controlled than within an institution and therefore the range of situations faced will be greater and potentially more exacting. Community-based care may also come to have far-reaching consequences for the skills required of individual professions. Because the patient is 'at home', his or her needs will not be constrained by a particular professional appointment. Increasingly, a patient, such as one recovering from a stroke, may require simultaneous inputs from the occupational therapist, physiotherapist, nurse and social worker. Either the professions will insist on professional barriers being maintained and hence engender expensive successive visits, or the 'skill-mix' will change and multi-skilled carers evolve. This is a major challenge of the next few years.

Some recognition of this broadening role may be seen in the development of

Project 2000 (UKCC, 1987) of this pattern of future nurse training in that nurses should receive a broader education incorporating sociology, psychology, philosophy, law, health education and counselling. The aim is to equip the young nurse with a better understanding of the patient's whole environment and therefore be better able to provide for these needs. Similarly, Weinman and Medlik (1985) describe programmes where interpersonal skills and awareness of the psychological dimensions of health care are provided for general practitioners, nurses and paramedic groups. These are valuable initiatives but it is important to recognize that they are training-oriented approaches. The training strategy is certainly a valid option for promoting the sort of interpersonal skills necessary in caring professions. It may also be the most appropriate, for these types of characteristics have proved notoriously elusive in all types of selection contexts.

Earlier sections of this handbook have discussed current selection processes and so they will not be reviewed here. However, it is worth pointing out that in almost all the professions discussed in this chapter, selection into the caring professions is heavily reliant upon the interview as the entry hurdle. Some institutions do include a piece of written work, and very few some form of objective test. Despite mounting evidence over a number of years that it is an unreliable and invalid assessment method, the interview remains in the ascendancy as the dominant selection technique.

Current selection practice would suggest that the qualities of the type sought here are most likely to be detected via an assessment centre process. However, these are relatively expensive to develop and, furthermore, are most appropriate to final selection once some prior filtering of candidates has occurred. Within the caring professions highlighted here there are often very large numbers of applicants (for example, between 90 000 and 130 000 nurse applicants) and therefore the development of assessment centres would need to be integrated with a procedure for reducing numbers earlier in the recruitment activity. Even if a full assessment centre process was deemed impracticable it would seem worth considering some elements.

A recent review of selection procedures in other professions (Borrill, 1987) concluded that nursing was not alone in the selection problems it faced. It showed that of the institutions cooperating in the survey, 100 per cent used the interview with 95 per cent of these using it as the sole method of assessment. Despite the fact that many institutions were very unhappy with the quality of this assessment, only 5 per cent used other activities such as discussion groups or spending time on wards.

This research also focused upon the need to ensure that applicants were committed, motivated and fully aware of what was involved in the job. In order to do this the technique of Job Information Checklists was developed. These consist of a number of detailed statements about the nature of nursing tasks and activities. The potential candidate answers as to whether he or she believes the statements to be 'true' or 'false'. Thereby his or her own perception of the job of the nurse can be tested against reality, and misconceptions modified. This material is referred to as 'Self-Selection Materials' and is geared to enabling the potential applicant to decide whether the job in question is really for him or her. Clearly it is a vital ingredient of pre-screening and the concept could readily be adapted to other professions.

The type of personal qualities one is seeking may be susceptible to measurement by personality questionnaires or inventories. However, it was concluded that research evidence thus far had failed to define reliably any consistent set of qualities. Moreover, the range of subsequent nursing contexts or specialities indicated that no consistently successful pattern would emerge.

Instead it was recommended that a limited form of assessment centre be developed including group exercises where critical interpersonal skills might be assessed and some type of work sample where patient interaction is involved. The methods and approaches recommended are currently being validated.

CONCLUSION

There is no easy way to improve selection into the caring professions. The qualities required can develop with experience and maturity and therefore may be very difficult to detect as potential at the selection stage. However, as the population of eligible 18-year-olds declines, it is even more vital that selection practice is effective, since wastage is even more damaging under these circumstances. Furthermore, as the professional and personal demands increase it is essential that those able to meet the challenges are recruited. Recent approaches do offer some intriguing possibilities by blending effective self-selection (screening) with the established benefits of assessment centre principles.

REFERENCES

Barclay Report (1980), *Social workers: their role and tasks*. Institute of Social Work, Bedford Square Press, London.
Birch, J.A. (1975). *To Nurse or Not to Nurse*, Royal College of Nursing, London.
Birch, J.A. (1983). Anxiety and conflict in nurse education, in B.D. Davis, (ed.). *Research into Nurse Education*. Croom Helm, London.
Borrill, C. (1987). The chosen ones, *Nursing Times*, **83**(4), 52–3.
Burton, M. (1985). The environment, good interactions and interpersonal skills in nursing, in C.M. Kagan, (ed.). *Interpersonal Skills in Nursing: Research and Applications*. Croom Helm, London.
Caney, D. (1983). Competence—can it be assessed? *Physiotherapy*, **69**(8) (September).
Combs, A.W., Avila, D.C., and Purkey, W.W. (1974). *Helping Relationships. Basic Concept for the Helping Professions*. Allyn and Bacon, Boston.
Davis, B. (1985). The clinical effect of interpersonal skills: the implementation of pre-operative information giving, in C.M. Kagan (ed.). *Interpersonal Skills in Nursing: Research and Applications*. Croom Helm, London.
Department of Health and Social Security (1972). Report on the Committee on Nursing (Chairman Professor Asa Briggs), Cmnd 5115. HMSO, London.
Dickson, D.A., and Maxwell, M. (1985). The interpersonal dimension of physiotherapy, *Implications for Training Physiotherapy*, **71**(7), 306–10.
Gott, M. (1983). The preparation of the student for learning in the clinical setting, in B.D. Davis (ed.). *Research into Nurse Education*. Croom Helm, London.
Henderson, V. (1966). *The Nature of Nursing*. Collier-Macmillan, London.

Kratz, C.R. (ed.) (1979). *The Nursing Process*. Bailliere Tindall, London.

Lewis, B.R. (1983). Personality and intellectual characteristics of trainee nurses and their assessment, in B.D. Davis, (ed.). *Research into Nurse Education*. Croom Helm, London.

Lewis, B.R., and Cooper, C.L. (1976). Personality measurement among nurses: a review, *International Journal of Nursing Studies*, **13**, 209–29.

Ley, P. (1977). Psychological studies of doctor–patient communication, in S. Rachman (ed.). *Contributions to Medical Psychology*. Pergamon, Oxford.

Macleod Clark, J. (1984). Verbal communication in nursing, in A. Faulkner (ed.). *Recent Advances in Nursing. 7, Communication*, Churchill Livingstone, Edinburgh.

Maguire, P. (1985). Deficiencies in key interpersonal skills, in C. Kagan (ed.). *Interpersonal Skills in Nursing: research and applications*, Croom Helm, London.

Niehouse, O.L. (1981). Burnout! A real threat to human resources managers, *Personnel (USA)*, **58**(5), 25–32.

Occupational Therapy (1986). College of Occupational Therapists, London.

Perlman, B., and Hartman, E.A. (1983). Burnout: summary and future research, *Human Relations*, **35**, 283–305.

Shaw, I. (1977). Selecting for social work, *British Journal of Social Work*, **7**, 55–72.

Shaw, I. (1985). A closed profession? Recruitment to social work, *British Journal of Social Work*, **15**, 261–80.

Social Workers: their role and tasks (1982). Report of Working Party set up by the National Institute for Social Work under the Chairmanship of Mr Peter M. Barclay. Bedford Square Press, London.

Squires, A., and Livesley, E. (1984). Beware of burnout, *Physiotherapy*, **70**(6) (June).

Tait, A. (1985). Interpersonal skill issues arising from mastectomy nursing contexts, in C.M. Kagan (ed.). *Interpersonal Skills in Nursing: research and application*. Croom Helm, London.

UKCC (United Kingdom Control Council for Nursing, Midwifery and Health Visitors) (1987). *Project 2000: the only option*. London.

Weinman, J., and Medlik, L. (1985). Sharing psychological skills in the general practice setting, *British Journal of Medical Psychology*, **58**, 223–30.

Chapter 4.7

Selection for Creative Occupations

PAUL THORNE

Bristow Design Systems Ltd, 50/54 Southampton Row, London WC1B 4AR, UK

INTRODUCTION

Systematic study of the nature of creativity in people goes back to Francis Galton, with his *Hereditary Genius* (1869) and beyond. Any substantial research into the nature of occupations which demand at least some element of creative output has yet to begin. Most of the modern interest in creativity among psychologists was stimulated by J.P. Guilford beginning in 1950 but while there have been many attempts to measure creativity in individuals, these have had little effect upon organizational recruitment practices. It would seem that most recruitment into creative occupations is done almost exclusively by those to whom the recruits will report.

The creative director of a design company is both the person to whom applicants would expect to relate, and whose judgement of their merit and potential would be felt the most weightily. It is the research and development director and his or her specialist staff who would be most likely to assess both the relevance of the research thrust of a senior potential recruit as well as its technical and creative merit. In these kinds of environment, few personnel specialists contribute much more than a judicious exploration of personal references.

Only the senior specialists, it would often appear, are believed to have the necessary insight and depth of understanding to know who from outside would be a likely contributor. For example, Ogilvy in *Confessions of an Advertising Man* (1987) confessed:

> Whenever I see a remarkable advertisement or television commercial, I find out who wrote it. Then I call the writer on the telephone and congratulate him (*sic*) on his work. Sometimes, I call on my victim at home; ten minutes after crossing the threshold I can

---

Handbook of Assessment in Organizations   Edited by P. Herriot
© 1989 John Wiley & Sons Ltd

tell whether he has a richly furnished mind, what kind of taste he has and whether he is happy enough to sustain pressure.

In the experience of the author, most of the science-based research activities, whether state sponsored or not, are managed in this way, with word-of-mouth recommendation, past loyalties and associations, and chance meetings at conferences playing at least as great a part as studies of published learned papers, so-called tests of creative ability, or investigations of prior creative works.

There is much debate about creativity but little certainty. The debate revolves around brain laterality (the discovery that the left and right hemispheres have differing areas of specialization); the core notion of convergency and divergency in thinking and decision making; and the social environment which constantly accelerates the demands on the active members of our society to adjust and invent rather than to conform and perpetuate. The so-called creative occupations, such as designers, researchers, artists and inventors, are probably becoming relatively less creative, while the creativity expected of the population at large is increasing. The number of occupations which could be proposed as being creative continues to increase rapidly along with the major changes in industrial infrastructure. The move away from the work ethic and low productivity manufacture to labour intensive services and leisure has its effects. Thus, where once there were only architects and their assistants, there are now space planners, interior and exterior designers, landscape architects, and even exhibition designers. Where there were once just writers, producers and performers within the creative area of broadcasting, there are now many more subsets and specialisms which could not have existed twenty years ago, each of which has its own measure of merit, career ladder and determining characteristics for success.

WHAT IS CREATIVITY?

It is useful to separate out the concept of creativity into product (outcome), process (activity) or person (as an expectation or a probability of he or she being inventive). Researchers over many years have reinforced the view that in any of these, creativity can be represented just as much by the ultimate act of true genius, as it can by the most inconsequential, but none the less surprising, piece of trivial comment. If an outcome even causes surprise because of its freshness or unexpectedness, and has an added value to somebody other than the originator, then it is a creative product.

However, the definition of what is a *significantly* creative *product* causes some greater difficulties. The perception of creativity is itself so subjective that its measurement usually comes about almost solely through the application of competitive economics. A truly creative painting, for example, could be seen as such by very few. The measure of its uniqueness of value will only receive popular assessment when it is sold for a unique price. Assessment of the creative product of industries and nations has suffered the same fate. For example, attempts to reach a consensus as to which products were major innovations in the pharmaceutical world and which were not failed in a Senate Sub-Committee on Antitrust and Monopoly (Kefauver Hearings) (Comanor, 1966) because it developed into a confrontation between groups of experts each with their different lists.

The *process* of creation would seem to be best characterized as having three elements to it.

1. Novelty or originality.
2. Reality, in the sense that it impacted some aspect of the real world so as to improve on it.
3. Integration and realization in the sense that something is completed from disparate parts, which is not just the half-formed, nor the simple extension of an existing order.

The reason for including the latter two is to differentiate the process of creation from simple uniqueness. Some schizophrenics use original expressions in their speaking, and will give surprising answers. However, just being strange does not itself make for being creative.

By the time we reach out to define the occupationally creative *person*, we move into areas of concept bereft of quality data, and strewn with preconceptions and stereotypes. As often as not, having a 'creative' job defines the creative individual.

Thus, an artist is creative, as is a playwright, a novelist or a film maker. They are creative because their output is original, a one off, and hopefully will have an added value of some consequence. However, if we look at another occupational group, say architects, or research scientists, would we as readily accept that their product is creative? No one can be creative all of the time. If a creative person is occupied in a job which gives no opportunities for the expression of his or her creativity, then how will he or she be seen to be creative? If, on the other hand, a person is in a 'creative' job, but is not a creative person, does the fact that the job (and presumably the job context) is creative make that person become perceived as such?

The basic proposition that there is such a person as a creative person, or that it is possible to increase the degree of creativity exhibited in an individual irrespective of his or her context has yet to be demonstrated.

In the occupational context, creativity requires more than one flash of genius. If it is a creative occupation, it will ask that the individual incumbent persists in reaching novel conclusions, continues to refresh ideas, and confidently turns to new pastures for innovation once the old ones become well ploughed. The pressure should be on the individual to want to move on as soon as the subject of his or her activity has yielded its creative end. Routine would not normally be expected to be a significant component to the occupation. These two points will be revisited in a later section.

WHAT ARE CREATIVE OCCUPATIONS?

There are now very few of life's disciplines which do not have within them some component of occupational specialization which is creative. Every science has its share of occupations which can be considered to have a necessary element of novel investigation and creative resolution. Among the more prevalent of these outside of the public sector is in chemistry and in bioscience. Pharmaceutical companies spend up to 10 per cent of their revenues on research and development. In other science-based industries using chemistry, physics and engineering as core disciplines (e.g. oil and chemicals), it is likely to be less. Since the ascendancy of computer software technology, and the mini- and microcomputers, a whole new range of creative occupations has surfaced in the design and development activities supporting computer usage. The constant improvement in manufacturing technology has encouraged the extension of engineering more into development of existing plant operations. As machinery has been subjected to more and more sophisticated control devices, so the design becomes a greater component of its engineering than its regulation. Product design also has become a more common employment as product life cycles have shortened and technologies shift and re-shape.

The distribution of scientific and engineering research occupations has been subject to recent review. During 1987 the Department of Trade and Industry carried out a sample survey of expenditure and employment on research and development performed in UK industry in 1986. It included 74 enterprises accounting for 75 per cent of the total expenditure on R&D in 1985. The survey showed that from 1981 to 1986 R&D performed on 'active components and electronic sub-assemblies' nearly quadrupled, and on 'electronic data processing equipment' and 'motor vehicles', nearly doubled. The biggest single manufacturing industry category in expenditure terms was electronics. Of all expenditure an overall percentage of around 43 per cent was attributed to wages. Within this sample, occupations were categorized as scientists or engineers, technicians and technical assistants, and administrative staff (presumably this could represent the order of probability of being creative). About half of the 175 000 employed were classified in the top group. Given that of this 175 000 only a small proportion would need to be creative for a significant part of their employment (say at best 20 per cent), then the prevalence of creative occupations in the manufacturing working population could be very small (at most 75 000 employees in the United Kingdom).

But products are not just physical goods and industrial R&D is not the only place where innovation is needed. We now include financial packages, new ways of trade, new ways of financing new ventures, both international and domestic, and new ways of saving and insuring.

Outside of manufacturing, creative occupations are represented in the graphic arts, where, for example, space design includes a growing number of new specialisms. Architects and other designers of physical space have long been seen as among the creative occupations. With modern technologies such as computer-aided design they are expanding horizons. The designers of film sets now can thank scientific invention for the opportunity to create special effects.

In journalism, and throughout the media, including advertising and public relations, there are many occupations which are traditionally high in the list of those which we would call creative. It could be argued that the opportunities to be so creative within these occupations are increasing thanks to the power of the computer and physical communications to influence working lives.

Within the management field, competition for markets and for successful growth could be seen as placing demand for a greater degree of creativity from such people as marketing managers, especially where there is a fast moving or high technology market place. The essential problem of definition is that, taken to its limits, it would be difficult to identify any occupation above the purely routine, where at least an element of creativity could be described as inessential. Conversely, the most obviously creative occupational category could turn out many examples where pure routine was the only component over many years.

For example, the Industrial Relations Manager at Ford, dealing with multi-cultural and multi-union conflict as a first order King Solomon could well need all of the talents of ideational fluency, originality, and persistence normally associated with creative minds in the face of attack from orthodoxy. On the other hand, a research fellow could well for years follow an investigative paradigm from which even occasional deviation was discouraged. Similarly, the hospital manager manoeuvring his or her resources under an increasing demand and a reducing budget, or a politician seeking to find new ways of raising local taxes, could each need to be more creative than any ten advertising copywriters who were obliged to play with words under heavy supervision and within a very limited set of parameters.

Thus the list of creative occupations could be defined as a very large one, or a very small one, the only certainty being that it is a constantly changing one. Furthermore, there is the overlap of multi-disciplinarism, where one set of knowledge and skills needs input from another or more to find answers to complex problems. The creativity is not in the occupation but in the organization of the varied personnel and occupations, for instance in space research.

The inclusion criterion for creative occupations is thus enormously complicated by the problems of definitions at each level. Perhaps this is best presented in the form of a triangle as shown here:

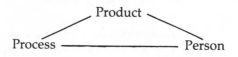

Interactivity of creative components

For an occupation to offer the potential to a creative person, there has to be the possibility of the product of the organizational unit to which the occupational category belongs being a creative one. There also has to be the possibility that there are processes of innovation that can be engaged. If any of the three is absent then the probability of there being an occupation within the observed organization which can be termed creative is effectively zero. This argument leads us directly to the conclusion that there are no creative occupations, only creative opportunities or otherwise for all occupations. In looking for criteria or otherwise, we might be missing the most important point, which is how do we make all occupations more open to creative acts.

Abraham Maslow put it best:

> I had unconsciously confined creativeness to certain conventional areas only of human endeavour, unconsciously assuming that any painter, any poet, any composer was leading a creative life. Theorists, artists, scientists, inventors, writers could be creative. Nobody else could be. . . . For instance, one woman, uneducated, poor, a full-time housewife and mother, did none of these conventionally creative things and yet was a marvellous cook, mother, wife and homemaker. She was in all of her ideas original, novel, ingenious, unexpected, inventive. I just had to call her creative. I learned from her and others like her that a first-rate soup is more creative than a second-rate painting. (Maslow, 1968, p. 135)

THE PERSONAL CHARACTERISTICS OF THE CREATIVE PERSON

Much research has been undertaken over the years seeking to find a correlation between data relating to creative performance and personal attributes. In almost all cases the definition of the more-or-less creative person was reached either through peer or other form of assessment of a general nature. A typical early effort was reported by Jones (1964). In this study, 25 managers rated the creative performance of a representative sample of 88 industrial scientists and technologists within a large company. According to his test results, the typically more creative scientist or engineer was found to be

> highly capable of reasoning well with words and other symbols, fluent in the output of ideas, original in the quality of ideas, emotionally stable, determined to master his working environment, adventurous in outlook, high in degree of scientific curiosity and low in indication of general anxiety. (Jones, 1964, p. 134)

Almost all studies of the characteristics of the features of a creative person have included both intellectual and attitudinal, value and behavioural measures, neither one nor the other being sufficient to explain enough of the variability.

Indicators of creative persons include the following:

1. Their perception of the world is more open-ended and active. Barron (1963) found a preference for the complex and the asymmetrical in the more creative population, an openness to experiences even where this might result in confusion. Contrast the normal reaction to the first hearing of Blake's poem 'Tiger, Tiger', with that of Bertrand Russell, who was reported to have passed out as a result of the experience. Creative thinkers often report avoiding logic or words to the last, preferring inconclusive images. Also they do not place as many boundaries on their range of interests.
2. Their thinking is more often divergent. The concept of divergent thinking, of expanding, generating and building on ideas as against convergent, which is to close down on the one right answer, is fundamental to all beliefs about creativity.
3. Their self-images show high independence, individualism and determination.

In a well-known study, Vernon (1973) asked professors to draw up a list of the 40 most creative architects in the United States. These highly outstanding professionals saw themselves especially as being creative. The control group used words such as responsible, sincere, reliable and tolerant.

4. Their work behaviour is characterized by industry and devotion to their discipline. Anecdotal and research evidence combine to show that most innovations result from the individual pursuit of an area of enquiry against conventional understanding and with an absolute determination to get to the end.

Clearly there is a need for creative people to be intelligent but correlation studies have shown every number from 0.0 to 0.7 in seeking to show relationships between measures of creativity and of 'intelligence'. This range of correlations is probably related to the sample of those studied. If they are all of well above average intelligence, then the correlation between intelligence and creativity is going to be lower than if intelligence is more widely introduced. Finally, to be creative, the individual needs to have a wide range of available knowledge from which to draw. In most occupations, the knowledge takes considerable time to acquire, in some it is less important. For example, for medicinal chemists in the pharmaceutical business to reach a point where they are likely to make any significant discovery, they would need to have spent seven years in post-school education, and probably three years detailed study within the specific area of investigation that their employing company has placed them. On the other hand, in an occupation which is based on the languages of, say, English or mathematics, inventiveness can come very much earlier, because there is relatively little contextual and informational constraint, and learning would have started so much earlier in life.

THE IDENTIFICATION OF CREATIVE TALENT

The pervasive use of the interview in selection is more likely to be misleading in the selection for creativity than it is in many other areas. Intelligence testing is of value only in so far as those people who are below average in intelligence for their occupation are not likely to contribute creatively. Ability tests are very often used, but most frequently they seek to find characteristics of divergency and of fluency.

The Guilford Tests are the originals in this area and include questions of:

1. Unusual uses, where candidates are asked to record in five minutes as many unusual ways they can of using common objects, e.g. a pencil.
2. Consequences, where probable outcomes of hypothetical major changes or events are requested, e.g. 'all the lead in the world turns to gold, what outcomes can you suggest?'
3. Stories, explanations, completions, or titles where candidates are asked to make up sentences or stories in response to ambiguous presentations, e.g. there are more fatal accidents on Thursday than on any other day of the week. How many ways can this be explained?

Other tests of this general style, but of a less verbal nature are:

4. Tangrams, where a number of irregular shapes have to be rearranged to make representations of known objects.
5. Abstract concrete tests—using blocks and asking for them to be rearranged in ways subject to different criteria for the group.

None of these on its own has been shown to have great predictive validity, although each is quite high on face validity.

Problems exist in scoring. For example, which is the more important, originality or fluency? What is the reference group? There are still methodological concerns. For example, is the time-pressure really necessary to the measurement as it is seen to be with IQ tests? How do you measure the quality levels of creative outcomes?

The evaluation of personal characteristics can be undertaken using any of the popular general instruments, for example the 16PF. Cattell got numbers of people who were judged to be creative to complete his inventory and compared their scores. He found they differed on 10 of the 16 scales. Emotional stability, venturesomeness and experimenting were seen to discriminate. Belbin (1981) used the 16PF results to predict creativity in experiment teams with some success. Studies of criterion groups of creative persons found high scores in five scales of the California Personality Inventory (CPI) which characterized both creative writers and architects. These were flexibility, achievement through independence, self-acceptance, sociability and capacity for status. The writers were high on psychological mindedness (interest in the internal workings of others) where the architects were higher on dominance (social initiative). There are also some specialized instruments. The Q-sorts, used to separate the creative from the non-creative architects, showed the creative to go for the words enthusiastic, industrious and independent about themselves, more often than virtuous, sympathetic or concerned for others.

Biographical reports are probably more useful in assessing creativity than in respect of most other aspects of occupational attributes. Most creative people are said to show evidence of creativity from an early age. The relevance of the early creativity to that required within the occupation needs to be taken into account, but in general people who are creative now can be expected to have written more inventive essays, explored more of their potential talents, and have had higher ratings for creativity in school.

Work samples are more often the most important aspect of selection for creative occupations. Portfolios, research papers, copy, product licences and inventions are all asked for as evidence of innovation. The subjectivity of the evaluator is an intrinsic weakness in this process, but can be overcome to some extent by peer checks and by expert ratings. Situational exercises are often possible in the more verbal, graphic or musical ends of the occupational scales, but with effort could be derived for the scientific. The instant generation of work samples in this way can further illustrate the response to pressure, and go some way to eliminating the possibility of the candidates' creativity coming from their past situation and not from their intrinsic ability.

The tentative conclusion as to the validity of these tests is that there is a moderate degree of predictability reached by each of the means of assessing creative potential as measured by subsequent creative products. The best route would seem to be to go for 'creative' portfolio (Treffinger, 1980) which includes assessments of creative thinking, dispositional and biographical characteristics and representative creative products. Only through such breadth of sampling would the relatively weak validity of each of these methods separately be overcome.

For all these evaluative procedures, the doubt will continue as to whether there is a true dimension of creativity, or that there are occupations which are intrinsically more or less creative. The fact that one of the landmark enquiries into American architects shows up significant self-report differences between the creative and the others, seems in itself to deny that architecture is a totally creative occupation. If it is, how come it has non-creative incumbents?

The research practitioner is not encouraged to look for creativity where staffing of research in pharmaceutical companies is discussed. For example G. Vita of the R&D organization of the Bristol-Meyers company R&D operation in New York said:

> When hiring, it is important to consider: (a) the scientific knowledge required; (b) analytical qualities, judgement, and degree of open-mindedness; (c) self-reliance and self-assertion; (d) sensitivity to others; and (e) emotional stability.

A colleague at the same conference, J.B. Fitzgerald, who was from the R&D of ICI Pharmaceuticals, suggested that the factors that contribute to scientific environments are:

> Departmental structure, scientific autonomy, rewards and recognition, risk and ability of the organization to tolerate conflict, warmth and support, scientific standards, a clear identity and feeling of belonging, and good information and communications.

In both cases, no mention is made of creative potential.

In later discussion (p. 224), Dr Vita added

> . . . that you need a certain number of people who have a little bit of genius. When you have too many, then your organization is in trouble again. Your creativity, your inventiveness is in trouble.

The senior professional in this research environment cannot but be excused from having some doubts as to whether assessments of creativity are either competent or welcome.

CONCLUSION

Selection for creative occupations is at best a hazardous process and at worst a futile one. The major issues that need to be confronted are threefold.

1. *When is an occupation not creative?* A sample of activity could show as much pre-programmed, orthodox and confirmed activity in a primary research scientist's

job as it could show up complex problem solving requiring frequent intuitive and lateral thinking in the position of a local government administrator.

2. *Is a creative person always creative*? The factors that encourage people to make innovations could be as often in their environment as in themselves or it could be an accident of circumstances. A casual read through James H. Austin's (1977) book, especially his 'cast of characters'—the people who influenced his successful innovation in brain research, who number over 75—is enough to realize how much the individual needs highly active random stimulus from others to show his or her creative output. Does the strongly individualistic attribute of perceived creativity simply mean that creativity has to break through social resistance to show itself? Could it yet be something everyone has, awaiting the right environment to come to the surface?

3. *Is creative thinking really different*? It could be a matter of perception.

The most powerful, but least used word in expressing a core aspect of creativity is 'imagination'. To William Wordsworth imagination is 'reason in her most exalted mood'. A great poet felt that creativity was an extension of rationality.

A great rationalist, Dr Johnson, on the other hand, had this to say: 'Imagination, a licentious and vagrant facility, insusceptible of limitations and impatient of restraint, has always endeavoured to baffle the logician, to perplex the confines of distinction, and burst the enclosures of regularity.'

REFERENCES AND FURTHER READING

Amabile, T.M. (1984). *The Social Psychology of Creativity*. Springer-Verlag, New York.

Austin, J.H. (1977). *Chase, Chance and Creativity*. Columbia, New York.

Barron, F. (1963). The disposition toward originality, in C.W. Taylor and F. Barron (eds). *Scientific Creativity its Recognition and Development*. Wiley, New York.

Barron, F. (1969). *Creative Person and Creative Process*. Holt, Rinehart & Winston, New York.

Barron, F., and Harington, D.M. (1981). Creativity, intelligence and personality, *Annual Review of Psychology*, **32**, 439-76.

Belbin, R.M. (1981). *Management Teams*. Heinemann, London.

Chastor, A.H. (1961). Creativity in self-actualizing people, in A.H. Maslow (ed.) *Toward a Psychology of Being*. Macmillan, New York.

Comanor, W.S. (1966). The drug industry and medical research. The economics of the Kefauver Committee investigation, *Journal of Business*.

Eiduson, B.T. (1962). *Scientists, Their Psychological World*. Basic Books, New York.

Gross, F. (ed.) (1983). *Decision Making in Drug Research*. Raven Press, New York.

Guilford, J.P. (1950). Creativity, *American Psychologist*, **5**, 444–54.

Guilford, J.P. (1967). *The Nature of Human Intelligence*. McGraw-Hill, New York.

MacKinnon, D.W. (1962). The nature and nurture of creative talent, *American Psychologist*, **17**, 484–95.

Maslow, A.H. (1968) (ed.). In *Toward a Psychology of Being*. Van Nostrand, Reinhold, New York.

Ogilvy, D. (1963/87). *Confessions of an Advertising Man*. Pan Books, London.

Treffinger, D.J. (1980). The progress and peril of identifying creative talent among gifted and talented students, *Journal of Creative Behaviour*, **14**.

Vernon, P.E. (ed.) (1973). *Creativity*. Penguin, Harmondsworth, London.

Chapter 4.8

Computer/Systems Personnel

GEORGE PENNEY

National Computing Centre, Oxford Road, Manchester M1 1BD

INTRODUCTION

More and more of the jobs performed in any developed country are computer related. At one extreme of the technology is the word processor (WP) or VDU operator; at another the telecommunications engineer. Neither of these extremes would come within the normal understanding of computing jobs, though they do fall within the broader and now generally used term *Information Technology* (IT). This chapter confines itself to jobs generally thought of as computing (even though many of these would have less direct interaction with the computer than, say, the VDU operator, and would demand less technical understanding of computers than that demanded of the telecommunications engineer).

Figure 1 shows the range of jobs generally included in the statistics of IT—for instance, the UK Department of Trade and Industry reports (1984, 1985)—with the exception of the vast and essentially unrelated electronics industry which looms large in these reports. In the absence of any comprehensive information, the relative sizes of the segments represent the author's best estimates. Note that most of the jobs relate to *software,* with only the extreme minority concerned with *hardware;* that most software jobs are in *data processing;* that most of these are with *computer users* and in the *commercial/administrative* (as opposed to the scientific/ engineering) area. This majority occupational field is known by the term DP. The meaning of all these terms should become clear as the jobs are described, but for a fuller explanation see Lynch (1987).

Computing (IT) is not a homogeneous set of jobs, there being quite different career paths, and virtually no interchange, between DP and the rest. These minority (non-DP) occupations are grouped here as hi-tech, industrial control and

Handbook of Assessment in Organizations   Edited by P. Herriot

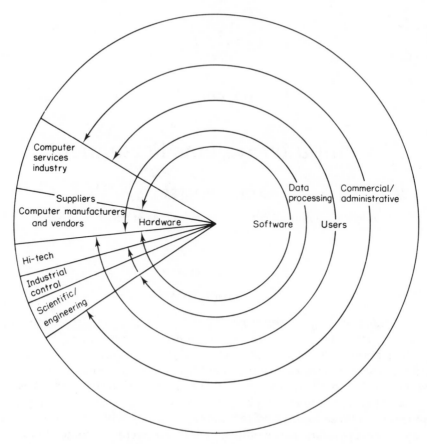

Figure 1   Divisions within computing employment (author's estimates).

scientific/engineering. Again, each of these demands different skills, and so there is little interchange of personnel between them.

NON-DP OCCUPATIONS

Hi-tech

Though small in numbers, these are the most difficult jobs to fill, since they require knowledge, in some depth, of hardware, software and electronics. Until recently, most associated degree courses were in either computer science or electronic engineering, with each side having little or no grasp of the field of knowledge of the other. A first degree course, now available, giving proper coverage to the whole area, takes four years, which means that short-term shortages can be catered for only by re-training. A possible way of alleviating the current shortages would seem to be for the hi-tech companies actively to recruit degree holders from the one area and fund them on specialist post-graduate courses in the other.

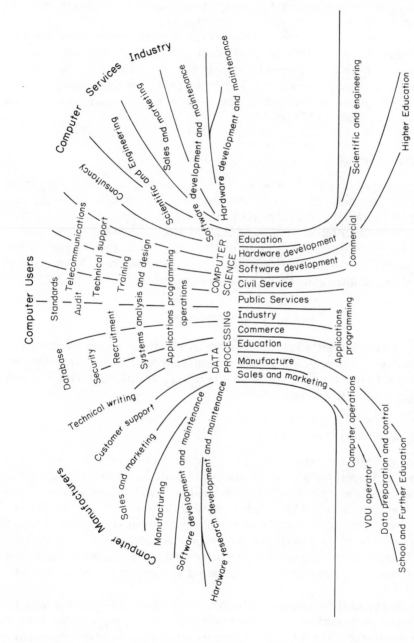

Figure 2   Ways up the computing tree (from Penney, 1979)

Industrial control

In industrial applications of computers, the computer may be controlling any-thing from a single machine tool to a complete manufacturing process. Some of the data produced are fed back into the process as a regulating mechanism; other data may be output for managerial or supervisory control, while a third category may be fed directly into the DP system. While all industrial applications have to be programmed, full-time programmers in this field would be rare, most of the programs being written as a part-time activity by people directly concerned with the process—engineers or technicians. The programming languages used would normally be Assembler or FORTRAN.

Scientific/engineering

While there are full-time specialist scientific programmers, working mainly in the computer services industry (p. 610), the majority of scientific/engineering pro-gramming is incidental to the main job activity—from computer-aided engineer-ing design to weather forecasting—and is performed as required by the (mainly graduate) scientists or engineers concerned. FORTRAN is the established lan-guage, though Pascal and others are making some impression. The career path tends to be tied to main activity, rather than to computing.

MAIN DP OCCUPATIONS

The only clear division within the mainstream DP jobs is into computer operations and systems development. All others are minority occupations, mainly with hardware or software suppliers (pp. 609 and 610). Figure 2 illustrates the degree of interchange within DP occupations.

Computer operations

Operations is a fairly straightforward area, when confined to medium to large computers. However, outside what would normally be regarded as computer operations come the operators of small business machines (micros). At one extreme, they may have the knowledge and skills to introduce and modify new software, and, at the other, may be no more than keyboard operators. A typical entry age would be 16–18, possibly direct from school or from further education—National Certificate in Computer Studies or, more usually, the double-sandwich course of that level, described by Penney and Lazzerini (1979), the NCC Threshold Scheme.

They would be likely to interact with several colleagues, and possibly with the general public, and employers therefore have a preference for someone with an outgoing personality. The job has not existed long enough for any clear career path to have emerged, but the most likely next step is into a broader business function rather than further computing specialization. The number of such opportunities is constantly increasing, and is likely to continue to do so.

Operators in mini/mainframe environments would tend to come from the same variety of sources, but with quite different activities and expectations.

Employers provide little, if any, off-the-job training for operators. New operators are expected to begin in such jobs as loading printer stationery and gradually progress to the more responsible and demanding job of console operator.

Whereas the small business machine operator may well be the only person in the firm with any computer knowledge, a computer operator in a larger installation is usually a member of a shift, under the control of a shift leader, or senior operator. This is the normal next step, after trainee/junior operator and then operator. Shift leader by the age of 20 is quite common.

During batch processing (as distinct from on-line) the operators are changing program and data disks and continuous stationery, as well as keeping an eye on the console messages, and solving any problems as they appear. The job can be a combination of prolonged inactivity with bursts of concentrated activity. The shift leader carries considerable responsibility, since any delay can cause business disruption.

In an on-line environment, where all the necessary disks are in place the whole time, the cost of disruption may be even greater. The operator must have the concentration, presence of mind and knowledge to avoid the computer being 'down' for the vital minutes or seconds which could put the company's operations, public image, physical safety or, in extreme cases, its continued existence, at risk.

Some computer rooms work, to all appearances, totally without operators. So long as there are enough disk drives to allow any user access to any file or program which might be required, the operator can be in a different room or different building, simply keeping an eye on a screen for something to go wrong and giving any necessary instructions through a keyboard. This could become the pattern for the day shift, or even round the clock, where the computer is permanently accessible on-line, as in the leisure/travel industry. The gradual change to operator-less working has not so far involved any overall reduction in the number of operators employed; it has just meant a lower rate of increase. There is a distinct tendency to employ female operators on small business computers and, for different reasons—principally shift work—males on large machines.

Weatherley *et al.* (1979), in a study carried out on 1000 DP staff, found that 15 per cent of the programmers had previously been operators. Figure 4 shows typical and possible career paths, from operating and from programming up to possible board level.

System development

A first level breakdown of system development tasks is into: (*a*) specifying requirements; (*b*) designing; and (*c*) installing and maintaining a system to meet those requirements.

Type (*a*) involves the collection and analysis of facts about the system—either existing or new. Type (*b*) consists of successive breakdowns into subsystems down to the level of statements which the available machine software is capable of accepting. Type (*c*) is a process of fitting the computing system and the external system together, making them work and continue working.

The confusion of job titles is briefly discussed in Chapter 1.6. Type (*a*) tasks may be performed under the title business analyst, information analyst, systems analyst, analyst designer, programmer/analyst or analyst programmer. Either of the last two, or a programmer, or a software engineer, may perform Type (*b*). People holding any of these job titles may participate in Type (*c*). Finally, the whole cycle may be carried out by an information engineer. A distinction must be made between systems programming (or software programming) and applications programming. A systems program is the layer of software resident on the hardware, converting it from a set of electrical, electronic and mechanical components into a functioning machine, and making it amenable to the needs of the applications programmer.

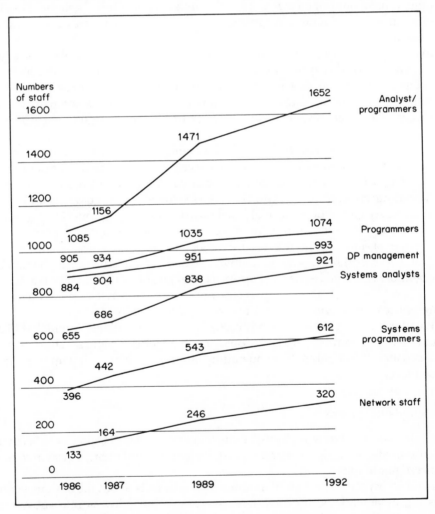

Figure 3 Numbers of IT personnel employed in 1986 and 1987 and predictions for 1989 and 1992 (540 respondents to 1987 NCC salary survey) (NCC, 1987b)

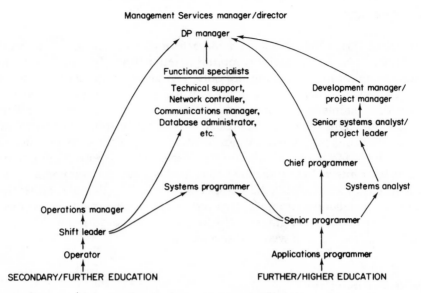

Figure 4   Career paths in medium to large DP installations

Systems programmers are needed, not simply to develop the software, but also to implement, maintain and keep abreast of successive versions, to advise and support the applications programmers.

The majority of entrants to DP start as trainee applications programmers, often with only a minimum of formal training.

CLASSES OF EMPLOYER

As indicated in Figure 1, the majority class of employer is the computer user, with hardware and software suppliers employing an extreme minority. The balance is tending to change as more use is made of packaged software.

Computer users

Any medium to large organization, as well as many small ones, in both private and public sectors (and including the hardware and software suppliers), may come within this category. All but the smallest, using exclusively packaged software, can be expected to have both operations and development functions. As noted on p. 607, development includes a wide variety of job titles. While the types of task divide roughly into analysis, design and programming, there is an increasing tendency, as shown in Figure 3, to adopt the single title of analyst programmer. Figure 4 shows typical career paths, including the separate functions of programming and analysis (which continue to exist, in many DP departments, in spite of the prevailing use of a single job title).

Hardware suppliers

Some hardware vendors do no manufacturing, and may have no particular recruitment policy. The major computer manufacturers take part in the under-graduate 'milk round', looking not only for trainee programmers, but also for trainees in every other function of their business, their future managers in R&D, production, maintenance, sales, marketing, personnel and accounting. For most of these functions, they are interested in graduates from any discipline; the exceptions being physics/electronics for R&D, engineering for production and maintenance, and mainly maths/computer science for systems programming. As well as their internal DP staff, they have analysts and programmers, in contact with the customers, helping the salesperson to conclude the sale and set the new computer installation running. This job is known alternatively as 'customer support' or 'systems engineer'. The training offered varies widely between employers, from several weeks to several years.

The service industry

The computer services industry, starting out from computer bureaux and soft-ware houses, now takes in a wide variety of services, including a complete 'turnkey' operation, general management consultancy service, and specialized hardware/software maintenance. The larger service companies, like the computer manufacturers and some users, have an annual intake of graduates from almost any discipline.

As opposed to the hardware suppliers, they tend not to employ specialist sales personnel. Every consultant, every systems programmer and every hardware maintenance engineer represents the outward face of the company and is expected to be spotting future business opportunities and opening doors. In this, there may be a great contrast, in terms of required personality, between the 'back-room' systems programmer, employed by the computer manufacturer, develop-ing, say, a new operating system, and the outward-looking software house systems programmer—another warning to the job seeker not to rely on job titles.

FUTURE EMPLOYMENT TRENDS

As shown by Figure 3, the number of jobs in all aspects of system development is expected to continue growing, in existing installations alone, for many years ahead. Of computer operations and routine data input, not shown in this diagram, the former is predicted by NCC (1988) as remaining fairly constant, while the latter, as a specialized computing job, is rapidly disappearing. There are still instances of this as a section of the computing function, but most data input has moved out into the user departments, and become combined with more general clerical functions.

The Salary Survey of NCC (1988, p. 66) reports as follows:

Employment and Growth

Respondents were asked to indicate the numbers of IT staff employed last year and this year, and the numbers they expect (or hope) to employ in 1989 and 1991.

The strongest growth in demand, albeit from a small base, is for staff with networking and communications skills. Within the sample, the numbers of network staff have grown by 23% over the last year, and respondents expect their demand for network staff almost to double over the next five years. This is clearly in response to the increasing use of on-line DP systems, office automation implementation to provide such facilities as electronic mail and a number of other communications-based IT applications such as financial dealing systems.

Systems development staff are divided into three broad categories: systems analysts, analyst/programmers and programmers. All categories are experiencing growth, but the growth is concentrated in the combined analyst/programmer role (43% over the next five years) and the systems analyst (34% over the same period). By contrast the five-year growth rate for applications programmers was only 15%. This trend has been observed in successive NCC Salary Surveys over the last three years.

There are a number of likely factors which are contributing to this trend. The growing use of applications generators and 4th generation languages is one factor that is likely to diminish the load of pure programming or coding in a department. Another factor is the increasing number of personal and departmental systems which are developed. These are often small systems, where the traditional division of labour between programmer and analyst is not worth while. The provision of support for 'end-user computing' is another area where the combined skills of an analyst and a programmer are the most useful.

Systems programming and technical support skills are still an area of rapid growth. As a specialist job, the systems programmer is found mainly in the large organisations and installations. However, as smaller departments grow and mature there is often a need for specialist systems programmers, hence the growing demand for their skills.

The operations job group is now virtually static in terms of employment growth, with a slight downturn in the numbers of operators employed forecast for the period 1989–1992. The numbers of data preparation and data entry staff employed within the IT department continue to fall, with the spread of on-line systems.

Predicted growth rates are closely related to the size of the installation, with highest rates of growth predicted in the smaller installations.

Such skill areas as networking and communications, referred to in that extract, are well up the career path, possibly from senior programmer or senior operator, or possibly, and exceptionally, from a specialist post-graduate course. These, and other specializations, offer many mid-career opportunities outside the conventional pyramid, for those with specialized interests and aptitudes—though when the present job holders were recruited into DP, such jobs were non-existent.

TRAINING AND QUALIFICATIONS

The majority of employers of DP staff take little, if any, notice of computing qualifications. This is unfortunate, and stems to some extent, in the view of the author, from the totally non-DP orientation of the traditional university computer science degree. Nowadays, most polytechnics, and a few universities, include a highly practical DP content in their computing degree courses, as those employers who have been converted, and who use them regularly, are well aware. In a review of the success of their TOPS training programme, the Manpower

Services Commission (MSC) (1983) found that the only computing qualification receiving any substantial recognition was the NCC Systems Analysis Certificate [Section 7.8(iii)]. A majority of candidates for this NCC qualification are graduates, though possession of a degree is not an absolute entry requirement.

Most employers who take part in the annual 'milk round' are looking for people with a flexible approach and good communication ability, rather than any particular degree subject, with, as reported by Spurgeon, Patrick and Michael (1984) 'a slight bias against computer science graduates' (p. 34). The author has met employers, some of whom prefer business studies or accountancy, some maths, some classics, etc. University computer science graduates tend to find jobs with the computer manufacturers, or the software houses, or in the hi-tech industry, rather than with computer users.

While most DP employers send employees on courses from time to time on different aspects of the technology, this method of keeping up to date cannot be relied on, as diverse developments occur so rapidly. Individuals have to be prepared to give a significant amount of their own time to reading the journals and new books, in order to be prepared for the next promotion or move. A willingness to work unsocial hours in an emergency is necessary; even the data processing manager is not immune from frantic telephone calls at midnight!

REQUIRED ATTRIBUTES

In selecting computer operators, employers look for evidence of reliability, attention to detail, an orientation towards things mechanical and common sense. For all jobs in development, they look for a combination of logic (with words and diagrams as well as numbers), patience, persistence and, again, attention to detail. For systems programming, maths has always been a strong recommendation; if anything, the demands made on modern systems software reinforce this need. However, there is a myth that you must be strong in maths to do any kind of work with computers. Programming in machine code, in which every instruction consists only of a series of numbers, no doubt is less mind-boggling to a mathematician than to a non-mathematician, but present-day programming commands, consisting mainly of English words, make no such demand. A fall-back position is 'programming is logical: maths is logical'—implying the non-existence of verbal or diagrammatic logic, which is ludicrous. The myth persists, however, with successive waves of teachers and careers advisers, and has undoubtedly deterred many suitable candidates from considering DP as a career.

The common mathematical symbols, of course, occur routinely in applications programs—but this hardly merits a course in higher mathematics. Graphical presentation is useful in any business context, and both the programmer and the analyst find a good understanding of statistical concepts more useful than a traditional maths education. A study by Penney and Lazzerini (1979) on 500 computing trainees showed that five groups with differing degrees of academic qualification in English language differed significantly in continuous assessment $F_{(df4)} = 4.11$, $p < 0.001$. Academic achievement in mathematics showed no significant prediction (p. 28). However, in a study by Weatherley *et al.* (1979) of

1000 DP staff, all the management groups liked maths 'and some groups opted for sub-branches of the subject'—though this could reflect simply the results of earlier selection policies. On other school subjects, 'DP managers were shown to like English composition, modern languages and literature, whereas the other three groups of managers (systems, programming and operations) opted only for mathematical subjects' (p. 19) (a reason, perhaps, why they had reached only the position below DP manager?).

> On personal characteristics, DP managers differ from [the] other managers, in that they show strong belief in themselves, in their ability to have novel ideas, preference for working alone rather than in committees, being able to write good reports, being able to smooth out disagreements and putting drive into the organisation. Other groups [of managers] only had one positive point: systems analysts felt they could write good reports, programming managers thought themselves to be patient in teaching, and operations managers considered themselves able to smooth out disagreements (p. 20).

Spurgeon, Patrick and Michael (1984) found interview result ranked first by employers in selecting trainees (p. 57). Since most development staff start out as trainee programmers, there is a problem. Weatherley *et al.* (1979), using the Strong–Campbell Vocational Interest Questionnaire, found programming managers, in common with applications programmers (and in contrast with systems analysts and data processing managers) preferring to avoid interviewing for selection—as well as other people-related activities.

> All those in programming jobs, and analyst programmers, agreed on dislikes for jobs relating to people, and particularly children. . . . Dislikes for religious, fashion and military activities were shown, and arty, religious and aggressive people were disliked. . . . Systems programmers were similar . . . but showed an almost total indifference to many types of people, and in addition, unconventional people were liked, whilst emotional, ill and old people were not liked. In general, there are real differences between systems programmers and applications programmers (pp. 20 and 21).

The systems programmers were unique in that not one expressed dislike of the job; in every other job there were some expressing dislike. (The sample was drawn entirely from computer users, i.e. not from computer manufacturers or software houses.)

The nature of the systems analyst's job demands skill in the use of language and the ability to reason critically with words, recognizing assumptions, false inferences, invalid conclusions etc. A programming language, though it uses, for most commands, words taken from normal language, requires only a very limited vocabulary: the programmer may be highly educated, with a large vocabulary, but not much interest in using it in live human relationships, while the analyst will make use of whatever vocabulary comes to hand as an aid to resolving a business or human problem.

Sex-related differences

Weatherley *et al.* (1979) found a number of differences between male and female DP staff. Females were more enterprising: 'High scores [on the factor "Enterprising"] for female systems managers contrast with average for male systems managers. Average scores for female programming managers, female analyst-programmers, female programmers and female systems programmers, contrast with modestly low enterprising score for their male counterparts' (p. 22).

Female systems, programming and operations managers were found to be more conventional than the remainder of the sample. 'It would appear that the higher score on the "conventional" scale for female managers is not a function of their gender, but more because their role requires them to act in conventional ways' (p. 23). A study by Penney (1985) showed substantial differences in job satisfiers between the sexes. The respondents, all in DP development, were asked to choose between: (*a*) very important; (*b*) fairly important; and (*c*) not at all important, to 30 sources of job satisfaction. A ranking was obtained by deducting the total of (*c*) responses on a given item from the (*a*) responses for that item. The most striking sex-related differences were as shown in Table 1.

Table 1   Rank order of job satisfiers for male and female DP staff*

	Male	Female
Job security	3	11
Promotion prospects	11	4
Money	4	7
Training policy	4	2
Starting a new project	15	4
Personal freedom	8	15
Helping people	10	18
Respect in professional field	14	6

* Lowest number = highest rank

Thus, for instance, Male rank 3 for 'Job security' shows that the result of (*a*)−(*c*) for this item was slightly greater than for 'Money' or 'Training policy' and much greater than for 'Starting a new project'.

SELECTION PROCEDURES

Brotherton *et al.* (1981) found employers making use of several stages of interviewing. 'The preliminary selection of graduate entrants . . . is often carried out within Universities, as part of the annual "Milk Round". . . . Most organisations have an idea of what constitutes an "acceptable" or "suitable" employee and this "image" is often used as a guide in pre-selection . . . it is usually framed in terms of educational level, training or experience (age), or in terms of personality.' 'Over the years a tendency to administer psychometric tests during this stage appears to have developed . . .' (p. 12). 'The final employment decision is often made by a selection board . . .' (p. 13).

On the use of tests, Spurgeon, Patrick and Michael (1984) report, 'Given that aptitude test result was ranked by employers as the second most important factor in the selection of trainee programmers (the first being interview result), it is surprising that currently only just over half (52%) of the organizations replying to the survey actually used aptitude tests . . .' (p. 39). As distinct from the staged approach of graduate selection, it is the author's impression that the final selection interview tends to be with the immediate manager and that manager's boss, with little or no involvement by specialist personnel staff. A problem is that few line managers in DP receive any training in interviewing, or in any other selection technique. Since the interview is a two-way transaction, an untrained interviewer may not only miss important clues but also unwittingly influence the applicant against the job or the organization.

PREDICTORS AND THEIR VALIDITY

Qualifications

Spurgeon *et al.* (1984) report that 'The majority of employers currently require at least "A" level passes when recruiting computer personnel at trainee level. However, only 5% of employers specified that they require a degree as a minimum qualification for trainee programmers and analyst programmers, and just 6% do so for trainee systems analysts.'

Little attempt is made by employers to validate their selection procedures. Sneath, Thakur and Medjuck (1976) found that only 5 per cent of respondents had conducted validation exercises of a statistical nature. Brotherton *et al.* (1981) found that 'organizations' (personnel) records were rarely complete' (in spite of the fact that all the organizations taking part were household names).

An exception is the Threshold Scheme, reported by Penney and Lazzerini (1979). A first job in programming was obtained by 23.2 per cent of trainees. In contrast to the requirement (above) by employers for 'at least "A" level passes', few of these trainees had even one 'A' level, and five had no 'O' levels. The mode was three 'O' levels, with a mean of 4.65, SD 2.63 (p. 40).

> Only seven of the programmer sample had the two ('A' level or Scottish Higher) passes which might have enabled them to enter programming without the benefit of Threshold, while a further seven had passed in one subject, and eighteen had failed in one or more subjects. In Computer Studies, there was one pass at 'A' grade, one at 'D' grade and one fail. There was one pass in Statistics, but none in Maths, while thirteen had failed, or been awarded a pass at 'O' level, in Maths or Maths/Statistics. In Physics, there were six passes and five fails. In English Language there were six passes and two fails.

There is no reason to believe that such results would be replicated in a study of the general DP population; selection for the Threshold Scheme is by a battery of psychometric tests and a structured interview format.

In a later study, Penney (1984) found that within two years of the end of the course, 7 per cent of those who had obtained a first job as computer operator had already migrated upwards to programming.

Tests v. other predictors

Penney and Lazzerini (1979) report as follows on the predictive value of the tests used in selection for the Threshold Scheme: For the trainee sample as a whole, AH2 (a test of general reasoning ability validated with a school-leaver population) was the test which gave the best prediction of course results ($r = 0.29$, p<0.001). For continuous assessment, however, while AH2 provided the best predictor for the operators, the test which best predicted programmer score was the letters section of Clerical Speed and Accuracy ($r = 0.31$, p<0.001). The test which best differentiated those who obtained programmer jobs from the remainder of the sample was the Standard Progressive Matrices (F (df3) = 16.0, p<0.001).

Equations were produced to predict each of the course assessments and the overall result (without regard to subsequent job direction), using educational attainment and all the test scores as predictors.

The simple correlations show that educational attainment is more predictive of course assessment, on average, than any of the tests. This is confirmed in the multiple regression equations; educational attainment proves to be about four times as effective a predictor as any single one of the tests. This finding could be said to follow from the fact that the tests were used as selectors, and hence subject to restriction of range, whereas educational attainment was not.

Further, the equations confirmed the previous finding that the different tests are fairly saturated with a 'g' component, and that it is this that is proving to be the effective predictor of course results. As soon as any one test had been included in the regression equation, no other test could significantly improve its predictive power. No test was found to be consistently a better predictor than any other tests. This is not to say that the tests do not measure anything other than general intelligence ('g'), only that their 'non-g' components were not effective in predicting course results.

In this study, no correction was made for restriction of range. Hunter and Hirsh (1987) recommend that such a correction should be made. Across a range of studies of different occupations, they show tests of cognitive ability predicting training success, after this correction, at the level $r = 0.63$; compared with college grades, $r = 0.33$; biodata, $r = 0.33$; education, $r = 0.27$; interview, $r = 0.11$; interest, $r = 0.20$; and age, $r = 0.02$ (p. 326). Concurrent validation studies by Crawley and Morris (1970) and Morris and Martin (1972) on systems analysts and programmers showed significant relationships between test scores and supervisor rankings on a number of factors, as shown in Tables 2 and 3.

Many tests which go under the title 'Programming Aptitude Test' lack any published validation. Crawley and Morris (1970) found that 'Some programmer aptitude tests are basically intelligence tests, and as such may have some relevance to the selection of systems analysts. [Others] have been devised without regard to accepted procedures for constructing psychological tests. Some

Table 2 Level of significance of relationships between programmer rankings and test scores

Test	Overall	Probability level					
		Program design	Coding	Test data preparation	Testing	Documentation	Maintenance
Letter series errors	0.05	0.05	0.03	0.007	0.04	0.0002	
Critical thinking	0.06	0.06	0.09	0.02	0.04	0.08	0.08
Sentence checking	0.08	0.1	0.09		0.07	0.1	
Verbal reasoning errors	0.05	0.02	0.004		0.004		
Numerical calculation	0.005	0.07	0.05	0.04		0.07	0.03
Spatial			0.1			0.06	
Clerical right errors			0.09				

Table 3 Level of significance of relationships between systems analyst ratings and test scores

| Test | Overall | Probability level | | |
		Fact finding	Information assessment	Report writing
Verbal reasoning		0.04		0.04
Diagrammatic reasoning	0.05	0.04	0.07	0.08
error score	0.03		0.07	0.05
Critical thinking	0.06	0.06	0.08	0.02

Source: Crawley and Morris (1970).

lack evidence of being a reliable measure of anything at all . . .' (p. 6). Many of the tests examined then are still used by some employers today. The author advises candidates who fail one such test to try another employer, who may well be using a different (if no better validated) test. The validated tests tend to have a substantial representation of questions of the general reasoning (IQ or 'g') nature. Examples of such questions are available in abundance in Eysenck (1962, 1969).

Brotherton et al. (1981) found that 'Overall, the various interviews were not as predictive as tests studied . . .' (p. 54).

Some managers believe that an interest in chess, bridge or crosswords is an indicator of programming potential. Penney and Lazzerini (1979) found that trainees claiming one or other of these interests showed the same or lower tendency to go towards programming than towards operating, while those with some other interests did have such a tendency. (The decision on direction was made initially by trainee and tutor jointly, and finally by an employer.) 'Whilst we cannot claim this as any firm indication that those who perform music or spot aircraft are more likely to get jobs as programmers, the received opinion on chess, bridge and crosswords receives no support at all' (p. 42). Weatherley et al. (1979) found DP personnel showing no more interest in chess, bridge or crosswords than the general population of similar educational level (p. 20).

Brotherton et al. (1981) say, in summing up:

The Selection Research Project has provided evidence that some aspects of current selection procedures are effective, but that there is much scope for their improvement. Interviews were shown to be no better than tests, and the selection of non-graduates was not obviously superior to that of graduates. The findings also show that:

1. There are tremendous differences in the apparent effectiveness of selection procedures both within and between organisations. The information needed to identify the good and to eliminate or improve the bad is usually available within the organisation, but is usually not used and in some cases not even recorded. The most obvious way to improve selection is to ensure that adequate records are kept and that selection procedures are continuously reviewed.
2. Selection procedures and later job assessments could be improved by careful study and planning. This should involve conscious decisions about the nature of the people to be employed, and the criteria of successful employment to be used.
3. The criteria of successful employment currently available are less than satisfactory. They could be improved by systematic job analysis in the context of the different needs of particular organisations.

4. There is a redundancy in the ability tests and non-test measures currently used in selection, and many are too complicated. They could probably be reduced in complexity in each situation. At the same time there is a need to increase the variety of instruments available to selectors as a whole. The greatest need here is for new tests to be devised which reflect the cultural background of applicants and the task demands of the job for which selection is being operated.

The report concludes:

Neither ability tests nor non-tests (interviews, Board decisions) as used in these studies are good predictors of job success. Various measures show acceptable correlations with different criteria, but there is no clear pattern to these.

Ability tests can, however, predict training performance, while the [Cattell] 16PF [a personality inventory] has some success against measures of training performance and job performance.

The best examples of effective prediction by selection tests exist in organisations which have carefully planned systems to deal with a particular population for skills training.

Psychometric testing in Britain is still dominated by instruments of American origin, and this in itself renders many tests less useful than they may appear.

Possibly owing something to those comments, many tests have been designed in the United Kingdom, since that report, addressing different kinds of ability and different educational levels, and the author has found them known, and used, in many other English-speaking countries since the mid-1980s.

Chapter 3.2 refers to computer-administered tests. The ones used in all the studies referred to in this chapter are pencil and paper. The author is not aware of any DP employer in the United Kingdom using computer-administered tests.

FAIRNESS

It is difficult, if not impossible, to achieve absolute fairness in selection, since the final choice is invariably made by an individual, and there is no person so perfect as to be without prejudice. The greater the extent to which objective criteria are employed, as distinct from such subjective measures as the interview, the greater the probability of fairness. But for DP jobs, as opposed to, say, weightlifters, there are no completely objective measures. A test which has been shown to be reliable and valid, in respect of the candidate group, the culture and the required abilities, gives a statistical probability—though not an absolute prediction—of success.

The majority of 'programming aptitude tests' in use in the United Kingdom were obtained originally from a computer manufacturer and most were designed in the United States. For these, there is no evidence of the existence of validity data, even for the US candidate population. Some unfairness (and ineffectiveness) can therefore be presumed. As shown by Weatherley *et al.* (1979), all DP jobs include a number of different kinds of task, each one demanding a different mix of abilities; a test of a single ability, however well validated for that ability, is unfair to the possessors of other relevant and independent, but untested, abilities. Tests of a single ability tend to favour those with a maths background; if used in selection for DP jobs, perhaps with the exception of systems programming (p. 608), they are *ipso facto* unfair.

Brotherton *et al.* (1981) point out that there is redundancy in the spread of tests being used by some employers. However, high inter-correlation between tests does not mean that any given individual who scores highly for one ability will necessarily score highly for other abilities. A given candidate may be in the 90th percentile for diagrammatic reasoning but only the 50th for verbal reasoning, and so on. Simply adding the scores together, as is the practice with those 'programming aptitude tests' which have questions covering a range of ability factors, will disguise both the strength and the weakness, and the candidate may be either selected, or rejected, for the wrong reason.

It is important, where a tendency has been shown for one sex to score higher for a given ability, to include a test for which the reverse holds true, and not to apply a cut-off on any individual test. For instance, numerous studies have shown males scoring higher for spatial ability and females for clerical speed and accuracy (e.g. Penney and Lazzerini, 1979).

If there are candidates from a different cultural background from that for which the test was validated, either re-validation is required or some allowance must be made. Penney and Lazzerini (1979) report 'an allowance is made in test scores for those whose native language is not English. . . . However, . . . we find no significant difference between the course results of the non-English native speakers and those of the native English speakers . . .' (p. 25). A pass/fail result, as practised by many DP employers, is almost bound to be unfair. However, Hunter and Hirsh (1987) report, as regards race, that 'the consensus conclusion . . . is that cognitive aptitude tests are not biased against minority (i.e. black) applicants' (p. 333) although 'bias' is a technical term whereas fairness is an evaluative judgement.

If reliable and valid psychometric tests are used, covering the range of abilities required for the job (and preferably for some subsequent jobs), the results are assessed by a competent person, and are weighed together with the assessment of a competent interviewer who is knowledgeable on the job content, the selection will be as fair as fallible humanity is likely to achieve. Most DP selection falls well short of this.

NEED FOR FURTHER WORK

Most validation studies reported, in the United States as well as in the United Kingdom, have either been concurrent or have followed the sample only as far as course grades. All such studies suffer from the restriction of range effect, since employers, having paid for tests, are not prepared to employ people regardless of test results.

In one of the few predictive studies following the accepted candidates for some years into employment, Brotherton *et al.* (1981) found some employers where test results and interview results predicted at a comparable level, but the finding that 'organisations' records were rarely complete' limited the value of the results and indicates a serious gap. A predictive study must be of value to any employer taking in large numbers of DP staff but, with incomplete personnel records, any attempt at systematic improvement of selection procedure and predictors must be in vain. Employers seeking to improve on current selection practices are advised to pay particular attention to this point.

EMPLOYMENT PRACTICES AND PROBLEMS

In spite of the growth, and reported shortages in the region of 12 to 15 per cent for some years past, the NCC Salary Surveys (1984–88) show some 65 to 70 per cent of employers regularly reporting the total absence of trainees or junior programmers. This includes some substantial companies, who have the overt policy of buying in trained staff—which is discouraging for those who do have a policy of offering training to inexperienced or untrained applicants.

Little is known, or is likely to be known, about the practices of the smaller employers. There is no reason to suppose that they have any different practice with computer staff from that for any other job category. If they are taking people who have been previously tested, for instance, from the NCC Threshold Scheme (Penney and Lazzerini, 1979) there is no point in any more sophisticated approach; if they are recruiting straight from school, it would undoubtedly be in their interests to obtain the objective information which relevant tests can provide.

The large employers who do take on trainees recruit mainly graduates, in yearly batches. The other main source of trainees is courses funded by the Department of Employment, of which the one nationally available is the Threshold Scheme.

For all computing jobs other than in operations, the market is a national one, with a tendency for the plum jobs, and the shortages, to be in London. However, in all the major conurbations, it is possible to move between employers without moving house. The big problem is getting a first foothold anywhere outside London (or the Civil Service), with the catch that no employer in London will offer a first job to someone lacking a London address. With two years' experience in any aspect of DP, jobs in all parts of the country—or the world for that matter—are plentiful. The Government, or a philanthropic institution, could soon cure the shortage of DP staff in the London area, by offering accommodation, for a limited period, at an affordable price.

Employers look for assurance from paper (essentially non-computing) qualifications, directly relevant experience, or recommendation from a known trainer. In any part of the United Kingdom, outside London, there are many more applicants for trainee positions than there are vacancies. A candidate with no experience is therefore well advised, if suitably qualified, to enter either higher education (and so have the benefit of the 'milk round') or a Government-funded course with an organization which can show a good placement record, or obtain a London address. The most difficult barrier is age. In general, training providers under the long-running MSC TOPS Programme applied 30 as the top age for programming training and 40 for systems analysis. The present author's discussions with employers find them generally most unwilling to accept someone into programming after the age of 30; the age limits generally applied to systems analysis are 25 to 40. Employers who are considering inexperienced but trained systems analysts look for evidence of good business or administrative—preferably management—experience. The author has become aware, through personal contact, of a small number of people outside these age groups entering DP. Other firms experiencing difficulty in filling vacancies, or suffering from a high staff turnover, would be well advised to consider people from older age groups. Employers would also do well to note the low correlation between age and training success (Hunter and Hirsh, 1987). The use of properly researched and standardized tests can be particularly useful with such a population, whose previous experience is most unlikely to give any clue as to their suitability. It is vital that the tests be administered and evaluated by qualified testers. An employer recruiting frequently may find it economic to have members of the DP or personnel department trained as testers, while other employers are likely to benefit from using an external testing agency/consultancy. This is not to say that a test, or a battery of tests, should be the sole selection criterion; personality, interests, attitude, motivation, all are important, and need to be assessed either by appropriate psychometric instruments or by skilled interviewers. Hunter and Hirsh (1987) report one study showing that an interview by a board has higher validity ($r = 0.24$) than an interview by a single interviewer ($r = 0.13$), and another in which a structured interview shows a validity of 0.40, as compared with 0.13 for an unstructured interview (pp. 330–1). Since all DP departments use the interview as a selection instrument, and recognizing that interviewing is a two-way process, any manager with responsibility for recruitment—not just personnel staff—should undergo training in interviewing. In the end, this is a function which no manager can safely delegate, and which no untrained person should undertake.

However, the competition, currently, from younger applicants for jobs in this high-profile and well-paid field, is such that the chances for older candidates who have no access to the 'milk round' are at present, regrettably, very slim. It is reasonable to suppose that employers' attitudes on this will eventually be affected by the demographic changes now beginning to show, unless, by the time these changes begin to bite, computer-aided system design fulfils its promise of making applications programming a redundant skill. The future, as ever, is uncertain.

REFERENCES

Brotherton, C.J., Cox, T.R., Howarth, C.I., Lazzerini, A.J., and Watts, J.A. (1981). *Studies of Selection in British Industry—Final Report of the Selection Research Project*. NCC, Manchester.

Crawley, M., and Morris, J. (1970). *Personnel Selection: 1 Systems Analysts*. NCC, Manchester.

Dept of Industry (1984). *The Human Factor. The Supply Side Problem*. Dept of Industry, London.

Dept of Industry (1985). *Changing Skills*. Dept of Industry, London.

Eysenck, H.J. (1962). *Know Your Own I.Q.* Penguin, London.

Eysenck, H.J. (1969). *Check Your Own I.Q.*. Penguin, London.

Hunter, J.E., and Hirsh, R.H. (1987). Applications of meta-analysis. In C.L. Cooper and I.T. Robertson (eds), *International Review of Industrial and Organisational Psychology*, Wiley, Chichester.

Lynch, Don B. (1987). *Dictionary of Computer and Information Technology Terms*. Chartwell Bratt, Kent.

Morris, J., and Martin, J. (1972). *Personnel Selection: 2 Programmers*. NCC, Manchester.

MSC (1983). Report of the Review Group on TOPS Computing Training. MSC, Sheffield.

NCC (1984) (1985) (1986) (1987a) (1988). *Salary Surveys*. NCC, Manchester.

NCC (1987b). Members Survey. NCC, Manchester.

Penney, G., and Lazzerini, A.J. (1979). *Data Processing Staff Selection—a Validation Study*. NCC, Manchester.

Penney, G. (1979). *A Career in Computing*. Input Two-Nine, London.

Penney, G. (1984). *Survey of Threshold Trainees 1981/2*. NCC, Manchester.

Penney, G. (1985). *DP Staff Selection and Retention*. NCC, Manchester.

Sneath, F., Thakur, M., and Medjuck, B. (1976). *Testing People at Work*. Institute of Personnel Management, London.

Spurgeon, P., Patrick, J., and Michael, I. (1984). *Training & Selection of Computer Personnel*. Occupational Services Ltd., Birmingham.

Weatherley, E., Blinkhorn, S., Penney, G., and Simpson, D. (1979). *An Investigation into the Career Structure, Job Content and Vocational Interests of British Data Processing Staff*. NCC, Manchester.

Chapter 4.9

Personnel Selection in the Military

N. M. HARDINGE

*Headquarters Royal Air Force Support Command, Brampton, Huntingdon,
Cambridgeshire PE18 8QL, UK**

INTRODUCTION

The principal task of the Armed Services, the one which sets it apart from other
occupations, is the direction, control and firing of weapons systems—from rifles
to nuclear submarines and supersonic aircraft. There are many additional tasks
encompassing the maintenance and logistic support of Service units and their
equipment, the command and control of the systems in wartime, and their
planning, procurement and administration in peacetime.

Some of the secondary functions are filled by civilian personnel and on both
sides of the Atlantic the current trend is for more of these functions to be
civilianized. However, bearing arms and operating in certain hostile environments will still be the Services' unique contribution. A wide range of tasks such as
fighter pilot, submarine captain, tank commander, etc., are high risk and stressful. It is of note, however, that Service selection and assessment in the United
Kingdom relies on conventional methods and techniques. Combat abilities are
not specifically addressed and the development of combat skills is entirely
dependent on training.

During post-war conscription, the UK Services allocated personnel to existing
jobs, largely guided by job vacancies. They provided the full technical training
needed to meet job requirements even though the training could take up to
eighteen months of a two-year conscription. Most other European countries still
rely on a cadre of career personnel and a much larger body of conscripts (80 per

---

* The views expressed in this chapter are those of the author only and do not necessarily
represent the views of the Ministry of Defence.

Handbook of Assessment in Organizations   Edited by P. Herriot
© 1989 John Wiley & Sons Ltd

cent of Sweden's wartime air force, for example, will be provided by conscripts and reserves). Even in peacetime, Service careers are very different from those of most civilian occupations. Service personnel are required to be highly mobile. They must move to wherever directed, often at short notice, and they are usually posted every two to three years. They must be flexible, being moved to any of a wide range of jobs in their specialization (of, for example, avionics maintenance). The Services strive for a high degree of flexibility and substitutability. The price paid is in terms of continuous and costly training, and perhaps in terms of lost opportunities to develop deeper, specialist, skills and knowledge. There will also be a personal cost, in terms of disrupted family life, and reduced options for personal career plans.

The Services can offer employment for a wide range of abilities, from non-qualified, non-technical jobs to specialist post-graduate jobs. They provide a fixed career structure with well-prescribed job levels, roles and rewards. Progress to some of the highest levels is offered but a combination of technical skill and experience and leadership skills is needed. Servicemen can choose to serve for a fixed term, usually six years or more, with options on either side for extending the engagement. However, a significant development in the United Kingdom has been the widespread introduction of notice engagements which allow a Service employee to leave before finishing his or her engagement by giving eighteen months' notice. Many aspects of lifestyle are predetermined, e.g. uniforms, accommodation, social and recreational activities, etc. In some ways, therefore, the Services offer a complete lifestyle: compatibility with that lifestyle is a major consideration.

ASSESSMENT PHILOSOPHY

The Second World War stimulated the application of standardized selection procedures to the military. Large numbers of enlisted men and women from all educational backgrounds had to be quickly and accurately assessed and then allocated to appropriate Service tasks. Academics and occupational practitioners were drafted into government service to apply their techniques; and the selection principles which had been developed for civilian careers guidance and assessment were adopted and modified for the Armed Services. These have been remarkably adaptable. The general approach was based on the following tenets (see Harradence, 1975).

1. The cooperation of the candidates in selection is essential. To this end they must always be given relevant information. If so, they will to a considerable extent select themselves.
2. The interview must for long remain the central selection technique, even if it adds little or nothing to the validity coefficient of objective selection instruments. It is unparalleled for acceptability, flexibility, speed and inclusiveness.
3. The best basis for the interview is a biographical questionnaire in which the candidate gives information about his or her initial opportunities, schooling, work record, technical and other interests and achievements, his or her

part in community and leadership activities and any special qualifications.

4. Simple, comprehensive, documentation of each person's career is often of far more value than any amount of testing. This carries the implication that staff must be capable of using records expertly.

5. In a large-scale classification programme, specialized tests, if they involve apparatus or complicated scoring, are of limited importance. The demands of training programmes give a tremendous primacy to general ability, or educability: and a classification test—if soundly constructed and simple to use—will do a remarkable proportion of the work which can be done by testing.

6. Interest and relevant previous experience can, where genuine, be even more important than intelligence. Tests of knowledge or trade experience to cover the main areas relevant to Service jobs are therefore exceedingly useful.

7. Finally, educational status and educational proficiencies are at least as relevant to classification as the results of 'pure' intelligence tests.

These principles still provide an accurate description of the present-day system. Developments in our models of intellectual ability would require us to review the assumptions about 'general ability' and 'pure intelligence', and these will be discussed later. Otherwise, the philosophy is still very relevant today.

Within many Western nations (such as the United Kingdom, the United States, Canada and Australia) there has been a steady move away from conscription towards all-volunteer forces. While retention, pay and training policies have been affected by such changes, there has been little effect so far on selection methods and procedures. Entry standards and allocation procedures have altered in order to get the best out of the available manpower, but the nature and content of the assessment tests has remained much the same. The development of new selection tests has been slow; however, the nature of many essential tasks is changing and this may require changes in the content of test batteries. Operating tasks, such as flying and driving, are changing from continuous psychomotor skills to serial information processing skills. They have become dominated by the need to handle high information workloads, assign priorities and make rapid choices. Equally, the skill requirements for technicians have substantially altered. The more manual skills of rectification and repair are being displaced by predominantly cognitive skills of fault diagnosis.

Shaped by the demands of conscription, selection and allocation processes form the central part of assessment in the Armed Services. The procedures are modelled on those of civilian assessment. While some tasks are quite unique to the Services, many of the jobs, especially in peacetime, are much the same as elsewhere; but the roles and social organization are very different. What kind of person, then, do the Armed Services look for?

WHAT KIND OF PERSON IS REQUIRED?

The three UK Services require different levels of ability and require different specialist skills. Career officers in the British Navy and Army must have minimum education qualifications of 2 'A' levels (the minimum requirement for tertiary education). In terms of general ability this roughly corresponds to the top 12 per cent of the population; for short career officers the minimum requirement is usually lower so that the top 20–25 per cent of the population is eligible. Educational qualifications are not necessary for recruitment to the ranks although they are required for entry to the more technical trades and branches. (The range of ability for recruits to the ranks is currently in the region of IQ 95–115 for the Royal Navy (RN).) The technical stream is a non-graduate population. Qualifications range from 'O' levels to 'A' levels and while the most technical branches will be almost as selective as the minimum requirement for officers the criteria for officer selection (especially in terms of personal qualities) are much more demanding.

Applicants are directly interested in the Armed Services or other uniformed Services; membership of this kind of Service is usually more important than the actual trade or job. Many people applying to join the Services have no job preference, and many others will be prepared to consider more than one option. Between 50 and 75 per cent of the young people interested in a career as an officer in one Service will have considered another. Only 10–20 per cent will have considered just the one Service (Jones, 1984a). However, there are relatively few applications to more than one Service and very few transfers between the Services. The early development of a sense of loyalty to the chosen Service is a notable feature of military induction. There is always a continuous core of Service applicants, whether the Armed Services are a fashionable career or not. However, recruitment is related to alternative job opportunities: Service applications increase as employment prospects reduce elsewhere.

What kind of person is attracted to the Services? The Services aim to reflect the broad spectrum of the wider society, but there is no doubt that they do have particular values and attitudes. Neil (1984) showed that Royal Air Force (RAF) officer entrants have a distinct personality profile. Subsequent research is examining the extent to which this is a characteristic of the applicant population or a consequence of selection-board decisions. However, the UK Services do not use personality tests to select or assess personnel. Apart from the generally lower reliability and validity of such tests, it is in no way certain what kind of personality types should be preferred. The person best suited to today's problems may not be the best to deal with tomorrow's.

Military training is often organized into two distinct stages. Because of the importance of organizational commitment, early training plays a special role. Basic training focuses very closely on the development of appropriate attitudes and Service skills—learning military discipline, physical fitness, drill and weapons proficiency—on the conversion of a civilian into a responsive member of an armed force. At this stage volunteer Services allow the individual or the organization a chance to reconsider the commitment.

Basic training for the lower ranks is simple, short (six weeks or so), rigorous, and has a minimal wastage rate (about 8 per cent). Initial officer training is longer (18–30 weeks). It too is rigorous, and focuses on attitude development. It may also include some aspects of technical training and generally has a much higher wastage rate (about 25 per cent). Training for special cadres like the Royal Marines and Parachute Regiment is much longer, much more demanding, and has significantly higher wastage rates (about 40 per cent). Technical training, which converts the proficient soldier, sailor or airman into a skilled specialist, takes much longer and is more intellectually demanding. Pilot training is like an extended selection process. The wastage is high (only 25 per cent become fast jet pilots); and the methods of assessment are quite different (a little like progressive job sample tests with subjective assessment based on performance checklists).

RECRUITMENT AND SELECTION ORGANIZATION

The scale of operations means that recruitment, selection and allocation is a full-time, year-round activity. The emphasis is job centred, and is therefore on selection. However, the need for fitting the man to the somewhat special organization requires an appropriate emphasis on the person-centred aspects of the placement process.

Brevity and reliability are key considerations for military selection. All nations would probably also wish to maintain the recruitment infrastructure necessary to provide for rapid expansion and mobilization if needed. The operating principle is to let servicemen select the individuals who will be working in their organization. They should know the range of individuals most suited to a military environment, and they should be best able to inform and advise applicants. Often, the military is accountable to some outside body for its selection system. In the United Kingdom, selection matters are frequently raised by parliamentary questions. In the United States, Congress requires a regular review and update of the Service test batteries. Within each nation the different Services also have separate recruitment and selection organizations and operate slightly different policies. Only Canada has an integrated defence force and uses a single selection system. The British Army and RAF rely on regular servicemen on a 2–3 year detachment for the selection of lower ranks: the RN relies on a separate Careers Service of permanent ex-NCOs. Different nations use different levels of civilian specialist (i.e. psychologist) support. Psychologists are widely used to develop and support the selection systems. Many nations include them as members of the selection board. Only a few nations—Belgium and Australia are among them—use civilian psychologists to make independent selection decisions. Only one or two nations (such as Canada) have a cadre of Service psychologists. Each Service in the United Kingdom has a nationwide network of recruiting offices. The RN and RAF select and allocate men for the ranks at these local offices; the British Army forwards its applicants to a central location for further testing and for allocation. For officer selection, the Services each have their own central assessment centre staffed by officers on a regular tour of duty. For historical reasons the recruitment and selection of officers and of other ranks are separate processes. There are, however, clear routes for progressing from one level to another. One of the results of today's more test-based selection system has been a reduction in the influence of class, education and social background as determinants of level of entry and of career progression.

Selection in the Armed Services is different from most private and commercial organizations in terms of scale and the degree of centralization. While the 'line manager' doesn't have a direct say in the selection of his own recruits, Service personnel are very strongly represented in the selection process. For officer selection, all three UK Services use the same kind of assessment centre process: slightly different structures are used for the selection of other ranks.

ASSESSMENT CENTRE SELECTION PROCESS

Officer selection procedures aim to identify both leadership qualities and specialist/professional abilities. The War Office Selection Board (WOSB) system set up in 1942 drew heavily upon selection techniques in the German Army (Harris, 1949). The Services' group exercises stemmed from this source; based on the belief that the personal qualities which are crucial to success as an officer can best be assessed by observing individuals interacting with others. Officer selection is still firmly based on the WOSB system—using the panel assessment of educational qualifications, psychometric tests, biodata, interviews, reference reports, and performance in group exercises. In essence it is an assessment centre model of selection. It is an extended process (two or three days at least): it is manpower intensive and costly. (It costs around £500 to assess an RN officer at the Admiralty Interview Board (AIB) and £1250 for the full selection of an officer at the Army's Regular Commission Board (RCB).) Overall, some 47 per cent of candidates will be rejected each year by the RCB; only about 35 per cent of the 2000–2500 AIB candidates will be successful. The assessment centre approach is used where the skills to be identified are felt to be rare and imprecise. With a central panel making the assessments, trade-offs can be made between an individual's strengths and weaknesses (as revealed by the different selection devices) and satisfactory levels of reliability and validity can still be achieved.

Miles (1986) provides an excellent international review of army officer selection methods. The assessment centre was the most common approach (used in eight countries). Academic qualifications and comprehensive personal histories were next (used in four countries). Three nations relied exclusively on psychometric techniques, and three carried out their selection during an extended period of initial training.

A SEQUENTIAL SELECTION PROCESS

The selection of UK other ranks is much briefer and cheaper. Psychometric tests, biodata and interviews are used, together with educational qualifications where they are available. The selection process is organized as a series of hurdles with minimum standards required in each part and the stages are sequenced for greatest efficiency. Typically, a candidate would first be asked to complete a biographical questionnaire (giving age, qualifications, family background, school or employment record, job preferences, etc.). The next step would be a series of paper-and-pencil aptitude tests. Candidates would then be interviewed. Clearly unsuitable candidates would be rejected; those marginally below the minimum test standard would be counselled to try again. Candidates meeting the minimum standards would be interviewed in more depth. The questionnaire and interview data will be recorded and rated by the selector and will provide the principal means of assessing personal qualities and motivation. Unsuccessful candidates should be given some form of careers advice (in so far as the selectors have the time and are able to advise on other careers). Successful candidates have the medical test to look forward to. After a candidate has passed the medical, employers' references will be called for. (These are used late in the sequence because not all employers will take kindly to an individual leaving his or her job.)

The proportion of candidates excluded at each stage of the process will be strongly influenced by the number of vacancies in the Service and the number of applicants. Because they represent the most reliable and valid single predictor, test standards will be adjusted up and down—within narrow limits—in response to changes in the recruiting climate. In the United Kingdom, the ratio of applicants to entrants might be in the region of 6:1 for other ranks. Approximately 22 per cent of applicants might be excluded on the basis of test scores, 40 per cent excluded after subsequent interview, and a further 7.5 per cent excluded on medical grounds. The essential unreliability of the interview is minimized by using highly structured interviews, by using standard assessment forms and rating scales, by intensive training and by using the Service personnel as effectively full-time selectors. However, the major part of the selection process depends on this one procedure. There is very little monitoring of the reliability of selection interviews: any data are usually the result of all-too-rare, special studies. Assessing the validity of the interview is easier because it can be based on the rating scales used and consistent correlations can be found between interview assessments and wastage in early training (Taylor, Hardy and Dodd, 1985). In any kind of organization, the routine monitoring of selection decisions and the final outcome are exceptional, and at best, rudimentary. The RN's advisers can track the outcome of each selector's decisions: they feed back this information and debrief an example interview from each selector as part of their regular (annual) inspection of the Careers Service.

The centralized, panel-based, approach allows the Services to use a more flexible, subjective integration of data for officer selection. A single board or panel means that the reliability of assessments can still be satisfactorily maintained—but it is expensive. A sequential process is much simpler and cheaper, and provides an acceptable level of reliability where there is a large number of selectors. There is less flexibility for giving a recruit the chance to compensate for one quality with another and it makes less economic use of manpower. To improve the allocation and reduce the shortfall in categories which are hard to fill, the British Army carries out its selection and allocation for the ranks in a central location. Nevertheless, it still uses a sequential approach rather than the more expensive assessment centre procedures.

THE TOOLS OF ASSESSMENT: WHAT IS USED

Section 3 in this volume gives a detailed description of the assessment methods which are generally available. A wide range of instruments is used in military selection (see Dennison, 1986 for a comprehensive review) but the most common tools are tests, group exercises, biodata and interviews. Given a wide range of reliable and valid instruments, the inter-correlations are such that any one of a vast number of combinations using just a small subset of devices will probably yield similar results. It is possible that national culture, as much as anything else, determines the collection of instruments that is finally used. The main considerations are what information is used, and how the information is integrated.

APTITUDE TESTS

In the United Kingdom assessment is based on general test batteries which permit both selection and allocation. These emphasize aptitude rather than achievement. They use power tests and timed tests. For the selection of other ranks, educational qualifications are not always available, and are often not required. The simple use of minimum scores determines acceptability for the Service: a profile of minimum test scores and personal preference is used to determine allocation. Educational qualifications are a prerequisite for all officers. Minimum test scores are not specified but test performance would be evaluated alongside other forms of data by the assessment board.

The test batteries are similar in composition for both officers and other ranks. This probably reflects selection technology and the assumed structure of human abilities as much as any generic task structures.

For officers, the tests are typically:

1. Non-verbal/spatial reasoning
2. Maths
3. Verbal reasoning
4. Speed and accuracy
5. General and/or service knowledge

There are additional aptitude tests for special duties (e.g. aircrew).

For other ranks, the tests are typically:

1. Spatial reasoning/practical knowledge
2. Maths
3. Verbal reasoning

The structure of the UK test batteries is very similar to the US's General Aptitude Test Battery (GATB) and Differential Aptitude Tests (DAT) (see Dunnette, 1976) which are non-Service test batteries. The pattern of tests is very much the 1940s model—a general ability or 'g' factor, made up of three or four content factors (maths, verbal, spatial, practical knowledge). Changes to circumstance and to test theory would allow a more flexible test model to be considered nowadays. The allocation requirements are much less pressing in an all-volunteer Service and individual preference must play a more important role. Today's peacetime Services are much smaller, and with present-day computer facilities this offers the prospect of profile matching for individual men and jobs. The prevailing education standards are high and the required range of abilities is relatively narrow. It is also quite likely that training will become more directly job/task related. Special aptitude tests, which are overshadowed by measures of general ability in heterogeneous conscript populations, may nevertheless be viable in more homogeneous volunteer Services. Assessment technology offers a wide variety of additional types of test (for example, psychomotor, trainability and work sample tests). Because these kinds of test are protracted, costly and complex they have only been used for limited forms of entry (e.g. pilot, direct entry technicians, etc.). The composition of US Service test batteries is more variable: they are regularly reviewed and reweighted. For the United Kingdom and other European nations, the revision of their test batteries will usually be driven by changes in the educational system—which are much less frequent. A review of the testing model to stress special aptitudes rather than 'educability' and 'general abilities' may, therefore, be long overdue.

INTERVIEWS

Biodata—historical and verifiable pieces of information about an individual—provide very effective predictors (see Anderson and Shackleton, 1986) and such items make up much of the content of selection interviews. The predictive validity of interviews is generally very low (Hunter and Hunter, 1984). This will mainly be due to low reliability—individual differences in the data collected and differences in the way they are weighted and combined. In order to tackle the first problem, every effort is made to structure Service selection interviews. All the interviewers are trained in the sequence of topics and the appropriate question format to use, in what kinds of information and what 'danger signs' and 'compensating qualities' to look for. Generally speaking, the interview will focus on the things it does best—elicit and check facts, resolve ambiguities, let the candidates state their goals and expectations and let them ask questions. The data are subjectively combined in some kind of rating scale. The assessors focus on motivation, and on suitability for Service life and chosen trade. Sometimes a global scale is used. Sometimes separate scales are used such as:

– Home background
– Educational record
– Interests
– Group activities
– Attitude to authority
– Positions of leadership and responsibility
– Motivation

Numerical ratings on these would simply be added together. The numerical ratings derived from such interviews show a consistent correlation with training wastage. Taylor, Hardy and Dodd (1985) found that 'leadership and responsibility' correlated 0.29 with voluntary withdrawal and 'motivation' correlated

0.18. The model used for these interviews relies heavily on past behaviour as a predictor of future performance: it tries to establish point-to-point correspondence between past behaviour and the requirements of the particular job and of general Service life. It does not draw upon a 'situational interviewing' model (for example, like that of Latham *et al.* 1980).

WEIGHTED APPLICATION BLANKS

In the United Kingdom, only the Royal Navy uses scored biodata items. The empirical combination of biodata (e.g. weighted application blanks) is more widely used by the US military. Drakeley and Jones (1987) conducted a meta-analysis of military studies using different methods of combining items. 'Intuitive' methods of integration yielded a mean validity of 0.04 (compared with 0.16 to 0.25 for the different empirical methods). The very poor performance of 'intuitive' methods compared with empirical methods highlights the unreliability of the way that interview data are traditionally utilized. Drakeley calculated mean validities for the three most popular military criteria:

- Achievement   0.31
- Turnover   0.26
- Military aptitude 0.22

Prompted by such results the RN developed a professional achievement predictor (PAP), and an early voluntary wastage predictor (EVWP). These yielded the following validity coefficients, and are now in use for officer selection:

Prediction of professional examination   0.50
Prediction of early voluntary wastage   0.24

Weighted application blanks (WABs) have much to offer—especially with the selection of lower ranks. We know how weak interviews are; and, given the interview model that is employed, WABs should be more widely used in support. As purely empirical devices however, they need to be reviewed and revalidated even more regularly than many other instruments.

PERSONALITY TESTS

Most personality tests were produced for clinical use or as research tools rather than as purpose-built tools for military selection. They present problems of faking and of adverse candidate reactions but foreign experience suggests that these are not insurmountable. Other nations use personality tests, often in place of group exercises. The Dutch Army, for instance, replaced group exercises in 1981 with measures of personality derived from personality tests, biodata and interviews. The UK Services do not use personality tests but rely on interview assessments, references, weighted application blanks, and, in the case of officer selection, group exercises. From time to time the Services try out new tests but so far

Table 1	Techniques of army officer selection

Used by	Method		
	Personality tests	Weighted application blanks	Group exercises
Australia	*		*
Belgium	*	*	*
Canada			*
France	*		*
Germany			*
Holland	*		
India	*		*
Israel	*		*
New Zealand	*		
Sweden			*
United Kingdom		*	*
United States (West Pt)			
United States (Marines)		*	*

Source: Miles (1986).

personality tests have not been able to add anything useful to the predictive power of the selection process.

Some measure of character and of leadership is invariably included—in the form of personality tests, group exercises, WABs, etc. Group exercises are the preferred method in UK selection. They tend to give a low level of prediction (see Table 1): however, their use is continued because they have a very high level of face validity and because they address areas of performance which are not adequately covered by any other measures. Table 1 identifies the devices used for army selection in different countries.

THE TOOLS OF ASSESSMENT: HOW ARE THEY USED?

In some instances assessment information is combined in a mechanistic way— perhaps by using weightings empirically derived from a multiple regression analysis—in others it is done more subjectively by individuals or by panels. A mechanistic approach may be advantageous where the predictors and the performance criteria are clear and relatively objective. Subjective integration is probably better suited when the performance criterion is more subjective and there is a wide, less well-defined range of predictors. The RAF utilizes a statistical combination of factors (interview assessment, test scores, age and flying experience) to provide a potent predictor of pilot suitability (Walker-Smith, 1985). Drakeley, Herriot and Jones (1988) showed that the subjective assessment of the RN's AIB was no better than a weighted application blank in predicting performance in a professional examination. However, it was superior in predicting a leadership criterion.

RELIABILITY AND VALIDITY

All countries expect that their system will be reliable, valid, effective and efficient. Hunter and Hunter (1984) report validity coefficients for different selection methods but this depends on the criterion used. Validity is usually assessed in relation to training performance, job proficiency or wastage. In the United States, as in Europe, virtually all of the validation of tests use training criteria—usually declarative knowledge. Drakeley *et al.* (1987) report a correlation of 0.45 between the RN test battery and professional examinations at the end of the first stage of officer training. (Ghiselli, 1966, quotes 0.35 for predicting training success with tests of intellectual ability.)

In another study Jones and Drakeley (1985) identify the correlations between component parts of centre assessments and two training criteria (see Table 2 below). Two components of the syllabus for initial officer training are routinely assessed and influence subsequent career decisions. Professional studies are assessed by formal examinations and leadership performance by ratings of 'officer-like qualities' (OLQ ratings).

The correlation between tests on entry and job performance is lower—typically 0.19 (Ghiselli, 1966): but some reduction in the correlations is to be expected if effective training moderates the impact of individual differences. Objective job performance criteria are hard to find: usually rank, or time to promotion is used as the yardstick. Only rarely is an objective measure of job proficiency available, and supervisors' formal assessments are the normal criterion. United Kingdom military selection usually sets itself the limited but clear goal of predicting success in the first stages of training. The RN is aiming to predict performance up to the first operational appointment and Jones (1987) reports a validity coefficient of 0.36 obtained for overall AIB assessment against first annual report and of 0.44 against several averaged annual assessments. He reviewed a number of validity studies which had used supervisor assessments in the RN and found that broad-based measurements (interview ratings, examination results and selection centre assessments) provided low to medium correlations (0.28 to 0.51). Single measures such as individual selection tests generally provided inconsistent results.

Table 2   Corrected validity coefficients for RN assessment centre marks and component parts

	Training criteria		
	Professional examination	OLQ ratings	Total (Prof.+OLQ)
Overall marks	0.55	0.37	0.52
Component parts:			
Command exercise	0.36	0.34	0.37
Discussion exercise	0.34	0.28	0.35
Headteachers' reference	0.31	0.29	0.34
Composite test score	0.45	0.13	0.37

Source: Jones and Drakeley (1985).

How reliable are these criterion assessments? Results are available from RAF experiments which were carried out when assessment forms based on behaviour expectancy scales were being developed to replace the trait-based scales. These showed inter-rater agreements of 0.81 to 0.89 between pairs assessing the same airmen (Childs, 1975). Correlations between assessments of overall promotablity were 0.62 and 0.88; agreement on long-term potential was much lower (0.09 and 0.22). Two distinct trades were being assessed (engineering and clerical) and the results suggest that the abilities required for success may be harder to identify in some jobs than in others, and that perhaps different abilities are required for short-term and long-term success.

The RN found that final selection centre mark (final board mark) correlated 0.44 with early average annual report marks and the British Army reports corresponding correlations between 0.22 and 0.43. Validity coefficients for assessment centres are typically in the region of 0.4. In their analysis of results from 21 assessment centres, Schmitt *et al.* (1984) reported an average correlation of 0.407. Reliability coefficients for overall ratings in assessment centres, including military assessment centres, are in the order of 0.7 (Anderson and Shackleton, 1986). Apart from overall panel assessments, only biodata seem to provide consistently significant prediction across the range of proficiency criteria.

A weak relationship between selection tests and early wastage is consistently reported. This arises almost entirely from their measurement of ability, and is found most strongly among trades which require lower levels of ability. Beyond a certain level of ability, motivational factors are more likely to affect the decision whether to leave or not. Wastage rates are a very simple index of how good is the selection. About 10 per cent of the lower ranks choose to leave the Services during the first six months (when it is virtually unrestricted). Another 5 per cent will be discharged as unfit for training in this period. Test scores and interview assessments predict some forms of wastage better than others. Taylor *et al.* (1985) found a reasonable correlation for overall interview assessments with compulsory withdrawal (0.37 when corrected for range restriction) but a weak one for voluntary withdrawal (0.09). This distinction between voluntary and non-voluntary wastage is also reflected in Drakeley, Herriot and Jones's study (1988).

MID-CAREER ASSESSMENT

All military services have extensive and formalized systems of performance assessment (probably to support and compensate for the pattern of short postings). Reports are completed annually, and again after changes in boss, job or unit. Appropriate training needs are highlighted then.

The Services have patterns of career and training development for the officers in each specialization. These are not fixed, but there is usually a series of recognized courses and valued postings which develop individual skills and experience and also provide a basis for assessment and career decisions. Military services differ from other organizations to the extent that personnel expect, and are expected, to be directed into jobs and locales—some of which are unpopular or dangerous. Personal preferences are elicited, and are considered as far as possible.

The Services provide a large number of training courses to help in the continuing technical and professional development of their personnel—the instruction being aimed at the needs of the next assignment. Often Service careers will develop in one of two directions—as a specialist or as a more generalist manager or policy maker. An increasingly broader career pattern will be developed as far as the individual's abilities and preferences will allow. High flyers are usually identified early on and will be steered towards a series of high-profile postings. The general aim is to provide wide experience and increasing responsibility as a preliminary to staff college training and to the higher positions of policy making or senior command that generally follow.

Attendance at junior staff college is usually widely available for all officers and is sometimes mandatory. Selection for senior staff college is much tougher. The usual criteria will include completion of the junior staff course, recommendation by commanding officers, completion of written examinations and subsequent vetting on the basis of past performance reports. A combination of all of these methods is used by the British Army's Senior Staff Course to select some 14 per cent of the pool.

Career patterns are probably less well defined for the lower ranks. There is not the same process for consultation over future postings and there is no real equivalent to staff college. Career progress is more a matter of increasing technical specialization and developing supervisory skills. A certain percentage of men are taken from the ranks for officer training. Initial selection is usually by special recommendation from commanding officers on the basis of outstanding performance revealed through annual assessments. Such individuals would then go through the normal officer assessment centre process and through initial officer training. For some branches, as much as one-third of the officer strength may have been commissioned that way. In particular cases, officers progress through the ranks—Israeli officers enter this way. In the Women's Royal Naval Service all officer entrants serve as ratings for a time.

As well as having a sophisticated selection and allocation system, the military has developed a very effective system of reporting and appraisal. However, there has been no corresponding development of formal mid-career assessment techniques and procedures. Because there are limited and strictly defined points of entry into the Services there is much less need to seek standardized assessments at a later stage. The procedures that exist have largely evolved from the administration of Service postings into an informal system of reviews and interviews based almost exclusively on the annual reports. These have been developed, and are administered, by desk officers. The officers would probably not see any need for a more formalized system or one which relied on outsiders and non-Service assessments. Some validation of these kinds of assessment decisions is probably urgently needed, but for the present, change and innovation are still directed towards improving selection and allocation.

NEW TECHNOLOGIES

Selection and assessment methods are developing on several fronts. Most notable is the general move towards using a broader basis for assessment which emphasizes the individual's occupational preferences. Much current work highlights the fact that recruitment is a two-way process; this creates ambiguities and lessens the validity of the interview (Herriot,1987). The Armed Services try to keep these processes separate in order to maximize interview validity. In the past this may have been somewhat at the expense of the applicant; however, several new measures are being used to assist the candidate in his choices. Wanous's work on realistic job previews (1976) was successfully applied to US marine selection. This highlighted how critical is the initial introduction into the Services and it has encouraged a wider use of self-selection procedures in the United Kingdom with new measures to provide 'acquaint' visits, short courses, exercises, etc., all giving the individual a better basis for making his or her career commitment. A simple but important development along these lines has been the introduction of job knowledge indices—a series of 'quizzes' which transmit key items of job information, describing the rough as well as the smooth (Bethell-Fox and Jones, 1986).

Work sample tests and trainability tests

Both kinds of tests are based on tasks that represent some of the core skills of a job: however, trainability tests include a controlled period of learning and are used to select for training rather than to choose people who are already competent. Work sample tests compare very favourably with conventional tests, and validities in excess of 0.5 have been obtained against training performance criteria (Robertson and Downs, 1979). Such tests are job specific, take a long time to administer and normally need to be administered on an individual basis; but, while much more costly than conventional written tests, they have been successfully used in some key areas of Armed Services selection. Flying screening—often a part of early training—is a common feature of pilot selection (see Burke, 1986) and validity coefficients of 0.4 are typical. For a brief period the RAF used a more rigorously designed trainability test and reported coefficients of 0.78–0.91 (Elshaw and Lidderdale, 1982). A trainability test recently introduced for helicopter navigators/tactical controllers in the RN yielded coefficients of 0.48. This application of trainability testing techniques to high-level, cognitive tasks represents an interesting new development (Jones, 1982).

Information tests

Conventional tests of aptitude and ability have frequently been supported by information tests which can provide a non-cognitive measure of interest and motivation. Such tests become outdated relatively quickly and therefore rarely find a permanent place in test batteries. Seen as a measure of motivation, the US Naval Knowledge Test was used to screen civilian applicants to the USN's Officer Candidate School (Glickman, 1956). Information tests also feature in the US Armed Services Vocational Aptitude Battery (ASVAB) and have been a longstanding feature of RAF technician selection. The RN equivalents played a key role in artificer apprentice (technician) selection. Dropped in 1975, when they became outdated, new versions are now being introduced. Information tests are also being used for RN officer selection: a test of naval knowledge has been shown to be predictive of performance in initial training (giving a correlation of 0.27 with examination results) and it adds to the level of prediction based on ability tests alone (Jones, 1984b).

Computer-based testing

Computer-based testing has not yet had its full impact. Initial applications focused on the cost benefits to be found in automated testing and scoring. Almost all involved the computerization of existing paper-and-pencil and psychomotor tests. As well as offering administrative advantages, computer-based testing overcomes the progressive unreliability of mechanically driven psychomotor tests. In addition to the simple cognitive/perceptual tests that we have at present, it opens the way to assess new aspects of dual-task performance (e.g. perceptual vigilance, scheduling, risk taking, etc.). Truly new and original tests which exploit the dynamic, interactive, visual aspects of computers have been slow to emerge but are being developed in the United States, and in the United Kingdom by Bartram (1987). The real-time capabilities of computers found an early application in the delivery of tailored tests (see Bryson, 1972). They use the computer to select which set of questions, from a pool of items, a candidate will be given: the selection is based on whether the candidate answered the last item correctly or not, and on its difficulty. Tailored tests are not widely used. While they can be shorter than conventional tests they are not necessarily more predictive (Sympson, *et al.*, 1982), and they leave the selectors open to complaints (however unjustified in practice) of inequality of treatment. For the same testing time as conventional tests they could offer a broader indication of ability by highlighting strengths and weaknesses in more detail. To gain real advantage, any such improved assessment profiles would have to be matched by detailed and improved job profiles.

Decision models

Cronbach and Gleser's (1965) classic examination of test validity highlighted some of the practical considerations that decision makers should bear in mind when using selection tests, emphasizing the need to consider test utility not just test validity. Even today relatively few organizations fully research the cost of alternative selection and prediction systems. This is an area of increasing importance and simple examples can be seen in models developed for problem areas of UK military selection. (Lidderdale and Bennett, 1977, describe a model for the cost evaluation of alternative selection and training systems for RAF pilots.) More recent studies (Drakeley and Jones, 1987; Jones, 1988) have provided cost estimates of the performance increase obtained from new selection procedures. It is to be hoped that these will encourage the Services to direct more resources towards modifying and improving selection procedures.

A PEEK INTO THE FUTURE

Shaped by the demands of conscription, selection and allocation processes form the central part of assessment in the Armed Services. As Services become all-volunteer, we can expect the emphasis to change. Perhaps we can see that non-cognitive factors are playing a bigger part in selection and allocation decisions already. Test batteries for general classification should give way to the testing of job-specific aptitudes and skills. It is likely that weighted application blanks will be more widely used. There should be more monitoring of selection interviews and decisions—not just for the purposes of validation but in order to prepare and coach the selectors. Mid-career assessment procedures and career development decisions could become more important—being oriented more towards the individual's needs and preferences, and extended to include the lower ranks. Retention issues and ways of widening the manpower base will become especially important as employment prospects become more attractive.

REFERENCES

Anderson, N., and Shackleton, V. (1986). Recruitment and selection: a review of developments in the 1980s, *Personnel Review*, **15**(4), 19–26.

Bartram, D. (1987). The development of an automated testing system for pilot selection: the Micropat Project, *Applied Psychology: An International Review*, **36**(3), 279–98.

Bethell-Fox, C.E., and Jones, A. (1986). Realistic job previews for the cost conscious employer, *Guidance and Assessment Review*, **2**, 6–7.

Bryson, R. (1972). Shortening tests: Effects of method used, length, and interval consistency on correlation with total score. *Proceedings 80th Annual Convention of the American Psychological Association*, Honolulu, **7**, 7–8.

Burke, E.F. (1986). Test validities, task breakdowns, and the integration of selection test research. *Proceedings of the 27th Military Testing Association*.

*Childs, A. (1975). *Airman Assessment Research Project: Phase 4 Final Report*. Science 4 (RAF) Note 17/75. CS(RAF), Ministry of Defence, London.

Cronbach, L.J., and Gleser, G. (1965). *Psychological Tests and Personnel Decisions*, 2nd edn. University of Illinois Press, Urbana, Ill.

*Dennison, D. (1986). *A Study of Army Officer Recruiting Procedures*. Report 86R001. Army Personnel Research Establishment, Ministry of Defence, c/o RAE Farnborough, Hants.

Drakeley, R.J., Herriot, P., and Jones, A. (1988). Biographical data, training performance and turnover, *Journal of Occupational Psychology*, **61**, 145–52.

*Drakeley, R.J., and Jones, A. (1987). *Final Report and Overview of the Use of Biographical Data in RN Officer Selection*. SP(N) Report R101. Naval Scientific Advisory Group, Ministry of Defence, London.

Drakeley, R.J., Wingrove, J., Herriot, P., and Jones, A. (1987). *Tales from the Darkside: Thoughts on the implementation of selection research*. Paper presented to the British Psychological Society Occupational Psychology Conference, Hull.

Dunnette, M.D. (1976). Aptitudes, abilities and skills, in M.D. Dunnette (ed.). *Handbook of Industrial and Organizational Psychology*. Rand McNally, Chicago.

Elshaw, C.C., and Lidderdale, I.G. (1982). Flying selection in the Royal Air Force, *Newsletter of the International Test Commission and of the Division of Psychological Assessment of the International Association of Applied Psychology*, No. 17, December 1982.

Ghiselli, E.E. (1966). *The Validity of Occupational Aptitude Tests*. Wiley, New York.

Glickman, A.S. (1956). The Naval Knowledge Test, *Journal of Applied Psychology*, **40**(6), 389–92.

*Harradence, J.D.F. (1975). *A Review of Selection Testing in the Royal Navy*. SP(N) Report R1. Naval Scientific Advisory Group, Ministry of Defence, London.

Harris, H. (1949). *The Group Approach to Leadership Testing*. Routledge & Kegan Paul, London.

Herriot, P. (1987). Graduate recruitment–getting it right, *Employment Gazette*, February 1987, 78–83.

Hunter, J.E., and Hunter, R.F. (1984). Validity and utility of alternative predictors of job performance, *Psychological Bulletin*, **96**, 72–98.

Jones, A. (1982). Providing the Man in the Back Seat. Paper presented to the 24th Conference of the Military Testing Association. San Antonio.

*Jones, A. (1984a). *One or Two Things We Know About Royal Navy Officer Recruitment From Market Research Studies*. SP(N) Report R71. Naval Scientific Advisory Group, Ministry of Defence, London.

Jones, A. (1984b). The role of occupational information in assessing and enhancing motivation for military service. *Proceedings of the 2nd Symposium on Motivation and Morale in the NATO Forces*, Brussels.

*Jones, A. (1987). *To the Fleet: III. Relationship Between Selection Variables, Training Results, and S206 Assessments*. SP(N) Report TR186. Naval Scientific Advisory Group, Ministry of Defence, London.

Jones, A. (1988). *Estimation of the Utility of an Assessment Centre against Training and Operational Outcomes*. Paper presented to the British Psychological Society Occupational Psychology Conference, Manchester.

*Jones, A., and Drakeley, R. (1985). *A Follow-up of 725 Entrants to RN Officer Training at BRNC, Dartmouth*. SP(N) Report R79, Naval Scientific Advisory Group, Ministry of Defence, London.

Latham, G.P., Saari, L.M., Pursell, E.D., and Campion, M.A. (1980). The situational interview, *Journal of Applied Psychology*, **65**, 422–7.

Lidderdale, I.G., and Bennett, L.V. (1977). *A Cost Benefit Analysis of a Simulator Test for Pilot Screening in the RAF*. HMSO Controller, London.

*Miles, R.J. (1986). *International Comparisons of Army Officer Selection Methods*. Memorandum 86M501. Army Personnel Research Establishment, Ministry of Defence, Royal Aircraft Establishment, Farnborough, Hants.

*Neil, G.W. (1984). *Officer Selection: the role of personality*. Research Note 20/84. Research Branch HQ RAF Support Command, RAF Brampton, Huntingdon, Cambs.

Robertson, I., and Downs, S. (1979). Learning and the prediction of performance: Development of trainability testing in the UK, *Journal of Applied Psychology*, **64**, 42–50.

Schmitt, N., Gooding, R.Z., Noe, R.A., and Kirsch, M. (1984). Meta-analysis of validity studies published between 1964 and 1982 and the investigation of study characteristics, *Personnel Psychology*, **37**, 407–22.

Sympson, J.B., Weiss, D.J., and Ree, M.J. (1982). *Predictive Validity of Conventional and Adaptive Tests in an Air Force Training Environment by Report No. AFHRL-TR-81-40*. Air Forces Human Resources Laboratory, Brooks Air Force Base, Texas.

*Taylor, J.S., Hardy, G.R., and Dodd, B.T. (1985). *An Investigation of the Personal Qualities Assessment Form in Ratings' Selection in the Royal Navy*. SP(N) Report TR158. Senior Psychologist (Naval), Ministry of Defence, London.

*Walker-Smith, G. (1985). Predicting success in flying training. Note for the Record 10/85. MOD Science 3(RAF), London.

Wanous, J.P. (1976). Organisational entry: From naive expectations to realistic beliefs, *Journal of Applied Psychology*, **61**, 22–9.

---

* Not available outside the Ministry of Defence.

Section 5:
Performance Appraisal and Counselling

Introduction to Section 5:
Performance Appraisal and Counselling

Victor Dulewicz

The history of performance appraisal is in one sense very short, though in another sense it stretches back for as long as people have worked together—for it is surely a basic human tendency to make judgements about those one is working with, as well as about oneself. In this respect, appraisal is an inevitable and probably universal activity, a fact that sometimes seems to get overlooked when it is discussed. If there are no formal appraisal systems, you can be sure that there will be informal assessments made, with little opportunity for the fairness or accuracy of them to be evaluated or scrutinized. However, the development of formal appraisal practices is a relatively recent phenomenon, and this introduction will begin by briefly trying to trace the origins of modern approaches to performance appraisal. This will help put the subsequent chapters into a broader context.

Much of the evolution of appraisal practices has taken place in the United States, though there have also been significant developments in Europe which have not always paralleled those across the Atlantic. Perhaps the clearest early contributor to the idea of formal appraisal was the American interest in job evaluation techniques after the First World War, which not surprisingly led on in the 1920s and 1930s to a consideration of ways of evaluating how managers were performing the jobs. After all, if you have gone to the trouble of assessing what a job is worth in terms of payment, it is only logical to try to assess whether the individual is doing it to a standard that justifies that payment. But the influence of the Hawthorne studies and of the Human Relations movement took the focus of appraisal wider than this. The aim became more than just assessment; morale raising was perceived as a function of the exercise. The notion was that high morale gave rise to high productivity. Even more unsound was the prevalent assumption that the goals of the organization were the goals of the individual. This kind of thinking persisted into the 1950s, and judging from some appraisal schemes, it is still around today.

In Europe, it took rather longer for formal appraisal practices to catch on. When they did, they tended to be linked to incentives, principally promotion. In the 1950s, American ideas about appraisal as a vehicle for management development began to creep in. On both sides of the Atlantic, letting people know where they stand—giving performance feedback—was seen as an important feature of appraisal, albeit for different reasons. In Europe it seems to have been a way of indicating recognition, which was supposed to be an incentive. In the United States, the belief was that knowing where you stood made you happier, and thus more likely to work hard and be productive. The form of the appraisal was also common to both America and Europe. The predominant approach was based on ratings, usually of personality attributes. The reasons behind this were the difficulty of measuring managerial performance and the perceived need for managers to have the right leadership qualities; the former problem is still with us, as later chapters will demonstrate, and the emphasis on personality factors is not only found in some present-day appraisal schemes, but is often implicit in the beliefs of individual managers.

The problems experienced with this kind of personality-rating-based appraisal were numerous, not least being the reluctance of managers to 'play God', as McGregor (1957) called it, in judging their colleagues. The result was a shift in the 1960s towards results-oriented appraisal, which was derived from the principles of Management by Objectives. With it came a shift towards greater openness; it had been common for appraisees not to be shown the actual appraisal report form prior to this. These changes meant that the appraisal became more concerned with problem solving and improving future performance than with assessment of the individual. Being a time of expanding opportunities, it was appropriate that appraisal should be more development centred.

Since that era, things have been a lot tougher economically, and this has also been reflected in appraisal practices. The recession has reduced promotion prospects and changed career expectations, while organizations have become even more dominated by bottom-line considerations. There is clear evidence (Long, 1986) that this is bringing a greater emphasis on performance issues and less on the developmental aspects of appraisal; the organization's needs are being put at the top of the list of priorities. Much the same pressures are forcing trade unions to take a greater interest in performance appraisal than they used to. If appraisal is once again becoming an important assessment device, with implications for reward strategies, then they are bound to have some views on the subject. And for good measure, there is the impact of equal opportunities legislation to be taken into account. In the United States, this has had a powerful impact on appraisal systems, forcing them to be more defensible in terms of job relevance. The same has not happened in all European countries, but an appraisal scheme that lays itself open to accusations of bias is inevitably a liability for the organization running it.

It is, of course, impossible in the space available to chart the development of appraisal in such a way as to reflect the individual variations to be found in each European country. Fortunately, the similarities seem to outweigh the differences

(Williams, Walker, and Fletcher, 1977). There are inevitably some contrasts to be found; for example, objectives-oriented appraisal does not appear to be as popular in the Netherlands as it is in the United Kingdom, and the former country has implemented appraisal in academic institutions well ahead of the latter (Drenth, 1984). Hopefully, however, it will be seen from this general account of some of the influences that have affected performance appraisal over the last half century that appraisal practice tends to some extent to mirror broader social movements.

Appraisal is not a highly dynamic subject and many of the issues which are critical today have been with us for many years. Some of the key issues currently facing managers with responsibility for designing and implementing appraisal schemes are as follows:

– Are the purposes and objectives clearly stated and realistic? Are they compatible with each other?
– Is the scheme technically sound and does it minimize the likelihood of rater error? Or does it in fact tell you more about the appraiser than the appraisee?
– Is it appropriate to appraise the degree to which the appraisee has met agreed objectives? Is it necessary to appraise personal qualities?
– Is the scheme used to reward staff financially and, if so, is it reliable enough, and how does this application fit in with any other purposes?
– Does the scheme put undue emphasis on one person, i.e. the boss's views?
– Is an appraisal interview carried out and, if so, how open is it? Does it encourage the appraisee to contribute fully? How effective is it?
– Can anything be done to increase the appraisee's self-awareness so that he or she can increase the value of the process?
– Are appraisers offered training and is it effective over the long term?
– Is it valid to appraise long-term potential on the basis of current performance?

In this section of the handbook, a number of leading European practitioners with extensive experience of the subject will address these issues, and many others. In Chapter 5.1, Victor Dulewicz and Clive Fletcher look at the aims of performance appraisal from the organization's point of view, and then examine the needs and motives of the participants, the appraiser and the appraisee. Finally, they discuss what possibilities there are for devising appraisal systems that are based on sound underlying assumptions and which can realistically offer something of value to all those involved. In the next chapter (5.2), John Handyside looks at the process of rating, and the design of rating scales. In the first part, he gives a useful summary of some of the problems commonly encountered when designing rating scales and then provides some valuable examples of measurement techniques and formats to help overcome these problems. He then turns his attention to the critical subject of rater error, and, in particular, the 'halo effect'. His own research findings present the reader with new insights into what is likely to cause the 'halo effect', and on what can be done to reduce it, as a consequence of better form design and appraiser training.

James Walker, in Chapter 5.3, looks at one of the crucial aspects of the total process—the appraisal interview. He begins by listing the numerous purposes of such interviews, and warns the reader about some of the problems which are likely to arise when some of the purposes are incompatible with each other, or when insufficient thought has been given to dealing with numerous potentially contentious issues. His review of research findings on the appraisal interview gives the reader some valuable pointers on what factors contribute to make an interview effective. Finally, he turns to the skills of interviewing, covering important aspects such as questioning technique, active listening, feedback and reflecting back, before concluding with the important subject of openness, and under what circumstances it is appropriate to encourage greater openness in the interview.

As already noted, one of the major advances over the last 25 years has been the introduction of Management by Objectives. In Chapter 5.4, Richard Macdonell describes the classical approach to MbO before outlining some of the major problems which have been encountered by organizations using the classical approach. He then goes on to identify those aspects of 'results-oriented' or 'outcome-oriented' performance review schemes which are still used to good effect by organizations and which are therefore worth retaining.

Self-awareness is a necessary, or at least a very valuable, condition for helping the appraisee—potentially a major beneficiary of appraisal processes—to achieve his or her objectives, such as improved work performance, increased job satisfaction, the identification of relevant strengths and the analysis of relevant training and development needs. In his chapter (5.5), Rowan Bayne draws an important distinction between inner and outer self-awareness and then describes four different approaches which appraisees (and staff generally) can use to increase their self-awareness: assertiveness; using a 'journal'; interpersonal process recall; and the Myers–Briggs psychological type indicator.

In the majority of appraisal systems, one person's judgement, i.e. the boss, is usually given far greater weighting than anyone else's views. While the boss normally has far greater contact with, and knowledge about, the appraisee's performance, these views can be highly subjective and biased. Often, the boss of the boss is also asked to give a view, but in many cases it is based on very limited direct knowledge. Richard Williams (Chapter 5.6) provides a critique of undue reliance on supervisors' ratings and then looks at other sources of performance data (self, peers, subordinates, personnel staff) which can be tapped in order to increase the total pool of evidence from which judgements can be made. He also looks at other methods, such as essays and critical incidents, which have been shown to be of value for some organizations.

It is now widely accepted that proper training of appraisers is a prerequisite for the success of an appraisal scheme. In Roger Pryor's chapter (5.7), he describes ten key criteria which a training course should meet if it stands a chance of being effective. He then describes the briefing which course members should receive before they attend the course, and the main skill components an appraisal course should cover. He concludes by giving some advice on the all-important matter of how one might evaluate effectiveness of the training.

Many appraisal schemes include an assessment of the appraisee's long-term potential. However, if jobs at a higher level in the organization require a range of skills and abilities which are significantly different from those required at the appraisee's current level, then it is highly questionable whether the appraisal scheme is the appropriate tool to use for assessing long-term potential. The method which has been shown in numerous studies to have the highest validity for this purpose is the assessment centre (AC). In a previous chapter (3.7) Rob Feltham looked at ACs for selection, and dealt with cost–benefit and utility issues. The final chapter in Section 5, by Jeroen Seegers, describes assessment centres which are designed for identifying long-term management potential and provides some valuable advice on how to set up such an AC. He also draws our attention to the power of the technique as a development tool. Participants obtain great benefits from feedback obtained from peers and assessors to help them improve their performance, and final results can help them to identify key training and development needs, which can feature in subsequent discussions and career planning. Seegers concludes by emphasizing the importance of integrating the AC into the broader appraisal and development processes of the organization.

There is no blueprint for the perfect appraisal scheme, nor are there easy answers to the questions posed earlier. The structure and cultures of organizations differ considerably, as do the purposes of any single scheme. In this section the authors have produced some general guidelines and advice, based on the research literature and their own considerable experience, to help readers address the main issues and, we trust, reach some conclusions which are relevant to their own situations and organizations.

REFERENCES

Drenth, P.J.D. (1984) Personnel appraisal, in P.J.D. Drenth, H. Thierry, P.J. Williams, and C.J. de Wolff (eds), *Handbook of Work and Organizational Psychology*. Wiley, Chichester.

Long, P. (1986). *Performance Appraisal Revisited*. Institute of Personnel Management, London.

McGregor, D. (1957). An uneasy look at performance appraisal, *Harvard Business Review*, **35**, 89–94.

Williams, R.S., Walker, J., and Fletcher, C. (1977). International review of staff appraisal practices: Current trends and issues, *Public Personnel Management*, January–February, 5–12.

Chapter 5.1

The Context and Dynamics of Performance Appraisal

VICTOR DULEWICZ[1] and CLIVE FLETCHER[2]

[1]*The Management College, Greenlands, Henley-on-Thames, Oxon RG9 3AU, UK, and*
[2]*Department of Psychology, University of London Goldsmiths' College, New Cross, London SE14 6NW, UK*

NEEDS OF THE ORGANIZATION

Although it is almost a cliché nowadays to claim that any organization's most important resource is its employees, such a claim is still valid. Moreover, the most important vehicle used by personnel departments when aiming to maximize the output of their human resources is the organization's appraisal and counselling scheme. Such schemes are normally used for assessing the performance of a company's employees and for developing their capacities, for rewarding them and for motivating them, so that the total sum of skills and energy available to the organization is growing steadily to meet its future requirements. To remain competitive and efficient it will probably need to develop its workforce.

Most appraisal and counselling schemes have been designed to produce different kinds of information for different purposes, and for different users. Furthermore, the purpose will often vary, depending on the level of employee being appraised. Management appraisal schemes are naturally likely to be more rigorous and wide ranging than those designed for, say, clerical staff, and shop-floor workers are less likely to be subjected to a formal appraisal scheme at all. Their performance is more likely to be appraised on the basis of how many widgets are produced and on how many days they have been absent, while their rewards are likely to be negotiated for them *en masse* by their union.

Appraisal schemes are thus designed usually for white-collar groups and often have a number of different purposes which will be described below:

Assessment and Selection in Organizations   Edited by P. Herriot
© 1989 John Wiley & Sons Ltd

1. *Performance review* This constitutes the core of most systems, largely because the information is the basis for so much else within it. The organization usually needs a record of how well an individual has performed over the last year, so as to reward and reinforce good performance and to improve aspects of poor performance. It needs a lasting record of an individual's performance so that, at some point in the future when being considered for another job, past job behaviour can be taken into account.

2. *Work planning* One of the main tasks of every manager should be to sit down with his or her subordinates and help them plan their work for, say, the next year or so. Nevertheless, we all know some managers who, if left to themselves, will not do this, for various reasons. Many appraisal schemes nowadays have work planning built in as a key component with a view to stretching the employee and to improving performance. Managers are required to plan overall objectives with their staff, and to set criteria whereby together they can measure the degree to which each objective has been met. The plan is then used at the end of the year as a basis for appraising performance. While managers should do this anyway, the organization is providing a procedure for ensuring that a minimal degree of work planning takes place and that such information is recorded. Formalizing such responsibilities is perhaps not the best way of getting the reluctant manager to plan, but it does at least ensure that employees do get some attention, and can be encouraged to persevere at the task and to try to improve. It is even better if the manager himself is appraised, and rewarded, for carrying out performance appraisal.

3. *Basis for compensation and benefits* This is probably the most contentious purpose of appraisal schemes, for reasons given later. Suffice to say that some organizations, mainly in the private sector but nowadays including public sector organizations such as the NHS, have a 'pay performance' policy. The objective of such policies is to give material rewards, usually in the form of salary and bonus incentives, to those who are performing very well, and little or no real increases in salary, and no bonuses to those whose performance is at a less than acceptable level. What better way of measuring performance than the formal appraisal system. This sounds initially to be very sensible, but the appraisal of performance in most jobs is a highly subjective matter, depending largely on the judgement of one or two appraisers. There are few jobs which have what appear to be objective criteria of performance, e.g. sales achieved in monetary terms, for salesmen, but on closer inspection one finds so many extraneous factors which have affected performance that even monetary criteria are often not especially reliable or valid indicators of performance. As we shall see later, incorporating reward into the appraisal process can have a very negative effect on appraisees, and can undermine the atmosphere in the appraisal process.

4. *Identification of training and development needs* The value of training is recognized by many organizations these days as a means of increasing the skills and

knowledge base of their employees. Performance appraisal is generally regarded as the appropriate vehicle for identifying an employee's areas of weakness, and for discussing which training courses might be appropriate for developing the skills or knowledge required to improve performance. Furthermore, development needs are also often identified. These are geared to adding to the individual's existing expertise, to equip the person to take on more demanding tasks or jobs. These requirements are usually recorded and eventually passed on to the department responsible for providing training.

5. *Transfer and promotion potential* Most organizations, especially those which have a policy of promoting from within, need to keep a record of those employees who have been performing consistently well over a long period and who are therefore no longer being really stretched in their current job or at their current level. It is important for them to know if someone has the capability to take on a job at a higher level or whether they need a transfer to a new job at the same level in order to broaden their experience and expertise. Once again the performance appraisal scheme is seen by most organizations as the best source of such information, and so ratings of potential to do a job at a higher level, or of the need for transfer at the same level, are usually incorporated into appraisal forms.

6. *Identification of long-term potential* In addition to appraising potential for the next level, many organizations, especially large ones, have sophisticated management development policies and programmes. In order to spot future senior managers early enough so they benefit from development programmes, and can progress rapidly through the various levels of management, some organizations use the performance appraisal system as one source of information about employees' long-term, or ultimate potential. Indeed, a few organizations appraise the ultimate potential of their white-collar staff from the day they join from school or university.

7. *Succession and career planning* Since managers tend to move jobs rapidly, sometimes at very short notice, it is a sign of good planning to have a system containing a list of suitable incumbents for every important management position in the organization. Even at lower levels, it is wise to have broad plans for the careers of its employees. The performance appraisal and counselling scheme yet again will often provide inputs to succession and career planning systems.

Long (1986) carried out a survey of a fairly representative cross-section of UK companies and asked what purpose their appraisal systems were designed to meet. The results appear in Table 1. This table shows quite an extensive range of different objectives, and in practice not all are usually met satisfactorily. Let us now turn to the important subject of the evaluation of the effectiveness of

Table 1.   Main Purposes of Performance Review Schemes

	1977 (%)	1985 (%)
To assess training and development needs	96	97
To help improve current performance	92	97
To review past performance	91	98
To assess future potential/promotability	87	71
To assist career planning decisions	81	75
To set performance objectives	57	81
To assess increases or new levels in salary	39	40
Others, e.g. updating personnel records	*	4
Base	230	250

* Not available in 1977

After P. Long. *Performance Appraisal Revisited*, IPM, 1986.

appraisal schemes and to what evidence exists that they do meet their objectives.

Studies of the appraisal process

One of the earliest systematic studies of the appraisal process was carried out by Meyer, Kay, and French (1965) in the General Electric Company in the United States. One major conclusion was that separate appraisal interviews should be held for different purposes, and in particular that counselling, in terms of coaching and goal setting, should be kept separate from the treatment of rewards and salary increases. They argued that it seems foolish to expect a manager to play the conflicting roles of counsellor (helping the subordinate to improve performance) and judge, presiding over the same person's salary action case. They also pointed out the potentially damaging effect that excessive criticism could have on the value of the discussions, and advocated that cooperative goal setting, and not criticism, should be used to improve performance.

Another study which was particularly rigorous (Dulewicz, Fletcher, and Walker, 1976) incorporated a before-and-after design. Around 500 employees of a government department completed a questionnaire dealing with attitudes to work, general supervision and communication with management, just before an appraisal system was introduced. Three years after its introduction, the same questionnaire, with additional items relating specifically to the appraisal scheme, was administered to a matched sample of 500 employees who had each received between one and four appraisal interviews. Results showed a statistically significant increase in the amount of discussion taking place between staff and their immediate bosses, and between staff and their managers. Furthermore, staff now felt much freer to talk to their managers than they had done before. While not providing conclusive proof, the introduction of the appraisal scheme was felt to be the most likely cause of improved communications. Another important finding was that, with each successive interview, discussions of work difficulties, ideas for improving work, future aspirations, good and poor performance and training needs were more likely to become of increasing value. Finally, those reporting that action points had in fact been followed up were more likely to report an improvement in their job performance.

One study has summarized the results of a number of evaluation studies carried out in seven different organizations in the public and private sectors (Fletcher and Williams, 1985). High response rates were achieved and altogether 5940 appraisees and 1332 appraisers responded. Results relating to overall reactions and points discussed in the interview, with the average percentage of respondents agreeing with the item, were as follows:

- The appraisee was against the whole scheme: 9 per cent.
- Performance weaknesses were discussed: 54 per cent.
- Training needs were discussed: 47 per cent.

Questions were also asked about the *perceived* link between the appraisal interview and both job satisfaction and performance. The results were:

- Appraisee reported job satisfaction increased by the interview: 30 per cent.
- Appraisee thought job performance had improved (or was likely to) as a result of the appraisal: 40 per cent.

These are the main findings relating to organizational purposes and objectives. Other studies relating to individual needs and more specific objectives will be dealt with in subsequent chapters in Section 5. What then are the main conclusions to be drawn from these studies? Meyer *et al.*'s (1965) work confirmed what writers such as McGregor and Maier had claimed before, that managers find it very difficult to be judge and counsellor, and that salary issues should be kept apart from the counselling aspects of appraisal such as reviewing past performance, setting goals for the future and identifying training needs. They also highlighted the potential problems of excessive criticism. Dulewicz *et al.* (1976) point out the benefits to be derived from appraisal in terms of increasing communication between boss and subordinate, the increased value of appraisal over time, and the beneficial effects on subsequent performance of seeing action points implemented. Further work on investigating how effective follow-up action proves to be would seem to be potentially valuable. Our experience suggests that follow-up on action points is very patchy, both within and between organizations. Fletcher and Williams (1985) reviewed the results from seven organizations which had relatively sophisticated appraisal schemes. Yet while only a small percentage of appraisees were against the schemes, performance weaknesses and training needs were only discussed in around one-half of the interviews. Furthermore, in terms of perceived effects, only about one-third of respondents reported that their job satisfaction had increased, and only 40 per cent claimed that their job performance had improved. It would appear to be important not only to spend much time and effort in the initial design and development of the appraisal process, but also to monitor its effectiveness closely and to try to ensure that it continues to meet its original purposes after managers have used it for a few years. Inevitably, some will become a bit lax and careless, while others will actually abuse the system in order to meet their own ends.

NEEDS OF THE PARTICIPANTS IN THE APPRAISAL PROCESS

There is, then, no shortage of organizational objectives which performance appraisal is meant to tackle. In the vast majority of cases, the nature of the appraisal scheme will entail some discussion of performance between managers and subordinates. It is here that the major problems tend to arise, for whatever the aims of appraisal outlined by the organization, the participants—the appraiser and appraisee—are likely to have their own agenda. As will be seen, those agendas not only frequently clash with each other, but they are by no means certain to line up with the objectives of the appraisal scheme as a whole.

Needs and motives of appraisees

There is little doubt that in all but the most simple jobs, people want feedback on how they are doing. Such feedback potentially satisfies the individual's need for information on progress, facilitates performance improvement and provides reassurance. The extent to which feedback is made available on a day-to-day basis varies greatly (Larson, 1984), but in the majority of instances it seems to be perceived as inadequate. Several studies reported by Anstey, Fletcher, and Walker (1976) showed that appraisees consistently rated this as the most important function of appraisal from their perspective.

However, wanting to discuss performance and to hear what the appraiser's view is does not imply willingness to accept that view. As Maier (1958) pointed out long ago, there is a considerable danger that criticism will lead to defensiveness on the part of the appraisee, particularly if important reward decisions are based on appraisal data (though not everyone has found that a link with pay is counterproductive; see Prince and Lawler, 1986). So, while subordinates may seek feedback, part of the reason for wanting it may be to refute any possible criticisms and to present themselves in a favourable light. Certainly, there is some evidence that appraisees' responses to critical feedback are often less than positive (Meyer, Kay, and French, 1965); much seems to depend on just how much criticism is conveyed and the style in which it is done (Fletcher, 1987).

This defensiveness is probably moderated by another pressure on the appraisees, namely to 'be reasonable' and to preserve the goodwill of their managers; reacting too strongly may make matters even worse. Nonetheless, the assessment arrived at through the appraisal process is likely to have a strong impact on the individual's self-esteem (Thompson and Dalton, 1970), which in turn has important implications for performance. It is not the case that the appraisees have to have performed particularly badly for adverse consequences to follow the appraisal. Pearce and Porter (1986) found that many appraisees were unhappy to be assessed as 'satisfactory', and that there was a significant and stable drop in organizational commitment for staff so rated after the introduction of an appraisal scheme. Viewed against the findings of Meyer (1975) that most employees perceived their work to be above average, this is not too surprising.

Apart from getting feedback, presenting themselves favourably, trying to sustain a good relationship with the appraiser, defending against criticism and maintaining self-esteem, appraisees may also want to use the appraisal situation to discuss career development issues with their managers. Thus, they have a variety of needs and motives in appraisal that may at times conflict with each other, as well as with the aims of the organization and the objectives of the appraiser.

Needs and motives of appraisers

It often seems to be assumed by those devising appraisal systems that the managers who will have the responsibility for carrying out the appraisals will automatically share their enthusiasm for the exercise—despite almost all the evidence being to the contrary. Ever since McGregor (1957) took his uneasy look at performance appraisal, the literature has reflected the common observation in organizations that managers often try to avoid carrying out appraisals. George (1986) poses the question 'Why is it that managers frequently reject the suggestion that appraisal can help them to manage better and that it represents a worthwhile investment of their time?' An examination of the likely gains and losses of the process from their perspective makes it easy to understand why.

Let us look initially at the various factors that together constitute a marked disincentive to appraisers. In the first place, there is frequently a degree of unease about being in a position to give a fair and accurate assessment. They may be aware of the subjective nature of appraisal and of the potential for it to be affected by bias of one kind or another; there is certainly good evidence to support such anxieties (Mitchell and Wood, 1980; Bernardin and Cardy, 1982). They may also feel less confident that they have seen enough of their subordinates' performance in the review period to make a balanced assessment of it; it is relevant to note that Fletcher (1978) found that managers who had more frequent day-to-day communications with their subordinates achieved more positive appraisal outcomes.

In the light of their own qualms, it is not surprising to find that managers are apprehensive when approaching the appraisal task. Of course, not all of them will feel this way, but the evidence suggests it will be true for the majority; ironically, it may be the ones who worry least who have most to be concerned about! The appraisees will have their own views on how well placed their managers are to form an accurate impression of their work, and if they are not impressed in this respect, the tendency to be defensive will be exacerbated and to some extent justified. As Ilgen and Favero (1985) point out, it is quite possible that an appraiser will give more favourable ratings than are actually warranted in order to avoid a confrontation. The appraisal is usually a brief annual event, but its effects can be detrimental to the working relationships between managers and subordinates for months if things go wrong. And they are quite likely to; the degree of openness required to handle such situations will probably not materialize without an atmosphere of mutual trust and respect—something which is conspicuously lacking in many employing organizations (George, 1986).

Even when appraisers are in the pleasant position of genuinely having only good things to say about subordinates, it may be a mixed blessing for them. They are often concerned about creating expectations that cannot be met, or, worse still in the eyes of some of them, the expectations will be met and they will lose their best people through transfer or promotion.

Surely, though, there are some positive aspects of appraisal for the managers involved. Is is not in their interests that their subordinates perform well (for which they need feedback)? Will not the organization reward managers who take their role in staff development seriously? From what has been said above, it can be seen that the appraisers may have considerable doubts about the value of the appraisal process for achieving the objectives set for it and for them. Napier and Latham (1986) found that many managers saw little or no practical value in conducting appraisals, regardless of whether the feedback given to subordinates is primarily favourable or unfavourable. Given that kind of jaundiced but not unreasonable view, one can hardly be surprised that appraisals are not taken seriously or are avoided altogether. For the majority of managers, they are rather a high-risk activity with little tangible reward. Organizations frequently pay lip service to the importance of developing subordinates, but little beyond that. The consequence of not carrying out appraisals is more often than not a deafening silence. When they are done, the amount of notice taken of them outside the two parties immediately involved tends to be limited.

In this section, we have looked at the needs and motives of the principal characters in the appraisal drama (and for some of them, that is what it tends to feel like). Just as there is no shortage of organizational objectives for appraisal, so there is an abundance of personal motivation inherent in the situation. Unfortunately, put together these present a promising scenario for conflict. Small wonder that appraisers and appraisees tend to come away from appraisal interviews with differing impressions and recollections (Sofer and Tuchman, 1970; Ilgen *et al.*, 1981), or that the whole exercise is inclined to become what George (1986) describes as 'a grand annual convulsion, more of a bureaucratic colossus than a means of ensuring continuing development of people'. What all this amounts to, however, is that appraisal schemes are too often poorly designed, over-ambitious in their aims yet inadequately resourced, and fail to take into account the participants. The next section will consider how something can be salvaged from the findings on the problems that appraisal systems have encountered. Thereby, more successful examples of such systems may be developed in the future.

DESIGNING AN EFFECTIVE APPRAISAL SYSTEM

An appraisal system should be at the very heart of an organization's overall human resources procedures. As we have seen, it has to meet not only a number of organizational objectives, but also a variety of the individual needs of employees. Furthermore, it has to be in tune with the prevailing culture of the organization if it is not to be quickly rejected by that body. Success is very difficult to achieve at the best of times, and cannot be assured by the design of a sound paperwork system. Appraisal and counselling are, after all, really about interpersonal relationships, not about form filling; they are about using the information collected on a continuing basis; and about ensuring action which will help the organization to manage its staff and its staff to develop.

George (1986) sets out six fundamental conditions which need to be satisfied if an appraisal system is to have any chance of being successful. It must:

1. demonstrably have the rigorous and wholehearted support of senior managers;
2. be organizationally valid and meet genuine organizational needs;
3. be socially acceptable, i.e. people must be willing to use it;
4. be administratively convenient;
5. fit the managerial style and overall culture of the organization;
6. be supported by extensive training and development work geared to building skills, knowledge, confidence and understanding.

He goes on to point out that it is mistaken to regard appraisal as merely a technique or a discrete process with an easily definable boundary. It is about how management is to be conducted 'in toto', part and parcel of the management process in the widest sense.

The context

So how do we go about designing such a wide ranging procedure? Two of the key processes to adopt from the outset are involvement and commitment. Not only does one need to have the support and commitment of senior management from the beginning, but one also needs to involve line managers in the design since they will in fact be the people who have to operate the system. They must be consulted, either *en masse* or a representative sample, so that the scheme accords with their style of management, has face validity and is administratively convenient for them to operate. It should also fit in with other existing procedures and practices. It is useless for an appraisal to recommend development opportunities if they are not available. Furthermore, the information generated must be used, especially by line managers if their staff are going to benefit, and if the system is going to encourage closer communication between managers and staff. In addition, managers responsible for compensation, training, staff development, career planning, etc., are also likely to receive parts of the total output of the system. Therefore, it is important to seek ideas and canvass opinions of all potential users during the development phase, and to gain the commitment to the final product of as many users as possible if the system is to have any chance of being accepted and integrated. Finally, if there are trade unions or staff associations representing employees within the organization, then they should be consulted and kept informed.

The prevailing culture of the organization should also have a major influence on the design of an appraisal system. If the climate is characterized by open communications and trust between managers and staff; if employees are motivated by positive rewards and encouragement, rather than by threats of punishment and criticism; and if the organization is flexible and unbureaucratic, then the appraisal system should reflect these values. If the organization is closed, punitive and bureaucratic, then an attempt to introduce a highly open and flexible system would be doomed to failure from the outset.

The organizational level of staff for whom the system is being devised is also highly relevant. A management appraisal system is likely to be designed to meet many more objectives and to be much more complex than one for, say, clerical staff or operators. The needs of the appraisees may well be different, while the appraisal and counselling skills of the appraisers might well need to be given special attention. These issues have a direct bearing on the content of the system, to which we will now turn.

Purposes of the system

As we have seen there is a wide range of possible purposes for any appraisal scheme. These relate both to organizational objectives and to the needs of the appraisees. Some of these have been shown to be incompatible with others, and one of the main reasons why systems have failed in the past has been that they were too ambitious and were designed to try to meet too many different, and sometimes conflicting objectives. One of the key design principles is to limit the number of purposes of the system, and to keep it as simple as possible.

We have already mentioned the problems arising from using appraisal for both performance review and for counselling and goal setting, since this puts appraisers in the role of judge and counsellor. This conflict typifies the traditional overall question of whether the system should be geared primarily to organizational needs such as rewarding performance and promoting talent, or primarily towards individual needs such as feedback and identifying development needs. If the answer is to both, then the solution is to maximize the time period between salary review and the appraisal interview and to remove salary issues from the agenda. However, some people have argued that a completely different vehicle is required for salary review purposes. This may be the ideal solution, but the increased administrative burden it entails has deterred most organizations from adopting it. This subject will be discussed further in Chapter 5.3 below.

Identification of long-term potential is another purpose which many organizations have divorced from the appraisal system. One reason is that, like salary, the discussion of long-term potential can be demotivating for the employee and undermine the basis for a constructive discussion. Furthermore, the appraiser is unlikely to be in a position to assess accurately the future requirements at much higher levels. Allied to this, however, is the argument that the requirements of jobs at a much higher level are very different to those at the current level, and so performance in the current job is not a reliable and valid guide anyway. Following this line of reasoning, some organizations have a totally separate appraisal system for appraising long-term potential, geared to the requirements of jobs at senior levels. Others have moved from appraisal to the assessment centre approach, whereby the requirements of senior jobs are simulated in a number of different situational exercises, and employees' performance and potential are assessed by senior managers. A detailed description of this approach appears in Chapters 3.7 (above) and 5.8. Yet another approach is to evaluate long-term potential by psychometric assessment. This usually involves the use of psychometric tests of mental ability, personality and motivation, and an in-depth interview by an occupational psychologist. Such psychometric testing may or may not form part of assessment centre procedures, so in some cases, psychometric assessment is a subset of the assessment centre process. This is another way of assessing the underutilized abilities and capacities of the individual.

Promotion potential for the next level is also a topic of some sensitivity, especially for those who have probably reached the limits of their likely advancement. While most organizations still utilize their appraisal system for assessing it, the subject is sometimes not put on the agenda for the appraisal interview. However, suitability for transfer to another job is often of great relevance to many employees, and is discussed. But it is advisable, if the organization's culture is not open, or if appraisers' skills are lacking, for promotability, like salary, to be kept separate from the appraisal.

Overall, it is desirable to minimize the number of purposes the scheme is designed to meet and to keep the evaluative components as separate as possible from those dealing with the individual's past performance, discussion of future objectives, ways of improving performance, training needs and future career. By doing this, the chances of the appraisal leading to real improvements in performance, skills and satisfaction will be greatly increased.

What is appraised

In the large majority of schemes, appraisees' performance is evaluated on the basis of specific competences, i.e. behaviours, skills, abilities, personality characteristics, or else on the basis of results and performance, i.e. the degree to which specific objectives, goals or targets have been attained. Indeed, some schemes embrace both approaches. Appraising results is widely used, especially at managerial levels, and has grown out of the work of Peter Drucker in the United States, and John Humble in the United Kingdom, whose Management by Objectives (MbO) approach was very popular in the 1960s and 1970s. At the beginning of the appraisal period the boss will sit down with the subordinate and agree a list of the main objectives (usually five or six) that should be achieved during the next twelve months. Objectives should be specified as clearly as possible, and quantifiable criteria established to enable the appraisal to be as precise and objective as possible. Since circumstances often change during the appraisal period, it is advisable to review objectives after about six months, to determine whether they need amending. At the end of the period, performance and results are usually discussed during the appraisal interview, and new objectives are set for the next period.

Establishing objectives and reviewing performance are particularly complex and demanding tasks if done effectively. Precision in defining objectives and criteria is difficult, circumstances often change during the period under review, external factors over which the appraisee has no control give ample opportunity for rationalization and defensiveness, and ultimately conclusions are highly subjective. A detailed description of this approach is presented in Chapter 5.4 below.

Most jobs below management level, and even some management jobs, do not require incumbents to meet clearly definable objectives anyway, so other characteristics need to be appraised. In the past, many schemes incorporated the appraisal of personality characteristics but this proved unsatisfactory for a number of reasons. First, descriptions of the traits are usually rather imprecise and so ratings tend to be highly subjective and unreliable. Problems such as halo, central tendency and leniency, which will be dealt with in the next chapter, become commonplace, and disagreements between appraisers and appraisees are very difficult to resolve. Another major criticism of using personality traits is that they tend to be, or should be, fairly enduring qualities of the individual which are not readily amenable to development. Therefore, it is difficult to derive action points and to discuss such weaknesses in a constructive way in a counselling interview. To avoid these shortcomings, the emphasis has shifted to the appraisal of job behaviours or competences. These characteristics should be derived from a systematic job analysis to identify what are the crucial elements of jobs to be covered in the appraisal scheme. Techniques such as repertory grid, critical incidents or structured questionnaires have proved to be particularly valuable for eliciting crucial job competences. Examples of such behaviours include: planning, organizing, analysis, communication skills, interpersonal skills, assertiveness, stress tolerance, and so on. Each one should be defined in clear behavioural terms, based on job analysis results, so as to convey a clear meaning and to relate to observable behaviour, thereby reducing the highly subjective nature of appraisal which can be so counterproductive. Competences should also be amenable to development. There is a large body of evidence available on the various appraisal methods and scales available, and some of this will be referred to in the chapters below.

Who appraises whom?

The next issue to address is who does the appraising? Usually it is the 'father', i.e. the immediate boss, who appraises performance and carries out the appraisal interview, since he or she is in the best position to do so, having far more direct knowledge of the individual's performance and of the job requirements and context. But to rely on one person's view can make the appraisal of performance rather too subjective and personal. The answer, of course, is to obtain views of the appraisee's performance from at least one other person who has had extensive contact with, and therefore detailed knowledge of, the individual's work. But here lies the problem, for in many jobs there is not another individual who has the requisite level of knowledge. Many organizations get the grandfather, i.e. the boss's boss, to act as the 'second rater' but, being much further removed from day-to-day contact, he or she can have either a very superficial or a highly selective view of the appraisee's performance. Hence these judgements can be at best of questionable value, and at worst highly misleading. The best compromise would appear to be to make the system highly flexible, and to give the 'father' the responsibility of getting additional appraiser(s) who have had close exposure to the appraisee to fill in an appraisal form. In a 'matrix organization' the problem should not arise, but even in other types of organization there is likely to be at least one other individual at a higher level, or even at the same level, who has had close contact over an extended period. There are also advantages in getting the appraisee to carry out a self-assessment and to share this information with the appraiser before the interview takes place. The subject of who appraises whom will be dealt with at greater length in Chapter 5.6.

Appraiser training

As noted above, performance appraisal is really about interpersonal relationships, and particularly the boss–subordinate relationship. To be an effective appraiser and counsellor, a boss needs a wide range of skills, many of which he or she does not possess at the outset of a career. This is probably the main reason why so many managers avoid doing appraisal, or if they do go through the motions, do it badly, with predictable consequences in terms of strained relationships, dissatisfaction, alienation and ultimately a lack of credibility in the appraisal scheme itself. Training courses for appraisal and counselling skills can make a dramatic improvement if they are well designed and include not only knowledge but also skills training, involving practice at completing performance review forms and carrying out appraisal interviews. These are usually based on role-plays, but a few training courses give trainees the opportunity to appraise performance and give feedback on actual, rather than on simulated, performance. Some key points on designing an effective training course and on the important skills which appraisers should acquire are covered in Chapter 5.7.

CONCLUSIONS

In this chapter we have provided an overview of the very extensive and complex subject of performance appraisal and counselling. We have looked at the subject from the organization's point of view, in terms of expected outcomes, and also from the individual's perspective. We have highlighted some of the available research evidence on the subject and have then identified some of the key issues which need to be tackled when designing and implementing an appraisal scheme. In Chapters 5.2 to 5.8, many of these issues will be covered in much greater detail.

REFERENCES

Anstey, E., Fletcher, C., and Walker, J. (1976). *Staff Appraisal and Development*. George Allen & Unwin, London.
Bernardin, H.J., and Cardy, R.L. (1982). Appraisal accuracy: The ability and motivation to remember the past, *Public Personnel Management*, **11**, 352–7.

Drenth, P.J.D. (1984). Personnel appraisal, in P.J.D. Drenth, H. Thierry, P.J. Willems, and C.J. de Wolff (eds), *Handbook of Work and Organizational Psychology*. Wiley, Chichester.

Dulewicz, V., Fletcher, C., and Walker, J. (1976). Job appraisal reviews three years on, *Management Services in Government*, **31**, August.

Fletcher, C. (1978). Manager/subordinate communication and leadership style; A field study of their relationship to perceived outcomes of appraisal interviews, *Personnel Review*, **7**, 59–62.

Fletcher, C. (1987). The effects of performance review in appraisal; evidence and implications, *Journal of Management Development*, **5**, 3–12.

Fletcher, C., and Williams, R. (1985). *Performance Appraisal and Career Development*. Hutchinson, London.

George, J. (1986). Appraisal in the public sector: Dispensing with the big stick, *Personnel Management*, May, 32–5.

Ilgen, D.R., Peterson, R.B., Martin, B.A., and Boeschen, D.A. (1981). Supervisor and subordinate reactions to performance appraisal sessions, *Organizational Behavior and Human Performance*, **28**, 311–20.

Ilgen, D.R., and Favero, J.L. (1985). Limits in generalization from psychological research to performance appraisal processes, *Academy of Management Review*, **10**, 311–21.

Larson, J.R. (1984). The performance feedback process; A preliminary model, *Organizational Behavior and Human Performance*, **33**, 42–76.

Long, P. (1986). *Performance Appraisal Revisited*. Institute of Personnel Management, London.

Maier, N.R.F. (1958). Three types of appraisal interview, *Personnel*, March–April, 27–40.

McGregor, D. (1957). An uneasy look at performance appraisal, *Harvard Business Review*, **35**, 89–94.

Meyer, H.H., Kay, E., and French, J.P.R. (1965). Split roles in performance appraisal, *Harvard Business Review*, **43**, 123–9.

Meyer, H.H. (1975). The pay-for-performance dilemma, *Organizational Dynamics*, **3**, 39–50.

Mitchell, T.R., and Wood, R.W. (1980). Supervisors' responses to subordinate poor performance: A test of the attributional model, *Organizational Behavior and Human Performance*, **25**, 123–8.

Napier, N.K., and Latham, G.P. (1986). Outcome expectancies of people who conduct performance appraisals, *Personnel Psychology*, **39**, 827–37.

Pearce, J.L., and Porter, L.W. (1986). Employee responses to formal performance appraisal feedback, *Journal of Applied Psychology*, **71**, 211–18.

Prince, J.B., and Lawler, E.E. (1986). Does salary discussion hurt the development performance appraisal? *Organizational Behavior and Human Performance*, **37**, 367–75.

Sofer, C., and Tuchman, M. (1970). Appraisal interviews and the structure of colleague relations, *Sociological Review*, **8**, 365–92.

Thompson, P.H., and Dalton, G.W. (1970). Performance appraisal: managers beware, *Harvard Business Review*, **48**, 149–57.

Williams, R.S., Walker, J., and Fletcher, C. (1977). International review of staff appraisal practices: current trends and issues, *Public Personnel Management*, January/February, 5–12.

Chapter 5.2

On Ratings and Rating Scales

JOHN D. HANDYSIDE

57 Gloucester Road, London SW7 4QN, UK

THE BASIC IDEA, AND SOME USEFUL FORMATS

The following simple rating form, which was used to short-list candidates for a
specialist managerial post, illustrates some of the issues that need to be dealt with.

	Low						High
Intellectual quality	1	2	3	4	5	6	7
Educational qualification	1	2	3	4	5	6	7
Professional qualification	1	2	3	4	5	6	7
Relevance of experience	1	2	3	4	5	6	7
Managerial abilities	1	2	3	4	5	6	7
Emotional balance	1	2	3	4	5	6	7
Drive and ambition	1	2	3	4	5	6	7
Health	1	2	3	4	5	6	7
Availability (salary: notice: etc)	1	2	3	4	5	6	7
Likeableness	1	2	3	4	5	6	7
Tough-minded realism and maturity	1	2	3	4	5	6	7
Overall rating	1	2	3	4	5	6	7

First, one needs to decide what assessment headings one is going to include—
and the extent and detail to which they will be defined.

Second, one needs to attach some sort of comparative format to the headings—
and again to decide the extent and detail of definition of the steps which will be
used.

Assessment and Selection in Organizations   Edited by P. Herriot
© 1989 John Wiley & Sons Ltd

And, finally, one may wish to state the basis on which the 'Overall rating' will be arrived at from the evidence of the separate assessment headings.

In this example all three of these requirements are dealt with at an extremely cursory level, and indeed the third is left entirely open.

Nonetheless in the actual situation in which two interviewers (sitting together) saw fourteen candidates for relatively brief interviews (i.e. about 40 minutes)— the candidates having been selected from a field of some 50 applicants on the basis of their letters of application and CV data on a standardized personal history form, this very simple and inexpensive rating form, which was completed independently by the two interviewers immediately after the interview, proved very useful in focusing the evaluation of the candidates and speeding up the process of deciding a final short-list of three strong candidates.

The reason why it worked effectively was that the selectors had discussed it in advance, and had agreed on what each of the headings would be taken to mean. On the 1 to 7 scale 4 meant 'what could reasonably be expected as the average for serious contenders for the post'; 1, 2, and 3 represented deficits below that level; 5, 6, and 7 would mean increasingly impressive quality, and that the distribution would approximate to 'normal', i.e. that 4 would be the most frequent, and 1 and 7 the least frequent levels.

In the majority of assessment situations, however, this preliminary agreement by the people who will be completing the rating forms cannot be taken for granted. Particularly in such cases as 'annual performance reviews' where large numbers of different raters are each reporting on quite small numbers of subordinates, it is rarely practicable to get all the raters to meet and agree on what the various headings are going to be taken to mean, and to agree on the metric of the various steps of the scales.

For this reason, in most situations, the obvious answer is to use the wording of the form itself to define the meaning of the headings, and of the steps in the comparative scale. This can result in formats such as the following, which comes from a validation study of the selection of research chemists.

Constructive imagination. Freshness of approach. Intuitive originality

| Text-bookish in his thinking. Sticks to precedents. Applies old approaches to new problems. Tends to get into and stay 'in a rut'. | ← Applies □ | Tends to ← □ | Neutral □ | Tends to → □ | → Applies □ | Comes up with novel ideas. Shows marked originality. Has an 'intuitive' facility — gets 'feelings' about possible ways of tackling things. |

Problem formulation. Ability to define research problems in fruitful ways

| Lacking in ability to sort out the issues. His initial statement of the problem tends to be complicated and untidy, and does not lead to clear insights. | ☐ | ☐ | ☐ | ☐ | ☐ | Defines problems incisively. Sorts out the crucial issues. Produces striking analogies which offer illuminating 'models'. Can 'structure' a complex problem so that its various parts and their inter-relationships are clear. |

Effectiveness with people. Ability to work well with others. Capacity to contribute to team effectiveness

| Upsets people needlessly. Sours the atmosphere. Drains other people's enthusiasm. Damages morale and hinders team achievement. | ☐ | ☐ | ☐ | ☐ | ☐ | An exceptionally good team worker. Wins respect for his contributions and for his ability to work cooperatively. People like to help and work with him. |

Accuracy. Carefulness. Scientific integrity

| Not sufficiently careful. Inclined to 'bodge' results. Lacking in absolute scientific standards. His work needs to be checked. | ☐ | ☐ | ☐ | ☐ | ☐ | Meticulous. Checks his results scrupulously. Absolute in his sense of scientific integrity. Never tries to 'cover up'. |

Energy. Finishing power. Ability to drive a project to completion

| Apt to lose momentum. Has difficulty in maintaining enough drive to carry projects through to completion. Tends to leave things without tying up the ends. | ☐ | ☐ | ☐ | ☐ | ☐ | Maintains energy effectively. Carries projects through to completion. Ties up the stray ends tidily. |

The form which was used for this validity study took four sides of A4 paper, and contained eighteen scales of this kind, each with both ends of the concept defined at about this length, and each given the same 'Applies; Tends to; Neutral; Tends to; Applies' scale of steps. A final 'Overall rating' was asked for as well, and had eleven boxes with simple adjective descriptions from 'Unsuitable' to 'Outstandingly excellent'. In practice the raters did not use the two extreme boxes, but spread their overall ratings from 'Barely adequate' to 'Excellent'.

An alternative format—and 'format' is a well-chosen word in this connection, since one often needs to decide on matters of typography and layout in order to keep the amount of paper that raters will have to handle within tolerable limits—is to use relatively short descriptive headings and to define the steps at greater length. This can produce scales of the form:

Drive. Application. Concentration on things that matter. Acceptance of responsibility

☐ Hard working and conscientious in normal duties, but inclined to take a limited view of the responsibilities of his post. Does not seem to see it as a part of his job to accept real responsibility for the achievement of broad business objectives. Inclined to limit himself to the fulfilment of day-to-day tasks and routines.

☐ Tough and combative in his perception of his responsibilities. Forces the achievement of short-term objectives, but at some cost of continuing cooperation and support from other people who get upset by his steam-roller methods.

☐ Doesn't seem to have much steam or ambition. Makes no special effort, and needs to be given detailed specific assignments and deadlines.

☐ Puts up an impressive front of activity and detailed plans and strategies, but the actual results tend to be disappointingly vague and wordy.

☐ Quietly and unobtrusively determined. Is deeply committed to the attainment of major business objectives. Gets results without making difficulties or fuss.

☐ Does not accept real responsibility. Shows little personal commitment to the achievement of work objectives. Significantly lacking in this respect.

Leadership of subordinates. Generation of response. Creation of morale and enthusiasm

☐ Delegates responsibility, but keeps the authority in his own hands. People carry him, but he takes the credit when things go well. Doesn't carry enough of the real load himself.

☐ Has little enthusiasm for taking a leadership role. Abdicates his responsibility for organizing and controlling the work of his subordinates.

☐ Is an exceptionally good leader. Is respected by his team for his technical competence, and for his fairness and objectivity in his dealings with people. Runs his unit happily and efficiently. His unit produces good people for promotion to more senior posts.

☐ Assigns tasks clearly and in a sensible way so that his people are using their abilities effectively and there are no muddles about who is responsible for what. Balances the work load. Is objective in judging individual performance, and counsels, trains, and develops his people effectively.

☐ Does not keep subordinates 'in the picture' sufficiently. Tends to be secretive about plans and projects in order to bolster up his position as 'the decision maker'. His people feel that they are being used as cogs in the machinery rather than as a self-motivating team.

☐ Ducks difficult decisions. Not prepared to exert control or discipline when he ought to. Does not intervene sufficiently to ensure that the work is evenly spread among his people.

Written work — Reports, Memoranda, Correspondence

☐ Not good at expressing himself on paper. His style lacks both clarity and conciseness. One has to struggle to find his meaning.

☐ Usually turns out a literate and understandable document. No special gifts of elegance or style, but he manages to get the facts across with reasonable clarity and brevity.

☐ Prolix and tortuous in the way he organizes material. Imposes too much on the reader's efforts and patience. Needs to learn to edit his drafts properly and stop wasting other people's time.

☐ Unfailingly lucid in his written work. His documents are clear, well organized, cogent, graceful in choice of phrase, and refreshingly succinct and to the point.

☐ Carries the virtue of brevity to the point of terse obscurity. One has to ask him to expand and explain his drafts.

☐ The style and presentation are usually fine, it is the intellectual quality of the content which is usually the problem!

☐ The intellectual quality is good, but the grammar and/or spelling are atrocious!

These three scales, which were among the ten which were used in a 4-page annual performance review form for managerial staff in a large organization, require the rater to tick the description which most nearly matches the typical performance of the person being rated.

They have the advantage that the descriptions tend to define the behaviour that the organization wishes to encourage and reward, and this can be salutary as much for the manager who is filling out the form as for the person who is being reported on!

The problem with this format is that the 'metric' is not readily apparent. Indeed the order in which the statements are printed is deliberately randomized. A necessary step in the method is to 'scale' the statements on a basis of their comparative desirability. This was done by the Thurstone technique, which required that all the statements, and substantial numbers of others which were drafted but which did not eventually get into the printed version, were each typed on cards and the packs of the resulting cards were given to a sample of raters with the instructions: 'Please sort these statements into six piles such that all the statements in any one pile are about equally favourable descriptions, and that the differences between the favourability of statements in each pile are about equal. You can also have a "reject" pile for statements that you wish to reject on the basis that they are unclear, or that their relative favourability is too difficult to decide. You can put as many or as few cards into each pile as you wish.'

This process of statement judging is repeated for up to about 30 different judges, and then the statements which show the least 'scatter', i.e. about which the judges agree as to the extent of favourability, are selected for use in the printed version of the form. A lay-over key is then produced which gives values from 0 to 5 for a tick in any particular box on the rating form. In this instance the 'score values' for the statements quoted above came out as 2, 3, 1, 1, 5, 0; and 1, 0, 5, 4, 1, 1; and 1, 3, 1, 5, 1, 2, 2.

There was also, in the case of this performance review form, a ten point 'Overall rating' using simple adjectival descriptions:

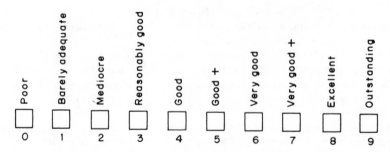

—which the raters were asked to complete after they had put their ticks for the sub-heading scales.

GOING FROM 'ASPECT' RATINGS TO AN 'OVERALL' RATING

As will be seen from these examples, the process of defining aspects of performance and then rating them separately, can be useful in concentrating the minds of raters on what they are being asked to do.

But for most purposes the final decision needs to be based on an amalgam of the component ratings, i.e. 'which of these candidates should the job be offered to?' or 'what salary adjustment should be made for this employee?' or even 'if we have to shed some employees, which are the ones we can best afford to dispense with?'

The 'Overall rating' is therefore usually the key issue, though the component ratings are the ones that are generally most acceptable as a basis for discussion with the employee in cases where there is 'open' reporting, as they indicate the particular aspects on which the employee can seek to improve his or her performance.

It is very rare to find any standard method of moving from the profile of the component ratings to an overall rating, set out on the form as a guide for the raters. They are expected to 'weight one thing with another, and come up with a sensible overall evaluation which takes account of all the evidence'—this is known as the 'clinical wholistic' method!

In fact it is possible to devise sensible and defensible methods of amalgamating the aspect ratings, which do not depend on the arbitrary 'clinical' insights of different raters. One such technique which has proved useful in quite large-scale applications is the 'importance-weighted vector-added' method.

This requires an additional rating to be given for each of the component scales. The rater is given an extra box for each sub-scale into which he is asked to enter an 'importance rating' or a 'visibility rating'—a four point scale of '0 = not called for in the job' or 'the job offers no scope for this sort of behaviour to be shown'; '1 = of some importance' or 'the job offers only a little scope for this to be shown'; '2 = of substantial importance' or 'the job calls for a moderate amount of this sort of behaviour'; '3 = very important in the job'—has been found to be appropriate for this purpose.

These qualifiers are inserted because it is often necessary to make one reporting system cover people in a variety of jobs within an organization, and what is important in one post may be of very little consequence in a different post.

An instruction is given that if a particular component rating is given zero importance or zero 'visibility', it is not necessary for the rater to give a rating for that scale. Apart from that no further demand is made on the way the rater completes the form.

The Personnel Department however carries out some simple calculations based on the ratings given, and is able to check the consistency of the 'overall rating' against the profile of the 'aspect' ratings. The way this is done makes use of 'vector addition'.

It is clear that simple addition of the scores on the aspect scales is not a logically defensible way of arriving at the 'overall rating'; to do so would mean that one would be perpetrating such nonsenses as assuming, for example, that high levels of drive and application compensate for deficits of such things as sound judgement and technical expertise—when clearly very energetic performance applied to ill-advised courses of action can be much more disastrous than less energetic application of ill-judged decisions.

To avoid this sort of nonsense which would be generated by simply adding up the component scores, one moves to vector addition. This involves the idea that conceptually independent aspects of performance can be treated as dimensions in a multi-dimensional space, and that what one wants to take as the 'overall assessment' is the total distance that the person is placed from the zero point— irrespective of the direction away from that zero point. The direction gives the qualitative answer, but the distance gives the quantitative answer.

The mathematics involved are straightforward; they follow directly from Pythagoras' theorem that the length of the third side of a right angled triangle is

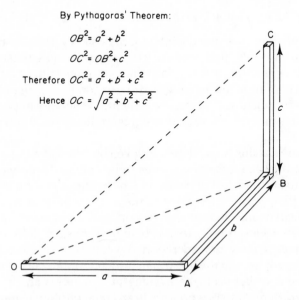

By Pythagoras' Theorem:

$$OB^2 = a^2 + b^2$$

$$OC^2 = OB^2 + c^2$$

Therefore $OC^2 = a^2 + b^2 + c^2$

Hence $OC = \sqrt{a^2 + b^2 + c^2}$

Figure 1   The principle of vector addition

the square root of the sum of the squares of the two sides which are at right angles to each other. This means that when one has a lot of 'conceptually independent' dimensions one can arrive at a defensible 'overall rating' by regarding it as the distance from the zero point, i.e. simply by quoting it as the square root of the sum of the squares of the scores on the various aspect scales (see Figure 1).

There is a slight complication introduced by the 'importance rating' element in arriving at the final 'vector added score'. The score on each sub-scale is multiplied by its importance weight (i.e. 0, 1, 2, or 3) before the square is calculated, then the squares are summed and divided by the sum of the squares of the weights. This gets rid of individual raters' tendencies to rate everything high or low for importance, but leaves in the relative weight effect. Finally, in order to get rid of decimal points it is convenient to multiply the final square root by a constant value of, say, 20 and quote it to the nearest whole number.

Thus the picture from the profile of the aspect ratings is converted to an index number, and this number can be compared against the 'overall rating' that has been awarded by the rater.

By this means two measures of 'overall performance' can be derived from the rater's answers, and if they agree reasonably closely they show that the rater was being consistent in his judgement. If they disagree the form can be referred back to the rater with a note 'Your comments about this chap don't really line up very well with the overall rating you gave him. Would you like to reconsider your judgement in this case?'

This technique was found to be effective and acceptable to both raters and ratees in one large company over a number of years, and is probably well worth consideration for use elsewhere.

USING MORE THAN ONE RATER PER RATEE

This sort of method of checking the internal consistency of the results of ratings is an advance, but it is a limited one. All that it does is show whether the rater is reasonably self-consistent. But suppose that a different rater had been asked to give a view—would he or she have agreed? It is a common-sense observation that some judges are harsh and some are lenient, so should important decisions affecting people's promotion or salary progress be made purely on the basis of one rater's answers?

The level of correlations between ratings given by different raters reporting on the performance of the same employees tends to be only of the order of 0.55 to 0.75, which shows that a good deal depends on which rater is making the report.

This means that, in the interests of fairness, there is lot to be said for getting ratings by more than one rater for each person, and either taking the average, or if the raters disagree substantially to ask them to reconsider their views and see if they can produce a more agreed report. By this means one can increase the reliability of the ratings, and the Spearman Brown formula can be used to estimate the likely agreement between the average of two raters and the hypothetical average of two different raters who were in an equal position to judge the persons who are being rated. The formula is that the expected correlation for the average of pairs of raters is $[2r/(1 + r)]$ where r is the correlation between individual raters, so if the correlation between two raters was 0.5 the probable correlation between the averages of pairs of raters would be 0.667, and 0.55 would become 0.71, and 0.6 would become 0.75, and 0.65 would become 0.788.

These are better, but they still leave quite a lot of chance effect in the results.

However, if one uses a double rating method such as the one described earlier, where one has both a vector-added score from the component scales, and an overall rating by each of the raters, one can compute the inter-correlations of all the four measures and use the results to estimate the reliability of the combination. In a study of this kind which used the performance ratings of 1566 senior staff from one company, the present author obtained the following correlation matrix:

	(1)	(2)	(3)	(4)
(1) Vector-added score by 1st rater	*	0.609	0.743	0.495
(2) Vector-added score by 2nd rater		*	0.552	0.694
(3) Overall rating by 1st rater			*	0.614
(4) Overall rating by 2nd rater				*

This meant that the combination of the four measures—two methods by each of two raters—gave an estimated reliability of 0.872, and this was indeed a much more respectable figure than the usual sort of level found for single-rater single-method applications of about 0.6!

When one can get a criterion measure with this sort of reliability one can really begin to run validation studies which will show the detail of the usefulness of various selection predictors, instead of getting the inconclusive and pessimistic indications that appear when correlations between test and criterion measures are heavily 'attenuated' because of the unreliability of the criterion.

HOW MANY STEPS SHOULD A RATING SCALE OFFER?

This is an obvious point which has been subjected to a number of research studies. Unfortunately, however, myths about the results of these studies have become a source of serious misdirection of efforts, and a cause of much wasted time and expense.

There is good evidence that the reliability of measurement increases up to some optimal number of scale steps, and then decreases if more than that number are offered to the raters. But what these experiments tend to overlook is the *purpose* for which the ratings are to be used. Reliability, in the sense of getting the same answer twice if you get the raters to give their judgements twice, is only one of the characteristics that one should seek. At least as important in practical applications is that the ratings should provide useful levels of *discrimination*.

One very large organization took some pride in the fact that it had taken account of the results of one such set of experiments which indicated that there was some loss of reliability when more than about six steps were used. So their exhaustive eight-page annual performance review form ended up with a six point 'overall' scale. The resultant distribution for over 8000 cases was:

Outstanding	4.7%
Very good	55.2%
Good	34.1%
Fair	5.5%
Not quite adequate	0.4%
Unsatisfactory	0.05%

—so they were obtaining virtually no trustworthy discrimination for about 90 per cent of the people who were being reported on! (Trustworthy here being taken in the sense that a one-step difference could very probably be due as much to the severity–leniency of the rater making the report as to real differences in the performance of the people being rated.)

Care should be taken to provide the opportunity for the raters to spread their ratings over a substantial number of steps. Raters can and do distinguish quite a wide range of judgement levels if they are given the opportunity to do so. (There is good evidence from studies that are now over a century old that 'discrimination' in the old-fashioned sense of being able to distinguish many rather than only a few levels of quality, is a part of what is generally regarded as good intellectual ability!)

If you give the raters ten or eleven points for an 'overall rating' you can always group up the results if there is evidence that the reliability is being reduced as a consequence. But if you give them only five or six points there is no way you can later break down the groupings if you find that the distribution you obtain does not allow you to pick out the sorts of proportion that you require for particular purposes, e.g. to select the top 10% or so for consideration for a programme of accelerated career development.

It is particularly important to see that ratings which are used for selection applications have sufficient spread to ensure that there are at the very least two or three steps which cover the range for the people who actually get selected. Otherwise it is impossible to do any validation because all the people who are hired will have the same rating, and there is no follow-up data on the people who were not hired.

The following tabulation shows how the 'normal curve' breaks up into proportions depending on the number of categories being offered. It can provide some guidance as to the number of steps that one should offer if one has a particular purpose in mind.

Proportions falling into each category when the 'normal curve' is divided into different numbers of equally spaced categories along the baseline.

Categories

2	50%	50%									
3	20%	60%	20%								
4	10%	40%	40%	10%							
5	6%	24%	40%	24%	6%						
6	4%	15%	31%	31%	15%	4%					
7	3%	10%	22%	29%	22%	10%	3%				
8	2½%	7%	16%	24%	24%	16%	7%	2½%			
9	2%	5%	12%	19%	23%	19%	12%	5%	2%		
10	2%	4%	9%	15%	20%	20%	15%	9%	4%	2%	
11	2%	3%	7%	12%	17%	18%	17%	12%	7%	3%	2%
12	1%	3%	5%	10%	14%	17%	17%	14%	10%	5%	3%	1%

However, one should also take account of the fact that in most rating applications the actual distributions that are obtained tend to 'skew' quite markedly towards the upper end of the scale, i.e. raters' reports on people usually discriminate much better among the less good performers, but only to a limited extent among the better performers.

As an indication of the sort of skewing that one can anticipate, the following was the distribution obtained with the ten-point 'overall' scale quoted earlier, for a sample of 1566 staff in one company:

Outstanding	16	1%
Excellent	235	15%
Very good+	532	34%
Very good	407	26%
Good+	235	15%
Good	91	6%
Reasonably good	31	2%
Mediocre	12	1%
Barely adequate	4	0.25%
Poor	3	0.20%

This explains the curious 'Very good+' and 'Good+' insertions into the adjectival scale. They were necessary in order to obtain discrimination within what would otherwise have been excessively large categories.

CONVERTING RATINGS TO CARDINAL MEASURES

For any important use of ratings it is almost always desirable to convert adjectival descriptions to numerical values. Adjectives provide 'ordinal' measures, i.e. 'very good' is better than 'good' and 'excellent' is better than 'very good'. That is, the *order* of the descriptions is agreed. But this *does not* necessarily mean that the amount of difference between the steps is equal. For cardinal measures one requires equal differences between the steps.

Cardinal measures are required if one is to be able accurately to carry out arithmetical calculations such as averaging ratings by different judges, or running correlations.

The Thurstone method of getting judges to sort cards bearing the verbal descriptions into piles, which was mentioned earlier, contains one way of obtaining 'equal appearing intervals' as the basic metric, but it is not suitable for simple adjectival 'overall scales'. The other classic psychophysics technique of 'just noticeable differences' as the basis of measurement is too cumbersome for use with most types of rating applications.

Fortunately there is a well-established technique called 'T scoring' which does the job effectively. The key idea is that one takes the total distribution of ratings as the basic information, and then calculates what values each of the adjectival descriptions would have if the distribution was a normal curve, with a mean of 50 and a standard deviation of 10.

An example is the easiest way of showing how this is done. Suppose that one has collected a lot of ratings for a large number of cases, and that the scale of steps which had been used by the raters was 'letter grades' of A+, A, B+, B, C+, C, D, and E, where A+ was the 'excellent' end of the scale, and E was the 'rotten' end of it.

Suppose that the accumulated ratings for a sample of 378 cases had the following distributions:

Characteristic	E	D	C	C+	B	B+	A	A+	(Blank)
Application diligence	7	9	23	194	78	32	19	14	(2)
Technical competence	5	16	60	153	62	36	27	11	(8)
Effectiveness with people	7	10	50	121	49	46	52	31	(12)
Quality of written work	12	27	60	86	125	39	7	4	(18)
TOTAL	31	62	193	554	314	153	105	60	(40)

(The column for 'Blanks' is necessary because in actual applications one virtually always finds that some raters have left some gaps in the forms that they have returned and pressures of deadlines rarely make it possible to chase them up to get them to supply the missing data!)

The first step is to compute the cumulative percentages for the total ratings starting at the lowest of the rating categories, thus:

Rating	Total ratings	Cumulative	Cumulative percent
A+	60	1472	100%
A	105	1412	95.92%
B+	153	1307	88.59%
B	314	1154	78.40%
C+	554	840	57.07%
C	193	286	19.43%
D	62	93	4.21%
E	31	31	2.11%

The next stage is to get the 'mid-point percent' values for each category. This is done by taking the cumulative percent for the step below and adding half of the cases in the category as a percent of the total. Thus for the C+ category the cumulative percent for the step below is 19.43 percent and there are 554 cases in C+ so the mid-point percent is $19.43 + [(\frac{1}{2} \times 544) \times (100/1472)]$ which is [19.43 per cent + 18.82 percent], to give 38.25 percent as the mid-point.

Table 1. 'T scores'

Mid-point percent	T score	Mid-point percent	T score
½	24	49 to 51	50
1	27	52 to 55	51
2	29	56 to 59	52
3	31	60 to 62	53
4	32	63 to 66	54
5 and 6	34	67 to 70	55
7	35	71 to 74	56
8	36	75 and 76	57
9 and 10	37	77 to 80	58
11 and 12	38	81 and 82	59
13 and 14	39	83 and 84	60
15 to 17	40	85 and 86	61
18 and 19	41	87 and 88	62
20 to 22	42	89 and 90	63
23 to 25	43	91 and 92	64
26 to 29	44	93	65
30 to 32	45	94 and 95	66
33 to 36	46	96	68
37 to 40	47	97	69
41 to 44	48	98	71
45 to 48	49	99	73
49 to 51	50	99½	76

(The apparent restriction to values from 24 to 76 is because the T score system is based on a normal distribution with a mean of 50 and a standard deviation of 10. With this SD the two most extreme cases in a sample of 1 million would score 1 and 99.)

Source: Based on the writings of W.A. McCall, *How to Measure in Education* (1929).

The final stage is to convert these 'mid-point percents' to T score values by using the table of T scores (Table 1). What this does is to give the baseline value of a normal distribution with a mean of 50 and a standard deviation of 10 that would cut off the actual percentage for the mid-point value thus:

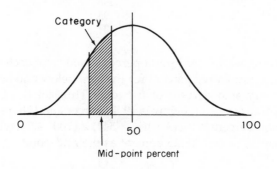

Doing this for our example we obtain:

Rating	Mid-point percent	T score from Table 1
A+	97.96	71
A	92.16	64
B+	83.60	60
B	67.74	55
C+	38.25	47
C	10.77	38
D	4.22	32
E	1.05	27

(**Note**: The T scores in Table 1 have been given for whole number values of the mid-point percents; this can introduce small rounding errors of up to ½ a point in the T scores obtained. If greater accuracy is required the whole of these calculations can conveniently be done on a computer or a programmable calculator by using a programme for the integral of the normal curve, in which case one does not require the Table given here. Exact calculation for this case gives a whole number value of 70 for A+, 39 for C, and 33 for D, but the others remain the same.)

What we now have are numerical values which can be substituted for the letter grades, and which can be averaged, used in calculating correlations, and so forth, as cardinal numbers.

Notice that the differences between adjacent categories are shown now as unequal: the difference between A and B+ is 4 points, whereas the difference between B and C+ is 8 points.

The method also shows up the differences of the distributions for the various headings in a convenient way. Substituting the T values one obtains the following means and SDs for the four characteristics:

	Mean	*SD*	*N*
Application, diligence	50.24	8.43	376
Technical competence	49.18	9.43	370
Effectiveness with people	52.13	10.87	366
Quality of written work	48.49	9.70	360
Total of all ratings	50.02	9.73	1472

Thus, for this example, the raters had reported on these people as being rather better, and also more varied, for effectiveness with people, than for written work.

Applying the method to the ten-point rating scale from 'Poor' to 'Outstanding' for the 1566 cases quoted earlier, one obtains T scores of Poor = 19, Barely adequate = 23, Mediocre = 26, Reasonably good = 30, Good = 35, Good+ = 40, Very good = 47, Very good+ = 54, Excellent = 64, and Outstanding = 76, so the difference between 'Excellent' and 'Outstanding' was nearly twice as large as the difference between 'Good+' and 'Very good'.

Incidentally, this sort of conversion to numbers underlines the inadvisability of using the word 'Average' as one of the rating categories—it nearly always comes out with a T score of substantially less than 50, so in practice raters tend to use it as a slightly derogatory description.

There is, too, a danger if simple numbers are set out as the 'steps' as they were in the first example in this chapter. Raters can, of course, use 1, 2, 3, etc., as rating labels, but this does not necessarily mean that the measurement is cardinal. Letter grades are therefore safer in this respect.

'. . . BUT WHAT ABOUT THE HALO EFFECT?'

Would-be users of ratings will almost certainly have been warned that there is something called the 'Halo Effect' which gives grounds for serious suspicion that ratings may be very questionable as genuine measures.

The suspicion was voiced over 80 years ago (Wells, 1907) that raters really *started* with a global impression of the 'general goodness' of the performance they were rating and the process of rating 'aspects' was already heavily contaminated by this general impression rather than that they were moving from a dispassionate evaluation of the separate aspects to a synthesis to arrive at their 'overall' rating.

A huge number of statistical studies since then have shown that there seem to be good grounds for this suspicion. The evidence for the 'Halo Effect' is indisputable, and it consists essentially of vast numbers of matrices of inter-correlations between ratings for 'aspects' which show that the inter-correlations are really too high to be accepted at their face value. They are just not credible on common-sense grounds. It is vanishingly rare to find zero or negative correlations appearing in such studies, even when reason cries out that they ought to be there.

Many attempts have been made to find cures—training the raters carefully with a lot of emphasis on getting them to separate the different aspects when they are giving their ratings, changing the format of the rating form—for example, by randomizing the order in which the 'steps' are presented, or by using elaborate techniques such as 'forced choice' methods, and so on. But the resultant rating inter-correlations have persisted in showing unreasonably high values.

More recently a lot of attention has been given to attempts to measure how much 'halo' is present, accepting in essence that it will be there whatever one does, and what one needs to do is to estimate how big an effect it is having. None of the methods which have so far been tried for this purpose has produced an unequivocal answer.

So right at the heart of the structure of even the most careful validation studies there is this worrying suspicion that the criterion measures are heavily contaminated by raters' tendency to generalize from their initial impression of the people they rate—i.e. that what is being measured is more an expression of their liking of the person than a dispassionate evaluation of the person's performance.

There are, however, good grounds for rejecting this view. In the first place if one looks at the rating forms that raters have produced it is clear that most of them show fairly varied profiles for the different aspects for each person rated. It is not the case that one usually gets flat profiles that vary only in respect of their average level. Raters do indicate that Smith does very well in some respects, but badly in others, not that he is just much the same for everything.

Secondly, if the halo effect is due to raters failing to distinguish adequately between various aspects of performance, one would expect that more careful explanation on the rating form of what the different aspects were would substantially reduce the effect—but the research evidence shows only a small improvement.

Thirdly, one would expect a reduction of halo as a result of appropriate training—but again the experiments have shown only very limited effects of training, and sometimes even a decrease in the accuracy of the ratings.

So in practice the explanation of the halo effect as being caused by the raters contaminating their 'aspect' judgements with large amounts of their initial 'global' evaluation just does not hold water.

A recent study by the present writer (Handyside, 1988), which was based on the analysis of ratings given in an assessment centre, described by Dulewicz (1982), pointed to a different explanation of the cause of the effect.

A total of over 8000 ratings had been obtained when 223 managerial candidates had gone through a series of simulation exercises, and had each been rated independently on an E to A+ scale, by each of two raters for a number of aspects of their performance in each of the various exercises. There were 19 different raters involved in making the ratings—the raters were rotated in such a way as to ensure that the people being assessed were always rated by a number of different raters, and nobody's fortune depended too much on which of the raters had acted as judges of their performance.

When the two ratings for each observation—i.e. of the same candidate in the same exercise, and for the same aspect of performance—were segregated into 'high' and 'low' it was found that the average for the high raters was 0.91 standard deviations higher than the average for the low raters—even though they correlated 0.7175.

Thus the lenient raters were producing a mean rating of C+, where the severe raters were producing a mean of C–.

In order to explore what effect this 'severity–leniency' was having on the intercorrelations of the ratings, the situation was simulated on a computer, and large numbers of simulated ratings were produced in such a way that the 'severity–leniency' bias could be manipulated for various values from zero to about 2½ times as much as had been found to be the value for the raters who had taken part in this assessment centre.

A large number of repetitions were necessary to cover a wide range of 'true correlations' from −1 to +1, and for various levels of severity–leniency bias in the raters. In fact over half a million simulated ratings were used in the analysis.

What the results showed was that the severity–leniency of the raters had a very clear-cut effect on the way that the underlying (i.e. zero severity–leniency) correlation became distorted, and that this distortion was both different in kind, and greater in magnitude, than the ordinary and well-known 'attenuation' effect which is produced when a measure with less than perfect reliability is correlated against an 'external criterion'.

Figure 2 shows the effects when the raters are entirely consistent in the amount of leniency–severity they show, i.e. they carry exactly the same amount of bias from rating one characteristic to rating another. The left-hand diagram shows the ordinary attenuation effect when the ratings are correlated against an external criterion that is not a rating by the same raters. Here all the correlations are *reduced in absolute magnitude but the sign remains the same.*

The right-hand diagram shows the effect on the size of the correlation when both ratings have been given by the same raters. Here the severity–leniency bias has the effect of shifting all the correlations towards being *more positive and larger* than the underlying values before the bias is introduced.

The severity–leniency bias therefore distorts the underlying correlations in such a way as to have a maximal effect on large negative correlations and a lesser effect on high positive correlations. It produces what looks exactly like the classical halo effect—which is that one obtains implausibly large and positive correlations between characteristics that on *a priori* grounds could be expected to be zero or even negative.

The picture becomes more complicated if the raters are less than perfectly consistent in the amount of bias that they show, so that they only have a tendency to be severe or lenient, but the amount of the bias differs from rating one characteristic to rating another. In this case the point of intersection of the lines in the right-hand diagram moves down and to the left from the +1, +1 coordinate, and the slope of the line is affected to some extent. But the general principle remains the same, that the effect is larger on low and negative correlations than it is on high positive ones, and that—except for very high positive correlations—the distortion increases the inter-rating correlations.

It looks, therefore, from these results that the cause of 'halo' is not necessarily

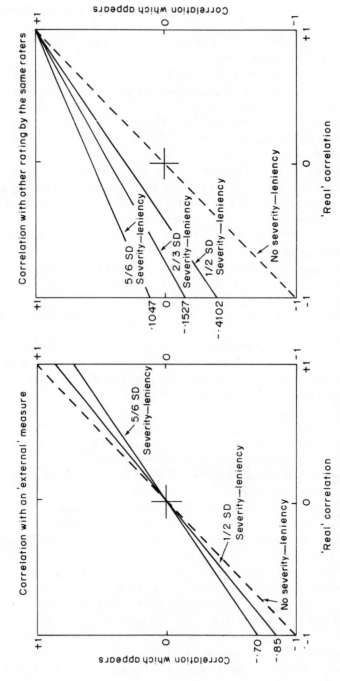

Figure 2 Distortions of correlations produced by severity–leniency of raters

that the individual raters fail adequately to distinguish between the 'aspects' that they are asked to rate. An important cause of the effect is that they have slightly different absolute standards of judgement, and that when the ratings by large numbers of raters are 'pooled' these small differences of standards combine in such a way as to produce higher correlations than would otherwise appear— particularly when the characteristics are 'really' largely independent of each other.

The likely cure for this effect will not be by efforts to get the raters to distinguish more strongly between different aspects, but by getting them to equate their absolute standards of judgement to a greater extent, i.e. by more precise definition of the meanings of the 'steps' in the rating scales, and by giving the raters training and practice aimed to get them all to have more nearly the same absolute standards of judgement. This has implications both for the design of rating scales and rating forms, and for the kind of training and practice that the raters are given. Most importantly, however, it indicates that criticisms that ratings are often more an expression of the raters' general liking of the individuals than a genuine measure of their job performance, can now be refuted as being unduly cynical.

REFERENCES

Dulewicz, V. (1982). The application of assessment centres, *Personnel Management*, September.

Handyside, J.D. (1988). Severity–leniency and the 'halo effect' in ratings, *Guidance and Assessment Review*, December.

McCall, W.A. (1929). *How to Measure in Education*. Macmillan, London.

Wells, F.L. (1907). A statistical study of literary merit, *Archives of Psychology*, **1**, 7.

Chapter 5.3

The Appraisal Interview

JAMES WALKER

City University Business School, Northampton Square, London EC1V 0HB, UK

Nearly all organizations have a formal appraisal scheme which generally consists of two main procedures: a staff performance report which is completed on staff annually; and an appraisal interview which is also usually an annual event. This chapter is concerned with the appraisal interview. Of course, appraisal is not an annual event, it is a continuous activity of managers—the manager is appraising staff from day to day as part of normal supervision. The manager will identify specific work that is well done and praise the employee, and the manager will draw the attention of the employee to poor performance or performance weaknesses. In fact, at the formal annual review the employee should hear nothing for the first time. Events which are brought up at the appraisal interview should have been discussed throughout the year.

Who conducts the appraisal interview? A survey of companies by the Institute of Personnel Management (Long, 1986) shows that in 98 per cent of organizations the immediate boss conducts the interview with the subordinate. As the interview is a job-related discussion, only the employee and the immediate boss are sufficiently aware of the employee's work over the past year to hold a discussion. In a few organizations the manager's manager, or 'grandfather', conducts the discussion with the employee. The senior manager is a safeguard against personal bias and possible reviewing inexperience. The other role of the 'grandfather' is to act as a countersigning manager to the report, and possibly to add comments. The senior managers will also act as moderators, ensuring that the managers under them observe common standards of appraisal so that undue leniency or harshness is corrected. Very occasionally the interview is conducted by a management development committee or the personnel manager, neither of whom is likely to be

Handbook of Assessment in Organizations   Edited by P. Herriot
© 1989 John Wiley & Sons Ltd

sufficiently aware of the details of the employee's performance to conduct an effective interview.

PURPOSES OF THE APPRAISAL INTERVIEW

The appraisal interview may have many purposes. Bailey and Parkinson (1985) list the following purposes of the appraisal interview from the point of view of the employee:

1. A chance to talk frankly with your manager.
2. A chance to discuss performance against your job description.
3. A chance to discuss problems and identify solutions to them.
4. A chance to find out how you are doing.
5. A chance to put forward your own good ideas.
6. A chance to find out more about the work of your section.
7. A chance to receive praise for work well done.
8. To receive constructive criticism of your work areas.
9. To agree a plan for the following year's work.
10. An opportunity to talk about strengths, opportunities, weaknesses and problems.
11. To talk about training needs and agree action on them.
12. To discuss the need for a change of job, or your wish to stay where you are and develop expertise.
13. A chance to discuss improvements.
14. To find our how promotable you are, short and long term.

Even this long list does not exhaust the possibilities. Many companies expect the manager to determine the employee's salary for the next year at the interview. Further, according to the company's commitment to management by objectives, the two parties may agree work objectives for the employee for the next year.

The many possible purposes of the interview raise several problems. Few interviews of half-an-hour to an hour can cover all the aims in the above list, since they are too numerous and complex. This makes the appraisal scheme too complicated and overloads the interview, which offends against the principle of a well-designed scheme, i.e. that it should be simple. The reason that many schemes fail is because they are so complex that managers are unwilling or unable to implement them (Allan and Rosenberg, 1980).

Some of these purposes or aims are conflicting. Most experts argue that salary determination should be kept separate from the appraisal interview. Anstey, Fletcher and Walker (1976) identify three purposes of reviews—performance, development and guidance. Randall and his colleagues (1972) arrived at much the same grouping, but named them the *reward review*, the *performance review* and the *potential review*. Randall suggested that these three groups of activities should be 'kept separate not only in time, but also in paperwork, procedure and responsibilities'. The argument is that the employee will not make a positive contribution to the appraisal discussion while waiting to hear of next year's salary. He or she will think 'all this talk of performance improvement is very well, but what I want to hear is my next year's salary award'. It may also be argued that employees are unlikely to refer to any difficulties they may be experiencing if their salary hinges upon the interview.

The same sort of argument applies to discussion of promotion and pro-motability, especially in career organizations. The employees may be waiting to hear about the possibility of promotion, and will not take any positive part in the discussion until this has been covered. Recent research (Prince and Lawler, 1986) has suggested that salary determination may not inhibit discussion as much as many experts believe. Splitting the appraisal procedure into three separate events runs the danger of making it too costly in time and effort. This splitting of the appraisal review may not be necessary as the manager has to change his or her style from time to time through the interview. At some time he or she may be listening and at other times doing rather more of the talking, other times he or she will be persuading or helping the employee to talk through ideas. The manager needs constantly to adjust the style of the interview according to the situation, and in this way should be able to cover all the relevant aspects.

Many managers are strong critics of the appraisal review for two main reasons. First, they say they are appraising all the time anyway as part of day-to-day supervision. They are encouraging their staff to improve their performance and pointing out any weaknesses, and are in constant communication with their staff and able to tackle problems before they develop. The managers may resent the introduction of a formal appraisal system as threatening their competence. The second main objection made by some managers is that pressure of work does not allow time for formal appraisal. They feel it would take too much of their time from the day-to-day tasks of management and supervision. They may doubt if they have sufficient skills to tackle appraisal interviews.

There may be some force in these criticisms, but they are contradictory and tend to cancel each other out. If communications between managers and subordinates are good and frequent there may not be so much to discuss at the appraisal interview, but experience suggests that managers are unduly sanguine about the effectiveness of their communications with their subordinates.

FEEDBACK AT THE INTERVIEW

The manager is expected to discuss with the employee performance weaknesses and areas of the work that have not been done so well, and if necessary draw them to the employee's attention quite firmly. In other words the manager is acting as a judge of the employee. This role is incompatible with acting as a helper and counsellor discussing with the employer how performance can be improved and soliciting suggestions from the employee. It is difficult to act as a judge and a counsellor at the same time (Maier, 1966; Meyer, Kay and French, 1965).

This conflict in the interview was particularly acute in the early days of appraisal, when there used to be long lists of personality characteristics on the appraisal form which the manager had to rate. It is meaningless to discuss personality; the employee is likely to reject ratings of personality traits and become defensive and frustrated. One reason is that a person cannot change his or her personality. It may be possible to change performance or the way work is done, but it is not possible to change personality. Also, the rating of personality traits tends to be unreliable. If two managers rate an employee on personality they are likely to disagree. For these reasons the rating of personality has fallen into disrepute, and only performance is rated. Fletcher and Williams (1985) give a sensitive account of the change in thinking about appraisal since the early days.

Even now the report forms of many companies have lists of personal qualities for rating, particularly in the report on potential. Personnel managers may disapprove of these ratings of personal qualities (Walker, 1983) but still retain them on the company's appraisal form. There is a certain tension between what people do and what they say. One reason why companies cling to the rating of personal qualities may be because when promotion is being considered management wishes to know what sort of a person the individual is as well as his or her performance. We have seen the elimination of personality traits from appraisal forms, and must expect to see the gradual dropping of personal qualities such as initiative, judgement and determination, etc. There are few difficulties with positive feedback when praise is pleasant to give and pleasant to receive. The worst that has been said of positive feedback is that it has no subsequent effect on performance (Meyer, Kay and French, 1965). The problems arise with negative feedback, which employees tend to reject, or become defensive when it is discussed. Managers do not like giving negative feedback and often neglect to do so. MacGregor wrote 'Managers do not like to play God . . .'. The evidence is that managers do not appraise unless there is some control to ensure that they have conducted the appraisal.

Not all employees have as good a chance as others of being appraised, as is shown in Table 1, taken from the Institute of Personnel Management Survey 1986. It demonstrates the proportions of companies which appraise staff of different levels. The results of a similar survey in 1977 are also included.

Junior levels in the United Kingdom are less likely to be appraised than more senior levels of employee, but generally there has been an increase in appraisal of employees who are not management. The evidence from American surveys is that a higher proportion of organizations appraise junior level staff than in the

Table 1   Percentage of organizations appraising staff

	1977	1986
Directors	*	52
Senior management	80	90
Middle management	90	96
Junior management	91	92
First line supervisors	60	78
Clerical/secretarial	45	66
Skilled/semi-skilled	2	24
Knowledge workers	*	55

(* Not available)

United Kingdom (PPF, 1974). Employers in the United States consider it cost-effective, in the United Kingdom they tend not to. Fletcher (in Anstey, Walker and Fletcher, 1976) describes the type of interview that evolves for junior staff. Most junior staff want to be covered by appraisal and find it useful when they are appraised. It appears that owing to the nature of the work there is less need than with senior staff to clarify the definition of the job. There is less scope for giving feedback as many junior staff get a fair idea from the work how they are doing. Typists know if work is rejected, and machine operators have the number of key depressions recorded, but many staff would still like reassurance, or some recognition of their performance. The interview tends to be shorter and simpler but the manager may have to do more of the talking.

RESEARCH INTO THE APPRAISAL INTERVIEW

There is a body of research into the dynamics of the appraisal interview. The method has been to ask the manager and/or the employee to complete a perceptual questionnaire some time after the interview. The questionnaire assesses such factors as whether the participants were satisfied with the interview, whether the employee felt encouraged to improve performance, whether the interviewer was friendly and the style of interviewing, whether performance had improved as a result of the interview, and so on. This method has its weaknesses. The measures are very subjective and are subject to distortion of memory. The questionnaire is sometimes completed months after the interview. There is also selective perception of what occurred at the interview and denial of anything unpleasant. If the managers and employees are asked what was discussed in the interview there is poor agreement between them (Sofer and Tuckman, 1970). Fletcher, in Anstey, Walker and Fletcher (1976), talks of a government department where 7 per cent of the employees said they had not participated in an interview although their managers had sent a note to the personnel department confirming that an interview had been held. Despite these weaknesses of the research method quite a lot has been discovered about the interview. A number of authors have written about what makes for a successful appraisal interview. Burke and Wilcox (1969) identify four factors:

1. A high level of subordinate participation in the appraisal process.
2. A helpful and constructive attitude (as opposed to a critical one) on the part of the superior.
3. The solution of job problems which may be hampering the subordinate's current job performance.
4. The mutual setting of specific goals to be achieved by the subordinate in the near future.

Fletcher (1973) has shown that a balanced approach to the discussion covering strengths and weaknesses led to the best outcomes. He contrasted two styles of interviewing, 'tell and sell' approach and 'problem-solving' approach after Maier (1958). In the tell and sell approach the manager conveys an assessment of the subordinate's performance and tries to persuade the appraisee to agree to it and to take whatever action the interviewer thinks necessary. In the problem-solving appraisal the manager's approach is less authoritarian and the employee is encouraged to do most of the talking. An interviewer usually does not convey an assessment in the appraisal but concentrates on helping the employee think the way through job problems and provide solutions. Fletcher's results showed that the problem-solving approach, with or without a discussion of performance weaknesses, elicited a favourable attitude to appraisal in a considerably greater number of cases than did the tell and sell approach, which suggests that appraisals in the problem-solving style probably cause greater willingness to implement action decided on.

Fletcher, working in twelve government departments—the biggest study ever conducted—found two other factors important in determining the success of the interview. First, the way the scheme had been introduced. If senior managers had been involved with a 'top-down' approach, that is if senior managers interviewed their own staff, had a favourable attitude and had attended training courses, the scheme was more likely to succeed. Second, when appraisers had been trained to interview using role-playing methods under skilled guidance, the interview was more successful. He also showed (1978) that the more frequently the two parties communicated before the interview, the more successful the interview was likely to be. Dulewicz, Fletcher and Walker (1976) showed that interviews had better outcomes if the participants had prepared, and if the employee was given some days' advance notice of the interview. Questionnaires were completed before the appraisal scheme was introduced and again three years afterwards. Significant improvements in the frequency, quality and degree of satisfaction of manager/subordinate communications were reported.

Metcalfe (1980) shows that managers in successful appraisals spent significantly more time inviting participation, in supportive behaviour, and in giving positive evaluations. They were also more friendly and ended the interview on a positive note. In the unsuccessful interviews managers spent more time expressing opinions and feelings, in disagreeing and attacking, and in giving negative evaluations of the subordinate and of his performance.

There is fairly general agreement that participation by the employee is associated with successful interviews. Greller (1975, 1978) shows that a sense of ownership at the interview leads to greater satisfaction with it. There is also some agreement that participation in goal setting or objective setting leads to greater commitment by the employee to follow up the interview with action agreed on (Meyer, Kay and French, 1956).

Dulewicz *et al.*'s (1976) results, showing that preparation is important for the success of the interview, and Fletcher's (1976) findings (in Anstey, Walker and Fletcher, 1976), that trained interviewers have more satisfactory interviews than untrained ones, both underline the importance of certain preliminaries to the interview.

PRELIMINARIES TO THE INTERVIEW

Both parties need to prepare for the interview.

The interviewer needs to be clear about what the organization's purpose of the interview is. In broad terms it may be any combination of the following (Bailey and Parkinson, 1985):

1. To motivate and encourage.
2. To reprimand.
3. To praise.
4. To counsel or guide.
5. To plan ahead.
6. To improve relations with a member of staff.
7. To improve standards of performance.

The manager will need to collect information about the employee and will consider the employee's performance against the job description and any objectives set in the past year, how the employee manages resources—whether staff, materials or money—any problems the employee may have had, and his or her strengths, weaknesses, hopes and ambitions. The manager has to know what has to be achieved in the coming year and how the employee can contribute.

The manager, the immediate boss, will have considerable knowledge of the employee before the interview, and they may have been very close throughout the year. The interviewer can consult the senior manager, the 'grandfather', and other people who know the employee. He should also be familiar with the record of the last year's interview and last year's staff report. After this preparation the interviewer should have an agenda for the interview, and know what has to be covered.

PREPARING THE ENVIRONMENT

The appraisal interview needs to be carried out somewhere quiet and private, without interruptions. Someone else can take telephone calls. If possible the interviewer should sit beside the interviewee. Face to face across a desk does not encourage a frank exchange of views, and it accentuates the boss/subordinate relationship. Allow enough time for the interview—it is not a brief chat, but takes on average between half-an-hour and an hour.

The interviewee should prepare for the interview as well as the interviewer. Some companies give employees an interview preparation form before the interview—an example is shown in Figure 1. The employee should be warned of the interview some days ahead of its occurrence to allow time for preparation. Where the appraisal scheme is open the employee may be given all or part of the report form to read. There should be plenty of time to digest it before the interview.

Performance Appraisal Interview - Jobholder Preparation Form

Appraisal discussion is more worthwhile if the jobholder has been encouraged to
prepare for the discussion by considering past performance and noting particular
points or queries. Below you will find a list of questions which will help your
preparation.

Against your Forward Job Plan what do you feel to be your main achievements since your last Appraisal?

As a result, what particular strengths do you believe you have shown in current job?

Are there any things that you feel you have not achieved satisfactorily?

In what way would you like to develop your strengths and abilities?

What training needs do you have?
How do these relate to your job performance?

Figure 1   Interview preparation form

What constraints, obstacles and difficulties have you encountered in your job?

What suggestions therefore do you have for improving the way in which your job is done?

What targets and standards do you plan for the next year?

What guidance or help would you like?

Additional comments

This preparation form is for **your own** use at the Performance Appraisal Interview. If **You** wish you can copy it to your Manager.

TRAINING IN INTERVIEWING

Most managers have had experience in interviewing, and although some are anxious that they do not have the competence to conduct an appraisal interview, after training nearly all are capable of conducting an adequate interview.

There are a number of techniques for training in appraisal interviewing:

1. Lecture plus discussion.
2. Demonstration role-playing interviews where the trainer conducts a role-playing interview in front of a class.
3. Film.
4. Practice interview under guidance.

All the experts are agreed that the best method of training is for managers to conduct practice interviews under skilled guidance. This may be supplemented by closed circuit television or audio tapes where the manager sees or hears the interview. In the practice interview the manager interviews a fellow course member or a 'guinea pig' who acts a role. To make the interview realistic the interviewee can complete a staff report on himself or herself and provide a job description. It is an advantage to have at least two practice interviews as it is usual to see an improvement from the first to the second.

The Institute of Personnel Management Survey (Long, 1986) showed that 53 per cent of organizations used role-playing training interviews. This compares with 22 per cent of organizations in the 1977 survey.

One criticism of the role-playing technique is that it is rather unrealistic. This may be overcome by conducting real-life exercises. The role plays are conducted in front of a skilled tutor and other members of the course who provide constructive criticism at the end of the interview. The aim is to suggest how to improve the conduct of the interview.

The main objectives of training are:

1. To explain the purpose of appraisal interviews, and to get students used to the situation and aware of problems likely to be met.
2. To bring about shifts in attitudes by increasing the confidence of the shy and nervous, and cautioning the over-confident. Only practice interviews can provide this experience.
3. To teach techniques, correct faults and develop skills.

THE STRUCTURE OF THE INTERVIEW

All interviews will be different, but most will have a similar structure which may cover the following ground.

Introduction

1. Break the ice with a friendly chat.

2. Discuss the purpose of the interview from the point of view of the organization, and how it can help the employee—it cannot be presumed that the employee knows this.
3. Explain the role of the appraisal in helping to manage the supervisor/subordinate relationship.
4. Suggest the benefits likely to be gained by both the manager and the job holder.
5. Encourage the job holder to refer to any notes and the interview preparation form, if this has been completed.

The main part of the interview

1. Discuss strengths and weaknesses, opportunities and problems.
2. Review what the job holder has achieved against the job description and any objectives set previously.
3. Explore any area of under-achievement. This may be introduced by asking the employee if anything has gone less well in the job. The interviewee may introduce areas of weakness which are safer to discuss than if they had been brought up by the interviewer. Do not discuss more than two areas of weakness, which is as much as most people can bear.
4. Ask about the job holder's ideas for change, and any other views on how performance might be maintained/improved.
5. Assess how well the employee uses resources.
6. Then move on and set any objectives for the period ahead.

The interviewer must not spoon feed the employee, but get the employee to suggest improvements and changes.

Conclusion

Towards the end one can provide an opportunity for widening the discussion and discuss promotability if requested, and wider career prospects, but the discussion should never concentrate solely around promotability as this is sterile. Promotion is something hypothetical which may or may not happen in the future; also in many organizations promotion may not be within the authority of the manager. For these reasons a discussion of promotion in the appraisal interview can be counter-productive.

Finally, summarize what the employee has agreed to do, and what the manager has agreed to do. Agree action which will need to be confirmed in writing later.

THE SKILLS OF INTERVIEWING

The skills of interviewing in the appraisal interview are similar to those used in other types of interview, e.g. the selection interview, or counselling. They will be dealt with under three headings: *questioning, active listening, giving feedback—summarizing and reflecting back*.

Questioning

What is needed are good open-ended questions which require the employee to answer at length and thus to achieve genuine two-way discussion. They are often prefixed by 'how', 'what' or 'why'. Open-ended questions encourage the employee to think carefully and produce an answer which is in no way suggested by the question. They are particularly useful during the early stages of the interview to promote a good atmosphere and to set the scene.

> 'What have you most enjoyed doing during the year?'
> 'What part of the work are you best at?'

They are also useful in introducing new topics later in the interview, or in opening up an area for deeper scrutiny.
Open questions can *extend* by prompting a fuller answer.

> 'How else could this be achieved?'
> 'Could you tell me more about that?'
> 'Could you explain that more fully?'

Link—a progressive flow of thought should be sustained, linking one thought to the next. Often a single word such as

> 'accordingly'
> 'then'
> 'nevertheless'

indicates the link. A phrase may help as a link.

> 'What did you do next?'
> 'How did the changes work out?'
> 'A bit earlier you said that . . . (the new system of filing led to some problems, how are they being resolved) . . . ?'

Compare—by, for instance, comparing on a before-and-after basis.

> 'How did your staff respond to the changes in organization last year?'

Clarify—the manager should not accept statements at their face value without clarifying what the employee feels or means.

> 'Are are you saying that his truculent attitude is a symptom of the real problem?'
> 'Do I understand the problem as you see it, two members of staff do not communicate?'

Poor questioning techniques

Closed-ended questions admit only a brief 'yes' or 'no' response and soon bring the discussion to a halt.

> 'Are you still coming to work by car?'
> 'Are you satisfied with the new word processor?'

Leading questions or loaded or provocative questions are to be avoided.

> 'You are willing to take responsibility, aren't you?'
> 'You would agree to that, wouldn't you?'

The question contains within its form the expected answer.

Multiple questions, where two or more questions are wrapped into one, and the employee will choose to answer the last question, or the easier one, should not be used.

> 'How does your new job compare with the old one, is it easier, do you enjoy it as well, or do you find it too busy?'

Active listening

There is a difference between hearing and active listening. Hearing is a physical response to sound, active listening is working with the mind.

About half the time spent in conversation is in listening, but it is not so clear how much is understood or remembered. Because we can think faster than we speak, the listener has spare capacity. This could be put to good effect by concentrating on what is said and trying to understand the underlying meaning.

The interviewer/manager must show that the employee is being listened to, partly by what the manager says but also by adopting an attentive posture, an interested expression on the face and eye contact. If the manager starts to lose interest this soon becomes apparent to the interviewee. The manager does not have to listen to everything, and must control the interview, for instance, if the employee starts to complain about a manager the interviewer should indicate understanding, but not approval—far less agreement. If the complaining continues, the interviewer can bring it to an end by asking 'What have you done to improve the situation?'

An active listener is in a good position to manage an interview and see that it runs along constructive lines while avoiding unnecessary repetition, or dwelling too long on one subject, Active listening is a skill which can be developed, but there are pitfalls to be avoided:

1. *Making hasty judgements*—showing impatience or 'tuning out' because nothing interesting is forthcoming.

2. *Selective listening*—listening only to certain people; turning a deaf ear to certain topics, and avoiding the unpleasant; ignoring the feelings which are being expressed as well as the facts; showing bias or prejudice because of a person's appearance, ethnic origin, gender, or beliefs.
3. *Interruptions*—by guessing the end of a sentence or remark; by allowing other people to interrupt.
4. *Attention*—daydreaming or mind-wandering; being easily disturbed by other sounds; or by trying to make the interviewee think that you are listening when you are not.

Feedback, summarizing and reflecting back

The manager needs to let the employees know that their remarks are being received. This is done as much by body language as verbally, as indicated earlier. Positive feedback is encouraging, negative feedback is discouraging, and if it is repeated may induce the employee to keep silent.

One technique that is very useful for providing feedback is summarizing and reflecting back, where the interviewer summarizes what the interviewee is saying. Perhaps he or she gathers up the meaning and reflects it back in one phrase. For example, if an employee is complaining that it is impossible to get down to the job because there is always something more urgent to do, and it is never possible to get a continuous period of work, the interviewer says 'So your job is rather bitty then'. When reflecting back it is effective to reflect the feeling which the interviewee has been expressing, as well as the facts.

Another example is an interviewee who says 'I prefer to work on my own initiative'. The manager says 'You like to organize things in your own way'. It is important to keep out any hint of disagreement or judgement.

Summarizing and reflecting back allows any misunderstandings to be cleared up. The employees know what they have said has been understood, and that their feelings as well as the facts have been communicated.

Because summarizing and reflecting back are not immediately obvious skills of interviewing, these techniques should feature on any training course on appraisal interviewing, or where tutoring at practice interview sessions take place (see Chapter 5.7).

OPENNESS AND THE APPRAISAL INTERVIEW

It is now customary to show employees what has been written about them on the performance report. In the Institute of Personnel Management Survey (Long, 1986) 92 per cent of organizations showed the performance report to employees. However, many organizations still keep a potential or promotability report closed. An argument is that performance is objective, it is something which has happened and can be discussed dispassionately, while promotion is speculative and may or may not happen. Also, some managements have said that opening the potential report would be too difficult for managers to handle. Some organizations, such as the British Civil Service, have found it difficult to move to open reporting. The fear of management is that when managers know that what they write about subordinates will be shown to them reports will become blander and more lenient to avoid unpleasantness. Research has shown that open reporting can lead to greater leniency, but does not always do so (Walker *et al.*, 1977). Another fear is that secondary closed systems would grow up, so the sealed envelope would accompany the open report.

Managers now practising openness 'who have experienced the change from closed reporting' say that they are more careful of what they write, not necessarily less frank. They tend to assemble evidence and examples to substantiate the written report, in case they are challenged after the employee has read it. One commonly used outlet for the employee is to provide a space on the report form to allow him or her to make comments.

When openness has been made voluntary there has been a very high take-up of employees wanting to see their reports. It is in keeping with a more open society and greater participation, extending sometimes to subordinates writing part of their reports and participating by self-appraisal. Organizations that have moved to open reporting are, on the whole, satisfied with it, and some say that the quality of reporting improves because managers are more careful about what they write. There grows up a greater trust between manager and subordinate, for the subordinate knows that the manager does not say one thing and then write something else.

The individual may make the psychological contract with the organization at the appraisal interview. Certainly, with the successful interview the individual will be committed to work plans for the next year. It is the manager's task to see that at the interview there is a reconciliation between the aims of the organization and the aims of the individual, and that the employee leaves the interview with commitment to the organization's aims. For these reasons many people believe the performance review and the interview are important procedures in the management of an organization's human resources.

REFERENCES

Allan, P., and Rosenberg, S. (1980). Getting a managerial performance appraisal system under way: New York City's experience, *Public Administration Review*, **40**, 372–9.

Anstey, E., Walker, J., and Fletcher, C.A. (1976). *Staff Appraisal and Development*. Allen and Unwin, London.

Bailey, D., and Parkinson, T. (1985). *Effective Appraisal Interviews*. Linneys Colour Print.

Burke, R.J., and Wilcox, J.S. (1969). Characteristics of effective employee performance review and development interviews, *Personnel Psychology*, **22**, 291–305.

Dulewicz, V., Fletcher, C.A., and Walker, J. (1976). Job appraisal reviews three years on, *Management Services in Government*, **31**, 1–10.

Fletcher, C.A. (1973). Interview style and the effectiveness of appraisal, *Occupational Psychology*, **47**, 225–50.

Fletcher, C.A. (1978). Manager–subordinate communication and leadership style, *Personnel Review*, **7**, 59–62.

Fletcher, C.A., and Williams, R. (1985). *Performance Appraisal and Career Development*. Hutchinson, London.

Fournies, F.F. (1973). *Management Performance Appraisal, A National Study*. Fournies Associates, Somerville, NJ.

Gill, D. (1977). *Appraisal Performance, Present Trends and the Next Decade*. Institute of Personnel Management, London.

Greller, M.M. (1975). Subordinate participation and reactions to the appraisal interview, *Journal of Applied Psychology*, **60**, 554–9.

Greller, M.M. (1978). The nature of subordinate participation in the appraisal interview, *Academy of Management Journal*, **21**, 646–58.

Long, P. (1986). *Performance Appraisal Revisited*. Institute of Personnel Management, London.

Maier, N.R.F. (1958). Three types of appraisal interview, *Personnel*, March/April, 27–40.

Maier, N.R.F. (1966). *The Appraisal Interview*. Wiley, Chichester.

McGregor, D. (1957). An uneasy look at performance appraisal, *Harvard Business Review*, **35**, 89–94.

Metcalfe, B.A. (1982). *Effective Appraisal Interviewing*, SAPU, Sheffield University.

Meyer, H.H., Kay, E., and French, J. (1965). Split roles in performance appraisal, *Harvard Business Review*, **43**, 123–9.

Prince, J., and Lawler, E. (1986). Does salary discussion hurt the developmental performance appraisal? *Organisational Behaviour and Human Decision Processes*, **37**, 357–75.

Randell, G., Packard, P., and Slater, J. (1984). *Staff Appraisal, a Step to Effective Leadership*, 3rd edn. Institute of Personnel Management, London.

Sofer, C., and Tuchman, N. (1970). *Sociological Review*, **8**, 365–6.

Walker, J. *et al.* (1977). Performance appraisal. An open or shut case? *Personnel Review*, **6**, 38–42.

Walker, J. (1983). *Outside Organisations Appraisal Arrangements. A survey of twenty-three organisations*. Management and Personnel Office, London.

Chapter 5.4

Management by Objectives

RICHARD MACDONELL

*Department of Business and Management Studies, University of Salford,
Salford M5 4WT, UK*

THE CLASSICAL THEORY OF MbO

Following a growing ground swell of discontent about the utility of traditional appraisal methods Management by Objectives (MbO) seemed to offer the opportunity of 'cracking the problem' in a way that both allowed for the employment of hard criteria while simultaneously linking appraisal with the practical day-to-day mechanics of running an enterprise.

Many writers still see MbO as providing an all embracing philosophy but there is a much wider body of opinion that believes it to have been a brave attempt to integrate many issues but one which has not really been able to survive the changing cultural, economic and organizational climates of the 1970s and 1980s.

If MbO has not lasted, the concept of mana*ging* by objectives is perhaps one that survives. It is common enough to bump into younger managers who talk naturally about their KRAs (Key Result Areas) without knowing much, if anything, about the background to the concept. In an endeavour to set 'objective appraisal' in a context that is useful in itself, as well as allowing comparisons to be made with other areas and chapters in the handbook, it seems useful to examine first the notion of appraisal in traditional MbO terms and then look to see how the data may be able to survive in a more free-standing fashion away from the rather rigid definitions that accompany what we might best call 'classical' MbO.

It is hard to think of any introduction to the term 'Management by Objectives' that does not start with a nod in the direction of Peter Drucker who coined the term in his influential book *The Practice of Management* (1954). He spoke of the need to obtain a principle of management which gave full scope to individual strengths

Assessment and Selection in Organizations.   Edited by P. Herriot
© 1989 John Wiley & Sons Ltd

and responsibilities while also serving to give direction and harmonization for individuals and teams alike.

Many authors have developed the original idea; 'standard' texts in this area include Mali (1972), Raia (1974) and, in the UK, Humble (1970). A definition that best encompasses what we are calling classical MbO can be attributed to Odiorne (1979) when he described it as

> a process whereby the superior and subordinate managers of an organization jointly identify its common goals, define each individual's major area of responsibility in terms of the results expected of him and use these measures as guides for operating the unit and assessing the contribution of each of its members.

If this makes it sound that MbO is a tightly defined area then such a view needs to be fairly immediately challenged. Indeed, many definitions of MbO exist and, as Kondrasuk (1982) has pointed out, there are many other titles in the managerial literature that are synonymous with MbO such as Management by Results, Individual Goal Setting, Accountability Management, and so on. Indeed, Kelly (1983) has pointed out that, to some extent, every manager manages by objectives in that one always has objectives to achieve in either the short or long term, however imprecisely these may be defined.

However, in general terms there is some broad agreement about the overall process of MbO. Raia (1974) suggested that it can be seen as consisting of four distinct stages:

- *Goal setting*   The 'cascading-down' effect of reducing long-term objectives to the level of organizational goals which in turn go down to the level of departmental objectives and finally to the level of individual targets.
- *Action planning*   The development of realistic plans for the attainment of these targets.
- *Self-control*   Implementation and the taking of corrective action.
- *Periodic progress reviews*   To appraise, reinforce and strengthen motivation.

The linkage between objective setting and appraisal was fairly quickly recognized by practitioners, for example Humble (1967), who set the relationship into the form of a cyclical process whereby a review linked into the next phase of goal-setting activity. Humble neatly summed this up in the form of a diagram (Figure 1).

The concentration on what an individual *does* provided by such an approach was an idea that was timely. Drucker's 1954 outline seemed to promise the provision of the key required to unlock many of the concerns about the subjective nature of appraisal that were beginning to be voiced and which were encapsulated in McGregor's seminal paper, published in 1957 and entitled with gentle understatement 'An uneasy look at appraisal'. In occupational psychology generally, the first stirrings that would ultimately lead to objective training techniques were evident and also in 1957 Wherry was emphasizing the importance of 'real' criteria in selection by suggesting that the approach of psychometricians up to

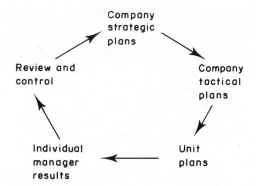

Figure 1   MbO as a continuous process

that time was something along the lines of: 'We do not know what we are doing but we are doing it very carefully and hope you are pleased with our unintelligent diligence.'

The clear potential advantage of linking organizationally defined goals with the assessment process offered a chance of moving away from inferential judgements about personal characteristics. These could only really be based upon a limited sample of observed behaviour and, taken in general, were only possible when a superior was in evidence, thus giving full rein for the possibility of 'Hawthorne Effects'. Thus, MbO appeared to offer a methodology which with its concentration upon that which was 'objective' simply had to be better than anything which was obviously 'subjective'.

Heynes (1978) outlined the main features of such an approach (Figure 2).

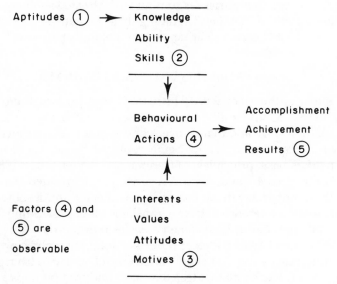

Figure 2   A perspective on factors to be appraised

Some features of classical MbO have obvious assessment advantages and implications:

- The identification and harmonization of individual and organizational goals become possible.
- Joint goal setting by individuals and superiors leads to commitment and ultimately to high levels of motivation.
- Organization and individual growth can go hand in hand.
- Objectives will have to be defined in measurable terms which include time for completion.

Perhaps a little less obviously but of significant practical importance, it was also recognized that:

- Possible environmental changes always need to be taken into account.
- Rewards could be allocated according to performance.
- The overall philosophy of MbO is 'proactive' rather than 'reactive' and looks to the future rather than concentrating simply upon the past.

This second list of issues has much in common with other forms of performance appraisal. Environmental issues will always need to be taken into account. What might have been an average level of performance for an ice cream salesman during the long hot summer of 1976 would have appeared positively outstanding in the years that followed. The extent to which salary is linked to performance has long been a contentious issue and will arise elsewhere in Section 5. In addition, Randall (1973) had alerted us to the need to be clear in making a distinction between performance reviews, reward reviews, potential reviews and organization reviews, and it is a source of continuing irritation and annoyance to many that the distinctions between these issues continue to be treated submerged under the umbrella description of 'appraisal'. The highly systematic and broadly ranging scope of classical MbO serves to bring such points into sharp relief.

SOME PROBLEMS WITH CLASSICAL MbO

Since the initial enthusiasm with which MbO was greeted there has been a continuing debate about its ultimate value. Seyna (1986) has argued that MbO reached its nadir in 1970 and that an over-concentration on bureaucratic systems and masses of paperwork is now being replaced by an appreciation of the applicability of its basic principles. O'Donnell and O'Donnell in 1983 posed the question 'Is MbO *passé*?' and, hardly surprisingly, concluded that it was not. However, this is not a view that is shared by all other authorities. Indeed, the fact that one managerial reference database translates MbO as standing for 'Management Buy Out' gives one at least some pause for reflection.

In the years since 1954 the idea of MbO as a total, all-embracing system that provides a universal panacea for every managerial ill has faded from prominence. In this respect it is like so many ideas that have endured perhaps a little longer than being 'flavours of the month' but which have not really lived up to all their earlier promise, Management Information Systems being perhaps the most up-to-date example of this (Heller, 1988). In addition, MbO has been criticized as lacking responsiveness to changes in climate or 'organizational visions' (Peters, 1982). It has been pointed out that MbO places particular emphasis on goal setting, feedback, interaction and participation (Welden, 1982) but that it may be a technique that requires such levels of trust, openness and maturity on the part of its users that it works best for those who need it least!

In writing about any general aspect of assessment or management it is fairly easy to slip into a dry listing of non-specific points. The import of the preceding few paragraphs that practical, everyday considerations should not be overlooked is nicely, if somewhat painfully, outlined in as realistic a satire as one could wish to find in the managerial literature. Hansen (1973) outlined what he called 'a model for subverting Management by Objectives' and the six headings he used were:

1. *Lampoon-tation* Essentially reducing the importance of objectives by name-calling—'Meandering by Objectives' or 'Muddling between Opportunities', missing no opportunity to emphasize the global and complex nature of the overall system—for example personalizing the issue by calling it something like 'Frank's Folly'.
2. *Concept isolation* Isolate the MbO concept from the rest of the management organization, deify it, have everything written down so that flexibility goes out of the window.
3. *Gandhian passive resistance* Follow a supervisor blindly. Ask no questions, give no feedback. Let him wander about in ignorance until he too will be happy to join the subversive movement.
4. *Overhead magnification* Add to the organizational energy that is required to maintain the MbO process. Plague everyone with notes, reports and copies that link everything with goals, e.g. 'see goal four' which recipients then have to look up to have the slightest idea what is being talked about.
5. *Feigned paranoia* Act as if you are a lamb being sacrificed on the altar of MbO. Blame your failures on it; give the concept breath, humanize it. Point out all the Theory X behaviour that is going on around you.
6. *Prophetic self-fulfilment* Keep the informal system filled by the power of suggestion. Start rumours to the effect that the chief proponent and ramrod of MbO will soon be leaving. Ask questions along the lines of 'Do you think MbO is just sick or is it dying?'

Of course, such a model could be applied to other assessment ideas in ways which might not kill them but would certainly slow them down. For our purposes, the subversive model indicates why many authors believe that classical MbO is unlikely ever to fulfil its early promise but we can still raise the question as to whether the assessment implications can be 'hived-off' and treated as a separate entity.

In any event, evaluating performance against objectives is always likely to face a number of common problems.

1. Is 'joint' goal setting between a manager and a subordinate ever going to be a practical possibility? The manager will often feel uncomfortably torn between a 'boss–judge' and a 'friend–helper' role (Kerr, 1976).
2. How can you tell whether goals are set with an easy or challenging or impossible ultimate measured criterion? The subversive model must at least alert us to the possibility that subordinates could 'bend' objectives to provide some form of slack or buffer. Or, more naturally impulsive and enthusiastic individuals could be easily carried away into biting off more than can realistically be chewed. This is of even more importance if payment systems are going to be linked to objective accomplishment.
3. How do you recognize when conditions are changing and what account needs to be taken of them? It has become, to say the least, something of a truism to talk about the accelerating rate of change but it is increasingly recognized that the only certainty, even in the short term, in most organizations is that the future will be different.
4. How do you treat the performer who *exceeds* the set objective? Geneen of ITT, with his 'let there be no surprises' philosophy, would have viewed over-achievement in the same light as under-achievement and it may require a rather sophisticated understanding of organizational finance before many people see the rationale behind such seemingly unfair criticism.
5. How will you cope with the issues that are not easy to set in objective terms? Production quotas, days lost due to absence or revenue generated may lend themselves fairly naturally to quantification but some topics really never get too far away from what is, ultimately, a set of value judgements or subjective analyses. Chief among these are the exercise of flair or creativity, the way in which resources are balanced and used in concert, the avoidance of conflict, unnecessary hostility and illegal or unethical practices. 'Thou shalt not get found out' is not an objective that everyone would be prepared to accept!

WORTHWHILE FEATURES OF MbO

As Kerr (1976) has pointed out there are some features of using objectives that are well worth the effort to employ:

– *Conscious emphasis on goal setting*. Because some things are not amenable to objective treatment it does not mean that we should overlook those that are and thereby lose the advantages of highlighting the improvements in performance that can come from following a results-orientated approach.
– *Frequent interaction and feedback between superior and subordinates*. It is often said that appraisal should be part of the continuing day-to-day relationship between a manager and a subordinate rather than an uneasy yearly fencing match with no obvious outcome or follow-up. An approach based on working towards specified objectives may often prevent every interaction seeming to be tinged with criticism on the part of either party and be particularly useful in building the confidence of younger or more cautious managers.

B. REVIEW OF PERFORMANCE

KEY ACCOUNTABILITIES (ranked in order of importance)	DESCRIBE PERFORMANCE-EXEMPLIFY IF NECESSARY (refer to criteria agreed in last year's Review)	CHANGES LIKELY IN 1989	AGAINST WHAT CRITERIA WILL PERFORMANCE BE JUDGED DURING THE COMING YEAR?	TRAINING AND DEVELOPMENT NEEDS TO MAINTAIN/IMPROVE PERFORMANCE OR COPE WITH ANTICIPATED CHANGES

OTHER FACTORS –
e.g additional/temporary responsibilities, major problems, team briefing, etc.

What of all the above has been done notably well in the 12 months under review, and why?

SUCCESSION
What has the job holder done to develop a successor? How does this compare with what was agreed at the last appraisal as needed to be done? What needs to be done in 1989?

Agreement reached on content of this form on _____ by _____

_____ (Job Holder) _____ (Immediate Superior)

What of all the above has been done less than adequately in the 12 months, and why?

TRAINING
What training which was entered on last year's Review Form has not been carried out, and why not?

This section is for the Immediate Superior, Grandfather and Operating Unit Manager

Provisional Overall Assessment

☐

_____ (Immediate Superior)

_____ (Grandfather)

Figure 3   An example assessment form

– *Opportunities for participation*. Although the boss/subordinate relationship will always be a reality it need not always get in the way of participation and the motivational results that can accrue (see, for example, Erez, Earley and Hulin, 1985).

Some companies do in fact use a form of objective assessment in conjunction with more conventional assessment techniques such as rating scales and free narrative reporting. The example shown here (Figure 3) from Fothergill and Harvey (a North Manchester division of the Courtaulds group) focuses very much on the reporting relationship between a manager and his subordinate but uses concepts such as Key Accountabilities and Performance Criteria in ways that are not necessarily linked to a 'top-down cascade' of objectives. Readers who are interested in these mixed approaches could usefully look at the periodic reviews of appraisal conducted under the auspices of the Institute of Personnel Management (for example Long, 1986 represents the most recent) which contain many useful examples of assessment forms as appendices.

We appear to be arriving at a conclusion that indicates simply (but none the worse for that) the advantages of being as objective as possible without necessarily having to 'buy-into' a broader, all-embracing philosophy. Before we let matters rest, it would be unfair to overlook an interesting recent development put forward by Kane and Freeman (1986, 1987). After a trenchant discussion of 'the harmful effects of basing appraisals on the achievement of objectives', they move on to describe a possible way of bringing together an objectively based approach with one that is rooted in more traditional performance appraisal.

Kane and Freeman point out that people are hired by organizations to fill positions which can be described as a series of functions which need to be performed on a regular, recurring basis in order to provide the products and services that define the business. Performance appraisal should, they argue, restrict itself to the assessment of how well job incumbents are carrying out their functions (Figure 4).

Work–unit objectives

	I	II	III	IV	V
A	x		x	x	
B		x	x		x
C	x	x		x	
D		x		x	x
E	x		x		x

Individual job functions

Roman numerals: objectives I to V

Letters: job functions A to E

Figure 4   Matrix of work unit objectives and individual job functions

An objective approach needs a more flexible perspective and may need also to consider how all the job functions being carried out within the work unit and the organization can be combined and coordinated to achieve outcomes that vary from one period to another. Thus, by plotting relationships on a matrix, it might be possible to get the best of both worlds, setting work unit objectives without 'game playing' or the need for constant re-negotiation and maintaining general standards that remain constant across periods of time. It will be interesting to see if this amalgam brings reports of practical success.

If this chapter has a simple message it is along the lines of trying to highlight the advantages that come from using objectives and quantification wherever possible without necessarily slipping into the strait-jacket of any single, overall 'philosophical approach'. The authors of surveys into methods and applications of performance appraisal in this country (Long, 1986) and the United States (Eichel and Bender, 1984) are given to categorizing MbO or objective methods of appraisal as 'results orientated' or 'outcome orientated' as opposed to other methods outlined in other chapters in this book. On the face of it, there is nothing particularly wrong with this but it does run the risk of suggesting that, once categorized, the issue is put to rest and there is nothing else that really could or should be done. The way forward to make appraisal less of an organizational chore or annual ritual is to concentrate more on defining activities with an eye to their temporal organizational reality. Semantics aside, it could be argued that there is a real distinction to be made between what is often loosely called 'annual appraisal' and what should be called *performance review*, which is where objectives might be of greatest use in that it should concentrate on a review of the past. What were the objectives? Have they been achieved? If not, why not? This, of course, to be followed by the setting of objectives for the next period of time. *Appraisal* is a term which is much better employed for the process whereby assessor and assessee can take a step away from the everyday hurly-burly and review implications of style, training and questions of general feedback. These either encompass or lead as a separate issue to *potential review* which clearly recognizes that trying to predict future performance must be partially based on past performance but with many other considerations coming into play. Finally, along the lines advocated by Randall (1973) a *salary review* should be seen as a distinctly different issue. Time consuming? Perhaps, but the issues are too important to be swept under the organizational carpet and a systematic recognition of the different steps will go a long way towards curing the headaches that are traditionally associated with trying, for example, to cope with the solid-citizen employee who needs to be motivated and maintained in a role where good performance is the norm but who has little real potential for the future as compared with the high flyer who has lots of scope for development but a lot to learn on the way. Too complex?—not really, and anyway who said being a manager was simple?

REFERENCES

Drucker, P. (1954). *The Practice of Management*. Heinemann, London.

Eichel, E., and Bender, H.E. (1984). *Performance Appraisal. A study of current techniques*. American Management Association, New York.

Erez, M., Earley, P.C., and Hulin, C.L. (1985). The impact of participation on goal acceptance and performance: a two-step model, *Academy of Management Journal*, **28**, 50–67.

Hansen, L.H. (1973). A model for subverting Management by Objectives, in E.F. Huse, J.L. Bowditch, and D. Fisher (eds), *Readings on Behavior in Organizations*. Addison-Wesley, Reading, Mass.

Heller, R. (1988). Really useful information, *Business Life*, **14**, April–May, 62–5.

Heynes, M.G. (1978). Developing an appraisal program, *Personnel Journal*, January, 14–19.

Humble, J.W. (1967). *Improving Business Results*. McGraw-Hill, London.

Humble, J.W. (1970). *Management by Objectives in Action*. McGraw-Hill, London.

Kane, J.S., and Freeman, K.A. (1986). MBO and performance appraisal: A mixture that's not a solution, Part 1, *Personnel*, December, 26–36.

Kane, J.S., and Freeman, K.A. (1987). MBO and performance appraisal: A mixture that's not a solution, Part 2, *Personnel*, February, 26–32.

Kelly, C.M. (1983). Remedial MBO, *Business Horizons*, **26**(5), 62–7.

Kerr, S. (1976). Overcoming the dysfunctions of MbO, in D.A. Kolb, I.M. Rubin, and J.M. McIntyre (eds), *Organizational Psychology*. Prentice-Hall, Englewood Cliffs, New Jersey, pp. 320–8.

Kondrasuk, J.N. (1982). Management by Objectives: Past, present and future, *Managerial Planning*, **30**(6), 31–6.

Long, P. (1986). *Performance Appraisal Revisited*. The Institute of Personnel Management, London.

Mali, P. (1972). *Managing by Objectives. An Operating Guide to Faster and More Profitable Results*. Wiley–Interscience, New York.

McGregor, D. (1957). An uneasy look at performance appraisal, *Harvard Business Review*, **35**(3), May–June, 89–94.

O'Donnell, M., and O'Donnell, R.J. (1983). MBO—Is it *passé*? *Hospital and Health Services Administration*, **28**(5), 46–58.

Peters, T.J. (1982). The rational model has led us astray, *Planning Review*, **10**(2), 16–23.

Raia, A.P. (1974). *Managing by Objectives*. Scott, Foresman and Co., New York.

Randall, G. (1974). Performance appraisal: purposes, practices and conflicts, *Occupational Psychology*, **47**, 221–4.

Weldon, D.J. (1982). MBO success or failure? *Leadership and Organizational Development Journal*, **3**(4), 2–8.

Wherry, R.J. (1957). The past and future of criterion evaluation, *Personnel Psychology*, **10**, 1–5.

Chapter 5.5

Four Approaches to Increasing Self-awareness

Rowan Bayne

Psychology Department, Polytechnic of East London, The Green, Stratford, London E15 4LZ, UK

INTRODUCTION

Self-awareness is relevant to appraisal interviews in two obvious and central ways. First, a formal outcome of the appraisal may be a decision to seek to increase self-awareness by, for example, going on a communication skills course of some kind or by trying out a new way of working. Second, the effectiveness of an appraisal interview depends in part on the appraisee's self-awareness. If he or she does not remember his or her thoughts and feelings about a particular difficulty, and what he or she actually did, for example, this is a severe handicap to increasing job satisfaction or performance! Similarly, if a question like 'Do you have any skills or talents which could be used more fully in your present job?' is posed (which it should be), considerable self-awareness is needed to answer it well.

Self-awareness then, in the senses implied above—and as defined in the next section—is a necessary or at least very helpful condition for achieving such aims of appraisal interviewing as improving work performance, increasing job satisfaction (or 'job excitement'), identifying strengths and using them more, and identifying areas for training and development. Other factors likely to be influential in achieving these aims include preparation for the interview, aims which emphasize communication and development more than appraisal, and the appraiser's interviewing skills and qualities. All seem likely to contribute to a constructive and accurate self-assessment (for discussion of relevant research see Fletcher and Williams, 1985). More specifically, they are likely to result in such

---

Handbook of Assessment in Organizations   Edited by P. Herriot
© 1989 John Wiley & Sons Ltd

desirable aspects of the interview itself as psychological involvement, maccep-
tance of accurate feedback and commitment to agreed outcomes—all problems in
appraisal interviews generally (Fletcher and Williams, 1985).

This chapter first briefly discusses the concept of self-awareness, and then
reviews four approaches which seek to increase self-awareness: assertiveness;
using a 'journal'; interpersonal process recall; and contemporary 'psychological
type' theory.

SELF-AWARENESS

Two general senses of self-awareness have been implied so far in this chapter.
More formally, the first can be called *inner self-awareness*, and refers to 'awareness
of one's own thoughts, feelings and reactions'. Inner self-awareness is strongly
related to accuracy of self-appraisal (Gibbons, 1983). A second meaning of self-
awareness is *outer self-awareness*, which refers to 'awareness of one's behaviour
and its impact on others'. Both kinds of self-awareness matter in organizations.
They, and the degree of congruence or incongruence between them, have direct
and indirect effects on job performance. Encounter or T-groups are probably the
purest recognition of their importance, and are a particularly direct approach to
both senses of self-awareness: sensitivity to inner experience and trying out new
ways of behaving. However, such group techniques are problematic in how well
any training effect generalizes to behaviour outside the group, and, for some
styles of group leadership, they may have adverse effects upon individuals (Bates
and Goodman, 1986).

The four training and development methods reviewed below share the aims of
encounter groups for employees and their organizations but are probably less
threatening. Moreover, they can be tried either on training courses, or more
informally by colleagues or friends, or by the individual on his or her own, the
latter practice in harmony with Fletcher and Williams's (1985) useful emphasis on
self-development. However, they share with encounter groups the problem of
deciding for whom each method is most appropriate, when it should be used and
for which purposes. At present, this is largely a matter of judgement and personal
experiment. The discussions below are therefore intended to help managers and
appraisees compare each method with their needs and choose accordingly. They
may also give a new perspective on a method which is already familiar. The
principle is very much the same as for different forms of exercise: swimming,
walking, yoga, etc., are suitable for different people at different times.

ASSERTIVENESS

In general terms, assertiveness is 'expressing and acting on your rights as a person
while respecting the rights of other people'. I will discuss assertiveness first in
terms of rights, then as broad categories of behaviour and, thirdly, as skills.

Most books on assertiveness give a list of 'basic human rights', with quite a lot of
variation. Four rights which seems to me key ones in organizations, and which
appear in nearly all the lists, are to ask others to do things, to decide whether to do

something or not, to express feelings, opinions, values, and to make mistakes. Note that the assertive rights are not about getting your own way all the time: they embody respect for yourself and others. If they seem quite ordinary, even obvious, Satir's (1978) estimate, based on wide experience of organizations, was that about 4 per cent of behaviour is assertive. If this is so, then the rights are acted upon only infrequently.

Another way of defining assertiveness is to contrast it with other styles of behaviour. For example, assertiveness can be defined as *not* being aggressive, passive or manipulative. Aggressive behaviour is expressing or acting on your rights at the expense of another person's. It is threatening, punishing, or 'putting down', saying something must happen, rather than wanting or preferring it to happen. Sometimes it is appropriate for managers to be aggressive in this sense, but the risk is that the other person tends to feel humiliated, hurt or aggressive, and therefore to work less effectively.

Passive behaviour is hoping you will get what you want, that it will just happen or that someone else will do it without your asking or without your asking clearly. It tends to go with 'bottling up' emotions, and the other person may well feel frustrated and resentful. Manipulative behaviour is also indirect. An example is using guilt (or trying to use guilt) as a weapon: 'It's not much to ask . . . I don't ask often'.

The styles touched on above are general ones. They need qualifying with notions like 'appropriate honesty' and a recognition that sometimes being aggressive or passive is the best option. Moreover, no one is *always* assertive and no one *always* chooses the best option.

Two examples of assertiveness skills

There are two particularly useful kinds of statement in most books on assertiveness. The first are arguments and perspectives for and against the value of each skill. (These perspectives are also often hypotheses which psychology has not yet tested.) The second are 'tips' on how to do a particular skill. Therefore, this section is organized as follows: some of the arguments and perspectives are put for the skills of (1) giving compliments and (2) receiving compliments; the basic skills are outlined; and refinements and subtleties are suggested.

The skills are outlined in the form of suggestions to try out, rather than in a mechanical or prescriptive way. Assertiveness is not just techniques. Indeed, a firm sense of what you like and dislike underlies effective assertive behaviour— most obviously in making requests and saying no—and an adequate degree of self-esteem is also necessary. Self-awareness, self-esteem and the successful use of assertiveness skills are processes, not once-and-for-all achievements. They interact with each other and tend to improve gradually and erratically.

Giving compliments

There are two main perspectives:

1. Reasons for not giving people compliments include fear of being seen as manipulative, thinking that the person knows already, and that he or she might get conceited.
2. On the other hand, compliments (accurate, genuine ones) may increase self-awareness and self-esteem, decrease resentment at being overlooked ('The only time anyone here takes any notice of me is when I do something wrong'), and make critical comments easier to accept and act upon.

The general issue is whether the results of not giving compliments are worse or better than those of giving them. The basic skill (if you decide to use it) is in giving compliments in such a way as to increase the chances of the positive results.

The basic skill

Giving compliments in an assertive way is a matter of being brief and specific ('I like the way you stand up to X' is more specific than 'You are working very well'), taking the risk, and, as with all assertiveness skills, sensitivity and timing.

Refinements and subtleties

- Looking for opportunities to give a compliment is itself a positive thing to do, and likely to have an effect on morale.
- Compliments can be non-verbal, e.g. a smile of appreciation.
- One aspect of timing is that it may sometimes be wise to give a compliment when you are not also asking for something!
- Complimenting yourself is an approach to increasing self-esteem (and also to managing stress).

Receiving compliments

In assertiveness terms, the most skilful way to respond is to thank the person straightforwardly and to enjoy the compliment, in particular to pause for a second or two, and to beware of being dismissive ('It was luck'), or complimenting quickly back ('I like your X too'). Both, it can be argued, *reject* the other person's compliment.

Refinements and subtleties

- Consider thanking the other person, pausing, and *then* saying your view, including 'It was luck' if you really think it was.
- Consider asking for detail, e.g. 'Thank you. Was there anything in particular you liked?' This refinement applies particularly if you suspect that the compliment was insincere and wish to challenge it.
- As a final aspect of this assertiveness skill, you may like to consider your unspoken 'rules' and those of your organization about giving and receiving compliments. As far as I know, organizational rules of this kind have not been

systematically studied, but my impression, first and second hand, of British organizations is that some common rules are: 'Do not give compliments, at least not easily', 'Be more ready to criticize than to give compliments', and 'Don't ask for positive feedback'. Another might be 'Don't refuse or challenge insincere compliments'. I think the effects of these rules on organizational climate and individual self-esteem might be quite marked and, conversely, that assertiveness theory suggests a relatively simple approach to positive change.

Other assertiveness skills

Perhaps the two main assertiveness skills are 'making requests' and 'saying no'. Two best sellers have used saying no in their title. Other skills include asking someone not to do something, developing self-esteem, giving criticism and receiving criticism. The most useful guide, and for both sexes despite its title, is Dickson (1987), but there are many 'self-help' books on assertiveness to choose from, some explicitly related to organizations, others more general. The books also differ dramatically in their definitions of assertiveness and their approaches, e.g. in their emphasis on inner versus outer self-awareness or on techniques versus qualities. Emphasis on the role of beliefs also varies. Some people appear to need to replace an irrational belief which is incompatible with assertiveness with a more rational, compatible one before, or as well as, changing their behaviour, e.g. 'I must never make mistakes. It's awful when I do' might be replaced with 'Mistakes happen and are unfortunate, but rarely terrible or awful' (Rakos, 1986).

The latter author reviews the hundreds of studies of assertiveness. In his view, early research established the effectiveness of assertiveness training, and current research is focusing on more sophisticated issues. Thus the main emphasis is on the role of situations, types of relationship, and cultural factors in the skilful and effective use of assertiveness skills. For example, one study was concerned with assertiveness by candidates in selection interviews: some assertive behaviours tended to be viewed more positively than others by prospective employers (cited in Rakos, 1986, p. 412).

Finally, it is worth emphasizing the large 'artistic' element in using assertiveness skills well: the attitudes and personal qualities of the person using them matter more than technical virtuosity. And further, part of the most useful attitude is being constructive towards *oneself*. This attitude is expressed very explicitly in the second approach considered here: using a 'journal'.

USING A 'JOURNAL'

The journal is a second approach to increasing inner and outer self-awareness, and therefore effectiveness at work and elsewhere. I will outline the method (which is 'common sense' in that it is logical, but, like assertiveness, does not appear to be commonly practised) and then discuss it briefly. The method is developed from various sources, including Walker (1985) and Egan (1975, 1986).

Method

Do the following, at least every few days:

1. Choose an experience that matters to you, e.g. a conversation or part of one, or something you've seen, done or read.
2. Describe the experience—in writing, or on tape—in a sentence or two, e.g. '21 July, very angry about extra work, said to X: "This sort of thing makes me feel like giving up." '
3. *Reflect* on your experience. Write or speak *as freely as you can*—not analysing at all, not concerned with literary merit!
4. Analyse your reactions and perhaps challenge them.
    (a) Be specific.
    (b) Is there a familiar feeling or pattern there?
    (c) Do your reactions tell you anything about yourself?
    (d) What other ways (however unlikely) are there of looking at what happened?
5. Consider action.
    (a) Is there any action you want to take now?
    (b) Is there anything which you might do differently next time?
    If either (a) or (b) applies, plan (small steps) and perhaps practise or rehearse.
6. If you have decided on action, choose time and place carefully.
7. Begin the cycle of reflection and analysis again. Describe the experience, etc., until step (8) is appropriate.
8. Summarize the overall outcome:
    (a) Have you learned anything about yourself?
    (b) Do you want to do anything further with this knowledge?

In a diagram the journal method can be depicted as shown in Figure 1. Ideally, it is a spiral of development, with self-awareness increased through actions as well as reflection.

There are many other ingenious and varied approaches to using a journal, e.g. Rainer (1980). A major strength of all of them is that the writer takes his or her inner self seriously. The approach outlined in this chapter avoids both what some people see as self-indulgence, and also introspection to the point of morbidity, by the constructive intent and rhythm of reflection and action. In effect, the approach asks a person to counsel himself or herself, where counselling means taking a problem—a difficult decision, a troubling experience—bringing a judicious combination of support and challenge to bear on it, and moving from sufficient clarification and understanding to action (Egan, 1975, 1986). It is also a useful counterbalance to the danger of superficiality in some approaches to assertiveness, i.e. an over-emphasis on technique and a neglect of 'inwardness'.

Walker (1985) offers some useful advice on the actual process. For example, he emphasizes using a journal in an individual way, e.g. using diagrams and pictures; selecting a few experiences to work on in depth; making a very clear

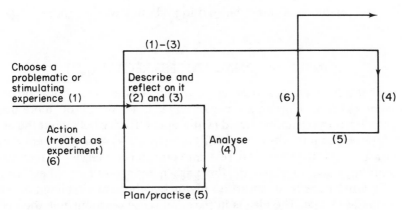

Figure 1   Diagram to depict the journal method for increasing self-awareness

separation between reflection and analysis; perhaps setting aside a regular time; and perhaps showing an extract to someone for comment.

An example of a journal entry may help to 'bring alive' the skeleton and advice sketched above:

21 July, very angry about extra work, said to D: 'This sort of thing makes me feel like giving up.' (*Steps 1 and 2.*)

I was furious and reacted at once. Rare event. The next four months are *packed*, and I don't want to feel overworked. Stressed. Hated feeling that way last year. Why me anyway? I should know how much I'm doing. Is he trying to get at me? Doubt it. Glad I did react strongly and quickly: it's good being spontaneous. One of the charms of football. (*End of step 3*—reflection—at least on this occasion. The next step is a much more considered analysis.)

What I actually did was speak forcefully and briefly. I didn't throw or break anything. I then just shrugged and said something general. I don't *know* what he thought. I was most angry about (*a*) not being consulted (it was a shock) and (*b*) becoming too stressed. What else? The new work has some possibilities, not just a burden! (*End of step 4.* The next step is to list some possible actions.)

I'll (*a*) ask J's advice, (*b*) say something to D about consultation, and perhaps about cutting back my work in another area (I'll look at the assertiveness book for suggestions on how to put this), (*c*) think about my reaction to sudden requests to take on new responsibilities, (*d*) consider putting less effort into Y and cancelling X, (*e*) plan *re* the possibilities in the new work. Do (*a*) today. (*End of step 5.*)

Comment on the (part) example

The steps overlap but the distinctions are still useful and generally followed in the example. Walker's (1985) advice to 'record less and reflect more' (steps 2 and 3) has been followed. Feelings are expressed. Some 'distance' from the incident has been achieved. The actions are feasible, but some need to be expressed more specifically. Medium term is included—not just 'fire fighting'. On a more general note, the writer will follow steps 6–8 (or whatever variations he or she chooses) when appropriate, and may be writing about two or more experiences concurrently.

INTERPERSONAL PROCESS RECALL (IPR)

The emphasis in using a journal is (in useful contrast to most approaches to assertiveness) on developing a sense of one's 'inner world' or, more matter of factly, on directing attention inwards with more effective behaviour the eventual result. Interpersonal process recall (IPR) (Kagan, 1984) shares this emphasis.

In the aspect of IPR discussed here, a conversation or interview is recorded, and the recording used to stimulate the participant's recall of what happened, especially what happened inwardly: his or her thoughts, feelings, intentions, images, fantasies, etc. The idea is in part that these reactions will then be more available to the person next time, perhaps giving him or her a wider range of things to say, and therefore a greater chance of communicating clearly and well.

Perhaps the most generally useful variation of IPR is to work with an 'inquirer'. This is a special and surprisingly difficult role for the other person. The difficulty lies on the one hand in *not* criticizing or commenting, and on the other in timing, manner and choice of question. When the person doing IPR stops the tape, the inquirer encourages him or her to recall his or her experience at the time by (*a*) listening hard, (*b*) asking questions like:

- Did you have any thoughts about that?
- Did you want to say anything further?
- How attractive was he/she to you?
- Did any pictures go through your mind?

and (*c*) doing nothing else.

Kagan (e.g. 1984) has found that IPR increases a person's sense of responsibility for his or her behaviour and motivation to change. Barker (1985) evaluated the empirical evidence on IPR as a training method as so far 'merely suggestive', but is optimistic about its likely value and cost-effectiveness.

PSYCHOLOGICAL TYPE

Psychological type is the fourth approach considered here. Like the others, it can be used in its own right or in a complementary way. It is an approach to self-awareness in both senses, but at a 'deeper', more organized level of personality.

Psychological type theory is the contemporary development of some of Jung's (1923) ideas about personality. He saw the types as 'compass points . . . in the wilderness of the psyche', ways of helping people understand themselves and others. It is an extremely positive approach—almost glowingly so—and thus obviously does not attempt to account for all aspects of personality. However, it does appear to explain a great deal and to have many applications in training, team building, career development, counselling, etc. (Hirsh, 1985; Myers and McCaulley, 1985). In this section I will outline the theory, first as a way of describing aspects of personality, and second as a model of personality development. Finally, I will suggest some implications of the approach for decision making and for communication.

Type as personality description

Psychological type is concerned with strengths and potential strengths. It suggests sixteen types of people, each with different combinations of strengths. The types are *not* regarded as static or as 'boxes'; the term 'style' captures this part of the tone of the theory better but lacks type's underlining of what the theory sees as *profound* differences between people: not just different but in some respects opposite.

Type is about preferences. These are elements of inner self-awareness which may or may not be expressed in behaviour. Consequences of expressing or not expressing preferences are suggested. For example, taking one of the preferences, the theory suggests that people with a preference for extraversion tend to behave in an extraverted way: to be more active, outgoing, sociable and expressive. However, a few people will have a preference for extraversion but not have developed—used and trusted—it sufficiently actually to behave extravertedly much of the time. In effect they will be 'unfulfilled extraverts': predominantly quiet, private, reserved and inward, behaving, at least to the casual observer, like genuine introverts. They—and 'unfulfilled introverts'—will also, according to the theory, have less 'sense of self' and be less effective.

There are three other pairs of preferences which, with *introversion* (I)/*extraversion* (E), form the sixteen types. First, *sensing* (S) and *intuition* (N)—tending, respectively, to be more practical and 'down to earth', to like flexible use of familiar skills, to be more aware of the present (S), versus tending to be more imaginative, more likely to look for general patterns and links to other ideas, to like inspiration and possibilities (N).

Second, *thinking* (T) and *feeling* (F). These terms are used in a particular sense by Jung and Myers and are *not* meant to be construed as indices of how intelligent (academically or otherwise) or how in touch with their emotions people are.

Thinking and feeling are seen broadly as two ways of making decisions: a tendency to decide more by logic and analysis, to criticize first, to be cool and sceptical (T), versus a tendency to decide more on the basis of likes and dislikes, to appreciate first, to need harmony, and to be warm and trusting (F). The final pair of preferences are *judging* (J) and *perceiving* (P). These preferences are associated with being more organized and decisive (J) rather than more flexible and easy-going (P).

The theory suggests that each of us is more comfortable and more skilful with one of each pair of preferences, and can usefully be described as, for example, ISFP, ESTJ, or another of the sixteen possible combinations. Descriptions of the resulting types take interactions between the preferences into account. For example, F in an ESFJ plays a different role to F in an INFP, though the two types do also have something in common. For the best descriptions of each type so far developed, see Hirsh and Kummerow (1987) and Myers and McCaulley (1985). I have given only a bare indication here.

Type as a model of development

As implied above, type theory suggests what each type is like at its best, and what sort of activities each type finds fulfilling. It also proposes different developmental routes for each type: which preferences will ideally be developed most and in which sequence (Myers, 1980; Bayne, 1988). Particularly provocative is the idea that in mid-life many people want to develop 'other sides of themselves'; in terms of type theory, the 'other sides' are the relatively neglected preferences. An application, directly relevant to appraisal interviews, will illustrate this idea: it is concerned with being somewhat more specific about the kind of activity each type should in theory find most fulfilling and also do most effectively, particularly between about 20 and 40 years old, and quite possibly throughout life. However, type is flexible, not prescriptive about such matters. For instance, someone in what is in theory an unsuitable kind of work may (*a*) do it in an unusual and valuable way and (*b*) use his or her own preferences much more in life outside work.

Simpler levels of organizing the types than the basic sixteen are quite often more useful. In this example, J and P are omitted, leaving eight combinations. People whose preferences are for I and S will in theory be most fulfilled and most effective working in a quiet and systematic way, mainly in their inner world. Obviously this leaves many options including, say, accounting, computing and artistic activities. It should, however, be obviously practical. In contrast, E and S is a more outgoing combination, more likely to enjoy working with machinery or selling, or some other interaction with the external world.

More briefly, and just to give a sense of the theory, main motives for each of the other combinations are as follows:

- I and N: developing new ideas and theories; E and N: changing the situation.
- I and T: analysing and understanding ideas; E and T: analysing, criticizing and organizing a situation.
- I and F: working quietly and individually on something highly valued; E and F: helping others.

These general motives are systematically related to the careers people of different types choose (Myers and McCaulley, 1985)—to date the best evidence for the validity of this approach. Bayne (1988) provides an exercise on self-development of one's 'true type' and Hirsh (1985) numerous exercises on type in organizations. The key references are Myers (1980) and Myers and McCaulley (1985), the latter being only available to psychologists or people who have passed an introductory course on the Myers–Briggs Type Indicator (run by OPP and the Myers–Briggs Users' Group (UK)).*

---

* Oxford Psychologists Press, Lambourne House, 311–321 Banbury Road, Oxford OX27 7JH, UK. The Myers–Briggs Users' Group (UK), Emmaus House, Clifton, Bristol BS8 4PD, UK.

Type and decision making

Expanding on the example above, the preferences suggest a model of problem management and decision making. As Myers (1980) points out, each step in the model will be easier for some (developed) types than others.

The first step is a 'sensing' one: gather the facts, and check you have them all. This is, in theory, unlikely unless your S is very well developed. Second, use 'intuition' to 'brainstorm' strategies for dealing with the problem. Third, use 'thinking' to analyse costs and benefits of each strategy. Fourth, use 'feeling' to judge how much each strategy and outcome matters to you and others. All the above is largely an introverted process, but the final stage is to act, to use extraversion (unless the strategy is internal, e.g. a change of attitude).

Type and communication

The implications of type for communication provide a third perspective on type theory. Difference in type can cause misunderstandings, rejection and hostility. Similarity in type can mean a too easy or even stultifying togetherness. Myers's primary concern in developing Jung's work and the Myers–Briggs Type Indicator, was to encourage 'the constructive use of differences'; she wanted people to appreciate and benefit from both their own types and those of other people, especially those with opposite preferences. For example, as an INFP, I show a draft of politically risky memos to a colleague and friend, INTP: I want to see what someone who is at his best analysing ideas (the opposed preference to my F), suggests are the consequences of sending the draft. I then integrate these new data—they are often new!—and make a decision, still relying most on F (my best developed preference) but with more information to go on. Of course, type or development of a complementary preference is only one factor in choosing whom to ask for advice.

In more general terms, type theory explains some miscommunications (and some rapport). A useful starting point is 'X and Y are different, and that might suggest a way of communicating better', rather than 'I just can't stand ESTJs'! All types *can* communicate well with each other. The general sources of conflict between I and E are sociability and privacy (see, e.g. in next paragraph). Between S and N, they are S's being seen as or feeling slow and mundane, N's as impractical and unobservant. Similarly, F's can see T's as unsympathetic and critical, T's can see F's as illogical and too soft. For example, someone who preferred F might make a request on the basis of 'I'd like to . . .' when his T manager would (typically) want *reasons*. J's and P's tend to clash on issues of order and autonomy. Meetings are excellent arenas for observing these differences.

As a final example, consider an extravert colleague who found introverts dull and boring. After studying her own type, and type theory, she changed this view to 'introverts tend to be reflective and to need more time alone'. She also changed her behaviour. Instead of bouncing in spontaneously to see an introverted colleague, quite often being disappointed by the result, and ascribing it to dullness on the part of the colleague, she now warns the colleague of an intended visit and, if appropriate, of the purpose of the visit. Their relationship has improved. The changes in this particular extrovert also illustrate one way inner self-awareness and outer self-awareness interact with and complement each other.

SUMMARY AND CONCLUSIONS

Two senses of self-awareness were distinguished, focusing respectively on inner experience (*within* the person) and behaviour (*between* one person and others in the organization). Greater self-awareness is a factor in more effective appraisal interviews (as well as more generally, e.g. need for coping with change in managerial and other work). Four complementary approaches to increasing self-awareness—in both senses—were briefly discussed. Assertiveness places most emphasis on new ways of behaving towards colleagues. Using a journal and interpersonal process recall (IPR) can be seen as providing a firmer basis for effective use of assertiveness and other actions. Contemporary psychological type theory is also very practical, but its particular value in this chapter may be in providing a theoretical basis for describing central aspects of inner self-awareness and for explaining its relationships with effective and less effective behaviour at work and elsewhere.

REFERENCES

Barker, C. (1985). Interpersonal process recall in clinical training and research, in F.N. Watts (ed.). *New Developments in Clinical Psychology*. BPS/Wiley, Chichester.

Bates, B., and Goodman, A. (1986). The effectiveness of encounter groups: Implications of research for counselling practice, *British Journal of Guidance and Counselling*, **14**, 240–51.

Bayne, R. (1988). Psychological type as a model of personality development, *British Journal of Guidance and Counselling*, **16**(2), 167–75.

Dickson, A. (1987). *A Woman in Your Own Right, Assertiveness and You*. Quartet, London.

Egan, G. (1975, 1986). *The Skilled Helper*, 1st and 3rd edns. Brooks/Cole, Monterey.

Fletcher, C., and Williams, R. (1985). *Performance Appraisal and Career Development*. Hutchinson, London.

Gibbons, F.C. (1983). Self-attention and self-report: the 'veridicality hypothesis', *Journal of Personality*, **51**(3), 517–42.

Hirsh, S.K. (1985). *Using the Myers–Briggs Type Indicator in Organizations. A Resource Book*. Consulting Psychologists Press.

Hirsh, S.K. and Kummerow, J.M. (1987). *Introduction to Type in Organizational Settings*. Consulting Psychologists Press.

Jung, C. (1923/1971). *Psychological Types*. Routledge Kegan Paul, London.

Kagan, N. (1984). Interpersonal process recall: Basic methods and recent research, in D. Larsen (ed.). *Teaching Psychological Skills*. Brooks/Cole, Monterey.

Myers, I.B. (1980). *Gifts Differing*. Consulting Psychologists Press.

Myers, B., and McCaulley, M. (1985). *Manual: A guide to the development and use of the MBTI*. Consulting Psychologists Press.

Rainer, T. (1980). *The New Diary*. Angus and Robertson, London.

Rakos, R.F. (1986). Asserting and confronting, in O. Hargie (ed.). *A Handbook of Communication Skills*. Croom Helm, London.

Satir, V. (1978). *Peoplemaking*. Souvenir Press, London.

Walker, D. (1985). Writing and reflection, in D. Boud, R. Keogh, and D. Walker (eds). *Reflection: Turning Experience into Learning*. Kogan Page, London.

Chapter 5.6

Alternative Raters and Methods

RICHARD S. WILLIAMS

*Middlesex Business School, Middlesex Polytechnic, The Burroughs, Hendon,
London NW4 4BT, UK*

In the typical appraisal scheme the principal rater is the immediate supervisor: a recent survey in the United Kingdom by the Institute of Personnel Management (IPM) (Long, 1986) showed that in 98 per cent of responding organizations the immediate superior was responsible for carrying out the appraisal. The manager the next level up often has a role too, but usually a much lesser one—namely, that of a second-level reviewer. But there are many others who could have a part to play in the rating process. Most obvious is the individual being appraised, yet self-appraisal is rare: the IPM survey reports a figure of 28 per cent but it is not clear what kind of self-review is involved. As to the involvement of others (peers, subordinates, clients, personnel specialists) as raters, there are few figures available which in itself perhaps suggests that these others rarely have a formal role as raters. Also, the quantity of evidence about the different sources varies. The most is known about self- and peer appraisal; very little is known about subordinates, personnel specialists and clients as sources of ratings. Indeed, such is the dearth of evidence about clients it perhaps is only worth noting that they exist as a potential source.

As regards methods, the most commonly used are the work-planning/results-orientated approaches and rating scales (see Chapters 5.2 and 5.4). A third method often used is the essay approach. This chapter will review the two main variants of this method, looking at their strengths and weaknesses as appraisal techniques.

However, the chapter will focus primarily on the contribution that different parties can make to the rating process. It will examine the evidence (where available) about the technical properties of ratings made by sources other than the

Handbook of Assessment in Organizations   Edited by P. Herriot
© 1989 John Wiley & Sons Ltd

immediate supervisor, and will review the strengths and weaknesses of the different raters. Finally, various operational issues will be considered; the psycho-metric properties of peer ratings, for example, may be encouraging but how in practice does an organization make use of such ratings in its appraisal system?

WHAT IS WRONG WITH THE IMMEDIATE SUPERVISOR AS THE SOURCE OF RATINGS?

Immediate supervisors (indeed, any single source) have a number of limitations as raters. First, the immediate supervisor cannot observe all of the job holder's work performance. So, the ratings will at best be based on only a partial view of an individual's behaviour. Second, the supervisor may be more interested in certain aspects of work behaviour than in others; for example, the supervisor may place more emphasis on end results and rather less on the means by which the results are achieved. Third, there may be some settings, e.g. where 'management by exception' is practised, in which job holders have relatively little contact with their supervisors—perhaps only when things go wrong. Fourth, in many of the newer work or organizational structures, such as matrix structures, it is not always clear who the immediate supervisor is; in these circumstances a job holder may have two or more bosses. Who does the appraisal? Perhaps both, or all, contribute in some way.

None of these points is meant to imply that the immediate supervisor should be discarded as a rater; this is scarcely conceivable. Rather, the point is that the immediate supervisor's view is a partial one. For a more composite appraisal others need to be involved. But, before going on to examine the different sources, it is necessary first to mention the criteria against which their ratings will be assessed.

CRITERIA FOR ASSESSING RATINGS

In reviews (Kane and Lawler, 1978; Thornton, 1980) of peer and self-assessment several different measurement properties have been examined. These include *reliability, validity, freedom from bias, leniency* and *halo*. In addition, Kane and Lawler (1978) identify other, non-technical, criteria for assessing the different rating sources: these are *practicability* and *acceptability*, and will be dealt with in the final section which examines operational issues. The two types of criteria are relevant to the *utility* of appraisal.

SELF-RATING

Whether officially encouraged by the organization or not, self-appraisal happens. At appraisal time people inevitably will make some judgements about their performance during the past year. Increasingly, organizations are formally en-couraging some measure of self-appraisal. In some organizations this means completing some kind of preparation form before the appraisal interview takes place. This is hardly self-rating but it is one means of focusing the appraisee's attention on what the organization considers to be important aspects of perform-ance. True self-rating, in which the appraisee completes a version of the appraisal form, is rare (Long, 1986). The most likely reason for this, assuming that organizations have thought of self-rating in the first place, is the fear that appraisees' own ratings will be higher than those made by their managers. There is some evidence to show that such leniency effects can occur, but the findings are not conclusive.

Thornton (1980) has reviewed the psychometric properties of self-appraisals of job performance; the evidence about these technical characteristics is far from clear cut. Thornton (1980) himself concluded that:

> . . . self-appraisals tend to manifest *more* leniency, *less* agreement with other sources, *less* discriminant validity, and *less* reliability than ratings by supervisors and peers. Self-appraisals display *less* halo and adequate construct validity in a few studies. Existing data do not allow any conclusion whether the quality of self-appraisals is a function of scale format, amount of rater training, type of judgment, or purpose of appraisal.

Other, more recent, reviews (Shrauger and Osberg, 1981; Mabe and West, 1982; Fletcher, 1985), which are wider ranging in their examinations of self-assessment, take a more optimistic view; Fletcher (1985) concludes that 'self-assessments of ability and performance can be very accurate and can even be superior to other, more conventional, assessment techniques in prediction'.

However, the conditions under which self-appraisals are carried out are one factor which may influence the ratings. For example, appraisal schemes often are used for reward purposes. Under such circumstances leniency effects would hardly be surprising. Indeed, using appraisals in this way may have an inflation-ary effect on ratings whatever the source. Also, what is noteworthy about much of the evidence on which these conclusions are based, is that self-ratings often are compared with ratings made by others. But there is another type of self-rating—where job holders provide a self-assessment of different aspects of their job performance relative to one another rather than in comparison to other job holders. With this kind of self-appraisal it has been shown (Meyer, 1980) that the assessments are less prone to 'halo' effects; in other words, appraisees can be discriminating in giving a profile of their relative strengths and weaknesses.

The main dangers with self-rating centre on the risks of lower reliability and of leniency. The latter may be fuelled by appraisals being used for reward purposes and it may be a danger to which those lacking in self-analytical capacity are prone. But these dangers seem not to be inevitable and the risks need also to be set against the advantages claimed for self-assessment.

As was noted,earlier, self-appraisal will happen anyway. Encouraging it in a formal way does something to help ensure that the appraisee's perspective is not overlooked. After all, no single source observes so much of our behaviour at work as we do ourselves. And though our own explanations for the causes of our behaviour sometimes are suspect, allowing self-appraisal may reveal motiva-tional or situational factors affecting performance. As a consequence, others may come to realize that their explanations for our own behaviour may be mistaken; an unusual proneness to errors of detail may be a result of a preoccupation with a family health problem rather than due to lack of care. One fear is that self-appraisal may lead to discontent and disagreement being voiced in the appraisal interview. This possibility is, of course, ever present but it can be argued that the articulation and discussion of differences of opinion is beneficial; they are unlikely to be resolved if they are not brought out into the open. Though self-appraisal often is seen as threatening to the supervisor it may, in fact, be of benefit in conducting the appraisal interview. Bassett and Meyer (1969), for example, showed that appraisal interviews based on self-review (rather than a manager-prepared review) led to a 'more productive and constructive discussion' between the two parties. They also showed that such appraisals resulted in less defensiveness on the part of the subordinates. Furthermore, performance improvements were more likely from employees who had given lower ratings. Similarly, positive findings are reported by McHenry, Howard and McHatton (1984).

PEER APPRAISAL

Kane and Lawler (1978) identify three different types of peer appraisal. One is *peer nomination*: here each member of a work group, say, is asked to nominate the one (or some other specified number) member of the group who is highest on some particular aspect of performance. Nominations of the lowest on that aspect sometimes are requested also; self-nominations usually are excluded. Another method is *peer rating*: this is the same as supervisor rating or self-rating, only the source is different. Finally, there is *peer ranking*: each group member ranks all the other members of the work group in order from highest (best) to lowest (worst) on one or more dimensions of performance.

Kane and Lawler (1978) conclude that peer nomination '. . . effectively discriminates those group members who are extreme on a variable from those who are not with a relatively high degree of validity and reliability'. By contrast, the reliability and validity of peer ratings are much lower and they are prone to the usual rating biases. Peer rankings have been little researched, so it is inappropriate to make conclusive statements about their psychometric properties. But the general conclusion that Kane and Lawler (1978) draw about the technical characteristics of peer assessment is a positive one; indeed, on the face of it peer ratings would seem to be psychometrically superior to ratings from other sources. However, whether such assessments have a part to play in an appraisal system will depend at least as much (if not more) on considerations of practicability and acceptability.

Various strengths and weaknesses have been identified for peer assessment in general and for the particular methods. Using peers brings a perspective different from that of the supervisors and it makes it possible to get a number of independent judgements; the average of these may be superior to any single judgement. But the disadvantages weigh heavily against these strengths. A possible reason for the reliability of peer assessments is the frequency of interaction among peers; but this interaction may itself be threatened by the process of peer appraisal, particularly if those judgements are used for administrative/

reward purposes. Thus, there is the danger of creating friction among colleagues; existing social relationships may be damaged. It seems likely that for peer appraisal to work at all satisfactorily there needs to be an adequate level of interpersonal trust among the peers, but even if this exists there may be some reluctance to rate. There is also the possibility that friendship may bias the assessments, although the evidence (see Latham and Wexley, 1981) suggests that this danger may not be great. The issue of purpose is important. Using peer ratings for reward purposes only heightens the dangers already mentioned. This therefore points towards using peer assessments for developmental purposes. But here again caution must be exercised: it would be naive to suppose that very favourable or very unfavourable peer assessments would be ignored by the supervisor whose own assessment may consequently be influenced. There are implications here for the practicalities of how one operates an appraisal system incorporating peers.

OTHER SOURCES

Other sources—subordinates, personnel specialists—are considered together because relatively little is known about the psychometric characteristics of ratings made by these sources. Therefore, they are described here in terms of their likely advantages and disadvantages.

Subordinate appraisal

Subordinates are well placed to make judgements about their supervisors' competence on several dimensions of behaviour but especially at managing people. However, there are dangers. Subordinates may feel threatened; they may fear retribution from the supervisor should they give an unfavourable (albeit honest) rating. The supervisor may feel defensive about receiving assessments from this source. Subordinates may not be sure of what higher levels of management regard as acceptable standards of supervisory performance; the subordinates may well have their own views about this but do their views necessarily coincide with those of management? However, it may be of value to have these subordinate views exposed as a means of furthering team building. In addition, there are many operational issues (to be discussed below) which may work against upward appraisal in practice.

Field review

In field review (as described by Latham and Wexley, 1981) a representative of the personnel department interviews managers about their subordinates' performance. Evaluation reports are written by the personnel representative, reviewed (modified if necessary), and then approved by the managers. Henderson (1984) adds to this description; he states that one of the tasks of the field reviewer is to explain each performance dimension and the measurement method (rating scale or whatever) being adopted. Though it is not clear from either of these descriptions, the personnel specialist presumably also obtains evidence in support of the assessments provided by the managers.

Field review carried out in this way provides professional assistance to line managers in making appraisals and there is some training value deriving from this help. The approach may do something to cut down the amount of time which managers spend in writing appraisal reports and it may help in promoting a common standard of assessment across the organization. But there seem to be many drawbacks. On the face of it, it would appear to be a costly exercise; is it an efficient use of resources? Does the extra information which may be gained justify the expenditure? There is a danger that line managers may reject some of their responsibility for appraisal and may fail to accept the same degree of ownership for the final assessment report. How will the appraisal interview be affected if the document on which the feedback is based has been prepared by another person? Is there a danger that the personnel specialist's report will go beyond the information that has been given? Unfortunately, so little is known about field review in practice that it is not possible to give definitive answers to these questions.

MULTIPLE APPRAISAL

Two main conclusions may be drawn from the foregoing review of rating sources. First, it is worth re-stating that no one source can adequately assess a job holder's performance if only because no one source observes all of an individual's behaviour. Second, no one type (source) of rating has been shown conclusively to be psychometrically superior to any other source. Many writers (e.g. DeVries *et al.*, 1980; Landy and Farr, 1981) have pointed towards an approach based upon multiple sources, sometimes called multiple appraisal. In other words, if no single source is adequate, then use a combination of a number of different sources, as is done in assessment centres.

The approach has a number of advantages. The likelihood of obtaining a comprehensive picture of an employee's performance is increased; after all, different raters observe different aspects of performance. This should lead to a more valid rating. At the very least, there will be a large database—some say a more complex picture, but one which more accurately reflects organizational reality (Borman, 1978). The data generated may be practically more useful, depending on the purposes for which they will be used; but it should be remembered that purpose itself may have an influence on the quality of the data generated.

Then there are the disadvantages. Different sources may bring different perspectives and this may make it difficult to compare and reconcile differences in ratings. If there are differences are they due to perspective, or to bias? And even if the ratings are similar the different perspectives may mean that like is not being compared with like. The different ratings may none the less be equally valid. Combining or averaging ratings may mask important differences, hence the range of ratings needs also to be included in any feedback which is given.

Such uncertainties may deter organizations from using alternative sources, either singly or in combination. Further discouragement may also come from having to devise a workable system, in other words all the practical issues to do with how an organization actually operates an appraisal system based upon more than one source.

ESSAY OR NARRATIVE METHODS

There are two main techniques; these are *essays* and the *critical incident* (CI) technique. A third approach—*field review*—has been described already when personnel specialists were discussed as a rating source.

Essays

Perhaps the simplest kind of essay is where the appraiser writes a 'pen picture' of the subordinate's performance during the review period. This is tantamount to giving the appraiser a blank sheet of paper. A variant is to provide some headings on the sheet of paper to guide the appraiser on what is to be assessed.

Essays have a number of advantages. Appraisers have the freedom to concentrate on what they consider to be the most important aspects of appraisees and of their performance. They also allow appraisers to use their own words and, provided the narrative is well written, the resulting description can be a very vivid assessment of the person. But this points to one of the chief drawbacks of the essay method—its heavy dependence on the writing skills of appraisers and their conscientiousness in putting pen to paper.

Other drawbacks are that the approach requires considerable analytical skills on the part of the appraiser, otherwise important aspects of performance may be overlooked and not assessed. The approach (like others) also relies a lot on appraisers' memories, particularly their ability for recall, although the use of headings may serve as memory joggers. Narratives may suffer from many of the biasing effects to which other methods are prone and writing an essay may be seen as more time consuming than completing a series of rating scales. Also, the lack of standardization means that one narrative is not easily compared to another. A further danger with a well-written appraisal (whether favourable or unfavourable) is that it may be given excessive credence simply by virtue of its being well written. Hence, the appraisee may benefit (or suffer) because of the appraiser's writing skills.

Critical incidents

Perhaps the most basic way of using the CI technique is much as it is used for identifying training needs. Thus, at the end of the review period the appraiser would be required to describe two incidents—one where the appraisee had been particularly effective and the other an incident of less than effective performance. The appraisal form might provide some guidelines to aid completion, e.g. Who was involved? What actually happened? How did the incident come about? Have there been other similar incidents? What were the consequences?

This approach to the CI technique has many of the same advantages and disadvantages as the essay. However, it offers potential for a more balanced assessment—effective and ineffective incidents—but at the same time this concentration on extremes ignores a large part of the appraisee's typical performance.

One way of increasing the usefulness of the approach is to have appraisers record critical incidents throughout the year as they occur (see Williams, 1981, for one description). This may help to improve day-to-day performance management by providing feedback in a timely fashion as well as avoiding the danger of the 'recency effect' where appraisers base their appraisals on events taking place in the few weeks or months before the report is written. The maintenance of a written record of incidents throughout the year may lead to a better quality of appraisal (whatever method is used) but diary keeping of this kind may well meet with resistance from the affected staff; there is a danger of it working against the necessary climate of trust that is required for appraisal to work well. And given that appraisers often view appraisal as a chore, they too may baulk at such record keeping, seeing it as burdensome and time consuming.

ALTERNATIVE SOURCES AND METHODS IN PRACTICE

From the foregoing review several of the operational issues are evident, for example being clear about purpose. Also, many of the practical aspects are ones which apply to conventional supervisor appraisals; these are the familiar issues involving design and implementation. For example, what assessment method(s) will be used? What will be the content of the appraisal? Other concerns stem directly from involving other raters. Do the alternative sources make their appraisals on forms designed expressly for their perspective? Or is the normal supervisor appraisal form used? Do the alternative sources need to be trained? Will the alternative assessments be mandatory? What safeguards will there be about anonymity and confidentiality? How will the different assessments be integrated, particularly if ratings and narrative evaluations from several sources have to be combined? How will the information be used? To provide feedback? If so, who will provide the feedback? And how? For reward purposes? If so, what might be the effects on the quality of the data generated? Will the use of alternative ratings, especially for reward purposes, be acceptable to those affected?

The reported accounts of alternative methods and rating sources help to answer some of these questions, although for the most part organizations wishing to use additional sources will be in the position of having to experiment to develop a workable system. Many of the issues are ones which have to be faced in the design of any appraisal system, but using multiple sources does add to the complexity of developing and implementing a scheme.

The use of narratives seems certain to continue, particularly in conjunction with other approaches. It is likely that providing guidance on what is to be assessed will help appraisers to write more accurate narratives. Where such appraisals are to be used for feedback purposes there clearly is a need for specific, behavioural evidence. This is particularly necessary if someone other than the appraiser will be giving the feedback, as might be the case in multiple appraisal. The CI technique appears to offer the prospect of providing such richer data. Used on a regular basis critical incidents may be one approach to diary keeping, a method which Guion (1986) has suggested is a means of improving the quality of appraisals.

Using self-appraisal

For the foreseeable future appraisal systems are most likely to have supervisor ratings at their core. In many organizations, supervisor appraisal will remain the sole source but there will be increasing use of forms of self-appraisal. In particular, there will be more and more use of true self-appraisal, not just self-assessment as interview preparation. One approach to self-appraisal is that proposed by Teel (1978). Appraiser and appraisee each completes independently a copy of the appraisal form before the interview takes place. During the interview the forms are compared. Where there are discrepancies they are dealt with in the following manner: with a difference of one point between the two, the higher rating is accepted; a difference of two points, however, requires detailed discussion in order to identify the reasons for the difference.

Self-appraisal is not necessarily appropriate for everyone. It is less likely to work well with those lacking in self-insight. So, there is a need to train such people so that they become more competent in this respect (Fletcher and Williams, 1985; McHenry, Howard and McHatton, 1984): as Fletcher (1985) notes, individuals seem to improve with practice. Self-appraisal may also work less successfully where there is a dependency relationship between appraisee and manager or with authoritarian managers.

Furthermore, certain conditions need to be met in order to operate a system of self-appraisal (Fletcher, 1985). The purpose of the appraisal, especially how the information will be used, what *specifically* is to be appraised and how, all need to be made clear and explicit. As with conventional supervisor appraisal, motivation to rate is as important as ability to rate. Motivation to rate accurately and honestly may be fostered by emphasizing to the appraisees that confirmatory evidence will be sought. Accuracy may also be enhanced by encouraging appraisees to recall situations similar to the one currently being appraised: this may be one means of training to improve self-assessment. And as was suggested earlier the nature of the rating task is of significance; where an appraisee is asked for a profile of relative strengths and weaknesses there is less halo error and less leniency.

Using subordinate appraisal

Reports (e.g. Bernardin and Beatty, 1987) about subordinate appraisal show that one of the ways in which it is used is in instrumented survey feedback; the IBM employee opinion surveys represent an example of this. This type of usage is rather different from what one normally thinks of as appraisal but it has a lengthy history in the fields of organization development and team development. In many management development programmes, ratings are obtained from some or all of the manager's subordinates and used as a basis for providing feedback and for identifying development needs. There are many instruments available for obtaining subordinates' views about their managers but the psychometric properties of several of the questionnaires are inadequate (Morrison, McCall and DeVries, 1978). Morrison *et al.* (1978) also are cautious about whether such instruments work. They take the view that the evidence suggests that '. . . *some* managers have a positive reaction to receiving feedback from their subordinates and may even modify their behaviour as a result. The evidence, however, is hardly conclusive.'

Bernardin and Beatty (1987), in their account of company practices, are more enthusiastic although they note that subordinate appraisal stands more of a chance of getting off the ground in those organizations which have a climate of participativeness. They also list several other operational conditions which need to be met. Many of these apply whatever the type of appraisal system: being clear about objectives, particularly about why there should be subordinate appraisal and how the information will be used; being specific about what is to be rated; field testing the scheme, with cautious interpretation of the data at first; and careful monitoring. They stress the importance of tight administrative control and the need for anonymity and confidentiality. Where the data are to be used for feedback purposes, that feedback has to be provided quickly.

Clearly, there are resource implications with this, especially if the organization proceeds to a large-scale programme of survey feedback. All the administration involved in running a survey will have to be dealt with. Will the personnel department have the resources to cope? Computer analysis of data will be required. Does the organization have adequate facilities for this? And if the appraisal scheme incorporates narrative comments these too need to be integrated in some way; someone will have to do this.

Peer appraisal would very likely operate in a similar fashion to upward appraisal and all the points made here would therefore apply.

Bernardin and Beatty (1987) take the view that subordinate appraisals do have a part to play even where the ratings are used for reward purposes (see also Stinson and Stokes, 1980) provided that they are part of a multiple appraisal system. They also state that subordinate ratings should be interpreted along with other information about the manager, a view shared by Morrison *et al.* (1978). This then leads on to multiple appraisal.

Using multiple appraisal

Some writers (Latham and Wexley, 1981) have gone so far as to suggest that the ideal appraisal system is one based on multiple sources, and from what has already been said here the logic is easy enough to understand. There are a few reports of experiments but for the most part multiple appraisal remains untested. Organizations wishing to use multiple appraisal will need to observe the guidelines suggested in the two foregoing sections as well as those design principles applying to conventional supervisor appraisal. Over and above these there are practical issues to do with combining data from different sources and providing feedback. For example, in the experiment reported by Stinson and

Stokes (1980), peer and subordinate ratings were used, but because of the condition of anonymity it was not possible to identify the type of source. This leads to some difficulties in interpreting the data and consequently in providing feedback. To whom should the feedback be provided? Clearly, to the manager who is the subject of the appraisal; but what about the manager's manager? How should the feedback be provided? A written report, presumably prepared by personnel? But should there be provision for counselling? Again, by whom? And what are the resource implications?

IS IT WORTH IT?

These questions about resource implications lead on to one final issue—that of utility. In crude terms, is it worth using other sources as raters? There are two aspects to this. On the one hand there is the technical evidence about the different sources. This indicates that no one source is superior to any other and each source has deficiencies. Faced with this evidence the conclusion to use multiple sources is not surprising.

On the other hand, there are all the operational aspects of designing and implementing a scheme drawing on several sources. These are not insurmountable but they are certainly daunting, and the implementation of a multiple appraisal scheme requires a high degree of commitment from all levels involved. Using utility analysis, Landy and Farr (1983) have provided an illustration of the cost-effectiveness of appraisal but we simply do not have enough evidence to be able to make statements, in utility terms, about the relative worth of different rating sources. The decision to embark on some scheme of multiple appraisal must therefore remain one of managerial judgement. The importance attached to appraisal data and the costs (often overlooked) of poor data are among the factors which bear on this decision. Field review seems not to have much to recommend it, but given the acceptance of subordinate and peer appraisal as part of organization and management development programmes, this route may be one means of introducing these two sources. For the foreseeable future, the source most likely to be introduced to appraisal schemes is the appraisee; self-appraisal is being practised more and more already and is a trend which looks set to continue.

REFERENCES

Bassett, G.A., and Meyer, H.H. (1968). Performance appraisal based on self-review, *Personnel Psychology*, **21**, 421–30.

Bernardin, H.J., and Beatty, R.W. (1987). Can subordinate appraisals enhance managerial productivity? *Sloan Management Review*, 63–73.

Borman, W.C. (1978). Exploring upper limits of reliability and validity in job performance ratings, *Journal of Applied Psychology*, **63**, 135–44.

DeVries, D.L., Morrison, A.M., Shullman, S.L., and Gerlach, M.L. (1980). *Performance Appraisal on the Line*, Centre for Creative Leadership, Greensboro, NC.

Fletcher, C.A. (1985). Interviews, inventories and insight. Chairman's Address to the British Psychological Society's Occupational Psychology Conference, University of Sheffield.

Fletcher, C., and Williams, R. (1985). *Performance Appraisal and Career Development*. Hutchinson, London.

Guion, R.M. (1986). Personnel evaluation, in R.A. Berk (ed.). *Performance Assessment*. Johns Hopkins University Press, Baltimore, pp. 345–60.

Henderson, R.I. (1984). *Performance Appraisal*, 2nd edn, Reston Inc., Reston, VA.

Kane, J.S., and Lawler, E.E. (1978). Methods of peer assessment, *Psychological Bulletin*, **85**, 555–86.

Landy, F.J., and Farr, J.L. (1983). *The Measurement of Work Performance*. Academic Press, London.

Latham, G.P., and Wexley, K.N. (1981). *Increasing Productivity Through Performance Appraisal*. Addison-Wesley, Reading, Mass.

Long, P. (1986). *Performance Appraisal Revisited*. Institute of Personnel Management, London.

Mabe, P.A., and West, S.G. (1982). Validity of self-evaluation of ability: a review and meta-analysis, *Journal of Applied Psychology*, **67**, 280–96.

McHenry, R., Howard, J., and McHatton, M. (1984). Employee Driven Performance Appraisal. Paper delivered at the Institute of Personnel Management National Conference, Harrogate.

Meyer, H.H. (1980). Self-appraisal of job performance, *Personnel Psychology*, **33**, 291–5.

Morrison, A.M., McCall, M.W., and DeVries, D.L. (1978). *Feedback to Managers: a comprehensive review of twenty-four instruments*. Centre for Creative Leadership, Greensboro, NC.

Shrauger, J.S., and Osberg, T.M. (1981). The relative accuracy of self-predictions and judgements by others in psychological assessment, *Psychological Bulletin*, **90**, 322–51.

Stinson, J., and Stokes, J. (1980). How to multi-appraise, *Management Today*, June, 43–53.

Teel, K.S. (1978). Self-appraisal revisited, *Personnel Journal*, **57**, 364–7.

Thornton, G.C. (1980). Psychometric properties of self-appraisal of job performance, *Personnel Psychology*, **33**, 263–71.

Williams, R. (1981). *Career Management and Career Planning*. HMSO, London.

Chapter 5.7

Training for Performance Appraisal

ROGER PRYOR

Interactive Skills Ltd, Cygnet House, Market Place, Henley-on-Thames, Oxon RG9 2AH, UK

It has become well recognized that training is an essential part of launching an appraisal scheme. In fact it could be said that it is *fundamental* to success — a set of well-designed forms and clear policy statements does not guarantee effective appraisal discussions but well-trained, skilful appraisers can overcome the problems of poorly designed documentation.

In the early stages of implementing an appraisal scheme there is, naturally, a tendency to focus particularly on the forms and policy. This can lead to a situation where the paperwork is seen to drive the process rather than to support it. At its worst this leads to appraisal being viewed by appraisers as a 'form filling' exercise rather than as a useful opportunity for discussion, feedback and future planning. The problem is exacerbated if the 'training' provided is no more than a briefing on policy and how to complete forms. While briefing is necessary, effective appraisal training is much more concerned with the *process skills* involved in preparing for and handling an appraisal discussion.

WHO SHOULD BE TRAINED?

Historically the focus has been on training appraisers. More recently there has been a trend towards providing training for appraisees too. If the appraisal is to be an effective, in-depth, two-way dialogue there is a strong case for the argument that more effective outcomes will be achieved if both parties have developed the attitudes and skills necessary for participation.

Assessment and Selection in Organizations   Edited by P. Herriot
© 1989 John Wiley & Sons Ltd

WHAT ARE THE FEATURES OF GOOD APPRAISAL TRAINING?

Experience has shown that appraisal training is more likely to be effective if it is designed to meet the ten criteria listed below:

1. *Builds confidence* For a variety of reasons some appraisers are nervous about conducting honest, open discussions with appraisees. There may also be nervousness about attending an appraisal training course. It is important, therefore, that the training undertaken builds confidence rather than reduces it. This may be achieved by creating a course design which avoids embarrassing course members in front of colleagues, builds competence before practice and, in the provision of feedback, emphasizes the positive rather than the negative.

2. *Thorough coverage* A wide range of interpersonal skills are relevant to appraisal and these are discussed in the next section of this chapter. Careful thought needs to be given as to how best to treat these topics to achieve an adequate balance. Prior experience of course members will also need to be taken into account.

3. *Applied skills* Treating each of the skills of appraisal separately allows course participants to assimilate material in a gradual fashion, leading to better retention. Retention will be further enhanced if an opportunity is given to apply the skill through an appropriate exercise before moving on to a new area.

4. *Realistic practice* The conduct of at least one simulated appraisal provides an opportunity on a course to integrate the skills practised in individual exercises. It is preferable that the simulation be as close to a real-life appraisal as possible. For this reason role plays are less desirable as they tend to be seen as artificial by course members. A better alternative is to have participants set objectives for one another, to observe performance against those objectives, then to build the appraisal around the real-life observations made. This personalizes the practice a great deal more than a role play does and leads to better acceptance of feedback on how the appraisal was handled as the appraiser was not 'being somebody else'.

5. *Feedback provided* Practice without feedback is a very inefficient method of learning. To get the most from practice exercises in appraisal training necessitates a structured approach. Different learning points will need to be drawn out at different stages of the course; feedback needs to be provided in a way which maintains the self-esteem of the participant and relevant rather than irrelevant material needs to be focused on. The use of checklists containing descriptions of key behaviours can be useful as they also serve as a reminder for the participants post-course.

6. *Job related* Wherever possible linkages should be established between appraisal training and the 'back on the job' situation. This may be achieved in various ways. Questionnaires might be distributed to appraisers and their appraisees, prior to the training course, to gather real-life observations of the appraisers' approach or views on appraisal. An analysis might be made of

completed appraisal documentation to develop examples for use on the course. Potentially difficult appraisal situations might be identified for discussion.

7. *Participative approach* Effective appraisal practice is influenced as much by attitudes as it is by skills and knowledge of appraisal. Positive attitudes will be encouraged, in part, by building confidence and competence in handling the task and by ensuring the training is relevant to the job. This will be further assisted if the course design is participative, enabling members to voice concerns they may have, to share their experiences, and to debate and discuss material presented by the tutor. This style of teaching means that the tutor will need to be well versed in appraisal and able to respond in a helpful way to the concerns of participants. A thorough knowledge of the practices of other organizations and the appraisal literature together with the scheme being operated is important.

8. *Suitable handouts* As with other forms of skills training, the most useful handouts are ones that get the key points across in a succinct and orderly way and which are as useful after the course as they are during it. Lengthy narrative should be avoided as it is less likely to be referred back to by the busy appraiser. There should be a logical flow to the material and use made of indexing to make particular items easy to find. Ample space should be provided for the participants' own thoughts to be jotted down as the course progresses.

9. *Appropriate timing* It is preferable that appraisal training is conducted near to the time when appraisals are to be done. If this is not feasible, then a bridging mechanism needs to be developed as part of the course design to provide a link between training and application. At its simplest this could include reviewing of course handouts but preferably would also include the use of audio or video based refresher material.

   Another element of timing is to do with the length of the course offered. It is difficult to envisage any real development of skills and attitudes occurring in a course of less than two days' duration. Indeed, some organizations offer three- and four-day courses to less experienced personnel. It may, however, prove difficult to involve people at the top of the organization in a two-day course because of very real time constraints. A one-day overview might be offered as an alternative to this more experienced group, with the opportunity provided for individuals to attend a longer course according to their particular needs.

10. *Post-course follow-up* As mentioned earlier in this chapter it is desirable to establish links between appraisal training and the work situation. Precourse work will facilitate this and a good course design will provide for post-course follow-up. This might include a one-day appraisal 'clinic', after the next round of appraisals have been conducted, to review the experience and provide further support, follow-up coaching by the tutor on a one-to-one basis, monitoring of post-course action plans, the use of audio/video reinforcement materials, etc. Whatever the vehicle, follow-up is important to ensure the consolidation of learning. It can also serve as a

useful feedback mechanism on the effectiveness of the original training design.

WHAT AREAS SHOULD APPRAISAL TRAINING COVER?

It is best to separate briefing on the appraisal system and organizational policy on appraisal, from the skills training course or workshop. If this is not done there is a risk that debate about the system will distract from skills acquisition and that 'procedures' will replace 'process' as the centre of discussion.

The *Briefing* component of appraisal training will normally cover, *inter alia*:

- an overview on appraisal;
- the objectives of the specific scheme;
- how the scheme was developed;
- policy on matters such as confidentiality and access;
- the relationship (if any) between appraisal information, salary progression, career development, succession, training, etc.;
- the timings of the appraisal cycle;
- the role of the different parties involved in the appraisal scheme;
- procedures to be followed;
- the location and period of retention of completed documentation;
- the approach to be adopted for handling disagreements and policy on rights of appeal;
- the documentation itself, including a sample or model of effectively completed forms;
- other matters which will depend on the specific design of the appraisal scheme concerned.

Appraiser training

The *skills* component of appraiser training should include how to:

- select and use the most appropriate style for handling an appraisal;
- give feedback in a way which maintains the appraisee's self-esteem;
- identify the areas on which the appraisal is to be based (e.g. objective setting, key result areas, etc.);
- collect good quality observational material to use in the feedback process;
- document the appraisal form effectively;
- evaluate performance data objectively and accurately;
- prepare the 'process' aspect of the appraisal as well as the 'content';
- handle the opening and closing stages;
- use the discussion skills of listening, questioning, influencing and responding effectively;
- create a positive, open climate for the discussion;
- resolve problem areas and develop action plans leading to performance im-

provement, increased job satisfaction, personal development, career development, etc.;
- monitor and interpret the non-verbal components of interpersonal
  communication;
- confront effectively;
- put points of view assertively rather than aggressively;
- structure an appraisal discussion to best effect;
- handle potentially difficult appraisals, e.g. the person who has reached a career
  ceiling, the high flyer, etc.

As many of these skills also relate to day-to-day management of staff, appraisal
training can have a useful spin-off in terms of contributing to ongoing management effectiveness.

Perhaps it is useful at this stage to look at one of these areas in greater detail so
we will now focus on *'style of appraising'*, the first skill area identified above.

People differences

Some years ago it was inferred in the appraisal literature (Maier, 1976) that there
was a single best way of approaching an appraisal discussion. More recently a
great deal of publicity has been given to the concept of 'self-appraisal' for
everyone. The author's experience is that there is no single best style but rather
that different approaches seem to work well with different people and for
different purposes. Given the great variety of people, in terms of experience,
personality, ability and motivation, that appraisers have to contend with, then
this should come as no surprise. Yet some organizations still choose to mandate
that their appraisers should adopt a single style in preference to others.

The works of Reddin, Fiedler, Hersey and Blanchard (see Blanchard, Zigarmi,
and Zigarmi, 1986), all of whom have proposed contingency theories of leadership style, urge leaders to assess situations and to adopt the style most appropriate to the situation. This notion can usefully be applied to performance appraisal
too. When training appraisers it becomes important then to develop their skills in
diagnosing the development level of their appraisee, or their readiness for greater
or lesser involvement in the appraisal discussion. Coupled with learning diagnos-

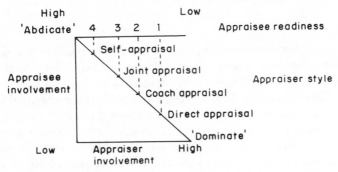

Figure 1   A model of appraisal

tic skills the appraiser also must learn the variety of behaviours that will be needed to achieve a flexibility of approach when handling different people. Several years ago (Pryor, 1985) I proposed a version of the appraisal model shown in Figure 1 as a means of describing the relationship between appraisee readiness and appraiser style.

The two extreme styles of 'abdication' and 'domination' are unlikely to be effective in any situation. But between the extremes are four styles, any of which may be effective if matched correctly to the needs and characteristics of the appraisee. In determining which style to adopt, apart from the purpose of the appraisal system, the appraiser needs to take account of the appraisee's:

- awareness of standards expected;
- knowledge and skill in the job;
- level of self-awareness and ability to be objective;
- ability to identify problems and develop responses to these;
- willingness to be open;
- maturity of judgement;
- degree of motivation and commitment.

The higher the appraisee is on these factors then the more likely it is that 'self-appraisal' will be an appropriate way of handling the discussion. The lower the appraisee is on these factors the more likely it is that he or she will be looking for, or need, direction, feedback and guidance on how to approach things, i.e. a direct appraisal. These factors and others may also affect the learning style of the individual and this too will need to be taken into account.

As part of a training course design, questionnaire materials may be used to identify the style the appraiser is most likely to use with his or her appraisee (as perceived by the appraiser and the appraisee). This preferred style will have been influenced by the appraiser's own personality and past experiences. The degree of fit between preferred style and most appropriate style can then be explored and ways of achieving flexibility discussed and practised.

To explain this concept simply as part of a briefing session would be inadequate as appraisers need the opportunity to assimilate and practise the approach. This is also true of the many other topics covered in appraiser training.

Purpose differences

Skills training for appraisal needs to take into account not only people differences but also the different purposes for which appraisal is used within organizations. If a system has a heavy bias towards assessment and evaluation applications, for example, with outputs linked to financial rewards, then it is essential that this is reflected in the training undertaken. This may mean greater in-depth coverage of topics such as sources of rating error and how to correct for them, the use of behaviourally anchored rating scales, goal setting and performance measurement techniques (McMaster, 1979), and so on. A bias towards use of appraisal data for predicting promotion potential may require special attention being paid to issues to do with equal employment opportunity, and ways to improve the reliability and validity of appraisal data for predicting potential (Kleiman and Durham, 1981). The linking of appraisal with performance improvement may change the emphasis yet again with special priority being given to action planning (Moravec, 1981).

Appraisee training

The skills component of appraisee training may include:

- preparing for the appraisal discussion;
- overcoming nervousness and anxiety;
- handling discussion effectively including listening;
- questioning, influencing and responding;
- participating assertively, rather than aggressively or submissively;
- responding to criticism and praise;
- recognizing and encouraging the giving of good quality feedback;
- handling difficult appraisals;
- responding to different styles of appraisal;
- giving feedback effectively to the appraiser;
- action planning;
- interpreting non-verbal communication;
- other related topics.

Courses for appraisees may vary considerably in length and are sometimes coupled with other subjects or included as part of induction training. Experience shows that they are warmly received by staff who are enabled to enter subsequent appraisal discussions more confidently and with a greater potential contribution to make.

HOW MIGHT APPRAISAL TRAINING BE EVALUATED?

Appraisal training may be evaluated in a variety of ways ranging from end-of-course questionnaires to collection of on-the-job evidence of application. The latter may be undertaken by interviewing both appraisees and appraisers after a round of appraisals have occurred. In rare instances it has been known for trainers to be able to observe directly an appraisal in progress and this has given valuable insights into the effectiveness of the original training. Other methods of evaluation have included the use of semantic differential questionnaires to measure attitude change as a result of training, knowledge-based questionnaires to test awareness of policy and procedures, and simulation exercises to observe skills being applied.

The biggest challenge still facing appraisal trainers is gaining recognition from management of the importance of adequate training when launching an appraisal scheme. The success of initial training events becomes crucial in building commitment and enthusiasm. This is considerably helped when people appreciate that appraisal training is relevant not only to the annual appraisal meeting but also to day-to-day interactions on the job.

REFERENCES

Blanchard, K., Zigarmi, P., and Zigarmi, D. (1986) *Leadership and the One Minute Manager*. Willow Books, Collins, London.

Kleiman, L.S., and Durham, R.L. (1981). Performance appraisal, promotion and the courts: a critical view, *Personnel Psychology*, **34**(1), 103–21.

McMaster, J.B. (1979). Designing an appraisal system that is fair and accurate, *Personnel Journal*, **58**(1), 38–40.

Maier, N.R.F. (1976). *The Appraisal Interview*. University Associates, San Diego, CA.

Moravec, M. (1981). Performance appraisal: a human resource management system with productivity payoffs, Arabian Bechtel Co Ltd, *Management Review*, **70**(6), 51–4.

Pryor, R.L. (1985). A fresh approach to performance appraisal, *Personnel Management*, June, 37–9.

Chapter 5.8

Assessment Centres for Identifying Long-term Potential and for Self-development

JEROEN J.J.L. SEEGERS

GITP/FOCUS, Bergen Dalseweg 127, Postbus 9043, 6500KC, Nijmegen, The Netherlands

INTRODUCTION

An assessment centre is a procedure (not a location) that uses multiple assessment techniques to evaluate employees for a variety of manpower purposes and decisions (Thornton and Byham, 1982). Assessment differs from psychometric prediction in both measurement techniques utilized and the process of making the prediction.

The assessment approach may use techniques like paper-and-pencil tests, questionnaires, and the use of background information. Particularly important in the assessment approach, however, is the focus on relevant behaviours displayed by the assessee in simulations.

The assessment centre method may be used to identify an individual's growth and development possibilities. The simulations in which the assessed person takes part represent as closely as possible the situations that the incumbent will be encountering in performing the job in question and they portray different aspects of that job. Thus, information is gathered, in a standardized and controllable manner, on behaviour that is representative for future job behaviour. This information is not communicated in psychological terminology, but expressed in terms easily recognized by management. The assessment centre method is conducted strictly step by step, with each phase basically forming an entity of itself. The effectiveness of the assessment centre method has already been proved in practice on numerous occasions, especially in cases concerned with potential assessment and career development.

Assessment and Selection in Organizations   Edited by P. Herriot
© 1989 John Wiley & Sons Ltd

ASSESSMENT CENTRE FOR IDENTIFYING POTENTIAL

The assessment centre method is used with particular success as a method for potential evaluation and management development. Evaluation of potential is based on gathering information on a range of aspects that is much wider than with evaluation of achievements and job performance. The latter types of evaluation may be restricted to evaluation of the knowledge, the capacities and skills that are necessary for successful performance of a particular job or of all jobs within a specific department. Potential evaluation should focus on the skills that are required for a great number of positions that may be within the reach of the assessee at some point in the future.

By using an *integrated* evaluation system composed of tests and simulations for the purpose of arriving at the best possible predictions, the assessment centre method is highly effective for the prevention of the most common assessment errors (Byham, 1981).

One of the objectives of application of the assessment centre method is to evaluate the growth potential of individual employees. The primary concern then is not information on the employee's performance of his present job and the resulting achievement over the last few months or years, but answering the question whether he or she would be able to fill other jobs, i.e. prediction. So the emphasis is not on the present or the past, but on the future, i.e. potential evaluation. The assessment centre method in its application for potential evaluation is based on the following assumptions:

- that every employee can develop his or her skills further;
- that the development possibilities of the assessees can be established, also those possibilities for which no evidence may be traced in the performance of the present job;
- that the organization is continually in need of people who can perform various kinds of jobs.

The organization benefits from using the assessment centre method for potential evaluation in that it offers an opportunity for human resource planning to meet the requirement of an appropriate number of suitable employees. The employees benefit from the potential evaluation in that they are given the opportunity to develop their capacities and use them in work situations.

Career policy

The assessment centre method as a technique to evaluate potential should be considered within the framework of a more comprehensive policy, i.e. career policy. Career policy is concerned with making three factors agree with each other: the potential skills of individual employees; their personal and professional interests; and the specific needs of the organization itself.

Career planning policy involves the following activities:

- determination of the establishment, i.e. the total number of positions of a particular type and level, based on the future organizational structure;
- recruitment and selection;
- development and training;
- potential evaluation.

For potential evaluation the following instruments may be used:

- performance appraisal and achievement evaluation;
- career interests registration: recording the wishes and aspirations of the employees regarding their future;
- suitability advice;
- results of special assignments, such as practical training period and teaching commitment;
- results of assessment exercises;
- advice based on psychological tests;
- advice based on a medical examination by the company physician.

The term 'suitability advice' denotes the prognosis given by managers and, if necessary, other personnel about the suitability of the employee to fill different—mainly higher level—positions. This suitability advice is the 'potential evaluation' in a narrower sense. It will be apparent from the above that there are also other ways to evaluate an employee's potential. Three types of evaluation have been summarized in Table 1, which shows that they differ in many respects.

Most assessment methods generally try to establish a person's suitability to hold a new position on the basis of behaviour and, above all, successful performance of previous jobs. This approach is workable if the new position does not greatly differ from the old one. However, if it does differ substantially, prediction of a person's future performance on the basis of his current performance proves to be a tricky business. A brilliant salesman does not necessarily make a good sales manager. In such cases, the assessment centre method may be applied.

Characteristics of the method

The assessment centre method is not to be looked upon as replacing all other methods and techniques used in the promotion and selection processes, such as interviews, psychological tests and performance appraisals, but as supplementing these tools of assessment. In combination with these traditional methods, assessment exercises supply the organization with a fairly complete picture of the competence of its (future) employees.

The term 'assessment centre' may be used to denote:

1. the assessment centre method in general;
2. a specific assessment centre programme designed for selection, evaluation or training purposes;

Table 1 Comparison of three types of evaluation*

TYPE OF EVALUATION	PERFORMANCE APPRAISAL	ACHIEVEMENT EVALUATION	POTENTIAL EVALUATION
evaluation interview	job performance interview	remuneration interview	assessment centres
general objective	improvement of job performance and work situation	establishment of remuneration	evaluation of growth potential
general question:	how does the employee perform his job?	how has the employee performed his job?	what other skills does the employee possess?
motive of the organization:	employment of available personnel	effective remuneration	securing of future staff
motive of the employee:	satisfactory job	justified remuneration	motivation for future
position:	present position	present position	other, mainly higher level positions
time perspective:	recent past and near future	recent past	future
object:	work behaviour	results	behavioural criteria
aspects:	qualitative aspects	output, effect	predictive aspects
stress on:	what may be improved	what is (specially) remunerated	what growth potential there may be

* *Source*: Proot and Dragstra, 1982 (adapted).

3. a specific assessment centre meeting in which the actual evaluation of the candidates takes place.

The following elements are characteristics of the assessment centre method:

– To evaluate a person's suitability for a particular position, use is made of previously formulated and defined criteria, resulting from a careful analysis of the job in question.
– Different techniques are employed for the establishment of a person's suitability for a specific job. Apart from interviews, tests and exercises may be used.
– The exercises are attuned to the content of the future job and they are often simulations of part of the job content (simulation exercises).
– A form of group selection is used in which the participants who are considered for a specific job meet and their mutual interaction is observed.
– Multiple assessors are involved. They are managers, preferably working in jobs that are several levels higher up in the organizational hierarchy than the job in question.

– The final judgement is based on a combination of the different evaluation methods.

In the United States the assessment centre method is used mainly as an alternative selection method. In Europe—where it is most frequently employed in the United Kingdom, the Netherlands and Germany—the assessment centre method is mainly used as a diagnostic instrument in potential evaluation, career planning, and management development. In particular, larger organizations use the method to give substance and direction to their often extensive training programmes for management trainees and intermediate and higher level staff.

ASSESSMENT CENTRE TECHNOLOGY

The assessment centre method or *technology* is characterized, among other things, by the use of multiple instruments:

– job practice simulations;
– interviews;
– tests.

The choice of instrument depends on:

– the critical situations in which the future incumbent is supposed to (re)act successfully;
– the data available from the participant's work experience;
– the criteria that are relevant for the job in question and in relation to which the participant's behaviour is to be assessed.

There is research evidence that a combination of assessment exercises and psychological tests provides a very powerful method for arriving at fairly accurate predictions about a person's future behaviour. The combination of the two instruments leads to considerably higher results than will be the case if only one of them is used (Moses and Byham, 1977). Tests tend to work mainly in-depth and can frequently provide explanations for certain behaviours that have been observed during the assessment meeting. Tests are occasionally also used for the pre-selection of candidates. The information resulting from the tests then forms the basis for the interview with individual candidates.

It is generally true that no single exercise exists that enables the assessment of *all* behavioural criteria. A specific group exercise may say something about a person's persistence, but little about his written skills. It is obvious that the best manner of predicting a person's future behaviour through exercises will be for that person to be put in a situation that closely resembles the future job. If it proves possible to simulate accurately the reality, the yield is a powerful instrument for evaluation. A disadvantage of this instrument is that more experienced candidates may be favoured above persons with more talents. Therefore, the assessment centre method makes frequent use of simulated job situations: so-called

Table 2   The use of assessment exercises

Assessment exercise	Frequency of use (%)
In-basket	95
Assigned-role leaderless group discussion	85
Interview simulation	75
Non-assigned-role leaderless group discussion	45
Scheduling (primarily for supervisory positions)	40
Analysis (primarily for higher level positions)	35
Management games	10
Background interview (as part of the assessment centre as opposed to being part of a promotion system)	5
Paper-and-pencil tests: – Intellectual – Reading – Mathematics and arithmetic – Personality	2 1 1 1
Projective tests	1

From: Thornton and Byham, 1982.

simulation exercises. In Table 2 the uses of the different types of exercises are listed by percentage (Thornton and Byham, 1982). This list was developed from a review of approximately 500 centres with which the authors have been associated. To be more accurate, it must be stated that the usage of psychological tests is very much larger in the United Kingdom and Benelux countries than in the United States.

The exercises

The in-basket (in-tray)

The exercise that is used most is the in-basket. It is an individual exercise in which the participant is provided with a basket or file containing letters, memos and other written notes, on the basis of which he needs to assess particular problem situations and make a number of decisions to solve the problems involved in a limited time. The problems that he will be handling are true-to-life simulations of everyday job practice. The in-basket may be used to elicit a candidate's management skills, such as planning, organization, written communication skill, and decisiveness. The evaluation of the results is the work of experts. Therefore, the results of this exercise are rated by experienced and trained assessors. Next, the assessor writes a report on the candidate's performance. It is often advisable to arrange for an interview with the candidate after the assignment has been completed: such an interview leads to a better understanding of the candidate's method of handling the different exercise items and greatly contributes to the acceptance of the findings by the candidate. The validity of the in-basket has been studied on numerous occasions (Crooks, 1968; Frederiksen, 1962, 1966).

Management game

A management game is excellently suited for simulation. These games can be designed to reflect the organization's own background. Thus, the candidates may be given the assignment to sell particular products or draw up a policy plan, cooperation with other members of the group or with the assessors themselves. Differences in professional experience within the group should be avoided. However, a management game is fairly complex and extensive, and therefore it is most effectively used in training situations and less suitable in assessment situations.

Criteria-based interviewing

The interview is conducted on the basis of a list of behavioural criteria. The interviewer puts specific questions to the participant to elicit information about a number of behavioural criteria that are relevant to the job in question.

This type of interviewing must not be confused with so-called 'situational interviews'. One of the major things you would *not* do is to put questions in a form like 'what would you do if . . .'? These questions are theoretical and will give you also theoretical answers: 'if I were my boss, I would . . .'. The following questions are examples of wrong questions because they are either leading questions or theoretical questions.

1. 'I suppose you enjoyed working in sales, didn't you?'
2. 'I guess you left that job because you needed more money?'
3. 'What makes you think you can sell?'
4. 'Are you well organized?'

Better questions are those which are non-leading behavioural questions. Examples are:

1. 'What was your biggest decision within the last two months?'
2. 'What did you do when you discovered he was not capable of handling that person?'
3. 'Tell me about the largest sale you made and how you did it.'

These questions may also relate to the participant's biographical criteria, such as education, work experience, interests, career progress, ambitions and aspirations. Such an interview can also be used effectively if a pre-selection of candidates (those who will and those who will not be invited to attend an assessment centre meeting) is desired.

Leaderless group discussions

There are different types of leaderless group discussions: those with and those without assigned roles. On some occasions the participants are asked to solve a number of problems in playing the part of a consultant; at other times each participant is assigned a role of his own and together they must carry out a specific task. The latter type of group discussion will inevitably call up more emotions and tension than is the case in group discussions in which the participants meet informally and which lack the element of competition.

The use of group discussions in which the participants are really competing with each other has been frequently criticized in the Netherlands. Roe and Daniels (1984) are right in stating that in view of the validity of the decisions it is fully justified to incorporate this type of exercise in the assessment programme if successful performance of a particular job requires the incumbent to act effectively in groups. For additional studies on the subject the reader is referred to Hinrichs and Haanpera (1974, 1976).

Fact-finding exercises

In a fact-finding exercise the participant is supplied with general information, e.g. relating to the fact that a particular employee has been fired. The participant must question a role player who is well informed and try to come to a judgement about the correctness of the decision taken in the past, after which he or she has to affirm or revoke it. No matter what his or her personal decision will be, it will subsequently be challenged by the role player. This exercise is an instrument to test the participant's listening skill, stress tolerance, judgement and problem analysis skill (Pigors and Pigors, 1961).

Analysis exercises

In these exercises complex situations and information must be analysed and different alternatives studied. Furthermore, participants must communicate the findings of their analysis to an assessor or a group of colleagues by means of a presentation. Here again, it is possible to simulate situations that occur in real job practice. The exercise is often followed by a group discussion. In these exercises the major stress is on analysis and interpretation of written material: stress which is usually covered less comprehensively in the exercise types mentioned before.

Interview simulation

Candidates are placed in an interview situation in which they are expected to play a specific role, e.g. that of customer complaint manager, or supervisor or foreman. The opponent is a trained and previously instructed role player. Behaviour relevant to dimensions such as interpersonal skill, behavioural flexibility and listening skill will be elicited in the course of the exercise.

The validity of assessment exercises

Designing good exercises and simulations that meet the demands is a time-consuming and complex activity. Many times a particular exercise is used without considering if that exercise really does what it ought to do, that is elicit job-relevant behaviour. In this connection it is essential that not only the job activity, but also the practical situation be simulated. Thus, using a group exercise just because it seems a nice thing to do, is a wrong approach. A group exercise should only be used if performing in groups constitutes an essential part of the job.

Similarly, a group discussion is not necessarily always required as an exercise in an assessment programme for managers, since it should be borne in mind that many managers only seldom find themselves acting in group situations, but most frequently maintain relationships on a person-to-person basis. Therefore, the stress in the assessment programme should be on that type of interaction.

A mistake that is frequently made when designing an exercise is that it proves either too easy or too difficult. The level of the exercise should correspond to the level of the job.

The criterion 'planning and organization' is important both for the job of sales manager and for the job of salesman, but for different reasons: the salesman needs planning and organization skills primarily because he must be able to schedule his sales calls and because he must make his personal list of priorities, whereas the sales manager needs his planning and organization skills primarily to make strategic plans and to set priorities both for his own activities and for those of his subordinates. The difference in level must be reflected in the exercise. Besides, they must be constructed in such a way that every candidate has an equal chance and that company candidates, or candidates who have experience in the type of business, will not be at an advantage over candidates who do not yet know the ins and outs of the organization.

Content validity

One bit of evidence supporting the content validity of assessment centres is provided in a unique study originally conducted by Byham and Byham (1976) and recently updated with new data. Over 1000 assessment reports in twelve large companies were examined to identify the number of assessors who were able to make a judgement of the participants' skill levels on the basis of behaviour observed relevant to each of 25 dimensions. In these programmes the assessors were instructed not to rate the dimension if insufficient behaviour was observed. Therefore, the assessment reports contain evidence of whether or not the exercise elicited adequate behaviour relevant to the dimensions. Table 3 presents the findings. A checkmark (✓) means the dimension was observable at least 90 per cent of the time it was sought, a star (*) means the dimension was observable at least 95 per cent of the time and (X) means the dimension was observable at least 90 per cent of the time it was sought, but in only some of the exercises in the category.

Table 3   Evidence of dimensions observable in several assessment exercises (a)

Job-related dimensions	Business game	In-basket and interview	Leaderless group discussion (assigned roles)	Leaderless group discussion (non-assigned roles)	Analysis	Scheduling	Background interview	Fact-finding and decision making	Interview simulation	Written presentation	Analysis/oral presentation
1. Impact			√	√			√		√		*
2. Oral communication skill	√	√	*	*			√		*		
3. Oral presentation skill			*		X						*
4. Written communication skill		*			√					*	
5. Creativity					X			√			
6. Tolerance for stress					X[b]	X[b]			√	√[c]	
7. Work standards		√			X			√		X	
8. Leadership	√		√	*				√		*	
9. Persuasiveness sales ability			√		√			√	X	X	*
10. Sensitivity		*	√	*					√		
11. Behavioral flexibility	X		√					√	√		
12. Tenacity			√					√	√	X	
13. Risk taking	√	√		X	√			√			√
14. Initiative	√	*	√	*				*		X	
15. Independence			√					√	X	X	
16. Planning and organizing	√	*			X	*		√			
17. Delegation		*						√		X	
18. Management control		*						√	√		
19. Analysis	√	*			*		√	*	√	X	*
20. Judgement		*		X	*	*	√	*	√		*
21. Decisiveness		*		X	*		X	*	√		*
22. Development of subordinates		X						√	X		
23. Adaptability	√							√			
24. Technical translation		X			X					*	√
25. Organizational sensitivity		X			X			√	X		X

a. From 'Effectiveness of Assessment Center Exercises in Producing Behavior' by R.N. Byham and W.C. Byham Assessment & Development. March 1976 9−10 Copyright 1976 by Development Dimensions International Reprinted by permission

b Time stress.   c Interpersonal stress.   * means observed in 95% of the exercises
√ means observed in 90% of exercises. X means observed in 90% of certain exercises in category, but not all exercises.

Validity and cost effectiveness

Hardly any other psychological tool except tests of aptitude has a research basis as firm as the assessment centre methodology.

In 1970 the assessment centre method was unique in that extensive research had established its validity before it came into popular use. The assessment centre method, in its modern form, came into existence as a result of the AT&T Management Progress Study (Bray, Campbell, and Grant, 1974). In this study, which began in the late 1950s, individuals entering management positions in Bell Telephone operating companies were assessed and, from then on, their careers were followed-up. The study was unusual in that it was pure research. Neither the individuals assessed, nor their bosses, were given information about their performance in the centre. Nor was this information in any way allowed to affect participants' careers. Participants were assessed soon after they entered management as new college recruits or after being promoted from the ranks. The 1970 *Harvard Business Review* article presented the results from the first eight years of the study (Byham, 1970).

Additional data from this landmark study are now available. Not only have researchers followed participant advancement over the ensuing years, but a second assessment was conducted eight years after the first (Bray and Howard, 1983). Table 4 shows the validity of both assessment predictions. The criterion used was advancement to the fourth level of management in a seven-level hierarchy. The eight-year prediction is more valid—an expected finding since most individuals would have begun to consolidate their management skills after eight years in management. Yet the original assessment ratings were still valid— even after 20 years. Thornton and Byham (1982) reviewed 29 studies of the validity of assessment centre methodology. The authors found more support for the assessment centre method than other selection methods, while still lament-

Table 4   Ratings at original assessment and eight years later and management level attained at year 20

	Attained fourth level	
Original assessment rating of potential	N	
Predicted to achieve fourth level or higher	25	60%
Predicted to achieve third level	23	25%
Predicted to remain below third level	89	21%
	137	
Eight-year assessment rating of potential	N	
Predicted to achieve fourth level or higher	30	73%
Predicted to achieve third level	29	38%
Predicted to remain below third level	76	12%
	135	

ing the fact that most of the studies were done by a few large organizations (AT&T, GE, IBM, SOHIO, Sears). In 1985 Thornton and his associates at Colorado State University processed 220 validity coefficients from 50 studies using meta-analysis. They estimated the method's validity at 0.37 (Gaugler *et al.*, 1987). Working independently of Thornton, Cascio and Ramos (1984) arrived at the same figure (0.37) in studying the validity of first-level assessment centres in an operating company of the Bell System. Cascio's main interest, however, was to measure the 'bottom-line impact' of promotion decisions based on assessment centre information and decisions based on criteria extracted from other methods.

To determine the dollar impact of assessment centres, Cascio needed more than validity information; he needed cost data (fully loaded costs of the assessment process), plus job performance data expressed in dollars. Over a four-year period he developed a simple methodology for expressing in dollar terms the job-performance levels of managers. Using information provided by more than 700 line managers, Cascio combined data on the validity and cost of the assessment centre with the dollar-valued job performance of first-level managers. With these data, he produced an estimate of the organization's net gain in dollars resulting from the use of assessment centre information in the promotion process. Over a

Table 5   Starting up an assessment centre: a step-by-step approach

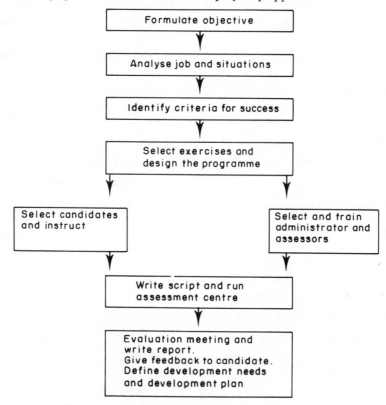

four-year period, the gain to the company in terms of improved job performance of new managers was estimated at $13.4 million, or approximately $2700 each year for each of the 1100 people promoted into first-level management jobs.

STARTING UP AN ASSESSMENT CENTRE

Basically, the assessment centre method is a very systematic and step-by-step approach (see Table 5), and that is just the reason why it is so widely applicable. Hereafter each phase will be discussed briefly and commented upon.

Inventory phase

Formulate objective

For what purpose is the assessment centre method going to be used: Selection? Management development? Evaluation? Education and training? Each objective calls for its own specific approach.

Introducing the assessment centre method should not be an aim in itself, but a *means* to handle certain processes in the organization more effectively and more efficiently. We do not intend to force an open door but we know from experience that only too frequently organizations are eager to introduce assessment centres because of the novelty, without applying the technique in the way that is best within the organization concerned. As a matter of fact there is no standard approach: every organization requires a specific approach that depends on the formulated objective. For example, an assessment programme for the purpose of selecting from large groups of applicants the best candidates for certain vacancies will be quite different from a programme designed to establish the potential of the current intermediate staff.

Job analysis and criteria

Some questions are crucial to this phase—which target group is involved: salespersons, trainees, specialists, executives? What elements are the jobs concerned made up of, and what are the essential characteristics of each job? About which dimension does the assessor wish to gather information: leadership skill, ability to organize, planning skill, communication skill or stress tolerance? Whether it be a matter of selection of external candidates or evaluation of internal candidates within the framework of management development and promotion, in both cases the criteria on which the candidates are assessed should be chosen in such a way that the crucial job elements may be traced back to them.

The main objective of personal selection and placement is to predict a person's behaviour in a new job. To be able to do so it is a prerequisite that the job in question is understood in all its detail and that the behavioural patterns, that must be shown by the candidate in order to be able to perform his future job successfully, are explicitly known. Therefore, when people are evaluated for the purpose of selection and promotion, job analysis should be considered as an essential component of the package of methods to be used. This means that the job analysis should lead to a sound understanding of what we would like to call 'job-related behaviour'. In the description of this behaviour we are concerned with finding out what kind of behaviour is required in any specific work situation

Often there is confusion about the difference between the criteria that need to be met for successful job performance and the specific 'requirements' that need to be met by the candidate. Criteria are accurate descriptions of the expectations that an organization has regarding a candidate in terms of behaviour, whereas many so-called 'job requirements' only so much as point in the direction of a criterion. An organization that only wants candidates with a complete academic training presumably looks for such specific recruits not just because it values an academic degree—preferably the highest possible—but primarily because it is interested in criteria such as 'ability to learn' and 'specialist knowledge'.

That a candidate has a college degree is information that may be relevant to these criteria, but no more than that. For most sales positions organizations are not really that much concerned about the length and range of experience that candidates can demonstrate, but basically they just want to know if they can sell. Experience from working as a salesperson may be an indication that a person really can sell, but does not necessarily mean that he or she will be able to do so in practice. In view of the above it may be concluded that job requirements should be used only if they are indispensable or if they are needed to restrict the number of applicants, and that criteria should always be used as much as possible to describe the job.

Table 6 shows the manner in which the behavioural criteria and the job requirements are derived from the job in question. The job is divided into tasks (job description): from these tasks different job requirements are derived from the job in question. The desired behaviour, however, leads us to which behavioural criteria are important for success. Finally, various assessment instruments are selected to elicit the behaviours related to each single behavioural criterion.

In summary, the following four 'conditions' related to proper job analysis need to be emphasized:

1. The method used to analyse the job and identify the criteria must be well elaborated.
2. The job analysis and criteria identification must have a fixed place in the entire selection or assessment procedure.
3. The criteria must be defined clearly and unambiguously.
4. There must be an objective and controllable method of determining the order of importance of the criteria.

Making the system operational

Select exercises and design the programme

Which exercises will be used and why? The exercises to be used in an assessment programme must simulate elements of the future job. They must resemble the

Table 6   Derivation of job requirements and behavioural criteria

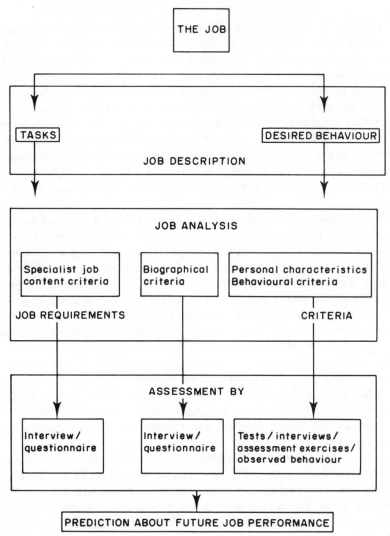

actual job practice, i.e. the problems and situations portrayed in the exercises must be of the same kind, of the same complexity and level of difficulty as encountered in the daily routine of that job.

The exercises are designed to elicit 'job-related behaviour'. This means first of all that the criteria on which the exercises are based should be directly derived from the job and contain all crucial and common elements of the job; secondly, that the exercises must simulate the most important and common job aspects; and, thirdly, that the exercises are constructed in such a way that they are actually able to evoke the desired behaviour, to enable the assessors to make statements on the candidate's behaviour concerning the criteria involved.

Select and train the administrator and the assessors

Which members of management will be assessing? How do you learn to assess purely on the basis of facts (what people do and say) and not on the basis of prejudice and presumptions? Who takes care of the coordination of the entire assessment process? Who controls the data, provides for feedback to the candidates and designs the programme? Most organizations using the assessment centre method employ their own managers as assessors of the candidates. Normally they are managers who work two levels higher up in the organizational hierarchy than the level of the job that the candidates are considered for.

Involving the immediate superior as an assessor is not recommended, as this might pose a threat to both parties. It is important, though, that the assessors are familiar with the job in question. As a rule, there is one assessor for every two candidates.

Sometimes, though, external consultants and psychologists are asked to act as assessors. This is often done when the job considered is top level or when the organization is too small to supply enough trained assessors of its own. Also, when an organization starts working with the assessment centre method for the first time, it will usually be dependent on outside assessment experts. Personnel departments should play a major role in the entire assessment centre process. In most cases, someone from the department is put in charge of the coordination and supervision of the process. From the very moment that the organization decides to start up an assessment programme to the final evaluation together with the candidates, this internal administrator supervises the assessment process. He or she gives advice on the preparation of job analysis and the selection of instruments; takes part in the pre-selection of the candidates; trains, occasionally together with other people, the assessors; controls and clusters all information and provides for follow-up. He or she supervises the final evaluation made by the assessors.

The assessors must receive adequate and thorough training in assessing the candidates. This is an item in the process that should really not be underestimated, because (in combination with the criteria and the exercises) it is a determining factor for the success of the programme. Training the assessor should usually take from three to five days. Training topics are: What is the aim of the intended programme? Which criteria do we select and why?, etc. The assessors are also asked to participate in all the exercises that will be used in the assessment programme. The results of their participation will be discussed in detail with the trainer.

Observing behaviour, evaluating it in relation to the criteria, writing reports and arriving at the final judgement (which includes establishing a candidate's training needs), are all essential elements of the assessor training.

The assessors must be made familiar with interview techniques and with eliciting behaviour by means of role play exercises. To be proficient in both, the assessor must first of all know the criteria. These criteria must be based on a thorough job analysis which the assessor understands and finds unambiguous. The assessor must learn which behaviour is related to which criterion, and become skilful in observing the often very subtle differences.

Pure observation, without any immediate judgement, is extremely difficult. In translating behaviour into criteria (classification) it is of the utmost importance that the assessor has a clear understanding of the criteria involved. This is the reason why accurate definition of the criteria is of vital importance.

Select and instruct the candidates

Who will be considered for participation in the assessment centre programme? Who will be asked to attend the meeting on how to conduct the pre-selection? Good pre-selection of the candidates for participation in the assessment centre programme is a primary concern. Here again, depending on the aim of the assessment programme, different problems may occur. The problems arising when the assessment method is used for the selection of external candidates are completely different from the problems accompanying use of the method for career planning, which involves internal candidates only.

In the case of external candidates, the problems are relatively limited after the pre-selection. It is possible to arrive at a first selection on the basis of reviewing of the application letters, review of the candidate's curriculum vitae and a first round of interviews. Using a structured criteria-based interview proves to be very helpful at this stage. During the pre-selection of internal candidates a number of problems may arise.

In fact judgements made by the direct superior count heavily in the decision regarding who is going to be considered for a specific development programme or for a certain promotion. It will be obvious that the superior's judgement is based on a mixture of facts, subjective impressions, vague feelings and prejudices.

A primary concern in the pre-selection of internal candidates must be to avoid a person being given the life-long label of either unsuitable for a management position or 'crown prince'. Make sure that the candidates who, at some point in the process, are no longer considered for participation in an assessment meeting or for promotion, are at any rate considered for participation in a different programme.

A psychological test or structured interview may be part of the pre-selection. More and more frequently some types of self-selection are used, in which potential candidates are helped to arrive at their own decision as to whether or not they will participate in an assessment programme. Afterwards they may again be considered for an assessment programme.

Implementation

Prepare script for the assessment centre

How will the assessment programme be implemented? How long will it be? Where will it be held? When will the meeting be? After the job has been analysed, when the exercises to be used have been selected, the number of candidates participating is known and an estimate has been made of the overall time

Table 7 Example of an assessment centre programme

Programme Day 1

Time	Activity
08.30 a.m.	Reception of candidates + coffee + checking into hotel
09.00 a.m.	General introduction
09.30 a.m.	Participants prepare for in-basket
11.30 a.m.	Participants fill in PEF (participant evaluation form) on in-basket
11.45 a.m.	Participants take part in group tests Assessors prepare for in-basket interview
12.45 p.m.	Joint lunch
1.30 p.m.	Participant 1 is interviewed on IB by team AB Participant 3 is interviewed on IB by team CD Participant 5 is interviewed on IB by team EF Participant 7 is interviewed on IB by team GH Participant 9 is interviewed on IB by team IJ Participant 2 is interviewed by psychologist X Participant 8 is interviewed by psychologist Y
2.30 p.m.	Participant 4 is interviewed by psychologist X Participant 7 is interviewed by psychologist Y
3.30 p.m.	Participant 3 is interviewed by psychologist X Participant 2 is interviewed on IB by team BA Participant 4 is interviewed on IB by team DC Participant 6 is interviewed on IB by team FE Participant 8 is interviewed on IB by team HG
4.10 p.m.	Participant 1 prepares for group discussion
4.30 p.m.	Participant 1 is interviewed by psychologist X
5.10 p.m.	Participants 2 to 9 prepare for group discussion
5.30 p.m.	Participants 1 to 4 conduct group discussion. Assessors AB and IJ Participants 5 to 9 conduct group discussion. Assessors CD, EF and GH

Programme Day 2

Time	Activity
08.30 a.m.	Participant 2 takes part in interview simulation with team GH Participant 4 takes part in interview simulation with team IJ Participant 6 takes part in interview simulation with team AB Participant 8 takes part in interview simulation with team CD Participant 5 is interviewed by psychologist X
09.30 a.m.	Participant 1 takes part in interview simulation with team HG Participant 3 takes part in interview simulation with team JI Participant 5 takes part in interview simulation with team BA Participant 7 takes part in interview simulation with team DC Participant 9 takes part in interview simulation with team FE
10.30 a.m.	Participant 6 is interviewed by psychologist X
11.30 a.m.	Participant 2 takes part in fact finding with team EF Participant 4 takes part in fact finding with team GH Participant 6 takes part in fact finding with team IJ Participant 8 takes part in fact finding with team AB Participant 9 is interviewed by psychologist X Participant 1 takes part in fact finding with team FE Participant 3 takes part in fact finding with team HG Participant 5 takes part in fact finding with team JI Participant 7 takes part in fact finding with team BA Participant 9 takes part in fact finding with team DC
12.45 p.m.	Debriefing and lunch
3.00 p.m.	Assessors meet for evaluation discussion
8.00 p.m.	Closing

involved, it is possible to prepare a script or programme. This script contains information on the day's timetable, the work programme, interviews and feed-back discussions, who should be where at what time, etc. It also contains information about the candidates, the job under consideration, the criteria, and the exercises. It sometimes may be necessary for the assessors to take part in a short refresher course, so that, among other things, they can study and go over the observation forms and evaluation forms once again and can brush up their knowledge and skills required for successful performance of their roles as assessors.

Table 7 presents an example of such a script. The choice of accommodation depends on the duration of the assessment centre programme, which may vary from one up to three days. If the session stretches over several days, it will usually be a hotel or conference facilities, although it is not strictly necessary to meet in a place completely secluded from the outside world. On the contrary, the accommodation chosen for an assessment programme should be no different from the place commonly used for training courses.

Evaluation

Final judgement and report writing

How do they arrive at a joint final decision and how do they report it to the candidates and to management? What happens with the information? After all the candidates have completed the exercises, they will be invited to a closing interview. They are informed then about the criteria on which they were assessed and why specific exercises had to be done. They are also told about the manner of report writing and about the time when the individual feedback discussions will take place. During this closing discussion the candidates have the opportunity to express their feelings and ideas about the programme.

All information gathered during the assessment meeting—both from the observations made by the different assessors and from the analysis of the handling of/approach to individual exercises is clustered and must result in a unanimous final judgement. This final judgement is not necessarily, nor need it be, equivalent to the average of the judgement of the individual assessors. The administrator clusters all information and conducts the discussion with the assessors. This discussion is very useful as it provides an opportunity to gain a good understanding of the weaknesses and strengths of each candidate. Weighing the different judgements against each other is of great importance, for certain criteria may be so crucial that a good score on one of these is an absolute prerequisite, if the candidate is to be considered for the specific job.

The evaluation discussion follows some simple rules:

- each individual participant will be discussed;
- no comparisons made between participants;
- criterion by criterion;
- through all exercises;

– no average scoring but evaluation based on behavioural evidence.

After the evaluation meeting has been concluded and once the final judgement of each candidate is known to the assessors and the administrator, the latter person can start writing the final reports. In each report the candidate's weaknesses and strengths are indicated in a manner readily understandable by the candidate, all based on actually demonstrated behaviour and familiar situations. Afterwards the administrator discusses the report with the candidate. The report may include suggestions for (further) development. Some weaknesses may be such that it will be relatively easy to reach the desired level of adequate behaviour on these dimensions; others may be of a structured nature and not amended so easily.

Careful follow-up and the presentation of alternative development opportunities and a realistic picture of the candidate's further career may ensure that the candidate does not feel badly about the assessment programme. Good follow-up is just as important as good report writing. Follow-up should be a task both for personnel and for management. In particular, management should not neglect its responsibilities in this respect.

DESIGNING A WELL-BALANCED SYSTEM

Common errors

The assessment centre method is used more and more frequently and successfully in different organizations and different forms. The strength of the method lies in the fact that it can always be tailored to the specific purpose envisaged by the organization. If the errors that are made before the actual assessment process starts are not counted, three errors are left that are commonly made in applying the assessment centre method:

1. The assessment centre method is not regarded as an element of a complete package of methods, but as an alternative to other techniques, such as psychological tests or interviews.
2. The criteria on which the evaluations are based are inadequately justified, because in analysing the job in question there has been too little attention to the search for the crucial elements.
3. The exercises used are insufficiently related to the crucial job elements, so that it is impossible to give reliable predictions about the future job performance.

In order to establish a well-balanced selection and promotion system it is necessary to base it on the criteria derived from the job. In such a system every method of evaluation will contribute to the overall evaluation.

It will be apparent from Table 8 that there is little sense in holding the same interview more than once, which is often the case. In fact the different general interviews should be replaced by more specific interviews and simulations. In Table 8 an example is given of such a programme containing only one general

Table 8   Example of a selection or evaluation programme

Criteria	Methods				
	Structured general interview	Criteria-based interview	Interview simulation	In-basket + interview	Psycho-logical test
Biographical criteria	X				X
(Professional) training	X				X
Practical experience	X				X
Expert knowledge	X				X
Planning and organization			(X)	X	
Delegation				X	
Problem analysis			X	X	X
Judgement			X	X	X
Persuasion	(X)		X		
Listening	X		X		X
Flexibility		X	X		X
Cooperation		X			X
Stress tolerance			X	X	X
Achievement motivation		X		X	X
Initiative		X	X	X	
Time	1 hour	1 hour depending on number of criteria	30 minutes	2 hours	depending on number of tests and on whether or not accompanied by interview with psychologist

interview, the other interviews having been replaced by alternative evaluation methods. After all, these alternative methods do not take more assessor time than the traditional interviews did, but because they have been specifically designed to elicit behaviour relevant to certain criteria, they contribute more to the overall evaluation. So each assessment technique helps to gather the information needed for final evaluation.

Part of a total process

Assessment exercises provide information on specific criteria; interviews, tests and performance appraisals provide information on yet other criteria. It is highly recommended, though, to plan the system in such a way that the same criteria

Table 9   The assessment centre method as an element of a total process

PERSONNEL ASSESSMENT

PERFORMANCE	*POTENTIAL*
– Curriculum vitae – References – Interviews – Technical tests – Performance appraisal	– Psychological tests – Assessment centres

past	present	future

may be observed for assessment on several occasions and to let various persons give their statements about the same set of criteria. This adds to the strength of the selection and promotion system, because there is an opportunity to compare opposite opinions with each other.

If the demands of the job for which the candidates are being assessed are different from those pertaining to the candidates' present position, the assessment centre method can be very helpful, as the method is eminently suited for the evaluation of potential, i.e. future capacities. The same holds for psychological tests. This is not the case with methods that are mainly used to evaluate a person's capacities as made explicit in the past, i.e. to evaluate his past job performance and achievements (see Table 9).

ASSESSMENT CENTRES FOR DEVELOPMENT

The most widely known application of the assessment centre method is for the selection of managers. Especially in the United States the method has always been used almost exclusively as an instrument in the selection of management personnel (Moses and Byham, 1977), and only recently has it come to be used for management development as well. However, in the United Kingdom and the Benelux countries the method is used mainly as support in the areas of management development, career planning and identification of potential.

The major reason for this may be found in the fact that the assessment centre method provides management with a system and language which allow better identification of the individual needs of employees. The system also enables management to guide and monitor more effectively the individual employee in his development.

Basically three different types of programmes are distinguished:

– Assessment centres with outside consultants/assessors.
– Assessment centres with inside assessors.
– Assessment centres with self-assessment.

Outside assessors

A number of organizations are using assessment centre programmes in which outside consultants act as independent assessors to the organization. They are usually one- or two-day assessment programmes on an individual basis and are used to obtain a comprehensive picture of the candidate by means of a mix of instruments (tests, simulations, interviews). The positions concerned are usually high-level positions within the organization and for political or practical reasons it is impossible to use inside assessors. The result of this type of comprehensive assessment centre is an overview of individual development needs. This overview will then be discussed with the human resource development manager and translated into an individual development plan. This development plan is more than just an enumeration and description of training courses, task forces and special assignments.

Inside assessors

Assessment centres with inside assessors are frequently used within larger organizations in order to improve the operation of their succession plans. For such organizations it is essential that they can make accurate judgements about the extent of the 'gap' between the individual's present job performance and future job requirements. The system is not only designed to identify future potential, but also creates opportunities for specific development.

In point of design, this type of assessment centre closely resembles the centres for selection purposes. The main difference is that in assessment centres with inside assessors the candidates are already employed in the organization and are assessed in view of a career rather than because they are considered for a specific position. Such a centre calls for a different choice of criteria and exercises.

Peer assessors

The third type involves self-assessment or peer-assessment. In such an assessment centre programme the assessees and assessors are the same persons. At a preliminary stage each candidate analyses his or her job. This analysis is then discussed with the candidate's manager. Next, the assessor takes part in an assessment centre programme. This centre will be videotaped from beginning to end. In the days following the centre the participants receive a 'crash course' assessor training that teaches them to view critically their own videotapes. They are also asked to look at videotapes made of a number of peers and provide feedback to each of these peers. On the basis of this self-assessment and peer assessment, the candidate can now draw up an analysis of his personal strengths and weaknesses and formulate his personal development plan. Finally, the candidate and his or her manager will meet to discuss this plan.

This type of programme, of which various versions are known to exist, proves to have a very strong effect. In particular, the 'peer rating' component seems a major influence.

DEVELOPMENT: A CONTINUOUS PROCESS OF ASSESSMENT AND APPRAISAL

Any development plan or management development process is doomed to fail if management does not commit itself. Several studies have led to the conclusion that training in itself seldom results in changes in behaviour unless there is some sort of reinforcement by management.

If follow-up is not included as part of the development assessment centre programme, the development character of the programme will soon lose its credibility.

Table 10 shows the results of a study by Dulewicz (1985) in which he describes the changes over time in attitudes towards a specific assessment programme called IMPACT (Identification of Management Potential and Counselling Techniques). Around three years after the event, management investigated development recommendations which had not been implemented and took action wherever appropriate.

From the foregoing it may be concluded that an effective system for human resource development should meet a number of primary conditions:

1. As soon as a person is employed by the organization, a specific development plan and introduction programme should be drawn up, both being based on a thorough analysis of the candidate's relative strengths and weaknesses in view of his or her future career.
2. The development plan must be part of the performance assessment and appraisal system within the organization.

Table 10   Specific attitudes to IMPACT: debriefing and follow-up

	Highly favourable or favourable	Highly unfavourable or unfavourable
(1) Assessments of my performance were accurate		
(immediate survey)	86	2
(follow-up survey)	72	5
(2) Feedback information will be/has been valuable for my personal development		
(immediate survey)	75	5
(follow-up survey)	56	20
(3) Feedback recommendations on career planning and development will be/have been valuable		
(immediate survey)	83	4
(follow-up survey)	34	31
(4) My career will benefit/has benefited from attendance		
(immediate survey)	65	6
(follow-up survey)	36	34
(5) In future my career will benefit from attendance		
(follow-up survey)	41	24

Table 11   The derivation of criteria and job requirements

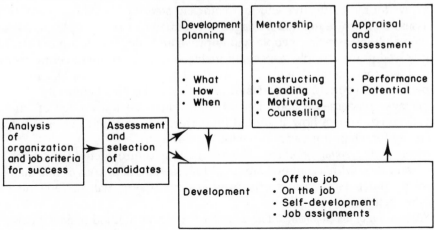

3. Managers must be asked to perform different roles, i.e. of planner and controller, of mentor and of assessor/appraiser. They should be trained in order to be able to perform these roles successfully.
4. Development of employees should be reinforced positively:

   (a) towards the employee so that he takes initiatives to develop himself (self-motivation and self-assessment);
   (b) towards the superior so that he will create the conditions that allow the employee to develop himself and to ensure the superior's mentorship to the employee;
   (c) towards the human resource development manager, so that he will provide for the appropriate means and resources for development and training.

ADVANTAGES AND PROBLEMS

On the basis of practical experience and extensive research the assessment centre method can be said to have the following advantages:

1. *More accurate evaluation*   The assessment centre method results in more accurate and sharper selection and evaluation of employees, which means that on fewer occasions will the wrong decisions be made with respect to promotion and placement.
2. *More specific training*   A more clearly criteria-based diagnosis enables more specific training: no investment in people who will not produce a profit after all and no investment in training which is too general.
3. *More effective use of human resources*   Use of the assessment centre method results in reduced job turnover caused by poor performance or by identifying the presence of potential too late.
4. *More effective management*   Use of the assessment centre method leads to a

better understanding of, and insight into, employee performance, which allows for more effective and more efficient steering by management. In the assessment centre method managers are trained to assess people. As a result, their skill in assessing people will improve and they will feel more strongly involved in the 'people' aspects of their job. The assessment centre method endows management with the responsibility for the decisions regarding personal placement, transfers and promotion. The idea behind it is that the manager possesses a good insight into, and wide knowledge of, the job concerned, knows how it should be performed, and that the final responsibility for job performance lies with the manager.

5. *More effective communication*   The assessment centre method provides the organization with a common language for assessment purposes; line management, and personnel and organization departments will understand each other better.

6. *Stimulation of development*   The assessment centre method makes it easier to give feedback and to stimulate training. Employees understand what is meant and will more readily accept the message. The assessment centre method ensures that employees assume part of the responsibility for their personal development, stimulating self-development through acceptance. The assessment centre method is more objective and more just, and therefore the employee is more likely to accept its results. The candidates can get a feeling of what it is like to perform the job that they are considered for. Because they take part in simulations they get a better understanding of what will be expected of them in the future job and it will be easier for them to make an accurate judgement about whether they will be able to fulfil these expectations.

7. *Change of organizational culture*   The assessment centre method helps organizations change their work style because the employees are taught to work in a different manner; thus, the change may be from non-profit to profit-based work.

Again based on practical experience and research we may mention as main problems:

1. *Acceptance by management*   How do I convince management that it, and not personnel, is responsible for the assessment?

2. *Fear of the unknown*   'Assessment centre' as a term is very obscure: it erroneously calls up visions of large-scale procedures and tremendous costs.

3. *Management time involved*   Because management time is condensed (in *one* day) the time involvement is made visible and, as a result, may be calculated.

4. *Costs*   The initial costs of starting up the system are often relatively high: the costs of job analysis, training and simulation development weigh heavily upon the first project. The costs of wrong decisions are often difficult to visualize (money value of personnel). In weighing the costs against the profit there is too much focus on the short-term impact. The yield (cost saving) of properly functioning management is difficult to visualize.

5. *Confusion with performance appraisal*   The assessment centre focuses primarily

on future job behaviour. It is not concerned with appraisal of the candidates' job performance in the past, but with their potential to perform successfully in a future job.

6. *Reactions to feedback* By means of the assessment centre method it is possible to make fairly accurate statements about a candidate's weaknesses (development needs). If this knowledge is not used afterwards, e.g. by providing for a good training programme or coaching by the superior, the person involved will get frustrated.
7. *Absence of policy* The assessment centre method as a method is very balanced and as such fits in well with a properly formalized personnel policy. Many organizations are still stuck in the 'bulldozer' phase and are not yet ready for a subtle approach. Absence of innovative thinking in the field of human resources policy acts prohibitively.

REFERENCES

Bray, D.W., and Howard, A. (1983). *The AT&T Longitudinal Studies of Managers. Longitudinal studies of adult psychological development*. The Guilford Press, New York.

Byham, W.C. (1970). Assessment center for spotting future managers, *Harvard Business Review*, **48**(4), 150–60, plus appendix.

Byham, R.N., and Byham, W.C. (1976). Effectiveness of assessment center exercises in producing behavior, *Assessment & Development*, **3**(1), 9–10.

Byham, W.C. (1987). Applying a systems approach to personnel activities, *Monograph IX* Development Dimensions International, Pittsburg.

Cascio, W. F., and Ramos, R. A. (1984). Development and application of a new method for assessing job performance in behavioral/economic terms, *Journal of Applied Psychology*.

Crooks, L.A. (1968). Issues in the development and validation of in-basket exercises for specific objectives (Research Memo 68–23), Educational Testing Service, Princeton.

Dulewicz, S.V. (1985). Assessment Centres: Practical issues and research findings. *Human and Industrial Relations* (Supplement 17).

Frederiksen, N. (1962). Factors in in-basket performance, *Psychological Monographs*, **76** (22, Whole No. 541).

Frederiksen, N. (1966). Validation of a simulation technique, *Organizational Behavior and Human Performance*, **1**, 87–109.

Gaugler, B.B., Rosenthal, D.B., Thornton III, G.C., and Bentson, C. (1987). *Journal of Applied Psychology Monograph: Meta-Analysis of Assessment Center Validity*, **72**(3), 493–511.

Harris, H. (1949). *The Group Approach to Leadership Testing*. Routledge and Kegan Paul, London.

Hinrichs, J.R., and Haanpera, S. (1974). A technical research report on management assessment in IBM World Trade Corporation (Personnel Research Study, No. 18), *IBM Europe*, March.

Hinrichs, J.R., and Haanpera, S. (1976). Reliability of measurement in situational exercises: An assessment of the assessment center method, *Personnel Psychology*, **29**, 31–40.

Moses, J.L., and Byham, W.C. (eds) (1977). *Applying the Assessment Center Method*. Pergamon Press, New York.

Pigors, P., and Pigors, F. (1961). *Case Method in Human Relations: The incident process*. McGraw-Hill, New York.

Proot, J.R., and Dragstra, H. (1982). *Personeelsbeoordeling*. GITP, Nijmegen.

Roe, R.A., and Daniels, M.J.M. (1984). *Personeelbeoordeling, achtergrond en toepassing*. Van Gorcum, Assen.

Thornton III, G.C., and Byham, W.C. (1982). *Assessment Centers and Managerial Performance*. Academic Press, New York and London.

Author Index

Subject Index